⟡ **P9-EDO-657**

"Our nation is moving
toward two societies,
one black, one white—
separate and unequal."

—*Report of the National Advisory
Commission on Civil Disorders*

Civil Rights and the American Negro documents
America's response to the Negroes' historic struggle
for freedom and equality. Here is the indispensable
record, proof that the roots of our divided society lie
deep in the practices and prejudices of white America
perpetuated for more than three hundred years.

From the first shipment of slaves in 1619 through the
omitted clause of the Declaration of Independence
condemning slavery, to post Civil War cases and
codes that canceled new guarantees of equality, and
culminating in the shocking facts and conclusions
of the President's Commission on Civil Disorders,
Civil Rights And The American Negro contains the
essential information for understanding the crisis
that faces our society today.

ALBERT P. BLAUSTEIN, Professor of Law at Rutgers,
the State University School of Law–Camden, New Jersey,
has written extensively for various legal publications.
He is co-author with Clarence Clyde Ferguson, Jr. of
Desegregation and the Law. He has also been a consultant
on segregation problems for the Philadelphia School
System and the U.S. Commission on Civil Rights.

ROBERT L. ZANGRANDO, Assistant Executive
Secretary of the American Historical Association, has
taught history at Rutgers, the University of Pennsylvania,
and Drexel Institute of Technology. Dr. Zangrando has
written articles on the civil rights movement and
conducted a television course on the Negro in America.

Civil Rights
and the
American
Negro

A DOCUMENTARY HISTORY

Edited by Albert P. Blaustein
and Robert L. Zangrando

WASHINGTON SQUARE PRESS, INC. • NEW YORK

CIVIL RIGHTS AND THE AMERICAN NEGRO
A Documentary History

A *Washington Square Press* edition

1st printing........................August, 1968

Published by

L

Washington Square Press, Inc., 630 Fifth Avenue, New York, N.Y.

WASHINGTON SQUARE PRESS editions are distributed in the U.S. by Simon & Schuster, Inc., 630 Fifth Avenue, New York, N.Y. 10020 and in Canada by Simon & Schuster of Canada, Ltd., Richmond Hill, Ontario, Canada.

Dedicated to:
Silvio J. Zangrando
and the memory of
Karl A. Blaustein,
Eugene J. Hoerdt, and
Irving C. Migden

Preface

The issue of civil rights for black Americans has become a major national challenge in our time. In order to come to grips with this challenge in effective and meaningful terms, Americans would do well to review current problems against a historical backdrop. In an effort to provide such a context, the editors researched hundreds of documents and extracted a representative selection to describe the changing status of the Negro in America from the earliest colonial days to the present. While the emphasis has been on official, legal documents, we have included some selections which have gained recognition as quasi-public pronouncements.

As we organized this material we were confronted with the overriding effects of the pattern of white dominance on the Negro minority. The white majority has been virtually the sole decision-maker regarding the Negro's destiny. Characterized in part by hostility to the Negro and in part by ambivalence about itself and its feelings toward the Negro, the dominant white majority in each historical period pulled back from the point of extensive reform. Through some process of myopic self-deception and wishful thinking, the dominant majority repeatedly convinced itself that it had "done right" by the Negro—that the minority was pleased with the reform. At its best, this is sheer hypocrisy on the part of the white majority; at its worst, it is the breeding ground for unrelenting anger and frustration on the part of the Negro.

Certainly there have been moments of high promise for the interracial situation in America—moments when the custom of repression was relieved by genuine efforts for unqualified civil rights. We seem to be living in an era when the pressures for reform are great. But will this period also fall short of the goal of interracial justice and interracial rapport?

A book of this type could not have been compiled and prepared without the cooperation of a great number of people, some of whom inevitably and inadvertently are neglected at the time of acknowledgment. Sincere appreciation is expressed for the thoughts, guidance, and efforts of Dean C. Clarence

Ferguson, Jr., of the Howard University School of Law; Joyce Falcone and Rosalyn Tomar, secretaries at Rutgers–The State University School of Law, Camden; Rutgers law students John Casarow and John W. Daniels; Lois DuBois, Kathleen MacSweeney, Marlene Van Meter, and Jean Vivian, all of the American Historical Association staff; and Jessie L. Matthews, assistant law librarian at Rutgers-Camden, who also prepared the index; and of course Phyllis Blaustein who provided encouragement and refreshment. Defects and short-comings, however, are solely the responsibility of the editors.

Albert P. Blaustein
   Professor of Law and Law Librarian
   Rutgers–The State University, School of Law, Camden
      and
Robert L. Zangrando
   Assistant Executive Secretary, American Historical Association, and Director of the Service Center for Teachers of History

March 15, 1968

NOTE ON THE TEXT:

The texts of the original documents in Part I (1619-1775) have been modernized for clarity and consistency. All other official governmental documents—cases, constitutions, statutes, treaties, and executive orders—appear exactly as first printed in the source cited, with the exception of modern typographical changes. Punctuation has been modernized in nongovernmental publications such as speeches, newspaper editorials and articles, and diaries to facilitate readability.

Contents

I

Slavery and the New World

1619–1775

The Negro has been part of the American experience from the earliest days of white European involvement in the New World.

Negroes accompanied the Europeans who first charted the New World, and they did so as explorers and not merely as servants or slaves. But from the middle of the sixteenth century the rapid growth of sugar cultivation in Latin America made the use of Negro slave labor particularly attractive and profitable. It was soon apparent that the European nations engaged in settlement and development would rely heavily on the use of Negro slaves to overcome the labor shortage that characterized the exploitation of the wealth and resources of the Western Hemisphere. The Dutch, French, and English became active in the Negro slave trade during the seventeenth century, and the competition for Negro slaves was a major cause of friction in the international rivalries and wars of the seventeenth and eighteenth centuries.

The five major powers of Western Europe successfully reconciled the traffic in human flesh with their stated religious and political ideologies. The rationalizations which they employed—such as supposed Negro inferiority and the duty to educate and Christianize so-called barbarians—were woven into the white mentality during the colonial period.

The first Negro laborers brought to the North American

colonies had the status of indentured servants. Their bondage was not perpetual, and, like their white counterparts, they could eventually earn their independence. Unfortunately, the rapid tempo of economic growth, coupled with the pressing labor shortage, proved too alluring an inducement to white colonists and European entrepreneurs: by the middle of the seventeenth century the status of the Negro from the Carolinas to New England began to undergo a marked change. Colonial legislatures in Virginia and Maryland limited the freedom and mobility of Negro labor, and Negro slavery was expressly established in the early laws of the Carolinas. The Massachusetts Bay Colony had nominally recognized slavery in 1641, and other northern and middle colonies similarly accommodated themselves to the phenomenon of Negro bondage in both theory and practice. The English government sustained this trend in part by the establishment of the Royal Adventurers into Africa and the Royal African Company, chartered by the Crown in 1660 and 1672, respectively, and in part by abrogating colonial laws which seemed to interfere with the English slave trade.

The imposition of slavery in the North American colonies was not universally accepted. To begin with, those Negroes who survived the terrible rigors of the "middle passage" from Africa to the New World not infrequently rebelled. Some chose self-inflicted death rather than enslavement, while others mutinied and fought for their freedom. Of those forced to labor in the North American colonies, some fled into the vast wilderness, others chose open rebellion. Slave revolts in New York in 1712, and in Stono, South Carolina, in 1739, for example, confirmed the fact that whites could not automatically enslave Negroes. The threat of such revolts induced colonial legislatures to intensify laws against Negro mobility, the assembling of Negroes, and the right of Negroes to hold property, bear arms, and secure liquor. The religious and humanitarian sentiments of the seventeenth and eighteenth centuries encouraged certain whites to protest openly against slavery. Quaker spokesmen John Woolman and Anthony Benezet were particularly vocal in their opposition. However, then as later, these protestors represented the voice of minority dissent on the question of interracial injustice.

By the end of the colonial period, the phenomenon of Negro slavery had become fastened on the English colonies in America, and the bases had been laid for the economic, political, social, and attitudinal complexities that would characterize the interracial situation in the new United States.

FIRST NEGROES AT JAMESTOWN (1619)

Negroes played a necessary and a vital role in the exploration and conquest of the New World. They participated in the expeditions of Balboa, Cortés, Pizarro, and Coronado, and they actively engaged with the French in the seventeenth-century discovery and settlement of Canada and the Mississippi Valley.

Perhaps the Negro best known for his activities in the exploration of the New World was Estévanico, or "Little Stephen." Estévanico was one of four surviving members of a larger party (originally headed by Pámfilo de Narvaez in 1527) which set out to explore the Florida coast and the lands bordering on the Gulf of Mexico. In 1539, Estévanico served Fray Marcos as guide, scout, and interpreter, and before his death at the hands of Indians, Little Stephen was reported to have reached the Seven Cities of Cibola.

For the English colonies, the great and terrible paradox that was to make the Negro first a servant, then a slave, and finally a second-class citizen began in 1619. In that year the first Negro "servants" were brought to Jamestown, Virginia; ironically, the Virginia colonists established the House of Burgesses that same year. The American people have not yet resolved the inherent contradictions of these two concurrent phenomena: condoning enforced labor and degradation along racial lines on the one hand, and insisting on the institutional framework of participatory government on the other.

In the early years of the seventeenth century, American planters and landlords would have preferred white European settlers and servants who could continue the patterns of labor and servitude familiar to the European rural scene; Negroes were not especially sought nor were they initially classified as slaves. Such classification would become fixed in time. (See Document 4.) Indeed, in 1619, Captain John Smith's casual reference to the first shipment of Negroes hardly portended what this momentous event would mean for the American experience.

DOCUMENT 1
*The first shipment of Negro slaves**

... the *George* also was sent to Newfoundland with the *Cape Merchant;* there she bought fish that defrayed her charges, and made a good voyage in seven weeks. About the last of August, came in a Dutch man-of-war that sold us twenty Negroes; and Japazous, king of Patawomeck, came to James-town to desire two ships to come trade in his river, for a more plentiful year of corn had not been in a long time, yet very contagious, and by the treachery of one Poule, in a manner turned heathen, we were very jealous the savages would surprise us.

PRIVILEGES AND EXEMPTIONS
FOR PATROONS (1629)

Quite unlike twentieth-century, automated America, the seventeenth-century colonial world was one of acute labor shortages. Commercial companies anxious to settle the New World solely for their own profit and the European investors who controlled land in America were understandably eager to establish permanent settlements as quickly as possible in order to begin reaping a steady return. While the English had their headright system and patterns of proprietorship, the Dutch West India Company devised the patroon system. Under this system wealthy individuals were authorized to obtain extensive holdings in New Netherland, in return for their guaranteeing the passage and settlement of at least fifty persons.

While not without some protections and rights, these early

---

* Captaine John Smith, *The Generall Historie of Virginia, New England and the Summer Isles, Vol. I* (Glasgow: James MacLehose & Sons, 1907), pp. 246–47.

settlers were very much under the authority of their sponsors. Experienced in the African slave trade, the Dutch merchants were prepared to aid the settlers by providing black labor, though—as in the case of Virginia—this was not originally viewed as a desired practice or one to be continued indefinitely. Nonetheless, it was clear that the new Negroes were to be of the lowest serving classes.

DOCUMENT 2

Privileges and exemptions for patroons, masters, and private individuals, who will settle any colonies and cattle in New Netherland resolved upon for the service of the General West India Company in New Netherland, and for the benefit of the patroons, masters, and individuals. *

1. Such participants in the said Company as may be inclined to settle any colonies in New Netherland shall be permitted to send in the ships of this Company going thither, three or fours persons to inspect the situation of the country, provided that they, with the officers and ship's company, swear to the articles, so far as they relate to them, and pay for provisions and for passage, going and coming, six stivers per diem (and such as desire to eat in the cabin, twelve stivers); and undertake to be subordinate and give assistance like others, in cases offensive and defensive; and if any ships be taken from the enemy, they shall receive, *pro rata*, their proportions with the ship's company, each according to his quality; that is to say, the colonists eating out of the cabin shall be rated with the sailors, and those who eat in the cabin with those of the Company's people who eat at table and receive the lowest wages.

. . . .

* J. Franklin Jameson, ed., *Narratives of New Netherland, 1609–1664* (New York: Charles Scribner's Sons, 1909), pp. 90–96.

III. All such shall be acknowledged patroons of New Netherland who shall undertake, within the space of four years next after they have given notice to any of the chambers of the Company here, or to the commander or council there, to plant a colony there of fifty souls, upwards of fifteen years old; one-fourth part within one year, and within three years after the sending of the first, making together four years, the remainder, to the full number of fifty persons, to be shipped from hence, on pain, in case of manifest neglect, of being deprived of the privileges obtained; but it is to be observed that the Company reserve the island of the Manhattes to themselves.

. . . .

XIX. That they will not take from the service of the patroons any of their colonists, either man or woman, son or daughter, man-servant or maid-servant; and, though any of these should desire the same, they will not receive them, much less permit them to leave their patroons and enter into the service of another, unless on consent obtained from their patroons in writing, and this for and during so many years as they are bound to their patroons; after the expiration whereof, it shall be in the power of the patroons to send hither all such colonists as will not continue in their service, and not to set them at liberty until then. And any colonist who shall enter into the service of another patroon, or shall, contrary to his contract, betake himself to freedom, we promise to do everything in our power to deliver the same into the hands of his patroon or attorney, that he may be proceeded against according to the customs of this country, as occasion may require.

. . . .

XXX. The Company shall use their endeavors to supply the colonists with as many blacks as they can, on conditions hereafter to be made, in such manner, however, that they shall not be bound or held to do it for a longer time than they shall think proper. . . .

MASSACHUSETTS BODY OF
LIBERTIES (1641)

New England, later a center of abolitionist spirit, early
gave evidence of ambivalence and expediency about matters
of servitude and enforced labor. Like their counterparts in
England, the Massachusetts Bay Puritans were concerned
about defining the limits of authority and establishing general
duties, rights, and privileges for their constituents. The Zion
Wilderness was to serve, in John Winthrop's words, as a
"City on the Hill," a model community of the Elect; but
those who were not members in good standing of the Congre-
gationalist Church were often left to the caprice of the
magistrates. Privileges and immunities were not universal,
as Quakers, Antinomians, and other dissenters would learn.

Section 91 of the Body of Liberties was itself so hedged
with implicit qualifications that Massachusetts found no great
difficulty over the years in accommodating its interests to
the slave trade. Despite the apparent prohibition against
bondage, historians would argue for generations whether
certain persons in a "servant" capacity were actually slaves.

DOCUMENT 3

The Liberties of the Massachusetts Colony
in New England*

The free fruition of such liberties, immunities, and privi-
ledges as humanity, civility, and Christianity call for as due
to every man in his place and proportion without impeach-
ment and infringement has ever been and ever will be the
tranquillity and stability of churches and commonwealths. And
the denial or deprival thereof, the disturbance if not the ruin
of both.

We hold it therefore our duty and safety while we are
about the further establishing of this Government to collect

* Old South Leaflets, No. 164 (Boston: Directors of the Old
South Work, 1905).

and express all such freedoms as for present we foresee may concern us, and our posterity after us, and to ratify them with our solemn consent.

We do therefore this day religiously and unanimously decree and confirm these following rites, liberties, and privileges concerning our churches and civil state to be respectively, impartially, and inviolably enjoyed and observed throughout our jurisdiction forever.

. . . .

Liberties of Foreigners and Strangers

89. If any people of other nations professing the true Christian religion shall flee to us from the tyranny or oppression of their persecutors, or from famin, wars, or the like necessary and compulsory cause, they shall be entertained and succored among us, according to that power and prudence God shall give us.

90. If any ships or other vessels, be it friend or enemy, shall suffer shipwreck upon our coast, there shall be no violence or wrong offered to their persons or goods. But their persons shall be harbored and relieved, and their goods preserved in safety till authority may be certified thereof, and shall take further order therein.

91. There shall never be any bond slavery, villinage or captivity among us unless it be lawful captives taken in just wars, and such strangers as willingly sell themselves or are sold to us. And these shall have all the liberties and Christian usages which the law of God established in Israel concerning such persons do morally require. This exempts none from servitude who shall be judged thereto by authority.

AN ACT CONCERNING NEGROES, MARYLAND (1664)

The harsh realities of a land-rich but labor-scarce economy had become increasingly apparent to the Maryland settlers and to their proprietor, Lord Baltimore. By 1664, the Maryland Colonial Assembly was ready to impose, by force of law, the status of perpetual slavery upon Negro slaves and their offspring. Clear overtones of racism likewise fixed the status of slavery upon the offspring of any freeborn English woman who produced a child by a Negro slave. While Negroes had formerly shared with other servants the opportunities for eventual freedom and independence, laws of this kind during the last third of the seventeenth century marked a sharp turning point in the Negro's legal position and marked the path to bondage, which he would begin walking in colonial America.

DOCUMENT 4

An act concerning Negroes and other slaves*

Be it enacted by the Right Honorable the Lord Proprietary by the advise and consent of the upper and lower house of this present Generall Assembly, that all Negroes or other slaves already within the province, and all Negroes and other slaves to be hereafter imported into the province, shall serve *durante vita*. And all children born of any Negro or other slave shall be slaves as their fathers were, for the term of their lives. And forasmuch as divers freeborn English women, forgetful of their free condition and to the disgrace of our nation, marry Negro slaves, by which also divers suits may arise touching the issue of such women, and a great damage befalls the masters of such Negroes for prevention whereof, for deterring such freeborn women from such shameful matches. Be it further enacted by the authority, advise, and consent aforesaid, that whatsoever freeborn woman shall marry any slave from and after the last day of this present Assembly shall serve the master of such slave during the life of her husband. And that all the issue of such freeborn women so married shall be slaves as their fathers were. And be it further enacted, that all the issues of English or other freeborn women that have already married Negroes shall serve the masters of their parents till they be thirty years of age and no longer.

* *Assembly Proceedings,* September, 1664, Liber WH & L, pp. 28–29, Maryland Archives, I, pp. 533–34.

PROTEST OF THE GERMANTOWN MENNONITES (1688)

Appropriately, William Penn's colony (founded nominally as a haven for the oppressed Quakers and purposefully advertised as tolerant of pluralistic national, ethnic, and religious groups) produced the first recorded protest against the traffic in Negro slaves. The protest of the Germantown Mennonites was grounded on their belief that the slave trade flaunted Christian principles. In the days immediately preceding the Declaration of Independence, the Quakers would once again take the lead in opposing slavery.

DOCUMENT 5

*The first vote against slavery: Resolutions of the Germantown Mennonites**

This is to the monthly meeting held at Richard Worrell's:

These are the reasons why we are against the traffic of men as follows: Is there any that would be done to or handled in this manner? viz., to be sold or made a slave for all the time of his life? How fearful and fainthearted are many at sea when they see a strange vessel, being afraid it should be a Turk, and they should be taken and sold for slaves in Turkey. Now, what is *this* better done than Turks do? Yea, rather it is worse for them which say they are Christians; for we hear that the most part of such Negroes are brought hither against their will and consent, and that many of them are stolen. Now, though they are black, we cannot conceive there is more liberty to have them slaves, as [than] it is to have other white ones. There is a saying that we should do to all men as we would be done to ourselves [it] making no difference what generation, descent, or color they are. And those who steal or rob men, and those who buy or purchase

---

* Minutes of the Monthly Meeting, February 18, 1688, *The Friend*, January 13, 1844; reprinted in George H. Moore, *Notes on the History of Slavery in Massachusetts* (New York: Appleton and Co., 1866) pp. 74–77.

them, are they not all alike? Here is liberty of conscience which is right and reasonable; here ought to be likewise liberty of the body, except of evildoers, which is another case. But to bring men hither, or to rob and sell them against their will, we stand against. In Europe, there are many oppressed for conscience sake; and here there are those oppressed who are of a black color. And we who know that men must not commit adultery—some commit adultery *in* others, separating wives from their husbands, and giving them to others. And some sell the children of these poor creatures to other men. Ah! consider well this thing, you who do it, if you would be done to in this manner—and if it is done according to Christianity! You surpass Holland and Germany in this thing. This makes an ill report in all those countries of Europe where they hear of [it], that the Quakers here handle men as they there handle the cattle. And for that reason some have no mind or inclination to come hither. And who shall maintain your cause or plead for it? Truly, we cannot do so, except that you shall inform us better hereof, viz., that Christians have liberty to practice these things. Pray, what thing in the world can be done worse toward us, than if men should rob or steal us away and sell us for slaves to strange countries, separating husbands from their wives and children. Now this is not done in the manner we would be done to; therefore, we contradict and are against this traffic of men. And we who profess that it is not lawful to steal, must, likewise, avoid purchasing things that are stolen, but rather help to stop this robbing and stealing, if possible. And such men ought to be delivered out of the hands of the robbers and set free, as in Europe. Then is Pennsylvania to have a good report; instead, it now has a bad one, for this sake, in other countries. Especially whereas the Europeans desire to know in what manner *the Quakers* rule in *their* province; and most of them look upon us with an envious eye. But if this is done well, what shall we say is done evil?

If once these slaves (whom they say are such wicked and stubborn men) should join themselves—fight for their freedom and handle their masters and mistresses as they handled them before—will these masters and mistresses take the sword in hand and war against these poor slaves, like, as we are able to believe, some will not refuse to do? Or, have these poor

Negroes not as much right to fight for their freedom as you have to keep them slaves?

Now consider well this thing, if it is good or bad. And in case you find it to be good to handle these blacks in that manner, we desire and require you hereby lovingly, that you may inform us herein, which at this time never was done, viz., that Christians have such a liberty to do so. To the end we shall be satisfied on this point, and satisfy likewise our good friends and acquaintances in our native country, to whom it is a terror, or fearful thing, that men should be handled so in Pennsylvania.

This is from our meeting at Germantown, held of the second month, 1688, to be delivered to the monthly meeting at Richard Worrell's.

GARRET HENDERICH
DERICK OP DE GRAEFF
FRANCIS DANIEL PASTORIUS
ABRAM OP DE GRAEFF

At our monthly meeting, at Dublin, the 30th [of the] second month, 1688, we having inspected the matter above mentioned, and considered of it, we find it so weighty that we think it not expedient for us to meddle with it *here,* but rather commit it to the consideration of the quarterly meeting; tenor of it being related to the truth.

On behalf of the monthly meeting,
JO. HART

THE FIRST ABOLITIONIST TRACT (1700)

It is a commentary on American values that Judge Samuel Sewall is more widely remembered for his part in and later repentance over the Salem Witch Trials than for his careful and logically developed denunciation of Negro enslavement. In his stand against slavery, he based his position on the concept of Christian humanism, as the New England abolitionists would do a century and a half later. Although he firmly believed that slavery was wrong, he still felt that black men were not the equal of whites. In this way, he served as a harbinger of many later critics of slavery who decried slavery as much because of its effects upon the white majority as because of its brutalizing injustices to the Negro. Judge Sewall argued that the inherent immorality of slavery outweighed any conceivable benefits which might result from a system of bondage. His *Selling of Joseph,* based upon an analysis of biblical passages from both the Old and New Testaments, stands as the first abolitionist tract in the American colonies.

DOCUMENT 6

*The Selling of Joseph**

Forasmuch as liberty is in real value next to life, none ought to part with it themselves, or deprive others of it, but upon most mature consideration.

The numerousness of slaves at this day in the province, and the uneasiness of them in their slavery has put many upon thinking whether the foundation of it be firmly and well laid, so as to sustain the vast weight that is built upon it. It is most certain that all men, as they are the sons of Adam, are co-heirs and have equal right to liberty, and all other outward comforts of life. "God hath given the Earth [with all its commodities] unto the Sons of Adam" (Psal. 115:16), "And hath made of one blood all nations of men, for to dwell on all the face of the earth, and hath determined the times before appointed, and the bounds of their habitation: that they should seek the Lord. Forasmuch then as we are the offspring of God," etc. (Acts 17:26, 27, 29) Now, although the title given by the last Adam does infinitely better men's estates, respecting God and themselves, and grants them a most beneficial and inviolable lease under the broad seal of heaven, who were before only tenants at will. Yet through the indulgence of God to our first parents after the fall, the outward estate of all and each of their children remains the same as to one another. So that originally and naturally, there is no such thing as slavery. Joseph was rightfully no more a slave to his brethren than they were to him; and they had no more authority to sell him than they had to slay him. And if

* Reprinted in George H. Moore, *Notes on the History of Slavery in Massachusetts* (New York: Appleton and Co., 1866), pp. 83–87.

they had nothing to do to sell him, the Ishmaelites, bargaining with them and paying down twenty pieces of silver, could not make a title. Neither could Potiphar have any interest in him than the Ishmaelites had. (Gen. 37:20, 27, 28) For he that shall in this case plead alteration of property seems to have forfeited a great part of his own claim to humanity. There is no proportion between twenty pieces of silver and liberty. The commodity itself is the claimer. If Arabian gold be imported in any quantities, most are afraid to meddle with it, though they might have it at easy rates; unless it should have been wrongfully taken from the owners, it should kindle a fire to the consumption of their whole estate. It is a pity there should be more caution used in buying a horse or a little lifeless dust than there is in purchasing men and women: Whereas they are the offspring of God and their liberty is *Auro pretiosior omni.*

And seeing that God has said, "He that stealeth a man, and selleth him, or if he be found in his hand, he shall surely be put to death." (Exod. 21:16) This law being of everlasting equity, wherein man-stealing is ranked among the most atrocious of capital crimes: What louder cry can there be made of that celebrated warning, *Caveat emptor!*

And all things considered, it would be more conducive to the welfare of the province to have white servants for a term of years than to have slaves for life. Few can endure hearing of a Negro's being made free, and indeed they can seldom use their freedom well; yet their continual aspiring after their forbidden liberty renders them unwilling servants. And there is such a disparity in their conditions, color, and hair that they can never embody with us and grow up in orderly families, to the peopling of the land, but still remain in our body politic as a kind of extravasate blood. As many Negro men as there are among us, so many empty places are there in our train bands and the places taken up of men that might make husbands for our daughters. And the sons and daughters of New England would become more like Jacob and Rachel if this slavery were thrust quite out of doors. Moreover, it is too well known what temptations masters are under to connive at the fornication of their slaves, unless they should be obliged to find them wives, or pay their fines. It seems to be practically pleaded that they might be lawless; it is thought much of that the law should have satisfaction for their thefts and other immoralities; by which means holiness to the Lord is more rarely engraven upon this sort of servitude. It is likewise most lamentable to think that in taking Negroes out of Africa, and selling them here, that which God has joined together, men do boldly rend asunder: men from their country, husbands from their wives, parents from their children. How horrible is the uncleanness, mortality, if not murder, that the ships are guilty of that bring great crowds of these miserable men and women. I think when we are be-moaning the barbarous usage of our friends and kinfolk in Africa, it might not be unreasonable to inquire whether we are not culpable in forcing the Africans to become slaves among ourselves. And it may be a question whether all the benefit received by Negro slaves will balance the account of cash laid out upon them, and for the redemption of our own enslaved friends out of Africa. Besides all the persons and estates that have perished there.

Obj. 1. *These blackamoors are of the posterity of Cham, and therefore are under the curse of slavery.* (Gen. 9:25, 26, 27)

Ans. Of all offices, one would not beg this, viz., uncalled for, to be an executioner of the vindictive wrath of God; the extent and duration of which is to us uncertain. If this ever was a commission, how do we know but that it is long since out of date? Many have found it to their cost that a prophetical denunciation of judgment against a person or people would not warrant them to inflict that evil. If it would, Hazael might justify himself in all he did against his master, and the Israelites from 2 Kings 8:10, 12.

But it is possible that by cursory reading, this text may have been mistaken. For Canaan is the person cursed three times over, without any mention of Cham. Good expositors suppose the curse entailed on him, and that this prophesy was accomplished in the extirpation of the Canaanites and in the servitude of the Gibeonites. *Vide Pareum.* Whereas the blackamoors are not descended of Canaan, but of Cush. (Psal. 68:31) "Princes shall come out of Egypt" [Mizraim]. "Ethiopia [Cush] shall soon stretch out her hands unto God." Under these names all Africa may be comprehended, and their promised conversion ought to be prayed for. (Jer. 13:23)

"Can the Ethiopian change his skin?" This shows that black men are the posterity of Cush. Who time out of mind have been distinguished by their color. And for want of the truth, Ovid assigns a fabulous cause of it:

> *Sanguine tum credunt in corpora summa vocato*
> *Æthiopum populos nigrum traxisse colorem.*
> *Metamorph. lib. 2*

Obj. 2. *The Negroes are brought out of a pagan country into places where the gospel is preached.*

Ans. Evil must not be done that good may come of it. The extraordinary and comprehensive benefit accruing to the church of God, and to Joseph personally, did not rectify his brethren's sale of him.

Obj. 3. *The Africans have wars one with another: our ships bring lawful captives taken in those wars.*

Ans. For aught is known, their wars are much such as were between Jacob's sons and their brother Joseph. If they be between town and town, provincial or national, every war is upon one side unjust. An unlawful war can't make lawful captives. And by receiving, we are in danger of promoting and partaking in their barbarous cruelties. I am sure if some gentlemen should go down to the Brewsters to take the air, and fish, and a stronger party from Hull should surprise them and sell them for slaves to a ship outward bound, they would think themselves unjustly dealt with, both by sellers and buyers. And yet it is to be feared, we have no other kind of title to our Negroes. "Therefore all things whatsoever ye would that men should do to you, do you even so to them: for this is the law and the prophets." (Matt. 7:12)

Obj. 4. *Abraham had servants bought with his money and born in his house.*

Ans. Until the circumstances of Abraham's purchase be recorded, no argument can be drawn from it. In the meantime, charity obliges us to conclude that he knew it was lawful and good.

It is observable that the Israelites were strictly forbidden the buying or selling of one another for slaves. (Levit. 25:39, 46; Jer. 34:8–22) And God gauged His blessing in lieu of any loss they might conceit they suffered thereby. (Deut. 15:18) And since the partition wall is broken down, inordinate self-love should likewise be demolished. God expects that Christians should be of a more ingenuous and benign frame of spirit. Christians should carry it to all the world, as the Israelites were to carry it toward one another. And for men obstinately to persist in holding their neighbors and brethren under the rigor of perpetual bondage seems to be no proper way of gaining assurance that God has given them spiritual freedom. Our Blessed Saviour has altered the measures of the ancient love song, and set it to a most excellent new tune, which all ought to be ambitious of learning. (Matt. 5:43, 44; John 13:34) These Ethiopians, as black as they are, seeing they are the sons and daughters of the first Adam, the brethren and sisters of the last Adam, and the offspring of God, they ought to be treated with a respect agreeable. . . .

REGULATIONS CONCERNING NEGROES, NEW JERSEY (1704)

Colonial legislatures were careful to state the conditions regulating both the conduct of the Negro and conduct toward the Negro. In many instances these statutes carried harsh physical penalties for the slave who exceeded certain bounds, and provided severe financial penalties for the freeman who traded with, made off with, or even associated with the slave beyond the prescribed limits. New Jersey was not alone in detailing these regulations, and the act that follows is an adequate representation of the Negro's position in the colonies.

In 1709, the Lords Commissioners for Trade and Plantations considered the New Jersey enactment and recommended its repeal on the ground that it called for "inhumane penalties on Negroes."

DOCUMENT 7

An act for regulating Negro, Indian, and mulatto slaves within this province of New Jersey[*]

Whereas it is found by daily experience, that Negro, Indian, and mulatto slaves, under pretense of trade, or liberty of traffic, frequently steal from their masters, mistresses, or others what they expose to sale at a difference from their habitations; and it being a known truth, that without a receiver, the thief would soon desert his practice, be it therefore enacted by the Governor, Council, and Assembly now met and assembled, and by the authority of the same, that all and every person or persons inhabiting within this province, who shall at any time after publication hereof buy, sell, barter, trade, or traffic with any Negro, Indian, or mulatto slaves, for any rum, wine, beer, cider, or other strong drink, or any other chattels, goods, wares, or commodities whatsoever within this province of Nova Casaria, or New Jersey, shall pay for the first offense five pounds, and for the second and every other offense, ten pounds current money of this province, one-half to the informer, the other half to the use of the poor of that place where the fact is committed; to be recovered by action of debt in any of Her Majesty's Courts of Record within this province where the fact shall arise.

And be it further enacted by the authority aforesaid, that if any Negro, Indian, or mulatto slaves of or belonging to any other province, without license under the hand of his or her master or mistress, shall be taken up by any person within this province, he, she, or they so taken up shall be whipped at the public whipping post belonging to the place where the said Negro, Indian, or mulatto slaves shall be taken up, not exceeding twenty lashes on the bare back, and to be committed by a warrant from a justice of the peace where the fact shall arise to the jail of that county; and the person so taking them up and carrying them to be whipped, shall have for his reward the sum of ten shillings for each slave, paid by the master or mistress of the said slaves, and to remain

---

[*] *Laws of New Jersey*, c. IX, 1704.

in prison till it be paid, with all other charges that shall accrue thereby.

And be it further enacted by the authority aforesaid, that if any Negro, Indian, or mulatto slave shall steal to the value of sixpence, or above, and under the sum of five shillings, and be thereof convicted before two justices of the peace, one whereof to be of quorum, upon the oath or solemn affirmation of one or more witnesses, such Negro, Indian, or mulatto slave shall be whipped on the bare back, at the public whipping place, with forty lashes by the constable of such township or place where the offense was committed, or by such person as he shall appoint. And, that if any Negro, Indian, or mulatto slave shall steal to the value of five shillings, or above, and under the sum of forty shillings, and be thereof convicted in manner as aforesaid, such Negro, Indian, or mulatto slave shall be whipped on the bare back with forty stripes, as aforesaid, and be likewise burned with a hot iron on the most visible part of the left cheek, near the nose, with the letter T, by the constable, as aforesaid; the said constable shall receive for the whipping of each Negro, Indian, or mulatto slave five shillings, and for burning each Negro, Indian, or mulatto slave ten shillings, to be paid by the master or mistress of the said slave; and in default of payment, to be levied by warrant from any justice of the peace, out of the goods of the said master or mistress; and that every constable who shall neglect or refuse to do his duty herein shall forfeit the sum of forty shillings, to be levied by warrant of any justice of the peace, directed to whom he shall appoint, out of the goods and chattels of the said constable.

And if any Negro, Indian, or mulatto slave shall attempt by force or persuasion to ravish or have carnal knowledge of any white woman, maid or child, and be thereof convicted by the verdict of twelve men of the neighborhood before two justices of the peace, one whereof to be of the quorum, such Indian, Negro, or mulatto shall be castrated at the care and charge of his master or mistress, and the Negro to continue in jail at the charge of his master or mistress till execution be performed.

And whereas the baptizing of slaves is thought by some to be a sufficient reason to set them at liberty, which being a groundless opinion and prejudicial to the inhabitants of this province, be it further enacted by the authority aforesaid, that the baptizing of any Negro, Indian, or mulatto slave shall not be any reason or cause for setting them, or any of them, at liberty; nor shall they nor any of them have or procure their or any of their liberty by virtue thereof.

And be it enacted by the authority aforesaid, that all the children that have been or shall be born in the county of such Negro, Indian, or mulatto slaves as have been formerly or may hereafter be set at liberty, and all their posterity shall be and are hereby forever after rendered incapable of purchasing or inheriting any lands and tenements within this province.

And be it further enacted by the authority aforesaid, that any person or persons within this province, who shall knowingly keep or entertain any Negro, Indian, or mulatto slave in his or their house, or otherwise, for above the space of two hours, without their master's or mistress' leave, or some other reasonable cause or occasion, shall forfeit the sum of one shilling for each hour to the master or mistress of such slave, to be recovered before any one of Her Majesty's justices of the peace, in the manner aforesaid; and if above forty shillings, then before the Court of Common Pleas, as aforesaid.

SMITH V. BROWN AND COOPER (1705)

While the slave trade was not abolished in England until 1807, and slavery was not abolished in the Empire until 1833, the English courts had rendered numerous judgments against the existence of slavery during the period preceding the American Revolution.

Three legal maxims became significant in the English position on slavery. The first of these was that "England was too pure an Air for Slaves to breathe in." (*Cartwright's Case*, 2 Rushworth's Historical Collections 468 [1569].) This pronouncement was quoted by Hargrave, counsel for the Negro, in the *Somerset* case. (See Document 12.) The second of these maxims, "Once free for an hour, free for ever!" dates back to the early days of the English system of villeinage.

The most significant of the three maxims embodied the principle that a slave was free the moment he set foot on English soil. This maxim lay at the heart of the *Somerset* case. It had been set forth initially by Lord Chief Justice John Holt in *Smith* v. *Brown and Cooper*, reproduced here, and in the companion case of *Smith* v. *Gould*, 2 Salk. 666, 97 Eng. Rep. 567 (1705), 2 Ld. Raym. 1274, 92 Eng. Rep. 338 (1705). However, Justice Holt was quick to explain that the law in England would have no effect upon the existence of slavery in Virginia.

DOCUMENT 8

*Smith v. Brown and Cooper**

The plaintiff declared in an *indebitatus assumpsit* [a suit alleging debt] for twenty pounds for a Negro sold by the plaintiff to the defendant, *viz.* . . . and verdict for the plaintiff; and, on motion in arrest of judgment, Holt, C. J. held, that as soon as a Negro comes into England, he becomes free: one may be a villein in England, but not a slave.

Et per Powell, J.: In a villein the owner has a property, but it is an inheritance; in a ward he has a property, but it is a chattel real; the law took no notice of a Negro.

Holt, C. J.: You should have averred in the declaration, that the sale was in Virginia, and, by laws of that country, Negroes are saleable; for the laws of England do not extend to Virginia. Being a conquered country, their law is what the King pleases, and we cannot take notice of it but as set forth. Therefore he directed that the plaintiff should amend, and the declaration should be made, that the defendant was indebted to the plaintiff for a Negro sold here at London, but that the said Negro at the time of sale was in Virginia, and that Negroes, by the laws and statutes of Virginia, are saleable as chattels.

Then the Attorney General coming in, said, they were inheritances, and transferrable by deed, and not without: and nothing was done.

* 2 Salk. 666, 2 Ld. Raym. 1274, 91 Eng. Rep. 566 (1705).

THE ASSIENTO (1713)

Signed in 1713, the Treaty of Utrecht ended Queen Anne's War, known in England as the War of the Spanish Succession. It was that conflict which marked the beginning of the end of the French empire in North America, and the beginning of a period of more than two hundred years in which England was the world's one great seapower.

By the terms of the treaty, England received Newfoundland, Acadia (Nova Scotia), and the Hudson Bay region from France, and Gibraltar and Minorca from Spain.

As a prelude to the treaty, England and Spain signed the Assiento (*El Pacto del Assiento de Negro*) in March, 1713. Under this agreement, British subjects were granted the right to provide Negro slaves for Spanish America.

DOCUMENT 9

*The Assiento, or contract, for allowing to the subjects of Great Britain the liberty of importing Negroes into Spanish America**

The Assiento adjusted between their Britannic and Catholic Majesties for the English Company's obliging itself to supply the Spanish West Indies with black slaves for the term of thirty years, to commence on the first day of May of this present year, 1713, and to end on the like day in the year 1743.

The King

Whereas the Assiento agreed on with the Royal Guinea Company, settled in France, for the introducing of Negro

---

* Signed by the Catholic king at Madrid, the twenty-sixth day of March, 1713. Reprinted from the copy published by the Queen's authority; Charles Jenkinson, compiler, *A Collection of All the Treaties of Peace, Alliance, and Commerce, between Great Britain and Other Powers, from the Treaty at Munster in 1648, to the Treaties Signed at Paris in 1783*, Vol. I, 1648–1713 (London: J. Debrett, 1785), p. 375–99.

slaves into the Indies, is determined; and the Queen of Great Britain, being desirous of coming into this commerce, and in her name the English Company, as is stipulated in the preliminaries of the peace, and that this Assiento should continue for the time and space of thirty years; Don Manuel Menasses Gilligan, deputed by Her Majesty of Great Britain, did, in pursuance thereof, put into my hands a draft, made for that purpose, containing forty-two articles, for the regulating of this contract, which I referred to the consideration of a junta of three ministers of my Council of the Indies, that upon perusal thereof, they might report to me what should occur to them upon each article or condition. Which being done, and several points remaining upon this examination undetermined and controverted, I referred it back to another junta; and being fully informed of the whole matter, notwithstanding the objections made by both juntas, it being my intention to conclude and finish this Assiento, with all possible condescention and complacency towards the Queen of Great Britain, I have thought fit, by my royal decree of the twelfth of this present month, to admit and approve of the said forty-two articles contained in the forementioned draft, in the manner hereafter specified, with the enlargement, which over and above I have of my own free will resolved to grant to the said Company by my said decree. All which is in the manner following:

1. First then, to procure by this means a mutual and reciprocal advantage to the sovereigns and subjects of both crowns, Her British Majesty does offer and undertake for the persons, whom she shall name and appoint, that they shall oblige and charge themselves with the bringing into the West Indies of America, belonging to His Catholic Majesty, in the space of the said thirty years, to commence on the first day of May, one thousand seven hundred and thirteen, and determine on the like day, which will be in the year one thousand seven hundred and forty-three, viz., one hundred and forty-four thousand Negroes, *piezas de India,* of both sexes and of all ages, at the rate of four thousand and eight hundred Negroes, *piezas de India,* in each of the said thirty years, with this condition, that the persons who shall go to the West Indies to take care of the concerns of the Assiento shall avoid giving any offense, for in such case they shall be prosecuted and punished in the same manner as they would

have been in Spain, if the like misdemeanors had been committed there.

2. That for each Negro, *pieza de India,* of the regular standard of seven quarters, not being old or defective, according to what has been practiced and established hitherto in the Indies, the assientists shall pay thirty-three pieces of eight (*escudos*) and one-third of a piece of eight, in which sum shall be accounted to be, and shall be comprehended, all and all manner of duties of *alcavala, siza, union de armas, boqueron,* or any other duty whatsoever, of importation or regalia, that now are, or hereafter shall be imposed, belonging to His Catholic Majesty, so that nothing more shall be demanded; and if any should be taken by the governors, royal officers, or other ministers, they shall be made good to the assientists on account of the duties which they are to pay to His Catholic Majesty, of thirty-three and one-third pieces of eight, as aforesaid, the same being made appear by an authentic certificate, which shall not be denied by any public notary, thereunto required on the part of the assientists; for which purpose a general order (*cédula*) shall be issued in the most ample form.

. . . .

6. That the said assientists, after they shall have imported the four thousand eight hundred Negroes yearly, according to their contract, if they find it necessary for His Catholic Majesty's service, and that of his subjects, to import a greater number, they shall have liberty to do it during the first twenty-five years of this contract (for as much as in the five last years they shall import no more than the four thousand eight hundred agreed upon); with condition that they shall pay no more than sixteen pieces of eight and two-thirds of a piece of eight for all duties on each Negro, *pieza de India,* which they shall import, over and above the said four thousand eight hundred, that being half of thirty-three pieces of eight, and one-third above mentioned; and this payment also shall be made in this court.

7. That the said assientists shall be at liberty to employ, in this commerce for the carrying of their cargoes, Her Majesty of Great Britain's own ships, or those of her subjects, or any belonging to His Catholic Majesty's subjects (paying

them their freight, and with the consent of their owners), navigated with English or Spanish mariners, at their choice, care being taken that neither the commanders of those ships employed by the assientists, nor the mariners, do give any offense, or cause any scandal to the exercise of the Roman Catholic religion, under the penalties and pursuant to the regulations established by the first article of this Assiento. And also it shall be lawful for the said assientists, and they shall have power to introduce their black slaves contracted for into all the ports of the North Sea, and of Buenos Aires, in any of the aforementioned ships, in like manner as has been granted to any former assientists, however, always with this assurance, that neither the commanders nor seamen shall occasion any scandal to the Roman Catholic religion, under the penalties already mentioned.

• • • •

19. That the said assientists, their factors and agents, shall have power to navigate and import their Negro slaves, according to their contract, to all the northern ports of His Catholic Majesty's West Indies, including the river of Plata, with prohibition to all others, whether subjects of the crown or strangers, to carry and introduce thither any Negroes, under the penalties established by the laws that relate to this contract of trade; and His Catholic Majesty obliges himself by his faith and royal word to maintain the said assientists in the entire and full possession and performance of all the articles thereof, during the time agreed on, without allowing or conniving at anything that may be contrary to the punctual and exact fulfilling thereof, His Majesty considering it as his own concern; with this condition, that they shall not import into the said river of Plata, or Buenos Aires, more than the twelve hundred *piezas de negroes* allowed by the eighth article.

20. That in case the said assientists be molested in the execution and performance of this Assiento, and that their proceedings and rights be disturbed by way of suits at law, or in any other manner whatsoever, His Catholic Majesty declares that he will reserve to himself alone the cognizance thereof, and of all causes that may be moved thereupon, with an inhibition to all and whatsoever judges and justices to take to themselves the examination and cognizance of the

said causes, or of the suits, omissions, or defects that may happen in the performance of this Assiento.

. . . .

35. For the refreshing and preserving in health the Negro slaves which they shall import into the West Indies, after so long and painful voyage, and to prevent any contagious illness or distemper among them, the factors of this Assiento shall be allowed to hire such parcels of land as they shall think fit, in the neighborhood of the places where the factories shall be established, in order to cultivate the said lands and make plantations, in which they may raise fresh provisions for their relief and subsistence; which cultivating and improvement is to be performed by the inhabitants of the country and the Negro slaves, and not by any others, nor may any ministers of His Catholic Majesty hinder them, provided they keep to this rule. . . .

SLAVERY IN GEORGIA: FROM PROHIBITION TO ACCEPTANCE (1734–1750)

Georgia, the last of the original thirteen colonies, was established in 1732 as a haven for the indebted and oppressed. It was also seen by the Crown as an advantageous buffer colony against Spanish incursions into the Carolinas from the South.

In 1734, the Georgia Trustees, resident in England, submitted an enactment (accepted by the Crown) "for rendering the Colony of Georgia more Defensible by Prohibiting the Importation and use of Black Slaves or Negroes into the same." (*Colonial Records of Georgia*, I, 48–52.) Four years later, the Georgia settlers, arguing on the basis of the benefits that slave labor had brought to neighboring colonies, petitioned the Trustees to lift the ban on the importation and use of slaves. Their plea was grounded on the prediction of impending ruin if such action were not taken and on the optimistic assumption that Negro slaves would make a considerable difference in the economic prospects of the colony. Certain that the change would harm the colony, the Trustees denied the petition. It was their view that the only group which would benefit from such a step would be the slave traders.

In 1750, the Trustees finally yielded to the pleas for the importation of Negroes into Georgia—but only under certain conditions. They required compliance with a set of regulations, including the registration of all Negroes and the setting of a ratio quota between the number of Negroes and the number of white male servants capable of bearing arms. The new code also contained provisions prohibiting interracial marriage and insisting upon religious instruction for all Negro slaves. One of the reasons why it was no longer possible to bar Negroes from the colony was the fact that many settlers had migrated from South Carolina and brought their own Negro slaves into Georgia.

DOCUMENT 10

An act for repealing an act . . . and for per-
mitting the importation and use of . . .
[black slaves or Negroes] in the colony,
under proper restrictions and regulations
*. . . (1750)**

May it please Your Majesty.

* * * *

Whereas an act was passed by His Majesty in council, in the eighth year of his reign, entitled "an act for rendering the Colony of Georgia more Defensible by Prohibiting the Importation and use of Black Slaves or Negroes into the same," by which act the importation and use of black slaves or Negroes in the said colony was absolutely prohibited and forbid, under the penalty therein mentioned. And whereas at the time of passing the said act, the said colony of Georgia, being in its infancy, the introduction of black slaves or Negroes would have been of dangerous consequence; but at present it may be a benefit to the said colony and a convenience and encouragement to the inhabitants thereof to permit the importation and use of them into the said colony,

---

* *Colonial Records of Georgia*, I, pp. 56–62.

under proper restrictions and regulations, without danger to the said colony, as the late war has been happily concluded and a general peace established. Therefore, we, the trustees for establishing the colony of Georgia in America, humbly beseech Your Majesty that it may be enacted. And be it enacted, that the said act and every clause and article therein contained be from henceforth repealed and made void and of no effect. And be it further enacted, that from and after the first day of January, in the year of Our Lord one thousand seven hundred and fifty, it shall and may be lawful to import or bring black slaves or Negroes into the province of Georgia in America and to keep and use the same therein, under the restrictions and regulations hereinafter mentioned and directed to be observed concerning the same. And for that purpose be it further enacted, that from and after the said first day of January, in the year of Our Lord one thousand seven hundred and fifty, it shall and may be lawful for every person inhabiting and holding and cultivating lands within the said province of Georgia and having and constantly keeping one white man-servant on his own lands, capable of bearing arms and aged between sixteen and sixty-five years, to have and keep four male Negroes or blacks upon his plantation there; and for every person inhabiting and holding and cultivating lands within the said province of Georgia and having and constantly keeping two white men-servants, capable of bearing arms and aged between sixteen and sixty-five years, to have and keep eight male Negroes or blacks upon his plantation there; and so in proportion to the number of such white men-servants, capable of bearing arms and of such age as aforesaid, as shall be kept by every person within the said province. And be it further enacted, that every person who shall from and after the said first day of January, in the year of Our Lord one thousand seven hundred and fifty, have and keep more than four male Negroes or blacks to every such male servant as aforesaid, contrary to the intent and true meaning of this act, shall forfeit the sum of ten pounds sterling money of Great Britain for every such male Negro or black which he shall have and keep above the said number, and shall also forfeit the further sum of five pounds of like money for each month after, during which he shall retain and keep such male Negro or black; the said several sums of ten pounds and five pounds to be recovered and applied in such manner as is hereinafter mentioned. And be it further enacted, that no artificer within the said province of Georgia (coopers only excepted) shall take any Negro or black as an apprentice, nor shall any planter or planters within the said province lend or let out to any other planter or planters within the same, any Negro or Negroes, black or blacks to be employed otherwise than in manuring and cultivating their plantations in the country. And be it further enacted, that if any proprietor or proprietors of Negroes or blacks, which shall be imported or brought into or used within the said province, shall inflict any chastisement endangering the limb of a Negro or black, shall for the first offense forfeit not less than the sum of five pounds sterling money of Great Britain, and for the second offense not less than the sum of ten pounds of like money, to be recovered and applied in such manner as is hereinafter mentioned. But in the case of murder of a Negro or black, the criminal [is] to be tried according to the laws of Great Britain. And be it further enacted, that all and every Negro and Negroes, black and blacks, which shall be imported into or born within the said province of Georgia shall be registered in a proper office or offices to be kept for that purpose within the said province, and that no sale of any such Negro or Negroes, black or blacks, shall be good or valid unless the same be duly registered as aforesaid. And that inquisitions shall be made and taken once in every year (or oftener if need be), into the several registers thereof, by juries to be impaneled for that purpose, within the several districts of the said province, who shall immediately after such inquisition make their several reports and returns to the President and magistrates of the said province. And whereas permitting ships with Negroes or blacks to send them on shore when ill of contagious distempers (particularly the yellow fever) must be of the most dangerous consequence. Therefore, for the prevention of so great a calamity be it further enacted, that no ship which shall bring any Negroes or blacks to the said province shall land any Negro or Negroes, black or blacks, within the said province until such ship shall have been visited by the proper officer or officers of the said province for the purpose, and shall have obtained a certificate of health. And that no ship which shall come to the said province with Negroes or blacks shall come nearer to the said province than Cockspur, at the mouth of the River Savannah, but that every such ship shall first anchor and remain there until such ship shall have been visited by the proper officer or officers. And if upon inspection any such ship shall be found to be infected, such ship shall perform such quarantine in Tybee Creek, in the River Savannah, as by the President and assistants of the said province shall be from time to time ordered and directed. And to the end that due care may be taken of the crews of such infected ships and of the Negroes brought therein be it further enacted, that a lazaretto be forthwith built within the said province, under the direction and inspection of the President and magistrates thereof, on the west side of Tybee Island, in the said River Savannah, for the use and convenience of the said colony, where the whole crews of such infected ships and the Negroes brought therein may be conveniently lodged and assisted with medicines and accommodated with refreshments for their more speedy recovery; such medicines and refreshments to be provided at the expense of the captain of the ship. And in case any master of a ship shall attempt to land any Negroes in any other part of the colony, except as aforesaid, he shall for the said offense forfeit the sum of five hundred pounds sterling money of Great Britain. And in case he shall land any Negroes before his ship is visited and the proper certificate of health obtained, or not perform the full quarantine directed, he shall for the said offense not only forfeit the like sum of five hundred pounds, but also the Negroes on board the said ship. The said forfeitures to be recovered and applied in such manner as is hereinafter mentioned. And be it further enacted, that if any person or persons shall not permit or even oblige his or their Negro or Negroes, black or blacks, to attend at some time on the Lord's Day, for instruction in the Christian religion, in such place and places as the Protestant ministers of the gospel within the said province shall be able to attend them, contiguous to the residence of such Negro or Negroes, black or blacks, such person or persons shall for every such offense forfeit the sum of ten pounds sterling money of Great Britain, to be recovered and applied in such manner as is hereinafter mentioned. And be it further enacted, that all and every intermarriage and intermarriages between the white people and the Negroes or blacks within the said province shall be deemed unlawful marriages, and the same are hereby declared to be absolutely null and void. And that if any white man shall be convicted of lying with a female Negro or black, or if any white woman shall be convicted of lying with a male Negro or black, such white man or woman so offending shall on every such conviction forfeit the sum of ten pounds sterling money of Great Britain, to be recovered and applied in such manner as is hereinafter mentioned. Or otherwise, such white man or woman so convicted shall receive such corporal punishment as the court, before whom such conviction shall be, shall judge proper to inflict, and such male or female, black or Negro, shall also receive such corporal punishment as the said court shall order and direct. And whereas great advantages may arise to the inhabitants of the said colony of Georgia and to the British nation by the culture and raising of silk within the said province be it therefore further enacted, that every planter within the said colony who shall at anytime hereafter have or keep any male Negroes or blacks shall have and keep for every four male Negroes or blacks one female Negro or black, and so in proportion to such greater number of male Negroes or blacks as every such planter shall keep. And that every such planter shall instruct their female Negroes or blacks, or cause them to be well instructed in the art of winding or reeling silk from the silk balls or cocoons, and shall at the proper season in every year send their female Negroes or blacks to Savannah in order to learn the said art, or to such other place or places within the said province as the President and magistrates thereof shall from time to time appoint for that purpose. . . .

BLACKSTONE'S COMMENTARIES ON THE LAW OF ENGLAND (1765–1769)

It was a lawyer—Thomas Jefferson—who drafted the Declaration of Independence, and lawyers were prominent in writing the Constitution of the United States. The principal book which these lawyers read and studied was Sir William Blackstone's *Commentaries on the Law of England*. The influence of these writings on the entire body of American jurisprudence cannot be overestimated. Blackstone began lecturing in law at Oxford, in 1753; and his *Commentaries*, published in four volumes from 1765 to 1769, were the final form of those lectures.

In only three places in his *Commentaries* did Blackstone present legal principles applicable to slavery. Setting forth the "Absolute Rights of Individuals," he emphasized the principle that a slave became free as soon as he landed on English soil. This followed the decision of Lord Holt in *Smith* v. *Brown and Cooper*. (See Document 8.) In discussing the law of "Master and Servant," Blackstone took the position that slavery contracts were invalid. Finally, in commenting on "The Countries Subject to the Laws of England," he stated that the common law of England did not automatically extend to the colonies. Thus, despite Blackstone's arguments that slavery was violative of the English spirit of liberty and the English law of contracts, he held that the institution of slavery could be legally maintained in America.

DOCUMENT 11

*Of the Absolute Rights of Individuals**

The idea and practice of this political or civil liberty flourish in their highest vigor in these kingdoms, where it falls little short of perfection and can only be lost or destroyed by the folly or demerits of its owner—the legislature, and of course the laws of England, being peculiarly adapted to the preservation of this inestimable blessing, even in the meanest subject. Very different from the modern constitutions of other states on the continent of Europe, and from the genius of the imperial law, which in general are calculated to vest an arbitrary and despotic power, of controlling the actions of the subject, in the prince, or in a few grandees. And this spirit of liberty is so deeply implanted in our constitution, and rooted even in our very soil, that a slave or a Negro, the moment he lands in England, falls under the protection of the laws, and so far becomes a freeman; though the master's right to his service may *possibly* still continue.

* *Chitty's Blackstone*, Bk. I, Chap. I (Philadelphia: Lippincott, 1908), pp. 126-27.

Of Master and Servant[*]

In discussing the relation of master and servant, I shall first consider the several sorts of servants, and how this relation is created and destroyed; secondly, the effect of this relation with regard to the parties themselves; and, lastly, its effect with regard to other persons.

1. As to the several sorts of servants: I have formerly observed that pure and proper slavery does not, nay cannot, subsist in England: such I mean, whereby an absolute and unlimited power is given to the master over the life and fortune of the slave. And indeed it is repugnant to reason and the principles of natural law that such a state should subsist anywhere. The three origins of the right of slavery, assigned by Justinian, are all of them built upon false foundations. As, first, slavery is held to arise *jure gentium,* from a state of captivity in war, whence slaves are called *mancipia, quasi manu capti.* The conqueror, say the civilians, had a right to the life of his captive and, having spared that, has a right to deal with him as he pleases. But it is an untrue position, when taken generally, that by the law of nature, or nations, a man may kill his enemy: he has only a right to kill him in particular cases, in cases of absolute necessity, for self-defense; and it is plain this absolute necessity did not subsist, since the victor did not actually kill him, but made him a prisoner. War is itself justifiable only on principles of self-preservation, and therefore it gives no other right over prisoners but merely to disable them from doing harm to us, by confining their persons: much less can it give a right to kill, torture, abuse, plunder, or even to enslave an enemy when the war is over. Since therefore the right of *making* slaves by captivity depends on a supposed right of slaughter, that foundation failing, the consequence drawn from it must fail likewise. But, secondly, it is said that slavery may begin *jure civili;* when one man sells himself to another. This, if only meant of contracts to serve or work for another, is very just: but when applied to strict slavery, in the sense of the laws of old Rome or modern Barbary, it is also impossible. Every sale implies a

---

[*] *Chitty's Blackstone,* Bk. I, Chap. XIV (Philadelphia: Lippincott, 1908), pp. 423–25.

price, a *quid pro quo*, an equivalent given to the seller in lieu of what he transfers to the buyer: but what equivalent can be given for life and liberty, both of which, in absolute slavery, are held to be in the master's disposal? His property also, the very price he seems to receive, devolves *ipso facto* to his master the instant he becomes his slave. In this case, therefore, the buyer gives nothing and the seller receives nothing: of what validity then can a sale be, which destroys the very principles upon which all sales are founded? Lastly, we are told, that besides these two ways by which slaves *fiunt*, or are acquired, they may also be hereditary: *servi nascuntur;* the children of acquired slaves are *jure naturæ*, by a negative kind of birthright, slaves also. But this, being built on the two former rights, must fall together with them. If neither captivity nor the sale of one's self can by the law of nature and reason reduce the parent to slavery, much less can they reduce the offspring.

Upon these principles, the law of England abhors and will not endure the existence of slavery within this nation; so that when an attempt was made to introduce it, by Statute 1 Edw. VI. c. 3 [1547], which ordained that all idle vagabonds should be made slaves, and fed upon bread and water, or small drink and refuse meat, should wear a ring of iron around their necks, arms, or legs, and should be compelled by beating, chaining, or otherwise, to perform the work assigned them, were it never so vile, the spirit of the nation could not brook his condition, even in the most abandoned rogues; and therefore this statute was repealed two years afterwards. And now it is laid down that a slave or Negro, the instant he lands in England, becomes a freeman; that is, the law will protect him in the enjoyment of his person and his property. Yet, with regard to any right which the master may have lawfully acquired to the perpetual service of John or Thomas, this will remain exactly in the same state as before: for this is no more than the same state of subjection for life, which every apprentice submits to for the space of seven years, or sometimes for a longer term. Hence, too, it follows, that the infamous and unchristian practice of withholding baptism from Negro servants, unless they should thereby gain their liberty, is totally without foundation, as well as without excuse. The law of England acts upon general and extensive principles: it gives liberty, rightly understood, that is, protection to a Jew, a Turk, or a heathen, as well as to those who profess the true religion of Christ; and it will not dissolve a civil obligation between master and servant on account of the alteration of faith in either of the parties: but the slave is entitled to the same protection in England before, as after, baptism; and, whatever service the heathen Negro owed of right to his American master, by general not by local law, the same, whatever it be, is he bound to render when brought to England and made a Christian.

*Of the countries subject to the laws of England**

Plantations or colonies in distant countries are either such where the lands are claimed by right of occupancy only, by finding them desert and uncultivated, and peopling them from the mother country, or where, when already cultivated, they have been either gained by conquest or ceded to us by treaties. And both these rights are founded upon the law of nature, or at least upon that of nations. But there is a difference between these two species of colonies, with respect to the laws by which they are bound. For it has been held, that if an uninhabited country be discovered and planted by English subjects, all the English laws then in being, which are the birthright of every subject, are immediately there in force. But this must be understood with very many and very great restrictions. Such colonists carry with them only so much of the English law as is applicable to their own situation and the condition of an infant colony; such, for instance, as the general rules of inheritance and of protection from personal injuries. The artificial refinements and distinctions incident to the property of a great and commercial people, the laws of police and revenue (such especially as are enforced by penalties), the mode of maintenance for the established clergy, the jurisdiction of spiritual courts, and a multitude of other provisions are neither necessary nor convenient for them, and therefore are not in force. What shall be admitted and what rejected, at what times, and under

---

* *Chitty's Blackstone* (Philadelphia: Lippincott, 1908), Intro., Sec. 4, pp. 106–08.

what restrictions, must, in case of dispute, be decided in the first instance by their own provincial judicature, subject to the revision and control of the king in council: the whole of their constitution being also liable to be new-modeled and reformed by the general superintending power of the legislature in the mother country. But in conquered or ceded countries, that have already laws of their own, the king may indeed alter and change those laws; but, till he does actually change them, the ancient laws of the country remain, unless such as are against the law of God, as in the case of an infidel country. Our American plantations are principally of this latter sort, being obtained in the last century either by right of conquest and driving out the natives (with what natural justice I shall not at present inquire), or by treaties. And therefore the common law of England, as such, has no allowance or authority there, they being no part of the mother country, but distinct, though dependent, dominions. They are subject, however, to the control of the parliament; though (like Ireland, Man, and the rest) not bound by any acts of parliament, unless particularly named.

THE SOMERSET CASE (1772)

Reported variously as the *Somerset case*, *Somersett's Case*, the *Case of James Sommersett*, and *Somerset v. Stewart*, this was the most significant and far-reaching decision on slavery ever handed down by an English court.

Rendered in 1772, by Lord Chief Justice William Murray Mansfield, it freed the 14,000 Negro slaves then in Great Britain and ended the auction sales of human beings in the British Isles.

The court took the position that slavery, by its very nature, was so odious that it could not exist in the absence of a "positive law" creating such an institution. This decision was well known to the colonial bar on the eve of the Declaration of Independence.

DOCUMENT 12

*Somerset v. Stewart**

[*The Facts*]

On the third of December, 1771, affidavits were made by Thomas Walklin, Elizabeth Cade, and John Marlow that James Sommersett, a Negro, was confined in irons on board a ship called the *Ann and Mary*, John Knowles commander, lying in the Thames, and bound for Jamaica; and Lord Mansfield, on an application supported by these affidavits, allowed a writ of habeas corpus, directed to Mr. Knowles, and requiring him to return the body of Sommersett before his lordship with the cause of detainer.

Mr. Knowles, on the ninth of December, produced the body of Sommersett before Lord Mansfield and returned for cause of detainer, that Sommersett was the Negro slave of Charles Steuart, Esq., who had delivered Sommersett into Mr. Knowles's custody in order to carry him to Jamaica, and there sell him as a slave. Affidavits were also made by Mr. Steuart and two other gentlemen to prove that Mr. Steuart had purchased Sommersett as a slave in Virginia and had afterward brought him into England, where he left his master's service; and that his refusing to return was the occasion of his being carried on board Mr. Knowles's ship. [20 How. 1]

[*Statement of the Court*]

Lord Mansfield—The question is, if the owner had a right to detain the slave, for the sending of him over to be sold in Jamaica. In five or six cases of this nature, I have known it to be accommodated by agreement between the parties: on its first coming before me, I strongly recommended it here. But if the parties will have it decided, we must give our opinion. Compassion will not, on the one hand, nor inconvenience on the other, be to decide; but the law: in which the difficulty will be principally from the inconvenience on both sides. Contract for sale of a slave is good here; the sale

---

* Lofft. 1, 98 Eng. Rep. 499, 20 How. St. Tr. 1 (1772).

is a matter to which the law properly and readily attaches, and will maintain the price according to the agreement. But here the person of the slave himself is immediately the object of inquiry, which makes a very material difference. The now question is, whether any dominion, authority, or coercion can be exercised in this country on a slave according to the American laws? The difficulty of adopting the relation, without adopting it in all its consequences, is indeed extreme; and yet, many of those consequences are absolutely contrary to the municipal law of England. We have no authority to regulate the conditions in which law shall operate. On the other hand, should we think the coercive power cannot be exercised: it is now about fifty years since the opinion given by two of the greatest men of their own or any times (since which no contract has been brought to trial, between the masters and slaves); the service performed by the slaves without wages is a clear indication they did not think themselves free by coming hither. The setting 14,000 or 15,000 men at once loose by a solemn opinion is very disagreeable in the effects it threatens. There is a case in Hobart (Coventry and Woodfall), where a man had contracted to go as a mariner: but the now case will not come within that decision. Mr. Steuart advances no claims on contract; he rests his whole demand on a right to the Negro as slave and mentions the purpose of detainure to be the sending of him over to be sold in Jamaica. If the parties will have judgment *fiat justitia, ruat coelum,* let justice be done whatever the consequence. Fifty pounds a head may not be a high price; then a loss follows to the proprietors of above 700,000 pounds sterling. How would the law stand with respect to their settlement, their wages? How many actions for any slight coercion by the master? We cannot in any of these points direct the law; the law must rule us. In these particulars, it may be matter of weighty consideration what provisions are made or set by law. Mr. Steuart may end the question, by discharging or giving freedom to the Negro. I did think at first to put the matter to a more solemn way of argument: but if my brothers agree, there seems no occasion. I do not imagine, after the point has been discussed on both sides so extremely well, any new light could be thrown on the subject. If the parties choose to refer it to the Common Pleas, they can give themselves that satisfaction whenever they think fit. An application to parliament, if the merchants think the question of great commercial concern, is the best and perhaps the only method of settling the point for the future. The court is greatly obliged to the gentlemen of the bar who have spoken on the subject, and by whose care and abilities so much has been effected, that the rule of decision will be reduced to a very easy compass. I cannot omit to express particular happiness in seeing young men, just called to the bar, have been able so much to profit by their reading. I think it right the matter should stand over; and if we are called on for a decision, proper notice shall be given. [20 How.]

[Final Judgment]

Trinity term, June 22, 1772

LORD MANSFIELD—On the part of Somerset, the case which we gave notice should be decided this day, the court now proceeds to give its opinion. I shall recite the return to the writ of habeas corpus as the ground of our determination, omitting only words of form. The captain of the ship, on board which the Negro was taken, makes his return to the writ in terms signifying that there have been, and still are, slaves to a great number in Africa; and that the trade in them is authorized by the laws and opinions of Virginia and Jamaica; that they are goods and chattels, and, as such, saleable and sold. That James Somerset is a Negro of Africa, and long before the return of the King's writ was brought to be sold, and was sold to Charles Stewart, Esq., then in Jamaica. And he has not been manumitted since; that Mr. Stewart, having occasion to transact business, came over hither [in 1769], with an intention to return, and brought Somerset to attend and abide with him, and to carry him back as soon as the business should be transacted. That such intention has been, and still continues; and that the Negro did remain till the time of his [Somerset's] departure [October 1, 1771] in the service of his master, Mr. Stewart, and quitted it without his consent; and thereupon [November 26, 1771], before the return of the King's writ, the said Charles Stewart did commit the slave on board the *Ann and Mary* to safe custody, to be kept till he [Knowles] should set sail, and then to be taken with him to Jamaica, and there sold as a slave. And this is the cause why he, Captain Knowles, who was then and now is, commander of the above vessel, then and now lying in the river of Thames, did the said Negro, committed to his custody, detain; and on which he now renders him to the orders of the court. We pay all due attention to the opinion of Sir Philip Yorke and Lord Chief Justice Talbot, whereby they pledged themselves to the British planters for all the legal consequences of slaves coming over to this kingdom or being baptized, recognized by Lord Hardwicke, sitting as Chancellor on the nineteenth of October, 1749, that trover would lie: that a notion had prevailed, if a Negro came over, or became a Christian, he was emancipated, but no ground in law; that he and Lord Talbot, when Attorney and Solicitor General, were of the opinion that no such claim for freedom was valid; that though the Statute of Tenures had abolished villains regardant to a manor, yet he did not conceive but that a man might still become a villain in gross, by confessing himself such in open court. We are so well agreed, that we think there is no occasion of having it argued (as I intimated an intention at first), before all the judges, as is usual, for obvious reasons, on a return to a habeas corpus; the only question before us is, whether the cause on the return is sufficient? If it is, the Negro must be remanded; if it is not, he must be discharged. Accordingly, the return states that the slave departed and refused to serve; whereupon he was kept to be sold abroad. So high an act of dominion must be recognized by the law of the country where it is used. The power of a master over his slave has been extremely different in different countries. The state of slavery is of such a nature that it is incapable of being introduced on any reasons, moral or political, but only [by] positive law, which preserves its force long after the reasons, occasion, and time itself, from whence it was created, is erased from memory: it's so odious, that nothing can be suffered to support it, but positive law. Whatever inconveniences, therefore, may follow from a decision, I cannot say this case is allowed or approved by the law of England; and therefore the black must be discharged. [Lofft. 18]

II

Slavery During the Revolutionary and National Periods

1776–1820

The years 1776 to 1820 reveal the general ambivalence of the white majority regarding the status of the Negro. The period began with assertions of liberty outlined in the Declaration of Independence—a document of freedom that made no reference to the Negro's right to be free. The tragedies of this paradox were portended in Thomas Jefferson's attempt to write a condemnation of slavery into the Declaration of Independence and in the success of southern delegates' insistence to the Continental Congress that these particular passages be struck.

This was not the end of ambivalence and hesitation on the part of white society. In 1787, the Congress under the Articles of Confederation promulgated the Northwest Ordinance, which outlawed slavery and involuntary servitude in those states which would be carved from the Northwest Territory. Ironically, the Founding Fathers, sitting that same year in Philadelphia to draft the new national constitution, legitimized slavery by their compromises and acquiescence in the institution of bondage.

The paradoxes and contradictions seem almost endless during this crucial transitional period. The same generation that could pledge itself to abolish the importation of slaves from abroad by the year 1807, also enacted a federal law in 1793 to assist in the recapture of fugitive slaves. Furthermore, while eight northern and mid-Atlantic states abolished slavery in the period 1777 to 1804, the invention of the cotton gin, coupled with the heady opportunities for agricultural and economic exploitation of the transmontane Lower South, served to intensify the domestic slave trade and to extend and perpetuate slavery as an institution.

If the years 1776 to 1820 were replete with endless examples of hesitation and uncertainty over the question of the Negro, free or slave, the period had opened with a classic example of deliberate action—taken for the wrong reasons. From July to November, 1775, General George Washington and the Continental Congress agreed on a policy of barring both slaves and free Negroes from the American Army. After Lord Dunmore, the deposed Royal Governor of Virginia, issued a proclamation promising freedom to male slaves who joined in the defense of the Crown, Washington retreated from his position, and the Continental Congress approved the enlistment of free Negroes. In this instance, as in many future instances, the Negro would gain rights only in response to the threat of external and internal pressures, rather than on the basis of inherent justice.

DECLARATION OF INDEPENDENCE (1776)

The issue of slavery was conspicuous by its absence in the final text of the Declaration of Independence. But an assault on slavery had been included in Thomas Jefferson's original draft as part of his criticism of the king. The paragraph expressed Jefferson's own sense of justice and what he believed would gain the support of those who professed the concept of liberty. However, at the insistence of southern representatives in the Continental Congress, the key section on slavery was struck from the Declaration.

DOCUMENT 13

The Declaration of Independence, original draft*

When in the Course of human Events, it becomes necessary for one People to dissolve the Political Bands which have connected them with another, and to assume among the Powers of the Earth, the separate and equal Station to which the Laws of Nature and of Nature's God entitle them, a decent Respect to the Opinions of Mankind requires that they should declare the causes which impel them to the Separation.

WE hold these Truths to be self-evident, that all Men are created equal, that they are endowed by their Creator with [inherent and] *certain* unalienable Rights, that among these are Life, Liberty, and the Pursuit of Happiness—That to secure these Rights, Governments are instituted among Men, deriving their just Powers from the Consent of the Governed, that whenever any Form of Government becomes destructive of these Ends, it is the Right of the People to alter or to abolish it, and to institute new Government, laying its Foundation on such Principles, and organizing its Powers in such Form, as to them shall seem most likely to effect their Safety and Happiness.

· · · ·

[He (George III) has incited treasonable insurrections of our fellow citizens, with the allurements of forfeiture and confiscation of our property.

He has waged cruel war against human nature itself, violating its most sacred rights of life and liberty in the persons of a distant people who never offended him, captivating and carrying them into slavery in another hemisphere, or to incur miserable death in their transportation thither. This piratical warfare, the opprobrium of INFIDEL powers, is the warfare of the CHRISTIAN King of Great-Britain. Determined to keep open a market where MEN should be bought and sold, he has prostituted his negative for suppressing every legislative attempt to

* As reprinted in *We the States* (Richmond, Va.: Virginia Commission on Constitutional Government, 1964), pp. 11, 15.

prohibit or to restrain this execrable commerce. And that this assemblage of horrors might want no fact of distinguished die, he is now exciting those very people to rise in arms among us, and to purchase that liberty of which he has deprived them, by murdering the people on whom he also obtruded them: thus paying off former crimes committed against the LIBERTIES of one people with crimes which he urges them to commit against the LIVES of another.]

DELAWARE CONSTITUTION (1776)

Of the thirteen original colonies transformed into states at the time of the American Revolution, Delaware was alone in making clear and detailed reference to the question of the Negro and slavery in its constitution. The passage did not prohibit slavery; it merely outlawed the importation of slaves and their sale within the state.

DOCUMENT 14

Delaware Constitution[*]

ARTICLE 26

No person hereafter imported into this State from Africa ought to be held in slavery under any pretence whatever; and no negro, Indian, or mulatto slave ought to be brought into this State, for sale, from any part of the world.

THE QUOCK WALKER CASE (1783)

It was the judiciary, rather than the executive or the legislature, which ended slavery in Massachusetts as a le-

---

* Francis Newton Thorpe, ed., *The Federal and State Constitutions*, Vol. I (Washington, D.C.: U.S. Government Printing Office, 1909), p. 567.

galized institution. And it was done in one of the earliest decisions in the country applying a written constitution directly as law.

What became known nationwide as the *Quock Walker* case was officially entitled *Commonwealth* v. *Jennison*. It was never set down in the law reports. In fact, no opinion was ever written in the case. All that has been preserved—and often reprinted—is the charge to the jury by Chief Justice William Cushing, analyzing the law of liberty and slavery.

Before the court was an indictment, charging that Nathaniel Jennison had committed assault and battery on one Quacks (or, as he is variously called in other comments on the case, Quaco, Quack, Quork, Quork Walker, or Quock Walker). The justification, Jennison maintained, was that Quacks was his slave; therefore he had a right to bring him home when he ran away, and he only took proper measures for that purpose. The verdict, however, was *Guilty*.

DOCUMENT 15

*Commonwealth v. Jennison**

Charge of Chief Justice Cushing

As to the doctrine of slavery and the right of Christians to hold Africans in perpetual servitude, and sell and treat them as we do our horses and cattle, that (it is true) has been heretofore countenanced by the Province Laws formerly, but nowhere is it expressly enacted or established. It has been a usage—a usage which took its origin from the practice of some of the European nations, and the regulations of British government respecting the then Colonies, for the benefit of trade and wealth. But whatever sentiments have formerly prevailed in this particular or slid in upon us by the example of others, a different idea has taken place with the people of America, more favorable to the natural rights of mankind, and to that natural, innate desire of Liberty, with which Heaven (without regard to color, complexion, or shape of noses—features) has inspired all the human race. And upon

* A. B. Hart ed., *Commonwealth History of Massachusetts*, Vol. IV (New York: States History Co., 1929, 1930), pp. 37-38.

this ground our Constitution of Government, by which the people of this Commonwealth have solemnly bound themselves, sets out with declaring that all men are born free and equal—and that every subject is entitled to liberty, and to have it guarded by the laws, as well as life and property—and in short is totally repugnant to the idea of being born slaves. This being the case, I think the idea of slavery is inconsistent with our own conduct and Constitution; and there can be no such thing as perpetual servitude of a rational creature, unless his liberty is forfeited by some criminal conduct or given up by personal consent or contract. . . .

Verdict Guilty.

NORTHWEST ORDINANCE (1787)

For the one hundred eighty years from Jamestown to 1787 and for the next seventy-four years until the Civil War, questions of use and exploitation and authority over western lands plagued administrators, politicians, settlers, and sectional spokesmen alike. The Northwest Ordinance was an outstanding attempt to bring some rational order to the question. It may indeed be viewed as the greatest handiwork of the Congress under the Articles of Confederation. Article VI incorporated Jefferson's suggestion of 1784, that slavery be eventually outlawed in the lands recently ceded to the national government. However, the Ordinance still permitted the recapture and return of fugitive slaves apprehended in the Northwest Territory.

DOCUMENT 16

An ordinance for the government of the territory of the United States northwest of the river Ohio[*]

---

[*] Charles C. Tansill, ed., *Documents Illustrative of the Formation of the Union of the American States* (Washington, D.C.: U.S. Government Printing Office, 1927), p. 54.

ARTICLE 6

There shall be neither slavery nor involuntary servitude in the said territory, otherwise than in the punishment of crimes whereof the party shall have been duly convicted: *Provided, always,* That any person escaping into the same, from whom labor or service is lawfully claimed in any one of the original States, such fugitive may be lawfully reclaimed and conveyed to the person claiming his or her labor or service as aforesaid.

CONSTITUTION OF THE UNITED STATES (1787–1788)

Major compromises on the structure of the federal legislature, regulation of commerce, and questions of representation and taxation characterized the deliberations of the fifty-five delegates who sat in Philadelphia from May to September, 1787, to draft a new frame of government for the United States.

The best record of the Convention's debates, the "Notes" taken by delegate James Madison, indicate that the participants had to wrestle with the question of Negro slavery at several crucial points in their deliberations. (See Charles C. Tansill, ed., *Documents Illustrative of the Formation of the Union of the American States* [Washington, D.C.: U.S. Government Printing Office, 1927], especially pp. 508, 588–89, 616–18, 631, and 719). The Founding Fathers were inclined to treat the question of slavery as an economic and political matter—particularly so in light of the sensitivity of southern delegates, who would brook no interference with their institution. Nonetheless, the delegates apparently recognized that slavery was, in the final analysis, incompatible with the doctrines of freedom and liberty that characterized this "Revolutionary Generation" at the close of the eighteenth century. The Constitution artfully avoids the use of the term slavery, and refers to "persons" whom the States shall think it proper to import, or "persons" bound to service or labor.

The portions of the Constitution touching on the question

of slavery merit examination because they would become, in varying degrees, matters of irritation and dispute during the subsequent seven decades leading to the Civil War. The compromise over the status of Negro slaves as an element in the determination of taxation and representation seemed to work well enough in a procedural sense, but antislavery advocates were never reconciled to its substantive implications. Congress did legislate, in 1807, against the further importation of slaves (see Document 19), but this act had, of course, no effect upon the domestic slave trade.

A number of theories were advanced about the meaning of the "privileges and immunities" clause of Article IV. One of these, since rejected, asserted that the citizen of any state was guaranteed the rights he enjoyed at home when traveling in any other state. That would presumably have allowed him to maintain his property and slaves, regardless of where he took them. More inmportant, however, was the question of whether or not the clause could be held to include one-time slaves claiming residence in a free state as a source of their freedom. The Supreme Court answered that in the negative in *Dred Scott* v. *Sandford*. (See Document 34.)

Clause 3, Section 2 of Article IV referred to fugitive slaves, and Congress enacted legislation on that point in 1793 (Document 18) and again in 1850, as part of the famous Compromise (Document 31). The authority of Congress to determine the status of slavery in the territories and in the new states carved from those federal territories became a matter of dispute in the years preceding the Civil War. (See, for example, Documents 23, 30, 31, and 33.)

The following sections of the United States Constitutions are repeated in Document 38, together with the comparable portions of the Constitution of the Confederate States of America, adopted in 1861.

DOCUMENT 17

Constitution of the United States*

ARTICLE I

SECTION 2. Clause 3. Representatives and direct Taxes shall be apportioned among the several States which may be included within this Union, according to their respective Numbers, which shall be determined by adding to the whole Number of free Persons, including those bound to Service for a Term of Years, and excluding Indians not taxed, three-fifths of all other Persons. The actual Enumeration shall be made within three Years after the first Meeting of the Congress of the United States, and within every subsequent Term of ten Years, in such Manner as they shall by Law direct. The Number of Representatives shall not exceed one for every thirty Thousand, but each State shall have at Least one Representative; and until such enumeration shall be made, the State of New Hampshire shall be entitled to chuse three, Massachusetts eight, Rhode-Island and Providence Plantations one, Connecticut five, New-York six, New Jersey four, Pennsylvania eight, Delaware one, Maryland six, Virginia ten, North Carolina five, South Carolina five, and Georgia three.

• • • •

SECTION 9. Clause 1. The Migration or Importation of such Persons as any of the States now existing shall think proper to admit, shall not be prohibited by the Congress prior to the Year one thousand eight hundred and eight, but a Tax or duty may be imposed on such Importation, not exceeding ten dollars for each Person.

• • • •

* Norman J. Small, Lester S. Jayson, and Edward S. Corwin, eds., *The Constitution of the United States of America* (Washington, D.C.: U.S. Government Printing Office, 1964), pp. 120–21, 362, 775, 786, 791–92.

Article IV

SECTION 2. Clause 1. The Citizens of each State shall be entitled to all Privileges and Immunities of Citizens in the several States.

. . . .

SECTION 2. Clause 3. No person held to Service or Labour in one State, under the Laws thereof, escaping into another, shall, in Consequence of any Law or Regulation therein, be discharged from such Service or Labour, but shall be delivered up on Claim of the Party to whom such Service or Labour may be due.

. . . .

SECTION 3. Clause 2. The Congress shall have Power to dispose of and make all needful Rules and Regulations respecting the Territory or other Property belonging to the United States; and nothing in this Constitution shall be so construed as to Prejudice any Claims of the United States, or of any particular State.

FUGITIVE SLAVE ACT (1793)

Constitutional provisions are by no means entirely self-executing. Article IV, Section 2 of the U.S. Constitution (Document 17) contained the basic law on the right to re-possess fugitive slaves, but an act of Congress was necessary to set up the machinery for their return. Such an act was passed by the Second Congress on February 12, 1793. Its constitutionality was later upheld by the Supreme Court in 1842 in *Prigg* v. *Pennsylvania*, 16 Pet. (41 U.S.) 539. The act was later amended as part of the Compromise package of 1850. (See Document 31.)

DOCUMENT 18

*An act respecting fugitives from justice, and persons escaping from the service of their masters**

SECTION 1. *Be it enacted by the Senate and House of Representatives of the United States of America in Congress assembled,* That whenever the executive authority of any state in the Union, or of either of the territories northwest or south of the river Ohio, shall demand any person as a fugitive from justice, of the executive authority of any such state or territory to which such person shall have fled, and shall moreover produce the copy of an indictment found, or an affidavit made before a magistrate of any state or territory as aforesaid, charging the person so demanded, with having committed treason, felony, or other crime, certified as authentic by the governor or chief magistrate of the state or territory from whence the person so charged fled, it shall be the duty of the executive authority of the state or territory to which such person shall have fled, to cause him or her to be arrested and secured, and notice of the arrest to be given to the executive authority making such demand, or to the agent of such authority appointed to receive the fugitive, and to cause the fugitive to be delivered to such agent when he shall appear: But if no such agent shall appear within six months from the time of the arrest, the prisoner may be discharged. And all costs or expenses incurred in the apprehending, securing, and transmitting such fugitive to the state or territory making such demand, shall be paid by such state or territory.

SEC. 2. *And be it further enacted,* That any agent, appointed as aforesaid, who shall receive the fugitive into his custody, shall be empowered to transport him or her to the state or territory from which he or she shall have fled. And if any person or persons shall by force set at liberty, or rescue the fugitive from such agent while transporting, as aforesaid, the person or persons so offending shall, on conviction, be fined not exceeding five hundred dollars, and be imprisoned not exceeding one year.

---

* 1 Stat. 302 (1793).

SEC. 3. *And be it also enacted,* That when a person held to labour in any of the United States, or in either of the territories on the northwest or south of the river Ohio, under the laws thereof, shall escape into any other of the said states or territory, the person to whom such labour or service may be due, his agent or attorney, is hereby empowered to seize or arrest such fugitive from labour, and to take him or her before any judge of the circuit or district courts of the United States, residing or being within the state, or before any magistrate of a county, city or town corporate, wherein such seizure or arrest shall be made, and upon proof to the satisfaction of such judge or magistrate, either by oral testimony or affidavit taken before and certified by a magistrate of any such state or territory, that the person so seized or arrested, doth, under the laws of the state or territory from which he or she fled, owe service or labour to the person claiming him or her, it shall be the duty of such judge or magistrate to give a certificate thereof to such claimant, his agent or attorney, which shall be sufficient warrant for removing the said fugitive from labour, to the state or territory from which he or she fled.

SEC. 4. *And be it further enacted,* That any person who shall knowingly and willingly obstruct or hinder such claimant, his agent or attorney in so seizing or arresting such fugitive from labour, or shall rescue such fugitive from such claimant, his agent or attorney when so arrested pursuant to the authority herein given or declared; or shall harbor or conceal such person after notice that he or she was a fugitive from labour, as aforesaid, shall, for either of the said offences, forfeit and pay the sum of five hundred dollars. Which penalty may be recovered by and for the benefit of such claimant, by action of debt, in any court proper to try the same, saving moreover to the person claiming such labour or service, his right of action for or on account of the said injuries or either of them.

APPROVED, February 12, 1793.

ACT TO PROHIBIT THE IMPORTATION
OF SLAVES (1807)

From the ratification of the Constitution in 1788 to the final resolution of the Missouri Compromise in 1821 (Document 23), Congress enacted seven statutes on the slave trade. By far the most important was the act passed pursuant to Article I, Section 9, Clause 1 of the Constitution—one of the great Compromise provisions. It stated specifically that Congress could pass no law prohibiting the importation of slaves "as any of the States now existing shall think proper to admit . . . prior to the year one thousand eight hundred and eight." Congress had a statute ready for that deadline date. Such an act was approved on March 2, 1807, to go into effect on January 1, 1808.

The first of these seven statutes was passed in 1794, entitled "An Act to prohibit the carrying on the Slave Trade from the United States to any foreign place or country." (1 Stat. 347) It was supplemented in 1800. (2 Stat. 70) Then, in 1803, Congress passed "An Act to prevent the importation of certain persons into certain states, where, by the laws thereof, their admission is prohibited." (2 Stat. 205) The fourth of these statutes was the important act of 1807, supplemented and strengthened by further statutes in 1818 (3 Stat. 450) and in 1819 (3 Stat. 532). The 1820 statute (3 Stat. 600) defined certain slave-trading activities as acts of piracy, punishable by death.

DOCUMENT 19

An act to prohibit the importation of slaves into any port or place within the jurisdiction of the United States, from and after the first day of January, in the year of our Lord one thousand eight hundred and eight *

Be it enacted by the Senate and House of Representatives of the United States of America in Congress assembled, That from and after the first day of January, one thousand eight hundred and eight, it shall not be lawful to import or bring into the United States or the territories thereof from any foreign kingdom, place, or country, any negro, mulatto, or person of colour, with intent to hold, sell, or dispose of such negro, mulatto, or person of colour, as a slave, or to be held to service or labour.

SEC. 2. *And be it further enacted,* That no citizen or citizens of the United States, or any other person, shall, from and after the first day of January, in the year of our Lord one thousand eight hundred and eight, for himself, or themselves, or any other person whatsoever, either as master, factor, or owner, build, fit, equip, load or otherwise prepare any ship or vessel, in any port or place within the jurisdiction of the United States, nor shall cause any ship or vessel to sail from any port or place within the same, for the purpose of procuring any negro, mulatto, or person of colour, from any foreign kingdom, place, or country, to be transported to any port or place whatsoever, within the jurisdiction of the United States, to be held, sold, or disposed of as slaves, or to be held to service or labour: and if any ship or vessel shall be so fitted out for the purpose aforesaid, or shall be caused to sail so as aforesaid, every such ship or vessel, her tackle, apparel, and furniture, shall be forfeited to the United States, and shall be liable to be seized, prosecuted, and condemned in any of the circuit courts or district courts, for the district where the said ship or vessel may be found or seized.

. . . .

---

* 2 Stat. 426 (1807).

SEC. 4. *And be it further enacted,* If any citizen or citizens of the United States, or any person resident within the jurisdiction of the same, shall, from and after the first day of January, one thousand eight hundred and eight, take on board, receive or transport from any of the coasts or kingdoms of Africa, or from any other foreign kingdom, place, or country, any negro, mulatto, or person of colour, in any ship or vessel, for the purpose of selling them in any port or place within the jurisdiction of the United States as slaves, or to be held to service or labour, or shall be in any ways aiding or abetting therein, such citizen or citizens, or person, shall severally forfeit and pay five thousand dollars, one moiety thereof to the use of any person or persons who shall sue for and prosecute the same to effect; and every such ship or vessel in which such negro, mulatto, or person of colour, shall have been taken on board, received, or transported as aforesaid, her tackle, apparel, and furniture, and the goods and effects which shall be found on board the same, shall be forfeited to the United States, and shall be liable to be seized, prosecuted, and condemned in any of the circuit courts or district courts in the district where the said ship or vessel may be found or seized. And neither the importer, nor any person or persons claiming from or under him, shall hold any right or title whatsoever to any negro, mulatto, or person of colour, nor to the service or labour thereof, who may be imported or brought within the United States, or territories thereof, in violation of this law, but the same shall remain subject to any regulations not contravening the provisions of this act, which the legislatures of the several states or territories at any time hereafter may make, for disposing of any such negro, mulatto, or person of colour.

• • • •

SEC. 7. *And be it further enacted,* That if any ship or vessel shall be found from and after the first day of January, one thousand eight hundred and eight, in any river, port, bay, or harbor, or on the high seas, within the jurisdictional limits of the United States, or hovering on the coast thereof, having on board any negro, mulatto, or person of colour, for the purpose of selling them as slaves, or with intent to land the same, in any port or place within the jurisdiction of the United States, contrary to the prohibition of this act, every such ship or vessel, together with her tackle, apparel, and furniture, and the goods or effects which shall be found on board the same, shall be forfeited to the use of the United States, and may be seized, prosecuted, and condemned, in any court of the United States, having jurisdiction thereof. And it shall be lawful for the President of the United States, and he is hereby authorized, should he deem it expedient, to cause any of the armed vessels of the United States to be manned and employed to cruise on any part of the coast of the United States, or territories thereof, where he may judge attempts will be made to violate the provisions of this act, and to instruct and direct the commanders of armed vessels of the United States, to seize, take, and bring into any port of the United States all such ships or vessels, and moreover to seize, take, and bring into any port of the United States all ships or vessels of the United States, wheresoever found on the high seas, contravening the provisions of this act, to be proceeded against according to law, and the captain, master, or commander of every such ship or vessel, so found and seized as aforesaid, shall be deemed guilty of a high misdemeanor, and shall be liable to be prosecuted before any court of the United States, having jurisdiction thereof; and being thereof convicted, shall be fined not exceeding ten thousand dollars, and be imprisoned not less than two years, and not exceeding four years. And the proceeds of all ships and vessels, their tackle, apparel, and furniture, and the goods and effects on board of them, which shall be so seized, prosecuted and condemned, shall be divided equally between the United States and the officers and men who shall make such seizure, take, or bring the same into port for condemnation, whether such seizure be made by an armed vessel of the United States, or revenue cutters thereof, and the same shall be distributed in like manner, as is provided by law, for the distribution of prizes taken from an enemy: *Provided,* that the officers and men, to be entitled to one half of the proceeds aforesaid, shall safe keep every negro, mulatto, or person of colour, found on board of any ship or vessel so by them seized, taken, or brought into port for condemnation, and shall deliver every such negro, mulatto, or person of colour, to such person or persons as shall be appointed by the respective states, to receive the same; and if no such person or persons shall be appointed by the respective states, they shall deliver every such negro, mulatto, or person of colour, to the overseers of the poor of the port or place where such ship or vessel may be brought or found, and shall immediately transmit to the governor or chief magistrate of the state, an account of their proceedings, together with the number of such negroes, mulattoes, or persons of colour, and a descriptive list of the same, that he may give directions respecting such negroes, mulattoes, or persons of colour.

. . . .

APPROVED, March 2, 1807.

MISSISSIPPI AND ALABAMA STATE CONSTITUTIONS (1817, 1819)

The constant press westward during the first quarter of the nineteenth century saw a balanced admission of free and slave states. In turn, Indiana in 1816 and Illinois in 1818 entered the Union as free states, and the lush cotton-growing territories along the Gulf produced two new southern states, the slave states of Mississippi in 1817 and Alabama in 1819.

The constitutions of Mississippi and Alabama confirm the care taken by lawmakers in the South to protect the interests of the slaveholder and the institution of slavery. The slave was without legal rights and his guarantees of justice less than minimal: his fate was left to the caprice of the dominant white society, both in law and in practice.

DOCUMENT(S) 20

The Mississippi Constitution (1817)*

Slaves

SECTION 1. The general assembly shall have no power to pass laws for the emancipation of slaves, without the consent of their owners, unless where a slave shall have rendered to the State some distinguished service, in which case the owner shall be paid a full equivalent for the slaves so emancipated. They shall have no power to prevent immigrants to this State from bringing with them such persons as are deemed slaves by the laws of any one of the United States, so long as any person of the same age or description shall be continued in slavery by the laws of this State: *Provided,* That such person or slave be the *bona-fide* property of such immigrants; *And provided also,* That laws may be passed to prohibit the introduction into the State of slaves who may have committed high crimes in other States. They shall have power to pass laws to permit the owners of slaves to emancipate them, saving the rights of creditors, and preventing them from becoming a public charge. They shall have full power to prevent slaves from being brought into this State as merchandise; and also to oblige the owners of slaves to treat them with humanity, to provide for them necessary clothing and provision, to abstain from all injuries to them extending to life or limb, or in case of their neglect or refusal to comply with the directions of such laws, to have such slave or slaves sold for the benefit of the owner or owners.

SEC. 2. In the prosecution of slaves for crimes, no inquest by a grand jury shall be necessary, but the proceedings in such cases shall be regulated by law; except that, in capital cases, the general assembly shall have no power to deprive them of an impartial trial by a petit jury.

---

* Francis Newton Thorpe, ed., *The Federal and State Constitutions, Colonial Charters, and Other Laws of the States, Territories, and Colonies Now or Hitherto Forming the United States of America*, Vol. IV (Washington, D.C.: U.S. Government Printing Office, 1909), p. 2045.

The Alabama Constitution (1819)*

Slaves

SECTION 1. The general assembly shall have no power to pass laws for the emancipation of slaves, without the consent of their owners, or without paying their owners, previous to such emancipation, a full equivalent in money for the slaves so emancipated. They shall have no power to prevent emigrants to this State from bringing with them such persons as are deemed slaves by the laws of any one of the United States, so long as any person of the same age or description shall be continued in slavery by the laws of this State: *Provided*, That such person or slave be the *bona-fide* property of such emigrants: *And provided, also*, That laws may be passed to prohibit the introduction into this State of slaves who have committed high crimes in other States or Territories. They shall have power to pass laws to permit the owners of slaves to emancipate them, saving the rights of creditors, and preventing them from becoming a public charge. They shall have full power to prevent slaves from being brought into this State as merchandise, and also to oblige the owners of slaves to treat them with humanity, to provide for them necessary food and clothing, to abstain from all injuries to them extending to life or limb, and, in case of their neglect, or refusal to comply with the directions of such laws, to have such slave or slaves sold for the benefit of the owner or owners.

SEC. 2. In the prosecution of slaves for crimes, of higher grade than petit larceny, the general assembly shall have no power to deprive them of an impartial trial by a petit jury.

SEC. 3. Any person who shall maliciously dismember or deprive a slave of life, shall suffer such punishment as would be inflicted in case the like offence had been committed on a free white person, and on the like proof; except in case of insurrection of such slave.

. . . .

* Thorpe, ed., *The Federal and State Constitutions . . .*, Vol. I, pp. 111–12.

Schedule

. . . .

Sec. 6. Every white male person above the age of twenty-one years, who shall be a citizen of the United States, and resident in this State at the time of the adoption of this constitution, shall be deemed a qualified elector at the first election to be holden in this State. And every white male person who shall reside within the limits of this State at the time of the adoption of this constitution, and shall be other-wise qualified, shall be entitled to hold any office or place of honor, trust, or profit under this State; anything in this constitution to the contrary notwithstanding.

VIRGINIA STATUTE ON SLAVES, FREE NEGROES, AND MULATTOES (1819)

In 1819, the state of Virginia recodified into one major act its various laws and regulations concerning the Negro, both slave and free. The stipulations indicate the far-reaching regulations which a society imposes upon itself by accepting a system of bondage. The law restricted the mobility and conduct of free Negroes, imposed harsh penalties upon slaves who traveled about without special passes or who assembled for educational purposes, and even required certain regulatory actions on the part of whites. Committed to the concept of racial distinctions, the lawmakers also utilized the Act of 1819 to set a blood-ratio by which to identify mulattoes.

The law contained a provision to punish free Negroes who spoke provocatively to whites. Less dramatic, but compatible with the economy of the times, were the numerous sections of the act devoted to the purchase and sale of slaves, the gift of Negroes from one master to another, and the dispo-sition of slave property upon the death of the master. That a Negro was considered a slave inherently is evident in Section 61, which stipulated that manumitted slaves could lose their freedom if they remained within the state for more than a year following their emancipation.

While these regulations seem excessive, they were relatively temperate compared with the tightened restrictions visited upon the Negro throughout the South during the generation immediately preceding the Civil War.

DOCUMENT 21

An act reducing into one, the several acts concerning slaves, free Negroes, and mulattoes[*]

1. *Be it enacted by the General Assembly,* That no persons shall henceforth be slaves within this Commonwealth, except such as were so on the seventeenth day of October, in the year one thousand seven hundred and eighty-five, and the descendants, of the females of them, "and such persons and their descendants, being slaves, as since have been, or hereafter may be brought into this State, or held therein pursuant to law."

2. Hereafter it shall be lawful to bring into this State, and "to hold therein, any slave or slaves, born within the United States, or any territory thereof, or within the District of Columbia, except such slaves as, at the time of their removal, were resident out of the limits aforesaid, and such as shall have been convicted of any offence, and transported therefor, under the laws of this State, or of any other state, territory, or district."

3. "It shall not be lawful for any person whatsoever, to bring into this State, or to hold therein, any slave or slaves born or resident out of the limits aforesaid, or any slave or slaves that shall have been convicted of any offence, and therefor transported by the laws of this State, or of any state, territory, or district aforesaid; and, if any person shall bring into this State, contrary to the provisions of this act, any such slave or slaves, or shall sell, purchase, or hold, in this State, any such slave or slaves, knowing such slave or slaves to have been brought into this State contrary to the provisions of this act, every such offender shall forfeit and pay to the

* *Revised Code of the Laws of Virginia* . . . , Vol. I (Richmond: T. Ritchie, 1819), pp. 421–44.

Commonwealth, for the use of the literary fund, for each slave so brought in, sold, purchased, or held, a fine of one thousand dollars: *Provided, however,* That the penalty aforesaid shall not be incurred by any person bringing into this State any slave or slaves for the purpose only of passing through, or for a short time abiding therein, if such slave or slaves be not kept within this State for one whole year, or sold or offered for sale therein.

4. "If any person shall heretofore have brought into this State, or held therein, any slave or slaves, such as, under the provisions of this act, he might lawfully bring or hold therein, and shall thereby have incurred any penalty or forfeiture not yet recovered or enforced, such penalty or forfeiture shall be, and the same is hereby remitted."

5. Any negro or mulatto, bond or free, shall be a good witness in pleas of the Commonwealth for or against negroes or mulattoes, bond or free, or in civil pleas where free negroes or mulattoes shall alone be parties, and in no other cases whatever.

6. No slave shall go from the tenements of his master or other person with whom he lives, without a pass or some letter or token, whereby it may appear that he is proceeding by authority from his master, employer or overseer: if he does, it shall be lawful for any person, to apprehend and carry him before a justice of the peace, to be by his order punished with stripes, or not, in his discretion. And, if any slave shall presume to come and be upon the plantation of any person whatsoever, without leave in writing from his or her owner, employer or overseer, not being sent upon lawful business, it shall be lawful for the owner or overseer of such plantation, to give or order such slave, ten lashes on his or her bare back for every such offence: "and, if any negro or mulatto bond or free, shall furnish a pass or permit to any slave, without the consent of the master, employer or overseer of such slave, he or she so offending shall, on conviction thereof before any magistrate of this Commonwealth, receive on his or her bare back, well laid on, any number of lashes not exceeding thirty-nine, at the discretion of such magistrate."

7. No negro or mulatto slave whatsoever shall keep or carry any gun, powder, shot, club, or other weapon whatsoever, offensive or defensive, but all and every gun, weapon, and ammunition found in the possession or custody of any

negro or mulatto may be seized by any person, and, upon due proof thereof, made before any justice of the peace of the county or corporation where such seizure shall be, shall by his order be forfeited to the seizer for his own use; and, moreover, every such offender shall have and receive, by order of such justice, any number of lashes not exceeding thirty-nine, on his or her bare back, well laid on, for every such offence: *Provided,* That slaves living at any frontier plantation, may be permitted to keep and use guns, powder, shot, and weapons, offensive or defensive, by license from a justice of the peace of the county wherein such plantation lies, to be obtained upon application of the owners of such slaves.

8. No free negro or mulatto, shall be suffered to keep or carry any fire-lock of any kind, any military weapon, or any powder, or lead, without first obtaining a license from the court of the county or corporation in which he resides, which license may, at any time, be withdrawn by an order of such court. Any free negro or mulatto who shall so offend, shall, on conviction before a justice of the peace, forfeit all such arms and ammunition to the use of the informer.

9. It shall be the duty of every constable, to give information against, and prosecute, every free negro or mulatto, who shall keep or carry arms or ammunition, contrary to this act.

10. If any free negro or mulatto, who shall have been convicted of keeping or carrying arms or ammunition, shall a second time offend in like manner, he shall, in addition to the forfeiture aforesaid, be punished with stripes, at the discretion of a justice, not exceeding thirty-nine.

11. Every person other than a negro, of whose grandfathers or grandmothers any one is, or shall have been a negro, although all his other progenitors, except that descending from the negro, shall have been white persons, shall be deemed a mulatto; and so, every such person, who shall have one-fourth part or more of negro blood, shall in like manner be deemed a mulatto.

12. Riots, routs, unlawful assemblies, trespasses and seditious speeches, by a slave or slaves, shall be punished with stripes, at the discretion of a justice of the peace, "and should any quarrel or fight take place with any free negro or mulatto and any slave or slaves, such free negro or mulatto, being

proved before a justice of the peace to be the aggressor in such quarrel or fight, shall be punished with stripes, at the discretion of said justice, not exceeding thirty lashes, and he who will may apprehend and carry him, her, or them, before such justice."

13. And to prevent the inconveniences arising from the meeting of slaves; *Be it further enacted,* That if any master, mistress, or overseer of a family, merchant, tavern-keeper, or any other person, shall knowingly permit or suffer any slave, not belonging to him or her, to be and remain upon his or her plantation, "lot or tenement," above four hours at any one time, without leave of the owner or overseer of such slave, he or she, so permitting, shall forfeit and pay three dollars for every such offence; and every owner or overseer of a plantation, merchant, tavern-keeper, or other person, who shall so permit or suffer more than five negroes or slaves, other than his or her own, to be and remain upon his or her plantation or quarter, lot or tenement, at any one time, shall forfeit and pay one dollar for each negro or slave above that number; which said several forfeitures shall be to the informer, and recoverable with costs, before any justice of the peace of the county or corporation where such offence shall be committed.

14. *Provided, always,* That nothing herein contained shall be construed to prohibit the negroes or slaves of one and the same owner, though seated at different quarters, from meeting with their owner's or overseer's leave, upon any plantation to such owner belonging; nor to restrain the meeting of slaves on their owner's or overseer's business, at any public mill, so as such meeting be not in the night time, nor on a Sunday; nor to prohibit their meeting on any other lawful occasion, by license in writing from their owner or overseer; nor their going to church and attending divine service on the Lord's day, or any other day of public worship.

15. And, whereas it is represented to the General Assembly, that it is a common practice, in many places within this Commonwealth, for slaves to assemble in considerable numbers, at meeting-houses, and places of religious worship, in the night, "or at schools for teaching them reading or writing," which, if not restrained, may be productive of considerable evil to the community;

Be it therefore enacted, That all meetings or assemblages

of slaves, "or free negroes or mulattoes mixing and associating with such slaves," at any meeting-house or houses, or any other place or places, in the night, "or at any school or schools for teaching them reading or writing, either in the day or night," under whatsoever pretext, shall be deemed and considered as an unlawful assembly; and any justice of the county or corporation wherein such assemblage shall be, either from his own knowledge, or the information of others, of such unlawful assemblage or meeting, may issue his warrant directed to any sworn officer or officers, authorising him or them to enter the house or houses, where such unlawful assemblages or meetings may be, for the purpose of apprehending or dispersing such slaves, and to inflict corporal punishment on the offender or offenders, at the discretion of any justice of the peace, not exceeding twenty lashes.

16. And the said officer or officers shall have power to summon any person, to aid and assist in the execution of any warrant or warrants directed to him or them, for the purpose aforesaid, who, on refusal, shall be subject to a fine at the discretion of the justice, not exceeding ten dollars: *Provided,* That nothing herein contained shall be so construed as to prevent the masters or owners of slaves from carrying or permitting his, her or their slave or slaves to go with him, her or them, or with any part of his, her or their white family, to any places whatever, for the purpose of religious worship; *provided,* that such worship be conducted by a regularly ordained or licensed white minister; nor shall any thing herein contained be considered as in any manner affecting white persons, who may happen to be present at any meeting or assemblage, for the purpose of religious worship, so conducted by a white minister as aforesaid, at which there shall be such a number of slaves, as would, as the law has been heretofore construed, constitute an unlawful assembly of slaves.

17. If any white person, free negro, mulatto, or Indian, shall, at any time be found in company with slaves at any unlawful meeting, such person, being thereof convicted before any justice of the peace, shall forfeit and pay three dollars for every such offence, to the informer, recoverable with costs, before such justice; or, on failure of present payment, shall receive on his or her bare back, twenty lashes, well laid

on, by order of the justice, before whom such conviction shall be.

18. And every justice of the peace, upon his knowledge of such unlawful meeting, or information thereof to him made within ten days after, shall issue his warrant to apprehend the persons so met or assembled, and cause them to be brought before himself, or any other justice of his county or corporation, to be dealt with as this act directs; and every justice failing herein, shall forfeit and pay eight dollars for every such failure; and every sheriff, or other officer, who shall fail, upon knowledge or information of such meeting, to endeavor to suppress the same, and bring the offenders before some justice of the peace, to receive due punishment, shall be liable to the like penalty of eight dollars; both which penalties shall be to the informer, and recoverable with costs, before any justice of the county or corporation, wherein such failure shall be; and every under-sheriff, serjeant or constable, who, upon knowledge or information of such meeting, shall fail to perform his duty in suppressing the same, and apprehending the persons so assembled, shall forfeit and pay four dollars for every such failure, to the informer, recoverable with costs, before any justice of the county or corporation wherein such failure shall be.

. . . .

22. If any negro or mulatto, bond or free, shall at any time "use abusive and provoking language to, or" lift his or her hand in opposition to any person not being a negro or mulatto, he or she so offending shall, for every such offence, proved by the oath of the party before a justice of the peace of the county or corporation where such offence shall be committed, receive such punishment as the justice shall think proper, not exceeding thirty lashes, on his or her bare back, well laid on; except in those cases, where it shall appear to such justice, that such negro or mulatto was wantonly assaulted, and lifted his or her hand in his or her defence.

23. If any negro or other slave shall, at any time, consult, advise or conspire to rebel, or make insurrection, or shall plot or conspire the murder of any "free white" person or persons whatsoever, every such consulting, plotting or conspiring, shall be adjudged and deemed felony, and the slave or slaves,

convicted thereof in manner herein-after directed, shall suffer death, and be utterly excluded all benefit of clergy.

24. If any free person shall advise or conspire with a slave to rebel or make insurrection, or shall in any wise aid, assist, or abet any slave or slaves making rebellion or insurrection, or shall advise or assist such slave in the murder of any person whatsoever, or shall consult, advise or conspire with any other free person, or with any negro or other slave, to induce, entice or excite any slave or slaves to rebel or make insurrection, every such free person so counselling, advising, plotting or conspiring, or so aiding, assisting or abetting, on conviction of any of the said offences, shall be held and deemed a felon, and shall suffer death without benefit of clergy, by hanging by the neck.

. . . .

32. The justices of every county or corporation shall be justices of *oyer* and *terminer,* for trying slaves charged with felony; which trials shall be by five at least, without juries, upon legal evidence, at such times as the sheriffs or other officers shall appoint, not being less than five, nor more than ten days after the offenders shall have been committed to jail. No slave shall be condemned in any such case, unless all of the justices, sitting upon his or her trial, shall agree in opinion, that the prisoner is guilty, after assigning him or her counsel, in his or her defence, whose fee, amounting to not less than five, nor more than twenty-five dollars, at the discretion of the justices sitting upon said trial, shall be paid by the owner of the slave; *Provided always,* That, when judgment of death shall be passed upon any such offender, there shall be thirty days at least between the time of passing judgment and the day of execution, except in cases of conspiracy, insurrection or rebellion.

. . . .

53. It shall be lawful for any person, by his or her last will and testament, or by any other instrument in writing, under his or her hand and seal, attested and proved, in the county or corporation court, by two witnesses, or acknowledged by the party in the court of the county where he or she

resides, to emancipate and set free his or her slaves, or any of them, who shall thereupon be entirely and fully discharged from the performance of any contract entered into during servitude, and enjoy as full freedom as if they had been particularly named and freed by this act.

54. *Provided, nevertheless,* That all slaves so emancipated shall be liable to be taken by execution, to satisfy any debt contracted by the person emancipating them, before such emancipation is made.

. . . .

61. If any slave hereafter emancipated, shall remain within this Commonwealth more than twelve months after his or her right to freedom shall have accrued, he or she shall forfeit all such right, and may be apprehended and sold by the overseers of the poor of any county or corporation, in which he or she shall be found, for the benefit of the literary fund: "But this provision shall not extend to any infant slave or slaves who shall be emancipated, until such slave or slaves shall have remained within this Commonwealth twelve months after he, she or they have attained the age of twenty-one years."

. . . .

64. It shall not be lawful for any free negro or mulatto, to migrate into this Commonwealth; and every free negro or mulatto, who shall come into this Commonwealth, contrary to this act, shall and may be apprehended and carried by any citizen before some justice of the peace of the county where he shall be taken; which justice is hereby authorised to examine, send and remove every such free negro or mulatto out of this Commonwealth, into that state or island, from whence it shall appear he or she last came; and for this purpose, the sheriff or other officer, and other persons, may, by such justice, be employed within the Commonwealth, upon the same terms as are by law directed, in the removal of criminals from one county to another; "and the expenses and charges of such removal, to be audited and paid out of the treasury as other public charges." And every free negro or mulatto, who shall come, or be brought into this Commonwealth by water, from any country, state or island, may and shall be exported to the place, from whence he or she came,

or was brought; and the charges attending the same shall be paid by the importer; to be recovered by motion in the name of the Commonwealth, upon ten days previous notice thereof, in any court of record; "and every free negro or mulatto so removed or exported, and thereafter returning to this Commonwealth (unless it be in consequences of shipwreck or some other unavoidable necessity), upon proof thereof made before any magistrate of this Commonwealth, shall receive, by order of such magistrate, thirty-nine lashes on his or her bare back well laid on; which punishment may, at the discretion of any magistrate, be repeated once in every week, so long as such free negro or mulatto shall remain within the Commonwealth."

. . . .

AMERICAN COLONIZATION SOCIETY MEMORIAL (1820)

The idea that the Negro problem might be solved or ameliorated by the transportation of blacks to Africa drew support from an otherwise disparate collection of spokesmen. Antislavery advocates saw some justice in establishing free Negroes in a land of their own in Africa, and many expected that the practice might hasten emancipation in the United States. The latter possibility alarmed the slaveholding interests, and yet many of them saw in colonization an opportunity to remove the free Negro as a source of unrest and a core of leadership against the slave system.

To the majority of the public, however, the colonization scheme probably represented a comfortable, intermediate way between slavery and emancipation. Leaders of the American Colonization Society played upon the sentiments of this majority by intimating that colonization would rid the United States of an inferior and undesirable element, and that it would complement the provisions of the Act of 1819 (3 Stat. 532) against the international slave trade. Although the colonization movement could later point to the establishment of Liberia as a tangible product of its work, the movement had little real effect on the status of the Negro in America.

DOCUMENT 22

American Colonization Society: a memorial to the United States Congress*

To the Senate and House of Representatives of the United States:

The President and Board of Managers of the American Colonization Society respectfully represent that, being about to commence the execution of the object to which their views have been long directed, they deem it proper and necessary to address themselves to the legislative council of their country. They trust that this object will be considered, in itself, of great national importance, will be found inseparably connected with another, vitally affecting the honor and interest of this nation, and leading, in its consequences, to the most desirable results.

Believing that examination and reflection will show that such are its connexions and tendency, they are encouraged to present themselves, and their cause, where they know that a public measure, having these advantages, cannot fail to receive all the countenance and aid it may require.

The last census shows the number of free people of color of the United States, and their rapid increase. Supposing them to increase in the same ratio, it will appear how large a proportion of our population will, in the course of even a few years, consist of persons of that description.

No argument is necessary to show that this is very far indeed from constituting an increase of our physical strength; nor can there be a population, in any country, neutral as to its effects upon society. The least observation shows that this description of persons are not, and cannot be, either useful or happy among us; and many considerations, which need not be mentioned, prove, beyond dispute, that it is best, for all the parties interested, that there should be a separation; that

---

* *Annals of Congress,* 16th Congress, 1st Session (February 3, 1820), pp. 1047–51.

those who are now free, and those who may become so hereafter, should be provided with the means of attaining to a state of respectability and happiness, which, it is certain, they have never yet reached, and, therefore, can never be likely to reach, in this country.

. . . .

The two last reports of the Society, to which your memorialists beg leave to refer, show the success of their mission to Africa, and the result of their inquiries upon that continent. From those it is manifest that a situation can be readily obtained, favorable to commerce and agriculture, in a healthy and fertile country, and that the natives are well disposed to give every encouragement to the establishment of such a settlement among them. Thus, it appears, that an object of great national concern, already expressly desired by some of the States, and truly desirable to all, receiving, also, the approbation of those upon whom it is more immediately to operate, is brought within our reach.

But this subject derives, perhaps, its chief interest from its connexion with a measure which has, already, to the honor of our country, occupied the deliberations of the Congress of the United States.

Your memorialists refer, with pleasure, to the act, passed at the last session of Congress, supplementary to the act formerly passed for the suppression of the slave trade. The means afforded, by the provisions of that act, for the accomplishment of its object, are certainly great; but the total extirpation of this disgraceful trade cannot, perhaps, be expected from any measures which rely alone upon the employment of a maritime force, however considerable.

The profits attending it are so extraordinary, that the cupidity of the unprincipled will still be tempted to continue it, as long as there is any chance of escaping the vigilance of the cruisers engaged against them. From the best information your memorialists have been able to obtain, of the nature, causes, and course of this trade, and of the present situation of the coast of Africa, and the habits and dispositions of the natives, they are well assured that the suppression of the African slave trade, and the civilization of the natives, are measures of indispensable connexion. . . .

Since the establishment of the English settlement at Sierra Leone, the slave trade has been rapidly ceasing upon that part of the coast.

Not only the kingdoms in its immediate neighborhood, but those upon the Sherbro and Bagroo rivers, and others with whom the people of that settlement have opened a communication, have been prevailed upon to abandon it, and are turning their attention to the ordinary and innocent pursuits of civilized nations.

That the same consequences will result from similar settlements cannot be doubted. When the natives there see that the European commodities, for which they have been accustomed to exchange their fellow-beings, until vast and fertile regions have become almost depopulated, can be more easily and safely obtained by other pursuits, can it be believed that they will hesitate to profit by the experience? Nor will the advantages of civilization be alone exhibited. That religion, whose mandate is "peace on earth and good will towards men," will "do its errand"; will deliver them from the bondage of their miserable superstitions, and display the same triumphs which it is achieving in every land.

. . . .

No nation has it so much in its power to furnish proper settlers for such establishments as this; no nation has so deep an interest in thus disposing of them. By the law passed at the last session, and before referred to, the captives who may be taken by our cruisers, from the slave ships are to be taken to Africa, and delivered to the custody of agents appointed by the President. There will then be a settlement of captured negroes upon the coast, in consequence of the measures already adopted. And it is evidently most important, if not necessary, to such a settlement, that the civilized people of color of this country, whose industry, enterprise, and knowledge of agriculture and the arts, would render them most useful assistants, should be connected with such an establishment.

When, therefore, the object of the Colonization Society is viewed in connexion with that entire suppression of the slave trade which your memorialists trust it is resolved shall be effected, its importance becomes obvious in the extreme.

The beneficial consequences resulting from success in such a measure, it is impossible to calculate. To the general cause of humanity it will afford the most rich and noble contribution, and for the nation that regards that cause, that employs its power in its behalf, it cannot fail to procure a proportionate reward. It is by such a course that a nation insures to itself the protection and favor of the Governor of the World. Nor are there wanting views and considerations, arising from our peculiar political institutions, which would justify the sure expectation of the most signal blessings to ourselves from the accomplishment of such an object. If one of these consequences shall be the gradual and almost imperceptible removal of a national evil, which all unite in lamenting, and for which, with the most intense, but, hitherto, hopeless anxiety, the patriots and statesmen of our country have labored to discover a remedy, who can doubt, that, of all the blessings we may be permitted to bequeath to our descendants, this will receive the richest tribute of their thanks and veneration?

Your memorialists cannot believe that such an evil, universally acknowledged and deprecated, has been irremovably fixed upon us. Some way will always be opened by Providence by which a people desirous of acting justly and benevolently may be led to the attainment of a meritorious object. And they believe that, of all the plans that the most sagacious and discerning of our patriots have suggested, for effecting what they have so greatly desired, the colonization of Africa, in the manner proposed, presents the fairest prospects of success. But if it be admitted to be ever so doubtful, whether this happy result shall be the reward of our exertions, yet, if great and certain benefits immediately attend them, why may not others, still greater, follow them?

In a work evidently progressive, who shall assign limits to the good that zeal and perseverance shall be permitted to accomplish? Your memorialists beg leave to state that, having expended considerable funds in prosecuting their inquiries and making preparations, they are now about to send out a colony, and complete the purchase, already stipulated for with the native kings and chiefs of Sherbro, of a suitable territory for their establishment. The number they are now enabled to transport and provide for, is but a small proportion of the people of color who have expressed their desire to go; and without a larger and more sudden increase of their funds than can be expected from the voluntary contributions of individuals, their progress must be slow and uncertain. They have always flattered themselves with the hope that when it was seen they had surmounted the difficulties of preparation, and shown that means applied to the execution of their design would lead directly and evidently to its accomplishment, they would be able to obtain for it the national countenance and assistance. To this point they have arrived; and they, therefore, respectfully request that this interesting subject may receive the consideration of your honorable body, and that the Executive Department may be authorized, in such way as may meet your approbation, to extend to this object such pecuniary and other aid as it may be thought to require and deserve.

Your memorialists further request, that the subscribers to the American Colonization Society may be incorporated, by act of Congress, to enable them to act with more efficiency in carrying on the great and important objects of the Society, and to enable them, with more economy, to manage the benevolent contributions intrusted to their care.

Signed by John Mason, W. Jones, E. B. Caldwell, and F. S. Key, committee.

WASHINGTON
February 1, 1820

III

Expansion and the Anti-Slavery Controversy

1820–1860

The forty-year period from 1820 to 1860 opened with the bitter controversy over slavery in Missouri. Although that dispute was temporarily resolved by the Compromise of 1820, the period itself ended in armed hostility—with the North and the South arguing the same issues debated in regard to Missouri. The pessimistic views of Thomas Jefferson were thus confirmed, for he had observed at the time of the Missouri controversy that "this momentous question, like a fire bell in the night, awakened and filled me with terror. I consider it at once as the knell of the Union."

The forty years preceding the American Civil War represented a time of unprecedented development and expansion. But national growth led the country into a seemingly irreconcilable domestic conflict. Whether touching on trade and economic development or on the opening of new territories, the slavery question could not be removed from the center of the public arena. Politicians sought endless means of compromise, but they learned to their dismay, and that of their constituents, that the basic issue could not be avoided. There existed a certain compelling necessity that forced this nominally free society to confront the slavery issue head on.

Whether or not the Civil War was unavoidable is still an open historical question; but that the fundamental issue of slavery and racial injustice was, by definition, an irrepressible problem for a democratic society seems beyond dispute.

During the years 1820 to 1860, the North and the South seemed increasingly to move in divergent directions. For its part, the South dramatized the fears of Negro insurrections and slave revolts, and used those fears as justification for tightening the slave codes that limited the Negro's mobility, educational opportunities, and contacts with the world beyond his immediate environment. At the same time, the South interpreted northern pressures, whether in the form of political action in Congress or independent antislavery agitation, as hostile and unrelenting opposition to its way of life. In part to meet the criticism of its peculiar institution from without, and in part to assuage its own conscience, the South developed a positive defense of slavery—an assertion that it represented an absolute good for Negroes and whites alike.

On the political front, the southern states increasingly voiced the arguments of states' rights and local control over economic and social questions, and took the constitutional position that it was the responsibility of the federal government to protect the individual property rights of slaveholders and to guarantee the capture of fugitive slaves. In this, the South evidenced an increasing tendency toward myopic regionalism, and its obdurate defense of slavery as an indisputable right flew in the face of trends throughout the Western world toward the emancipation of slaves and serfs and the irresistible liberalizing pressures of nineteenth-century thought.

The people of the North did not initially take a strong position on the Negro—free or slave. But as the northern states grew in population, wealth, and diversity of attitudes, they emphasized national political adjustments on the basis of majority rule. The South, on the other hand, increasingly adhered to a political philosophy designed to protect its minority status within Congress. At the same time that the South was seeking to justify slavery, the North was becoming increasingly dissatisfied with the institution. In part, this was born of a fear that the extension of slavery into the new western territories would work to the detriment of northern, free, white labor; in part, it was also bred of a moral revulsion of slavery held by the abolitionists of the antebellum period.

The Negro, himself, had been ill prepared to take a full role in the political controversies of the dominant white majority. Increasingly after 1830, the position of the slaves deteriorated in both the Old and the New South; even in the North, the status of free Negroes was restricted by state statutes. Yet the Negro was not content to accept a fate arbitrarily handed him by the white society. During the forty-year period preceding the Civil War, numerous slave revolts, runaway slaves, and the Underground Railroad all gave witness to the determination of southern Negroes to reject the inheritance of bondage. At the same time, leading Negro abolitionists in the North, such as Sojourner Truth, Harriet Tubman, and Frederick Douglass, allied themselves with white abolitionists in bringing pressure upon both North and South alike to recognize the evils of slavery.

Amendments, provisos, and compromises could not reconcile the extreme views of North and South. The nation moved to civil war.

THE MISSOURI COMPROMISE (1819, 1820)

When the territory of Missouri applied for admission to statehood, the Congress and the nation were confronted with a unique substantive question that had far-reaching implications both for the settlement and for the future political status of all the states that might be carved from the vast area acquired from France in the Louisiana Purchase of 1803.

Should slavery be allowed in the new state of Missouri? The fact that southern slaveholders had already migrated into the Missouri territory made the question more than academic. When the bill for admission came before the House, Congressman James Tallmadge of New York offered an amendment that would have prohibited the further introduction of slavery and would have eventually freed the progeny of slaves then in the territory. Tallmadge's remarks in defense of his amendment refer to the excitement and bitterness that his proposition elicited from slavery advocates. While he justified his position on the grounds of Congressional authority, there was also an indication of northern reluctance to see the extension of southern political advantage by inflated representation (tied to the three-fifths compromise of the federal Constitution). The Tallmadge amendment passed the House but was rejected by the Senate.

The issue was resolved by a two-part compromise. First, Missouri gained admission to the Union as a slave state, with a provision that portions of the Louisiana Territory lying north of 36° 30′ north latitude would be free. (This limitation was later overturned by the 1854 Kansas-Nebraska Act [Document 33] and by the 1857 *Dred Scott* case, 19 How. 393 [Document 34].) Second, Maine was simultaneously admitted to statehood, which enabled the Senate to maintain the balance between slave and free state representation— twelve of each. The enabling act of March 6, 1820, made it clear, however, that fugitive slaves could be apprehended north of the compromise line and returned to their owners.

DOCUMENT(S) 23

*Remarks of Congressman Tallmadge in support of the Amendment**

Mr. Tallmadge, of New York, rose. Sir, said he, it has been my desire and my intention to avoid any debate on the present painful and unpleasant subject. When I had the honor to submit to this House the amendment now under consideration, I accompanied it with a declaration, that it was intended to confine its operation to the newly acquired territory across the Mississippi; and I then expressly declared that I would in no manner intermeddle with the slaveholding States, nor attempt manumission in any one of the original States in the Union. Sir, I even went further, and stated that I was aware of the delicacy of the subject, and that I had learned from Southern gentlemen the difficulties and the dangers of having free blacks intermingling with slaves; and, on that account, and with a view to the safety of the white population of the adjoining States, I would not even advocate the prohibition of slavery in the Alabama Territory; because,

---

* *Annals of Congress*, 15th Congress, 2nd Session (February 16, 1819), pp. 1203–15.

surrounded as it was by slaveholding States, and with only imaginary lines of division, the intercourse between slaves and free blacks could not be prevented, and a *servile* war might be the result. While we deprecate and mourn over the evil of slavery, humanity and good morals require us to wish its abolition, under circumstances consistent with the safety of the white population. Willingly, therefore, will I submit to an evil which we cannot safely remedy. I admitted all that had been said of the danger of having free blacks visible to slaves, and therefore did not hesitate to pledge myself that I would neither advise nor attempt coercive manumission. But, sir, all these reasons cease when we cross the banks of the Mississippi, a newly acquired territory, never contemplated in the formation of our Government, not included within the compromise or mutual pledge in the adoption of our Constitution, a new territory acquired by our common fund, and ought justly to be subject to our common legislation.

Sir, when I submitted the amendment now under consideration, accompanied with these explanations, and with these avowals of my intentions and of my motives, I did expect that gentlemen who might differ from me in opinion would appreciate the liberality of my views, and would meet me with moderation, as upon a fair subject for general legislation. Sir, I did expect at least that the frank declaration of my views would protect me from harsh expressions, and from the unfriendly imputations which have been cast out on this occasion. But, sir, such has been the character and the violence of this debate, and expressions of so much intemperance and of an aspect so threatening have been used, that continued silence on my part would ill become me, who had submitted to this House the original proposition. While this subject was under debate before the Committee of the Whole, I did not take the floor, and I avail myself of this occasion to acknowledge my obligations to my friends (Messrs. Taylor and Mills) for the manner in which they supported my amendment, at a time when I was unable to partake in the debate. I had only on that day returned from a journey long in its extent and painful in its occasion; and, from an affection of my breast, I could not then speak; I cannot yet hope to do justice to the subject, but I do hope to say enough to assure my friends that I have not *left* them in the controversy, and to convince the opponents of the measure, that their violence has not driven me from the debate.

Sir, the honorable gentleman from Missouri (Mr. Scott), who has just resumed his seat, has told us of the *ides of March*, and has cautioned us to *"beware of the fate of Cæsar and of Rome."* Another gentleman (Mr. Cobb), from Georgia, in addition to other expressions of great warmth, has said, "that, if we persist, the Union will be dissolved"; and, with a look fixed on me, has told us, "we have kindled a fire which all the waters of the ocean cannot put out, which seas of blood can only extinguish."

Sir, language of this sort has no effect on me; my purpose is fixed, it is interwoven with my existence, its durability is limited with my life, it is a great and glorious cause, setting bounds to a slavery, the most cruel and debasing the world ever witnessed; it is the freedom of man; it is the cause of unredeemed and unregenerated human beings.

Sir, if a dissolution of the Union must take place, let it be so! If civil war, which gentlemen so much threaten, must come, I can only say, let it come! My hold on life is probably as frail as that of any man who now hears me; but, while that hold lasts, it shall be devoted to the service of my country—to the freedom of man. If blood is necessary to extinguish any fire which I have assisted to kindle, I can assure gentlemen, while I regret the necessity, I shall not forbear to contribute my mite. Sir, the violence to which gentlemen have resorted on this subject will not move my purpose, nor drive me from my place. I have the fortune and the honor to stand here as the representative of freemen, who possess intelligence to know their rights, who have the spirit to maintain them. Whatever might be my own private sentiments on this subject, standing here as the representative of others, no choice is left me. I know the will of my constituents, and, regardless of consequences, I will avow it; as their representative, I will proclaim their hatred to slavery in every shape; as their representative, here will I hold my stand, until this floor, with the Constitution of my country which supports it, shall sink beneath me. If I am doomed to fall, I shall at least have the painful consolation to believe that I fall, as a fragment, in the ruins of my country.

· · · ·

Sir, has it already come to this; that in the Congress of the United States—that, in the legislative councils of republican America, the subject of slavery has become a subject of so much feeling—of such delicacy—of such danger, that it cannot safely be discussed? Are members who venture to express their sentiments on this subject to be accused of talking to the galleries, with intent to excite a servile war, and of meriting the fate of Arbuthnot and Ambrister? Are we to be told of the dissolution of the Union, of civil war, and of seas of blood? And yet, with such awful threatenings before us, do gentlemen, in the same breath, insist upon the encouragement of this evil, upon the extension of this monstrous scourge of the human race? An evil so fraught with such dire calamities to us as individuals, and to our nation, and threatening, in its progress, to overwhelm the civil and religious institutions of the country, with the liberties of the nation, ought at once to be met, and to be controlled. If its power, its influence, and its impending dangers have already arrived at such a point that it is not safe to discuss it on this floor, and it cannot now pass under consideration as a proper subject for general legislation, what will be the result when it is spread through your widely extended domain? Its present threatening aspect, and the violence of its supporters, so far from inducing me to yield to its progress, prompts me to resist its march. Now is the time. It must now be met, and the extension of the evil must now be prevented, or the occasion is irrecoverably lost, and the evil can never be contracted.

Sir, extend your view across the Mississippi, over your newly acquired territory; a territory so far surpassing in extent the limits of your present country, that that country which gave birth to your nation, which achieved your Revolution, consolidated your Union, formed your Constitution, and has subsequently acquired so much glory, hangs but as an appendage to the extended empire over which your republican Government is now called to bear sway. Look down the long vista of futurity. See your empire, in extent unequalled, in advantageous situation without a parallel, and occupying all the valuable part of our continent. Behold this extended empire, inhabited by the hardy sons of American freemen—knowing their rights, and inheriting the will to protect them—owners of the soil on which they live, and interested in the institutions which they labor to defend—with two oceans laving your shores, and tributary to your purposes, bearing on their bosoms the commerce of your people. Compared to yours, the Governments of Europe dwindle into insignificance, and the whole world is without a parallel. But, sir, reverse this scene; people this fair dominion with the slaves of your planters; extend slavery—this bane of man, this abomination of heaven—over your extended empire, and you prepare its dissolution; you turn its accumulated strength into positive weakness; you cherish a canker in your breast; you put poison in your bosom; you place a vulture on your heart—nay, you whet the dagger and place it in the hands of a portion of your population, stimulated to use it, by every tie, human and divine. The envious contrast between your happiness and their misery, between your liberty and their slavery, must constantly prompt them to accomplish your destruction. Your enemies will learn the source and the cause of your weakness. As often as internal dangers shall threaten, or internal commotions await you, you will then realize, that, by your own procurement, you have placed amidst your families, and in the bosom of your country, a population producing at once the greatest cause of individual danger and of national weakness. With this defect, your Government must crumble to pieces, and your people become the scoff of the world.

Sir, we have been told, with apparent confidence, that we have no right to annex conditions to a State on its admission into the Union; and it has been urged that the proposed amendment, prohibiting the further introduction of slavery, is unconstitutional. This position, asserted with so much confidence, remains unsupported by any argument, or by any authority derived from the Constitution itself. The Constitution strongly indicates an opposite conclusion and seems to contemplate a difference between the old and the new States. The practice of the Government has sanctioned this difference in many respects.

The third section of the fourth article of the Constitution says, "new States may be admitted by the Congress into this Union," and it is silent as to the terms and conditions upon which the new States may be so admitted. The fair inference from this silence is that the Congress which might admit should prescribe the time and the terms of such admission.

The tenth section of the first article of the Constitution says, "the migration or importation of such persons as any of the States now existing shall think proper to admit, shall not be prohibited by the Congress prior to the year 1808." The words "now existing" clearly show the distinction for which we contend. The word *slave* is nowhere mentioned in the Constitution, but this section has always been considered as applicable to them, and unquestionably reserved the right to prohibit their importation into any new State before the year 1808.

Congress, therefore, have power over the subject, probably as a matter of legislation, but more certainly as a right, to prescribe the time and the condition upon which any new State may be admitted into the family of the Union. Sir, the bill now before us proves the correctness of my argument. It is filled with conditions and limitations. The territory is required to take a census, and is to be admitted only on condition that it have forty thousand inhabitants. I have already submitted amendments preventing the State from taxing the lands of the United States, and declaring all navigable waters shall remain open to the other States and be exempt from any tolls or duties. And my friend (Mr. Taylor) has submitted amendments prohibiting the State from taxing soldiers' lands for the period of five years. And to all these amendments we have heard no objection; they have passed unanimously. But now, when an amendment prohibiting the further introduction of slavery is proposed, the whole House is put in agitation, and we are confidently told that it is unconstitutional to annex conditions on the admission of a new State into the Union. The result of all this is that all amendments and conditions are proper, which suit a certain class of gentlemen, but whatever amendment is proposed, which does not comport with their interests or their views, is unconstitutional, and a flagrant violation of this sacred charter of our rights. In order to be consistent, gentlemen must go back and strike out the various amendments to which they have already agreed. The Constitution applies equally to all, or to none. . . .

An act to authorize the people of the Missouri territory to form a constitution and state government, and for the admission of such state into the Union on an equal footing with the original states, and to prohibit slavery in certain territories*

Be it enacted by the Senate and House of Representatives of the United States of America, in Congress assembled, That the inhabitants of that portion of the Missouri territory included within the boundaries hereinafter designated, be, and they are hereby, authorized to form for themselves a constitution and state government, and to assume such name as they shall deem proper; and the said state, when formed, shall be admitted into the Union, upon an equal footing with the original states, in all respects whatsoever.

SEC. 2. *And be it further enacted,* That the said state shall consist of all the territory included within the following boundaries, to wit: Beginning in the middle of the Mississippi river, on the parallel of thirty-six degrees of north latitude; thence west, along that parallel of latitude, to the St. Francois river; thence up, and following the course of that river, in the middle of the main channel thereof, to the parallel of latitude of thirty-six degrees and thirty minutes; thence west, along the same, to a point where the said parallel is intersected by a meridian line passing through the middle of the mouth of the Kansas river, where the same empties into the Missouri river, thence, from the point aforesaid north, along the said meridian line, to the intersection of the parallel of latitude which passes through the rapids of the river Des Moines, making the said line to correspond with the Indian boundary line; thence east, from the point of intersection last aforesaid, along the said parallel of latitude, to the middle of the channel of the main fork of the said river Des Moines; thence down and along the middle of the main channel of the said river Des Moines, to the mouth of the same, where it empties into the Mississippi river; thence, due east, to the middle of the main channel of the Mississippi

---

* 3 Stat. 545 (1820).

river; thence down, and following the course of the Mississippi river, in the middle of the main channel thereof, to the place of beginning. . . .

SEC. 3. *And be it further enacted,* That all free white male citizens of the United States, who shall have arrived at the age of twenty-one years, and have resided in said territory three months previous to the day of election, and all other persons qualified to vote for representatives to the general assembly of the said territory, shall be qualified to be elected, and they are hereby qualified and authorized to vote, and choose representatives to form a convention.

. . . .

SEC. 8. *And be it further enacted,* That in all that territory ceded by France to the United States, under the name of Louisiana, which lies north of thirty-six degrees and thirty minutes north latitude, not included within the limits of the state, contemplated by this act, slavery and involuntary servitude, otherwise than in the punishment of crimes, whereof the parties shall have been duly convicted, shall be, and is hereby, forever prohibited: *Provided always,* That any person escaping into the same, from whom labour or service is lawfully claimed, in any state or territory of the United States, such fugitive may be lawfully reclaimed and conveyed to the person claiming his or her labour or service as aforesaid.

APPROVED, March 6, 1820.

ELKISON V. DELIESSELINE (1823)

Under the terms of an 1820 South Carolina statute, free Negroes aboard vessels entering the harbors of that state were imprisoned on shore for the period their ships were in port. The constitutional validity of this enactment was challenged in an 1823 habeas corpus proceeding in Charleston before United State Supreme Court Justice William Johnson. It was heard under the then prevailing practice requiring the justices to spend a portion of their time "riding circuit" to preside in the lower federal courts.

The act was declared unconstitutional, and the Negroes were freed. But the implications of the case went far beyond the striking down of that particular enactment. Justice Johnson's decision marked the first time that the commerce clause was used as a basis for invalidating state legislation. The decision presaged Johnson's concurring opinion in the following year in *Gibbons* v. *Ogden*, 9 Wheat. (22 U.S.) 1 (1824). Another important aspect of the case was the justice's broad construction of the federal treaty power as paramount to state legislation.

During the course of the trial, Justice Johnson was shocked by the argument of one of the attorneys speaking for South Carolina. The southern lawyer asserted that rather than see the state surrender such powers over Negroes he would prefer the dissolution of the Union.

DOCUMENT 24

*Elkison v. Deliesseline (1823)**

Johnson, Circuit Justice . . .

Two questions have now been made in argument; the first on the law of the case, the second on the remedy. On the unconstitutionality of the law under which this man is confined, it is not too much to say, that it will not bear argument; and I feel myself sanctioned in using this strong language, from considering the course of reasoning by which it has been defended. Neither of the gentlemen has attempted to prove that the power therein assumed by the state can be exercised without clashing with the general powers of the United States to regulate commerce; but they have both strenuously contended, that ex necessitate it was a power which the state must and would exercise, and, indeed, Mr. Holmes concluded his argument with the declaration, that, if a dissolution of the Union must be the alternative, he was ready to meet it. Nor did the argument of Col. Hunt deviate at all from the same course. Giving it in the language of his own summary, it was this: South Carolina was a sovereign state when she adopted the constitution; a sovereign state

---

* Brunner, Col. Cas. 431, 2 Wheeler Cr. Cas. 56, Case No. 4,366, 8 Fed. Cas. 493 (Cir. Ct., D.S.C. 1823).

cannot surrender a right of vital importance; South Carolina, therefore, either did not surrender this right, or still possesses the power to resume it, and whether it is necessary, or when it is necessary, to resume it, she is herself the sovereign judge. But it was not necessary to give this candid exposé of the grounds which this law assumes; for it is a subject of positive proof, that it is altogether irreconcilable with the powers of the general government; that it necessarily compromits the public peace, and tends to embroil us with, if not separate us from, our sister states; in short, that it leads to a dissolution of the Union, and implies a direct attack upon the sovereignty of the United States.

Let it be observed that the law is, "if any vessel (not even the vessels of the United States excepted) shall come into any port or harbor of this state," etc., bringing in free colored persons, such persons are to become "absolute slaves," and that, without even a form of trial, as I understand the act, they are to be sold. By the next clause the sheriff is vested with absolute power, and expressly enjoined to carry the law into effect, and is to receive the one half of the proceeds of the sale. The object of this law, and it has been so acknowledged in argument, is to prohibit ships coming into this port employing colored seamen, whether citizens or subjects of their own government or not. But if this state can prohibit Great Britain from employing her colored subjects (and she has them of all colors on the globe), or if at liberty to prohibit the employment of her subjects of the African race, why not prohibit her from using those of Irish or of Scottish nativity? If the color of his skin is to preclude the Lascar or the Sierra Leone seaman, why not the color of his eye or his hair exclude from our ports the inhabitants of her other territories? In fact it amounts to the assertion of the power to exclude the seamen of the territories of Great Britain, or any other nation, altogether. With regard to various friendly nations it amounts to an actual exclusion in its present form. Why may not the shipping of Morocco or of Algiers cover the commerce of France with this country, even at the present crisis? Their seamen are all colored, and even the state of Massachusetts might lately, and may perhaps now, expedite to this port a vessel with her officers black, and her crew composed of Nantucket Indians, known to be among the best seamen in our service. These might all become slaves under this act. If this law were enforced upon such vessels, retaliation would follow; and the commerce of this city, feeble and sickly, comparatively, as it already is, might be fatally injured. Charleston seamen, Charleston owners, Charleston vessels, might, eo nomine, be excluded from their commerce, or the United States involved in war and confusion. I am far from thinking that this power would ever be wantonly exercised, but these considerations show its utter incompatibility with the power delegated to congress to regulate commerce with foreign nations and our sister states.

Apply the law to the particular case before us, and the incongruity will be glaring. The offense, it will be observed, for which this individual is supposed to forfeit his freedom, is that of coming into this port in the ship Homer, in the capacity of a seaman. I say this is the whole of his offense; for I will not admit the supposition that he is to be burdened with the offense of the captain in not carrying him out of the state. He is himself shut up, he cannot go off; his removal depends upon another. It is true the sale of him is suspended upon the conviction of the captain, and the captain has the power to rescue him from slavery. But suppose the captain, as is very frequently the case, may find it his interest or his pleasure to get rid of him, and of the wages due him, his fate is suspended on the captain's caprice in this particular; but it is the exercise of the dispensing power in the captain, and nothing more. The seaman's crime is complete, and the forfeiture incurred by the single act of coming into port; and this even though driven into port by stress of weather, or forced by a power which he cannot control into a port for which he did not ship himself; the law contains no exception to meet such contingencies. The seaman's offense, therefore, is coming into the state in a ship or vessel; that of the captain consists in bringing him in, and not taking him out of the state, and paying all expenses. Now, according to the laws and treaties of the United States, it was both lawful for this seaman to come into this port, in this vessel, and for the captain to bring him in the capacity of a seaman; and yet these are the very acts for which the state law imposes these heavy penalties. Is there no clashing in this? It is in effect a repeal of the laws of the United States, pro tanto, converting a right into a crime.

And here it is proper to notice that part of the argument

against the motion, in which it was insisted on that this law was passed by the state in exercise of a concurrent right. "Concurrent" does not mean "paramount," and yet, in order to divest a right conferred by the general government, it is very clear that the state right must be more than concurrent. But the right of the general government to regulate commerce with the sister states and foreign nations is a paramount and exclusive right; and this conclusion we arrive at, whether we examine it with reference to the words of the constitution, or the nature of the grant. That this has been the received and universal construction from the first day of the organization of the general government is unquestionable; and the right admits not of a question any more than the fact. In the constitution of the United States, the most wonderful instrument ever drawn by the hand of man, there is a comprehension and precision that is unparalleled; and I can truly say, that after spending my life in studying it, I still daily find in it some new excellence. It is true that it contains no prohibition on the states to regulate foreign commerce. Nor was such a prohibition necessary, for the words of the grant sweep away the whole subject, and leave nothing for the states to act upon. Wherever this is the case, there is no prohibitory clause interposed in the constitution. Thus, the states are not prohibited from regulating the value of foreign coins or fixing a standard of weights and measures, for the very words imply a total, unlimited grant. The words in the present case are, "to regulate commerce with foreign nations, and among the several states, and with the Indian tribes." If congress can regulate commerce, what commerce can it not regulate? And the navigation of ships has always been held, by all nations, to appertain to commercial regulations.

But the case does not rest here. In order to sustain this law, the state must also possess a power paramount to the treaty-making power of the United States, expressly declared to be a part of the supreme legislative power of the land; for the seizure of this man, on board a British ship, is an express violation of the commercial convention with Great Britain of 1815. Our commerce with that nation does not depend upon the mere negative sanction of not being prohibited. A reciprocal liberty of commerce is expressly stipulated for and conceded by that treaty; to this the right of navigating their ships in their own way, and particularly by their own subjects, is necessarily incident. If policy requires any restriction of this right, with regard to a particular class of subjects of either contracting party, it must be introduced by treaty. The opposite party cannot introduce it by a legislative act of his own. Such a law as this could not be passed even by the general government, without furnishing a just cause of war.

But to all this the plea of necessity is urged; and of the existence of that necessity we are told the state alone is to judge. Where is this to land us? Is it not asserting the right in each state to throw off the federal constitution at its will and pleasure? If it can be done as to any particular article it may be done as to all; and, like the old confederation, the Union becomes a mere rope of sand. But I deny that the state surrendered a single power necessary to its security, against this species of property. What is to prevent their being confined to their ships, if it is dangerous for them to go abroad? This power may be lawfully exercised. To land their cargoes, take in others, and depart, is all that is necessary to ordinary commerce, and is all that is properly stipulated for in the convention of 1815, so far as relates to seamen. If our fears extend also to the British merchant, the supercargo, or master, being persons of color, I acknowledge that, as to them, the treaty precludes us from abridging their rights to free ingress and egress, and occupying houses and warehouses for the purposes of commerce. As to them, this law is an express infraction of the treaty. No such law can be passed consistently with the treaty, and unless sanctioned by diplomatic arrangement, the passing of such a law is tantamount to a declaration of war. But if the policy of this law was to keep foreign free persons of color from holding communion with our slaves, it certainly pursues a course altogether inconsistent with its object. One gentleman likened the importation of such persons to that of clothes infected with the plague, or of wild beasts from Africa; the other to that of fire-brands set to our own houses only to escape by the light. But surely if the penalty inflicted for coming here is in its effect that of being domesticated, by being sold here, then we ourselves inoculate our community with the plague; we ourselves turn loose the wild beast in our streets, and we put the fire-brand under our own houses. If there are evil persons abroad who would steal to this place in order to do us this mischief (and the whole provisions of this act are founded in that supposition), then this method of disposing of offenders by detaining them here presents the finest facilities in the world for introducing themselves lawfully into the very situation in which they would enjoy the best opportunities of pursuing their designs. Now, if this plea of necessity could avail at all against the constitution and laws of the United States, certainly that law cannot be pronounced necessary which may defeat its own ends; much less when other provisions of unexceptionable legality might be resorted to, which would operate solely to the end proposed, viz., the effectual exclusion of dangerous characters. On the fact of the necessity for all this exhibition of legislation and zeal, I say nothing; I neither admit nor deny it. In common with every other citizen, I am entitled to my own opinion; but when I express it, it shall be done in my private capacity.

But what shall we say to the provisions of this act as they operate on our vessels of war? Send your sheriff on board one of them, and would the spirited young men of the navy submit to have a man taken? It would be a repetition of the affair of the "Chesapeake." The public mind would revolt at the idea of such an attempt; and yet it is perfectly clear that there is nothing in this act which admits of any exception in their favor.

Upon the whole, I am decidedly of the opinion that the third section of the state act now under consideration is unconstitutional and void, and that every arrest made under it subjects the parties making it to an action of trespass. . . .

GARRISON'S LIBERATOR (1831)

A controversial personality both to his contemporaries and to future historians, William Lloyd Garrison and his newspaper, *The Liberator,* have come to represent the extreme in antebellum abolitionist spirit. Attitudes toward slavery were considerably sharpened in the early 1830's by the circulation of David Walker's *Appeal,* Nat Turner's insurrection (Document 26), the abolition of slavery by the British Parliament (3 & 4 Wm. IV, c.73 [1833]), and the heightened efforts of American antislavery groups. Garrison intensified the senti-

ments of North and South, Negro and white, by his outspoken
and uncompromising position. He demanded the immediate
and total end of slavery.

DOCUMENT 25

*To the Public**

In the month of August, I issued proposals for publishing *The Liberator* in Washington City; but the enterprise,
though hailed in different sections of the country, was palsied
by public indifference. Since that time, the removal of the
Genius of Universal Emancipation to the Seat of Government
has rendered less imperious the establishment of a similar
periodical in that quarter.

During my recent tour for the purpose of exciting the minds
of the people by a series of discourses on the subject of
slavery, every place that I visited gave fresh evidence of the
fact, that a greater revolution in public sentiment was to be
effected in the free States—*and particularly in New England*
—than at the South. I found contempt more bitter, opposition
more active, detraction more relentless, prejudice more stubborn, and apathy more frozen, than among slave-owners
themselves. Of course, there were individual exceptions to the
contrary. This state of things afflicted, but did not dishearten
me. I determined, at every hazard, to lift up the standard of
emancipation in the eyes of the nation, *within sight of Bunker
Hill and in the birthplace of liberty.* That standard is now
unfurled; and long may it float, unhurt by the spoliations of
time or the missiles of a desperate foe—yea, till every chain
be broken, and every bondman set free! Let Southern oppressors tremble—let their secret abettors tremble—let their
Northern apologists tremble—let all the enemies of the perse-
cuted blacks tremble.

I deem the publication of my original Prospectus unnecessary, as it has obtained a wide circulation. The principles
therein inculcated will be steadily pursued in this paper, ex-
cepting that I shall not array myself as the political partisan
of any man. In defending the great cause of human rights, I
wish to derive the assistance of all religions and of all parties.

---

* *The Liberator*, Vol. I, No. 1 (January 1, 1831), 1:1-2.

Assenting to the "self-evident truth" maintained in the American Declaration of Independence, "that all men are created equal, and endowed by their Creator with certain inalienable rights—among which are life, liberty and the pursuit of happiness," I shall strenuously contend for the immediate enfranchisement of our slave population. In Park Street Church, on the Fourth of July, 1829, in an address on slavery, I unreflectingly assented to the popular but pernicious doctrine of *gradual* abolition. I seize this opportunity to make a full and unequivocal recantation, and thus publicly to ask pardon of my God, of my country, and of my brethren the poor slaves, for having uttered a sentiment so full of timidity, injustice, and absurdity. A similar recantation, from my pen, was published in the *Genius of Universal Emancipation* at Baltimore, in September, 1829. My conscience is now satisfied.

I am aware that many object to the severity of my language; but is there not cause for severity? I *will be* as harsh as truth, and as uncompromising as justice. On this subject, I do not wish to think, or speak, or write, with moderation. No! no! Tell a man whose house is on fire to give a moderate alarm; tell him to moderately rescue his wife from the hands of the ravisher; tell the mother to gradually extricate her babe from the fire into which it has fallen;—but urge me not to use moderation in a cause like the present. I am in earnest— I will not equivocate—I will not excuse—I will not retreat a single inch—AND I WILL BE HEARD. The apathy of the people is enough to make every statue leap from its pedestal, and to hasten the resurrection of the dead.

It is pretended, that I am retarding the cause of emancipation by the coarseness of my invective and the precipitancy of my measures. *The charge is not true.* On this question my influence,—humble as it is,—is felt at this moment to a considerable extent, and shall be felt in coming years—not perniciously, but beneficially—not as a curse, but as a blessing; and posterity will bear testimony that I was right. I desire to thank God, that he enables me to disregard "the fear of man which bringeth a snare," and to speak his truth in its simplicity and power. And here I close with this fresh dedication:

Oppression! I have seen thee, face to face,
And met thy cruel eye and cloudy brow;

But thy soul-withering glance I fear not now—
For dread to prouder feelings doth give place
Of deep abhorrence! Scorning the disgrace
Of slavish knees that at thy footstool bow,
I also kneel—but with far other vow
Do hail thee and thy herd of hirelings base:—
I swear, while life-blood warms my throbbing veins,
Still to oppose and thwart, with heart and hand,
Thy brutalising sway—till Afric's chains
Are burst, and Freedom rules the rescued land,—
Trampling Oppression and his iron rod:
Such is the vow I take—SO HELP ME GOD!

WILLIAM LLOYD GARRISON

BOSTON,
1 January 1831

NAT TURNER'S INSURRECTION AND "CONFESSION" (1831)

The specter of a Negro insurrection had always held a horrible fascination for southern whites, and the famous plot of the free Negro, Denmark Vesey, in South Carolina in 1822 seemed to affirm the slaveholders' worst fears. The bloody Nat Turner insurrection in Virginia nine years later demonstrated that plantation slaves could rebel, and the South bent every effort thereafter toward the harsher repression of slaves and of those whites seeking to ameliorate the Negro's condition.

Thomas Gray alleged that he took Nat Turner's own confession prior to the latter's trial and conviction. In publishing these materials, Gray assured the reader that Turner and his fellow slaves bore no connection with any grander scheme of rebellion. The "confession" is occasionally interrupted by Gray's own interpretive remarks. When it sentenced Nat Turner, the court deliberately reminded him that ". . . your hands were often imbrued in the blood of the innocent; and your own confession tells us that they were stained with the blood of a master, in your own language, 'too indulgent.'"

DOCUMENT 26

Thomas Gray's Introduction and Interview[*]

To the Public

The late insurrection in Southampton has greatly excited the public mind, and led to a thousand idle, exaggerated, and mischievous reports. It is the first instance in our history of an open rebellion of the slaves, and attended with such atrocious circumstances of cruelty and destruction, as could not fail to leave a deep impression, not only upon the minds of the community where this fearful tragedy was wrought, but throughout every portion of our country, in which this population is to be found. Public curiosity has been on the stretch to understand the origin and progress of this dreadful conspiracy, and the motives which influence its diabolical actors. The insurgent slaves had all been destroyed, or apprehended, tried, and executed (with the exception of the leader), without revealing anything at all satisfactory as to the motives which governed them, or the means by which they expected to accomplish their object. Every thing connected with the sad affair was wrapt in mystery, until Nat Turner, the leader of this ferocious band, whose name has resounded throughout our widely extended empire, was captured. This "great Bandit" was taken by a single individual, in a cave near the residence of his late owner, on Sunday, the thirtieth of October, without attempting to make the slightest resistance, and on the following day safely lodged in the jail of the County. His captor was Benjamin Phipps, armed with a shotgun well charged. Nat's only weapon was a small light sword which he immediately surrendered, and begged that his life might be spared. Since his confinement, by permission of the Jailor, I have had ready access to him, and finding that he was willing to make a full and free confession of the origin, progress, and consummation of the insurrectory movements of the slaves of which he was the contriver and head, I determined for the gratification of

[*] Thomas R. Gray, ed., *The Confessions of Nat Turner, The Leader of the Late Insurrection in Southampton, Va.* (Richmond: Thomas R. Gray, 1832), pp. 1–15. [Copy in the Rare Book Room, Library of Congress.]

public curiosity to commit his statements to writing, and publish them, with little or no variation, from his own words. That this is a faithful record of his confessions, the annexed certificate of the County Court of Southampton, will attest. They certainly bear one stamp of truth and sincerity. He makes no attempt (as all the other insurgents who were examined did), to exculpate himself, but frankly acknowledges his full participation in all the guilt of the transaction. He was not only the contriver of the conspiracy, but gave the first blow towards its execution. . . .

Believing the following narrative, by removing doubts and conjectures from the public mind which otherwise must have remained, would give general satisfaction, it is respectfully submitted to the public by their ob't serv't,

T. R. GRAY

Confession

. . . Sir, You have asked me to give a history of the motives which induced me to undertake the late insurrection, as you call it. To do so I must go back to the days of my infancy, and even before I was born. I was thirty-one years of age the 2nd of October last, and born the property of Benj. Turner, of this county. In my childhood a circumstance occurred which made an indelible impression on my mind, and laid the groundwork of that enthusiasm which has terminated so fatally to many, both white and black, and for which I am about to atone at the gallows. It is here necessary to relate this circumstance—trifling as it may seem; it was the commencement of that belief which has grown with time, and even now, sir, in this dungeon, helpless and forsaken as I am, I cannot divest myself of. Being at play with other children, when three or four years old, I was telling them something, which my mother overhearing, said it had happened before I was born. I stuck to my story, however, and related some things which went, in her opinion, to confirm it. Others being called on were greatly astonished, knowing that these things had happened, and caused them to say in my hearing, I surely would be a prophet, as the Lord had shewn me things that had happened before my birth. And my father and mother strengthened me in this my first impression, saying in my presence, I was intended for some great purpose, which they had always thought from certain marks on my head and breast. . . . My grandmother, who was very religious, and to whom I was much attached—my master, who belonged to the church, and other religious persons who visited the house and whom I often saw at prayers, noticing the singularity of my manners, I suppose, and my uncommon intelligence for a child, remarked I had too much sense to be raised, and if I was, I would never be of any service to any one as a slave. To a mind like mine, restless, inquisitive, and observant of everything that was passing, it is easy to suppose that religion was the subject to which it would be directed, and although this subject principally occupied my thoughts, there was nothing that I saw or heard of to which my attention was not directed. The manner in which I learned to read and write, not only had great influence on my own mind, as I acquired it with the most perfect ease, so much so, that I have no recollection whatever of learning the alphabet; but to the astonishment of the family, one day, when a book was shewn to me to keep me from crying, I began spelling the names of different objects—this was a source of wonder to all in the neighborhood, particularly the blacks—and this learning was constantly improved at all opportunities. When I got large enough to go to work, while employed, I was reflecting on many things that would present themselves to my imagination, and whenever an opportunity occurred of looking at a book, when the school children were getting their lessons, I would find many things that the fertility of my own imagination had depicted to me before; all my time, not devoted to my master's service, was spent either in prayer, or in making experiments in casting different things in moulds made of earth, in attempting to make paper, gun-powder, and many other experiments, that although I could not perfect, yet convinced me of its practicablity if I had the means. I was not addicted to stealing in my youth, nor have ever been. Yet such was the confidence of the negroes in the neighborhood, even at this early period of my life, in my superior judgment, that they would often carry me with them when they were going on any roguery, to plan for them.

. . . .

Question: Do you not find yourself mistaken now?

Answer: Was not Christ crucified? And by signs in the heavens that it would make known to me when I should commence the great work—and until the first sign appeared, I should conceal it from the knowledge of men. And on the appearance of the sign (the eclipse of the sun last February), I should arise and prepare myself, and slay my enemies with their own weapons. And immediately on the sign appearing in the heavens, the seal was removed from my lips, and I communicated the great work laid out for me to do, to four in whom I had the greatest confidence (Henry, Hark, Nelson, and Sam). It was intended by us to have begun the work of death on the 4th July last. Many were the plans formed and rejected by us, and it affected my mind to such a degree, that I fell sick; and the time passed without our coming to any determination how to commence. Still forming new schemes and rejecting them, when the sign appeared again, which determined me not to wait longer.

Since the commencement of 1830, I had been living with Mr. Joseph Travis, who was to me a kind master, and placed the greatest confidence in me; in fact, I had no cause to complain of his treatment to me. On Saturday evening, the 20th of August, it was agreed between Henry, Hark, and myself to prepare a dinner the next day for the men we expected, and then to concert a plan, as we had not yet determined on any. Hark, on the following morning, brought a pig, and Henry brandy, and being joined by Sam, Nelson, Will, and Jack, they prepared in the woods a dinner, where, about three o'clock, I joined them.

Q. Why were you so backward in joining them?

A. The same reason that had caused me not mix with them for years before.

I saluted them on coming up and asked Will how came he there; he answered, his life was worth no more than others, and his liberty as dear to him. I asked him if he thought to obtain it? He said he would, or lose his life. This was enough to put him in full confidence. Jack, I knew, was only a tool in the hands of Hark; it was quickly agreed we should commence at home (Mr. J. Travis') on that night, and until we had armed and equipped ourselves and gathered sufficient force, neither age nor sex was to be spared (which was invariably adhered to). We remained at the feast, until about two hours in the night, when we went to the house and found Austin; they all went to the cider press and drank, except myself. On returning to the house, Hark went to the door with an axe for the purpose of breaking it open, as we knew we were strong enough to murder the family if they were awaked by the noise; but reflecting that it might create an alarm in the neighborhood, we determined to enter the house secretly, and murder them whilst sleeping. Hark got a ladder and set it against the chimney, on which I ascended, and hoisting a window, entered and came downstairs, unbarred the door, and removed the guns from their places. It was then observed that I must spill the first blood. On which, armed with a hatchet and accompanied by Will, I entered my master's chamber; it being dark, I could not give a deathblow. The hatchet glanced from his head; he sprang from the bed and called his wife. It was his last word. Will laid him dead with a blow of his axe, and Mrs. Travis shared the same fate as she lay in bed. The murder of this family, five in number, was the work of a moment; not one of them awoke. There was a little infant sleeping in a cradle, that was forgotten, until we had left the house and gone some distance, when Henry and Will returned and killed it; we got here four guns that would shoot and several old muskets, with a pound or two of powder. We remained some time at the barn, where we paraded. I formed them in a line as soldiers, and after carrying them through all the manoeuvres I was master of, marched them off to Mr. Salathul Francis', about six hundred yards distant. Sam and Will went to the door and knocked. Mr. Francis asked who was there. Sam replied it was him, and he had a letter for him; on which he got up and came to the door. They immediately seized him, and dragging him out a little from the door, he was dispatched by repeated blows on the head. There was no other white person in the family. We started from there for Mrs. Reese's, maintaining the most perfect silence on our march, where finding the door unlocked, we entered, and murdered Mrs. Reese in her bed, while sleeping; her son awoke, but it was only to sleep the sleep of death. He had only time to say who is that, and he was no more.

. . . .

Our number amounted now to fifty or sixty, all mounted and armed with guns, axes, swords, and clubs. On reaching Mr. James W. Parker's gate, immediately on the road leading to Jerusalem, and about three miles distant, it was proposed to me to call there, but I objected, as I knew he was gone to Jerusalem, and my object was to reach there as soon as possible; but some of the men having relations at Mr. Parker's, it was agreed that they might call and get his people. I remained at the gate on the road, with seven or eight, the others going across the field to the house, about half a mile off. After waiting some time for them, I became impatient and started to the house for them; and on our return we were met by a party of white when [sic], who had pursued our blood-stained track, and who had fired on those at the gate, and dispersed them, which I knew nothing of, not having been at that time rejoined by any of them. Immediately on discovering the whites, I ordered my men to halt and form, as they appeared to be alarmed. The white men, eighteen in number, approached us in about one hundred yards, when one of them fired (this was against the positive orders of Captain Alexander P. Peete, who commanded, and who had directed the men to reserve their fire until within thirty paces). And I discovered about half of them retreating; I then ordered my men to fire and rush on them. The few remaining stood their ground until we approached within fifty yards, when they fired and retreated.

. . . .

CALHOUN'S RESOLUTIONS (1837–1838)

John C. Calhoun was the chief architect of the southern legal position on slavery, anchoring his arguments on his states' rights interpretation of the Constitution. The nation, he contended, was a compact of states, and thus the ultimate jurisdiction over domestic issues such as slavery was subject to state authority, rather than to the authority of either the federal government or the citizens of the nation as a whole. He took the position that the basic task of the national government was to resist aggression against a state's institutions by forces from outside that state.

The South Carolina Senator adroitly pictured slavery as an institution essential to the nation's welfare, as well as one sanctioned by the Founding Fathers. Accordingly, abolitionist efforts to bar slavery from the territories or from the District of Columbia violated the national interests in addition to basic constitutional rights. In presenting his resolutions to the Senate, Calhoun announced that he wanted them adopted by his colleagues as a test of good faith.

DOCUMENT 27

*Mr. Calhoun's Resolutions**

The following is a copy of these resolutions, as they passed the Senate:

I. *Resolved*, That, in the adoption of the Federal Constitution, the States adopting the same acted, severally, as free, independent, and sovereign States; and that each, for itself, by its own voluntary assent, entered the Union with the view to its increased security against all dangers, *domestic* as well as foreign, and the more perfect and secure enjoyment of its advantages, natural, political, and social.

II. *Resolved*, That in delegating a portion of their powers to be exercised by the Federal Government, the States retained, severally, the exclusive and sole right over their own domestic institutions and police to the full extent to which those powers were not thus delegated, and are alone responsible for them; and that any intermeddling of any one or more States, or a combination of their citizens, with the domestic institutions and police of the others, on any ground, political, moral, or religious, or under any pretext whatever, with the view to their alteration or subversion, is not warranted by the Constitution, tending to endanger the domestic peace and tranquillity of the States interfered with, subversive of the objects for which the Constitution was formed, and, by necessary consequence, tending to weaken and destroy the Union itself.

* *Congressional Globe*, Appendix, 25th Congress, 2nd Session, (January 12, 1838), p. 98.

III. *Resolved*, That this Government was instituted and adopted by the several States of this Union as a common agent, in order to carry into effect the powers which they had delegated by the Constitution for their mutual security and prosperity; and that in fulfilment of this high and sacred trust, this Government is bound so to exercise its powers, as not to interfere with the stability and security of the domestic institutions of the States that compose the Union; and that it is the solemn duty of the Government to resist, to the extent of its constitutional power, all attempts by one portion of the Union to use it as an instrument to attack the domestic institutions of another, or to weaken or destroy such institutions.

IV. *Resolved*, That domestic slavery, as it exists in the Southern and Western States of this Union, composes an important part of their domestic institutions, inherited from their ancestors, and existing at the adoption of the Constitution, by which it is recognised as constituting an important element in the apportionment of powers among the States, and that no change of opinion or feeling, on the part of the other States of the Union in relation to it, can justify them or their citizens in open and systematic attacks thereon, with the view to its overthrow; and that all such attacks are in manifest violation of the mutual and solemn pledge to protect and defend each other, given by the States respectively, on entering into the constitutional compact which formed the Union, and as such are a manifest breach of faith, and a violation of the most solemn obligations.

V. *Resolved*, That the interference by the citizens of any of the States, with the view to the abolition of slavery in this District, is endangering the rights and security of the people of the District; and that any act or measure of Congress designed to abolish slavery in this District, would be a violation of the faith implied in the cessions by the States of Virginia and Maryland, a just cause of alarm to the people of the slaveholding States, and have a direct and inevitable tendency to disturb and endanger the Union.

And resolved, That any attempt of Congress to abolish slavery in any Territory of the United States in which it exists would create serious alarm, and just apprehension, in the States sustaining that domestic institution; would be a violation of good faith towards the inhabitants of any such

Territory who have been permitted to settle with, and hold slaves therein, because the people of any such Territory have not asked for the abolition of slavery therein, and because when any such Territory shall be admitted into the Union as a State, the people thereof will be entitled to decide that question exclusively for themselves.

THE AMISTAD CASE (1841)

As a result of an unexpected decision of the lower federal courts in Connecticut, the Supreme Court had on its docket in 1841 the appeal of the United States Government involving the Spanish schooner *Amistad* and its cargo of "fresh African negroes." Captured in Africa and en route from one Cuban port to another, the Negroes had successfully revolted and seized the vessel. What was their status?

Despite the intervention of President Martin Van Buren to turn these Negroes over to the Spanish authorities, the Supreme Court declared them to be free. Justice Joseph Story reached the conclusion that they were "free native Africans" rather than slaves. He took the position that they had the status of kidnapped free men and thus had the same rights as other kidnapped persons.

DOCUMENT 28

*United States Appellants v. the Libellants and Claimants of the Schooner Amistad**

Mr. Justice Story, delivered the opinion of the court.

This is the case of an appeal from the decree of the circuit court of the district of Connecticut, sitting in admiralty. The leading facts, as they appear upon the transcript of the proceedings, are as follows: On the 27th of June 1839, the schooner "L'Amistad," being the property of Spanish subjects, cleared out from the port of Havana, in the island of Cuba,

---

* Supreme Court of the United States, 15 Pet. (40 U.S.) 518, 587 (1841).

for Puerto Principe, in the same island. On board of the schooner were the master, Ramon Ferrer, and Jose Ruiz and Pedro Montez, all Spanish subjects. The former had with him a negro boy, named Antonio, claimed to be his slave. Jose Ruiz had with him forty-nine negroes, claimed by him as his slaves, and stated to be his property, in a certain pass or document, signed by the governor-general of Cuba. Pedro Montez had with him four other negroes, also claimed by him as his slaves, and stated to be his property, in a similar pass or document, also signed by the governor-general of Cuba.

On the voyage, and before the arrival of the vessel at her port of destination, the negroes rose, killed the master, and took possession of her. On the 26th of August, the vessel was discovered by Lieutenant Gedney, of the United States brig "Washington," at anchor on the high seas, at the distance of half a mile from the shore of Long Island. A part of the negroes were then on shore, at Culloden Point, Long Island, who were seized by Lieutenant Gedney, and brought on board. The vessel, with the negroes and other persons on board, was brought by Lieutenant Gedney into the district of Connecticut, and there libelled for salvage in the district court of the United States. A libel for salvage was also filed by Henry Green and Pelatiah Fordham, of Sag Harbor, Long Island. On the 18th of September, Ruiz and Montez filed claims and libels, in which they asserted their ownership of the negroes as their slaves, and of certain parts of the cargo, and prayed that the same might be "delivered to them, or to the representatives of her Catholic Majesty, as might be most proper." On the 19th of September, the attorney of the United States for the district of Connecticut filed an information or libel, setting forth, that the Spanish minister had officially presented to the proper department of the government of the United States, a claim for the restoration of the vessel, cargo, and slaves, as the property of Spanish subjects, which had arrived within the jurisdictional limits of the United States, and were taken possession of by the said public armed brig of the United States, under such circumstances as made it the duty of the United States to cause the same to be restored to the true proprietors, pursuant to the treaty between the United States and Spain; and praying the court, on its being made legally to appear that the claim of the Spanish minister was well founded, to make such order for the disposal of the vessel, cargo and slaves, as would best enable the United States to comply with their treaty stipulations. But if it should appear, that the negroes were persons transported from Africa, in violation of the laws of the United States, and brought within the United States, contrary to the same laws; he then prayed the court to make such order for their removal to the coast of Africa, pursuant to the laws of the United States, as it should deem fit. . . .

On the 7th of January 1840, the negroes, Cinque and others, with the exception of Antonio, by their counsel, filed an answer, denying that they were slaves, or the property of Ruiz and Montez, or that the court could, under the constitution or laws of the United States, or under any treaty, exercise any jurisdiction over their persons, by reason of the premises; and praying that they might be dismissed. They specially set forth and insisted in this answer, that they were native-born Africans; born free, and still, of right, ought to be free and not slaves; that they were, on or about the 15th of April 1839, unlawfully kidnapped, and forcibly and wrongfully carried on board a certain vessel, on the coast of Africa, which was unlawfully engaged in the slave-trade, and were unlawfully transported in the same vessel to the island of Cuba, for the purpose of being there unlawfully sold as slaves; that Ruiz and Montez, well knowing the premises, made a pretended purchase of them; that afterwards, on or about the 28th of June 1839, Ruiz and Montez, confederating with Ferrer (master of the Amistad), caused them, without law or right, to be placed on board of the Amistad, to be transported to some place unknown to them, and there to be enslaved for life; that, on the voyage, they rose on the master, and took possession of the vessel, intending to return therewith to their native country, or to seek an asylum in some free state; and the vessel arrived, about the 26th of August 1839, off Montauk Point, near Long Island; a part of them were sent on shore, and were seized by Lieutenant Gedney, and carried on board; and all of them were afterwards brought by him into the district of Connecticut. . . .

No question has been here made, as to the proprietary interests in the vessel and cargo. It is admitted, that they belong to Spanish subjects, and that they ought to be restored.

The only point on this head is, whether the restitution ought to be upon the payment of salvage, or not? The main controversy is, whether these negroes are the property of Ruiz and Montez, and ought to be delivered up; and to this, accordingly, we shall first direct our attention.

It has been argued on behalf of the United States, that the court are bound to deliver them up, according to the treaty of 1795, with Spain, which has in this particular been continued in full force, by the treaty of 1819, ratified in 1821. The sixth article of that treaty seems to have had, principally in view, cases where the property of the subjects of either state had been taken possession of within the territorial jurisdiction of the other, during war. The eighth article provides for cases where the shipping of the inhabitants of either state are forced, through stress of weather, pursuit of pirates or enemies, or any other urgent necessity, to seek shelter in the ports of the other. There may well be some doubt entertained, whether the present case, in its actual circumstances, falls within the purview of this article. But it does not seem necessary, for reasons hereafter stated, absolutely to decide it. The ninth article provides, "that all ships and merchandize, of what nature soever, which shall be rescued out of the hands of any pirates or robbers, on the high seas, shall be brought into some port of either state, and shall be delivered to the custody of the officers of that port, in order to be taken care of and restored, entire, to the true proprietor, as soon as due and sufficient proof shall be made concerning the property thereof." This is the article on which the main reliance is placed on behalf of the United States, for the restitution of these negroes. To bring the case within the article, it is essential to establish: 1st, That these negroes, under all the circumstances, fall within the description of merchandize, in the sense of the treaty. 2d, That there has been a rescue of them on the high seas, out of the hands of the pirates and robbers; which, in the present case, can only be, by showing that they themselves are pirates and robbers: and 3d, That Ruiz and Montez, the asserted proprietors, are the true proprietors, and have established their title by competent proof.

If these negroes were, at the time, lawfully held as slaves, under the laws of Spain, and recognised by those laws as property, capable of being lawfully bought and sold; we see no reason why they may not justly be deemed, within the intent of the treaty, to be included under the denomination of merchandize, and as such ought to be restored to the claimants; for upon that point the laws of Spain would seem to furnish the proper rule of interpretation. But admitting this, it is clear, in our opinion, that neither of the other essential facts and requisites has been established in proof; and the *onus probandi* of both lies upon the claimants to give rise to the *casus fœderis*. It is plain, beyond controversy, if we examine the evidence, that these negroes never were the lawful slaves of Ruiz or Montez, or of any other Spanish subjects. They are natives of Africa, and were kidnapped there, and were unlawfully transported to Cuba, in violation of the laws and treaties of Spain, and the most solemn edicts and declarations of that government. By those laws and treaties, and edicts, the African slave-trade is utterly abolished; the dealing in that trade is deemed a heinous crime; and the negroes thereby introduced into the dominions of Spain, are declared to be free. Ruiz and Montez are proved to have made the pretended purchase of these negroes, with a full knowledge of all the circumstances. And so cogent and irresistible is the evidence in this respect, that the district-attorney has admitted in open court, upon the record, that these negroes were native Africans, and recently imported into Cuba, as alleged in their answers to the libels in the case. The supposed proprietary interest of Ruiz and Montez is completely displaced, if we are at liberty to look at the evidence, or the admissions of the district-attorney.

If then, these negroes are not slaves, but are kidnapped Africans, who, by the laws of Spain itself, are entitled to their freedom, and were kidnapped and illegally carried to Cuba, and illegally detained and restrained on board the Amistad; there is no pretence to say, that they are pirates or robbers. We may lament the dreadful acts by which they asserted their liberty, and took possession of the Amistad, and endeavored to regain their native country; but they cannot be deemed pirates or robbers, in the sense of the law of nations, or the treaty with Spain, or the laws of Spain itself; at least, so far as those laws have been brought to our knowledge. Nor do the libels of Ruiz or Montez assert them to be such.

This posture of the facts would seem, of itself, to put an end to the whole inquiry upon the merits. But it is argued, on behalf of the United States, that the ship and cargo, and negroes, were duly documented as belonging to Spanish subjects, and this court have no right to look behind these documents; that full faith and credit is to be given to them; and that they are to be held conclusive evidence in this cause, even although it should be established by the most satisfactory proofs, that they have been obtained by the grossest frauds and impositions upon the constituted authorities of Spain. To this argument, we can, in no wise, assent. There is nothing in the treaty which justifies or sustains the argument. We do not here meddle with the point, whether there has been any connivance in this illegal traffic, on the part of any of the colonial authorities or subordinate officers of Cuba; because, in our view, such an examination is unnecessary, and ought not to be pursued, unless it were indispensable to public justice, although it has been strongly pressed at the bar. What we proceed upon is this, that although public documents of the government, accompanying property found on board of the private ships of a foreign nation, certainly are to be deemed *prima facie* evidence of the facts which they purport to state, yet they are always open to be impugned for fraud; and whether that fraud be in the original obtaining of these documents, or in the subsequent fraudulent and illegal use of them, when once it is satisfactorily established, it overthrows all their sanctity, and destroys them as proof. Fraud will vitiate any, even the most solemn, transactions; and an asserted title to property, founded upon it, is utterly void. The very language of the ninth article of the treaty of 1795, requires the proprietor to make due and sufficient proof of his property. And how can that proof be deemed either due or sufficient, which is but a connected and stained tissue of fraud? This is not a mere rule of municipal jurisprudence. Nothing is more clear in the law of nations, as an established rule to regulate their rights and duties, and intercourse, than the doctrine, that the ship's papers are but *prima facie* evidence, and that, if they are shown to be fraudulent, they are not to be held proof of any valid title. This rule is familiarly applied, and, indeed, is of every-day's occurrence in cases of prize, in the contests between belligerents and neutrals, as is apparent from numerous cases to be found in the reports of this court; and it is just as applicable to the transactions of civil intercourse between nations, in times of peace. If a private ship, clothed with Spanish papers, should enter the ports of the United States, claiming the privileges and immunities, and rights, belonging to *bona fide* subjects of Spain, under our treaties or laws, and she should, in reality, belong to the subjects of another nation, which was not entitled to any such privileges, immunities or rights, and the proprietors were seeking, by fraud, to cover their own illegal acts, under the flag of Spain; there can be no doubt, that it would be the duty of our courts to strip off the disguise, and to look at the case, according to its naked realities. In the solemn treaties between nations, it can never be presumed, that either state intends to provide the means of perpetrating or protecting frauds; but all the provisions are to be construed as intended to be applied to *bona fide* transactions. The 17th article of the treaty with Spain, which provides for certain passports and certificates, as evidence of property on board of the ships of both states, is, in its terms, applicable only to cases where either of the parties is engaged in a war. This article required a certain form of passport to be agreed upon by the parties, and annexed to the treaty; it never was annexed; and therefore, in the case of *The Amiable Isabella*, 6 Wheat. 1, it was held inoperative.

It is also a most important consideration, in the present case, which ought not to be lost sight of, that, supposing these African negroes not to be slaves, but kidnapped, and free negroes, the treaty with Spain cannot be obligatory upon them; and the United States are bound to respect their rights as much as those of Spanish subjects. The conflict of rights between the parties, under such circumstances, becomes positive and inevitable, and must be decided upon the eternal principles of justice and international law. If the contest were about any goods on board of this ship, to which American citizens asserted a title, which was denied by the Spanish claimants, there could be no doubt of the right of such American citizens to litigate their claims before any competent American tribunal, notwithstanding the treaty with Spain. *A fortiori*, the doctrine must apply, where human life and human liberty are in issue, and constitute the very essence of the controversy. The treaty with Spain never could have intended to take away the equal rights of all foreigners, who should contest their claims before any of our courts, to equal justice; or to deprive such foreigners of the protection given them by other treaties, or by the general law of nations. Upon the merits of the case, then, there does not seem to us to be any ground for doubt, that these negroes ought to be deemed free; and that the Spanish treaty interposes no obstacle to the just assertion of their rights. . . .

ROBERTS V. BOSTON (1844–1855)

State-imposed racial segregation in the schools eventually led to the most important of all the judicial decisions on the civil rights of the American Negro: *Brown* v. *Board of Education of Topeka*. (See Document 78.)

But the problem was before the Massachusetts courts more than a century earlier. The Negroes of Boston had long struggled against segregation in public education and had held a number of mass meetings to register their protest. Their position was set forth in a series of resolutions to the Boston school committee in 1844. The failure of the school committee to act resulted in the litigation of *Roberts* v. *Boston* in 1849. It was in this case that Charles Sumner, arguing on behalf of the Negro plaintiff, delivered one of the most famous of all the addresses attacking racial discrimination.

Despite the provision of the Massachusetts Constitution that "all men, without distinction of color or race, are equal before the law," the Massachusetts courts held that the school regulation separating the races was neither illegal nor even unreasonable.

What was not solved by judicial decision, was, however, solved by legislative action. In 1855, the Massachusetts legislature passed a statute ending school segregation throughout the state.

DOCUMENT(S) 29

*Protest against school segregation**

Resolved, That, impelled by a deep sense of gratitude, we tender to Dr. H. Storer our unfeigned thanks for his successful efforts in instituting the late investigation of affairs connected with the Smith School [for Negroes], and for his unremitting attention to the same from the commencement to the close.

Resolved, That we present our most grateful acknowledgements to the Hon. John C. Park, for the late voluntary and disinterested devotion of his time and eminent talents in the cause of the wronged and neglected colored children of this city.

Whereas, we, the colored citizens of the city of Boston, have recently sent a petition to the School Committee, respectfully praying for the abolition of the separate schools for colored children, and asking for the rights and privileges extended to other citizens in respect to the common school system—viz. the right to send our children to the schools established in the respective districts in which we reside; and

Whereas, the School Committee, at their last meeting, passed a vote saying, in substance, that the prayer of our petition would not be granted, and that the separate schools for colored children would be continued; and

Whereas, we believe, and have the opinion of eminent counsel, that the institution and support of separate schools, at the public charge, for any one class of the inhabitants in exclusion of any other class, is contrary to the laws of this Commonwealth; therefore,

Resolved, That we consider the late action of the School Committee, in regard to our petition asking for the entire abolition of separate schools for colored children, as erroneous and unsatisfactory.

Resolved, That while we would not turn aside from our main object, the abolition of the separate colored schools, we cannot allow this occasion to pass without an expression of our surprise and regret at the recent acquittal by the School

---

* "The Smith School," *The Liberator,* Vol. XIV, No. 26 (June 28, 1844), 103: 3–4.

Committee of Abner Forbes, Principal of the Smith School, and of our deep conviction that he is totally unworthy of his present responsible station; and that the colored parents of this city are recommended to withdraw their children from the exclusive school established in contravention of that equality of privileges which is the vital principle of the school system of Massachusetts.

Resolved, That a copy of the above preamble and resolutions be sent to the Chairman of the School Committee, with a request that the petition heretofore presented may be reconsidered, and that we be allowed a hearing on said petition before them.

Resolved, That the heartfelt thanks of the colored citizens of Boston are due to Messrs. George S. Hillard and John T. Sargent for the humane and independent stand recently taken by them in the School Committee, in behalf of the rights and welfare of the colored children.

Resolved, That the expression of the sense of this meeting be transmitted to the several gentlemen named in the foregoing resolutions, and be also published in the city papers.

JOHN T. HILTON, *President*

Henry L. W. Thacker ⎫
Jonas W. Clark   ⎬ *Vice Presidents*

William C. Nell ⎫
Robert Morris   ⎬ *Secretaries*

Counsel Charles Sumner's oral argument before the Supreme Court of Massachusetts on behalf of the plaintiff in Roberts v. Boston[*]

May it please your Honors:

Can any discrimination, on account of color or race, be made, under the Constitution and Laws of Massachusetts, among the children entitled to the benefit of our public schools? This is the question which the Court is now to hear, to consider, and to decide.

———

[*] Delivered on December 4, 1849 (Boston: B. F. Roberts, 1849).

Or, stating the question with more detail, and with a more particular application to the facts of the present case, are the Committee, having the superintendence of the public schools of Boston, entrusted with the *power*, under the constitution and laws of Massachusetts, to exclude colored children from these schools, and to compel them to resort for their education to separate schools, set apart for colored children only, at distances from their homes less convenient than those open to white children?

This important question arises in an action by a colored child, only five years old, who, by her next friend, sues the city of Boston for damages, on account of a refusal to receive her into one of the public schools. . . .

I. I begin with the principle, that, according to the spirit of American institutions, and especially of the Constitution of Massachusetts, *all men, without distinction of color or race, are equal before the law.* . . .

The equality which was declared by our fathers in 1776, and which was made the fundamental law of Massachusetts in 1780, was *equality before the law.* Its object was to efface all political or civil distinctions, and to abolish all institutions founded upon *birth.* "All men are *created* equal," says the Declaration of Independence. "All men are *born* free and equal," says the Massachusetts Bill of Rights. These are not vain words. Within the sphere of their influence no person can be *created*, no person can be *born*, with civil or political privileges, not enjoyed equally by all his fellow-citizens, nor can any institution be established recognizing any distinctions of birth. This is the Great Charter of every person who draws his vital breath upon this soil, whatever may be his condition, and whoever may be his parents. He may be poor, weak, humble, black—he may be of Caucasian, of Jewish, of Indian, or of Ethiopian race—he may be of French, of German, of English, of Irish extraction—but before the Constitution of Massachusetts all these distinctions disappear. He is not poor, or weak, or humble, or black—nor Caucasian, nor Jew, nor Indian, nor Ethiopian—nor French, nor German, nor English, nor Irish; he is a MAN,—the equal of all his fellow-men. He is one of the children of the State, which, like an impartial parent, regards all its offspring with an equal care. . . .

II. I now pass to the second stage of this argument, and

ask attention to this proposition. The legislature of Massachusetts, in entire harmony with the Constitution, has made no discrimination of color or race, in the establishment of Public Schools.

If such discrimination were made by the laws, they would be unconstitutional and void. But the legislature of Massachusetts has been too just and generous, too mindful of the Bill of Rights, to establish any such privilege of *birth*. The language of the statutes is general, and applies equally to all children, of whatever color or race. . . .

III. The Courts of Massachusetts have never recognized any discrimination, founded on color or race, in the administration of the Public Schools, but have recognized the equal rights of all the inhabitants. . . .

IV. The exclusion of colored children from the Public Schools, open to white children, is a source of practical inconvenience to them and their parents, to which white persons are not exposed, and is, therefore, a violation of Equality. The black and the white are not equal before the law. . . .

V. The separation of children in the Public Schools of Boston, on account of color or race, is in the nature of *Caste*, and is a violation of Equality. . . .

VI. The Committee of Boston, charged with the superintendence of the Public Schools, have no *power* under the Constitution and laws of Massachusetts, to make any discrimination on account of color or race, among children in the Public Schools. . . .

The fact that a child is black, or that he is white, cannot of itself be considered a qualification, or a disqualification. It is not to the skin that we can look for the criterion of fitness for our Public Schools.

But it is said that the Committee are intrusted with a discretion, in the exercise of their power, and that, in this discretion, they may distribute, assign, and classify all children belonging to the schools of the city, *according to their best judgment*, making, if they think proper, a discrimination of color or race. Without questioning that they are intrusted with a discretion, it is outrageous to suppose that it can go to this extent. The Committee can have no discretion which is not in harmony with the Constitution and laws. Surely, they cannot, in their mere discretion, nullify a sacred and dear-bought principle of Human Rights, which is expressly guaranteed by the Constitution.

Still further—and here I approach a more technical view of the subject—it is an admitted principle, that the regulations and by-laws of municipal corporations must be *reasonable,* or they are inoperative and void. . . .

And here we are brought once more, in another form, to the question of the validity of the discrimination on account of color by the School Committee of Boston. Is this *legally reasonable?* Is it reasonable, in the exercise of their discretion, to separate the descendants of the African race from the white children, in consequence of their descent merely? Passing over now those principles of the Constitution, and those provisions of the law, which of themselves would decide the question, constituting as they do *the highest reason,* but which have been already amply considered, look for a moment at the Educational system of Massachusetts, and it will be seen that practically no discrimination of color is made by law in any part of it. A descendant of the African race may be Governor of the Commonwealth, and as such, with the advice and consent of the Council, may select the *Board of Education.* As Lieutenant Governor, he may be, *ex officio,* a member of the Board. He may be the *Secretary* of the Board, with the duty imposed on him by law of seeing "that *all* children in this Commonwealth, who depend upon common schools for instruction, may have the best education which those schools can be made to impart." He may be a member of any School Committee, or a teacher in any public school of the State. As a legal voter, he can vote in the selection of any School Committee. . . .

It is clear that the Committee may classify scholars, according to their age and sex; for the obvious reasons that these distinctions are inoffensive, and especially recognized as *legal* in the law relating to schools. (Revised Statutes, c. 23, § 63.) They may also classify scholars according to their moral and intellectual qualifications, because such a power is necessary to the government of schools. But the Committee cannot assume, *a priori,* and without individual examination, that an *entire race* possess certain moral or intellectual qualities, which shall render it proper to place them all in a class by themselves. Such an exercise of the discretion with which the Committee are intrusted, must be unreasonable, and therefore illegal.

But it is said that the Committee, in thus classifying the children, have not violated any principle of Equality, inasmuch as they provided a school with competent instructors for the colored children, where they have equal advantages of instruction with those enjoyed by the white children. It is said that in excluding the colored children from the Public Schools open to white children, they furnish them an equivalent.

To this there are several answers. I shall touch upon them only briefly, as the discussion, through which we have now travelled, substantially covers the whole ground.

1st. The separate school for colored children is not one of the schools established by the law relating to Public Schools. (Revised Statutes, Chap. 23.) It is not a Public School. As such, it has no legal existence, and, therefore cannot be a legal equivalent. . . .

2d. The second is, that, in point of fact, it is not an equivalent. We have already seen that it is the occasion of inconvenience to the colored children and their parents, to which they would not be exposed, if they had access to the nearest public schools, besides inflicting upon them the stigma of Caste. Still further, and this consideration cannot be neglected, the matters taught in the two schools may be precisely the same; but a school, exclusively devoted to one class, must differ essentially, in its spirit and character, from that public school known to the law, where all classes meet together in equality. It is a mockery to call it an equivalent.

3d. But there is yet another answer. Admitting that it is an equivalent, still the colored children cannot be compelled to take it. Their rights are Equality before the law; nor can they be called upon to renounce one jot of this. They have an equal right with white children to the general public schools. A separate school, though well endowed, would not secure to them that precise Equality, which they would enjoy in the general public schools. The Jews in Rome are confined to a particular district, called the Ghetto. In Frankfort they are condemned to a separate quarter, known as the Jewish quarter. It is possible that the accommodations allotted to them are as good as they would be able to occupy, if left free to choose throughout Rome and Frankfort; but this compulsory segregation from the mass of citizens is of itself an *inequality* which we condemn with our whole souls. It is a vestige of ancient intolerance directed against a despised people. It is of the same character with the separate schools in Boston.

Thus much for the doctrine of equivalents, as a substitute for equality. . . .

Who can say, that this does not injure the blacks? Theirs, in its best estate, is an unhappy lot. Shut out by a still lingering prejudice from many social advantages, a despised class, they feel this proscription from the Public Schools as a peculiar brand. Beyond this, it deprives them of those healthful animating influences which would come from a participation in the studies of their white brethren. It adds to their discouragements. It widens their separation from the rest of the community, and postpones that great day of reconciliation which is sure to come.

The whole system of public schools suffers also. It is a narrow perception of their high aim which teaches that they are merely to furnish to all the scholars an equal amount in knowledge, and that, therefore, provided all be taught, it is of little consequence where, and in what company it be done. The law contemplates not only that they shall all be taught, but that they shall be taught *all together*. They are not only to receive equal quantities of knowledge, but all are to receive it in the same way. All are to approach together the same common fountain; nor can there be any exclusive source for any individual or any class. The school is the little world in which the child is trained for the larger world of life. It must, therefore, cherish and develop the virtues and the sympathies which are employed in the larger world. And since, according to our institutions, all classes meet, without distinction of color, in the performance of civil duties, so should they all meet, without distinction of color, in the school, beginning there those relations of equality which our Constitution and laws promise to all. . . .

*Sarah C. Roberts v. The City of Boston**

The opinion was delivered at the March term, 1850.

SHAW, C. J. The plaintiff, a colored child of five years of age, has commenced this action, by her father and next friend, against the city of Boston, upon the statute of 1845, c. 214, which provides, that any child unlawfully excluded from public school instruction, in this commonwealth, shall recover damages therefore, in an action against the city or town, by which such public school instruction is supported. The question therefore is, whether, upon the facts agreed, the plaintiff has been unlawfully excluded from such instruction. . . .

By the agreed statement of facts, it appears, that the defendants support a class of schools called primary schools, to the number of about one hundred and sixty, designed for the instruction of children of both sexes, who are between the ages of four and seven years. Two of these schools are appropriated by the primary school committee, having charge of that class of schools, to the exclusive instruction of colored children, and the residue to the exclusive instruction of white children.

The plaintiff, by her father, took proper measures to obtain admission into one of these schools appropriated to white children, but pursuant to the regulations of the committee, and in conformity therewith, she was not admitted. Either of the schools appropriated to colored children was open to her; the nearest of which was about a fifth of a mile or seventy rods more distant from her father's house than the nearest primary school. It further appears, by the facts agreed, that the committee having charge of that class of schools had, a short time previously to the plaintiff's application, adopted a resolution, upon a report of a committee, that in the opinion of that board, the continuance of the separate schools for colored children, and the regular attendance of all such children upon the schools, is not only legal and just, but is best adapted to promote the instruction of that class of the population. . . .

---

* Supreme Judicial Court of Massachusetts, 59 Mass. (5 Cush.) 198 (1849).

The great principle, advanced by the learned, and eloquent advocate of the plaintiff, is, that by the constitution and laws of Massachusetts, all persons without distinction of age or sex, birth or color, origin or condition, are equal before the law. This, as a broad general principle, such as ought to appear in a declaration of rights, is perfectly sound; it is not only expressed in terms, but pervades and animates the whole spirit of our constitution of free government. But, when this great principle comes to be applied to the actual and various conditions of persons in society, it will not warrant the assertion, that men and women are legally clothed with the same civil and political powers, and that children and adults are legally to have the same functions and be subject to the same treatment; but only that the rights of all, as they are settled and regulated by law, are equally entitled to the paternal consideration and protection of the law, for their maintenance and security. What those rights are, to which individuals, in the infinite variety of circumstances by which they are surrounded in society, are entitled, must depend on laws adapted to their respective relations and conditions.

Conceding, therefore, in the fullest manner, that colored persons, the descendants of Africans, are entitled by law, in this commonwealth, to equal rights, constitutional and political, civil and social, the question then arises, whether the regulation in question, which provides separate schools for colored children, is a violation of any of these rights.

Legal rights must, after all, depend upon the provisions of law; certainly all those rights of individuals which can be asserted and maintained in any judicial tribunal. The proper province of a declaration of rights and constitution of government, after directing its form, regulating its organization and the distribution of its powers, is to declare great principles and fundamental truths, to influence and direct the judgment and conscience of legislators in making laws, rather than to limit and control them, by directing what precise laws they shall make. The provision, that it shall be the duty of legislatures and magistrates to cherish the interests of literature and the sciences, especially the university at Cambridge, public schools, and grammar schools, in the towns, is precisely of this character. Had the legislature failed to comply with this injunction, and neglected to provide public schools in the towns, or should they so far fail in their duty as to repeal all laws on the subject, and leave all education to depend on private means, strong and explicit as the direction of the constitution is, it would afford no remedy or redress to the thousands of the rising generation, who now depend on these schools to afford them a most valuable education, and an introduction to useful life.

We must then resort to the law, to ascertain what are the rights of individuals, in regard to the schools. By the Rev. Sts. *c.* 23, the general system is provided for. This chapter directs what money shall be raised in different towns, according to their population; provides for a power of dividing towns into school districts, leaving it however at the option of the inhabitants to divide the towns into districts, or to administer the system and provide schools, without such division. The latter course has, it is believed, been constantly adopted in Boston, without forming the territory into districts.

The statute, after directing what length of time schools shall be kept in towns of different numbers of inhabitants and families, provides (§ 10) that the inhabitants shall annually choose, by ballot, a school committee, who shall have the general charge and superintendence of all the public schools in such towns. There being no specific direction how schools shall be organized; how many schools shall be kept; what shall be the qualifications for admission to the schools; the age at which children may enter; the age to which they may continue; these must all be regulated by the committee, under their power of general superintendence. . . .

The power of general superintendence vests a plenary authority in the committee to arrange, classify, and distribute pupils, in such a manner as they think best adapted to their general proficiency and walfare. If it is thought expedient to provide for very young children, it may be, that such schools may be kept exclusively by female teachers, quite adequate to their instruction, and yet whose services may be obtained at a cost much lower than that of more highly qualified male instructors. So if they should judge it expedient to have a grade of schools for children from seven to ten, and another for those from ten to fourteen, it would seem to be within their authority to establish such schools. So to separate male and female pupils into different schools. It has been found necessary, that is to say, highly expedient, at times, to establish special schools for poor and neglected children, who have passed the age of seven, and have become too old to attend the primary school, and yet have not acquired the rudiments of learning, to enable them to enter the ordinary schools. If a class of youth, of one or both sexes, is found in that condition, and it is expedient to organize them into a separate school, to receive the special training, adapted to their condition, it seems to be within the power of the superintending committee, to provide for the organization of such special school. . . .

In the absence of special legislation on this subject, the law has vested the power in the committee to regulate the system of distribution and classification; and when this power is reasonably exercised, without being abused or perverted by colorable pretences, the decision of the committee must be deemed conclusive. The committee, apparently upon great deliberation, have come to the conclusion, that the good of both classes of schools will be best promoted, by maintaining the separate primary schools for colored and for white children, and we can perceive no ground to doubt, that this is the honest result of their experience and judgment.

It is urged, that this maintenance of separate schools tends to deepen and perpetuate the odious distinction of caste, founded in a deep-rooted prejudice in public opinion. This prejudice, if it exists, is not created by law, and probably cannot be changed by law. Whether this distinction and prejudice, existing in the opinion and feelings of the community, would not be as effectually fostered by compelling colored and white children to associate together in the same schools, may well be doubted; at all events, it is a fair and proper question for the committee to consider and decide upon, having in view the best interests of both classes of children placed under their superintendence, and we cannot say, that their decision upon it is not founded on just grounds of reason and experience, and in the results of a discriminating and honest judgment.

The increased distance, to which the plaintiff was obliged to go to school from her father's house, is not such, in our opinion, as to render the regulation in question unreasonable, still less illegal.

On the whole the court are of opinion, that upon the facts stated, the action cannot be maintained.

Plaintiff nonsuit.

*An act in amendment of "An act concerning public schools," passed March twenty-fifth, eighteen hundred and forty-five**

Be it enacted by the Senate and House of Representatives, in the General Court assembled, and by the authority of the same, as follows:

SECTION 1. In determining the qualifications of scholars to be admitted into any public school or any district school in the Commonwealth, no distinction shall be made on account of the race, color or religious opinions, of the applicant or scholar.

SEC. 2. Any child who, on account of his race, color or religious opinions, shall be excluded from any public or district school in the Commonwealth, for admission to which he may be otherwise qualified, shall recover damages therefor in an action of tort, to be brought in the name of said child by his guardian or next friend, in any court of competent jurisdiction to try the same, against the city or town by which such school is supported.

SEC. 3. In filing interrogatories for discovery in any such action, the plaintiff may examine any number of the school committee, or any other officer of the defendant city or town, in the same manner as if he were a party to the suit.

SEC. 4. Every person belonging to the school committee, under whose rules or directions any child shall be excluded from such school, and every teacher of any such school, shall, on application by the parent or guardian of any such child, state in writing the grounds and reasons of such exclusion.

SEC. 5. This act shall take effect from and after the first day of September next.

[APPROVED by the Governor, April 28, 1855.]

---

* *Massachusetts Acts and Resolves, c. 256, 1855, pp. 674-75.*

WILMOT PROVISO (1846-1847)

In the course of a debate on President Polk's appropriations bill for the Mexican War (1846–1847), David Wilmot introduced and argued for his famous "Proviso." The Pennsylvania Congressman proposed an amendment to prohibit the extension of slavery into any of the new territories that might be acquired as a result of the war. In his arguments he reminded his colleagues that he had supported the annexation of Texas as a slave state. Like so many other northern spokesmen, he felt that, while slavery should be permitted to continue in those states in which it had been practiced, its extension into new territories would be contrary to the interests of free labor.

DOCUMENT 30

*Congressman Wilmot's arguments against the extension of slavery**

Sir, it will be recollected by all present, that, at the last session of Congress, an amendment was moved by me to a bill of the same character as this, in the form of a proviso, by which slavery should be excluded from any territory that might subsequently be acquired by the United States from the republic of Mexico.

Sir, on that occasion, that proviso was sustained by a very decided majority of this House. Nay, sir, more, it was sustained, if I mistake not, by a majority of the Republican party on this floor. I am prepared, I think, to show that the entire South were then willing to acquiesce in what appeared to be, and, in so far as the action of this House was concerned, what was the legislative will and declaration of the Union on this subject. It passed this House. Sir, there were no threats of disunion sounded in our ears. It passed here and went to the Senate, and it was the judgment of the public, and of men well informed, that, had it not been defeated

---

* *Congressional Globe*, Appendix, 29th Congress, 2nd Session (February 8, 1847), p. 315.

there for want of time, it would have passed that body and become the established law of the land. . . .

There was then no cry that the Union was to be severed in consequence. The South, like brave men defeated, bowed to the voice and judgment of the nation. No, sir, no cry of disunion then. Why now? The hesitation and the wavering of northern men on this question has encouraged the South to assume a bolder attitude. This cry of disunion proceeds from no resolve of the South. It comes, sir, from the cowardice of the North. . . .

But, sir, the issue now presented is not whether slavery shall exist unmolested where it now is, but whether it shall be carried to new and distant regions, now free, where the footprint of a slave cannot be found. This, sir, is the issue. Upon it I take my stand, and from it I cannot be frightened or driven by idle charges of abolitionism. I ask not that slavery be abolished. I demand that this Government preserve the integrity of free territory against the aggressions of slavery— against its wrongful usurpations. Sir, I was in favor of the annexation of Texas. . . . The Democracy of the North, almost to a man, went for annexation. Yes, sir, here was an empire larger than France given up to slavery. Shall further concessions be made by the North? Shall we give up free territory, the inheritance of free labor? Must we yield this also? Never, sir, never, until we ourselves are fit to be slaves. The North may be betrayed by her Representatives, but upon this great question she will be true to herself—true to posterity. Defeat! Sir, there can be no defeat. Defeat to-day will but arouse the teeming millions of the North, and lead to a more decisive and triumphant victory to-morrow.

But, sir, we are told, that the joint blood and treasure of the whole country being expended in this acquisition, therefore it should be divided, and slavery allowed to take its share. Sir, the South has her share already; the installment for slavery was paid in advance. We are fighting this war for Texas and for the South. I affirm it—every intelligent man knows it—Texas is the primary cause of this war. For this, sir, northern treasure is being exhausted, and northern blood poured out upon the plains of Mexico. We are fighting this war cheerfully, not reluctantly—cheerfully fighting this war for Texas; and yet we seek not to change the character of her institutions. Slavery is there: there let it remain. . . .

Now, sir, we are told that California is ours; that New Mexico is ours—won by the valor of our arms. They are free. Shall they remain free? Shall these fair provinces be the inheritance and homes of the white labor of freemen or the black labor of slaves? This, sir, is the issue—this is the question. The North has the right, and her representatives here have the power. . . . But the South contend, that in their emigration to this free territory, they have the right to take and hold slaves, the same as other property. Unless the amendment I have offered be adopted, or other early legislation is had upon this subject, they will do so. Indeed, they unitedly, as one man, have declared their right and purpose so to do, and the work has already begun. Slavery follows in the rear of our armies. Shall the war power of our Government be exerted to produce such a result? Shall this Government depart from its neutrality on this question, and lend its power and influence to plant slavery in these territories? There is no question of abolition here, sir. Shall the South be permitted, by aggression, by invasion of the right, by subduing free territory, and planting slavery upon it, to wrest these provinces from northern freemen, and turn them to the accomplishment of their own sectional purposes and schemes? This is the question. Men of the North answer. Shall it be so? Shall we of the North submit to it? If we do, we are coward slaves, and deserve to have the manacles fastened upon our own limbs.

. . . .

THE COMPROMISE OF 1850

The annexation of Texas, the accession of new territories as a result of the Mexican War, and the intensified activities of the abolitionists set the stage for a lengthy season of controversy and sectional conflict in the years 1849 and 1850. Again another stalemate was reached in the debate over slavery that began with the Constitutional Convention of 1787 and continued through the Missouri crisis of 1819–1820.

Once again the ingenuity of the nation and its lawmakers was challenged to shape solutions acceptable to the majorities within the South and the North alike. This would be the last major set of issues engaging the elder statesmen, Henry Clay, John C. Calhoun, and Daniel Webster, and the first to test the junior Senators, Stephen Douglas, William Seward, and Salmon Chase.

In an effort to achieve Congressional accord on a number of diverse but related issues, Clay offered a series of resolutions in January, 1850. These dealt with the admission of California as a free state, the political organization of the territories carved from the Mexican Cession, the adjustment of the Texas debt and the Texas boundary line, the status of slavery and the slave trade in the District of Columbia, and the stiffening of the fugitive slave law. The heated Congressional debates which followed were widely publicized. In September, 1850, the basic elements in Clay's compromise package were enacted into law. The most important of the statutes affecting the Negro and his rights were the new fugitive slave law and the act ending the slave trade in the District of Columbia.

One of the key elements in the Compromise of 1850 was the passage of a new and much more stringent Fugitive Slave Act. Designed to amend and strengthen the provisions of the Act of 1793 (Document 18) this new law placed enforcement exclusively under federal jurisdiction. The law provided for the appointment of federal commissioners, whose authority to pass judgment on the status of fugitives was complemented by the power to invoke the aid of federal marshals and even of private citizens in capturing, retaining, and returning Negroes to their declared owners or their agents. The fugitive was not allowed to testify in his own behalf, and a transcript of the owner's claim of loss, that had been filed with a court, was deemed sufficient proof of ownership. Moreover, the commissioners received fees on a differential basis: five dollars in those cases where the Negro was released, and ten dollars when the fugitive was successfully remanded to the declared owner or his agent. The act was a signal victory for the South. To the angry abolitionists, the national government had now become an agent of the slaveholders.

As a sop to the antislavery forces, the 1850 Compromise included an act to end the slave trade in the District of

Columbia. Since abolitionists had long argued that Congress had the power to outlaw both the slave trade and the institution of slavery itself within the District, the opponents of slavery regarded this measure as insufficient in light of the over-all dilemma facing the country.

Those who endorsed the compromise package hoped that its several parts would serve to quiet the controversy. But the next ten years showed the futility of such a compromise in light of the tremendous social, moral, political, and economic dimensions of the slavery question.

DOCUMENT(S) 31

An act to amend, and supplementary to, the act entitled "An act respecting fugitives from justice, and persons escaping from the service of their masters," approved February twelfth, one thousand seven hundred and ninety-three[*]

Be it enacted by the Senate and House of Representatives of the United States of America in Congress assembled, That the persons who have been, or may hereafter be, appointed commissioners, in virtue of any act of Congress, by the Circuit Courts of the United States, and who, in consequence of such appointment, are authorized to exercise the powers that any justice of the peace, or other magistrate of any of the United States, may exercise in respect to offenders for any crime or offence against the United States, by arresting, imprisoning, or bailing the same under and by virtue of the thirty-third section of the act of the twenty-fourth of September seventeen hundred and eighty-nine, entitled "An Act to establish the judicial courts of the United States," shall be, and are hereby, authorized and required to exercise and discharge all the powers and duties conferred by this act.

· · · ·

[*] 9 Stat. 462 (1850).

Sec. 5. *And be it further enacted,* That it shall be the duty of all marshals and deputy marshals to obey and execute all warrants and precepts issued under the provisions of this act, when to them directed; and should any marshal or deputy marshal refuse to receive such warrant, or other process, when tendered, or to use all proper means diligently to execute the same, he shall, on conviction thereof, be fined in the sum of one thousand dollars, to the use of such claimant, on the motion of such claimant, by the Circuit or District Court for the district of such marshal; and after arrest of such fugitive, by such marshal or his deputy, or whilst at any time in his custody under the provisions of this act, should such fugitive escape, whether with or without the assent of such marshal or his deputy, such marshal shall be liable, on his official bond, to be prosecuted for the benefit of such claimed, for the full value of the service or labor of said fugitive in the State, Territory, or District whence he escaped: and the better to enable the said commissioners, when thus appointed, to execute their duties faithfully and efficiently, in conformity with the requirements of the Constitution of the United States and of this act, they are hereby authorized and empowered, within their counties respectively, to appoint, in writing under their hands, any one or more suitable persons, from time to time, to execute all such warrants and other process as may be issued by them in the lawful performance of their respective duties; with authority to such commissioners, or the persons to be appointed by them, to execute process as aforesaid, to summon and call to their aid the bystanders, or *posse comitatus* of the proper county, when necessary to ensure a faithful observance of the clause of the Constitution referred to, in conformity with the provisions of this act; and all good citizens are hereby commanded to aid and assist in the prompt and efficient execution of this law, whenever their services may be required, as aforesaid, for that purpose; and said warrants shall run, and be executed by said officers, any where in the State within which they are issued.

Sec. 6. *And be it further enacted,* That when a person held to service or labor in any State or Territory of the United States, has heretofore or shall hereafter escape into another State or Territory of the United States, the person or persons to whom such service or labor may be due, or his, her, or their agent or attorney, duly authorized, by power of attorney, in writing, acknowledged and certified under the seal of some legal officer or court of the State or Territory in which the same may be executed, may pursue and reclaim such fugitive person, either by procuring a warrant from some one of the courts, judges, or commissioners aforesaid, of the proper circuit, district, or county, for the apprehension of such fugitive from service or labor, or by seizing and arresting such fugitive, where the same can be done without process, and by taking, or causing such person to be taken, forthwith before such court, judge, or commissioner, whose duty it shall be to hear and determine the case of such claimant in a summary manner; and upon satisfactory proof being made, by deposition or affidavit, in writing, to be taken and certified by such court, judge, or commissioner, or by other satisfactory testimony, duly taken and certified by some court, magistrate, justice of the peace, or other legal officer authorized to administer an oath and take depositions under the laws of the State or Territory from which such person owing service or labor may have escaped, with a certificate of such magistracy or other authority, as aforesaid, with the seal of the proper court or officer thereto attached, which seal shall be sufficient to establish the competency of the proof, and with proof, also by affidavit, of the identity of the person whose service or labor is claimed to be due as aforesaid, that the person so arrested does in fact owe service or labor to the person or persons claiming him or her, in the State or Territory from which such fugitive may have escaped as aforesaid, and that said person escaped, to make out and deliver to such claimant, his or her agent or attorney, a certificate setting forth the substantial facts as to the service or labor due from such fugitive to the claimant, and of his or her escape from the State or Territory in which such service or labor was due, to the State or Territory in which he or she was arrested, with authority to such claimant, or his or her agent or attorney, to use such reasonable force and restraint as may be necessary, under the circumstances of the case, to take and remove such fugitive person back to the State or Territory whence he or she may have escaped as aforesaid. In no trial or hearing under this act shall the testimony of such alleged fugitive be admitted in evidence; and the certificates in this and the first [fourth] section mentioned, shall be conclusive of the right of the person or persons in whose favor granted, to remove such fugitive to the State or Territory from which he escaped, and shall prevent all molestation of such person or persons by any process issued by any court, judge, magistrate, or other person whomsoever.

SEC. 7. *And be it further enacted,* That any person who shall knowingly and willingly obstruct, hinder, or prevent such claimant, his agent or attorney, or any person or persons lawfully assisting him, her, or them, from arresting such a fugitive from service or labor, either with or without process as aforesaid, or shall rescue, or attempt to rescue, such fugitive from service or labor, from the custody of such claimant, his or her agent or attorney, or other person or persons lawfully assisting as aforesaid, when so arrested, pursuant to the authority herein given and declared; or shall aid, abet, or assist such person so owing service or labor as aforesaid, directly or indirectly, to escape from such claimant, his agent or attorney, or other person or persons legally authorized as aforesaid; or shall harbor or conceal such fugitive, so as to prevent the discovery and arrest of such person, after notice or knowledge of the fact that such person was a fugitive from service or labor as aforesaid, shall, for either of said offences, be subject to a fine not exceeding one thousand dollars, and imprisonment not exceeding six months, by indictment and conviction before the District Court of the United States for the district in which such offence may have been committed, or before the proper court of criminal jurisdiction, if committed within any one of the organized Territories of the United States; and shall moreover forfeit and pay, by way of civil damages to the party injured by such illegal conduct, the sum of one thousand dollars, for each fugitive so lost as aforesaid, to be recovered by action of debt, in any of the District or Territorial Courts aforesaid, within whose jurisdiction the said offence may have been committed.

SEC. 8. *And be it further enacted,* That the marshals, their deputies, and the clerks of the said District and Territorial Courts, shall be paid, for their services, the like fees as may be allowed to them for similar services in other cases; and where such services are rendered exclusively in the arrest, custody, and delivery of the fugitive to the claimant, his or her agent or attorney, or where such supposed fugitive may be discharged out of custody for the want of sufficient proof as aforesaid, then such fees are to be paid in the whole by such claimant, his agent or attorney; and in all cases where the proceedings are before a commissioner, he shall be entitled to a fee of ten dollars in full for his services in each case, upon the delivery of the said certificate to the claimant, his or her agent or attorney; or a fee of five dollars in cases where the proof shall not, in the opinion of such commissioner, warrant such certificate and delivery, inclusive of all services incident to such arrest and examination, to be paid, in either case, by the claimant, his or her agent or attorney. The person or persons authorized to execute the process to be issued by such commissioners for the arrest and detention of fugitives from service or labor as aforesaid, shall also be entitled to a fee of five dollars each for each person he or they may arrest and take before any such commissioner as aforesaid, at the instance and request of such claimant, with such other fees as may be deemed reasonable by such commissioner for such other additional services as may be necessarily performed by him or them; such as attending at the examination, keeping the fugitive in custody, and providing him with food and lodging during his detention, and until the final determination of such commissioner; and, in general, for performing such other duties as may be required by such claimant, his or her attorney or agent, or commissioner in the premises, such fees to be made up in conformity with the fees usually charged by the officers of the courts of justice within the proper district or county, as near as may be practicable, and paid by such claimants, their agents or attorneys, whether such supposed fugitives from service or labor be ordered to be delivered to such claimants by the final determination of such commissioners or not.

Sec. 9. *And be it further enacted,* That, upon affidavit made by the claimant of such fugitive, his agent or attorney, after such certificate has been issued, that he has reason to apprehend that such fugitive will be rescued by force from his or their possession before he can be taken beyond the limits of the State in which the arrest is made, it shall be the duty of the officer making the arrest to retain such fugitive in his custody, and to remove him to the State whence he fled, and there to deliver him to said claimant, his agent, or attorney. And to this end, the officer aforesaid is hereby authorized and required to employ so many persons as he may deem necessary to overcome such force, and to retain them in his service so long as circumstances may require. The said officer and his assistants, while so employed, to receive the same compensation, and to be allowed the same expenses, as are now allowed by law for transportation of criminals, to be certified by the judge of the district within which the arrest is made, and paid out of the treasury of the United States.

SEC. 10. *And be it further enacted,* That when any person held to service or labor in any State or Territory, or in the District of Columbia, shall escape therefrom, the party to whom such service or labor shall be due, his, her, or their agent or attorney, may apply to any court of record therein, or judge thereof in vacation, and make satisfactory proof to such court, or judge in vacation, of the escape aforesaid, and that the person escaping owed service or labor to such party. Whereupon the court shall cause a record to be made of the matters so proved, and also a general description of the person so escaping, with such convenient certainty as may be; and a transcript of such record, authenticated by the attestation of the clerk and of the seal of the said court, being produced in any other State, Territory, or district in which the person so escaping may be found, and being exhibited to any judge, commissioner, or other officer authorized by the law of the United States to cause persons escaping from service or labor to be delivered up, shall be held and taken to be full and conclusive evidence of the fact of escape, and that the service or labor of the person escaping is due to the party in such record mentioned. And upon the production by the said party of other and further evidence if necessary, either oral or by affidavit, in addition to what is contained in the said record of the identity of the person escaping, he or she shall be delivered up to the claimant. And the said court, commissioner, judge, or other person authorized by this act to grant certificates to claimants of fugitives, shall, upon the production of the record and other evidences aforesaid, grant to such claimant a certificate of his right to take any such person identified and proved to be owing service or labor as aforesaid, which certificate shall authorize such claimant to seize or arrest and transport such person to the State or Territory from which he escaped: *Provided,* That nothing herein contained shall be construed as requiring the production of a transcript of such record as evidence as aforesaid. But in its absence the claim shall be heard and determined upon other satisfactory proofs, competent in law.

APPROVED, September 18, 1850.

An act to suppress the slave trade in the District of Columbia*

Be it enacted by the Senate and House of Representatives of the United States of America in Congress assembled, That from and after the first day of January, eighteen hundred and fifty-one, it shall not be lawful to bring into the District of Columbia any slave whatever, for the purpose of being sold, or for the purpose of being placed in depot, to be subsequently transferred to any other State or place to be sold as merchandize. And if any slave shall be brought into the said District by its owner, or by the authority or consent of its owner, contrary to the provisions of this act, such slave shall thereupon become liberated and free.

SEC. 2. *And be it further enacted,* That it shall and may be lawful for each of the corporations of the cities of Washington and Georgetown, from time to time, and as often as may be necessary, to abate, break up, and abolish any depot or place of confinement of slaves brought into the said District as merchandize, contrary to the provisions of this act, by such appropriate means as may appear to either of the said corporations expedient and proper. And the same power is hereby vested in the Levy Court of Washington county, if any attempt shall be made, within its jurisdictional limits, to establish a depot or place of confinement for slaves brought into the said District as merchandize for sale contrary to this act.

APPROVED, September 20, 1850.

---

* 9 Stat. 467 (1850).

TEACHING NEGROES TO READ (1853)

As was common throughout the antebellum South, Virginia had a statute imposing criminal penalties on those who taught Negroes to read or write. These laws were grounded on the fear that literacy would result in increased discontent with slave status and would facilitate acts of rebellion. (See, for example, Document 21.)

DOCUMENT 32

The trial of Mrs. Margaret Douglass for teaching colored children to read, Norfolk, Virginia*

The Narrative

A Southern lady living with a daughter in Norfolk, Virginia, sixty-six years ago and being greatly interested in the religious and moral instruction of colored children and finding that the Sunday school where they were allowed to attend was not sufficient, invited them to come to her house, where in a back room upstairs she and her daughter taught them to read and write. She knew that it was against the law to teach slaves, and so she was careful to take none in her school but free colored children. One day a couple of city constables entered with a warrant and marched the two teachers and the children to the Mayor's office, where she was charged with teaching them to read, contrary to law. She explained that none of the children were slaves and that she had no idea that a child could not be taught to read simply because it was black. But the Mayor told her that this was the law, but as she had acted in good faith he would dismiss the case.

---

* 7 Am. State Trials 45 (1853).

But the Grand Jury heard of it and indicted her, and at the next term of court she was tried for a violation of the Virginia code which provided that every assemblage of negroes for the purpose of religious worship, where it was conducted by a negro, and every assemblage of negroes for instruction in reading and writing, or in the night time, for any purpose, was unlawful, and if a white person assembled with negroes to instruct them to read and write, he should be fined and imprisoned. She refused the services of a lawyer and defended herself, and though she called several witnesses to show that the same thing had been done for years in the Sunday schools in the city, the jury convicted her, but placed the penalty at a fine of only one dollar. But this was overruled by the judge, who sentenced her to be imprisoned for a month, which sentence was duly carried out.

The Verdict and Sentence

November 13 [1853]

The Jury this morning returned into court with a verdict of *Guilty,* and fixing the penalty at a fine of one dollar. The Court then adjourned for the term.

January 10, 1854

After the adjournment of the Court on November 13, Mrs. Douglass obtained permission from the Judge and the Sheriff to visit New York, where she remained several weeks, returning to Norfolk with her daughter. She appeared today for sentence.

JUDGE BAKER . . .
There are persons, I believe, in our community, opposed to the policy of the law in question. They profess to believe that universal intellectual culture is necessary to religious instruction and education, and that such culture is suitable to a state of slavery; and there can be no misapprehension as to your opinions on this subject, judging from the indiscreet freedom with which you spoke of your regard for the colored race in

general. Such opinions in the present state of our society I regard as manifestly mischievous. It is not true that our slaves cannot be taught religious and moral duty, without being able to read the Bible and use the pen. Intellectual and religious instruction often go hand in hand, but the latter may well exist without the former; and the truth of this is abundantly vindicated by the well-known fact that in many parts of our own Commonwealth, as in other parts of the country in which among the whites one-fourth or more are entirely without a knowledge of letters, respect for the law, and for moral and religious conduct and behavior, are justly and propely appreciated and practiced.

A valuable report or document recently published in the city of New York by the Southern Aid Society sets forth many valuable and important truths upon the condition of the Southern slaves, and the utility of moral and religious instruction, apart from a knowledge of books. I recommend the careful perusal of it to all whose opinions concur with your own. It shows that a system of catechetical instruction, with a clear and simple exposition of Scripture, has been employed with gratifying success; that the slave population of the South are peculiarly susceptible of good religious influences. Their mere residence among a Christian people has wrought a great and happy change in their condition: they have been raised from the night of heathenism to the light of Christianity, and thousands of them have been brought to a saving knowledge of the Gospel.

Of the one hundred millions of the negro race, there cannot be found another so large a body as the three millions of slaves in the United States, at once so intelligent, so inclined to the Gospel, and so blessed by the elevating influence of civilization and Christianity. Occasional instances of cruelty and oppression, it is true, may sometimes occur, and probably will ever continue to take place under any system of laws: but this is not confined to wrongs committed upon the negro; wrongs are committed and cruelly practiced in a like degree by the lawless white man upon his own color; and while the negroes of our town and State are known to be surrounded by most of the substantial comforts of life, and invited both by precept and example to participate in proper, moral and religious duties, it argues, it seems to me, a sickly sensibility towards them to say their persons, and feelings, and interests are not sufficiently respected by our laws, which, in effect, tend to nullify the act of our Legislature passed for the security and protection of their masters.

The law under which you have been tried and found guilty is not to be found among the original enactments of our Legislature. The first legislative provision upon this subject was introduced in the year 1831, immediately succeeding the bloody scenes of the memorable Southampton insurrection; and that law being found not sufficiently penal to check the wrongs complained of, was re-enacted with additional penalties in the year 1848, which last mentioned act, after several years' trial and experience, has been re-affirmed by adoption, and incorporated into our present code. After these several and repeated recognitions of the wisdom and propriety of the said act, it may well be said that bold and open opposition to it is a matter not to be slightly regarded, especially as we have reason to believe that every Southern slave state in our country, as a measure of self-preservation and protection, has deemed it wise and just to adopt laws with similar provisions.

There might have been no occasion for such enactments in Virginia, or elsewhere, on the subject of negro education, but as a matter of self-defense against the schemes of Northern incendiaries, and the outcry against holding our slaves in bondage. Many now living well remember how, and when, and why the anti-slavery fury began, and by what means its manifestations were made public. Our mails were clogged with abolition pamphlets and inflammatory documents, to be distributed among our Southern negroes to induce them to cut our throats. Sometimes, it may be, these libelous documents were distributed by Northern citizens professing Southern feelings, and at other times by Southern people professing Northern feelings. These, however, were not the only means resorted to by the Northern fanatics to stir up insubordination among our slaves. They scattered far and near pocket handkerchiefs, and other similar articles, with frightful engravings, and printed over with anti-slavery nonsense, with the view to work upon the feeling and ignorance of our negroes, who otherwise would have remained comfortable and happy. Under such circumstances there was but one measure of protection for the South, and that was adopted. . . .

For these reasons, as an example to all others in like cases disposed to offend, and in vindication of the policy and justness of our laws, which every individual should be taught to respect, the judgment of the Court is, in addition to the proper fine and costs, that you be imprisoned for the period of one month in the jail of this city.

THE KANSAS–NEBRASKA TERRITORIES (1854)

In 1854, Stephen A. Douglas, Illinois Democrat and chairman of the Senate Committee on Territories, set off anew the national controversy over slavery when he proposed a bill to organize the Kansas and Nebraska territories for settlement and admission into the Union.

Reactions to the Kansas–Nebraska Act were sharply divided along sectional lines; furthermore, the measure split the Democrats, hastened the demise of the faltering Whig party, and sired as its replacement a major political entity in the form of the new Republican party. Issues supposedly settled by the Missouri Compromise of 1820 (Document 23) and wounds apparently healed by the Compromise of 1850 (Document 31) were reopened, never to close again short of war. Contemporaries of Douglas and later historians alike assigned a variety of motives to his sponsoring the bill. Some accused him of pandering to southern pressures within the Senate, led by pro-slavery Democrat David Atchison of Missouri; some noted Douglas's need of southern support for his own political, presidential aspirations, or for his intended transcontinental railroad legislation favoring Illinois cities. Others saw his eagerness, as an advocate of national expansion, to get on with the settlement and development of the West as quickly as possible; while others cited his desire to pull the Democratic party together in preparation for future political campaigns. If the last were an objective, the Senator failed miserably. Because he harbored no personal aversion to slavery, Douglas did not fully comprehend the extent to which northern sentiments favored maintenance of the Missouri

Compromise line. Withal, the Illinois Democrat badly miscalculated, and it cost him—and the nation—dearly.

The Kansas–Nebraska Act permitted the occupants of the two territories to decide for themselves whether they would enter the Union as slave or free states. Douglas defended this concept of popular, or squatter, sovereignty as the true test of democratic procedures. Such an arrangement had been incorporated into the Compromise of 1850 for the Territories of Utah and New Mexico, but the status of Kansas and Nebraska was quite different; each of them lay above 36° 30′ north latitude and should not, by the terms of the Missouri Compromise of 1820, have been open to slavery. The Act of 1854 affirmed the applicability of the Fugitive Slave Law within the two territories, but specifically declared Section 8 of the Missouri Compromise—which had established the line 36° 30′—null and void. Congressional authority to regulate territorial affairs was thus negated, and the South rejoiced in its victory.

The Kansas–Nebraska Act actually posed for the nation a more searching question than the immediate one concerning the organization of the territories and their admission to statehood. That is, on what grounds and under what circumstances may basic human principles and moral issues be left to the caprice of the ballot box? In an effort to control Kansas and Nebraska, antislavery and pro-slavery advocates sought frantically—with violent results—to settle the territories and dominate the elections that would determine the fate of the two emerging states. The basic question persisted, however: when are certain principles so enduring as not to be susceptible, even under the best procedural, democratic guarantees, to resolution by strict majority will?

Almost immediately upon the introduction by Senator Douglas of his initial bill for organizing the Kansas and Nebraska Territories, an antislavery coalition formed to announce its opposition to altering the arrangements that had, since 1820, barred slavery from the area. Signed by the senators and a majority of the representatives from Ohio, it was published in *The New York Times* and was widely circulated throughout the country as "An Appeal to the People" and as an "Appeal to Independent Democrats." An instrument that helped to focus broad public resentment against the Douglas bill, the Appeal condemned the proposed legislation as a violation of a sacred and long-standing pledge, and as a slave-holders' plot pure and simple. The Appeal reflected and further dramatized political discontent with the Democrats and with the atrophied Whigs, and helped markedly to rally the individuals and groups who later formed the new Republican party in the summer of 1854.

DOCUMENT(S) 33

An act to organize the territories of Nebraska and Kansas, May 30, 1854[*]

Be it enacted by the Senate and House of Representatives of the United States of America in Congress assembled, That all that part of the territory of the United States included within the following limits, except such portions thereof as are hereinafter expressly exempted from the operations of this act, to wit: beginning at a point in the Missouri River where the fortieth parallel of north latitude crosses the same; thence west on said parallel to the east boundary of the Territory of Utah, on the summit of the Rocky Mountains; thence on said summit northward to the forty-ninth parallel of north latitude; thence east on said parallel to the western boundary of the territory of Minnesota; thence southward on said boundary to the Missouri River; thence down the main channel of said river to the place of beginning, be, and the same is hereby, created into a temporary government by the name of the Territory of Nebraska; and when admitted as a State or States, the said Territory, or any portion of the same, shall be received into the Union with or without slavery, as their constitution may prescribe at the time of their admission: *Provided,* That nothing in this act contained shall be construed to inhibit the government of the United States from dividing said Territory into two or more Territories, in such manner and at such times as Congress shall deem convenient and proper, or from attaching any portion of said Territory to any other State or Territory of the United States:

---

[*] 10 Stat. 277 (1854).

Provided further, That nothing in this act contained shall be construed to impair the rights of person or property now pertaining to the Indians in said Territory, so long as such rights shall remain unextinguished by treaty between the United States and such Indians, or to include any territory which, by treaty with an Indian tribe, is not, without the consent of said tribe, to be included within the territorial limits or jurisdiction of any State or Territory; but all such territory shall be excepted out of the boundaries, and constitute no part of the Territory of Nebraska, until said tribe shall signify their assent to the President of the United States to be included within the said Territory of Nebraska, or to affect the authority of the government of the United States to make any regulations respecting such Indians, their lands, property, or other rights, by treaty, law, or otherwise, which it would have been competent to the government to make if this act had never passed.

. . . .

Sec. 9. *And be it further enacted,* That the judicial power of said Territory shall be vested in a Supreme Court, District Courts, Probate Courts, and in Justices of the Peace. The Supreme Court shall consist of a chief justice and two associate justices, any two of whom shall constitute a quorum, and who shall hold a term at the seat of government of said Territory annually, and they shall hold their offices during the period of four years, and until their successor shall be appointed and qualified. The said Territory shall be divided into three judicial districts, and a district court shall be held in each of said districts by one of the justices of the Supreme Court, at such times and places as may be prescribed by law; and the said judges shall, after their appointments, respectively, reside in the districts which shall be assigned them. The jurisdiction of the several courts herein provided for, both appellate and original, and that of the probate courts and of justices of the peace, shall be as limited by law: *Provided,* That justices of the peace shall not have jurisdiction of any matter in controversy when the title or boundaries of land may be in dispute, or where the debt or sum claimed shall exceed one hundred dollars; and the said supreme and districts courts, respectively, shall possess chancery as well as common law jurisdiction. Each District Court, or the judge thereof, shall appoint its clerk, who shall also be the register in chancery, and shall keep his office at the place where the court may be held. Writs of error, bills of exception, and appeals, shall be allowed in all cases from the final decisions of said district courts to the Supreme Court, under such regulations as may be prescribed by law; but in no case removed to the Supreme Court shall trial by jury be allowed in said court. The Supreme Court, or the justices thereof, shall appoint its own clerk, and every clerk shall hold his office at the pleasure of the court for which he shall have been appointed. Writs of error, and appeals from the final decisions of said Supreme Court, shall be allowed, and may be taken to the Supreme Court of the United States, in the same manner and under the same regulations as from the circuit courts of the United States, where the value of the property, or the amount in controversy, to be ascertained by the oath or affirmation of either party, or other competent witness, shall exceed one thousand dollars; except only that in all cases involving title to slaves, the said writs of error, or appeals shall be allowed and decided by the said Supreme Court, without regard to the value of the matter, property, or title in controversy; and except also that a writ of error or appeal shall also be allowed to the Supreme Court of the United States, from the decision of the said Supreme Court created by this act, or of any judge thereof, or of the district courts created by this act, or of any judge thereof, upon any writ of *habeas corpus*, involving the question of personal freedom: *Provided*, that nothing herein contained shall be construed to apply to or affect the provisions to the "act respecting fugitives from justice, and persons escaping from the service of their masters," approved February twelfth, seventeen hundred and ninety-three, and the "act to amend and supplementary to the aforesaid act," approved September eighteen, eighteen hundred and fifty; and each of the said district courts shall have and exercise the same jurisdiction in all cases arising under the Constitution and Laws of the United States as is vested in the Circuit and District Courts of the United States; and the said Supreme and District Courts of the said Territory, and the respective judges thereof, shall and may grant writs of *habeas corpus* in all cases in which the same are granted by the judges of the United States in the District of Columbia; and the first six days of every term of said courts, or so much thereof as shall be necessary, shall be appropriated to the trial of causes arising under the said constitution and laws, and writs of error and appeal in all such cases shall be made to the Supreme Court of said Territory, the same as in other cases. The said clerk shall receive in all such cases the same fees which the clerks of the district courts of Utah Territory now receive for similar services.

SEC. 10. *And be it further enacted,* That the provisions of an act entitled "An act respecting fugitives from justice, and persons escaping from the service of their masters," approved February twelve, seventeen hundred and ninety-three, and the provisions of the act entitled "An act to amend, and supplementary to, the aforesaid act," approved September eighteen, eighteen hundred and fifty, be, and the same are hereby, declared to extend to and be in full force within the limits of said Territory of Nebraska.

. . . .

SEC. 14. *And be it further enacted,* That a delegate to the House of Representatives of the United States, to serve for the term of two years, who shall be a citizen of the United States, may be elected by the voters qualified to elect members of the Legislative Assembly, who shall be entitled to the same rights and privileges as are exercised and enjoyed by the delegates from the several other Territories of the United States to the said House of Representatives, but the delegate first elected shall hold his seat only during the term of the Congress to which he shall be elected. The first election shall be held at such time and places, and be conducted in such manner, as the Governor shall appoint and direct; and at all subsequent elections the times, places, and manner of holding the elections, shall be prescribed by law. The person having the greatest number of votes shall be declared by the Governor to be duly elected; and a certificate thereof shall be given accordingly. That the Constitution, and all Laws of the United States which are not locally inapplicable, shall have the same force and effect within the said Territory of Nebraska as elsewhere within the United States, except the eighth section of the act preparatory to the admission of Missouri into the Union, approved March sixth, eighteen hundred and twenty, which, being inconsistent with the principle of non-intervention by Congress with slavery in the States and Territories, as recognized by the legislation of eighteen hundred and fifty, commonly called the Compromise Measures, is hereby declared inoperative and void; it being the true intent and meaning of this act not to legislate slavery into any Territory or State, nor to exclude it therefrom, but to leave the people thereof perfectly free to form and regulate their domestic institutions in their own way, subject only to the Constitution of the United States: *Provided,* That nothing herein contained shall be construed to revive or put in force any law or regulation which may have existed prior to the act of sixth March, eighteen hundred and twenty, either protecting, establishing, prohibiting, or abolishing slavery.*

* Sections 27, 28, and 32 make the identical provisions for Kansas.

. . . .

*An appeal to the people, January 19, 1854**

Fellow-Citizens: As Senators and Representatives in the Congress of the United States, it is our duty to warn our constituencies whenever imminent danger menaces the Freedom of our institutions or the Permanency of our Union.

Such danger, as we firmly believe, now impends, and we earnestly solicit your prompt attention to it.

. . . .

At the present session, a new Nebraska bill has been reported by the Senate Committee on Territories, which, should it unhappily receive the sanction of Congress, will open all the unorganized territory of the Union to the ingress of slavery.

We arraign this bill as a gross violation of a sacred pledge;

* "The Nebraska Bill in Congress, Address to the People," *The New York Times* (January 24, 1854). 2: 4–6.

as a criminal betrayal of precious rights; as part and parcel of an atrocious plot to exclude from a vast unoccupied region, emigrants from the Old World and free laborers from our own States, and convert it into a dreary region of despotism, inhabited by masters and slaves.

Take your maps, fellow-citizens, we entreat you, and see what country it is which this bill gratuitously and recklessly proposes to open to slavery.

. . . .

This immense region, occupying the very heart of the North American Continent, and larger, by thirty-three thousand square miles, than all the existing Free States, excluding California . . . this immense region, embracing all the unorganized territory of the nation, except the comparatively insignificant district of Indian territory north of Red River and between Arkansas and Texas, and now for more than thirty years regarded by the common consent of the American people as consecrated to Freedom, by statute and by compact—this immense region, the bill now before the Senate, without reason and without excuse, but in flagrant disregard of sound policy and sacred faith, proposes to open to Slavery.

. . . .

It is a strange and ominous fact, well calculated to awaken the worst apprehensions, and the most fearful forebodings of future calamity, that it is now deliberately proposed to repeal this prohibition [the Missouri Compromise], by implication or directly—the latter certainly the manlier way—and thus to subvert this compact, and allow Slavery in all the yet unorganized territory.

. . . .

We appeal to the People. We warn you that the dearest interests of Freedom and the Union are in imminent peril. Servile demagogues may tell you that the Union can be maintained only by submitting to the demands of Slavery. We tell you that the safety of the Union can only be insured by the full recognition of the just claims of Freedom and

Man. The Union was formed to establish justice, and to secure the blessings of liberty. When it fails to accomplish these ends it will be worthless and when it becomes worthless it cannot long endure.

. . . .

Whatever apologies may be offered for the toleration of Slavery in the States, none can be urged for its extension into Territories where it does not exist, and where the extension involves the repeal of ancient law, and the violation of solemn compact. Let all protest earnestly and emphatically, by correspondence, through the press, by memorials, by resolutions of public meetings and legislative bodies, and in whatever other mode may seem expedient against this enormous crime.

. . . .

[Signed by the senators and a majority of the representatives from Ohio.]

THE DRED SCOTT CASE (1857)

Second only to the decision in *Brown* v. *Board of Education of Topeka* (Document 78) in its impact on race relations, the *Dred Scott* case was the most far-reaching judicial statement of the nineteenth century. This was the case that set the stage for the Civil War.

Twenty years before the date of the final decision, Dr. John Emerson left his home in Missouri to spend four years as an army surgeon in Illinois and in that part of the Louisiana Purchase Territory which is now Minnesota. He took with him his slave, Dred Scott. Under the Northwest Ordinance of 1787, Illinois was a free state; under the Missouri Compromise, that part of the Louisiana Territory in which Dred Scott had lived with Dr. Emerson was likewise free, while Missouri was a slave state.

In 1847, following his return to Missouri, Dred Scott sued

for his freedom in the state courts. Although these actions were largely prohibited in the Deep South, legal arguments of a Negro that he had been born free or had been set free were heard regularly in the courts of Missouri and the other Border States.

Dred Scott was denied his freedom. Although the Circuit Court of St. Louis County had rendered judgment in his favor, the decision was reversed by the Missouri Supreme Court. The Court ruled that residence in a free territory did not make a slave free. Dred Scott then prepared to bring a similar action in the federal courts. But could such an action be instituted? Federal courts would hear cases only in which there was diversity of citizenship—where the litigants were "citizens of different states," as provided in Article III, Section 2, Clause 1 of the Constitution.

Since Dr. Emerson had died meanwhile, his widow became Scott's lawful owner. Her second husband, Congressman Calvin C. Chaffee, the well-known Massachusetts abolitionist, was eager to bring this test case to the Supreme Court. The Congressman could not, of course, allow himself to be known publicly as a slave owner, and Scott was therefore "sold" to Mrs. Emerson-Chaffee's brother, John F. A. Sanford of New York (mistakenly spelled "Sandford" in the Supreme Court Reports). The necessary diversity of citizenship was established.

Still, two questions had to be answered in Scott's favor before the Court would take up the key question of whether residence in a free state or free territory resulted in emancipation. The first question before the Court was whether Scott was constitutionally a Missouri "citizen." The second question was whether Scott's action was precluded because he had already lost a similar lawsuit in the Missouri state courts.

The issues were argued in 1856. Chief Justice Taney ordered re-argument to avoid rendering an opinion during the Presidential campaign of 1856. It was not until February 15, 1857, that the judges met in conference to discuss the case. According to the leading Supreme Court historian, "An agreement was then reached that the Court should give no opinion upon the constitutionality of the Missouri Compromise Act, but should decide the case upon the point that, whatever effect the negro's residence in Illinois and in the

Northwest Territory had upon his status there, his status in Missouri, after his return to that State, must depend upon the law of Missouri; and that Missouri, by its law as laid down by its Supreme Court, regarded him as a slave, and hence incapable of maintaining suit in the Federal Circuit Court." (Charles Warren, *The Supreme Court in United States History*, Vol. III [Boston: Little, Brown and Company, 1923], p. 15.) Thus the case would have been disposed of on the second point alone.

Within a few days, however, it was learned that dissenting Justices John McLean and Benjamin R. Curtis planned to write opinions sustaining the power exercised in the Missouri Compromise. This led the majority to the conclusion that they should discuss this point as well.

Outstanding lawyers argued the case before the Supreme Court: Montgomery Blair on behalf of Dred Scott and H. S. Geyer for the defendant were the principal spokesmen. Their briefs gave emphasis, first, to the meaning of "citizenship" as applied to Negroes, and, second, to the powers of Congress over the territories.

The technical basis of decision was the Supreme Court's denial that it had jurisdiction to determine the merits of the controversy and its conclusion that it must abide by the state court's decree that Dred Scott remain a slave. Specifically, the Court held: (1) that Dred Scott, a Negro, was not a citizen of Missouri within the meaning of the Constitution and thus could not invoke the diversity jurisdiction of the federal courts; (2) that the prior decision of the Missouri Supreme Court was conclusive; (3) that Scott's temporary residence in free territory had not made him free; and (4) that the Missouri Compromise was unconstitutional since it violated substantive rights in property under the Fifth Amendment's due process clause.

The determination on the Missouri Compromise marked the second time in American history that the Supreme Court declared an act of Congress unconstitutional (the first had occurred in 1803 in *Marbury* v. *Madison*). Thus Congress was denied the power to exclude slavery from any part of the unorganized western territories. Furthermore, the case in effect deprived even the Negroes in free states of the rights of citizenship under the Constitution.

The majority in the *Dred Scott* case assumed that it was

limited to the construction placed on constitutional words by the framers. And in this respect the Court in *Dred Scott* was in error, even in its own time.

Unnecessary to the decision was the famous—and infamous —dictum in the opinion by Chief Justice Roger B. Taney that the Negro "had no rights which the white man was bound to respect." "This statement comprised no part of the holding of the case, but it symbolized in the public mind what the Supreme Court said and did. Continued repetition of this phrase provided the basic theme of a vigorous and successful attack upon the prestige of the Court. . . . The [actual] law of the case was lost in the maelstrom which engulfed North and South." (Albert P. Blaustein and C. Clyde Ferguson, Jr., *Desegregation and the Law*, 1st ed. [New Brunswick, N. J.: Rutgers University Press, 1957], pp. 84–85.)

DOCUMENT(S) 34

*Dred Scott vs. Alex. Sandford, Saml. Russell, and Irene Emerson** *

To the Honorable, the Circuit Court within and for the County of St. Louis:

Your petitioner, Dred Scott, a man of color, respectfully represents that sometime in the year 1835 your petitioner was purchased as a slave by one John Emerson, since deceased, who afterwards, to-wit, about the year 1836 or 1837, conveyed your petitioner from the State of Missouri to Fort Snelling, a fort then occupied by the troops of the United States and under the jurisdiction of the United States, situated in the territory ceded by France to the United States under the name of Louisiana, lying north of 36 degrees and 30' North latitude, not included within the limits of the State of Missouri, and resided and continued to reside at said Fort Snelling for upwards of one year, and holding your petitioner in slavery at said Fort during all that time in violation of the Act of Congress of March 6th, 1820, entitled An Act to Authorize the People of Missouri Territory to Form a Constitu-

* *Dred Scott Papers*, Missouri Historical Society, St. Louis, Missouri.

tion and State Government, and for the admission of such State into the Union on an equal footing with the original states, and to Prohibit Slavery in Certain Territories.

Your petitioner avers that said Emerson has since departed this life, leaving his widow Irene Emerson and an infant child whose name is unknown to your petitioner; and that one Alexander Sandford has administered upon the estate of said Emerson and that your petitioner is now unlawfully held in slavery by said Sandford as said administrator and said Irene Emerson who claims your petitioner as part of the estate of said Emerson, and by one Samuel Russell.

Your petitioner therefore prays your Honorable Court to grant him leave to sue as a poor person, in order to establish his right to freedom, and that the necessary orders may be made in the premises.

DRED SCOTT

State of Missouri
County of St. Louis $\Big\}$ ss.

This day personally came before me, the undersigned, a Justice of the Peace, Dred Scott, the person whose name is affixed to the foregoing petition, and made oath that the facts set forth in the above petition are true to the best of his knowledge and belief, that he is entitled to his freedom. Witness my hand this 1st day of July, 1847.

his
Dred X Scott
mark

Sworn to and subscribed before me this 1st day of July, 1847.

PETER W. JOHNSTONE
Justice of the Peace.

Argument of Montgomery Blair, of counsel for the plaintiff in error [Dred Scott]*

The argument most relied on by those who deny the citizenship of free colored men is, that the acts of Congress on the

---

* From the Briefs in *Dred Scott* v. *Sandford,* filed in the Library of the Supreme Court of the United States.

subject of naturalization provide for naturalizing white persons only, and thus, it is contended, marked the national sentiment, that none but white persons were citizens. . . .

The Constitution commits the subject of naturalization to Congress without limitation; and although in general it has been confined to white persons, yet, as we have seen, it has been extended to both Indians and negroes. The favorite argument, therefore, of the adversaries of negro citizenship is turned against them; and, if it had been valid, the facts would be conclusive against them. But, as Judge Gaston says, there is no connection between the subject of citizenship as acquired by birth and that acquired under the laws of Congress; and "it would be a dangerous mistake to confound them." . . .

If there be limitations on a principle adopted in the United States, which is of universal application in the mother country, it is for those who insist on the limitations to show affirmatively that such limitations have been established here. The Constitution of the United States certainly recognises no such limitations on this subject; it recognises but two kinds of free persons—citizens and aliens;—nobody supposes that free negroes are aliens; they are, therefore, necessarily citizens, and are, in fact, so regarded and treated. Thus, they are permitted to hold property in all the States; to carry on commerce under the laws of the United States; are entitled to bounties and pre-emptions; (see opinion of Legaré, Att'y Gen'l, vol. 4, p. 147.) All these rights are held by them as "citizens;" and even where the laws discriminate against them as respects political functions or privileges, it is still as a class of citizens they are excluded. . . .

Free blacks are thus recognised as citizens in all the States. Where the law does not prescribe, as one of the qualifications of an elector, that he shall be *white*, they vote as other citizens, and they are excepted nowhere from any duty or privilege appertaining to citizens, unless by express provision of law. And so of the United States. . . .

In the organization of the Western Territory, first by the resolutions adopted 23d April, 1784, the organization was committed to the *"free males of full age"*; afterwards, by the ordinance of 1787, to "the free male inhabitants of full age," residents in the Territory for a specified time, and to "the citizens of the States" resident there. The 4th article provides for the admission of the States to be formed out of the territory into the Union on an equal footing with the original States, and the celebrated and long contested 6th article abolished slavery. The ordinance, therefore, distinctly contemplated not only the establishment of civil and political equality in Territories, but designed that its "free inhabitants," including those made free by the ordinance, should "be entitled to the privileges and immunities of *citizens* of the several States."

These proceedings show, 1st, that Congress refused emphatically to allow any distinction to be made between the *white* and other inhabitants in the privileges to be extended to them by the several States; and 2d, that others were recognised as citizens besides whites; and together demonstrate that the substitution which was made in the Constitution without debate or objection, of the word "*citizen*" for "*free inhabitant,*" used in the articles of Confederation, was not done to exclude such "*other citizens*" from the privileges conferred by the Constitution. . . .

The laws of Missouri, accordingly, (see Rev. Laws of 1845, p. 755,) permit "free negroes or mulattoes, who produce a certificate of citizenship from some one of the United States," to reside in the State; and by the code of 1835, "free negroes who were citizens of other States" were excepted from the exclusion imposed on others, and were to be released if arrested, on producing a certificate of citizenship from any court of record. In reply to this recognition of citizenship, it was argued that this law of Missouri was an invasion of the requirements of the fundamental condition upon which the State was admitted, as it required *naturalization certificates* from the States, when it was well known the Constitution had taken the power of naturalization from the States; and it was stated by counsel that, in point of fact, no such certificates had ever been produced.

The answer to this is easy. The law does not purport to require naturalization certificates, but merely certificates attesting the citizenship of the parties in some of the States. This would be an easy condition, on the part of a free negro going from almost any of the Northern States, in which they are under no disabilities; as, for instance, from New York, where Chancellor Kent says they are recognised as citizens, both by the constitution and laws. That no such certificate was ever produced, may be accounted for by the notorious fact that the law has not been enforced.

The plea to the jurisdiction alleges that Dred was not a citizen, because he was a negro. But the law of Missouri admits that negroes may be citizens, and prescribes the evidence which shall be required.

. . . .

The plaintiff's claim of citizenship is consistent with this [additional] view of the subject. He is not eligible to office, and is not a voter, and therefore is not, according to these cases, a citizen entitled to all the privileges secured by the fourth article; but that he is a *quasi* citizen, or citizen in that sense of the term which enables him to acquire and hold property under the States and under the United States, is universally admitted; and it would seem to follow, necessarily, that all the incidents to these acknowledged rights of person and property, or all the rights necessary to maintain them, and which are allowed to others in the same circumstances as parts of such rights, attached also to these persons. No one can be said to have title to property who cannot maintain an action to defend it against trespassers; and, accordingly, these persons can sue and be sued as other citizens in the State court, and so suits have been heretofore maintained in the courts of the United States, without question—an instance of which is the suit of Legrand vs. Darnell, hereinafter referred to for other purposes, (reported 2 Peters, 670,) brought by the present Chief Justice of the Supreme Court, in which the defendant is described in the bill as a negro, and in which that fact also appears by the subject-matter. They are embraced in the class of citizens, without question, in the construction of the laws regulating commerce, the holding and acquisition of property, &c. The laws of the United States regulating judicial proceedings follow the same division of free persons into citizens and aliens, observed in legislating on other subjects aiming to provide for all cases under this division. Why should not the classification allowed on other subjects hold in judicial proceedings? . . .

Although the point under consideration has not been expressly decided by this court, suits have been entertained, and here, as already shown, without question, in which free persons of color were parties in character of "citizens."

• • • •

The section [of the Missouri Compromise] in question is in these words: "*And be it further enacted,* That in all that Territory, ceded by France to the United States, which lies north of thirty-six degrees and thirty minutes north latitude, not included within the limits of the State contemplated by this act, slavery and involuntary servitude, otherwise than in the punishment of crimes whereof the parties shall have been duly convicted, shall be and the same is hereby forever prohibited; *Provided always,* that any person escaping into the same, from whom labor or service is lawfully claimed in any State or Territory of the United States, such fugitive may be lawfully reclaimed and conveyed to the person claiming his or her labor or service as aforesaid."

The validity of this section is denied, on the ground that Congress possessed no power to prohibit slavery in the Territories.

This is a question of more importance, perhaps, than any which was ever submitted to this court; and the decision of the court is looked for with a degree of interest by the country which seldom attends its proceedings. It is, indeed, the great question of our day and times, and is, substantially, the issue on which the great political divisions among men is founded in all times and countries. It is in form here a question on the construction of a few words in our fundamental law. But it is the principle involved that shapes the conclusions of political men and parties, rather than the force or meaning of the language which constitutes properly the legal question.

• • • •

To limit the meaning of the words merely to a grant of power to make rules and regulations for disposition of the public lands in a particular region, under such circumstances, would be to grant no power at all. The power to grant or to hold lands presupposes the existence of a government to protect the property and the grantee in the rights granted to him. And the possession and disposition of land by a govern-

ment, being in a region of country lying outside of the jurisdiction of any other government, cannot be conceived of,
unassociated with the idea of political sovereignty, to be
exercised under the limitations and according to the nature
of its own constitution. To deny, therefore, that territory
under such conditions means a district of country subject to
be governed by the United States, is to deny all meaning and
effect whatever to the clause. And, therefore, when the chief
justice, in Canter's case, (1 Peters, 546,) speaks of Congressional legislation over such a Territory, as legislation "in
virtue of the general right of sovereignty which exists in the
Government, or in virtue of that clause which enables Congress to make all needful rules and regulations respecting the
territory belonging to the United States," he does not talk
"loosely," as has been said, but with his accustomed
precision. . . .

What are needful rules and regulations, and whether any
particular law was indispensable as such, is a question not
within the scope of judicial inquiry. When there is a substantive power vested in Congress, the laws passed in the
exercise of it cannot be questioned in the courts, unless they
violate some of the constitutional limitations of the legislative
power; as, for example, provisions against "religious tests,"
"bills of attainder," "trial by jury," &c., &c. If the power is
conceded at all, whether derived from the clause I have
considered, or from the treaty-making or war-making power,
it is necessarily what the chief justice described it in Canter's
case, "the combined power of a General and a State government."

As it is conceded generally that Congress has such a
power—and it is questioned only when applied to a particular
subject—the only legal question involved is, whether this
application violates any of the express restrictive provisions
of the Constitution on the legislative power. Nothing of the
sort is pretended. It is only contended that its operation is
prejudicial to one section of the country, and therefore violative of the *spirit* of the Constitution, which recognises the
equality of the States. But this, if true in fact, is not one of
those *"inevitable consequences"* which are alone the subjects
of judicial consideration. If the operation of the prohibition
is unequal or discriminating against any State; or against any
peculiar individual rights or institutions created or recognised

by the law of such State, this may be a conflict in the policy of the two governments in reference to such institutions; but to call it a violation of the constitution of either government would be to make the constitution of one government dependent on the legislation of the other; and where the policy of the States differed among themselves, as they do on many subjects, there would of necessity result a multitude of violations of the Constitution of the United States. Thus, if it is a violation of the Constitution to forbid slavery in the Territories because it is allowed in some of the States, it would be equally a violation of the Constitution to permit it to go there when other States prohibit it, and it would cease to be a violation of the Constitution if all the States should prohibit the institution, and again become so if any of them should re-establish it.

Case for defendant in error [by] H. S. Geyer*

. . . The averment that the plaintiff is a citizen of the State of Missouri, is a necessary averment. If it had been omitted, or defectively stated, it would have been error in the Circuit Court to entertain jurisdiction, even though the defendant had not traversed the averment, but pleaded to the merits. . . .

Citizens within the meaning of art. 3, sec. 2, are citizens of the United States who are citizens of the States in which they respectively reside. . . .

Citizens are natives or naturalized. All persons born in the United States are not citizens; the exceptions are, first, children of foreign ambassadors; secondly, Indians; and thirdly, in general, persons of color. . . .

"Negroes or other slaves born within and under the allegiance of the United States are *natural born subjects, not citizens*. Citizens under our constitution mean free inhabitants born within the United States, or naturalized under the law of Congress." (2 Kent's Com., p. 258, note *b*.)

. . . .

---

* *Ibid.*

No residence of a slave at Fort Snelling could change his condition or divest the title of his owner. Slavery existed by law in all the territory ceded by France to the United States, and Congress has not the constitutional power to repeal that law, or abolish or prohibit slavery within any part of that territory.

The power of Congress to institute municipal governments for the territory within the United States, and not within any particular State, is not denied. It has been often exercised by Congress and recognized by this court; but the power is raised only by implication, and, from whatever source derived, does not carry with it supreme, universal and unlimited power over the persons and property of the inhabitants, to abolish slavery, or to interfere with the local law of property in any form.

The 8th section of the act of the 6th March, 1820, is the first and almost the only instance of an assumption by Congress of the power to abolish slavery in a Territory. It has never been recognized by this court. It is understood to be claimed, that authority of Congress to erect Territorial governments is conferred by Art. 4, sect. 3, of the Constitution, which gives the "power to dispose of and make all needful rules and regulations respecting the *territory or other property belonging to the United States,*" or to result from the power to acquire territory; and in either case, it comprehends a power of legislation, exclusive, universal, absolute and unlimited. . . .

The subject of the power conferred by art. 4, sec. 3, is *property*, and the property *only* of the United States, not of the inhabitants of the States or Territories. Whatever Congress may regulate under that clause, it may dispose of absolutely. It is a power over the *territory*—that is, the *unappropriated lands*—of the United States, whether within a State or Territory. The power attaches to the territory and other property belonging to the United States wherever situate.

To organize a municipal government or corporation for a district of country, to prohibit slavery, or to interfere in any way with the law of property, is not to make needful rules and regulations respecting the territory or other property belonging to the United States within such district. Therefore the power to institute such a government, and more especially an unlimited power to *legislate* in all cases whatsoever over the inhabitants of a Territory and their property, can not be deduced from the clause under consideration. . . .

Finally. A temporary government is necessary, but it is not necessary to that end to abolish slavery or change the local law of property. Nor is it just or defensible, much less necessary and proper, to deprive any citizen of his right to remove to a country open to all others, with any property recognized by the constitution of the United States and protected by the local laws.

The Opinion[*]

MR. CHIEF JUSTICE TANEY delivered the opinion of the Court.

This case has been twice argued. After the argument at the last term, differences of opinion were found to exist among the members of the court; and as the questions in controversy are of the highest importance, and the court was at that time much pressed by the ordinary business of the term, it was deemed advisable to continue the case, and direct a re-argument on some of the points, in order that we might have an opportunity of giving to the whole subject a more deliberate consideration. It has accordingly been again argued by counsel, and considered by the court; and I now proceed to deliver its opinion. . . .

The plaintiff was a negro slave, belonging to Dr. Emerson, who was a surgeon in the army of the United States. In the year 1834, he took the plaintiff from the State of Missouri to the military post at Rock Island, in the State of Illinois, and held him there as a slave until the month of April or May, 1836. At the time last mentioned, said Dr. Emerson removed the plaintiff from said military post at Rock Island to the military post at Fort Snelling, situated on the west bank of the Mississippi river, in the Territory known as Upper Louisiana, acquired by the United States of France, and

---

[*] Supreme Court of the United States, 19 How. (60 U.S.) 393 (1857).

situated north of the latitude of thirty-six degrees thirty minutes north, and north of the State of Missouri. Said Dr. Emerson held the plaintiff in slavery at said Fort Snelling, from said last-mentioned date until the year 1838.

In the year 1835, Harriet, who is named in the second count of the plaintiff's declaration, was the negro slave of Major Taliaferro, who belonged to the army of the United States. In that year, 1835, said Major Taliaferro took said Harriet to said Fort Snelling, a military post, situated as hereinbefore stated, and kept her there as a slave until the year 1836, and then sold and delivered her as a slave, at said Fort Snelling, unto the said Dr. Emerson hereinbefore named. Said Dr. Emerson held said Harriet in slavery at said Fort Snelling until the year 1838.

In the year 1836, the plaintiff and Harriet intermarried, at Fort Snelling, with the consent of Dr. Emerson, who then claimed to be their master and owner. Eliza and Lizzie, named in the third count of the plaintiff's declaration, are the fruit of that marriage. Eliza is about fourteen years old, and was born on board the steamboat Gipsey, north of the north line of the State of Missouri, and upon the river Mississippi. Lizzie is about seven years old, and was born in the State of Missouri, at the military post called Jefferson Barracks.

In the year 1838, said Dr. Emerson removed the plaintiff and said Harriet, and their said daughter Eliza, from said Fort Snelling to the State of Missouri, where they have ever since resided.

Before the commencement of this suit, said Dr. Emerson sold and conveyed the plaintiff, and Harriet, Eliza, and Lizzie, to the defendant, as slaves, and the defendant has ever since claimed to hold them, and each of them, as slaves. . . . .

There are two leading questions presented by the record:

1. Had the Circuit Court of the United States jurisdiction to hear and determine the case between these parties? And

2. If it had jurisdiction, is the judgment it has given erroneous or not?

The plaintiff in error, who was also the plaintiff in the court below, was, with his wife and children, held as slaves by the defendant, in the State of Missouri; and he brought this action in the Circuit Court of the United States for that district, to assert the title of himself and his family to freedom.

The declaration is in the form usually adopted in that State to try questions of this description, and contains the averment necessary to give the court jurisdiction; that he and the defendant are citizens of different States; that is, that he is a citizen of Missouri, and the defendant a citizen of New York.

The defendant pleaded in abatement to the jurisdiction of the court, that the plaintiff was not a citizen of the State of Missouri, as alleged in his declaration, being a negro of African descent, whose ancestors were of pure African blood, and who were brought into this country and sold as slaves. . . .

The question is simply this: Can a negro, whose ancestors were imported into this country, and sold as slaves, become a member of the political community formed and brought into existence by the Constitution of the United States, and as such become entitled to all the rights, and privileges, and immunities, guaranteed by that instrument to the citizen? One of which rights is the privilege of suing in a court of the United States in the cases specified in the Constitution. . . .

We proceed to examine the case as presented by the pleadings.

The words "people of the United States" and "citizens" are synonymous terms, and mean the same thing. They both describe the political body who, according to our republican institutions, form the sovereignty, and who hold the power and conduct the Government through their representatives. They are what we familiarly call the "sovereign people," and every citizen is one of this people, and a constituent member of this sovereignty. The question before us is, whether the class of persons described in the plea in abatement compose a portion of this people, and are constituent members of this sovereignty? We think they are not, and that they are not included, and were not intended to be included, under the word "citizens" in the Constitution, and can therefore claim none of the rights and privileges which that instrument provides for and secures to citizens of the United States. On the contrary, they were at that time considered as a subordinate and inferior class of beings, who had been subjugated by the dominant race, and, whether emancipated or not, yet remained subject to their authority, and had no rights or privileges but such as those who held the power and the Government might choose to grant them. . . .

In discussing this question, we must not confound the rights of citizenship which a State may confer within its own limits, and the rights of citizenship as a member of the Union. It does not by any means follow, because he has all the rights and privileges of a citizen of a State, that he must be a citizen of the United States. He may have all of the rights and privileges of the citizen of a State, and yet not be entitled to the rights and privileges of a citizen in any other State. For, previous to the adoption of the Constitution of the United States, every State had the undoubted right to confer on whomsoever it pleased the character of citizen, and to endow him with all its rights. But this character of course was confined to the boundaries of the State, and gave him no rights or privileges in other States beyond those secured to him by the laws of nations and the comity of States. Nor have the several States surrendered the power of conferring these rights and privileges by adopting the Constitution of the United States. Each State may still confer them upon an alien, or any one it thinks proper, or upon any class or description of persons; yet he would not be a citizen in the sense in which that word is used in the Constitution of the United States, nor entitled to sue as such in one of its courts, nor to the privileges and immunities of a citizen in the other States. The rights which he would acquire would be restricted to the State which gave them. The Constitution has conferred on Congress the right to establish an uniform rule of naturalization, and this right is evidently exclusive, and has always been held by this court to be so. Consequently, no State, since the adoption of the Constitution, can by naturalizing an alien invest him with the rights and privileges secured to a citizen of a State under the Federal Government, although, so far as the State alone was concerned, he would undoubtedly be entitled to the rights of a citizen, and clothed with all the rights and immunities which the Constitution and laws of the State attached to that character. . . .

It becomes necessary, therefore, to determine who were citizens of the several States when the Constitution was adopted. And in order to do this, we must recur to the Governments and institutions of the thirteen colonies, when they separated from Great Britain and formed new sovereignties, and took their places in the family of independent nations. We must inquire who, at that time, were recognised as the people or citizens of a State, whose rights and liberties had been outraged by the English Government; and who declared their independence, and assumed the powers of Government to defend their rights by force of arms.

In the opinion of the court, the legislation and histories of the times, and the language used in the Declaration of Independence, show, that neither the class of persons who had been imported as slaves, nor their descendants, whether they had become free or not, were then acknowledged as a part of the people, nor intended to be included in the general words used in that memorable instrument.

It is difficult at this day to realize the state of public opinion in relation to that unfortunate race, which prevailed in the civilized and enlightened portions of the world at the time of the Declaration of Independence, and when the Constitution of the United States was framed and adopted. But the public history of every European nation displays it in a manner too plain to be mistaken.

They had for more than a century before been regarded as beings of an inferior order, and altogether unfit to associate with the white race, either in social or political relations; and so far inferior, that they had no rights which the white man was bound to respect; and that the negro might justly and lawfully be reduced to slavery for his benefit. He was bought and sold, and treated as an ordinary article of merchandise and traffic, whenever a profit could be made by it. This opinion was at that time fixed and universal in the civilized portion of the white race. It was regarded as an axiom in morals as well as in politics, which no one thought of disputing, or supposed to be open to dispute; and men in every grade and position in society daily and habitually acted upon it in their private pursuits, as well as in matters of public concern, without doubting for a moment the correctness of this opinion.

And in no nation was this opinion more firmly fixed or more uniformly acted upon than by the English Government and English people. They not only seized them on the coast of Africa, and sold them or held them in slavery for their own use; but they took them as ordinary articles of merchandise to every country where they could make a profit on them, and were far more extensively engaged in this commerce than any other nation in the world.

The opinion thus entertained and acted upon in England was naturally impressed upon the colonies they founded on this side of the Atlantic. And, accordingly, a negro of the African race was regarded by them as an article of property, and held, and bought and sold as such, in every one of the thirteen colonies which united in the Declaration of Independence, and afterwards formed the Constitution of the United States. The slaves were more or less numerous in the different colonies, as slave labor was found more or less profitable. But no one seems to have doubted the correctness of the prevailing opinion of the time.

The legislation of the different colonies furnishes positive and indisputable proof of this fact. . . .

The language of the Declaration of Independence is equally conclusive: . . .

This state of public opinion had undergone no change when the Constitution was adopted, as is equally evident from its provisions and language. . . .

Indeed, when we look to the condition of this race in the several States at the time, it is impossible to believe that these rights and privileges were intended to be extended to them.

It is very true, that in that portion of the Union where the labor of the negro race was found to be unsuited to the climate and unprofitable to the master, but few slaves were held at the time of the Declaration of Independence; and when the Constitution was adopted, it had entirely worn out in one of them, and measures had been taken for its gradual abolition in several others. But this change had not been produced by any change of opinion in relation to this race; but because it was discovered, from experience, that slave labor was unsuited to the climate and productions of these States: for some of the States, where it had ceased or nearly ceased to exist, were actively engaged in the slave trade, procuring cargoes on the coast of Africa, and transporting them for sale to those parts of the Union where their labor was found to be profitable, and suited to the climate and productions. And this traffic was openly carried on, and fortunes accumulated by it, without reproach from the people of the States where they resided. And it can hardly be supposed that, in the States where it was then countenanced in its worst form—that is, in the seizure and transportation—

the people could have regarded those who were emancipated as entitled to equal rights with themselves. . . .

The legislation of the States therefore shows, in a manner not to be mistaken, the inferior and subject condition of that race at the time the Constitution was adopted, and long afterwards, throughout the thirteen States by which that instrument was framed; and it is hardly consistent with the respect due to these States, to suppose that they regarded at that time, as fellow-citizens and members of the sovereignty, a class of beings whom they had thus stigmatized; whom, as we are bound, out of respect to the State sovereignties, to assume they had deemed it just and necessary thus to stigmatize, and upon whom they had impressed such deep and enduring marks of inferiority and degradation; or, that when they met in convention to form the Constitution, they looked upon them as a portion of their constituents, or designed to include them in the provisions so carefully inserted for the security and protection of the liberties and rights of their citizens. It cannot be supposed that they intended to secure to them rights, and privileges, and rank, in the new political body throughout the Union, which every one of them denied within the limits of its own dominion. More especially, it cannot be believed that the large slaveholding States regarded them as included in the word citizens, or would have consented to a Constitution which might compel them to receive them in that character from another State. For if they were so received, and entitled to the privileges and immunities of citizens, it would exempt them from the operation of the special laws and from the police regulations which they considered to be necessary for their own safety. It would give to persons of the negro race, who were recognised as citizens in any one State of the Union, the right to enter every other State whenever they pleased, singly or in companies, without pass or passport, and without obstruction, to sojourn there as long as they pleased, to go where they pleased at every hour of the day or night without molestation, unless they committed some violation of law for which a white man would be punished; and it would give them the full liberty of speech in public and in private upon all subjects upon which its own citizens might speak; to hold public meetings upon political affairs, and to keep and carry arms wherever they went. And all of this would be done in the face of the subject race of the same color, both free and slaves, and inevitably producing discontent and insubordination among them, and endangering the peace and safety of the State. . . .

No one, we presume, supposes that any change in public opinion or feeling, in relation to this unfortunate race, in the civilized nations of Europe or in this country, should induce the court to give to the words of the Constitution a more liberal construction in their favor than they were intended to bear when the instrument was framed and adopted. Such an argument would be altogether inadmissible in any tribunal called on to interpret it. If any of its provisions are deemed unjust, there is a mode prescribed in the instrument itself by which it may be amended; but while it remains unaltered, it must be construed now as it was understood at the time of its adoption. It is not only the same in words, but the same in meaning, and delegates the same powers to the Government, and reserves and secures the same rights and privileges to the citizen; and as long as it continues to exist in its present form, it speaks not only in the same words, but with the same meaning and intent with which it spoke when it came from the hands of its framers, and was voted on and adopted by the people of the United States. Any other rule of construction would abrogate the judicial character of this court, and make it the mere reflex of the popular opinion or passion of the day. This court was not created by the Constitution for such purposes. Higher and graver trusts have been confided to it, and it must not falter in the path of duty. . . .

And upon a full and careful consideration of the subject, the court is of opinion, that, upon the facts stated in the plea in abatement, Dred Scott was not a citizen of Missouri within the meaning of the Constitution of the United States, and not entitled as such to sue in its courts; and, consequently, that the Circuit Court had no jurisdiction of the case, and that the judgment on the plea in abatement is erroneous.

We are aware that doubts are entertained by some of the members of the court, whether the plea in abatement is legally before the court upon this writ of error; but if that plea is regarded as waived, or out of the case upon any other ground, yet the question as to the jurisdiction of the Circuit Court is presented on the face of the bill of exception itself, taken by the plaintiff at the trial; for he admits that he and his wife were born slaves, but endeavors to make out his title to freedom and citizenship by showing that they were taken by their owner to certain places, hereinafter mentioned, where slavery could not by law exist, and that they thereby became free, and upon their return to Missouri became citizens of that State.

Now, if the removal of which he speaks did not give them their freedom, then by his own admission he is still a slave; and whatever opinions may be entertained in favor of the citizenship of a free person of the African race, no one supposes that a slave is a citizen of the State or of the United States. If, therefore, the acts done by his owner did not make them free persons, he is still a slave, and certainly incapable of suing in the character of a citizen.

The principle of law is too well settled to be disputed, that a court can give no judgment for either party, where it has no jurisdiction; and if, upon the showing of Scott himself, it appeared that he was still a slave, the case ought to have been dismissed, and the judgment against him and in favor of the defendant for costs, is, like that on the plea in abatement, erroneous, and the suit ought to have been dismissed by the Circuit Court for want of jurisdiction in that court.

But, before we proceed to examine this part of the case, it may be proper to notice an objection taken to the judicial authority of this court to decide it; and it has been said, that as this court has decided against the jurisdiction of the Circuit Court on the plea in abatement, it has no right to examine any question presented by the exception; and that anything it may say upon that part of the case will be extra-judicial, and mere obiter dicta.

This is a manifest mistake; there can be no doubt as to the jurisdiction of this court to revise the judgment of a Circuit Court, and to reverse if for any error apparent on the record, whether it be the error of giving judgment in a case over which it had no jurisdiction, or any other material error; and this, too, whether there is a plea in abatement or not. . . .

We proceed, therefore, to inquire whether the facts relied on by the plaintiff entitled him to his freedom. . . .

In considering this part of the controversy, two questions arise: 1. Was he, together with his family, free in Missouri by reason of the stay in the territory of the United States hereinbefore mentioned? And 2. If they were not, is Scott himself free by reason of his removal to Rock Island, in the State of Illinois, as stated in the above admissions?

We proceed to examine the first question.

The act of Congress, upon which the plaintiff relies, declares that slavery and involuntary servitude, except as a punishment for crime, shall be forever prohibited in all that part of the territory ceded by France, under the name of Louisiana, which lies north of thirty-six degrees thirty minutes north latitude, and not included within the limits of Missouri. And the difficulty which meets us at the threshold of this part of the inquiry is, whether Congress was authorized to pass this law under any of the powers granted to it by the Constitution; for if the authority is not given by that instrument, it is the duty of this court to declare it void and inoperative, and incapable of conferring freedom upon any one who is held as a slave under the laws of any one of the States.

The counsel for the plaintiff has laid much stress upon that article in the Constitution which confers on Congress the power "to dispose of and make all needful rules and regulations respecting the territory or other property belonging to the United States"; but, in the judgment of the court, that provision has no bearing on the present controversy, and the power there given, whatever it may be, is confined, and was intended to be confined, to the territory which at that time belonged to, or was claimed by, the United States, and was within their boundaries as settled by the treaty with Great Britain, and can have no influence upon a territory afterwards acquired from a foreign Government. It was a special provision for a known and particular territory, and to meet a present emergency, and nothing more. . . .

But the power of Congress over the person or property of a citizen can never be a mere discretionary power under our Constitution and form of Government. The powers of the Government and the rights and privileges of the citizen are regulated and plainly defined by the Constitution itself. And when the Territory becomes a part of the United States, the Federal Government enters into possession in the character impressed upon it by those who created it. It enters upon it with its powers over the citizen strictly defined, and limited by the Constitution, from which it derives its own existence, and by virtue of which alone it continues to exist and act as a Government and sovereignty. It has no power of any kind beyond it; and it cannot, when it enters a Territory of the United States, put off its character, and assume discretionary or despotic powers which the Constitution has denied to it. It cannot create for itself a new character separated from the citizens of the United States, and the duties it owes them under the provisions of the Constitution. The Territory being a part of the United States, the Government and the citizen both enter it under the authority of the Constitution, with their respective rights defined and marked out; and the Federal Government can exercise no power over his person or property, beyond what that instrument confers, nor lawfully deny any right which it has reserved. . . .

Now, as we have already said in an earlier part of this opinion, upon a different point, the right of property in a slave is distinctly and expressly affirmed in the Constitution. The right to traffic in it, like an ordinary article of merchandise and property, was guaranteed to the citizens of the United States, in every State that might desire it, for twenty years. And the Government in express terms is pledged to protect it in all future time, if the slave escapes from his owner. This is done in plain words—too plain to be misunderstood. And no word can be found in the Constitution which gives Congress a greater power over slave property, or which entitles property of that kind to less protection than property of any other description. The only power conferred is the power coupled with the duty of guarding and protecting the owner in his rights.

Upon these considerations, it is the opinion of the court that the act of Congress which prohibited a citizen from holding and owning property of this kind in the territory of the United States north of the line therein mentioned, is not warranted by the Constitution, and is therefore void; and that neither Dred Scott himself, nor any of his family, were made free by being carried into this Territory; even if they had been carried there by the owner, with the intention of becoming a permanent resident.

We have so far examined the case, as it stands under the Constitution of the United States, and the powers thereby delegated to the Federal Government.

But there is another point in the case which depends on State power and State law. And it is contended, on the part of the plaintiff, that he is made free by being taken to Rock

Island, in the State of Illinois, independently of his residence in the territory of the United States; and being so made free, he was not again reduced to a state of slavery by being brought back to Missouri. . . .

The plaintiff, it appears, brought a similar action against the defendant in the State court of Missouri, claiming the freedom of himself and his family upon the same grounds and the same evidence upon which he relies in the case before the court. The case was carried before the Supreme Court of the State; was fully argued there; and that court decided that neither the plaintiff nor his family were entitled to freedom, and were still the slaves of the defendant; and reversed the judgment of the inferior State court, which had given a different decision. If the plaintiff supposed that this judgment of the Supreme Court of the State was erroneous, and that this court had jurisdiction to revise and reverse it, the only mode by which he could legally bring it before this court was by writ of error directed to the Supreme Court of the State, requiring it to transmit the record to this court. If this had been done, it is too plain for argument that the writ must have been dismissed for want of jurisdiction in this court. . . .

Upon the whole, therefore, it is the judgment of this court, that it appears by the record before us that the plaintiff in error is not a citizen of Missouri, in the sense in which that word is used in the Constitution; and that the Circuit Court of the United States, for that reason, had no jurisdiction in the case, and could give no judgment in it. Its judgment for the defendant must, consequently, be reversed, and a mandate issued, directing the suit to be dismissed for want of jurisdiction.

THE LINCOLN–DOUGLAS DEBATES (1858)

The 1858 campaign to return a United States Senator from Illinois pitted Abraham Lincoln against the Democratic incumbent, Stephen A. Douglas. The nation watched with intense interest as these two men dramatized the slavery issue in an extended canvass of the state.

Immediately upon receiving the Republican nomination at the party's state convention in Springfield, June 17, 1858, Lincoln took the offensive. His "House Divided" speech deftly linked the Senator, as author of the Kansas–Nebraska Act, with a preconceived plot to advance the slaveholders' interests. According to the Republican challenger, Democrats Stephen Douglas, Franklin Pierce, Roger Taney, and James Buchanan had consorted by degrees to throw the mantle of federal protection over slavery and affix the institution to all parts of the nation. The charge was without foundation in fact, but this would not be the last time Lincoln would hammer away at a false accusation designed to inflame the voters against his adversary. Where the Illinois Republican truly scored in this campaign, both in the minds of objective contemporaries and later analysts, was in his assertion that Douglas's failing lay in his inability to recognize and admit that slavery did, indeed, represent a crucial moral issue to the nation. By the time Lincoln had finished with his opponent, Douglas's assertion that he cared not whether slavery was "voted up or voted down" would seem callous and cavalier at best, cruel and unprincipled at worst.

In addition to their separate appearances throughout the state, Lincoln and Douglas engaged in seven debates between late August and mid-October. The best known of the seven debates took place at Freeport on August 27. Lincoln replied to a series of inquiries put to him by Douglas, but he was careful to distinguish between his "pledged" position and his "tendencies." He then threw the burden back upon the Senator by asking four questions of his own. Douglas's response to one of these became known as his "Freeport Doctrine," in which he admitted that, despite the *Dred Scott* decision (Document 34), slavery could not exist without the protection of local police power sustained by majority will. Douglas thus affirmed his popular sovereignty concept, but in so doing he further alienated southern support and added to the likelihood of a sectional rupture within the Democratic party.

Douglas sought to discredit his opponent by identifying him with Negro and abolitionist interests from outside the state. In the fourth joint debate, held at Charleston on September 18, 1858, Lincoln disavowed any such identification and took a position that placed him squarely with the vast majority of northern whites on the question of race relations.

In the seventh and final debate, held on October 15, 1858, at Alton, Lincoln repeated his attack upon Douglas's disregard for the moral aspects of slavery and its extension and perpetuation. At the same time, the Republican challenger continued to show paramount concern for the interests of *white* labor when examining the slavery controversy.

DOCUMENT(S) 35

*Lincoln at Charleston, Illinois, September 18, 1858**

Ladies and gentlemen: It will be very difficult for an audience so large as this to hear distinctly what a speaker says, and consequently it is important that as profound silence be preserved as possible.

While I was at the hotel to-day, an elderly gentleman called upon me to know whether I was really in favor of producing a perfect equality between the negroes and white people. While I had not proposed to myself on this occasion to say much on that subject, yet as the question was asked me I thought I would occupy perhaps five minutes in saying something in regard to it. I will say, then, that I am not, nor ever have been, in favor of bringing about in any way the social and political equality of the white and black races; that I am not, nor ever have been, in favor of making voters or jurors of negroes, nor of qualifying them to hold office, nor to intermarry with white people; and I will say, in addition to this, that there is a physical difference between the white and black races which I believe will forever forbid the two races living together on terms of social and political equality. And inasmuch as they cannot so live, while they do remain together there must be the position of superior and inferior, and I as much as any other man am in favor of having the

---

* Arthur Brooks Lapsley, ed., *The Writings of Abraham Lincoln*, Vol. IV (New York: Lamb Publishing Company, 1906), pp. 1–3.

superior position assigned to the white race. I say upon this occasion I do not perceive that because the white man is to have the superior position the negro should be denied everything. I do not understand that because I do not want a negro woman for a slave I must necessarily want her for a wife. My understanding is that I can just let her alone. I am now in my fiftieth year, and I certainly never have had a black woman for either a slave or a wife. So it seems to me quite possible for us to get along without making either slaves or wives of negroes. I will add to this that I have never seen, to my knowledge, a man, woman, or child who was in favor of producing a perfect equality, social and political, between negroes and white men. I recollect of but one distinguished instance that I ever heard of so frequently as to be entirely satisfied of its correctness, and that is the case of Judge Douglas's old friend Colonel Richard M. Johnson. I will also add to the remarks I have made (for I am not going to enter at large upon this subject), that I have never had the least apprehension that I or my friends would marry negroes if there was no law to keep them from it; but as Judge Douglas and his friends seem to be in great apprehension that they might, if there were no law to keep them from it, I give him the most solemn pledge that I will to the very last stand by the law of this State which forbids the marrying of white people with negroes. I will add one further word, which is this: that I do not understand that there is any place where an alteration of the social and political relations of the negro and the white man can be made, except in the State Legislature,—not in the Congress of the United States; and as I do not really apprehend the approach of any such thing myself, and as Judge Douglas seems to be in constant horror that some such danger is rapidly approaching, I propose as the best means to prevent it that the Judge be kept at home, and placed in the State Legislature to fight the measure. I do not propose dwelling longer at this time on this subject. . . .

Lincoln at Alton, Illinois, October 15, 1858*

. . . .

I have stated upon former occasions, and I may as well state again, what I understand to be the real issue in this controversy between Judge Douglas and myself. On the point of my wanting to make war between the free and the slave States, there has been no issue between us. So, too, when he assumes that I am in favor of introducing a perfect social and political equality between the white and black races. These are false issues, upon which Judge Douglas has tried to force the controversy. There is no foundation in truth for the charge that I maintain either of these propositions. The real issue in this controversy—the one pressing upon every mind—is the sentiment on the part of one class that looks upon the institution of slavery *as a wrong*, and of another class that *does not* look upon it as a wrong. The sentiment that contemplates the institution of slavery in this country as a wrong is the sentiment of the Republican party. It is the sentiment around which all their actions, all their arguments, circle, from which all their propositions radiate. They look upon it as being a moral, social, and political wrong; and while they contemplate it as such, they nevertheless have due regard for its actual existence among us, and the difficulties of getting rid of it in any satisfactory way, and to all the constitutional obligations thrown about it. Yet, having a due regard for these, they desire a policy in regard to it that looks to its not creating any more danger. They insist that it should, as far as may be, *be treated* as a wrong; and one of the methods of treating it as a wrong is to *make provision that it shall grow no larger*. They also desire a policy that looks to a peaceful end of slavery at some time, as being wrong. These are the views they entertain in regard to it as I understand them; and all their sentiments, all their arguments and propositions, are brought within this range. I have said, and I repeat it here, that if there be a man

---

* *Ibid.*, pp. 258–69.

amongst us who does not think that the institution of slavery is wrong in any one of the aspects of which I have spoken, he is misplaced, and ought not to be with us. And if there be a man amongst us who is so impatient of it as a wrong as to disregard its actual presence among us and the difficulty of getting rid of it suddenly in a satisfactory way, and to disregard the constitutional obligations thrown about it, that man is misplaced if he is on our platform. We disclaim sympathy with him in practical action. He is not placed properly with us. . . .

INCIDENT AT HARPERS FERRY (1859)

Most fiery and fanatical of all the abolitionists, John Brown believed himself God's chosen instrument to end slavery and to struggle against pro-slavery forces.

Having obtained funds from New England and New York abolitionists to establish a stronghold in western Virginia to assist fugitive slaves, Brown armed himself and his followers for an attack on the United States arsenal at Harpers Ferry. The arsenal was seized on October 16, 1859, and then recaptured two days later by U.S. Marines under the command of the then Colonel Robert E. Lee. Brown was indicted and found guilty of "treason, conspiracy and advising with slaves and others to rebel, and murder in the first degree." He rejected his counsel's plea of insanity and was sentenced to hang.

John Brown's impassioned speech at the trial expressed the moral urgency of the slavery issue and helped inspire antislavery forces.

DOCUMENT 36

*The trial of John Brown—his last speech**

John Brown:

I have, may it please the Court, a few words to say. In the first place, I deny everything but what I have all

---

* 6 Am. State Trials 700,800 (1859).

along admitted, of a design on my part to free slaves. I intended certainly to have made a clean thing of that matter, as I did last winter when I went into Missouri, and there took slaves without the snapping of a gun on either side, moving them through the country, and finally leaving them in Canada. I designed to have done the same thing again on a larger scale. That was all I intended to do. I never did intend murder or treason, or the destruction of property, or to excite or incite the slaves to rebellion, or to make insurrection. I have another objection, and that is that it is unjust that I should suffer such a penalty. Had I interfered in the manner, which I admit, and which I admit has been fairly proved—for I admire the truthfulness and candor of the greater portion of the witnesses who have testified in this case—had I so interfered in behalf of any of the rich, the powerful, the intelligent, the so-called great, or in behalf of any of their friends, either father, mother, brother, sister, wife, or children, or any of that class, and suffered and sacrificed what I have in this interference, it would have been all right, and every man in this court would have deemed it an act worthy of reward rather than punishment. This Court acknowledges, too, as I suppose, the validity of the law of God. I see a book kissed, which I suppose to be the Bible, or at least the New Testament, which teaches me that all things whatsoever I would that men should do to me, I should do even so to them. It teaches me further to remember them that are in bonds, as bound with them. I endeavored to act up to that instruction. I say I am yet too young to understand that God is any respecter of persons. I believe that to have interfered as I have done, as I have always freely admitted I have done in behalf of His despised poor, is no wrong, but right. Now, if it is deemed necessary that I should forfeit my life for the furtherance of the ends of justice, and mingle my blood further with the blood of my children and with the blood of millions in this slave country whose rights are disregarded by wicked, cruel, and unjust enactments, I say let it be done.

Let me say one word further. I feel entirely satisfied with the treatment I have received on my trial. Considering all the circumstances, it has been more generous than I expected. But I feel no consciousness of guilt. I have stated from the first what was my intention, and what was not. I never had any design against the liberty of any person, nor any disposition to commit treason or excite slaves to rebel or make any general insurrection. I never encouraged any man to do so, but always discouraged any idea of that kind. Let me say also in regard to the statements made by some of those who were connected with me, I fear it has been stated by some of them that I have induced them to join me; but the contrary is true. I do not say this to injure them, but as regretting their weakness. Not one but joined of his own accord, and the greater part at their own expense. A number of them I never saw, and never had a word of conversation with till the day they came to me, and that was for the purpose I have stated. Now, I am done.

THE MISSISSIPPI LEGISLATURE ON THE RIGHT OF SECESSION (1860)

While temperate southerners as well as northern abolitionists realized that the President-elect had no intention of interfering with slavery where it had existed legally, fire-eaters throughout the South declared that they would never tolerate the incumbency of a "Black Republican." Seizing upon Lincoln's election as a justification for direct and deliberate action, the Mississippi Legislature in November, 1860, proclaimed its endorsement of secession. The resolution cited a mixture of causes, including the violation of the compact among the several states, interference with the internal affairs of the southern states, obstruction of the Fugitive Slave Law, abolitionist propaganda, and the intent of the North, or so the legislators averred, to gain control of the national government and outlaw slavery in the states.

DOCUMENT 37

Resolution of the Mississippi Legislature, November 30, 1860[*]

Whereas, The Constitutional Union was formed by the several States in their separate sovereign capacity for the purpose of mutual advantage and protection;

That the several States are distinct sovereignties, whose supremacy is limited so far only as the same has been delegated by voluntary compact to a Federal Government, and when it fails to accomplish the ends for which it was established, the parties to the compact have the right to resume, each State for itself, such delegated powers;

That the institution of slavery existed prior to the formation of the Federal Constitution, and is recognized by its letter, and all efforts to impair its value or lessen its duration by Congress, or any of the free States, is a violation of the compact of Union and is destructive of the ends for which it was ordained, but in defiance of the principles of the Union thus established, the people of the Northern States have assumed a revolutionary position towards the Southern States;

That they have set at defiance that provision of the Constitution which was intended to secure domestic tranquillity among the States and promote their general welfare, namely: "No person held to service or labor in one State, under the laws thereof, escaping into another, shall, in consequence of any law or regulation therein, be discharged from such service or labor, but shall be delivered up on claim of the party to whom such service or labor may be due";

That they have by voluntary associations, individual agencies and State legislation interfered with slavery as it prevails in the slave-holding States;

That they have enticed our slaves from us, and by State intervention obstructed and prevented their rendition under the fugitive slave law;

---

[*] *Laws of Mississippi, 1860,* pp. 43–45.

That they continue their system of agitation obviously for the purpose of encouraging other slaves to escape from service, to weaken the institution in the slave-holding States by rendering the holding of such property insecure, and as a consequence its ultimate abolition certain;

That they claim the right and demand its execution by Congress to exclude slavery from the Territories, but claim the right of protection for every species of property owned by themselves; . . .

That they thus seek by an increase of abolition States "to acquire two-thirds of both houses" for the purpose of preparing an amendment to the Constitution of the United States, abolishing slavery in the States, and so continue the agitation that the proposed amendment shall be ratified by the Legislatures of three-fourths of the States;

That they have in violation of the comity of all civilized nations, and in violation of the comity established by the Constitution of the United States, insulted and outraged our citizens when travelling among them for pleasure, health or business, by taking their servants and liberating the same, under the forms of State laws, and subjecting their owners to degrading and ignominious punishment;

That to encourage the stealing of our property they have put at defiance that provision of the Constitution which declares that fugitives from justice (escaping) into another State, on demand of the Executive authority of that State from which he fled, shall be delivered up;

That they have sought to create domestic discord in the Southern States by incendiary publications;

That they encouraged a hostile invasion of a Southern State to excite insurrection, murder and rapine;

That they have deprived Southern citizens of their property and continue an unfriendly agitation of their domestic institutions, claiming for themselves perfect immunity from external interference with their domestic policy; . . .

That they have elected a majority of Electors for President and Vice-President on the ground that there exists an irreconcilable conflict between the two sections of the Confederacy in reference to their respective systems of labor and in pursuance of their hostility to us and our institutions, thus declaring to the civilized world that the powers of this Government are to be used for the dishonor and overthrow of the Southern Section of this great Confederacy. Therefore,

Be it resolved by the Legislature of the State of Mississippi, That in the opinion of those who now constitute the said Legislature, the secession of each aggrieved State is the proper remedy for these injuries.

IV

Civil War and Reconstruction

1861–1883

While the Civil War was nominally fought to preserve the Union and free the Negro, the victors pursued the former objective only. Although released from bondage, the Negro eventually paid the price of national unification. By the mid-1880's, he became a pawn of the white majority—North and South. It was they who decided that it was better to reconcile the sections to each other rather than to pursue full equality for Negro Americans.

At first, prospects of Union military victory implied not only the end of slavery, but also suggested that the nation might take the opportunity to incorporate its Negro citizens fully into the civic and political life of the country. Action by Congress during and immediately after the war, and certain measures taken by President Lincoln, seemed to confirm that notion. However, it was soon apparent that federal government actions from 1861 to 1875 were grounded on a number of motives, only one of which was the goal of Negro equality and racial justice. The young Republican party of 1860, nominally dedicated to the limitation of slavery if not necessarily to its abolition, became by the mid-1870's the spokesman for industrial growth and financial interests rather than the protector of the freedmen. And, the Congressional coalition which had passed such far-reaching measures as the Freedmen's Bureau Act, the Thirteenth, Fourteenth, and Fifteenth Amendments, and the major Civil Rights Acts from 1866 to 1875, had, by the latter year, become primarily concerned with political and economic advances.

By the mid-1880's, the Supreme Court had rendered a series of decisions which overturned the bright promises of Reconstruction legislation and confirmed the indifference of white America to the future of the Negro. If the tragedy of the Revolutionary era and the National period had been the nation's ambivalence in striking a firm position on interracial justice, the real calamity of the Civil War and the Reconstruction period rested on the nation's decision to turn its back on the plight of the freedmen.

CONFEDERATE STATES OF AMERICA— CONSTITUTION (1861)

Virtually copied from the Constitution of the United States, the 1861 Confederate Constitution was less guarded in its references to Negroes and considerably more specific in its provisions concerning property in slaves. The Confederate Constitution was careful to protect slave property in whatever territories the Confederacy might acquire, and the three-fifths rule for taxation and representation was incorporated into the new document.

In an attempt to attract the upper South and the Border States to its cause, the Confederacy excluded the slaveholding states and territories of the United States from its constitutional prohibition against importing Negroes from abroad.

For purposes of comparison, parallel sections dealing with Negroes and slavery which appear in the two constitutions are given here.

DOCUMENT(S) 38

The Constitution of the United States, 1788*

ARTICLE I

SEC. 2. . . . Clause 3. Representatives and direct taxes shall be apportioned among the several States which may be included within this Union, according to their respective numbers, which shall be determined by adding to the whole number of free persons, including those bound to service for a term of years, and excluding Indians not taxed, three fifths of all other persons. The actual enumeration shall be made within three years after the first meeting of the Congress of the United States, and within every subsequent term of ten years, in such manner as they shall by law direct. The number of Representatives shall not exceed one for every thirty thousand, but each State shall have at least one Representative; and until such enumeration shall be made, the State of *New Hampshire* shall be entitled to choose three, *Massachusetts* eight, *Rhode Island and Providence Plantations* one, *Connecticut* five, *New York* six, *New Jersey* four, *Pennsylvania* eight, *Delaware* one, *Maryland* six, *Virginia* ten, *North Carolina* five, *South Carolina* five, and *Georgia* three.

ARTICLE I

SEC. 9. Clause 1. The migration or importation of such persons as any of the States now existing shall think proper to admit shall not be prohibited by the Congress prior to the year one thousand eight hundred and eight, but a tax or duty may be imposed on such importation, not exceeding ten dollars for each person. . . .

---

* Small, Jayson, and Corwin, eds., *The Constitution of the United States of America* (Washington, D.C.: U.S. Government Printing Office, 1964), pp. 120–21, 362, 775, 786, 791–92.

The Constitution of the Confederate States of America, 1861*

ARTICLE I

SEC. 2. . . . (3) Representatives and direct taxes shall be apportioned among the several States which may be included within this Confederacy according to their respective numbers, which shall be determined by adding to the whole number of free persons, including those bound to service for a term of years, and excluding Indians not taxed, three-fifths of all slaves. The actual enumeration shall be made within three years after the first meeting of the Congress of the Confederate States, and within every subsequent term of ten years, in such manner as they shall by law direct, The number of Representatives shall not exceed one for every fifty thousand, but each State shall have at least one Representative; and until such enumeration shall be made, the State of South Carolina shall be entitled to choose six; the State of Georgia ten; the State of Alabama nine; the State of Florida two; the State of Mississippi seven; the State of Louisiana six; and the State of Texas six. . . .

ARTICLE I

SEC. 9. (1) The importation of negroes of the African race, from any foreign country, other than the slaveholding States or Territories of the United States of America, is hereby forbidden; and Congress is required to pass such laws as shall effectually prevent the same.

(2) Congress shall also have power to prohibit the introduction of slaves from any State not a member of, or Territory not belonging to, this Confederacy. . . .

(4) No bill of attainder, or *ex post facto* law, or law denying or impairing the right of property in negro slaves shall be passed. . . .

---

* Frank Moore, ed., *The Rebellion Record*, Vol. II (New York: G. P. Putnam, 1862), pp. 321–27.

The Constitution of the United States

ARTICLE IV

SEC. 2. (1) The citizens of each State shall be entitled to all privileges and immunities of citizens in the several States.

• • • •

(3) No person held to service or labor in one State, under the laws thereof, escaping into another, shall, in consequence of any law or regulation therein, be discharged from such service or labor, but shall be delivered up on claim of the party to whom such service or labor may be due.

ARTICLE IV

SEC. 3. . . . (2) The Congress shall have power to dispose of and make all needful rules and regulations respecting the territory or other property belonging to the United States; and nothing in this Constitution shall be so construed as to prejudice any claims of the United States or of any particular State.

The Constitution of the Confederate States

ARTICLE IV

SEC. 2 (1) The citizens of each State shall be entitled to all the privileges and immunities of citizens of the several States, and shall have the right of transit and sojourn in any State of this Confederacy, with their slaves and other property; and the right of property in said slaves shall not be thereby impaired.

(3) No slave or other person held to service or labor in any State or Territory of the Confederate States, under the laws thereof, escaping or unlawfully carried into another, shall, in consequence of any law or regulation therein, be discharged from such service or labor; but shall be delivered up on claim of the party to whom such slave belongs, or to whom such service or labor may be due.

ARTICLE IV

SEC. 3. (2) The Congress shall have power to dispose of and make all needful rules and regulations concerning the property of the Confederate States, including the lands thereof.

(3) The Confederate States may acquire new territory; and Congress shall have power to legislate and provide governments for the inhabitants of all territory belonging to the Confederate States lying without the limits of the several States, and may permit them, at such times and in such manner as it may by law provide, to form States to be admitted into the Confederacy. In all such territory the institution of negro slavery, as it now exists in the Confederate States, shall be recognized and protected by Congress and by the territorial government; and the inhabitants of the several Confederate States and Territories shall have the right to take to such territory any slaves lawfully held by them in any of the States or Territories of the Confederate States.

FEDERAL CONFISCATION ACTS (1861, 1862)

Seizing the property of rebels is not an unusual step for an established government dealing with insurrection, but the situation facing federal authorities in the 1860's was unique in one vital sense: the "property" of the rebellious persons included human beings in perpetual bondage. The situation was compounded by the continued existence of slavery throughout the Border States that remained loyal to the Union. Accordingly, Congress and President Lincoln had to devise legislation that would legalize the expropriation and freeing of slaves held by those aiding the Confederacy, while not interfering with the same type of "property" within the Border States. With the distinctive criterion—support of the Union cause—fugitive slave laws were honored for slave-owners residing in states committed to the Union. In addition, the Act of 1862 made provision for settling newly freed slaves in "some tropical country beyond the limits of the United States."

DOCUMENT(S) 39

An act to confiscate property used for insurrectionary purposes*

Be it enacted by the Senate and House of Representatives of the United States of America in Congress assembled, That if, during the present or any future insurrection against the Government of the United States, after the President of the United States shall have declared, by proclamation, that the laws of the United States are opposed and the execution thereof obstructed by combinations too powerful to be suppressed by the ordinary course of judicial proceedings, or by the power vested in the marshals by law, any person or persons, his, her, or their agent, attorney, or employee, shall purchase or acquire, sell or give, any property of whatsoever kind or description, with intent to use or employ the same, or

---

* 12 Stat. 319 (1861).

suffer the same to be used or employed, in aiding, abetting, or promoting such insurrection or resistance to the laws, or any person or persons engaged therein; or if any person or persons, being the owner or owners of any such property, shall knowingly use or employ, or consent to the use or employment of the same as aforesaid, all such property is hereby declared to be lawful subject of prize and capture wherever found; and it shall be the duty of the President of the United States to cause the same to be seized, confiscated, and condemned.

SEC. 2. And be it further enacted, That such prizes and capture shall be condemned in the district or circuit court of the United States having jurisdiction of the amount, or in admiralty in any district in which the same may be seized, or into which they be taken and proceedings first instituted.

SEC. 3. And be it further enacted, That the Attorney-General, or any district attorney of the United States in which said property may at the time be, may institute the proceedings of condemnation, and in such case they shall be wholly for the benefit of the United States; or any person may file an information with such attorney, in which case the proceedings shall be for the use of such informer and the United States in equal parts.

SEC. 4. And be it further enacted, That whenever hereafter, during the present insurrection against the Government of the United States, any person claimed to be held to labor or service under the law of any State shall be required or permitted by the person to whom such labor or service is claimed to be due, or by the lawful agent of such person, to take up arms against the United States, or shall be required or permitted by the person to whom such labor or service is claimed to be due, or his lawful agent, to work or to be employed in or upon any fort, navy-yard, dock, armory, ship, intrenchment, or in any military or naval service whatsoever, against the Government and lawful authority of the United States, then and in every such case the person to whom such labor or service is claimed to be due shall forfeit his claim to such labor, any law of the State or of the United States to the contrary notwithstanding. And whenever thereafter the person claiming such labor or service shall seek to enforce his claim, it shall be a full and sufficient answer to such claim that the person whose service or labor is claimed had been employed in hostile service against the Government of the United States, contrary to the provisions of this act.

APPROVED, August 6, 1861.

An act to suppress insurrection, to punish treason and rebellion, to seize and confiscate the property of rebels, and for other purposes[*]

Be it enacted by the Senate and House of Representatives of the United States of America in Congress assembled, That every person who shall hereafter commit the crime of treason against the United States, and shall be adjudged guilty thereof, shall suffer death, and all his slaves, if any, shall be declared and made free; or, at the discretion of the court, he shall be imprisoned for not less than five years and fined not less than ten thousand dollars, and all his slaves, if any, shall be declared and made free; said fine shall be levied and collected on any or all of the property, real and personal, excluding slaves, of which the said person so convicted was the owner at the time of committing the said crime, any sale or conveyance to the contrary nothwithstanding.

SEC. 2. *And be it further enacted,* That if any person shall hereafter incite, set on foot, assist, or engage in any rebellion or insurrection against the authority of the United States, or the laws thereof, or shall give aid or comfort thereto, or shall engage in, or give aid and comfort to, any such existing rebellion or insurrection, and be convicted thereof, such person shall be punished by imprisonment for a period not exceeding ten years, or by a fine not exceeding ten thousand dollars, and by the liberation of all his slaves, if any he have; or by both of said punishments, at the discretion of the court.

SEC. 3. *And be it further enacted,* That every person guilty of either of the offences described in this act shall be forever incapable and disqualified to hold any office under the United States.

SEC. 4. *And be it further enacted,* That this act shall not be construed in any way to affect or alter the prosecution,

[*] 12 Stat. 589 (1862).

conviction, or punishment of any person or persons guilty of treason against the United States before the passage of this act, unless such person is convicted under this act.

SEC. 5. *And be it further enacted,* That, to insure the speedy termination of the present rebellion, it shall be the duty of the President of the United States to cause the seizure of all the estate and property, money, stocks, credits, and effects of the persons hereinafter named in this section, and to apply and use the same and the proceeds thereof for the support of the army of the United States, that is to say:

First. Of any person hereafter acting as an officer of the army or navy of the rebels in arms against the government of the United States.

Secondly. Of any person hereafter acting as President, Vice-President, member of Congress, judge of any court, cabinet officer, foreign minister, commissioner or consul of the so-called confederate states of America.

Thirdly. Of any person acting as governor of a state, member of a convention or legislature, or judge of any court of any of the so-called confederate states of America.

Fourthly. Of any person who, having held an office of honor, trust, or profit in the United States, shall hereafter hold an office in the so-called confederate states of America.

Fifthly. Of any person hereafter holding any office or agency under the government of the so-called confederate states of America, or under any of the several states of the said confederacy, or the laws thereof, whether such office or agency be national, state, or municipal in its name or character: *Provided,* That the persons, thirdly, fourthly and fifthly above described shall have accepted their appointment or election since the date of the pretended ordinance of cecession of the state, or shall have taken an oath of allegiance to, or to support the constitution of the so-called confederate states.

Sixthly. Of any person who, owning property in any loyal State or Territory of the United States, or in the District of Columbia, shall hereafter assist and give aid and comfort to such rebellion; and all sales, transfers, or conveyances of any such property shall be null and void; and it shall be a sufficient bar to any suit brought by such person for the possession or the use of such property, or any of it, to allege and prove that he is one of the persons described in this section.

SEC. 6. *And be it further enacted,* That if any person within any State or Territory of the United States, other than those named as aforesaid, after the passage of this act, being engaged in armed rebellion against the government of the United States, or aiding or abetting such rebellion, shall not, within sixty days after public warning and proclamation duly given and made by the President of the United States, cease to aid, countenance, and abet such rebellion, and return to his allegiance to the United States, all the estate and property, moneys, stocks, and credits of such person shall be liable to seizure as aforesaid, and it shall be the duty of the President to seize and use them as aforesaid or the proceeds thereof. And all sales, transfers, or conveyances, of any such property after the expiration of the said sixty days from the date of such warning and proclamation shall be null and void; and it shall be a sufficient bar to any suit brought by such person for the possession or the use of such property, or any of it, to allege and prove that he is one of the persons described in this section.

· · · ·

SEC. 9. *And be it further enacted,* That all slaves of persons who shall hereafter be engaged in rebellion against the government of the United States, or who shall in any way give aid or comfort thereto, escaping from such persons and taking refuge within the lines of the army; and all slaves captured from such persons or deserted by them and coming under the control of the government of the United States; and all slaves of such persons found *on* [or] being within any place occupied by rebel forces and afterwards occupied by the forces of the United States, shall be deemed captives of war, and shall be forever free of their servitude, and not again held as slaves.

SEC. 10. *And be it further enacted,* That no slave escaping into any State, Territory, or the District of Columbia, from any other State, shall be delivered up, or in any way impeded or hindered of his liberty, except for crime, or some offence against the laws, unless the person claiming said fugitive shall first make oath that the person to whom the labor or service of such fugitive is alleged to be due is his lawful owner, and has not borne arms against the United States in the present rebellion, nor in any way given aid and comfort thereto; and no person engaged in the military or naval service of the United States shall, under any pretence whatever, assume to decide on the validity of the claim of any person to the service or labor of any other person, or surrender up any such person to the claimant, on pain of being dismissed from the service.

SEC. 11. *And be it further enacted,* That the President of the United States is authorized to employ as many persons of African descent as he may deem necessary and proper for the suppression of this rebellion, and for this purpose he may organize and use them in such manner as he may judge best for the public welfare.

SEC. 12. *And be it further enacted,* That the President of the United States is hereby authorized to make provision for the transportation, colonization, and settlement, in some tropical country beyond the limits of the United States, of such persons of the African race, made free by the provisions of this act, as may be willing to emigrate, having first obtained the consent of the government of said country to their protection and settlement within the same, with all the rights and privileges of freemen. . . .

APPROVED, July 17, 1862.

LINCOLN'S WARTIME OBJECTIVE (1862)

Lincoln, a practical politician as well as a dedicated nationalist, did not want to do anything drastic to alter the status of slavery in the Border States. He feared that such action would precipitate anti-Union feeling in those areas and feed the rebellion. Abolitionists chafed at what they considered Presidential indecision and acquiescence in the perpetuation of an immoral institution. They became increasingly incensed as Union forces penetrated portions of the Confederacy—in Virginia, Tennessee, and Louisiana—and seemed thereby to offer the President an excellent opportunity to end slavery in areas under federal control. In mid-August, 1862, Horace Greeley came forward as the spokesman for this dissatisfaction.

Greeley's *Tribune,* published daily in New York City and widely circulated in a weekly edition throughout the North and West, was the leading Republican paper of its day; and its salty editor was never averse to thrusting himself into the vanguard of a controversial position. Slavery nurtured treason and must therefore be struck down, he declared. Lincoln's immediate reply did little to pacify the critics, but it did serve to clarify and redefine his public aims and to elicit broad northern support. Meanwhile, the President had privately apprised his Cabinet of his intention to issue a proclamation on slavery in those areas controlled by the Confederacy (Document 41).

DOCUMENT(S) 40

*Horace Greeley's editorial: "To Abraham Lincoln, President of the United States"**

Dear Sir: I do not intrude to tell you—for you must know already—that a great proportion of those who triumphed in your election, and of all who desire the unqualified suppression of the rebellion now desolating our country, are sorely disappointed and deeply pained by the policy you seem to be pursuing with regard to the slaves of rebels. I write only to set succinctly and unmistakably before you what we require, what we think we have a right to expect, and of what we complain.

I. We require of you, as the first servant of the Republic charged especially and preeminently with this duty, that you EXECUTE THE LAWS. . . .

II. We think you are strangely and disastrously remiss in the discharge of your official and imperative duty with regard to the emancipating provisions of the new Confiscation Act. Those provisions were designed to fight Slavery with Liberty. They prescribe that men loyal to the Union, and willing to shed their blood in her behalf, shall no longer be held, with the nation's consent, in bondage to persistent, malignant traitors, who for twenty years have been plotting and for sixteen months have been fighting to divide and destroy our

* *The New York Tribune,* August 20, 1862, p. 4.

country. Why these traitors should be treated with tenderness by you, to the prejudice of the dearest rights of loyal men, we cannot conceive.

III. We think you are unduly influenced by the councils, the representations, the menaces, of certain fossil politicians hailing from the Border Slave States. . . .

IV. We think timid counsels in such a crisis calculated to prove perilous, and probably disastrous. It is the duty of a Government so wantonly, wickedly assailed by rebellion as ours has been, to oppose force to force in a defiant, dauntless spirit. It cannot afford to temporize with traitors, nor with semi-traitors. It must not bribe them to behave themselves, nor make them fair promises in the hope of disarming their causeless hostility. Representing a brave and high-spirited people, it can afford to forfeit any thing else better than its own self-respect, or their admiring confidence. For our Government even to seek, after war has been made on it, to dispel the affected apprehensions of armed traitors that their cherished privileges may be assailed by it, is to invite insult and encourage hopes of its own downfall. The rush to arms of Ohio, Indiana, Illinois is the true answer at once to the rebel raids of John Morgan and the traitorous sophistries of Beriah Magoffin.

V. We complain that the Union cause has suffered, and is now suffering immensely, from mistaken deference to rebel Slavery. Had you, sir, in your Inaugural Address, unmistakably given notice that, in case the rebellion already commenced, were persisted in, and your efforts to preserve the Union and enforce the laws should be resisted by armed force, *you would recognize no loyal person as rightfully held in Slavery by a traitor*, we believe the rebellion would therein have received a staggering if not fatal blow. . . .

VI. We complain that the Confiscation Act which you approved is habitually disregarded by your Generals, and that no word of rebuke for them from you has yet reached the public ear. Frémont's Proclamation and Hunter's Order favoring Emancipation were promptly annulled by you; while Halleck's Number Three, forbidding fugitives from slavery to rebels to come within his lines—an order as unmilitary as inhuman, and which received the hearty approbation of every traitor in America—with scores of like tendency, have never provoked even your remonstrance. . . .

And finally, we complain that you, Mr. President, elected as a Republican, knowing well what an abomination Slavery is, and how emphatically it is the core and essence of this atrocious rebellion, seem never to interfere with these atrocities, and never give a direction to your military subordinates, which does not appear to have been conceived in the interest of Slavery rather than of Freedom.

VIII. On the face of this wide earth, Mr. President, there is not one disinterested, determined, intelligent champion of the Union cause who does not feel that all attempts to put down the rebellion and at the same time uphold its inciting cause are preposterous and futile; that the rebellion, if crushed out to-morrow, would be renewed within a year if Slavery were left in full vigor; that army officers who remain to this day devoted to Slavery can at best be but half-way loyal to the Union; and that every hour of deference to Slavery is an hour of added and deepened peril to the Union. I appeal to the testimony of your ambassadors in Europe. It is freely at your service, not at mine. Ask them to tell you candidly whether the seeming subserviency of your policy to the slaveholding, slavery-upholding interest is not the perplexity, the despair of statesmen of all parties, and be admonished by the general answer!

IX. I close as I began with the statement that what an immense majority of the loyal millions of your countrymen require of you is a frank, declared, unqualified, ungrudging execution of the laws of the land, more especially of the Confiscation Act. That act gives freedom to the slaves of rebels coming within our lines, or whom those lines may at any time inclose—we ask you to render it due obedience by publicly requiring all your subordinates to recognize and obey it. The rebels are everywhere using the late anti-negro riots in the North, as they have long used your officers' treatment of negroes in the South to convince the slaves that they have nothing to hope from a Union success—that we mean in that case to sell them into a bitter bondage to defray the cost of the war. Let them impress this as a truth on the great mass of their ignorant and credulous bondmen, and the Union will never be restored—never. We cannot conquer ten millions of people united in solid phalanx against us powerfully aided by Northern sympathizers and European allies. We must have scouts, guides, spies, cooks, teamsters, diggers and choppers from the blacks of the South, whether we allow them to fight for us or not, or we shall be baffled and repelled. As one of the millions who would gladly have avoided this struggle at any sacrifice but that of principle and honor, but who now feel that the triumph of the Union is indispensable not only to the existence of our country but to the well-being of mankind, I entreat you to render a hearty and unequivocal obedience to the law of the land.

Yours,
HORACE GREELEY

Lincoln's Reply to Greeley, August 22, 1862 *

Hon. Horace Greeley

Dear Sir:

I have just read yours of the nineteenth instant, addressed to myself through the *New York Tribune.*

If there be in it any statements or assumptions of facts which I may know to be erroneous, I do not now and here controvert them.

If there be any inferences which I may believe to be falsely drawn, I do not now and here argue against them.

If there be perceptible in it an impatient and dictatorial tone, I waive it in deference to an old friend whose heart I have always supposed to be right.

As to the policy I "seem to be pursuing," as you say, I have not meant to leave any one in doubt. I would save the Union. I would save it in the shortest way under the Constitution.

The sooner the national authority can be restored, the nearer the Union will be—the Union as it was.

If there be those who would not save the Union unless they could at the same time save slavery, I do not agree with them.

If there be those who would not save the Union unless

* Arthur Brooks Lapsley, ed., *The Writings of Abraham Lincoln,* Vol. VIII (New York: Lamb Publishing Company, 1888), pp. 305–07.

they could at the same time destroy slavery, I do not agree with them.

My paramount object is to save the Union, and not either to save or destroy slavery.

If I could save the Union without freeing any slave, I would do it: if I could save it by freeing all the slaves, I would do it; and if I could do it by freeing some and leaving others alone, I would also do that.

What I do about slavery and the colored race, I do because I believe it helps to save this Union; and what I forbear, I forbear because I do not believe it would help to save the Union.

I shall do less whenever I shall believe what I am doing hurts the cause, and I shall do more whenever I believe doing more will help the cause.

I shall try to correct errors when shown to be errors, and I shall adopt new views so fast as they shall appear to be true views.

I have here stated my purpose according to my views of official duty, and I intend no modification of my oft-expressed personal wish that all men everywhere could be free.

Yours,
A. LINCOLN

EMANCIPATION PROCLAMATION—A WARTIME MEASURE (1862, 1863)

Lincoln's Emancipation Proclamation was a response to northern radical pressures that the end of slavery be designated the main objective of the Civil War. At the same time, the Proclamation served as a practical wartime measure designed to improve diplomatic negotiations with European governments who were scrutinizing the Union naval blockade of southern ports and reviewing the sensitive question of diplomatic recognition for the Confederacy.

In late September, 1862, Lincoln took advantage of General George McClellan's Union victory at Antietam to issue his preliminary proclamation on emancipation. Like the more famous companion document of January 1, 1863, this preliminary proclamation pertained only to those slaves resident in areas under Confederate control; its implementation, therefore, depended upon the force of Union troops in the field. By his action, Lincoln complemented earlier Congressional measures ending slavery in the District of Columbia (12 Stat. 376) (April, 1862), and in the national territories (12 Stat. 432) (June, 1862). The President was placing slavery on "the course of ultimate extinction"—as he had once urged in his Illinois Senatorial campaign of 1858—and providing a means to enable former slaves to enter with dignity into the Union cause.

DOCUMENT(S) 41

Lincoln's preliminary Emancipation Proclamation (September 22, 1862)[*]

A Proclamation, 22 September 1862

I, Abraham Lincoln, President of the United States of America, and commander-in-chief of the army and navy thereof, do hereby proclaim and declare that hereafter, as heretofore, the war will be prosecuted for the object of practically restoring the constitutional relation between the United States and each of the States, and the people thereof, in which States that relation is or may be suspended or disturbed.

That it is my purpose, upon the next meeting of Congress, to again recommend the adoption of a practical measure tendering pecuniary aid to the free acceptance or rejection of all slave States, so called, the people whereof may not then be in rebellion against the United States, and which States may then have voluntarily adopted, or thereafter may voluntarily adopt, immediate or gradual abolishment of slavery within their respective limits; and that the effort to colonize persons of African descent with their consent upon this continent or elsewhere, with the previously obtained consent of the governments existing there, will be continued.

That on the first day of January, in the year of our Lord

---

[*] James D. Richardson, *Messages and Papers of the Presidents,* Vol. VI (Bureau of National Literature and Art, 1904), pp. 96–98.

one thousand eight hundred and sixty-three, all persons held as slaves within any State or designated part of a State the people whereof shall then be in rebellion against the United States, shall be then, thenceforward, and forever free; and the Executive Government of the United States, including the military and naval authority thereof, will recognize and maintain the freedom of such persons, and will do no act or acts to repress such persons, or any of them, in any efforts they may make for their actual freedom.

That the Executive will, on the first day of January aforesaid, by proclamation designate the States and parts of States, if any, in which the people thereof, respectively, shall then be in rebellion against the United States; and the fact that any State, or the people thereof, shall on that day be in good faith represented in the Congress of the United States by members chosen thereto at elections wherein a majority of the qualified voters of such State shall have participated, shall, in the absence of strong countervailing testimony, be deemed conclusive evidence that such State, and the people thereof, are not then in rebellion against the United States.

That attention is hereby called to an Act of Congress entitled "An Act to make an additional article of war," approved 13 March 1862, and which Act is in the words and figures following:

Be it enacted by the Senate and House of Representatives of the United States of America in Congress assembled, That hereafter the following shall be promulgated as an additional article of war, for the government of the army of the United States, and shall be obeyed and observed as such:

ARTICLE .—All officers or persons in the military or naval service of the United States are prohibited from employing any of the forces under their respective commands for the purpose of returning fugitives from service or labor who may have escaped from any person to whom such service or labor is claimed to be due; and any officer who shall be found guilty by a court martial of violating this article shall be dismissed from the service.

SEC. 2. And be it further enacted, That this Act shall take effect from and after its passage.

Also to the ninth and tenth sections of an Act entitled "An Act to suppress insurrection, to punish treason and rebellion, to seize and confiscate property of rebels, and for other purposes," approved 17 July 1862, and which sections are in the words and figures following:

SEC. 9. And be it further enacted, That all slaves of persons who shall hereafter be engaged in rebellion against the Government of the United States, or who shall in any way give aid or comfort thereto, escaping from such persons and taking refuge within the lines of the army; and all slaves captured from such persons or deserted by them, and coming under the control of the Government of the United States; and all slaves of such persons found *on* [or] being within any place occupied by rebel forces and afterwards occupied by the forces of the United States, shall be deemed captives of war, and shall be forever free of their servitude, and not again held as slaves.

SEC. 10. And be it further enacted, That no slave escaping into any State, Territory, or the District of Columbia, from any other State, shall be delivered up, or in any way impeded or hindered of his liberty, except for crime, or some offense against the laws, unless the person claiming said fugitive shall first make oath that the person to whom the labor or service of such fugitive is alleged to be due is his lawful owner, and has not borne arms against the United States in the present rebellion, nor in any way given aid and comfort thereto; and no person engaged in the military or naval service of the United States shall, under any pretense whatever, assume to decide on the validity of the claim of any person to the service or labor of any other person, or surrender up any such person to the claimant, on pain of being dismissed from the service.

And I do hereby enjoin upon and order all persons engaged in the military and naval service of the United States to observe, obey, and enforce, within their respective spheres of service, the Act and sections above recited.

And the Executive will in due time recommend that all citizens of the United States who shall have remained loyal thereto throughout the rebellion shall (upon the restoration of the constitutional relation between the United States and their respective States and people, if that relation shall have been suspended or disturbed) be compensated for all losses by Acts of the United States, including the loss of slaves.

In witness whereof, I have hereunto set my hand and caused the seal of the United States to be affixed.

Done at the city of Washington, this twenty-second day of September, in the year of our Lord one thousand [L.S.] eight hundred and sixty-two, and of the independence of the United States the eighty-seventh.

ABRAHAM LINCOLN

The Emancipation Proclamation (January 1, 1863)*

Whereas, on the twenty-second day of September, in the year of our Lord one thousand eight hundred and sixty-two, a Proclamation was issued by the President of the United States, containing among other things the following, to wit:

"That on the First Day of January, in the Year of our Lord One Thousand Eight Hundred and Sixty-three, all persons held as Slaves within any State, or designated part of a State, the people whereof shall there be in rebellion against the United States, shall be then thenceforth and FOREVER FREE, and the Executive Government of the United States, including the Military and Naval authority thereof, will recognize and maintain the freedom of such persons, and will do no act or acts to repress such persons, or any of them, in any effort they may make for their actual freedom.

"That the Executive will, on the first day of January aforesaid, by Proclamation, designate the States and parts of States, if any, in which the people therein respectively shall then be in Rebellion against the United States, and the fact that any State, or the people thereof, shall on that day be in good faith represented in the Congress of the United States by Members chosen thereto at elections wherein a majority of the qualified voters of such State shall have participated, shall, in the absence of strong countervailing testimony, be deemed conclusive evidence that such State and the people thereof are not then in Rebellion against the United States."

Now, therefore, I, Abraham Lincoln, President of the United States, by virtue of the power vested in me as Commander-in-Chief of the Army and Navy of the United

---

* *The New York Tribune*, January 2, 1863, 4:5–6.

States, in time of actual armed rebellion against the authority and Government of the United States, and as a fit and necessary war measure for suppressing said Rebellion, do, on this first day of January, in the year of our Lord one thousand eight hundred and sixty-three, and in accordance with my purpose so to do, publicly proclaim for the full period of one hundred days from the date of the first above-mentioned order, and designate, as the States and parts of States wherein the people thereof, respectively, are this day in rebellion against the United States, the following, to wit: Arkansas, Texas, Louisiana—except the Parishes of St. Bernard, Palquemines, Jefferson, St. John, St. Charles, St. James, Ascension, Assumption, Terre Bonne, Lafourch, St. Mary, St. Martin and Orleans, including the City of New-Orleans—Mississippi, Alabama, Florida, Georgia, South Carolina, North Carolina, and Virginia—except the forty-eight counties designated as West Virginia, and also the counties of Berkley, Accomac, Northampton, Elizabeth City, York, Princess Ann, and Norfolk, including the cities of Norfolk and Portsmouth—and which excepted parts are, for the present, left precisely as if this Proclamation were not issued.

And by virtue of the power and for the purpose aforesaid, I do order and declare that ALL PERSONS HELD AS SLAVES within said designated States and parts of States ARE, AND HENCEFORWARD SHALL BE FREE; and that the Executive Government of the United States, including the Military and Naval Authorities thereof, will recognize and maintain the freedom of said persons.

And I hereby enjoin upon the people so declared to be free, to abstain from all violence, unless in necessary self-defense; and I recommend to them that in all cases, when allowed, they labor faithfully for reasonable wages.

And I further declare and make known, that such persons, of suitable condition, will be received into the armed service of the United States, to garrison forts, positions, stations, and other places, and to man vessels of all sorts in said service.

And, upon this, sincerely believed to be an act of justice, warranted by the Constitution, upon military necessity, I invoke the considerate judgment of mankind and the gracious favor of Almighty God. . . .

JEFFERSON DAVIS ON THE NEGRO
IN WARTIME (1863, 1864)

Addressing a joint session of the Confederate Congress
in Richmond, Virginia, on January 12, 1863, President
Jefferson Davis damned Lincoln's Emancipation Proclamation as a contemptible interference with the rights of Confederate citizens. Davis claimed that the worst and most
evil intentions of the Black Republican Administration were
now revealed, and the justification for southern rebellion was
fully confirmed. While Davis's remarks were flavored with
the expedient ritualisms of politics and diplomacy, they
revealed two themes incessantly on the southern mind: the
conviction of Negro inferiority and the fear of a Negro
uprising.

Few statements so clearly revealed the South's capacity
for self-deception on the topics of race and white dominance
as did Jefferson Davis's remarks to the Confederate Congress
in November of 1864.

The Confederate States of America had not achieved
diplomatic recognition by the major powers of Europe,
Sherman and his army had taken Atlanta and were in the
process of bisecting the lower South, Sheridan had devastated
the Shenandoah Valley, and Grant was pressing forward in
the East to seal the Confederacy's fate; Davis's government
would collapse within five months.

Although in dire peril on every hand, the South continued
to accede to the demands of states' rights and slavery. Slave-
owners had opposed taxation on and expropriation of slaves to
meet wartime crises, and the white southern mind could not
accept the logic of fully utilizing its slave manpower as a
mobile labor force or as a reservoir of military strength.
Davis declared it was premature and ill-advised to press
Negroes into uniform, but in the South's hour of need he was
discovering that the Negro could be seen as a "person" and
that military service by slaves might someday gain them
freedom.

DOCUMENT (S) 42

*Reaction to the Emancipation Proclamation**

. . . .

The public journals of the North have been received, containing a proclamation, dated on the 1st day of the present month, signed by the President of the United States, in which he orders and declares all slaves within ten of the States of the Confederacy to be free, except such as are found within certain districts now occupied in part by the armed forces of the enemy. We may well leave it to the instincts of that common humanity which a beneficent Creator has implanted in the breasts of our fellowmen of all countries to pass judgment on a measure by which several millions of human beings of an inferior race, peaceful and contented laborers in their sphere, are doomed to extermination, while at the same time they are encouraged to a general assassination of their masters by the insidious recommendation "to abstain from violence unless in necessary self-defense." Our own detestation of those who have attempted the most execrable measure recorded in the history of guilty man is tempered by profound contempt for the impotent rage which it discloses. So far as regards the action of this Government on such criminals as may attempt its execution, I confine myself to informing you that I shall, unless in your wisdom you deem some other course more expedient, deliver to the several State authorities all commissioned officers of the United States that may hereafter be captured by our forces in any of the States embraced in the proclamation, that they may be dealt with in accordance with the laws of those States providing for the punishment of criminals engaged in exciting servile insurrection. The enlisted soldiers I shall continue to treat as unwilling instruments in the commission of these crimes, and shall direct their discharge and return to their homes on the proper and usual parole.

In its political aspect this measure possesses great significance, and to it in this light I invite your attention. It affords

* James D. Richardson, *Messages and Papers of the Confederacy,* Vol. I (Nashville, Tenn.: U.S. Publishing Co., 1905), pp. 290–93.

to our whole people the complete and crowning proof of the true nature of the designs of the party which elevated to power the present occupant of the Presidential chair at Washington and which sought to conceal its purpose by every variety of artful device and by the perfidious use of the most solemn and repeated pledges on every possible occasion. I extract in this connection as a single example the following declaration, made by President Lincoln under the solemnity of his oath as Chief Magistrate of the United States, on the 4th of March, 1861:

Apprehension seems to exist among the people of the Southern States that by the accession of a Republican Administration their property and their peace and personal security are to be endangered. There has never been any reasonable cause for such apprehension. Indeed, the most ample evidence to the contrary has all the while existed and been open to their inspection. It is found in nearly all the published speeches of him who now addresses you. I do but quote from one of those speeches when I declare that I have no purpose, directly or indirectly, to interfere with the institution of slavery in the States where it exists. I believe I have no lawful right to do so; and I have no inclination to do so. Those who nominated and elected me did so with full knowledge that I had made this and many similar declarations and had never recanted them; and more than this, they placed in the platform for my acceptance and as a law to themselves and to me the clear and emphatic resolution which I now read:

"*Resolved*, That the maintenance inviolate of the rights of the States, and especially the right of each State to order and control its own domestic institutions according to its own judgment exclusively, is essential to that balance of power on which the perfection and endurance of our political fabric depend; and we denounce the lawless invasion by armed force of the soil of any State or Territory, no matter under what pretext, as among the gravest of crimes."

Nor was this declaration of the want of power or disposition to interfere with our social system confined to a state of peace. Both before and after the actual commencement of hostilities the President of the United States repeated in formal official communication to the Cabinets of Great Britain and France that he was utterly without constitutional power to do the act which he has just committed, and that in no possible event, whether the secession of these States resulted in the establishment of a separate Confederacy or in the restoration of the Union, was there any authority by virtue of which he could either restore a disaffected State to the Union by force of arms or make any change in any of its institutions. I refer especially for verification of this assertion to the dispatches addressed by the Secretary of State of the United States, under direction of the President, to the Ministers of the United States at London and Paris, under date of 10th and 22d of April, 1861.

The people of this Confederacy, then, cannot fail to receive this proclamation as the fullest vindication of their own sagacity in foreseeing the uses to which the dominant party in the United States intended from the beginning to apply their power, nor can they cease to remember with devout thankfulness that it is to their own vigilance in resisting the first stealthy progress of approaching despotism that they owe their escape from consequences now apparent to the most skeptical. This proclamation will have another salutary effect in calming the fears of those who have constantly evinced the apprehension that this war might end by some reconstruction of the old Union or some renewal of close political relations with the United States. These fears have never been shared by me, nor have I ever been able to perceive on what basis they could rest. But the proclamation affords the fullest guarantee of the impossibility of such a result; it has established a state of things which can lead to but one of three possible consequences—the extermination of the slaves, the exile of the whole white population from the Confederacy, or absolute and total separation of these States from the United States.

This proclamation is also an authentic statement by the Government of the United States of its inability to subjugate the South by force of arms, and as such must be accepted by neutral nations, which can no longer find any justification in withholding our just claims to formal recognition. It is also in effect an intimation to the people of the North that they must prepare to submit to a separation, now become inevitable, for that people are too acute not to understand a restoration of the Union has been rendered forever impossible by the adoption of a measure which from its very nature neither admits of retraction nor can coexist with union. . . .

On the use of Negroes in wartime*

The employment of slaves for service with the Army as teamsters or cooks, or in the way of work upon the fortifications, or in the Government workshops, or in hospitals and other similar duties, was authorized by the act of 17th of February last, and provision was made for their impressment to a number not exceeding 20,000, if it should be found impracticable to obtain them by contract with the owners. The law contemplated the hiring only of the labor of these slaves, and imposed on the Government the liability to pay for the value of such as might be lost to the owners from casualties resulting from their employment in the service.

This act has produced less result than was anticipated, and further provision is required to render it efficacious; but my present purpose is to invite your consideration to the propriety of a radical modification in the theory of the law.

Viewed merely as property, and therefore as the subject of impressment, the service or labor of the slave has been frequently claimed for short periods in the construction of defensive works. The slave, however, bears another relation to the State—that of a person. The law of last February contemplates only the relation of the slave to the master and limits the impressment to a certain term of service.

But for the purposes enumerated in the act, instruction in the manner of encamping, marching, and parking trains is needful; so that even in this limited employment length of service adds greatly to the value of the negro's labor. Hazard is also encountered in all the positions to which negroes can be assigned for service with the Army, and the duties required of them demand loyalty and zeal. In this respect the relation of person predominates so far as to render it doubtful whether the private right of property can consistently and beneficially be continued, and it would seem proper to acquire for the public service the entire property in the labor

---

* *Ibid.* pp. 493–96.

of the slave, and to pay therefor due compensation rather than to impress his labor for short terms; and this the more especially as the effect of the present law would vest this entire property in all cases where the slave might be recaptured after compensation for his loss had been paid to the private owner. Whenever the entire property in the service of a slave is thus acquired by the Government, the question is presented by what tenure he should be held. Should he be retained in servitude, or should his emancipation be held out to him as a reward for faithful service, or should it be granted at once on the promise of such service; and if emancipated, what action should be taken to secure for the freedman the permission of the State from which he was drawn to reside within its limits after the close of the public service? The permission would doubtless be more readily accorded as a reward for past faithful service, and a double motive for a zealous discharge of duty would thus be offered to those employed by the Government—their freedom and the gratification of the local attachment which is so marked a characteristic of the negro, and forms so powerful an incentive to his action. The policy of engaging to liberate the negro on his discharge after service faithfully rendered seems to me preferable to that of granting immediate manumission, or that of retaining him in servitude. If this policy should recommend itself to the judgment of Congress, it is suggested that, in addition to the duties heretofore performed by the slave, he might be advantageously employed as pioneer and engineer laborer, and in that event that the number should be augmented to 40,000.

Beyond these limits and these employments it does not seem to me desirable, under existing circumstances, to go. A broad moral distinction exists between the use of slaves as soldiers in defense of their homes and the incitement of the same persons to insurrection against their masters. The one is justifiable, if necessary, the other is iniquitous and unworthy of a civilized people; and such is the judgment of all writers on public law, as well as that expressed and insisted on by our enemies in all wars prior to that now waged against us. By none have the practices of which they are now guilty been denounced with greater severity than by themselves in the two wars with Great Britain, in the last and in the present century; and in the Declaration of Independence of 1776, when enumeration was made of the wrongs which justified the revolt from Great Britain, the climax of atrocity was deemed to be reached only when the English monarch was denounced as having "excited domestic insurrections amongst us."

The subject is to be viewed by us, therefore, solely in the light of policy and our social economy. When so regarded, I must dissent from those who advise a general levy and arming of the slaves for the duty of soldiers. Until our white population shall prove insufficient for the armies we require and can afford to keep in the field, to employ as a soldier the negro, who has merely been trained to labor, and as a laborer [under] the white man, accustomed from his youth to the use of firearms, would scarcely be deemed wise or advantageous by any; and this is the question now before us. But should the alternative ever be presented of subjugation or of the employment of the slave as a soldier, there seems no reason to doubt what should then be our decision. Whether our view embraces what would, in so extreme a case, be the sum of misery entailed by the dominion of the enemy, or be restricted solely to the effect upon the welfare and happiness of the negro population themselves, the result would be the same. The appalling demoralization, suffering, disease, and death which have been caused by partially substituting the invader's system of police for the kind relation previously subsisting between the master and slave have been a sufficient demonstration that external interference with our institution of domestic slavery is productive of evil only. If the subject involved no other consideration than the mere right of property, the sacrifices heretofore made by our people have been such as to permit no doubt of their readiness to surrender every possession in order to secure their independence. But the social and political question, which is exclusively under the control of the several States, has a far wider and more enduring importance than that of pecuniary interest. In its manifold phases it embraces the stability of our republican institutions, resting on the actual political equality of all its citizens, and includes the fulfillment of the task which has been so happily begun—that of Christianizing and improving the condition of the Africans who have, by the will of Providence, been placed in our charge. Comparing the results of our own experience with those of the experiments of others who have borne similar relation to the African race, the people of the several States of the Confederacy have abundant reason to be satisfied with the past, and will use the greatest circumspection in determining their course. These considerations, however, are rather applicable to the improbable contingency of our need of resorting to this element of resistance than to our present condition. If the recommendation above made, for the training of 40,000 negroes for the service indicated, shall meet your approval, it is certain that even this limited number, by their preparatory training in intermediate duties, would form a more valuable reserve force in case of urgency than three-fold their number suddenly called from field labor, while a fresh levy could, to a certain extent, supply their places in the special service for which they are now employed.

THE THIRTEENTH AMENDMENT (1865)

Slavery could not survive the Civil War. The Republican platform of 1864 had declared that:

. . . as slavery was the cause, and now constitutes the strength of the Rebellion, and as it must be, always and everywhere, hostile to the principles of Republican Government, justice and the National safety demand its utter and complete extirpation from the soil of the Republic; and that, while we uphold and maintain the acts and proclamations by which the Government, in its own defense, has aimed a deathblow at this gigantic evil, we are in favor, furthermore, of such an amendment to the Constitution, to be made by the people in conformity with its provisions, as shall terminate and forever prohibit the existence of Slavery within the limits of the jurisdiction of the United States.*

The Thirteenth Amendment, unlike the twelve that preceded it, was the first to effect broad, national reform of a substantive nature. Since the amendment process requires assent by three-fourths of the states, it was necessary to include eight of the former Confederate states, now operating

---

* Kirk H. Porter and Donald B. Johnson, eds., *National Party Platforms* (Urbana: University of Illinois Press, 1956), p. 31.

under reconstituted governments recognized by President Andrew Johnson, in the list of those endorsing ratification. The Amendment echoed the words of the Northwest Ordinance (Document 16) on slavery and made them applicable to the entire United States.

DOCUMENT 43

*Thirteenth Amendment**

SEC. 1. Neither slavery nor involuntary servitude, except as a punishment for crime whereof the party shall have been duly convicted, shall exist within the United States, or any place subject to their jurisdiction.

SEC. 2. Congress shall have power to enforce this article by appropriate legislation.

FREEDMEN'S BUREAU (1865, 1866)

In an effort to protect and aid the former slaves released from bondage by the disruptions of war or by federal legislation, Congress established the Freedmen's Bureau in early March, 1865. (The Bureau also helped displaced southern whites.) Designed to function under the aegis of the War Department, the Bureau was headed by General O. O. Howard, and its activities were marked by a wide range of assistance that provided, among other things, food, clothing and supplies, job placement, educational facilities, and homestead land. Created initially for the duration of the war and for one year thereafter, the Bureau was continued and its powers extended by act of Congress, over President Johnson's veto, in mid-July of 1866 (14 Stat. 173).

The Bureau's work represented an unprecedented and extraordinary outlay of direct federal aid to individuals. Widely applauded for its successful humanitarian activities, the Bureau was simultaneously denounced as an instrument

---

* Small, Jayson, and Corwin, eds., *The Constitution of the United States of America* (Washington, D.C: U.S. Government Printing Office, 1964), p. 1061.

of questionable interference in local affairs and as an agent of Republican control throughout the South. Historians still argue over the mixed motives that impelled Congress to endorse the Bureau's continuation, although the need for its activities seems clear in retrospect.

When Congress returned to Washington in December, 1865, it found that President Johnson had taken a number of steps to return the former Confederate states to their position within the Union and accept their representatives in Congress. Basically, Johnson followed Lincoln's temperate scheme for swift reconstruction of these state governments. Northern Republicans, in complete disagreement, engaged the President in a two-and-one-half-year struggle designed to establish the harsher and more restrictive terms of Congressional reconstruction throughout the South. The controversy over the status and condition of the Negro raised political and constitutional, as well as social and economic, questions of major importance.

Though he had remained a strong Unionist throughout the Civil War, Andrew Johnson never lost the characteristics of a poor white, states' rights, southern Democrat that had marked his earlier political career in Tennessee. In vetoing the extension of the Freedmen's Bureau, he overlooked instances of repression and discrimination visited upon former slaves. He stressed, instead, his fears that the proposed measure violated constitutional authority and needlessly expanded federal powers.

DOCUMENT(S) 44

*An act to establish a bureau for the relief of freedmen and refugees**

Be it enacted by the Senate and House of Representatives of the United States of America in Congress assembled, That there is hereby established in the War Department, to continue during the present war of rebellion, and for one year thereafter, a bureau of refugees, freedmen, and abandoned lands, to which shall be committed, as hereinafter provided,

---

* 13 Stat. 507 (1865).

the supervision and management of all abandoned lands, and the control of all subjects relating to refugees and freedmen from rebel states, or from any district of country within the territory embraced in the operations of the army, under such rules and regulations as may be prescribed by the head of the bureau and approved by the President. The said bureau shall be under the management and control of a commissioner to be appointed by the President, by and with the advice and consent of the Senate, whose compensation shall be three thousand dollars per annum, and such number of clerks as may be assigned to him by the Secretary of War, not exceeding one chief clerk, two of the fourth class, two of the third class, and five of the first class. And the commissioner and all persons appointed under this act, shall, before entering upon their duties, take the oath of office prescribed in an act entitled "An act to prescribe an oath of office, and for other purposes," approved July second, eighteen hundred and sixty-two, and the commissioner and the chief clerk shall, before entering upon their duties, give bonds to the treasurer of the United States, the former in the sum of fifty thousand dollars, and the latter in the sum of ten thousand dollars, conditioned for the faithful discharge of their duties respectively, with securities to be approved as sufficient by the Attorney-General, which bonds shall be filed in the office of the first comptroller of the treasury, to be by him put in suit for the benefit of any injured party upon any breach of the conditions thereof.

SEC. 2. *And be it further enacted,* That the Secretary of War may direct such issues of provisions, clothing, and fuel, as he may deem needful for the immediate and temporary shelter and supply of destitute and suffering refugees and freedmen and their wives and children, under such rules and regulations as he may direct.

SEC. 3. *And be it further enacted,* That the President may, by and with the advice and consent of the Senate, appoint an assistant commissioner for each of the states declared to be in insurrection, not exceeding ten in number, who shall, under the direction of the commissioner, aid in the execution of the provisions of this act; and he shall give a bond to the Treasurer of the United States, in the sum of twenty thousand dollars, in the form and manner prescribed in the first section of this act. Each of said commissioners shall receive an annual salary of two thousand five hundred dollars in full compensation for all his services. And any military officer may be detailed and assigned to duty under this act without increase of pay or allowances. The commissioner shall, before the commencement of each regular session of congress, make full report of his proceedings with exhibits of the state of his accounts to the President, who shall communicate the same to congress, and shall also make special reports whenever required to do so by the President or either house of congress; and the assistant commissioners shall make quarterly reports of their proceedings to the commissioner, and also such other special reports as from time to time may be required.

SEC. 4. *And be it further enacted,* That the commissioner, under the direction of the President, shall have authority to set apart, for the use of loyal refugees and freedmen, such tracts of land within the insurrectionary states as shall have been abandoned, or to which the United States shall have acquired title by confiscation or sale, or otherwise, and to every male citizen, whether refugee or freedman, as aforesaid, there shall be assigned not more than forty acres of such land, and the person to whom it was so assigned shall be protected in the use and enjoyment of the land for the term of three years at an annual rent not exceeding six per centum upon the value of such land, as it was appraised by the state authorities in the year eighteen hundred and sixty, for the purpose of taxation, and in case no such appraisal can be found, then the rental shall be based upon the estimated value of the land in said year, to be ascertained in such manner as the commissioner may by regulation prescribe. At the end of said term, or at any time during said term, the occupants of any parcels so assigned may purchase the land and receive such title thereto as the United States can convey, upon paying therefor the value of the land, as ascertained and fixed for the purpose of determining the annual rent aforesaid.

SEC. 5. *And be it further enacted,* That all acts and parts of acts inconsistent with the provisions of this act, are hereby repealed.

APPROVED, March 3, 1865.

Johnson's veto of the Freedmen's Bureau Bill, February 19, 1866[*]

To the Senate of the United States:

I have examined with care the bill, which originated in the Senate and has been passed by the two Houses of Congress, to amend an act entitled "An act to establish a bureau for the relief of freedmen and refugees," and for other purposes. Having with much regret come to the conclusion that it would not be consistent with the public welfare to give my approval to the measure, I return the bill to the Senate with my objections to its becoming a law.

I might call to mind in advance of these objections that there is no immediate necessity for the proposed measure. The act to establish a bureau for the relief of freedmen and refugees, which was approved in the month of March last, has not yet expired. It was thought stringent and extensive enough for the purpose in view in time of war. Before it ceases to have effect further experience may assist to guide us to a wise conclusion as to the policy to be adopted in time of peace.

I share with Congress the strongest desire to secure to the freedmen the full enjoyment of their freedom and property and their entire independence and equality in making contracts for their labor, but the bill before me contains provisions which in my opinion are not warranted by the Constitution and are not well suited to accomplish the end in view.

. . . .

While the territory and the classes of actions and offenses that are made subject to this measure are so extensive, the bill itself, should it become a law, will have no limitation in point of time, but will form a part of the permanent legislation of the country. I can not reconcile a system of military jurisdiction of this kind with the words of the Constitution which declare that "no person shall be held to answer for a

[*] Richardson, *Messages and Papers of the Presidents,* Vol. VI, pp. 398–405.

capital or otherwise infamous crime unless on a presentment or indictment of a grand jury, except in cases arising in the land or naval forces, or in the militia when in actual service in time of war or public danger," and that "in all criminal prosecutions the accused shall enjoy the right to a speedy and public trial by an impartial jury of the State and district wherein the crime shall have been committed." The safeguards which the experience and wisdom of ages taught our fathers to establish as securities for the protection of the innocent, the punishment of the guilty, and the equal administration of justice are to be set aside, and for the sake of a more vigorous interposition in behalf of justice we are to take the risks of the many acts of injustice that would necessarily follow from an almost countless number of agents established in every parish or county in nearly a third of the States of the Union, over whose decisions there is to be no supervision or control by the Federal courts. The power that would be thus placed in the hands of the President is such as in time of peace certainly ought never to be intrusted to any one man.

· · · ·

The third section of the bill authorizes a general and unlimited grant of support to the destitute and suffering refugees and freedmen, their wives and children. Succeeding sections make provision for the rent or purchase of landed estates for freedmen, and for the erection for their benefit of suitable buildings for asylums and schools, the expenses to be defrayed from the Treasury of the whole people. The Congress of the United States has never heretofore thought itself empowered to establish asylums beyond the limits of the District of Columbia, except for the benefit of our disabled soldiers and sailors. It has never founded schools for any class of our own people, not even for the orphans of those who have fallen in the defense of the Union, but has left the care of education to the much more competent and efficient control of the States, of communities, of private associations, and of individuals. It has never deemed itself authorized to expend the public money for the rent or purchase of homes for the thousands, not to say millions, of the white race who are honestly toiling from day to day for their subsistence. A system for the support of indigent persons in the United States was never contemplated by the authors of the Constitution; nor can any good reason be advanced why, as a permanent establishment, it should be founded for one class or color of our people more than another. Pending the war many refugees and freedmen received support from the Government, but it was never intended that they should thenceforth be fed, clothed, educated, and sheltered by the United States. The idea on which the slaves were assisted to freedom was that on becoming free they would be a self-sustaining population. Any legislation that shall imply that they are not expected to attain a self-sustaining condition must have a tendency injurious alike to their character and their prospects.

. . . .

There is still further objection to the bill, on grounds seriously affecting the class of persons to whom it is designed to bring relief. It will tend to keep the mind of the freedman in a state of uncertain expectation and restlessness, while to those among whom he lives it will be a source of constant and vague apprehension.

Undoubtedly the freedman should be protected, but he should be protected by the civil authorities, especially by the exercise of all the constitutional powers of the courts of the United States and of the States. His condition is not so exposed as may at first be imagined. He is in a portion of the country where his labor can not well be spared. Competition for his services from planters, from those who are constructing or repairing railroads, and from capitalists in his vicinage or from other States will enable him to command almost his own terms. He also possesses a perfect right to change his place of abode, and if, therefore, he does not find in one community or State a mode of life suited to his desires or proper remuneration for his labor, he can move to another where that labor is more esteemed and better rewarded. In truth, however, each State, induced by its own wants and interests, will do what is necessary and proper to retain within its borders all the labor that is needed for the development of its resources. The laws that regulate supply and demand will maintain their force, and the wages of the laborer will be regulated thereby. There is no danger that the exceedingly great demand for labor will not operate in favor of the laborer.

Neither is sufficient consideration given to the ability of the freedmen to protect and take care of themselves. It is no more than justice to them to believe that as they have received their freedom with moderation and forbearance, so they will disinguish themselves by their industry and thrift, and soon show the world that in a condition of freedom they are self-sustaining, capable of selecting their own employment and their own places of abode, of insisting for themselves on a proper remuneration, and of establishing and maintaining their own asylums and schools. It is earnestly hoped that instead of wasting away they will by their own efforts establish for themselves a condition of respectability and prosperity. It is certain that they can attain to that condition only through their own merits and exertions. . . .

SOUTHERN BLACK CODES (1865)

Throughout the former Confederate area, state governments legitimized by the terms of Presidential reconstruction proceeded in 1865 and 1866 to pass legislation regulating the status and conduct of newly freed Negroes. Termed Black Codes, these laws were based on the explicit assumption of Negro inferiority and sharply restricted the mobility and personal liberties of former free Negroes and new freedmen alike. The codes set terms of employment that, in many instances, amounted to a reinstatement of master-slave conditions in practice if not in name: Negroes could be bound over for service and labor to white persons; and prohibitive fees were imposed upon Negroes who aspired to commercial and artisan occupations. Finally, the codes made provision for fines and physical punishment for Negroes who refused to comply with the new legislation.

Southerners justified the need for such measures as the only feasible way of reestablishing workable relations in a biracial society so recently disrupted by the ravages of war. Northerners, however, viewed the codes as a deliberate attempt by the South to void the results of the war and return

Negroes to a system of permanent bondage. The Black Codes helped induce northern support for the Congressional reconstruction program that superseded the Presidential plan.

DOCUMENT 45

South Carolina Black Code, December 21, 1865—An act to establish and regulate the domestic relations of persons of color, and to amend the law in relation to paupers and vagrancy[*]

Be it enacted by the Senate and House of Representatives, now met and sitting in General Assembly, and by the authority of the same, as follows:

Husband and Wife

I. The relation of husband and wife amongst persons of color is established.

II. Those who now live as such, are declared to be husband and wife.

III. In case of one man having two or more reputed wives, or one woman two or more reputed husbands, the man shall, by the first of April next, select one of his reputed wives, or the woman one of her reputed husbands, and the ceremony of marriage, between this man or woman, and the person so selected, shall be performed.

IV. Every colored child, heretofore born, is declared to be the legitimate child of his mother, and also of his colored father, if he is acknowledged by such a father. . . .

VIII. One who is a pauper, or a charge to the public, shall not be competent to contract marriage. Marriage between a white person and a person of color, shall be illegal and void.

IX. The marriage of an apprentice shall not, without the consent of the master, be lawful.

. . . .

[*] *Acts of the General Assembly of the State of South Carolina,* 1864–1865, pp. 291–304.

Master and Apprentice

xv. A child over the age of two years, born of a colored parent, may be bound by the father, if he be living in the District, or in case of his death or absence from the District, by the mother, as an apprentice, to any respectable white or colored person, who is competent to make a contract—a male until he shall attain the age of twenty-one years and a female until she shall attain the age of eighteen years.

xvi. Illegitimate children, within the ages above specified, may be bound by the mother.

xvii. Colored children, between the ages mentioned, who have neither father nor mother living in the District in which they are found, or whose parents are paupers, or unable to afford to them maintenance, or whose parents are not teaching them habits of industry and honesty, or are persons of notoriously bad character, or are vagrants, or have been, either of them convicted of an infamous offense, may be bound as apprentices by the District Judge, or one of the Magistrates for the aforesaid term.

xviii. Males of the age of twelve years, and females, of the age of ten years, shall sign the indenture of apprenticeship and be bound thereby.

xix. When the apprentice is under these ages, and in all cases of compulsory apprenticeship, where the infant refuses assent, his signature shall not be necessary to the validity of the apprenticeship. The master's obligation of apprenticeship in all cases of compulsory apprenticeship, and cases where the father or mother does not bind a child, shall be executed in the presence of the District Judge, or one of the Magistrates, certified by him, and filed in the office of the Clerk of the District Court. . . .

xxii. The master or mistress shall teach the apprentice the business of husbandry, or some other useful trade or business, which shall be specified in the instrument of apprenticeship; shall furnish him wholesome food and suitable clothing; teach him habits of industry, honesty and morality; govern and treat him with humanity; and if there be a school within a convenient distance, in which colored children are taught, shall send him to school at least six weeks in every year of his apprenticeship, after he shall be of the age of ten years: *Provided,* That the teacher of such school shall have the license of the District Judge to establish the same.

XXIII. The master shall have authority to inflict moderate chastisement and impose reasonable restraint upon his apprentice, and to recapture him if he depart from his service.

XXIV. The master shall receive to his own use the profits of the labor of his apprentice. The relation of master and apprentice shall be dissolved by the death of the master, except where the apprentice is engaged in husbandry, and may be dissolved by the District Judge, when both parties consent, or it shall appear to be seriously detrimental to either party. In the excepted case it shall terminate at the end of the year in which the master died.

. . . .

Contracts for Service

XXXV. All persons of color who make contracts for service or labor, shall be known as servants, and those with whom they contract shall be known as masters.

XXXVI. Contracts between masters and servants, for one month or more, shall be in writing, be attested by one white witness, and be approved by the Judge of the District Court, or by a Magistrate.

. . . .

XLIII. For any neglect of the duty to make a contract as herein directed, or the evasion of that duty by the repeated employment of the same persons for periods less than one month, the party offending shall be guilty of a misdemeanor, and be liable on conviction to pay a sum not exceeding fifty dollars, and not less than five dollars, for each person so employed. No written contract shall be required, when the servant voluntarily receives no remuneration, except food and clothing.

. . . .

Regulations of Labor on Farms

XLV. On farms or in out-door service, the hours of labor, except on Sunday, shall be from sun-rise to sun-set, with a reasonable interval for breakfast and dinner. Servants shall rise at the dawn in the morning, feed, water and care for the animals on the farm, do the usual and needful work about the premises, prepare their meals for the day, if required by the master, and begin the farm work or other work by sunrise. The servant shall be careful of all the animals and property of his master, and especially of the animals and instruments used by him, shall protect the same from injury by other persons, and shall be answerable for all property lost, destroyed or injured by his negligence, dishonesty or bad faith.

XLVI. All lost time, not caused by the act of the master, and all losses occasioned by neglect of the duties hereinbefore prescribed, may be deducted from the wages of the servant; and food, nursing and other necessaries for the servant, while he is absent from work on account of sickness or other cause, may also be deducted from his wages. Servants shall be quiet and orderly in their quarters, at their work and on the premises; shall extinguish their lights and fires, and retire to rest at seasonable hours. Work at night, and out-door work in inclement weather, shall not be exacted unless in case of necessity. Servants shall not be kept at home on Sunday, unless to take care of the premises, or animals thereupon, or for work of daily necessity, or on unusual occasions; and in such cases only so many shall be kept at home as are necessary for these purposes. Sunday work shall be done by the servants in turn, except in cases of sickness or other disability, when it may be assigned to them out of their regular term. Absentees on Sunday shall return to their homes by sun-set.

XLVII. The master may give to a servant a task at work about the business of the farm which shall be reasonable. If the servant complain of the task, the District Judge, or a Magistrate, shall have power to reduce or increase it. Failure to do a task shall be deemed evidence of indolence, but a single failure shall not be conclusive. When a servant is entering into a contract, he may be required to rate himself as a full hand, three-fourths, half, or one-fourth hand, and according to this rate inserted in the contract, shall be the task, and of course the wages.

XLVIII. Visitors or other persons shall not be invited, or allowed by the servant, to come or remain upon the premises of the master, without his express permission.

XLIX. Servants shall not be absent from the premises without the permission of the master.

Rights of Master as Between Himself and His Servant

L. When the servant shall depart from the service of the master without good cause, he shall forfeit the wages due to him. The servant shall obey all lawful orders of the master or his agent, and shall be honest, truthful, sober, civil, and diligent in his business. The master may moderately correct servants who have made contracts, and are under eighteen years of age. He shall not be liable to pay for any additional or extraordinary services or labor of his servant, the same being necessary, unless by his express agreement.

Causes of Discharge of a Servant

LI. The master may discharge his servant for wilful disobedience of the lawful order of himself or his agent; habitual negligence or indolence in business; drunkenness, moral or legal misconduct; want of respect and civility to himself, his family, guests or agents; or for prolonged absence from the premises, or absence on two or more occasions without permission.

LII. For any acts or things herein declared to be causes for the discharge of a servant, or for any breach of contract or duty by him, instead of discharging the servant, the master may complain to the District Judge, or one of the Magistrates, who shall have power, on being satisfied of the misconduct complained of, to inflict, or cause to be inflicted, on the servant suitable corporal punishment, or impose upon him such pecuniary fine as may be thought fit, and immediately to remand him to his work; which fine shall be deducted from his wages, if not otherwise paid.

LIII. If a master has made a valid contract with a servant, the District Judge or a Magistrate may compel such servant to observe his contract, by ordering infliction of the punishment, or imposition of the fine herein before authorized. . . .

Rights of Servant as Between Himself and Master

LXI. The servant may depart from the master's service for an insufficient supply of wholesome food; for an unauthorized battery upon his own person, or one of his family, not committed in defence of the person, family, guests or agents of the master, nor to prevent a crime or aggravated misdemeanor; invasion by the master of the conjugal rights of the servant; or his failure to pay wages when due; and may recover wages due for services rendered to the time of his departure.

LXII. The contract for service shall not be terminated by the death of the master, without the assent of the servant. Wages due to white laborers and to white and colored servants, shall rank as rent does in case of the insufficiency of the master's property, to pay all debts and demands against him, but not more than one year's wages shall be so preferred. When wrongfully discharged from service, the servant may recover wages for the whole period of service according to the contract. If his wages have not been paid to the day of his discharge, he may regard his contract rescinded by the discharge, and recover wages up to that time.

. . . .

Mechanics, Artisans and Shop-keepers

LXXII. No person of color shall pursue or practice the art, trade or business of an artisan, mechanic or shop-keeper, or any other trade, employment or business (besides that of husbandry, or that of a servant under a contract for services or labor) on his own account and for his own benefit, or in partnership with a white person, or as agent or servant of any person, until he shall have obtained a license therefor from the Judge of the District Court, which license shall be good for one year only. This license the Judge may grant upon petition of the applicant, and upon being satisfied of his skill and fitness, and of his good moral character, and upon payment, by the applicant, to the Clerk of the District Court of one hundred dollars, if a shop-keeper or pedlar, to be paid annually, and ten dollars if a mechanic artisan, or to engage in any other trade, also to be paid annually: *Provided, however,* That upon complaint being made and proved to the District Judge of an abuse of such license, he shall revoke the same, and: *Provided, also,* That no person of color shall practice any mechanical art or trade, unless he shows that he has served an apprenticeship in such trade or art, or is now practicing such trade or art.

. . . .

Vagrancy and Idleness

xcv. These are public grievances, and must be punished as crimes.

xcvi. All persons who have not some fixed and known place of abode, and some lawful and reputable employment; those who have not some visible and known means of a fair, honest and reputable livelihood; all common prostitutes; those who are found wandering from place to place, vending, bartering, or peddling any articles or commodities, without a license from the District Judge, or other proper authorities; all common gamblers; persons who lead idle or disorderly lives, or keep or frequent disorderly or disreputable houses or places; those who, not having sufficient means of support, are able to work and do not work; those who, (whether or not they own lands, or are lessees or mechanics,) do not provide a reasonable and proper maintenance for themselves and families; those who are engaged in representing publicly or privately, for fee or reward, without license, any tragedy, interlude, comedy, farce, play, or other similar entertainment, exhibition of the circus, sleight of hand, wax work or the like; those who for private gain, without license, give any concert or musical entertainment of any description; fortune tellers; sturdy beggars; common drunkards; those who hunt game of any description, or fish on the land of others, or frequent the premises, contrary to the will of the occupants; shall be deemed vagrants, and be liable to the punishment hereinafter provided.

xcvii. Upon information, or oath, of another, or upon his own knowledge, the District Judge or a Magistrate shall issue a warrant for the arrest of any person of color known or believed to be a vagrant, within the meaning of this Act. The Magistrate may proceed to try, with the assistance of five freeholders, or call into his aid another Magistrate, and the two may proceed to try, with the assistance of three freeholders, as provided by the Act of 1787, concerning vagrants; or the Magistrate may commit the accused to be tried before the District Court. On conviction, the defendant shall be liable to imprisonment, and to hard labor, one or both, as shall be fixed by the verdict, not exceeding twelve months.

xcviii. The defendant, if sentenced to hard labor after conviction, may, by order of the District Judge, or Magistrate, before whom he was convicted, be hired for such wages as can be obtained for his services, to any owner or lessee of a farm, for the term of labor to which he was sentenced, or be hired for the same labor on the streets, public roads, or public buildings. The person receiving such vagrant shall have all the rights and remedies for enforcing good conduct and diligence at labor that are herein provided in the case of master and servant.

THE FOURTEENTH AMENDMENT (1868)

No part of the Constitution has aroused more controversy or spurred more litigation than the Fourteenth Amendment. Southern states, in particular, have passed innumerable laws and instituted numerous practices designed to avoid, evade, and delay its effectiveness.

The Fourteenth Amendment was drafted and passed by the first Reconstruction Congress in response to expressed doubts as to the constitutionality of the Civil Rights Act of April 9, 1866 (Document 47). There were many complications over ratification. Since ratification was made a condition of reinstatement into the Union, the Southern states did ratify the Amendment during the two years between Congressional action and final adoption. During this period, however, New Jersey, Ohio, and Oregon rescinded their ratification. Delaware, Kentucky, and Maryland rejected the proposal, and California ignored it completely.

The most important part of the Fourteenth Amendment is its first section with its three generic clauses: "privileges or immunities," "due process of law," and "equal protection of the laws." Rights under these clauses were guaranteed by the federal government against state encroachment. Interpretations of the dimensions of these rights and their enforcement have produced a century of litigation.

For most of its history, the Amendment has been more important in safeguarding property rights than in protecting civil rights. The dissenting view in the Slaughter-House Cases (Document 50) ultimately became the law in practice, providing a corporate sanctuary from state regulation. While the Amendment primarily sought to insure the rights of freedmen, Sections 3 and 4 confirmed the illegitimacy of the southern rebellion and voided the financial obligations undertaken by the Confederacy.

DOCUMENT 46

Fourteenth Amendment*

SEC. 1. All persons born or naturalized in the United States, and subject to the jurisdiction thereof, are citizens of the United States and of the State wherein they reside. No State shall make or enforce any law which shall abridge the privileges or immunities of citizens of the United States; nor shall any State deprive any person of life, liberty, or property, without due process of law; nor deny to any person within its jurisdiction the equal protection of the laws.

SEC. 2. Representatives shall be apportioned among the several States according to their respective numbers, counting the whole number of persons in each State, excluding Indians not taxed. But when the right to vote at any election for the choice of electors for President and Vice President of the United States, Representatives in Congress, the Executive and Judicial officers of a State, or the members of the Legislature

---

* Small, Jayson, and Corwin, *op. cit.*, pp. 1073ff.

thereof, is denied to any of the male inhabitants of such State, being twenty-one years of age, and citizens of the United States, or in any way abridged, except for participation in rebellion, or other crime, the basis of representation therein shall be reduced in the proportion which the number of such male citizens shall bear to the whole number of male citizens twenty-one years of age in such State.

SEC. 3. No person shall be a Senator or Representative in Congress, or elector of President and Vice President, or hold any office, civil or military, under the United States, or under any State, who, having previously taken an oath, as a member of Congress, or as an officer of the United States, or as a member of any State legislature, or as an executive or judicial officer of any State, to support the Constitution of the United States, shall have engaged in insurrection or rebellion against the same, or given aid or comfort to the enemies thereof. But Congress may be a vote of two-thirds of each House, remove such disability.

SEC. 4. The validity of the public debt of the United States, authorized by law, including debts incurred for payment of pensions and bounties for services in suppressing insurrection or rebellion, shall not be questioned. But neither the United States nor any State shall assume or pay any debt or obligation incurred in aid of insurrection or rebellion against the United States, or any claim for the loss or emancipation of any slave; but all such debts, obligations and claims shall be held illegal and void.

SEC. 5. The Congress shall have power to enforce, by appropriate legislation, the provisions of this article.

THE CIVIL RIGHTS ACTS (1866–1875)

Congress passed seven Civil Rights Acts during the Reconstruction era, 1866 to 1875. And while two of these are only of passing historical interest, the other five were of great significance in the struggle to secure civil rights for the American Negro. One act was passed over a Presidential veto, and three were in large measure struck down by the Supreme Court as unconstitutional. Congress did not again enact substantial civil rights legislation until 1957. (Document 81.)

Designed to safeguard the new freedmen from such discrimination as exemplified by the Black Codes (Document 45), the first of these acts (14 Stat. 27) was passed on March 13, 1866, and repassed on April 9 of that same year, over President Andrew Johnson's veto. It bore the expansive title of "An Act to protect all Persons in the United States in their Civil Rights, and furnish the Means of their Vindication." This act overturned the *Dred Scott* decision (Document 34) by giving Negroes "full and equal benefit of all laws and proceedings . . . as is enjoyed by white citizens." Whether or not it was unconstitutional became a moot point with the adoption of the Fourteenth Amendment in 1868 (Document 46), incorporating the more salient features of the earlier legislation.

Of less importance were the next two Civil Rights Acts. On May 21, 1866, a statute (14 Stat. 50) was passed, making it a criminal offense to "kidnap or carry away any other person, whether negro, mulatto, or otherwise, with the intent that such other person shall be sold or carried into involuntary servitude, or held as a slave." It was also made a crime to transport any Negro to a foreign country "to be held or sold as a slave." On March 2, 1867, Congress passed "An Act to abolish and forever prohibit the System of Peonage in the Territory of New Mexico and other Parts of the United States" (14 Stat. 546).

Because of constitutional criticisms leveled against the 1866 act, Congress relied upon the implementation powers of the Fourteenth and Fifteenth Amendments to reenact provisions in Section 18 of the fourth of the Civil Rights Acts. This was the Act of May 31, 1870 (16 Stat. 140), known as the Enforcement Act.

The main thrust of the 1870 Enforcement Act was the imposition of criminal sanctions for interference with the right of Negro suffrage, granted under the Fifteenth Amendment (Document 48). Section 6 of the 1870 act specified criminal penalties for those who "go in disguise upon the public highway" to violate the civil rights of another. As such it was the precursor of the sixth Civil Rights Act, the so-called Ku Klux Act, adopted on April 20, 1871 (17 Stat. 13).

The Act of 1870, the fourth act, had a stormy judicial history. Sections 3 and 4 were declared unconstitutional in

1876, in *United States* v. *Reese*, 92 U.S. 214; Section 5 was declared unconstitutional in 1903, in *James* v. *Bowman*, 190 U.S. 127; and Section 16 was declared unconstitutional in 1906 in *Hodges* v. *United States*, 203 U.S. 1.

Most far-reaching was the sixth or Ku Klux Act, which in Section 2 imposed penalties upon those who deprived "any person or any class of persons of the equal protection of the laws, or of equal privileges or immunities under the laws." Designated "An Act to enforce the Provisions of the Fourteenth Amendment" (17 Stat. 13), this statute also met with judicial disfavor. Section 2 was declared unconstitutional in two cases: *United States* v. *Harris*, 106 U.S. 629 (1883) and *Baldwin* v. *Franks*, 120 U.S. 678 (1887).

Once more in the post-Civil War period—and for the last time until 1957—Negro equality was "the appropriate object of legislation." So reads the preamble to the Civil Rights Act of March 1, 1875 (18 Stat. 335). But once more the Supreme Court was to nullify Congressional action. The basic "accommodations" section was held not to be supported by the Thirteenth or Fourteenth Amendments in the Civil Rights Cases (Document 54). Struck down was the provision "That all persons within the jurisdiction of the United States shall be entitled to the full and equal enjoyment of the accommodations, advantages, facilities, and privileges of inns, public conveyances on land or water, theaters, and other places of public amusement; subject only to the conditions and limitations established by law, and applicable alike to citizens of every race and color, regardless of any previous condition of servitude."

DOCUMENT(S) 47

An act to protect all persons in the United States in their civil rights, and furnish the means of their vindication[*]

Be it enacted by the Senate and House of Representatives of the United States of America in Congress assembled, That all persons born in the United States and not subject to any

---

[*] 14 Stat. 27 (1866).

foreign power, excluding Indians not taxed, are hereby declared to be citizens of the United States; and such citizens, of every race and color, without regard to any previous condition of slavery or involuntary servitude, except as a punishment for crime whereof the party shall have been duly convicted, shall have the same right, in every State and Territory in the United States, to make and enforce contracts, to sue, be parties, and give evidence, to inherit, purchase, lease, sell, hold, and convey real and personal property, and to full and equal benefit of all laws and proceedings for the security of person and property, as is enjoyed by white citizens, and shall be subject to like punishment, pains, and penalties, and to none other, any law, statute, ordinance, regulation, or custom, to the contrary notwithstanding.

SEC. 2. *And be it further enacted*, That any person who, under color of any law, statute, ordinance, regulation, or custom, shall subject, or cause to be subjected, any inhabitant of any State or Territory to the deprivation of any right secured or protected by this act, or to different punishment, pains, or penalties on account of such person having at any time been held in a condition of slavery or involuntary servitude, except as a punishment for crime whereof the party shall have been duly convicted, or by reason of his color or race, than is prescribed for the punishment of white persons, shall be deemed guilty of a misdemeanor, and, on conviction, shall be punished by fine not exceeding one thousand dollars, or imprisonment not exceeding one year, or both, in the discretion of the court.

. . . .

SEC. 4. *And be it further enacted*, That the district attorneys, marshals, and deputy marshals of the United States, the commissioners appointed by the circuit and territorial courts of the United States, with powers of arresting, imprisoning, or bailing offenders against the laws of the United States, the officers and agents of the Freedmen's Bureau, and every other officer who may be specially empowered by the President of the United States, shall be, and they are hereby, specially authorized and required, at the expense of the United States, to institute proceedings against all and every person who shall violate the provisions of this act, and cause him or them to be arrested and imprisoned, or bailed, as the case may be, for trial before such court of the United States or territorial court as by this act has cognizance of the offence. And with a view to affording reasonable protection to all persons in their constitutional rights of equality before the law, without distinction of race or color, or previous condition of slavery or involuntary servitude, except as a punishment for crime, whereof the party shall have been duly convicted, and to the prompt discharge of the duties of this act, it shall be the duty of the circuit courts of the United States and the superior courts of the Territories of the United States, from time to time, to increase the number of commissioners, so as to afford a speedy and convenient means for the arrest and examination of persons charged with a violation of this act; and such commissioners are hereby authorized and required to exercise and discharge all the powers and duties conferred on them by this act, and the same duties with regard to offences created by this act, as they are authorized by law to exercise with regard to other offences against the laws of the United States.

· · · ·

SEC. 6. *And be it further enacted,* That any person who shall knowingly and wilfully obstruct, hinder, or prevent any officer, or other person charged with the execution of any warrant or process issued under the provisions of this act, or any person or persons lawfully assisting him or them, from arresting any person for whose apprehension such warrant or process may have been issued, or shall rescue or attempt to rescue such person from the custody of the officer, other person or persons, or those lawfully assisting as aforesaid, when so arrested pursuant to the authority herein given and declared, or shall aid, abet, or assist any person so arrested as aforesaid, directly or indirectly, to escape from the custody of the officer or other person legally authorized as aforesaid, or shall harbor or conceal any person for whose arrest a warrant or process shall have been issued as aforesaid, so as to prevent his discovery and arrest after notice or knowledge of the fact that a warrant has been issued for the apprehension of such person, shall, for either of said offences, be subject to a fine not exceeding one thousand dollars, and imprisonment not exceeding six months, by indictment and conviction before the district court of the United States for the district in which said offence may have been committed, or before the proper court of criminal jurisdiction, if committed within any one of the organized Territories of the United States.

. . . .

SEC. 9. *And be it further enacted,* That it shall be lawful for the President of the United States, or such person as he may empower for that purpose, to employ such part of the land or naval forces of the United States, or of the militia, as shall be necessary to prevent the violation and enforce the due execution of this act.

SEC. 10. *And be it further enacted,* That upon all questions of law arising in any cause under the provisions of this act a final appeal may be taken to the Supreme Court of the United States.

SCHUYLER COLFAX
Speaker of the House of Representatives
LA FAYETTE S. FOSTER
President of the Senate, *pro tempore*

In the Senate of the United States, April 6, 1866

The President of the United States having returned to the Senate, in which it originated, the bill entitled "An act to protect all persons in the United States in their civil rights, and furnish the means of their vindication," with his objections thereto, the Senate proceeded, in pursuance of the Constitution, to reconsider the same; and,

Resolved, That the said bill do pass, two-thirds of the Senate agreeing to pass the same.

Attest: J. W. FORNEY
Secretary of the Senate

In the House of Representatives U. S. April 9th, 1866

The House of Representatives having proceeded, in pursuance of the Constitution, to reconsider the bill entitled "An act to protect all persons in the United States in their civil rights, and furnish the means of their vindication," returned to the Senate by the President of the United States, with his objections, and sent by the Senate to the House of Representatives, with the message of the President returning the bill:

Resolved, That the bill do pass, two-thirds of the House of Representatives agreeing to pass the same.

Attest: EDWARD McPHERSON, Clerk
by CLINTON LLOYD, Chief Clerk

*An act to enforce the right of citizens of the United States to vote in the several states of this Union, and for other purposes**

Be it enacted by the Senate and House of Representatives of the United States of America in Congress assembled, That all citizens of the United States who are or shall be otherwise qualified by law to vote at any election by the people in any State, Territory, district, county, city, parish, township, school district, municipality, or other territorial subdivision, shall be entitled and allowed to vote at all such elections, without distinction of race, color, or previous condition of servitude; any constitution, law, custom, usage, or regulation of any State or Territory, or by or under its authority, to the contrary notwithstanding.

SEC. 2. *And be it further enacted,* That if by or under the authority of the constitution or laws of any State, or the laws of any Territory, any act is or shall be required to be done as a prerequisite or qualification for voting, and by such constitution or laws persons or officers are or shall be charged with the performance of duties in furnishing to citizens an opportunity to perform such prerequisite, or to become qualified to vote, it shall be the duty of every such person and officer to give to all citizens of the United States the same and equal opportunity to perform such prerequisite, and to become qualified to vote without distinction of race, color, or previous condition of servitude; and if any such person or officer shall refuse or knowingly omit to give full effect to this section, he shall, for every such offence, forfeit and pay the sum of five hundred dollars to the person aggrieved thereby, to be recovered by an action on the case, with full costs, and such

---

* 16 Stat. 140 (1870).

allowance for counsel fees as the court shall deem just, and shall also, for every such offence, be deemed guilty of a misdemeanor, and shall, on conviction thereof, be fined not less than five hundred dollars, or be imprisoned not less than one month and not more than one year, or both, at the discretion of the court.

. . . .

SEC. 4. *And be it further enacted,* That if any person, by force, bribery, threats, intimidation, or other unlawful means, shall hinder, delay, prevent, or obstruct, or shall combine and confederate with others to hinder, delay, prevent, or obstruct, any citizen from doing any act required to be done to qualify him to vote or from voting at any election as aforesaid, such person shall for every such offence forfeit and pay the sum of five hundred dollars to the person aggrieved thereby, to be recovered by an action on the case, with full costs, and such allowance for counsel fees as the court shall deem just, and shall also for every such offence be guilty of a misdemeanor, and shall, on conviction thereof, be fined not less than five hundred dollars, or be imprisoned not less than one month and not more than one year, or both, at the discretion of the court.

SEC. 5. *And be it further enacted,* That if any person shall prevent, hinder, control, or intimidate, or shall attempt to prevent, hinder, control, or intimidate, any person from exercising or in exercising the right of suffrage, to whom the right of suffrage is secured or guaranteed by the fifteenth amendment to the Constitution of the United States, by means of bribery, threats, or threats of depriving such person of employment or occupation, or of ejecting such person from rented house, lands, or other property, or by threats of refusing to renew leases or contracts for labor, or by threats of violence to himself or family, such person so offending shall be deemed guilty of a misdemeanor, and shall, on conviction thereof, be fined not less than five hundred dollars, or be imprisoned not less than one month and not more than one year, or both, at the discretion of the court.

SEC. 6. *And be it further enacted,* That if two or more persons shall band or conspire together, or go in disguise upon the public highway, or upon the premises of another, with intent to violate any provision of this act, or to injure, oppress, threaten, or intimidate any citizen with intent to prevent or hinder his free exercise and enjoyment of any right or privilege granted or secured to him by the Constitution or laws of the United States, or because of his having exercised the same, such persons shall be held guilty of felony, and, on conviction thereof, shall be fined or imprisoned, or both, at the discretion of the court,—the fine not to exceed five thousand dollars, and the imprisonment not to exceed ten years,—and shall, moreover, be thereafter ineligible to, and disabled from holding, any office or place of honor, profit, or trust created by the Constitution or laws of the United States.

. . . .

SEC. 8. *And be it further enacted*, That the district courts of the United States, within their respective districts, shall have, exclusively of the courts of the several States, cognizance of all crimes and offences committed against the provisions of this act, and also, concurrently with the circuit courts of the United States, of all causes, civil and criminal, arising under this act, except as herein otherwise provided, and the jurisdiction hereby conferred shall be exercised in conformity with the laws and practice governing United States courts; and all crimes and offences committed against the provisions of this act may be prosecuted by the indictment of a grand jury, or, in cases of crimes and offences not infamous, the prosecution may be either by indictment or information filed by the district attorney in a court having jurisdiction.

. . . .

SEC. 16. *And be it further enacted*, That all persons within the jurisdiction of the United States shall have the same right in every State and Territory in the United States to make and enforce contracts, to sue, be parties, give evidence, and to the full and equal benefit of all laws and proceedings for the security of person and property as is enjoyed by white citizens, and shall be subject to like punishment, pains, penalties, taxes, licenses, and exactions of every kind, and none other, any law, statute, ordinance, regulation, or custom to the contrary notwithstanding. No tax or charge shall be imposed or enforced by any State upon any person immigrating thereto from a foreign country which is not equally imposed and enforced upon every person immigrating to such State from any other foreign country; and any law of any State in conflict with this provision is hereby declared null and void.

Sec. 17. *And be it further enacted,* That any person who, under color of any law, statute, ordinance, regulation, or custom, shall subject, or cause to be subjected, any inhabitant of any State or Territory to the deprivation of any right secured or protected by the last preceding section of this act, or to different punishment, pains, or penalties on account of such person being an alien, or by reason of his color or race, than is prescribed for the punishment of citizens, shall be deemed guilty of a misdemeanor, and, on conviction, shall be punished by fine not exceeding one thousand dollars, or imprisonment not exceeding one year, or both, in the discretion of the court.

Sec. 18. *And be it further enacted,* That the act to protect all persons in the United States in their civil rights, and furnish the means of their vindication, passed April nine, eighteen hundred and sixty-six, is hereby re-enacted; and sections sixteen and seventeen hereof shall be enforced according to the provisions of said act.

. . . .

Sec. 23. *And be it further enacted,* That whenever any person shall be defeated or deprived of his election to any office, except elector of President or Vice-President, representative or delegate in Congress, or member of a State legislature, by reason of the denial to any citizen or citizens who shall offer to vote, of the right to vote, on account of race, color, or previous condition of servitude, his right to hold and enjoy such office, and the emoluments thereof, shall not be impaired by such denial; and such person may bring any appropriate suit or proceeding to recover possession of such office, and in cases where it shall appear that the sole question touching the title to such office arises out of the denial of the right to vote to citizens who so offered to vote, on account of race, color, or previous condition of servitude, such suit or proceeding may be instituted in the circuit or district court of the United States of the circuit or district in which such person resides. And said circuit or district court shall have, concurrently with the State courts, jurisdiction thereof so far as to determine the rights of the parties to such office by reason of the denial of the right guaranteed by the fifteenth article of amendment to the Constitution of the United States, and secured by this act.

APPROVED, May 31, 1870.

An act to enforce the provisions of the Fourteenth Amendment to the Constitution of the United States, and for other purposes[*]

Be it enacted by the Senate and House of Representatives of the United States of America in Congress assembled, That any person who, under color of any law, statute, ordinance, regulation, custom, or usage of any State, shall subject, or cause to be subjected, any person within the jurisdiction of the United States to the deprivation of any rights, privileges, or immunities secured by the Constitution of the United States, shall, any such law, statute, ordinance, regulation, custom, or usage of the State to the contrary notwithstanding, be liable to the party injured in any action at law, suit in equity, or other proper proceeding for redress; such proceeding to be prosecuted in the several district or circuit courts of the United States, with and subject to the same rights of appeal, review upon error, and other remedies provided in like cases in such courts, under the provisions of the act of the ninth of April, eighteen hundred and sixty-six, entitled "An act to protect all persons in the United States in their civil rights, and *to* furnish the means of their vindication"; and the other remedial laws of the United States which are in their nature applicable in such cases.

SEC. 2. That if two or more persons within any State or Territory of the United States shall conspire together to overthrow, or to put down, or to destroy by force the government of the United States, or to levy war against the United States, or to oppose by force the authority of the government of the

---

[*] 17 Stat. 13 (1871).

United States, or by force, intimidation, or threat to prevent, hinder, or delay the execution of any law of the United States, or by force to seize, take, or possess any property of the United States contrary to the authority thereof, or by force, intimidation, or threat to prevent any person from accepting or holding any office or trust or place of confidence under the United States, or from discharging the duties thereof, or by force, intimidation, or threat to induce any officer of the United States to leave any State district, or place where his duties as such officer might lawfully be performed, or to injure him in his person or property on account of his lawful discharge of the duties of his office, or to injure his person while engaged in the lawful discharge of the duties of his office, or to injure his property so as to molest, interrupt, hinder, or impede him in the discharge of his official duty, or by force, intimidation, or threat to deter any party or witness in any court of the United States from attending such court, or from testifying in any matter pending in such court fully, freely, and truthfully, or to injure any such party or witness in his person or property on account of his having so attended or testified, or by force, intimidation, or threat to influence the verdict, presentment, or indictment, of any juror or grand juror in any court of the United States, or to injure such juror in his person or property on account of any verdict, presentment, or indictment lawfully assented to by him, or on account of his being or having been such juror, or shall conspire together, or go in disguise upon the public highway or upon the premises of another for the purpose, either directly or indirectly, of depriving any person or any class of persons of the equal protection of the laws, or of equal privileges or immunities under the laws, or for the purpose of preventing or hindering the constituted authorities of any State from giving or securing to all persons within such State the equal protection of the laws, or shall conspire together for the purpose of in any manner impeding, hindering, obstructing, or defeating the due course of justice in any State or Territory, with intent to deny to any citizen of the United States the due and equal protection of the laws, or to injure any person in his person or his property for lawfully enforcing the right of any person or class of persons to the equal protection of the laws, or by force, intimidation, or threat to prevent any citizen of the United States lawfully entitled to vote from giving his support or advocacy in a lawful manner towards or in favor of the election of any lawfuly qualified person as an elector of President or Vice-President of the United States, or as a member of the Congress of the United States, or to injure any such citizen in his person or property on account of such support or advocacy, each and every person so offending shall be deemed guilty of a high crime, and, upon conviction thereof in any district or circuit court of the United States or district or supreme court of any Territory of the United States having jurisdiction of similar offences, shall be punished by a fine not less than five hundred nor more than five thousand dollars, or by imprisonment, with or without hard labor, as the court may determine, for a period of not less than six months nor more than six years, as the court may determine, or by both such fine and imprisonment as the court shall determine. And if any one or more persons engaged in any such conspiracy shall do, or cause to be done, any act in furtherance of the object of such conspiracy, whereby any person shall be injured in his person or property, or deprived of having and exercising any right or privilege of a citizen of the United States, the person so injured or deprived of such rights and privileges may have and maintain an action for the recovery of damages occasioned by such injury or deprivation of rights and privileges against any one or more of the persons engaged in such conspiracy, such action to be prosecuted in the proper district or circuit court of the United States, with and subject to the same rights of appeal, review upon error, and other remedies provided in like cases in such courts under the provisions of the act of April ninth, eighteen hundred and sixty-six, entitled "An act to protect all persons in the United States in their civil rights, and to furnish the means of their vindication."

Sec. 3. That in all cases where insurrection, domestic violence, unlawful combinations, or conspiracies in any State shall so obstruct or hinder the execution of the laws thereof, and of the United States, as to deprive any portion or class of the people of such State of any of the rights, privileges, or immunities, or protection, named in the Constitution and secured by this act, and the constituted authorities of such State shall either be unable to protect, or shall, from any cause, fail in or refuse protection of the people in such rights, such facts shall be deemed a denial by such State of the equal protection of the laws to which they are entitled under the Constitution of the United States; and in all such cases, or whenever any such insurrection, violence, unlawful combination, or conspiracy shall oppose or obstruct the laws of the United States or the due execution thereof, or impede or obstruct the due course of justice under the same, it shall be lawful for the President, and it shall be his duty to take such measures, by the employment of the militia or the land and naval forces of the United States, or of either, or by other means, as he may deem necessary for the suppression of such insurrection, domestic violence, or combinations; and any person who shall be arrested under the provisions of this and the preceding section shall be delivered to the marshal of the proper district, to be dealt with according to law.

. . . .

Sec. 6. That any person or persons, having knowledge that any of the wrongs conspired to be done and mentioned in the second section of this act are about to be committed, and having power to prevent or aid in preventing the same, shall neglect or refuse so to do, and such wrongful act shall be committed, such person or persons shall be liable to the person injured, or his legal representatives, for all damages caused by any such wrongful act which such first-named person or persons by reasonable diligence could have prevented; and such damages may be recovered in an action on the case in the proper circuit court of the United States, and any number of persons guilty of such wrongful neglect or refusal may be joined as defendants in such action: *Provided*, That such action shall be commenced within one year after such cause of action shall have accrued; and if the death of any person shall be caused by any such wrongful act and neglect, the legal representatives of such deceased person shall have such action therefor, and may recover not exceeding five thousand dollars damages therein, for the benefit of the widow of such deceased person, if any there be, or if there be no widow, for the benefit of the next of kin of such deceased person.

Sec. 7. That nothing herein contained shall be construed to supersede or repeal any former act or law except so far as the same may be repugnant thereto; and any offences heretofore committed against the tenor of any former act shall be prosecuted, and any proceeding already commenced for the prosecution thereof shall be continued and completed, the same as if this act had not been passed, except so far as the provisions of this act may go to sustain and validate such proceedings.

APPROVED, April 20, 1871.

An act to protect all citizens in their civil and legal rights*

Whereas, it is essential to just government we recognize the equality of all men before the law, and hold that it is the duty of government in its dealings with the people to mete out equal and exact justice to all, of whatever nativity, race, color, or persuasion, religious or political; and it being the appropriate object of legislation to enact great fundamental principles into law: Therefore,

Be it enacted by the Senate and House of Representatives of the United States of America in Congress assembled, That all persons within the jurisdiction of the United States shall be entitled to the full and equal enjoyment of the accommodations, advantages, facilities, and privileges of inns, public conveyances on land or water, theaters, and other places of public amusement; subject only to the conditions and limitations established by law, and applicable alike to citizens of every race and color, regardless of any previous condition of servitude.

SEC. 2. That any person who shall violate the foregoing section by denying to any citizen, except for reasons by law applicable to citizens of every race and color, and regardless of any previous condition of servitude, the full enjoyment of any of the accommodations, advantages, facilities, or privileges in said section enumerated, or by aiding or inciting such denial, shall, for every such offense, forfeit and pay the sum of five hundred dollars to the person aggrieved thereby, to be recovered in an action of debt, with full costs; and shall also, for every such offense, be deemed guilty of a misde-

---

* 18 Stat. 335 (1875).

meanor, and, upon conviction thereof, shall be fined not less than five hundred nor more than one thousand dollars, or shall be imprisoned not less than thirty days nor more than one year: *Provided,* That all persons may elect to sue for the penalty aforesaid or to proceed under their rights at common law and by State statutes; and having so elected to proceed in the one mode or the other, their right to proceed in the other jurisdiction shall be barred. But this proviso shall not apply to criminal proceedings, either under this act or the criminal law of any State: *And provided further,* That a judgment for the penalty in favor of the party aggrieved, or a judgment upon an indictment, shall be a bar to either prosecution respectively.

SEC. 3. That the district and circuit courts of the United States shall have, exclusively of the courts of the several States, cognizance of all crimes and offenses against, and violations of, the provisions of this act; and actions for the penalty given by the preceding section may be prosecuted in the territorial, district, or circuit courts of the United States wherever the defendant may be found, without regard to the other party; and the district attorneys, marshals, and deputy marshals of the United States, and commissioners appointed by the circuit and territorial courts of the United States, with powers of arresting and imprisoning or bailing offenders against the laws of the United States, are hereby specially authorized and required to institute proceedings against every person who shall violate the provisions of this act, and cause him to be arrested and imprisoned or bailed, as the case may be, for trial before such court of the United States, or territorial court, as by law has cognizance of the offense, except in respect of the right of action accruing to the person aggrieved; and such district attorneys shall cause such proceedings to be prosecuted to their termination as in other cases: *Provided,* That nothing contained in this section shall be construed to deny or defeat any right of civil action accruing to any person, whether by reason of this act or otherwise; and any district attorney who shall willfully fail to institute and prosecute the proceedings herein required, shall, for every such offense, forfeit and pay the sum of five hundred dollars to the person aggrieved thereby, to be recovered by an action of debt, with full costs, and shall, on conviction thereof, be deemed guilty of a misdemeanor, and be fined not less than one thousand nor more than five thousand dollars: *And provided further,* That a judgment for the penalty in favor of the party aggrieved against any such district attorney, or a judgment upon an indictment against any such district attorney, shall be a bar to either prosecution respectively.

Sec. 4. That no citizen possessing all other qualifications which are or may be prescribed by law shall be disqualified for service as grand or petit juror in any court of the United States, or of any State, on account of race, color, or previous condition of servitude; and any officer or other person charged with any duty in the selection or summoning of jurors who shall exclude or fail to summon any citizen for the cause aforesaid shall, on conviction thereof, be deemed guilty of a misdemeanor, and be fined not more than five thousand dollars.

Sec. 5. That all cases arising under the provisions of this act in the courts of the United States shall be reviewable by the Supreme Court of the United States, without regard to the sum in controversy, under the same provisions and regulations as are now provided by law for the review of other causes in said court.

Approved, March 1, 1875.

THE FIFTEENTH AMENDMENT (1870)

The third and last of the Civil War amendments, the Fifteenth Amendment, has also had an unfortunate history. It was designed to grant Negroes the right of suffrage, and this was not, nor has it become, a universally popular idea. Ratification was demanded as a condition of readmittance for those few southern states still out of the Union, and it was only with their votes that the Amendment passed. New York rescinded her adoption of the Amendment, and it was rejected by California, Delaware, Kentucky, Maryland, Oregon, and Tennessee.

But mere passage of the Amendment and its enforcement legislation (Document 47) was not enough to guarantee franchise to the Negro. Poll taxes, literary tests, residence and registration requirements, and "grandfather clauses" all, in varying degrees, precluded equality at the polls in the years ahead. Supreme Court decisions enforcing Negro voting rights were eventually forthcoming (Documents 64, 76, and 93). But it was not until nearly a century later that the poll tax was outlawed by the Twenty-fourth Amendment, in 1964, and Congress passed the Voting Rights Act of 1965 (Document 92). Even then local practices made the Negro's right to vote a nullity in many areas.

DOCUMENT 48

Fifteenth Amendment*

SEC. 1. The right of citizens of the United States to vote shall not be denied or abridged by the United States or by any State on account of race, color, or previous condition of servitude.

SEC. 2. The Congress shall have power to enforce this article by appropriate legislation.

SENATOR BLANCHE K. BRUCE ON THE MISSISSIPPI ELECTION (1876)

The South remained unreconciled to the consequences of the Civil War and to the Reconstruction policies that included civil and political rights for Negroes. Despite the Fourteenth and Fifteenth Amendments and a series of federal enactments designed to protect Negro citizens and incorporate them on an equal footing into the body politic, white southerners regained local and state power. In so "redeeming" the South, these whites worked through the Democratic party and through a number of extra-legal organizations (such as the Ku Klux Klan, the Knights of the White Camelia, and the White League) committed to intimidation and violence as a means of suppressing Negroes.

Despite obstructionist activities, two Negroes did serve in the United States Senate during the Reconstruction period: Hiram R. Revels and Blanche K. Bruce, both from Mississippi.

---

* Small, Jayson, and Corwin, *op. cit.*, p. 1333.

At the end of March, 1876, Senator Bruce rose in the Senate to plead for a federal investigation of the violence which had stripped Mississippi Negroes of their civil and political rights. Bruce defended the Negro's role in public affairs and asked that existing laws be respected and enforced equitably.

DOCUMENT 49

*The Mississippi Election**

MR. BRUCE . . .

The conduct of the late election in Mississippi affected not merely the fortunes of partisans—as the same were necessarily involved in the defeat or success of the respective parties to the contest—but put in question and jeopardy the sacred rights of the citizen; and the investigation contemplated in the pending resolution has for its object not the determination of the question whether the offices shall be held and the public affairs of that State be administered by democrats or republicans, but the higher and more important end, the protection in all their purity and significance of the political rights of the people and the free institutions of the country. I believe the action sought is within the legitimate province of the Senate; but I shall waive a discussion of that phase of the question, and address myself to the consideration of the importance of the proposed investigation. . . .

The truth of the allegations relative to fraud and violence is strongly suggested by the very success claimed by the democracy. In 1873 the republicans carried the State by 20,000 majority; in November last the opposition claimed to have carried it by 30,000; thus a democratic gain of more than 50,000. Now, by what miraculous or extraordinary interposition was this brought about? I can conceive that a large State like New York, where free speech and free press operate upon intelligent masses—a State full of railroads, telegraphs, and newspapers—on the occasion of a great national contest, might furnish an illustration of such a thorough and general change in the political views of the people; but such a change of front is unnatural and highly

* *Congressional Record,* 44th Congress, 1st Session, March 31, 1876, pp. 2100–04.

improbable in a State like my own, with few railroads, and a widely scattered and sparse population. Under the most active and friendly canvass the voting masses could not have been so rapidly and thoroughly reached as to have rendered this result probable.

There was nothing in the character of the issues nor in the method of the canvass that would produce such an overwhelming revolution in the sentiments of the colored voters of the State as is implied in this pretended democratic success. The republicans—nineteen-twentieths of whom are colored—were not brought, through the press or public discussions, in contact with democratic influences to such an extent as would operate a change in their political convictions, and there was nothing in democratic sentiments nor in the proscriptive and violent temper of their leaders to justify such a change of political relations.

The evil practices so naturally suggested by this view of the question as probable will be found in many instances by the proposed investigation to have been actual. Not desiring to anticipate the work of the committee nor to weary Senators with details, I instance the single county of Yazoo as illustrative of the effects of the outrages of which we complain. This country gave in 1873 a republican majority of nearly two thousand. It was cursed with riot and bloodshed prior to the late election, and gave but seven votes for the republican ticket, and some of these, I am credibly informed, were cast in derision by the democrats, who declared that republicans must have some votes in the county. . . .

THE RECONSTRUCTION ERA CASES (1873–1883)

Overlapping the Reconstruction decade of 1865 to 1875 was a decade of Supreme Court decisions, from 1873 to 1883, which interpreted (and virtually paralyzed, both directly and indirectly) legislative action designed to enforce civil rights. The first of the major decisions was handed down in the Slaughter-House Cases (Document 50), and the last in the Civil Rights Cases (Document 54). In between were such landmark cases as *United States* v. *Cruikshank* (Document 51), *Hall* v. *DeCuir* (Document 52), and *Strauder* v. *West Virginia* (Document 53), with its companion cases *Virginia* v. *Rives,* 100 U.S. 313 (1880) and *Ex Parte Virginia,* 100 U.S. 339 (1880). Decisions were also handed down in *United States* v. *Reese,* 92 U.S. 214 (1876), which declared unconstitutional Sections 3 and 4 of the Enforcement Act of May 31, 1870 (Document 47), and *United States* v. *Harris,* 106 U.S. 629 (1883), which declared unconstitutional Section 2 of the Ku Klux Act of April 20, 1871 (Document 47).

Ironically, the Slaughter-House Cases involved neither racial discrimination nor Negroes. At issue was the constitutionality of a Louisiana statute granting to one particular slaughter-house syndicate the exclusive monopoly on butchering livestock in the New Orleans area. In the lawsuit which followed, it was argued that the monopoly legislation violated the privileges and immunities, due process, and equal protection clauses of the Fourteenth Amendment (Document 46).

The Supreme Court, in a five to four decision, held valid the Louisiana legislative grant. The majority took the position that the Fourteenth Amendment was solely designed to protect the newly freed Negroes from discrimination based on color and that the contesting New Orleans butchers did not come within that protected class.

What made this case so significant a barrier to civil rights enforcement was the Court's construction of the privileges and immunities clause. The Supreme Court denied that the Fourteenth Amendment had placed all issues of racial discrimination under federal control and held that only the privileges of *national* citizenship were protected. And national citizenship encompassed only such matters as, for example, access to seaports and travel to the District of Columbia, according to the majority of the Court. Thus few Negro rights could be enforced since equality in public education, public accommodations, and the like were deemed to be incidents of *state* citizenship.

DOCUMENT 50

The Butchers' Benevolent Association of New Orleans v. the Crescent City Live-Stock Landing and Slaughter-House Company, etc.*

Error to the Supreme Court of Louisiana. . . .

MR. JUSTICE MILLER . . . delivered the opinion of the court.

These cases are brought hereby writs of error to the Supreme Court of the State of Louisiana. They arise out of the efforts of the butchers of New Orleans to resist the Cresent City Live-Stock Landing and Slaughter-House Company in the exercise of certain powers conferred by the charter which created it, and which was granted by the legislature of that State.

The cases . . . were all decided by the Supreme Court of Louisiana in favor of the Slaughter-House Company, as we shall hereafter call it for the sake of brevity, and these writs are brought to reverse those decisions.

. . . .

It is not, and cannot be successfully controverted, that it is both the right and the duty of the legislative body—the supreme power of the State or municipality—to prescribe and determine the localities where the business of slaughtering for a great city may be conducted. To do this effectively it is indispensable that all persons who slaughter animals for food shall do it in those places *and nowhere else.*

The statute under consideration defines these localities and forbids slaughtering in any other. It does not, as has been asserted, prevent the butcher from doing his own slaughtering. On the contrary, the Slaughter-House Company is required, under a heavy penalty, to permit any person who wishes to do so, to slaughter in their houses; and they are bound to make ample provision for the convenience of all slaughtering for the entire city. The butcher then is still permitted to slaughter, to prepare, and to sell his own meats; but he is

---

* Supreme Court of the United States, 16 Wall. (83 U.S.) 36 (1873).

required to slaughter at a specified place and to pay reasonable compensation for the use of the accommodations furnished him at that place. . . .

It cannot be denied that the statute under consideration is aptly framed to remove from the more densely populated part of the city, the noxious slaughter-houses, and large and offensive collections of animals necessarily incident to the slaughtering business of a large city, and to locate them where the convenience, health, and comfort of the people require they shall be located. And it must be conceded that the means adopted by the act for this purpose are appropriate, are stringent, and effectual. But it is said that in creating a corporation for this purpose, and conferring upon it exclusive privileges—privileges which it is said constitute a monopoly—the legislature has exceeded its power. . . .

It may, therefore, be considered as established, that the authority of the legislature of Louisiana to pass the present statute is ample, unless some restraint in the exercise of that power be found in the constitution of that State or in the amendments to the Constitution of the United States adopted since the date of the decisions we have already cited.

If any such restraint is supposed to exist in the constitution of the State, the Supreme Court of Louisiana having necessarily passed on that question, it would not be open to review in this court.

The plaintiffs in error accepting this issue, allege that the statute is a violation of the Constitution of the United States in these several particulars:

That it creates an involuntary servitude forbidden by the thirteenth article of amendment;

That it abridges the privileges and immunities of citizens of the United States;

That it denies to the plaintiffs the equal protection of the laws; and,

That it deprives them of their property without due process of law; contrary to the provision of the first section of the fourteenth article of amendment.

This court is thus called upon for the first time to give construction to these articles.

• • • •

The institution of African slavery, as it existed in about half the States of the Union, and the contests pervading the public mind for many years, between those who desired its curtailment and ultimate extinction and those who desired additional safeguards for its security and perpetuation, culminated in the effort, on the part of most of the States in which slavery existed, to separate from the Federal government, and to resist its authority. This constituted the war of the rebellion, and whatever auxiliary causes may have contributed to bring about this war, undoubtedly the overshadowing and efficient cause was African slavery.

In that struggle slavery, as a legalized social relation, perished. It perished as a necessity of the bitterness and force of the conflict. When the armies of freedom found themselves upon the soil of slavery they could do nothing less than free the poor victims whose enforced servitude was the foundation of the quarrel. And when hard pressed in the contest these men (for they proved themselves men in that terrible crisis) offered their services and were accepted by thousands to aid in suppressing the unlawful rebellion, slavery was at an end wherever the Federal government succeeded in that purpose. The proclamation of President Lincoln expressed an accomplished fact as to a large portion of the insurrectionary districts, when he declared slavery abolished in them all. But the war being over, those who had succeeded in re-establishing the authority of the Federal government were not content to permit this great act of emancipation to rest on the actual results of the contest or the proclamation of the Executive, both of which might have been questioned in after times, and they determined to place this main and most valuable result in the Constitution of the restored Union as one of its fundamental articles. Hence the thirteenth article of amendment of that instrument. Its two short sections seem hardly to admit of construction, so vigorous is their expression and so appropriate to the purpose we have indicated.

. . . .

We repeat, then, in the light of this recapitulation of events, almost too recent to be called history, but which are familiar to us all; and on the most casual examination of the language of these amendments, no one can fail to be impressed with the one pervading purpose found in them all, lying at the foundation of each, and without which none of them would have been even suggested; we mean the freedom of the slave race, the security and firm establishment of that freedom, and the protection of the newly made freeman and citizen from the oppressions of those who had formerly exercised unlimited dominion over him. It is true that only the fifteenth amendment, in terms, mentions the negro by speaking of his color and his slavery. But it is just as true that each of the other articles was addressed to the grievances of that race, and designed to remedy them as the fifteenth.

We do not say that no one else but the negro can share in this protection. Both the language and spirit of these articles are to have their fair and just weight in any question of construction. Undoubtedly, while negro slavery alone was in the mind of the Congress which proposed the thirteenth article, it forbids any other kind of slavery, now or hereafter. If Mexican peonage or the Chinese coolie labor system shall develop slavery of the Mexican or Chinese race within our territory, this amendment may safely be trusted to make it void. And so, if other rights are assailed by the States which properly and necessarily fall within the protection of these articles, that protection will apply though the party interested may not be of African descent. But what we do say, and what we wish to be understood is, that in any fair and just construction of any section or phrase of these amendments, it is necessary to look to the purpose which we have said was the pervading spirit of them all, the evil which they were designed to remedy, and the process of continued addition to the Constitution until that purpose was supposed to be accomplished, as far as constitutional law can accomplish it.

The first section of the fourteenth article, to which our attention is more specially invited, opens with a definition of citizenship—not only citizenship of the United States, but citizenship of the States. No such definition was previously found in the Constitution, nor had any attempt been made to define it by act of Congress. It had been the occasion of much discussion in the courts, by the executive departments, and in the public journals. It had been said by eminent judges that no man was a citizen of the United States, except as he was a citizen of one of the States composing the Union. Those, therefore, who had been born and resided always in the District of Columbia or in the Territories, though within the United States, were not citizens. Whether this proposition was sound or not had never been judicially decided. But it had been held by this court, in the celebrated Dred Scott case, only a few years before the outbreak of the civil war, that a man of African descent, whether a slave or not, was not, and could not be a citizen of a State or of the United States. This decision, while it met the condemnation of some of the ablest statesmen and constitutional lawyers of the country, had never been overruled; and if it was to be accepted as a constitutional limitation of the right of citizenship, then all the negro race who had recently been made freemen, were still, not only not citizens, but were incapable of becoming so by anything short of an amendment to the Constitution.

To remove this difficulty primarily, and to establish a clear and comprehensive definition of citizenship which should declare what should constitute citizenship of the United States, and also citizenship of a State, the first clause of the first section was framed.

"All persons born or naturalized in the United States, and subject to the jurisdiction thereof, are citizens of the United States and of the State wherein they reside."

The first observation we have to make on this clause is, that it puts at rest both the questions which we stated to have been the subject of differences of opinion. It declares that persons may be citizens of the United States without regard to their citizenship of a particular State, and it overturns the Dred Scott decision by making *all persons* born within the United States and subject to its jurisdiction citizens of the United States. That its main purpose was to establish the citizenship of the negro can admit of no doubt. The phrase, "subject to its jurisdiction" was intended to exclude from its operation children of ministers, consuls and citizens or subjects of foreign States born within the United States.

The next observation is more important in view of the arguments of counsel in the present case. It is, that the distinction between citizenship of the United States and citizenship of a State is clearly recognized and established. Not only may a man be a citizen of the United States without being a citizen of a State, but an important element is necessary to convert the former into the latter. He must reside within the

State to make him a citizen of it, but it is only necessary that he should be born or naturalized in the United States to be a citizen of the Union.

It is quite clear, then, that there is a citizenship of the United States, and a citizenship of a State, which are distinct from each other, and which depend upon different characteristics or circumstances in the individual. . . .

Having shown that the privileges and immunities relied on in the argument are those which belong to citizens of the States as such, and that they are left to the State governments for security and protection, and not by this article placed under the special care of the Federal government, we may hold ourselves excused from defining the privileges and immunities of citizens of the United States which no State can abridge, until some case involving those privileges may make it necessary to do so.

But lest it be said that no such privileges and immunities are to be found if those we have been considering are excluded, we venture to suggest some which owe their existence to the Federal government, its National character, its Constitution, or its laws.

One of these is well described in the case of *Crandall* v. *Nevada* [6 Wall. (73 U.S.) 36 (1868)]. It is said to be the right of the citizen of this great country, protected by implied guarantees of its Constitution, "to come to the seat of government to assert any claim he may have upon that government, to transact any business he may have with it, to seek its protection, to share its offices, to engage in administering its functions. He has the right of free access to its seaports, through which all operations of foreign commerce are conducted, to the sub-treasuries, land offices, and courts of justice in the several states." And quoting from the language of Chief Justice Taney in another case, it is said "that *for all the great purposes for which the Federal government, was established, we are one people, with one common country, we are all citizens of the United States;*" and it is, as such citizens, that their rights are supported in this court in *Crandall* v. *Nevada.*

· · · ·

The adoption of the first eleven amendments to the Constitution so soon after the original instrument was accepted shows a prevailing sense of danger at that time from the Federal power. And it cannot be denied that such a jealousy continued to exist with many patriotic men until the breaking out of the late civil war. It was then discovered that the true danger to the perpetuity of the Union was in the capacity of the State organizations to combine and concentrate all the powers of the State, and of contiguous States, for a determined resistance to the General Government.

Unquestionably this has given great force to the argument, and added largely to the number who believe in the necessity of a strong National government.

But, however pervading this sentiment, and however it may have contributed to the adoption of the amendments we have been considering, we do not see in those amendments any purpose to destroy the main features of the general system. Under the pressure of all the excited feeling growing out of the war, our statesmen have still believed that the existence of the States with powers for domestic and local government, including the regulation of civil rights, the rights of person and of property, was essential to the perfect working of our complex form of government, though they have thought proper to impose additional limitations on the States, and to confer additional power on that of the Nation.

But whatever fluctuations may be seen in the history of public opinion on this subject during the period of our national existence, we think it will be found that this court, so far as its functions required, has always held, with a steady and an even hand, the balance between State and Federal power, and we trust that such may continue to be the history of its relation to that subject so long as it shall have duties to perform which demand of it a construction of the Constitution, or of any of its parts.

The judgments of the Supreme Court of Louisiana in these cases are AFFIRMED.

UNITED STATES V. CRUIKSHANK (1876)

Further whittling away the effectiveness of the Civil Rights Acts was the decision in *United States* v. *Cruikshank*. This case established the principle that the Fourteenth Amendment guarantees the rights of citizens only against encroachment by the *states*, and not against the actions of private individuals. In addition, it held that the violation by a private person of the civil rights of another could only be a crime when it interfered with an act connected with *national* citizenship. It also declared that the Constitution did not grant such rights as the right of assembly and the like; it merely forbade the Congress to infringe on such rights.

Before the Supreme Court were the convictions of three whites who were among a mob that had broken up a Negro meeting, killing two Negroes. The meeting had been convened to discuss local Louisiana elections.

Conviction had been based on Section 6 of the Enforcement Act of May 31, 1870. This was the general conspiracy section, which made it a federal crime for "two or more persons . . . [to] conspire together . . . to injure, oppress, threaten, or intimidate any citizen with intent to prevent or hinder his free exercise and enjoyment of any right or privilege granted or secured to him by the Constitution or laws of the United States." The Supreme Court ruled that the conviction could not stand.

While the Court refused to invoke this section to protect the right of assembly for a nonfederal purpose against encroachment by private persons, it did not declare it unconstitutional. Dicta hinted that the Court would have sustained the "right of the people peaceably to assemble for the purpose of petitioning Congress for a redress of grievances, or for any thing else connected with the powers or duties of the national government."

This fact was important to the Supreme Court decision in 1884 in *Ex parte Yarbrough*, 110 U.S. 651, involving the application of Rev. Stat. § 5508 (1875), which was derived from Section 6. The decision was also based on an interpretation of a similar provision, Rev. Stat. § 5520 (1875), derived from Section 2 of the Ku Klux Act of April 20, 1871 (Document 47). Here the Court upheld the conspiracy conviction of nine men who had beaten a Negro because he had votoed in a Congressional election.

DOCUMENT 51

*United States v. Cruikshank**

MR. CHIEF JUSTICE WAITE delivered the opinion of the court. . . .

The general charge in the first eight counts is that of "banding," and in the second eight, that of "conspiring" together to injure, oppress, threaten, and intimidate Levi Nelson and Alexander Tillman, citizens of the United States, of African descent and persons of color, with the intent thereby to hinder and prevent them in their free exercise and enjoyment of rights and privileges "granted and secured" to them "in common with all other good citizens of the United States by the constitution and laws of the United States." . . .

We have in our political system a government of the United States and a government of each of the several States. Each one of these governments is distinct from the others, and each has citizens of its own who owe it allegiance, and whose rights, within its jurisdiction, it must protect. The same person may be at the same time a citizen of the United States and a citizen of a State, but his rights of citizenship under one of these governments will be different from those he has under the other. *Slaughter-House Cases*, 16 Wall. 74. . . .

The first and ninth counts state the intent of the defendants to have been to hinder and prevent the citizens named in the free exercise and enjoyment of their "lawful right and privilege to peaceably assemble together with each other and with other citizens of the United States for a peaceful and lawful purpose." . . .

The particular amendment now under consideration assumes the existence of the right of the people to assemble for lawful purposes, and protects it against encroachment by Congress. The right was not created by the amendment; neither was its continuance guaranteed, except as against congressional interference. For their protection in its enjoyment, therefore, the people must look to the States. The power for that purpose was originally placed there, and it has never been surrendered to the United States.

---

* Supreme Court of the United States, 92 U.S. 542 (1876).

The right of the people peaceably to assemble for the purpose of petitioning Congress for a redress of grievances, or for any thing else connected with the powers or the duties of the national government, is an attribute of national citizenship, and, as such, under the protection of, and guaranteed by, the United States. The very idea of a government, republican in form, implies a right on the part of its citizens to meet peaceably for consultation in respect to public affairs and to petition for a redress of grievances. If it had been alleged in these counts that the object of the defendants was to prevent a meeting for such a purpose, the case would have been within the statute, and within the scope of the sovereignty of the United States. Such, however, is not the case. The offence, as stated in the indictment, will be made out, if it be shown that the object of the conspiracy was to prevent a meeting for any lawful purpose whatever. . . .

The third and eleventh counts are even more objectionable. They charge the intent to have been to deprive the citizens named, they being in Louisiana, "of their respective several lives and liberty of person without due process of law." This is nothing else than alleging a conspiracy to falsely imprison or murder citizens of the United States, being within the territorial jurisdiction of the State of Louisiana. . . . It is no more the duty or within the power of the United States to punish for a conspiracy to falsely imprison or murder within a State, than it would be to punish for false imprisonment or murder itself.

The fourteenth amendment prohibits a State from depriving any person of life, or property, without due process of law; but this adds nothing to the rights of one citizen as against another. . . .

The fourth and twelfth counts charge the intent to have been to prevent and hinder the citizens named, who were of African descent and persons of color, in "the free exercise and enjoyment of their several right and privilege to the full and equal benefit of all laws and proceedings, then and there before that time, enacted or ordained by the said State of Louisiana and by the United States; and then and there, at that time, being in force in the said State and District of Louisiana aforesaid, for the security of their respective persons and property, then and there, at that time enjoyed at and within said State and District of Louisiana by white persons, being citizens of said State of Louisiana and the United States, for the protection of the persons and property of said white citizens." There is no allegation that this was done because of the race or color of the persons conspired against. When stripped of its verbiage, the case as presented amounts to nothing more than that the defendants conspired to prevent certain citizens of the United States, being within the State of Louisiana, from enjoying the equal protection of the laws of the State and of the United States. . . .

The seventh and fifteenth counts are no better than the sixth and fourteenth. The intent here charged is to put the parties named in great fear of bodily harm, and to injure and oppress them, because, being and having been in all things qualified, they had voted "at an election before that time had and held according to law by the people of the said State of Louisiana, in said State, to wit, on the fourth day of November, A.D. 1872, and at divers other elections by the people of the State, also before that time had and held according to law." There is nothing to show that the elections voted at were any other than State elections, or that the conspiracy was formed on account of the race of the parties against whom the conspirators were to act. The charge as made is really of nothing more than a conspiracy to commit a breach of the peace within a State. Certainly it will not be claimed that the United States have the power or are required to do mere police duty in the States. If a State cannot protect itself against domestic violence, the United States may, upon the call of the executive, when the legislature cannot be convened, lend their assistance for that purpose. This is a guaranty of the Constitution (art. 4, sect. 4); but it applies to no case like this. . . .

The order of the Circuit Court arresting the judgment upon the verdict is, therefore, affirmed; and the cause remanded, with instructions to discharge the defendants.

HALL V. DECUIR (1878)

Prior to the passage of the Civil Rights Act of 1875 (Document 47), Louisiana had its own accommodations law. Louisiana's General Assembly passed a statute in 1869, requiring all common carriers operating in that state to give "equal rights and privileges in all parts of the conveyance, without distinction or discrimination on account of race or color."

The constitutionality of the federal act was not before the Supreme Court until 1883 in the Civil Rights Cases (Document 54). The constitutionality of the Louisiana law was in issue five years earlier. One Mrs. DeCuir, a Negro, was aboard a Mississippi steamboat that was en route from New Orleans to Vicksburg, Mississippi. Mrs. DeCuir's destination was Hermitage, Louisiana. Thus there existed a situation in which the vessel was in interstate commerce and the passenger was making an intrastate trip.

Because of her race, Mrs. DeCuir was refused accommodations in the cabin set apart for whites. She brought suit under the Louisiana act for the alleged mental and physical suffering resulting from that discrimination. The argument for the defense was that the statute was void as an attempt to "regulate commerce among the States"; this was in conflict with Article I, Section 8, Clause 3 of the Constitution. The Supreme Court declared the statute unconstitutional.

DOCUMENT 52

Hall v. DeCuir*

MR. CHIEF JUSTICE WAITE delivered the opinion of the court.

For the purposes of this case, we must treat the act of Louisiana of Feb. 23, 1869, as requiring those engaged in interstate commerce to give all persons travelling in that State, upon the public conveyances employed in such business, equal rights and privileges in all parts of the conveyance, without distinction or discrimination on account of race or color. Such was the construction given to that act in the courts below, and it is conclusive upon us as the construction of a State law by the State courts. It is with this provision of the statute alone that we have to deal. We have nothing whatever to do with it as a regulation of internal commerce,

---

* Supreme Court of the United States, 95 U.S. 485 (1878).

or as affecting any thing else than commerce among the States. . . .

But we think it may safely be said that State legislation which seeks to impose a direct burden upon inter-state commerce, or to interfere directly with its freedom, does encroach upon the exclusive power of Congress. The statute now under consideration, in our opinion, occupies that position. It does not act upon the business through the local instruments to be employed after coming within the State, but directly upon the business as it comes into the State from without or goes out from within. While it purports only to control the carrier when engaged within the State, it must necessarily influence his conduct to some extent in the management of his business throughout his entire voyage. His disposition of passengers taken up and put down within the State, or taken up within to be carried without, cannot but affect in a greater or lesser degree those taken up without and brought within, and sometimes those taken up and put down without. A passenger in the cabin set apart for the use of whites without the State must, when the boat comes within, share the accommodations of that cabin with such colored persons as may come on board afterwards, if the law is enforced.

It was to meet just such a case that the commercial clause in the Constitution was adopted. The river Mississippi passes through or along the borders of ten different States, and its tributaries reach many more. The commerce upon these waters is immense, and its regulation clearly a matter of national concern. If each State was at liberty to regulate the conduct of carriers while within its jurisdiction, the confusion likely to follow could not but be productive of great inconvenience and unnecessary hardship. Each State could provide for its own passengers and regulate the transportation of its own freight, regardless of the interests of others. Nay more, it could prescribe rules by which the carrier must be governed within the State in respect to passengers and property brought from without. On one side of the river or its tributaries he might be required to observe one set of rules, and on the other another. Commerce cannot flourish in the midst of such embarrassments. No carrier of passengers can conduct his business with satisfaction to himself, or comfort to those employing him, if on one side of a State line his passengers, both white and colored, must be permitted to occupy the same cabin, and on the other be kept separate. Uniformity in the regulations by which he is to be governed from one end to the other of his route is a necessity in his business, and to secure it Congress, which is untrammelled by State lines, has been invested with the exclusive legislative power of determining what such regulations shall be. If this statute can be enforced against those engaged in inter-state commerce, it may be as well against those engaged in foreign; and the master of a ship clearing from New Orleans for Liverpool, having passengers on board, would be compelled to carry all, white and colored, in the same cabin during his passage down the river, or be subject to an action for damages, "exemplary as well as actual," by any one who felt himself aggrieved because he had been excluded on account of his color.

. . . .

We confine our decision to the statute in its effect upon foreign and inter-state commerce, expressing no opinion as to its validity in any other respect.

Judgment will be reversed and the cause remanded, with instructions to reverse the judgment of the District Court, and direct such further proceedings in conformity with this opinion as may appear to be necessary; and it is

So ordered.

STRAUDER V. WEST VIRGINIA (1880)

Reviewing the course of judicial action on racial discrimination, Chief Justice Earl Warren used these words in *Brown* v. *Board of Education of Topeka* (Document 78): "In the first cases in this Court construing the Fourteenth Amendment, decided shortly after its adoption, the Court interpreted it as proscribing *all state-imposed* discrimination against the Negro race." (Emphasis supplied.) Four cases are then cited in Footnote 5 as authority for that statement. The first of these are the Slaughter-House Cases of 1873 (Document 50). The other three are decisions in which the Court invalidated *state action* practices restricting the right of Negroes to serve on juries. These were companion cases decided in 1880.

In the best known of the three opinions, *Strauder* v. *West Virginia,* the Court declared that a state statute barring Negroes from jury service violated the equal protection clause of the Fourteenth Amendment. Thus the Court reversed the murder conviction of a Negro who, under West Virginia law, was tried by an all-white jury.

The procedural structure in *Virginia* v. *Rives,* 100 U.S. 313 (1880), precluded judicial action to reverse the murder convictions of the Negroes tried by an all-white jury whose case was then before the Court. What the Supreme Court said, however, was significant as to Negro rights. While an accused does not have a legal right to a jury composed in whole or in part of members of his own race, jury commissioners are under obligation not to pursue a course of conduct in the administration of their office which would operate to discriminate in the selection of jurors on racial grounds.

Enforcement of Section 4 of the Civil Rights Act of 1875 (Document 47) was before the Supreme Court in *Ex parte Virginia,* 100 U.S. 339 (1880). A Virginia judge had been indicted under that section for excluding Negroes from the jury lists. The Court sustained the validity of the indictment, holding that the judge's conduct constituted state action. The Court noted:

We have said the prohibitions of the Fourteenth Amendment are addressed to the States. They are, "No *State* shall make or enforce a law which shall abridge the privileges or immunities of citizens of the United States, . . . nor deny to any person within its jurisdiction the equal protection of the laws." They have reference to actions of the political body denominated a State, by whatever instruments or in whatever modes that action may be taken. A State acts by its legislative, its executive, or its judicial authorities. It can act in no other way. The constitutional provision, therefore, must mean that no agency of the State, or of the officers or agents by whom its powers are exerted, shall deny to any person within its jurisdiction the equal protection of the laws. Whoever, by virtue of public position under a State government, deprives another of property, life, or liberty, without due process of law, or denies or takes away the equal protection of the laws, violates the constitutional inhibition; and as he acts in the name and for the State, and is clothed with the State's power, his act is that of the State. This must be so, or the constitutional prohibition has no meaning. Then the State has clothed one of its agents with power to annul or to evade it.

DOCUMENT 53

Strauder v. West Virginia*

Error to the Supreme Court of Appeals of the State of West Virginia.

MR. JUSTICE STRONG delivered the opinion of the court.

The plaintiff in error, a colored man, was indicted for murder in the Circuit Court of Ohio County, in West Virginia, on the 20th day of October, 1874, and upon trial was convicted and sentenced. The record was then removed to the Supreme Court of the State, and there the judgment of the Circuit Court was affirmed. The present case is a writ of error to that court, and it is now, in substance, averred that at the trial in the state court the defendant (now plaintiff in error) was denied rights to which he was entitled under the Constitution and laws of the United States.

In the Circuit Court of the State, before the trial of the indictment was commenced, the defendant presented his petition, verified by his oath, praying for a removal of the cause into the Circuit Court of the United States, assigning, as ground for the removal, that "by virtue of the laws of the State of West Virginia no colored man was eligible to be a member of the grand jury or to serve on a petit jury in the State; that white men are so eligible, and that by reason of his being a colored man and having been a slave, he had reason to believe, and did believe, he could not have the full and equal benefit of all laws and proceedings in the State of West Virginia for the security of his person as is enjoyed by white citizens, and that he had less chance of enforcing in the courts of the State his rights on the prosecution, as a citizen of the United States, and that the probabilities of a denial of them to him as such citizen on every trial which might take place on the indictment in the courts of the State

---

* Supreme Court of the United States, 100 U.S. 303 (1880).

were much more enhanced than if he was a white man." This petition was denied by the State court, and the cause was forced to trial. . . .

The law of the State to which reference was made in the petition for removal and in the several motions was enacted on the 12th of March, 1873 (Acts of 1872–73, p. 102), and it is as follows: "All white male persons who are twenty-one years of age and who are citizens of this State shall be liable to serve as jurors, except as herein provided." The persons excepted are State officials.

In this court, several errors have been assigned, and the controlling questions underlying them all are first, whether, by the Constitution and laws of the United States, every citizen of the United States has a right to a trial of an indictment against him by a jury selected and impanelled without discrimination against his race or color, because of race or color; and, second, if he has such a right, and is denied its enjoyment by the State in which he is indicted, may he cause the case to be removed into the Circuit Court of the United States?

It is to be observed that the first of these questions is not whether a colored man, when an indictment has been preferred against him, has a right to a grand or a petit jury composed in whole or in part of persons of his own race or color, but it is whether, in the composition or selection of jurors by whom he is to be indicted or tried, all persons of his race or color may be excluded by law solely because of their race or color, so that by no possibility can any colored man sit upon the jury.

The questions are important, for they demand a construction of the recent amendments of the Constitution. If the defendant has a right to have a jury selected for the trial of his case without discrimination against all persons of his race or color, because of their race or color, the right, if not created, is protected by those amendments, and the legislation of Congress under them. The Fourteenth Amendment ordains that: "all persons born or naturalized in the United States and subject to the jurisdiction thereof are citizens of the United States and of the State wherein they reside. No State shall make or enforce any laws which shall abridge the privileges or immunities of citizens of the United States, nor shall any State deprive any person of life, liberty, or property, without due process of law, nor deny to any person within its jurisdiction the equal protection of the laws."

This is one of a series of constitutional provisions having a common purpose; namely, securing to a race recently emancipated, a race that through many generations had been held in slavery, all the civil rights that the superior race enjoy. The true spirit and meaning of the amendments, as we said in the Slaughter-House Cases (16 Wall. 36), cannot be understood without keeping in view the history of the times when they were adopted, and the general objects they plainly sought to accomplish. At the time when they were incorporated into the Constitution, it required little knowledge of human nature to anticipate that those who had long been regarded as an inferior and subject race would, when suddenly raised to the rank of citizenship, be looked upon with jealousy and positive dislike, and that State laws might be enacted or enforced to perpetuate the distinctions that had before existed. Discriminations against them had been habitual. It was well known that in some States laws making such discriminations then existed, and others might well be expected. The colored race, as a race, was abject and ignorant, and in that condition was unfitted to command the respect of those who had superior intelligence. Their training had left them mere children, and as such they needed the protection which a wise government extends to those who are unable to protect themselves. They especially needed protection against unfriendly action in the States where they were resident. It was in view of these considerations the Fourteenth Amendment was framed and adopted. It was designed to assure to the colored race the enjoyment of all the civil rights that under the law are enjoyed by white persons, and to give to that race the protection of the general government, in that enjoyment, whenever it should be denied by the States. It not only gave citizenship and the privileges of citizenship to persons of color, but it denied to any State the power to withhold from them the equal protection of the laws, and authorized Congress to enforce its provisions by appropriate legislation. . . .

If this is the spirit and meaning of the amendment, whether it means more or not, it is to be construed liberally, to carry out the purposes of its framers. It ordains that no State shall make or enforce any laws which shall abridge the privileges or immunities of citizens of the United States (evidently referring to the newly made citizens, who, being citizens of the United States, are declared to be also citizens of the State in which they reside). It ordains that no State shall deprive any person of life, liberty, or property, without due process of law, or deny to any person within its jurisdiction the equal protection of the laws. What is this but declaring that the law in the States shall be the same for the black as for the white; that all persons, whether colored or white, shall stand equal before the laws of the States, and, in regard to the colored race, for whose protection the amendment was primarily designed, that no discrimination shall be made against them by law because of their color? The words of the amendment, it is true, are prohibitory, but they contain a necessary implication of a positive immunity, or right, most valuable to the colored race,—the right to exemption from unfriendly legislation against them distinctively as colored,—exemption from legal discriminations, implying inferiority in civil society, lessening the security of their enjoyment of the rights which others enjoy, and discriminations which are steps towards reducing them to the condition of a subject race.

That the West Virginia statute respecting juries—the statute that controlled the selection of the grand and petit jury in the case of the plaintiff in error—is such a discrimination ought not to be doubted. Nor would it be if the persons excluded by it were white men. If in those States where the colored people constitute a majority of the entire population a law should be enacted excluding all white men from jury service, thus denying to them the privilege of participating equally with the blacks in the administration of justice, we apprehend no one would be heard to claim that it would not be a denial to white men of the equal protection of the laws. Nor if a law should be passed excluding all naturalized Celtic Irishmen, would there be any doubt of its inconsistency with the spirit of the amendment. The very fact that colored people are singled out and expressly denied by a statute all right to participate in the administration of the law, as jurors, because of their color, though they are citizens, and may be in other respects fully qualified, is practically a brand upon them, affixed by the law, an assertion of their inferiority, and a stimulant to that race prejudice which is an impediment to securing to individuals of the race that equal justice which the law aims to secure to all others.

. . . .

We do not say that within the limits from which it is not excluded by the amendment a State may not prescribe the qualifications of its jurors, and in so doing make discriminations. It may confine the selection to males, to freeholders, to citizens, to persons within certain ages, or to persons having educational qualifications. We do not believe the Fourteenth Amendment was ever intended to prohibit this. Looking at its history, it is clear it had no such purpose. Its aim was against discrimination because of race or color. . . .

The Fourteenth Amendment makes no attempt to enumerate the rights it designed to protect. It speaks in general terms, and those are as comprehensive as possible. Its language is prohibitory; but every prohibition implies the existence of rights and immunities, prominent among which is an immunity from inequality of legal protection, either for life, liberty or property. Any State action that denies this immunity to a colored man is in conflict with the Constitution. . . .

Concluding, therefore, that the statute of West Virginia, discriminating in the selection of jurors, as it does, against negroes because of their color, amounts to a denial of the equal protection of the laws to a colored man when he is put upon trial for an alleged offence against the State, it remains only to be considered whether the power of Congress to enforce the provisions of the Fourteenth Amendment by approprite legislation is sufficient to justify the enactment of section 641 of the Revised Statutes. . . .

That the petition of the plaintiff in error, filed by him in the State court before the trial of his case, made a case for removal into the Federal Circuit Court, under sect. 641, is very plain, if, by the constitutional amendment and sect. 1977 of the Revised Statutes, he was entitled to immunity from discrimination against him in the selection of jurors, because of their color, as we have endeavored to show that he was. It set forth sufficient facts to exhibit a denial of that immunity, and a denial by the statute law of the State.

There was error, therefore, in proceeding to the trial of the indictment against him after his petition was filed, as also in overruling his challenge to the array of the jury, and in refusing to quash the panel.

The judgment of the Supreme Court of West Virginia will be reversed, and the case remitted with instructions to reverse the judgment of the Circuit Court of Ohio county; and it is

So ordered.

THE CIVIL RIGHTS CASES (1883)

With its decision in the Civil Rights Cases in 1883, the Supreme Court completed the virtual nullification of the Reconstruction era legislation designed to give equality to the Negro. Struck down as unconstitutional were Sections 1 and 2, the vital accommodations sections of the Civil Rights Act of March 1, 1875 (Document 47). This case, coupled with at least eight other decisions which had been handed down since 1873, permitted the maintenance of segregation-discrimination patterns throughout the nation, despite the Thirteenth, Fourteenth, and Fifteenth Amendments.

The five suits which made up the Civil Rights Cases were proceedings against private individuals who had denied the admission of "persons of color" to hotels and theaters. In quashing the indictments and in setting aside the convictions of the accused, the Court stated that the statutory provisions of the Civil Rights Act of 1875 went beyond the authority of Congress under both the Thirteenth and Fourteenth Amendments.

Here was the Court's reasoning: Denial of equal accommodations imposes no "badge of slavery" upon the person affected; and since the Thirteenth Amendment relates only to slavery, the Amendment is no source of power for the Congressional imposition of punishment for mere discriminatory practices. Further, since the Fourteenth Amendment speaks only to the states, Congress may only pass laws affecting discrimination by the states and not by private citizens.

Important to an understanding of the Civil Rights Cases and the later Supreme Court decisions on racial discrimination is the opinion of the lone dissenter, Justice John Marshall Harlan. In his words: "The [majority] opinion . . . proceeds . . . upon grounds entirely too narrow and artificial. . . . Constitutional provisions, adopted in the interest of liberty, . . . have been so construed as to defeat the ends the people desire to accomplish . . ." (109 U.S. 3, 26). Justice Harlan wrote an even more significant dissent thirteen years later in *Plessy v. Ferguson* (Document 58).

DOCUMENT 54

Civil Rights Cases[*]

These cases were all founded on the first and second sections of the Act of Congress, known as the Civil Rights Act, passed March 1st, 1875, entitled "An Act to protect all citizens in their civil and legal rights." 18 Stat. 335. Two of the cases, those against Stanley and Nichols, were indictments for denying to persons of color the accommodations and privileges of an inn or hotel; two of them, those against Ryan and Singleton, were, one on information, the other an indictment, for denying to individuals the privileges and accommodations of a theatre, the information against Ryan being for refusing a colored person a seat in the dress circle of Maguire's Theatre in San Francisco; and the indictment against Singleton was for denying to another person, whose color was not stated, the full enjoyment of the accommodations of the theatre known as the Grand Opera House in New York, "said denial not being made for any reasons by law applicable to citizens of every race and color, and regardless of any previous condition of servitude." The case of Robinson and wife against the Memphis & Charleston R. R. Company was an action brought in the Circuit Court of the United States for the Western District of Tennessee, to recover the penalty of five hundred dollars given by the second section of the act; and the gravamen was the refusal by the conductor of the railroad company to allow the wife to ride in the ladies' car, for the reason, as stated in one of the counts, that she was a person of African descent.

. . . .

Mr. Justice Bradley delivered the opinion of the court. After stating the facts in the above language he continued:

---

[*] Supreme Court of the United States, 109 U.S. 3 (1883).

It is obvious that the primary and important question in all the cases is the constitutionality of the law: for if the law is unconstitutional none of the prosecutions can stand. . . .

Are these sections constitutional? The first section, which is the principal one, cannot be fairly understood without attending to the last clause, which qualifies the preceding part.

The essence of the law is, not to declare broadly that all persons shall be entitled to the full and equal enjoyment of the accommodations, advantages, facilities, and privileges of inns, public conveyances, and theatres; but that such enjoyment shall not be subject to any conditions applicable only to citizens of a particular race or color, or who had been in a previous condition of servitude. In other words, it is the purpose of the law to declare that, in the enjoyment of the accommodations and privileges of inns, public conveyances, theatres, and other places of public amusement, no distinction shall be made between citizens of different race or color, or between those who have, and those who have not, been slaves. Its effect is to declare, that in all inns, public conveyances, and places of amusement, colored citizens, whether formerly slaves or not, and citizens of other races, shall have the same accommodations and privileges in all inns, public conveyances, and places of amusement as are enjoyed by white citizens; and *vice versa*. The second section makes it a penal offence in any person to deny to any citizen of any race or color, regardless of previous servitude, any of the accommodations or privileges mentioned in the first section.

Has Congress constitutional power to make such a law? Of course, no one will contend that the power to pass it was contained in the Constitution before the adoption of the last three amendments. The power is sought, first, in the Fourteenth Amendment, and the views and arguments of distinguished Senators, advanced whilst the law was under consideration, claiming authority to pass it by virtue of that amendment, are the principal arguments adduced in favor of the power. We have carefully considered those arguments, as was due to the eminent ability of those who put them forward, and have felt, in all its force, the weight of authority which always invests a law that Congress deems itself competent to pass. But the responsibility of an independent judgment is now thrown upon this court; and we are bound to exercise it according to the best lights we have.

The first section of the Fourteenth Amendment (which is the one relied on), after declaring who shall be citizens of the United States, and of the several States, is prohibitory in its character, and prohibitory upon the States. . . .

It is State action of a particular character that is prohibited. Individual invasion of individual rights is not the subject-matter of the amendment. It has a deeper and broader scope. It nullifies and makes void all State legislation, and State action of every kind, which impairs the privileges and immunities of citizens of the United States, or which injures them in life, liberty or property without due process of law, or which denies to any of them the equal protection of the laws. It not only does this, but, in order that the national will, thus declared, may not be a mere *brutum fulmen,* the last section of the amendment invests Congress with power to enforce it by appropriate legislation. To enforce what? To enforce the prohibition. To adopt appropriate legislation for correcting the effects of such prohibited State laws and State acts, and thus to render them effectually null, void, and innocuous. This is the legislative power conferred upon Congress, and this is the whole of it. It does not invest Congress with power to legislate upon subjects which are within the domain of State legislation; but to provide modes of relief against State legislation, or State action, of the kind referred to. It does not authorize Congress to create a code of municipal law for the regulation of private rights; but to provide modes of redress against the operation of State laws, and the action of State officers executive or judicial, when these are subversive of the fundamental rights specified in the amendment. Positive rights and privileges are undoubtedly secured by the Fourteenth Amendment; but they are secured by way of prohibition against State laws and State proceedings affecting those rights and privileges, and by power given to Congress to legislate for the purpose of carrying such prohibition into effect: and such legislation must necessarily be predicated upon such supposed State laws or State proceedings, and be directed to the correction of their operation and effect. A quite full discussion of this aspect of the amendment may be found in *United States* v. *Cruikshank,* 92 U.S. 542; *Virginia* v. *Rives,* 100 U.S. 313; and *Ex parte Virginia,* 100 U.S. 339. . . .

And so in the present case, until some State law has been passed, or some State action through its officers or agents has been taken, adverse to the rights of citizens sought to be protected by the Fourteenth Amendment, no legislation of the United States under said amendment, nor any proceeding under such legislation, can be called into activity: for the prohibitions of the amendment are against State laws and acts done under State authority. Of course, legislation may, and should be, provided in advance to meet the exigency when it arises; but it should be adapted to the mischief and wrong which the amendment was intended to provide against; and that is, State laws, or State action of some kind, adverse to the rights of the citizen secured by the amendment. Such legislation cannot properly cover the whole domain of rights appertaining to life, liberty and property, defining them and providing for their vindication. That would be to establish a code of municipal law regulative of all private rights between man and man in society. It would be to make Congress take the place of the State legislatures and to supersede them. It is absurd to affirm that, because the rights of life, liberty and property (which include all civil rights that men have), are by the amendment sought to be protected against invasion on the part of the State without due process of law, Congress may therefore provide due process of law for their vindication in every case; and that, because the denial by a State to any persons, of the equal protection of the laws, is prohibited by the amendment, therefore Congress may establish laws for their equal protection. In fine, the legislation which Congress is authorized to adopt in this behalf is not general legislation upon the rights of the citizen, but corrective legislation, that is, such as may be necessary and proper for counteracting such laws as the States may adopt or enforce, and which, by the amendment, they are prohibited from making or enforcing, or such acts and proceedings as the States may commit or take, and which, by the amendment, they are prohibited from committing or taking. It is not necessary for us to state, if we could, what legislation would be proper for Congress to adopt. It is sufficient for us to examine whether the law in question is of that character.

An inspection of the law shows that it makes no difference whatever to any supposed or apprehended violation of the Fourteenth Amendment on the part of the States. It is not predicated on any such view. It proceeds *ex directo* to declare that certain acts committed by individuals shall be deemed offences, and shall be prosecuted and punished by proceedings in the courts of the United States. It does not profess to be corrective of any constitutional wrong committed by the States; it does not make its operation to depend upon any such wrong committed. It applies equally to cases arising in States which have the justest laws respecting the personal rights of citizens, and whose authorities are ever ready to enforce such laws, as to those which arise in States that may have violated the prohibition of the amendment. In other words, it steps into the domain of local jurisprudence, and lays down rules for the conduct of individuals in society towards each other, and imposes sanctions for the enforcement of those rules, without referring in any manner to any supposed action of the State or its authorities.

If this legislation is appropriate for enforcing the prohibitions of the amendment, it is difficult to see where it is to stop. Why may not Congress with equal show of authority enact a code of laws for the enforcement and vindication of all rights of life, liberty and property? If it is supposable that the States may deprive persons of life, liberty and property without due process of law (and the amendment itself does suppose this), why should not Congress proceed at once to prescribe due process of law for the protection of every one of these fundamental rights, in every possible case, as well as to prescribe equal privileges in inns, public conveyances, and theatres? The truth is, that the implication of a power to legislate in this manner is based upon the assumption that if the States are forbidden to legislate or act in a particular way on a particular subject, and power is conferred upon Congress to enforce the prohibition, this gives Congress power to legislate generally upon that subject, and not merely power to provide modes of redress against such State legislation or action. The assumption is certainly unsound. It is repugnant to the Tenth Amendment of the Constitution, which declares that powers not delegated to the United States by the Constitution, nor prohibited by it to the States, are reserved to the States respectively or to the people.

. . . .

If the principles of interpretation which we have laid down are correct, as we deem them to be (and they are in accord with the principles laid down in the cases before referred to, as well as in the recent case of *United States* v. *Harris,* 106 U.S. 629), it is clear that the law in question cannot be sustained by any grant of legislative power made to Congress by the Fourteenth Amendment. That amendment prohibits the States from denying to any person the equal protection of the laws, and declares that Congress shall have power to enforce, by appropriate legislation, the provisions of the amendment. The law in question, without any reference to adverse State legislation on the subject, declares that all persons shall be entitled to equal accommodations and privileges of inns, public conveyances, and places of public amusement, and imposes a penalty upon any individual who shall deny to any citizen such equal accommodations and privileges. This is not corrective legislation; it is primary and direct; it takes immediate and absolute possession of the subject of the right of admission to inns, public conveyances, and places of amusement. It supersedes and displaces State legislation on the same subject, or only allows it permissive force. It ignores such legislation, and assumes that the matter is one that belongs to the domain of national regulation. Whether it would not have been a more effective protecton of the rights of citizens to have clothed Congress with plenary power over the whole subject, is not now the question. What we have to decide is, whether such plenary power has been conferred upon Congress by the Fourteenth Amendment; and, in our judgment, it has not.

· · · ·

Now, conceding, for the sake of the argument, that the admission to an inn, a public conveyance, or a place of public amusement, on equal terms with all other citizens, is the right of every man and all classes of men, is it any more than one of those rights which the states by the Fourteenth Amendment are forbidden to deny to any person? And is the Constitution violated until the denial of the right has some State sanction or authority? Can the act of a mere individual, the owner of the inn, the public conveyance or place of amusement, refusing the accommodation, be justly regarded as imposing any badge of slavery or servitude upon the applicant, or only as inflicting an ordinary civil injury, properly cognizable by the laws of the State, and presumably subject to redress by those laws until the contrary appears?

After giving to these questions all the consideration which their importance demands, we are forced to the conclusion that such an act of refusal has nothing to do with slavery or involuntary servitude, and that if it is violative of any right of the party, his redress is to be sought under the laws of the State; or if those laws are adverse to his rights and do not protect him, his remedy will be found in the corrective legislation which Congress has adopted, or may adopt, for counteracting the effect of State laws, or State action, prohibited by the Fourteenth Amendment. It would be running the slavery argument into the ground to make it apply to every act of discrimination which a person may see fit to make as to the guests he will entertain, or as to the people he will take into his coach or cab or car, or admit to his concert or theatre, or deal with in other matters of intercourse or business. Innkeepers and public carriers, by the laws of all the States, so far as we are aware, are bound, to the extent of their facilities, to furnish proper accommodation to all unobjectionable persons who in good faith apply for them. If the laws themselves make any unjust discrimination, amenable to the prohibitions of the Fourteenth Amendment, Congress has full power to afford a remedy under that amendment and in accordance with it.

When a man has emerged from slavery, and by the aid of beneficent legislation has shaken off the inseparable concomitants of that state, there must be some stage in the progress of his elevation when he takes the rank of a mere citizen, and ceases to be the special favorite of the laws, and when his rights as a citizen, or a man, are to be protected in the ordinary modes by which other men's rights are protected. There were thousands of free colored people in this country before the abolition of slavery, enjoying all the essential rights of life, liberty and property the same as white citizens; yet no one, at that time, thought that it was any invasion of his personal status as a freeman because he was not admitted to all the privileges enjoyed by white citizens, or because he was subjected to discriminations in the enjoyment of accommodations in inns, public conveyances and places of amusement. Mere discriminations on account of race or color were not regarded as badges of slavery. If, since that time, the enjoyment of equal rights in all these respects has become established by constitutional enactment, it is not by force of the Thirteenth Amendment (which merely abolishes slavery), but by force of the Thirteenth and Fifteenth Amendments.

On the whole we are of opinion, that no countenance of authority for the passage of the law in question can be found in either the Thirteenth or Fourteenth Amendment of the Constitution; and no other ground of authority for its passage being suggested, it must necessarily be declared void, at least so far as its operation in the several States is concerned. . . . *And it is so ordered.*

Mr. Justice Harlan dissenting.

The opinion in these cases proceeds, it seems to me, upon grounds entirely too narrow and artificial. I cannot resist the conclusion that the substance and spirit of the recent amendments of the Constitution have been sacrificed by a subtle and ingenious verbal criticism. "It is not the words of the law but the internal sense of it that makes the law, the letter of the law is the body; the sense and reason of the law is the soul." Constitutional provisions, adopted in the interest of liberty, and for the purpose of securing, through national legislation, if need be, rights inhering in a state of freedom, and belonging to American citizenship, have been so construed as to defeat the ends the people desired to accomplish, which they attempted to accomplish, and which they supposed they had accomplished by changes in their fundamental law. By this I do not mean that the determination of these cases should have been materially controlled by considerations of mere expediency or policy. I mean only, in this form, to express an earnest conviction that the court has departed from the familiar rule requiring, in the interpretation of constitutional provisions, that full effect be given to the intent with which they were adopted. . . .

I am of the opinion that such discrimination practised by corporations and individuals in the exercise of their public or quasi-public functions is a badge of servitude the imposition of which Congress may prevent under its power, by appropriate legislation, to enforce the Thirteenth Amendment; and, consequently, without reference to its enlarged power under the Fourteenth Amendment, the act of March 1, 1875, is not, in my judgment, repugnant to the Constitution.

It remains now to consider these cases with reference to the power Congress has possessed since the adoption of the Fourteenth Amendment. Much that has been said as to the power of Congress under the Thirteenth Amendment is applicable to this branch of the discussion, and will not be repeated.

Before the adoption of the recent amendments, it had become, as we have seen, the established doctrine of this court that negroes, whose ancestors had been imported and sold as slaves, could not become citizens of a State, or even of the United States, with the rights and privileges guaranteed to citizens by the national Constitution; further, that one might have all the rights and privileges of a citizen of a State without being a citizen in the sense in which that word was used in the national Constitution, and without being entitled to the privileges and immunities of citizens of the several States. Still, further, between the adoption of the Thirteenth Amendment and the proposal by Congress of the Fourteenth Amendment, on June 16, 1866, the statute books of several of the States, as we have seen, had become loaded down with enactments which, under the guise of Apprentice, Vagrant, and Contract regulations, sought to keep the colored race in a condition, practically, of servitude. It was openly announced that whatever might be the rights which persons of that race had, as freemen, under the guarantees of the national Constitution, they could not become citizens of a State, with the privileges belonging to citizens, except by the consent of such State; consequently, that their civil rights, as citizens of the State, depended entirely upon State legislation. To meet this new peril to the black race, that the purposes of the nation might not be doubted or defeated, and by way of further enlargement of the power of Congress, the Fourteenth Amendment was proposed for adoption. . . .

The assumption that this amendment consists wholly of prohibitions upon State laws and State proceedings in hostility to its provisions, is unauthorized by its language. The first clause of the first section—"All persons born or naturalized in the United States, and subject to the jurisdiction thereof, are citizens of the United States, and of the State wherein they reside"—is of a distinctly affirmative character. In its application to the colored race, previously liberated, it created and granted, as well citizenship of the United States, as citizenship of the State in which they respectively resided. It introduced all of that race, whose ancestors had been imported and sold as slaves, at once, into the political community known as the "People of the United States." They became, instantly, citizens of the United States, *and* of their respective States. Further, they were brought, by this supreme act of the nation, within the direct operation of that provision of the Constitution which declares that "the citizens of each State shall be entitled to all privileges and immunities of citizens in the several States." Art. 4, § 2.

The citizenship thus acquired, by that race, in virtue of an affirmative grant from the nation, may be protected, not alone by the judicial branch of the government, but by congressional legislation of a primary direct character; this, because the power of Congress is not restricted to the enforcement of prohibitions upon State laws or State action. It is, in terms distinct and positive, to enforce "the *provisions* of *this article*" of amendment; not simply those of a prohibitive character, but the provisions—*all* of the provisions—affirmative and prohibitive, of the amendment. It is, therefore, a grave misconception to suppose that the fifth section of the amendment has reference exclusively to express prohibitions upon State laws or State action. If any right was created by that amendment, the grant of power, through appropriate legislation, to enforce its provisions, authorizes Congress, by means of legislation, operating throughout the entire Union, to guard, secure, and protect that right. . . .

But what was secured to colored citizens of the United States—as between them and their respective States—by the national grant to them of State citizenship? With what rights, privileges, or immunities did this grant invest them? There is one, if there be no other—exemption from race discrimination in respect of any civil right belonging to citizens of the white race in the same State. That, surely, is their constitutional privilege when within the jurisdiction of other States. And such must be their constitutional right, in their own State, unless the recent amendments be splendid baubles, thrown out to delude those who deserved fair and generous treatment at the hands of the nation. Citizenship in this country necessarily imports at least equality of civil rights among citizens of every race in the same State. It is fundamental in American citizenship that, in respect of such rights, there shall be no

discrimination by the State, or its officers, or by individuals
or corporations exercising public functions or authority, against
any citizen because of his race or previous condition of servitude. . . .

This court has always given a broad and liberal construction
to the Constitution, so as to enable Congress, by legislation,
to enforce rights secured by that instrument. The legislation
which Congress may enact, in execution of its power to enforce the provisions of this amendment, is such as may be
appropriate to protect the right granted. The word appropriate
was undoubtedly used with reference to its meaning, as
established by repeated decisions of this court. Under given
circumstances, that which the court characterizes as corrective
legislation might be deemed by Congress appropriate and
entirely sufficient. Under other circumstances primary direct
legislation may be required. But it is for Congress, not the
judiciary, to say what legislation is appropriate—that is—best
adapted to the end to be attained. The judiciary may not,
with safety to our institutions, enter the domain of legislative
discretion, and dictate the means which Congress shall employ
in the exercise of its granted powers. That would be sheer
usurpation of the functions of a co-ordinate department,
which, if often repeated, and permanently acquiesced in,
would work a radical change in our system of government. . . .

It does not seem to me that the fact that, by the second
clause of the first section of the Fourteenth Amendment, the
States are expressly prohibited from making or enforcing laws
abridging the privileges and immunities of citizens of the
United States, furnishes any sufficient reason for holding or
maintaining that the amendment was intended to deny Congress the power, by general, primary, and direct legislation, of
protecting citizens of the several States, being also citizens of
the United States, against all discrimination, in respect of their
rights as citizens, which is founded on race, color, or previous
condition of servitude.

Such an interpretation of the amendment is plainly repugnant to its fifth section, conferring upon Congress power, by
appropriate legislation, to enforce not merely the provisions
containing prohibitions upon the States, but all of the provisions of the amendment, including the provisions, express
and implied, in the first clause of the first section of the article
granting citizenship. This alone is sufficient for holding that

Congress is not restricted to the enactment of laws adapted to counteract and redress the operation of State legislation, or the action of State officers, of the character prohibited by the amendment. It was perfectly well known that the great danger to the equal enjoyment by citizens of their rights, as citizens, was to be apprehended not altogether from unfriendly State legislation, but from the hostile action of corporations and individuals in the States. And it is to be presumed that it was intended, by that section, to clothe Congress with power and authority to meet that danger. If the rights intended to be secured by the act of 1875 are such as belong to the citizen, in common or equally with other citizens in the same State, then it is not to be denied that such legislation is peculiarly appropriate to the end which Congress is authorized to accomplish, viz., to protect the citizen, in respect of such rights, against discrimination on account of his race. . . .

It was said of the case of *Dred Scott* v. *Sandford,* that this court, there overruled the action of two generations, virtually inserted a new clause in the Constitution, changed its character, and made a new departure in the workings of the federal government. I may be permitted to say that if the recent amendments are so construed that Congress may not, in its own discretion, and independently of the action or non-action of the States, provide, by legislation of a direct character, for the security of rights created by the national Constitution; if it be adjudged that the obligation to protect the fundamental privileges and immunities granted by the Fourteenth Amendment to citizens residing in the several States, rests primarily, not on the nation, but on the States; if it be further adjudged that individuals and corporations, exercising public functions, or wielding power under public authority, may, without liability to direct primary legislation on the part of Congress, make the race of citizens the ground for denying them that equality of civil rights which the Constitution ordains as a principle of republican citizenship; then, not only the foundations upon which the national supremacy has always securely rested will be materially disturbed, but we shall enter upon an era of constitutional law, when the rights of freedom and American citizenship cannot receive from the nation that efficient protection which heretofore was unhesitatingly accorded to slavery and the rights of the master. . . .

In every material sense applicable to the practical enforcement of the Fourteenth Amendment, railroad corporations, keepers of inns, and managers of places of public amusement are agents or instrumentalities of the State, because they are charged with duties to the public, and are amenable, in respect of their duties and functions, to governmental regulation. It seems to me that, within the principle settled in *Ex parte Virginia*, a denial, by these instrumentalities of the State, to the citizen, because of his race, of that equality of civil rights secured to him by law, is a denial by the State, within the meaning of the Fourteenth Amendment. If it be not, then that race is left, in respect of the civil rights in question, practically at the mercy of corporations and individuals wielding power under the States. . . .

At every step, in this direction, the nation has been confronted with class tyranny, which a contemporary English historian says is, of all tyrannies, the most intolerable, "for it is ubiquitous in its operation, and weighs, perhaps, most heavily on those whose obscurity or distance would withdraw them from the notice of a single despot." To-day, it is the colored race which is denied, by corporations and individuals wielding public authority, rights fundamental in their freedom and citizenship. At some future time, it may be that some other race will fall under the ban of race discrimination. If the constitutional amendments be enforced, according to the intent with which, as I conceive, they were adopted, there cannot be, in this republic, any class of human beings in practical subjection to another class, with power in the latter to dole out to the former just such privileges as they may choose to grant. The supreme law of the land has decreed that no authority shall be exercised in this country upon the basis of discrimination, in respect of civil rights, against freemen and citizens because of their race, color, or previous condition of servitude. To that decree—for the due enforcement of which, by appropriate legislation, Congress has been invested with express power—every one must bow, whatever may have been, or whatever now are, his individual views as to the wisdom or policy, either of the recent changes in the fundamental law, or of the legislation which has been enacted to give them effect.

For the reasons stated I feel constrained to withhold my assent to the opinion of the court.

V

National Growth
and the Era
of Jim Crow
1884–1914

The Civil Rights Cases of 1883 confirmed the fact that the national government was officially abandoning the Negro to the caprice of state control. The next thirty years indicated the extent to which the Negro, though nominally freed from slavery, could be repressed and reduced to the status of second-class citizenship by the force of law and the force of custom sustained by that state control.

This was the era of Jim Crow. It was the period in which southern whites effected a common racial front against the Negro. Absorbed with industrial growth, cycles of economic prosperity and depression, further settlement of the West, and, finally, the challenge of colonial adventures, the nation at large proved indifferent to the status of the Negro. The dominant majority treated the Negro's lack of education, training, and wealth as confirmation of inferiority, and justified, on that basis, all forms of discriminatory behavior toward black Americans. State after state throughout the South and border areas changed their constitutions and instituted statutory measures designed to deprive the Negro of all opportunities for civic and political participation. Other laws imposed segregated facilities in education, travel, public accommodations, and the like; and the concept of Jim Crow was extended to all forms of public activity—frequently under the force of broadly structured laws, but also under the rubrics of "tradition" and "custom."

In addition to economic and political deprivation, the Negro was also subjected to the brutality of white terror and mob rule. From the early 1880's to the years immediately following World War I, lynching and mob violence went unchecked throughout the South, and this phenomenon was frequently matched by outbreaks of race rioting in the North and in the Midwest. Thanks to a generation of indifference to the Negro's plight, interracial violence had become a national problem.

Despite the promises of the Civil War and Reconstruction, the position of the Negro deteriorated to its nadir during the Jim Crow period, 1884 to 1914. Yet, there were those who fought this trend. In his declining years, Negro leader Frederick Douglass decried the wave of mob violence and suppression visited upon the Negro. And W. E. B. Du Bois and Monroe Trotter demanded full and unqualified justice through the mechanisms of equal educational and political and civil rights. Their short-lived Niagara Movement spoke to these very points.

An impressive array of white liberals, such as Joel and Arthur Spingarn, Oswald Garrison Villard, William English Walling, Charles Edward Russell, and Moorfield Storey, joined with Du Bois and other Negro activists to launch the Negro protest movement on a coordinated national basis with the founding of the National Association for the Advancement of Colored People in 1909.

The publication in 1903 of Du Bois's *The Souls of Black Folk* had served as the harbinger of Negro protest and a clear indication that black Americans would not long accept either the oppression of the dominant white majority or the accommodationist approach of Booker T. Washington. Jim Crow, in all its varied manifestations, would not go unchallenged.

FREDERICK DOUGLASS DENOUNCES
LYNCH LAW (1892)

At the end of the Reconstruction period, the Negro was thrown totally upon the caprice of the white southerner. The North, generally, and the Republican party, specifically (as the electoral compromise of 1877 indicated), were quite willing to turn their energies to other matters, such as economic and industrial growth, westward expansion and development, and, at the end of the century, international, imperialist ventures.

The white South used the Democratic party to regain control throughout the region, and political sanctions supplemented by physical intimidations were employed to remove the Negro as an effective element in public affairs. By the mid-1880's, an alarming tendency toward mob violence and lynching had come to characterize the southern whites' methods of suppression. Records going back to 1882 reveal increasing reliance upon lynching as an instrument of white dominance. Throughout the 1890's, the *reported* number of Negroes lynched exceeded one hundred in each year except two; the high of one hundred and sixty-one was reached in the year 1892. (*Statistical History of the United States from Colonial Times to the Present* [Stamford, Conn.: Fairfield Publishers, 1965], p. 218.)

To former abolitionists, both white and Negro, and to those of the later generation concerned with interracial justice and the maintenance of law and order, lynching had frightening implications. A one-time slave, who had become a leading abolitionist and an advisor to Presidents, Frederick Douglass was the most prominent Negro of his day. In 1892, he reviewed and analyzed the lynching phenomenon in an article that appeared in a nationally circulated journal. Douglass assessed the direct complicity of southern leaders and the tacit acquiescence of northerners generally in both abetting and condoning lynching practices. He emphasized the relationship between lynching and the prospects of Negro advancement, and lamented the corrosive effects that mob violence must inevitably have upon the entire community.

DOCUMENT 55

Lynch law in the South*

Whatever may be said of their weakness when required to hold a white man or a rich man, the meshes of the law are certainly always strong enough to hold or punish a poor man or a Negro. In this case there is neither color to blind, money to corrupt, nor powerful friends to influence court or jury against the claims of justice. All the presumptions of law and society are against the Negro. In the days of slavery he was presumed to be a slave, even if free, and his word was never taken against that of a white man. To be accused was to be condemned, and the same spirit prevails today. This state of opinion in the South not only assures by law the punishment of black men, but enables white men to escape punishment by assuming the color of the Negro in order to commit crime. It is often asserted that all Negroes look alike, and it is only necessary to bring one of the class into the presence of an accuser to have him at once identified as the criminal. . . .

I, however, freely confess that the present prospect has for me a gloomy side. When men sow the wind it is rational to expect that they will reap the whirlwind. It is evident to my mind that the Negro will not always rest a passive subject to the violence and bloodshed by which he is now pursued. If neither law nor public sentiment shall come to his relief, he will devise methods of his own. It should be remembered that the Negro is a man, and that in point of intelligence he is not what he was a hundred years ago. Whatever may be said of his failure to acquire wealth, it cannot be denied that he has made decided progress in the acquisition of knowledge; and he is a poor student of the natural history of civilization who does not see that the mental energies of this race, newly awakened and set in motion, must continue to advance. Character, with its moral influence; knowledge, with its power; and wealth, with its respectability, are possible to it as well as to other races of men. In arguing upon what will be the action of the Negro in case he continues to be the victim of lynch law I accept the statement often made in his disparagement, that he is an imitative being; that he will do what

---

* *North American Review*, CLV (July, 1892), pp. 117–24.

he sees other men do. He has already shown this facility, and he illustrates it all the way from the prize ring to the pulpit; from the plow to the professor's chair. The voice of nature, not less than the Book of books, teaches us that oppression can make even a wise man mad, and in such case the responsibility for madness will not rest upon the man but upon the oppression to which he is subjected.

How can the South hope to teach the Negro the sacredness of human life while it cheapens it and profanes it by the atrocities of mob law? The stream cannot rise higher than its source. The morality of the Negro will reach no higher point than the morality and religion that surround him. He reads of what is being done in the world in resentment of oppression and needs no teacher to make him understand what he reads. In warning the South that it may place too much reliance upon the cowardice of the Negro, I am not advocating violence by the Negro, but pointing out the dangerous tendency of his constant persecution. The Negro was not a coward at Bunker Hill; he was not a coward in Haiti; he was not a coward in the late war for the Union; he was not a coward at Harper's Ferry, with John Brown; and care should be taken against goading him to acts of desperation by continuing to punish him for heinous crimes of which he is not legally convicted.

. . . .

Now, where rests the responsibility for the lynch law prevalent in the South? It is evident that it is not entirely with the ignorant mob. The men who break open jails and with bloody hands destroy human life are not alone responsible. These are not the men who make public sentiment. They are simply the hangmen, not the court, judge, or jury. They simply obey the public sentiment of the South, the sentiment created by wealth and respectability, by the press and the pulpit. A change in public sentiment can be easily effected by these forces whenever they shall elect to make the effort. Let the press and the pulpit of the South unite their power against the cruelty, disgrace, and shame that is settling like a mantle of fire upon these lynch-law states, and lynch law itself will soon cease to exist.

Nor is the South alone responsible for this burning shame

and menace to our free institutions. Wherever contempt of race prevails, whether against African, Indian, or Mongolian, countenance and support are given to the present peculiar treatment of the Negro in the South. The finger of scorn in the North is correlated to the dagger of the assassin in the South. The sin against the Negro is both sectional and national, and until the voice of the North shall be heard in emphatic condemnation and withering reproach against these continued ruthless mob-law murders, it will remain equally involved with the South in this common crime.

BOOKER T. WASHINGTON AND COMPROMISE (1895)

Born a slave in Virginia, Booker T. Washington had been educated at Hampton Institute. In 1881, he founded the famous Tuskegee Institute in Alabama for the education of Negroes. With the death of Frederick Douglass, Washington became the leading Negro in the country. Because of sentiments such as those expressed in his Atlanta Address, Washington was readily acknowledged as a Negro spokesman by white southerners and by northern white philanthropists who helped maintain Tuskegee Institute.

Called upon to address the Cotton States and International Exposition in Atlanta in the fall of 1895, Washington said little that could unnerve white leaders and said much that pacified and assured them. His philosophy, implemented by the training courses at Tuskegee Institute, centered on the belief that the Negro must win dignity and respect by self-help and by the acquisition of manual skills that would fit him to play an essential economic role in the development of the New South. Washington's emphasis was on Negro responsibilities rather than rights, on the fulfillment of tasks rather than the enjoyment of privileges. In a period characterized by violence against and political suppression of the Negro, Washington made only oblique references to terrorism and civil disabilities. Anxious to confirm the Negro's utility to the white southerner, he intimated that black labor was superior to its immigrant counterpart for the development of the South.

Students of the period would later debate the wisdom of Washington's position on interracial affairs and his motives for striking an accommodationist position, but none could deny its historical importance in shaping national attitudes on race.

DOCUMENT 56

*The Atlanta Address, September 18, 1895**

Mr. President and Gentlemen of the Board of Directors and Citizens:

One-third of the population of the South is of the Negro race. No enterprise seeking the material, civic, or moral welfare of this section can disregard this element of our population and reach the highest success. I but convey to you, Mr. President and Directors, the sentiment of the masses of my race when I say that in no way have the value and manhood of the American Negro been more fittingly and generously recognized than by the managers of this magnificent Exposition at every stage of its progress. It is a recognition that will do more to cement the friendship of the two races than any occurrence since the dawn of our freedom.

Not only this, but the opportunity here afforded will awaken among us a new era of industrial progress. Ignorant and inexperienced, it is not strange that in the first years of our new life we began at the top instead of at the bottom; that a seat in Congress or the State Legislature was more sought than real estate or industrial skill; that the political convention or stump speaking had more attractions than starting a dairy farm or truck garden.

A ship lost at sea for many days suddenly sighted a friendly vessel. From the mast of the unfortunate vessel was seen a signal: "Water, water; we die of thirst!" The answer from the friendly vessel at once came back: "Cast down your bucket where you are." A second time the signal, "Water, water; send us water!" ran up from the distressed vessel, and was answered: "Cast down your bucket where you are." The captain of the distressed vessel, at last heeding the injunction,

---

* Booker T. Washington, *Up From Slavery* (New York: Doubleday, Page and Co., 1909), pp. 218–25.

cast down his bucket, and it came up full of fresh, sparkling water from the mouth of the Amazon River. To those of my race who depend upon bettering their condition in a foreign land, or who underestimate the importance of cultivating friendly relations with the Southern white man, who is his next door neighbor, I would say: "Cast down your bucket where you are"—cast it down in making friends in every manly way of the people of all races by whom we are surrounded.

Cast it down in agriculture, mechanics, in commerce, in domestic service, and in the professions. And in this connection it is well to bear in mind that whatever other sins the South may be called to bear, when it comes to business, pure and simple, it is in the South that the Negro is given a man's chance in the commercial world, and in nothing is this Exposition more eloquent than in emphasizing this chance. Our greatest danger is, that in the great leap from slavery to freedom we may overlook the fact that the masses of us are to live by the productions of our hands, and fail to keep in mind that we shall prosper in proportion as we learn to dignify and glorify common labor, and put brains and skill into the common occupations of life; shall prosper in proportion as we learn to draw the line between the superficial and the substantial, the ornamental gewgaws of life and the useful. No race can prosper till it learns that there is as much dignity in tilling a field as in writing a poem. It is at the bottom of life we must begin, and not at the top. Nor should we permit our grievances to overshadow our opportunities.

To those of the white race who look to the incoming of those of foreign birth and strange tongue and habits for the prosperity of the South, were I permitted I would repeat what I say to my own race, "Cast down your bucket where you are." Cast it down among the 8,000,000 Negroes whose habits you know, whose fidelity and love you have tested in days when to have proved treacherous meant the ruin of your firesides. Cast down your bucket among these people who have, without strikes and labor wars, tilled your fields, cleared your forests, built your railroads and cities, and brought forth treasures from the bowels of the earth, and helped make possible this magnificent representation of the progress of the South. Casting down your bucket among my people, helping and encouraging them as you are doing on these grounds, and, with education of head, hand and heart, you will find that they will buy your surplus land, make blossom the waste places in your fields, and run your factories. While doing this, you can be sure in the future, as in the past, that you and your families will be surrounded by the most patient, faithful, lawabiding, and unresentful people that the world has seen. As we have proved our loyalty to you in the past, in nursing your children, watching by the sick bed of your mothers and fathers, and aften following them with tear-dimmed eyes to their graves, so in the future, in our humble way, we shall stand by you with a devotion that no foreigner can approach, ready to lay down our lives, if need be, in defense of yours, interlacing our industrial, commercial, civil, and religious life with yours in a way that shall make the interests of both races one. In all things that are purely social we can be as separate as the fingers, yet one as the hand in all things essential to mutual progress.

There is no defense or security for any of us except in the highest intelligence and development of all. If anywhere there are efforts tending to curtail the fullest growth of the Negro, let these efforts be turned into stimulating, encouraging, and making him the most useful and intelligent citizen. Effort or means so invested will pay a thousand per cent interest. These efforts will be twice blessed—blessing him that gives and him that takes.

There is no escape through law of man or God from the inevitable:

> The laws of changeless justice bind
> Oppressor with oppressed;
> And close as sin and suffering joined
> We march to fate abreast.

Nearly sixteen millions of hands will aid you in pulling the load upwards, or they will pull against you the load downwards. We shall constitute one-third and more of the ignorance and crime of the South, or one-third its intelligence and progress; we shall contribute one-third to the business and industrial prosperity of the South, or we shall prove a veritable body of death, stagnating, depressing, retarding every effort to advance the body politic.

Gentlemen of the Exposition, as we present to you our

humble effort at an exhibition of our progress, you must not expect overmuch. Starting thirty years ago with ownership here and there in a few quilts and pumpkins and chickens (gathered from miscellaneous sources), remember the path that has led from these to the invention and production of agricultural implements, buggies, steam engines, newspapers, books, statuary, carving, paintings, the management of drug stores and banks has not been trodden without contact with thorns and thistles. While we take pride in what we exhibit as a result of our independent efforts, we do not for a moment forget that our part in this exhibition would fall short of your expectations but for the constant help that has come to our educational life, not only from the Southern States, but especially from Northern philanthropists, who have made their gifts a constant stream of blessing and encouragement.

The wisest among my race understand that the agitation of questions of social equality is the extremest folly, and that progress in the enjoyment of all the privileges that will come to us must be the result of severe and constant struggle rather than of artificial forcing. No race that has anything to contribute to the markets of the world is long in any degree ostracized. It is important and right that all privileges of the law be ours, but it is vastly more important that we be prepared for the exercise of those privileges. The opportunity to earn a dollar in a factory just now is worth infinitely more than the opportunity to spend a dollar in an opera house.

In conclusion, may I repeat that nothing in thirty years has given us more hope and encouragement, and drawn us so near to you of the white race, as this opportunity offered by the Exposition; and here bending, as it were, over the altar that represents the results of the struggles of your race and mine, both starting practically empty-handed three decades ago, I pledge that, in your effort to work out the great and intricate problem which God has laid at the doors of the South, you shall have at all times the patient, sympathetic help of my race; only let this be constantly in mind that, while from representations in these buildings of the products of field, of forest, of mine, of factory, letters, and art, much good will come, yet far above and beyond material benefits will be the higher good, that let us pray God will come, in a blotting out of sectional differences and racial animosities and suspicions, in a determination to administer absolute justice, in a willing obedience among all classes to the mandates of law. This, coupled with our material prosperity, will bring into our beloved South a new heaven and a new earth.

NEW YORK'S CIVIL RIGHTS ACT (1895)

With the Supreme Court decision in the Civil Rights Cases (Document 54), Congressional and executive action seeking equal rights for the American Negro came to an agonizing halt. Initiative passed to the states.

Some states enacted legislation to avoid and evade civil rights granted by the Thirteenth, Fourteenth, and Fifteenth Amendments, and the remnants of the Civil Rights Acts (Document 47) which survived Supreme Court declarations of unconstitutionality.

New York's statute, a prototype which was widely copied, was specifically designed to replace the stricken provisions of the Civil Rights Act of 1875 (Document 47) within the borders of the Empire State. Sections 1 and 2 of the New York law are obviously based on the first two sections of the 1875 federal enactment, and Section 3 of the state act is virtually the same as Section 4 of the federal act.

DOCUMENT 57

*An act to protect all citizens in their civil and legal rights**

The People of the State of New York, represented in Senate and Assembly, do enact as follows:

SECTION 1. That all persons within the jurisdiction of this State shall be entitled to the full and equal accommodations, advantages, facilities and privileges of inns, restaurants, hotels, eating-houses, bath-houses, barber-shops, theatres, music halls, public conveyances on land and water, and all other places of public accommodation or amusement, subject only to the conditions and limitations established by law and applicable alike to all citizens.

---

* *Laws of New York, 1895, ch. 1042, v. 1, p. 974.*

Sec. 2. That any person who shall violate any of the provisions of the foregoing section by denying to any citizens, except for reasons applicable alike to all citizens of every race, creed or color, and regardless of race, creed and color, the full enjoyment of any of the accommodations, advantages, facilities or privileges in said section enumerated, or by aiding or inciting such denial, shall for every such offense forfeit and pay a sum not less than one hundred dollars nor more than five hundred dollars to the person aggrieved thereby, to be recovered in any court of competent jurisdiction in the county where said offense was committed; and shall, also, for every such offense be deemed guilty of a misdemeanor, and upon conviction thereof shall be fined not less than one hundred dollars nor more than five hundred dollars, or shall be imprisoned not less than thirty days.

Sec. 3. That no citizen of the State possessing all other qualifications which are or may be required or prescribed by law, shall be disqualified to serve as grand or petit juror in any court of this State on account of race, creed or color, and any person charged with any duty in the selection or summoning of jurors who shall exclude or fail to summon any citizen for the cause aforesaid shall, on conviction thereof, be deemed guilty of a misdemeanor and be fined not less than one hundred dollars nor more than five hundred dollars, or imprisonment not less than thirty days, nor more than ninety days, or both such fine and imprisonment.

Sec. 4. This act shall take effect immediately.

PLESSY V. FERGUSON—THE DOCTRINE OF "SEPARATE BUT EQUAL" (1896)

For more than half a century, the 1896 Supreme Court decision in *Plessy* v. *Ferguson* stood as the principal legal obstacle to civil rights for the American Negro. This was the case which superimposed the "separate but equal" doctrine upon the law of the Constitution. It was a novel doctrine. It represented a substantial departure from what the Court had said and done in the first cases following the passage of the Civil Rights Acts (Document 47). Yet it provided a constitutional basis for a plethora of Jim Crow legislation that continued up to and beyond *Brown* v. *Board of Education of Topeka*, 1954 (Document 78). (The technical overruling of the *Plessy* case did not come until 1956 in *Gayle* v. *Browder*.)

Dissenting Justice John Marshall Harlan proved an apt prophet in expressing the view that the *Plessy* judgment "will, in time, prove to be quite as pernicious as the decision made by this tribunal in the *Dred Scott* case" (163 U.S. at 559).

The Court took the position that the Fourteenth Amendment "in the nature of things . . . could not have been intended to abolish distinctions based on color, or to enforce social, as distinguished from political equality, or a commingling of the two races upon terms unsatisfactory to either." This was far different language from that used by the Court in 1873 in the Slaughter-House Cases (Document 50), or in 1880 in *Strauder* v. *West Virginia* (Document 53).

The *Plessy* Court ignored the teaching of the Slaughter-House Cases that the "one pervading purpose" of the three post-Civil War Amendments was the "freedom of the slave race, the security and firm establishment of that freedom, and the protection of the newly made freeman and citizen from the oppressions of those who had formerly exercised unlimited dominion over him." Likewise ignored were the words in the *Strauder* case on the meaning of the Fourteenth Amendment: "What is this but declaring that the law in the States shall be the same for the black as for the white . . . [and] that no discrimination shall be made against them by law because of their color?"

Homer Adolph Plessy, one-eighth Negro and seven-eighths white, was arrested for his refusal to ride in the "colored" coach of a railroad train during the sixty-mile *intrastate* trip from New Orleans to Covington, Louisiana. Such refusal was a violation of the Louisiana law of 1890, requiring "equal but separate accommodations for the white, and colored races." Plessy then instituted an action to restrain enforcement of the statute on the grounds that it violated the Thirteenth and Fourteenth Amendments. Ferguson, the defendant, was the Louisiana judge designated to conduct the trial of Plessy on criminal charges. The plea to prohibit Ferguson from hearing the case was denied by the Louisiana Supreme Court. (*Ex parte Plessy*, 45 La. Ann. 80 [1893].) Less than a year before, however, the Court had held that this same statute could not constitutionally be applied to *interstate* passengers. (*State ex rel. Abbot* v. *Judge*, 44 La. Ann. 770 [1892].)

A group of Louisiana Negro leaders retained Albion W. Tourgée as counsel. An upstate New York lawyer (and some-time novelist), he had spent several years in North Carolina during the Reconstruction period, where he served briefly as a state judge.

Tourgée has often been given credit for the most famous and most quoted words to come from the Court in the course of decision. They appeared in the dissent of Justice John Marshall Harlan: "Our Constitution is color-blind," wrote the justice who had likewise dissented thirteen years earlier in the Civil Rights Cases. This was not, however, a direct quote from the Tourgée brief. The lawyer's exact words were: "Justice is pictured blind and her daughter, the Law, ought at least to be color-blind."

With the Plessy decision, the separate but equal formula became the law of the Constitution. *Plessy* v. *Ferguson* is cited again and again as the case which established this doctrine. And yet, oddly enough, there are no words in the Court's opinion which declare that segregation is to be permitted where equal facilities are provided. Such words were to come from lower court decisions which attempted to give meaning to the Plessy principle. What happened in the Plessy case was that the judges upheld what they believed to be the "reasonableness" of the Louisiana transportation laws without providing guidance for the other courts which had to decide these subsequent segregation cases. The principle propounded by the nine men of 1896—that a state could compel "reasonable" racial segregation—was strictly judge-made law, giving a hitherto unknown meaning to the Fourteenth Amendment. It was basic law, but it left unanswered two critical questions: What are the criteria for measuring equality? What is the proper judicial remedy where inequality is found to exist?" (Albert P. Blaustein and Clarence Clyde Ferguson, Jr., *Desegregation and the Law* [New Brunswick, N. J.: Rutgers University Press, 1957], p. 98.)

DOCUMENT(S) 58

Louisiana Railway Accommodations Act*

An Act to promote the comfort of passengers on railway trains; requiring all railway companies carrying passengers on their trains, in this State, to provide equal but separate accommodations for the white and colored races, by providing separate coaches or compartments so as to secure separate accommodations; defining the duties of the officers of such railways; directing them to assign passengers to the coaches or compartment set aside for the use of the race to which such passengers belong; authorizing them to refuse to carry on their train such passengers as may refuse to occupy the coaches or compartments to which he or she is assigned; to exonerate such railway companies from any and all blame or damages that might proceed or result from such a refusal; to prescribe penalties for all violations of this act; to put this act into effect ninety days after its promulgation, and to repeal all laws or parts of laws contrary to or inconsistent with the provisions of this act.

SEC. 1. *Be it enacted by the General Assembly of the State of Louisiana,* That all railway companies carrying passengers in their coaches in this State, shall provide equal but separate accommodations for the white, and colored races, by providing two or more passenger coaches for each passenger train, or by dividing the passenger coaches by a partition so as to secure separate accommodations; *provided* that this section shall not be construed to apply to street railroads. No person or persons, shall be permitted to occupy seats in coaches, other than the ones assigned to them on account of the race they belong to.

SEC. 2. *Be it further enacted etc.,* That the officers of such passenger trains shall have power and are hereby required to assign each passenger to the coach or compartment used for the race to which such passenger belongs; any passenger insisting on going into a coach or compartment to which by race he does not belong, shall be liable to a fine of twenty-five dollars or in lieu thereof to imprisonment for a period of not more twenty days in the parish prison and any officer

---

* *Louisiana Laws, 1890,* No. 111, pp. 152–54.

of any railroad insisting on assigning a passenger to a coach or compartment other than the one set aside for the race to which said passenger belongs shall be liable to a fine of twenty-five dollars or in lieu thereof to imprisonment for a period of not more than twenty days in the parish prison; and should any passenger refuse to occupy the coach or compartment to which he or she is assigned by the officer of such railway, said officer shall have power to refuse to carry such passenger on his train, and for such refusal neither he nor the railway company which he represents shall be liable for damages in any of the courts of this State.

SEC. 3. *Be it further enacted etc.*, That all officers and directors of railway companies that shall refuse or neglect to comply with the provisions and requirements of this act shall be deemed guilty of a misdemeanor and shall upon conviction before any court of competent jurisdiction be fined not less than one hundred dollars nor more than five hundred dollars; and any conductor or other employees of such passenger train, having charge of the same, who shall refuse or neglect to carry out the provisions of this act shall on conviction be fined not less than twenty-five dollars nor more than fifty dollars for each offense; all railroad corporations carrying passengers in this State other than street railroads shall keep this law posted up in a conspicuous place in each passenger coach and ticket office, provided that nothing in this act shall be construed as applying to nurses attending children of the other race.

SEC. 4. *Be it further enacted etc.*, That all laws or parts of laws contrary to or inconsistent with the provisions of this act be and the same are hereby repealed, and that this act shall take effect and be in full force ninety days after its promulgation.

*The Plessy Brief**

Statement of Case

The Plaintiff in Error was arrested on the affidavit of two witnesses charging him with violation of Act No. 111, of the

---

* Briefs and Records, Library of the Supreme Court of the United States.

Laws of Louisiana, session of 1890, averring that he was "a colored passenger on a train of the East Louisiana Railroad Company," who did "insist upon going into and remaining in a compartment of a coach of said train which had been assigned to white passengers." . . .

The language of the act is explicit: "should any passenger refuse to occupy"—not the coach used for the race to which he belongs but—"the coach or compartment *to which he or she is assigned by the officer of such railway,* said officer shall have power to refuse to carry such passenger on his train and *for such refusal,* neither he nor the railway company he represents, shall be liable for damage, *in any of the courts of this state.*" Is not this a clear denial to the person thus put off the train, of any right of action? Is it not that very denial of the "equal protection of the laws" which is clearly contemplated by the third restrictive provision of the Fourteenth Amendment?

If so, is this provision of such importance as to be essential to the validity of the law as a whole? Our contention is that no individual or corporation could be expected or induced to carry into effect this law, in a community where race admixture is a frequent thing and where the hazard of damage resulting from such assignment is very great, unless they were protected by such exemption. The State very clearly says to the railway, "You go forward and enforce this system of assorting the citizens of the United States on the line of race, and we will see that you suffer no loss through prosecution in OUR courts." Relying on this assurance, the company is willing to undertake the risk. Without it they might well shrink from such liability. The denial of the *right to prosecute,* then, becomes essential to the operation of the act, and if such "denial" is in derogation of the restriction of the Fourteenth Amendment, the whole act is null and void. It is a question for the Court to determine upon its knowledge of human nature and the conditions affecting human conduct, in regard to which it would be idle to cite authorities. If it is NOT a violation of this provision it would be difficult to imagine a statutory provision which could be violative of it. . . .

This provision authorizing and requiring the officer in charge of the train to pass upon and decide the question of race, is the very essence of the statute. If this is repugnant to the Constitutional provision, all the rest must fall.

There is no question that the law which puts it in the power of a railway conductor, at his own discretion, to require a man to ride in a "Jim Crow" car, that is, in the car "set apart exclusively for persons of the colored race," confers upon such conductor the power to deprive one of the reputation of being a white man, or at least to impair that reputation. The man who rides in a car set apart for the colored race, will inevitably be regarded as a colored man or at least be suspected of being one. And the officer has undoubtedly the power to entail upon him such suspicion. To do so, is to deprive him of "property" if such reputation *is* "property." Whether it is or not, is for the court to determine from its knowledge of existing conditions. Perhaps it might not be inappropriate to suggest some questions which may aid in deciding this inquiry. How much would it be *worth* to a young man entering upon the practice of law, to be regarded as a *white* man rather than a colored one? Six-sevenths of the population are white. Nineteen-twentieths of the property of the country is owned by white people. Ninety-nine hundredths of the business opportunities are in the control of white people. These propositions are rendered even more startling by the intensity of feeling which excludes the colored man from the friendship and companionship of the white man. Probably most white persons if given a choice, would prefer death to life in the United States *as colored persons.* Under these conditions, is it possible to conclude that the *reputation of being white* is not property? Indeed, is it not the most valuable sort of property, being the master-key that unlocks the golden door of opportunity? . . .

The plaintiff also contends that the provisions authorizing the officers of a train to require parties to occupy the particular cars or compartments set apart for distinct races, is a statutory grant of authority to interfere with natural domestic rights of the most sacred character.

A man may be white and his wife colored, a wife may be white and her children colored. Has the State the right to compel the husband to ride in one car and the wife in another? Or to assign the mother to one car and the children to another? Yet this is what the statute in question requires. In our case, it does not appear that the plaintiff may not have had with him a wife belonging to the other race, or children differing with him in the color of their skins. Has a State the right to order the mother to ride in one car and her young daughter, because her cheek may have a darker tinge, to ride alone in another? Yet such things as these, the act in question not only permits, but actually requires and commands to be done under penalty of fine and imprisonment, for failure or neglect. Are the courts of the United States to hold such things to be within the purview of a State's right to impose on citizens of the United States? . . .

The plaintiff also insists that a wholesale assortment of the citizens of the United States, resident in the state of Louisiana, on the line of race, is a thing wholly impossible to be made, equitably and justly by any tribunal, much less by the conductor of a train without evidence, investigation or responsibility.

The Court will take notice of the fact that, in all parts of the country, race-intermixture has proceeded to such an extent that there are great numbers of citizens in whom the preponderance of the blood of one race or another, is impossible of ascertainment, except by careful scrutiny of the pedigree. As slavery did not permit the marriage of the slave, in a majority of cases even an approximate determination of this preponderance is an actual impossibility, with the most careful and deliberate weighing of evidence, much less by the casual scrutiny of a busy conductor.

But even if it were possible to determine preponderance of blood and so determine racial character in certain cases, what should be said of those cases in which the race admixture is equal. Are they white or colored? . . .

In order to come within the scope of a "police regulation," even as defined in the "Slaughter House Cases," the act prohibited must be of a character to affect the general health or public morals of a whole community, not merely to minister to the wishes of one class or another. What is the act prohibited in the statute in question in this case? The sitting of a white man or woman in the car in which a colored man or woman sits or the sitting of a colored man or woman in the car in which white men or women are sitting,—is this dangerous to the public health? Does this contaminate public morals? If it does from whence comes the contamination? Why does it contaminate any more than in the house or on the street? Is it the white who spreads the contagion or the black? And if color breeds contagion in a railway coach, why exempt nurses from the operation of the Act?

The title of an Act does not make it a "police provision" and a discrimination intended to humiliate or degrade one race in order to promote the pride of ascendency in another, is not made a "police regulation" by insisting that the one will not be entirely happy unless the other is shut out of their presence. Haman was troubled with the same sort of unhappiness because he saw Mordecai the Jew sitting at the King's gate. He wanted a "police regulation" to prevent his being contaminated by the sight. He did not set out the real cause of his zeal for the public welfare: neither does this statute. He wanted to "down" the Jew: this act is intended to "keep the negro in his place." The exemption of nurses shows that the real evil lies not in the color of the skin but in the relation the colored person sustains to the white. If he is a dependent it may be endured: if he is not, his presence is insufferable. Instead of being intended to promote the *general* comfort and moral well-being, this act is plainly and evidently intended to promote the happiness of one class by asserting its supremacy and the inferiority of another class. Justice is pictured blind and her daughter, the Law, ought at least to be color-blind. . . .

The act in question in our case, proceeds upon the hypothesis that the State has the right to authorize and require the officers of a railway to assort the citizens who engage passage on its lines, according to race, *and to punish the citizen if he refuses to submit to such assortment,*

The gist of our case is the unconstitutionality of the assortment; *not* the question of equal accommodation; that much, the decisions of the court give without a doubt. We insist that the State has no right to compel us to ride in a car "set apart" for a particular race, whether it is as good as another or not. Suppose the provisions were that one of these cars should be painted white and the other black; the invidiousness of the distinction would not be any greater than that provided by the act.

But if the State has a right to distinguish between citizens according to race in the enjoyment of public privilege, by compelling them to ride in separate coaches, what is to prevent the application of the same principle to other relations? Why may it not require all red-headed people to ride in a separate car? Why not require all colored people to walk on one side of the street and the whites on the other? Why may it not require every white man's house to be painted white and every colored man's black? Why may it not require every white man's vehicle to be of one color and compel the colored citizen to use one of different color on the highway? Why not require every white business man to use a white sign and every colored man who solicits custom a black one? One side of the street may be just as good as the other and the dark horses, coaches, clothes and signs may be as good or better than the white ones. The question is not as to the *equality* of the privileges enjoyed, but *the right of the State to label one citizen as white and another as colored* in the common enjoyment of a public highway as this court has often decided a railway to be.

. . . .

The Declaration of Independence, with a far-reaching wisdom found in no other political utterance up to that time, makes the security of the individual's right to "the pursuit of happiness," a prime object of all government. This is the controlling idea of our institutions. It dominates the national as well as the state governments. In asserting national control over both state and national citizenship, in appointing the boundaries and distinctive qualities of each, in conferring on millions a status they had never before known and giving to every inhabitant of the country rights never before enjoyed and in restricting the rights of the states in regard thereto,—in doing this were the people consciously and actually intending to protect this right of the individual to the pursuit of happiness or not? If they were, was it the pursuit of happiness by all or by a part of the people which they sought to secure?

If the purpose was to secure the unrestricted pursuit of happiness by the four millions then just made free, now grown to nine millions, did they contemplate that they were leaving to the states the power to herd them away from her white citizens in the enjoyment of chartered privilege? Suppose a member of this court, nay, suppose every member of it, by some mysterious dispensation of providence should wake to-morrow with a black skin and curly hair—the two obvious and controlling indications of race—and in traveling through that portion of the country where the "Jim Crow Car" abounds, should be ordered into it by the conductor. It is easy to imagine what would be the result, the indignation, the protests, the assertion of pure Caucasian ancestry. But the conductor, the autocrat of Caste, armed with the power of the State conferred by this statute, will listen neither to denial or protest. "In you go or out you go," is his ultimatum.

What humiliation, what rage would then fill the judicial mind! How would the resources of language not be taxed in objurgation! Why would this sentiment prevail in your minds? Simply because you would then feel and know that such assortment of the citizens on the line of race was a discrimination intended to humiliate and degrade the former subject and dependent class—an attempt to perpetuate the caste distinctions on which slavery rested—a statute in the words of the Court "tending to reduce the colored people of the country to the condition of a subject race."

Because it does this the statute is a violation of the fundamental principles of all free government and the Fourteenth Amendment should be given that construction which will remedy such tendency and which is in plain accord with its words. Legal refinement is out of place when it seeks to find a way both to avoid the plain purport of the terms employed, the fundamental principle of our government and the controlling impulse and tendency of the American people.

ALBION W. TOURGÉE, *of Counsel for Plaintiff in Error.*

Plessy v. Ferguson[*]

MR. JUSTICE BROWN, after stating the case, delivered the opinion of the court.

This case turns upon the constitutionality of an act of the General Assembly of the State of Louisiana, passed in 1890, providing for separate railway carriages for the white and colored races. Acts 1890, No. 111, p. 152. . . .

The information filed in the criminal District Court

---

[*] Supreme Court of the United States, 163 U.S. 537 (1896).

charged in substance that Plessy, being a passenger between two stations within the State of Louisiana, was assigned by officers of the company to the coach used for the race to which he belonged, but he insisted upon going into a coach used by the race to which he did not belong. Neither in the information nor plea was his particular race or color averred.

The petition for the writ of prohibition averred that petitioneer was seven eighths Caucasian and one eighth African blood; that the mixture of colored blood was not discernible in him, and that he was entitled to every right, privilege and immunity secured to citizens of the United States of the white race; and that, upon such theory, he took possession of a vacant seat in a coach where passengers of the white race were accommodated, and was ordered by the conductor to vacate said coach and take a seat in another assigned to persons of the colored race, and having refused to comply with such demand he was forcibly ejected with the aid of a police officer, and imprisoned in the parish jail to answer a charge of having violated the above act.

The constitutionality of this act is attacked upon the ground that it conflicts both with the Thirteenth Amendment of the Constitution, abolishing slavery, and the Fourteenth Amendment, which prohibits certain restrictive legislation on the part of the States. . . .

A statute which implies merely a legal distinction between the white and colored races—a distinction which is founded in the color of the two races, and which must always exist so long as white men are distinguished from the other race by color—has no tendency to destroy the legal equality of the two races, or reëstablish a state of involuntary servitude. Indeed, we do not understand that the Thirteenth Amendment is strenuously relied upon by the plaintiff in error in this connection. . . .

The object of the [Fourteenth] amendment was undoubtedly to enforce the absolute equality of the two races before the law, but in the nature of things it could not have been intended to abolish distinctions based upon color, or to enforce social, as distinguished from political equality, or a commingling of the two races upon terms unsatisfactory to either. Laws permitting, and even requiring, their separation in places where they are liable to be brought into contact do not necessarily imply the inferiority of either race to the other, and have been generally, if not universally, recognized as within the competency of the state legislatures in the exercise of their police power. The most common instance of this is connected with the establishment of separate schools for white and colored children, which has been held to be a valid exercise of the legislative power even by courts of States where the political rights of the colored race have been longest and most earnestly enforced. . . .

The distinction between laws interfering with the political equality of the negro and those requiring the separation of the two races in schools, theatres and railway carriages has been frequently drawn by this court. Thus in *Strauder* v. *West Virginia*, 100 U.S. 303, it was held that a law of West Virginia limiting to white male persons, 21 years of age and citizens of the State, the right to sit upon juries, was a discrimination which implied a legal inferiority in civil society, which lessened the security of the right of the colored race, and was a step toward reducing them to a condition of servility. Indeed, the right of a colored man that, in the selection of jurors to pass upon his life, liberty and property, there shall be no exclusion of his race, and no discrimination against them because of color, has been asserted in a number of cases. *Virginia* v. *Rives*, 100 U.S. 313; *Neal* v. *Delaware*, 103 U.S. 370; *Bush* v. *Kentucky*, 107 U.S. 110; *Gibson* v. *Mississippi*, 162 U.S. 565. So, where the laws of a particular locality or the charter of a particular railway corporation has provided that no person shall be excluded from the cars on account of color, we have held that this meant that persons of color should travel in the same car as white ones, and that the enactment was not satisfied by the company's providing cars assigned exclusively to people of color, though they were as good as those which they assigned exclusively to white persons. *Railroad Company* v. *Brown*, 17 Wall. 445.

. . . [W]here a statute of Louisiana required those engaged in the transportation of passengers among the States to give to all persons travelling within that State, upon vessels employed in that business, equal rights and privileges in all parts of the vessel, without distinction on account of race or color, and subjected to an action for damages the owner of such a vessel, who excluded colored passengers on account of their color from the cabin set aside by him for the use of whites, it was held to be so far as it applied to interstate commerce, unconstitutional and void. *Hall* v. *DeCuir,* 95 U.S. 485. The court in this case, however, expressly disclaimed that it had anything whatever to do with the statute as a regulation of internal commerce, or affecting anything else than commerce among the States. . . .

It is claimed by the plaintiff in error that, in any mixed community, the reputation of belonging to the dominant race, in this instance the white race, is *property,* in the same sense that a right of action, or of inheritance, is property. Conceding this to be so, for the purposes of this case, we are unable to see how this statute deprives him of, or in any way affects his right to, such property. If he be a white man and assigned to a colored coach, he may have his action for damages against the company for being deprived of his so called property. Upon the other hand, if he be a colored man and be so assigned, he has been deprived of no property, since he is not lawfully entitled to the reputation of being a white man.

In this connection, it is also suggested by the learned counsel for the plaintiff in error that the same argument that will justify the state legislature in requiring railways to provide separate accommodations for the two races will also authorize them to require separate cars to be provided for people whose hair is of a certain color, or who are aliens, or who belong to certain nationalities, or to enact laws requiring colored people to walk upon one side of the street, and white people upon the other, or requiring white men's houses to be painted white, and colored men's black, or their vehicles or business signs to be of different colors, upon the theory that one side of the street is as good as the other, or that a house or vehicle of one color is as good as one of another color. The reply to all this is that every exercise of the police power must be reasonable, and extend only to such laws as are enacted in good faith for the promotion for the public good, and not for the annoyance or oppression of a particular class. . . .

So far, then, as a conflict with the Fourteenth Amendment is concerned, the case reduces itself to the question whether the statute of Louisiana is a reasonable regulation, and with respect to this there must necessarily be a large discretion on the part of the legislature. In determining the question of reasonableness it is at liberty to act with reference to the established usages, customs and traditions of the people, and with a view to the promotion of their comfort, and the preservation of the public peace and good order. Gauged by this standard, we cannot say that a law which authorizes or even requires the separation of the two races in public conveyances is unreasonable, or more obnoxious to the Fourteenth Amendment than the acts of Congress requiring separate schools for colored children in the District of Columbia, the constitutionality of which does not seem to have been questioned, or the corresponding acts of state legislatures.

We consider the underlying fallacy of the plaintiff's argument to consist in the assumption that the enforced separation of the two races stamps the colored race with a badge of inferiority. If this be so, it is not by reason of anything found in the act, but solely because the colored race chooses to put that construction upon it. The argument necessarily assumes that if, as has been more than once the case, and is not unlikely to be so again, the colored race should become the dominant power in the state legislature, and should enact a law in precisely similar terms, it would thereby relegate the white race to an inferior position. We imagine that the white race, at least, would not acquiesce in this assumption. The argument also assumes that social prejudices may be overcome by legislation, and that equal rights cannot be secured to the negro except by an enforced commingling of the two races. We cannot accept this proposition. If the two races are to meet upon terms of social equality, it must be the result of natural affinities, a mutual appreciation of each other's merits and a voluntary consent of individuals. As was said by the Court of Appeals of New York in *People* v. *Gallagher*, 93 N.Y. 438, 448, "this end can neither be accomplished nor promoted by laws which conflict with the general sentiment of the community upon whom they are designed to operate. When the government, therefore, has secured to each of its citizens equal rights before the law and equal opportunities for improvement and progress, it has accomplished the end for which it was organized and performed all of the functions respecting social advantages with which it is endowed." Legislation is powerless to eradicate racial instincts or to abolish distinctions based upon physical differences, and the attempt to do so can only result in accentuating the difficulties of the present situation. If the civil and political rights of both races be equal one cannot be inferior to the other civilly or politically. If one race be inferior to the other socially, the Constitution of the United States cannot put them upon the same plane. . . .

Affirmed.

Mr. Justice Harlan dissenting.

. . . However apparent the injustice of such legislation may be, we have only to consider whether it is consistent with the Constitution of the United States. . . .

If a white man and a black man choose to occupy the same public conveyance on a public highway, it is their right to do so, and no government, proceeding alone on grounds of race, can prevent it without infringing the personal liberty of each. . . .

The white race deems itself to be the dominant race in this country. And so it is, in prestige, in achievements, in education, in wealth and in power. So, I doubt not, it will continue to be for all time, if it remains true to its great heritage and holds fast to the principles of constitutional liberty. But in view of the Constitution, in the eye of the law, there is in this country no superior, dominant, ruling class of citizens. There is no caste here. Our Constitution is color-blind, and neither knows nor tolerates classes among citizens. In respect of civil rights, all citizens are equal before the law. The humblest is the peer of the most powerful. The law regards man as man, and takes no account of his surroundings or of his color when his civil rights as guaranteed by the supreme law of the land are involved. It is, therefore, to be regretted that this high tribunal, the final expositor of the fundamental law of the land, has reached the conclusion that it is competent for a State to regulate the enjoyment by citizens of their civil rights solely upon the basis of race.

In my opinion, the judgment this day rendered will, in time, prove to be quite as pernicious as the decision made by this tribunal in the *Dred Scott case*. It was adjudged in that case that the descendants of Africans who were imported into this country and sold as slaves were not included nor intended to be included under the word "citizens" in the Constitution, and could not claim any of the rights and privileges which that instrument provided for and secured to citizens of the United States; that at the time of the adoption of the Constitution they were "considered as a subordinate and inferior class of beings, who had been subjugated by the dominant race, and, whether emancipated or not, yet remained subject to their authority, and had no rights or privileges but such as those who held the power and the government might choose to grant them." 19 How. 393, 404. The recent amendments of the Constitution, it was supposed, had eradicated these principles from our institutions. But it seems that we have yet, in some of the States, a dominant race—a superior class of citizens, which assumes to regulate the enjoyment of civil rights, common to all citizens, upon the basis of race. The present decision, it may well be apprehended, will not only stimulate aggressions, more or less brutal and irritating, upon the admitted rights of colored citizens, but will encourage the belief that it is possible, by means of state enactments, to defeat the beneficient purposes which the people of the United States had in view when they adopted the recent amendments of the Constitution, by one of which the blacks of this country were made citizens of the United States and of the States in which they respectively reside, and whose privileges and immunities, as citizens, the States are forbidden to abridge. Sixty millions of whites are in no danger from the presence here of eight millions of blacks. The destinies of the two races, in this country, are indissolubly linked together, and the interests of both require that the common government of all shall not permit the seeds of race hate to be planted under the sanction of law. What can more certainly arouse race hate, what more certainly create and perpetuate a feeling of distrust between these races, than state enactments, which, in fact, proceed on the ground that colored citizens are so inferior and degraded that they cannot be allowed to sit in public coaches occupied by white citizens? That, as all will admit, is the real meaning of such legislation as was enacted in Louisiana. . . .

I am of opinion that the statute of Louisiana is inconsistent with the personal liberty of citizens, white and black, in that State, and hostile to both the spirit and letter of the Constitution of the United States. If laws of like character should be enacted in the several States of the Union, the effect would be in the highest degree mischievous. Slavery, as an institution tolerated by law would, it is true, have disappeared from our country, but there would remain a power in the States, by sinister legislation, to interfere with the full enjoyment of the blessings of freedom; to regulate civil rights, common to all citizens, upon the basis of race; and to place in a condition of legal inferiority a large body of American citizens, now constituting a part of the political community called the People of the United States, for whom, and by whom through representatives, our government is administered. Such a system is inconsistent with the guarantee given by the Constitution to each State of a republican form of government, and may be stricken down by Congressional action, or by the courts in the discharge of their solemn duty to maintain the supreme law of the land, anything in the constitution or laws of any State to the contrary notwithstanding.

For the reasons stated, I am constrained to withhold my assent from the opinion and judgment of the majority.

THE LOUISIANA CONSTITUTION (1898)

Like the rest of the nation, the South in the 1890's experienced a wave of reform in which liberal elements, identified with the Populist Movement, attempted to wrest control from conservative political and economic leaders. For a brief period there were indications that southern reformers would try to effect a united front between poor whites and Negroes as a basis for action against the established interests. The conservatives rallied with vigor and ingenuity. They convinced the liberal elements that total reform was less desirable than a union of whites to preserve the "purity" of the South.

Working across socio-economic lines, southern whites began to impose, through the sanction of law, a wide-ranging series of political, civil, economic, and social restrictions upon the Negro. Constitutions were rewritten and complementary statutes were enacted to formalize would-be legal patterns of segregation and discrimination. The courts concurred in support of Jim Crow legislation, and the Negro minority was powerless to protect itself.

One of the most devious instruments of white segregationists was the so-called "grandfather clause," which stipulated that no male of voting age who had not voted prior to 1867, or who was not the son or grandson of such a voter, could be eligible for political participation. The intent and promise of

the Fourteenth and Fifteenth Amendments were thus negated.
So strongly did Louisiana whites feel about suppressing the
Negro that they detailed restrictive procedures in their fundamental state document—their constitution. Other states acted
in similar fashion, and the abbreviated Oklahoma version came
before the United States Supreme Court in *Guinn and Beal*
v. *United States* (Document 64).

DOCUMENT 59

State Constitution of Louisiana, 1898[*]

Suffrage and Elections

ARTICLE 197

Every male citizen of this State and of the United States,
native born or naturalized, not less than twenty-one years of
age, and possessing the following qualifications, shall be an
elector, and shall be entitled to vote at any election in the
State by the people, except as may be herein otherwise
provided.

. . . .

SEC. 3. He shall be able to read and write, and shall
demonstrate his ability to do so when he applies for registration, by making, under oath administered by the registration
officer or his deputy, written application therefore, in the
English language, or his mother tongue, which application
shall contain the essential facts necessary to show that he is
entitled to register and vote, and shall be entirely written,
dated and signed by him, in the presence of the registration
officer or his deputy, without assistance or suggestion from any
person or any memorandum whatever, except the form of
application hereinafter set forth; provided, however, that if the
applicant be unable to write his application in the English
language, he shall have the right, if he so demands, to write
the same in his mother tongue from the dictation of an interpreter; and if the applicant is unable to write his application

---

[*] Thorpe, ed., *The Federal and State Constitutions . . .* , Vol.
III, pp. 1562–65.

by reason of physical disability, the same shall be written at his dictation by the registration officer or his deputy, upon his oath of such disability. . . .

SEC. 4. If he be not able to read and write, as provided by Section three of this article, then he shall be entitled to register and vote if he shall, at the time he offers to register, be the bona fide owner of property assessed to him in this State at a valuation of not less than three hundred dollars on the assessment roll of the current year in which he offers to register, or on the roll of the preceding year, if the roll of the current year shall not then have been completed and filed, and on which, if such property be personal only, all taxes due shall have been paid. The applicant for registration under this section shall make oath before the registration office or his deputy, that he is a citizen of the United States and of this State, over the age of twenty-one years; that he possesses the qualifications prescribed in section one of this article, and that he is the owner of property assessed in this State to him at a valuation of not less than three hundred dollars, and if such property be personal only, that all taxes due thereon have been paid.

SEC. 5. No male person who was on January 1st, 1867, or at any date prior thereto, entitled to vote under the Constitution or statutes of any State of the United States, wherein he then resided, and no son or grandson of any such person not less than twenty-one years of age at the date of the adoption of this Constitution, and no male person of foreign birth, who was naturalized prior to the first day of January, 1898, shall be denied the right to register and vote in this State by reason of his failure to possess the educational or property qualifications prescribed by this Constitution; provided, he shall have resided in this State for five years next preceding the date at which he shall apply for registration, and shall have registered in accordance with the terms of this article prior to September 1, 1898, and no person shall be entitled to register under this section after said date.

. . . .

ARTICLE 198

No person less than sixty years of age shall be permitted

to vote at any election in the State who shall not, in addition to the qualifications above prescribed, have paid on or before the 31st day of December, of each year, for the two years preceding the year in which he offers to vote, a poll tax of one dollar per annum, to be used exclusively in aid of the public schools of the parish in which such tax shall have been collected; which tax is hereby imposed on every male resident of this State between the age of twenty-one and sixty years. Poll taxes shall be a lien only upon assessed property, and no process shall issue to enforce the collection of the same except against assessed property.

. . . .

Article 200

No person shall vote at any primary election or in any convention or other political assembly held for the purpose of nominating any candidate for public office, unless he is at the time a registered voter. And in all political conventions in this State the apportionment of representation shall be on the basis of population. . . .

TENNESSEE'S JIM CROW LAW IN EDUCATION (1901)

The Tennessee Act of March 13, 1901, is typical of the Jim Crow legislation enacted throughout the South. Brief, but direct and comprehensive, the law prohibited Negroes and whites from being educated in the same classrooms and also forbade their attending the same schools. The act applied to all levels of education, and teachers and professors were subject to penalties for infractions. Unlike the more deviously worded Louisiana Constitution of 1898 (Document 59), the Tennessee statute bluntly and unequivocally identified the Negro.

DOCUMENT 60

An act to prohibit the co-education of the white and colored races and to prohibit the white and colored races from attending the same schools, academies, colleges or other places of learning in this state*

SECTION 1. *Be it enacted by the General Assembly of the State of Tennessee,* That hereafter it shall be unlawful for any school, academy, college or other place of learning to allow white and colored persons to attend the same school, academy, college or other place of learning.

SEC. 2. *Be it further enacted,* That it shall be unlawful for any teacher, professor or educator in the State, in any college, academy or school of learning, to allow the white and colored races to attend the same school or for any teacher or educator, or other person to instruct or teach both the white and colored races in the same class, school or college building, or in any other place or places of learning, or allow or permit the same to be done with their knowledge, consent or procurement.

SEC. 3. *Be it further enacted,* That any person or persons violating this Act or any of its provisions, when convicted shall be fined for each offense fifty ($50) dollars and imprisoned not less than thirty days nor more than six months, at the discretion of the Court.

SEC. 4. *Be it further enacted,* That Grand Juries shall have inquisitorial powers of all violations of the Act, and the same to be given in charge Circuit Court Judges to the Grand Juries.

SEC. 5. *Be it further enacted,* That this Act shall take effect from and after the first day of September, 1901, the public welfare requiring it.

APPROVED, March 13, 1901.

---

* *Laws of Tennessee, 1901,* Ch. 7, House Bill No. 7, p. 9.

CONGRESSIONAL VALEDICTORY OF THE NEGRO (1901)

George H. White of Tarboro, North Carolina, was the last Negro to sit in the United States Congress until the election of Chicago Republican Oscar DePriest in 1928. White's address to the House of Representatives in late January, 1901, represented, for over a quarter of a century, the Negro valedictory to Congress.

White traced the patterns of intimidation and fraud that had removed the Negro from effective participation in public affairs throughout the South, and he denounced the false myths and stereotypes employed by members of the dominant white majority to justify their conduct. The Negro, he asserted, wanted nothing more than equal justice through the conscientious execution of existing laws; however, the Fourteenth Amendment and complementary legislation, he lamented, had already become dead letters in practice. Supported by a sectional and embittered view of Reconstruction, southern Democrats had successfully convinced their region and the nation at large that the Negro must be suppressed and denied participation in public affairs. Although Congressman White could do little to reverse this course of events, he did at least trace its nature and decry its effects in a straightforward fashion.

DOCUMENT 61

Speech of Congressman George H. White*

. . . Now, Mr. Chairman, before concluding my remarks I want to submit a brief recipe for the solution of the so-called American negro problem. He asks no special favors, but simply demands that he be given the same chance for existence, for earning a livelihood, for raising himself in the scales of manhood and womanhood that are accorded to kindred nationalities. Treat him as a man; go into his home and learn of his

---

* *Congressional Record*, 56th Congress, 2nd Session, January 29, 1901, pp. 1635–38.

social conditions; learn of his cares, his troubles, and his hopes for the future; gain his confidence; open the doors of industry to him; let the word "negro," "colored," and "black" be stricken from all the organizations enumerated in the federation of labor.

Help him to overcome his weaknesses, punish the crime-committing class by the courts of the land, measure the standard of the race by its best material, cease to mold prejudicial and unjust public sentiment against him, and my word for it, he will learn to support, hold up the hands of, and join in with that political party, that institution, whether secular or religious, in every community where he lives, which is destined to do the greatest good for the greatest number. Obliterate race hatred, party prejudice, and help us to achieve nobler ends, greater results, and become more satisfactory citizens to our brother in white.

This, Mr. Chairman, is perhaps the negroes' temporary farewell to the American Congress; but let me say, Phœnix-like he will rise up some day and come again. These parting words are in behalf of an outraged, heart-broken, bruised, and bleeding, but God-fearing people, faithful, industrious, loyal people—rising people, full of potential force.

Mr. Chairman, in the trial of Lord Bacon, when the court disturbed the counsel for the defendant, Sir Walter Raleigh raised himself up to his full height and, addressing the court, said: "Sir, I am pleading for the life of a human being."

The only apology that I have to make for the earnestness with which I have spoken is that I am pleading for the life, the liberty, the future happiness, and manhood suffrage for one-eighth of the entire population of the United States. [Loud applause.]

THE CLASSIC SOUTHERN POSITION ON THE NEGRO (1907)

On the night of August 13–14, 1906, there occurred in Texas an incident later known as the "Brownsville Riot." Three entire companies of Negro infantrymen, stationed at Fort Brown on the outskirts of the town, were charged by

residents with both murder and the destruction of property.
President Theodore Roosevelt, later that fall, dishonorably
discharged every man in the three companies—although the
evidence justifying such stern action seemed then and seems
now circumstantial and inconclusive. In January, 1907, Senator Joseph B. Foraker of Ohio successfully sought a senatorial
investigation of the incident. Some of the soldiers were eventually reinstated with privileges and back pay.

It was in the course of debate on the Ohio Republican's
resolution that Democrat Benjamin R. Tillman of South Carolina rose to defend himself against criticisms by Wisconsin
Republican John C. Spooner, and to go on, at length, to
restate the classic southern position on the role of the Negro
in America.

Senator Tillman's remarks expressed the three major themes
justifying repression of the Negro: (1) the embittered mem-
ories of Reconstruction—as viewed through southern eyes—
with the inevitable conviction that Negroes must never again
be given a role in public affairs; (2) the concept of inherent
Negro inferiority; and (3) belief in the purity of the white
race, as epitomized in the sanctity of white womanhood. These
three elements, in the Senator's view, fully justified extra-legal
conduct that included manipulation of the ballot box, discriminatory Jim Crow legislation on both state and regional
levels, and, when necessary, recourse to lynching and mob
violence. Denying that racial considerations were limited
to the South, the Senator asked why northern Republicans
should object to the suppression of the Negro when the rest
of the nation had so readily concurred in racist discrimination
against Asian peoples.

DOCUMENT 62

Speech of Senator Benjamin R. Tillman*

. . . Now, what about those words of mine: "We shot them,"
etc. In what connection did I utter them? If I mistake not the
Senator from Wisconsin was in this Chamber when I used
that language. There were present a large number of leading

---

* *Congressional Record*, 59th Congress, 2nd Session, January 21,
1907, pp. 1440–44.

Republicans. I challenged each and every man here to show wherein the people of South Carolina were not justified, and no one dared reply. I will repeat the statement of fact and circumstances. It was in 1876, thirty years ago, and the people of South Carolina had been living under negro rule for eight years. There was a condition bordering upon anarchy. Misrule, robbery, and murder were holding high carnival. The people's substance was being stolen, and there was no incentive to labor. Our legislature was composed of a majority of negroes, most of whom could neither read nor write. They were the easy dupes and tools of as dirty a band of vampires and robbers as ever preyed upon a prostrate people. There was riotous living in the statehouse and sessions of the legislature lasting from year to year.

Our lawmakers never adjourned. They were getting a per diem. They felt that they could increase their income by remaining in session all the while. They were taxing us to death and confiscating our property. We felt the very foundations of our civilization crumbling beneath our feet, that we were sure to be engulfed by the black flood of barbarians who were surrounding us and had been put over us by the Army under the reconstruction acts. The sun of hope had disappeared behind a cloud of gloom and despair, and a condition had arisen such as has never been the lot of white men at any time in the history of the world to endure. Life ceased to be worth having on the terms under which we were living, and in desperation we determined to take the government away from the negroes.

We reorganized the Democratic party with one plank, and only one plank, namely, that "this is a white man's country and white men must govern it." Under that banner we went to battle. We had 8,000 negro militia organized by carpetbaggers. The carpetbag governor had come to Washington and had persuaded General Grant to transcend his authority by issuing to the State its quota of arms under the militia appropriation for twenty years in advance, in order to get enough to equip these negro soldiers. They used to drum up and down the roads with their fifes and their gleaming bayonets, equipped with new Springfield rifles and dressed in the regulation uniform. It was lawful, I suppose, but these negro soldiers or this negro militia—for they were never soldiers—growing more and more bold, let drop talk among themselves where the white children might hear their purpose, and it came to our ears. This is what they said: "The President is our friend. The North is with us. We intend to kill all the white men, take the land, marry the white women, and then these white children will wait on us."

Those fellows forgot that there were in South Carolina some forty-odd thousand ex-Confederate soldiers, men who had worn the gray on a hundred battlefields; men who had charged breastworks defended by men in blue; men who had held lines of battle charged by men in blue; men who had seen real battles, where heroes fought. They forgot that putting in uniform a negro man with not sense enough to get out of a shower of rain did not make him a soldier. So when this condition of desperation had reached the unbearable point; when, as I say, despair had come upon us, we set to work to take the government away from them.

. . . .

Have I ever advocated lynch law at any time or at any place? I answer on my honor, "Never!" I have justified it for one crime, and one only, and I have consistently and persistently maintained that attitude for the last fourteen years. As governor of South Carolina I proclaimed that, although I had taken the oath of office to support the law and enforce it, I would lead a mob to lynch any man, black or white, who had ravished a woman, black or white. This is my attitude calmly and deliberately taken, and justified by my conscience in the sight of God.

. . . .

Look at our environment in the South, surrounded, and in a very large number of counties and in two States outnumbered, by the negroes—engulfed, as it were, in a black flood of semi-barbarians. Our farmers, living in segregated farmhouses, more or less thinly scattered through the country, have negroes on every hand. For forty years these have been taught the damnable heresy of equality with the white man, made the puppet of scheming politicians, the instrument for the furtherance of political ambitions. Some of them have just enough education to be able to read, but not always to understand what they read. Their minds are those of children, while they have the passions and strength of men. Taught that they are oppressed, and with breasts pulsating with hatred of the whites, the younger generation of negro men are roaming over the land, passing back and forth without hindrance, and with no possibility of adequate police protection to the communities in which they are residing. . . .

VI

Emergence of
Negro Protest
1915–1941

The period that stretched from the First to the Second World War represented a subtle but basic turning point in the path of the American Negro. When the era opened, the condition of the Negro seemed almost hopeless. He had been deprived by law of nearly every basic individual and public right throughout the southern states; and he had been stripped, by acquiescence and custom, of many of these same rights throughout the rest of the country. His life was held cheaply, his chances for advancement restricted, and his own awareness of the means to effect change by concerted action was yet limited. By the time the nation was about to enter the Second World War, much of this had changed, or was just about to change.

The agency most responsible for the gradual emergence of the Negro protest movement was the National Association for the Advancement of Colored People. A product of the Progressive Era, the NAACP was pledged to a program of re-educating the American public to the need for and wisdom of interracial reform.

The Negro alone could not have moved white society to interracial reform, not even with the help of activist white liberals. It took the extensive disruptions of two world wars and a national depression to shatter the established patterns of society. The massive wartime migrations out of the rural

South into the urban areas of both the South and the North gave the Negro an opportunity to engage directly in the broader, more cosmopolitan features of American life and helped prepare him to organize for protest. In the interwar period, the wave of New Deal legislation also worked to the Negro's benefit. The depression had convinced many formerly complacent whites that reform on a broad front was in their interest, too.

There were other groups advocating change while seeking the endorsement of the Negro community. These included certain Socialist and Far Left organizations. Included in the latter category were the League of Struggle for Negro Rights and the National Negro Congress. While these groups had relatively minor impact upon the interracial situation, they helped to dramatize the plight of the Negro and forced the NAACP to take more vigorous action in the pursuit of reform. Finally, there were the black nationalists led by Marcus Garvey, who rejected interracial solutions in favor of a separatist position along racial lines.

While few Americans appreciated the extent to which the interracial situation had shifted from 1915 to 1941, there had indeed been a series of changes in conditions and attitudes that would not permit a perpetuation of Jim Crow.

W. E. B. DU BOIS'S PROGRAM FOR THE AMERICAN NEGRO (1915)

One of the founders of the National Association for the Advancement of Colored People in 1909, W. E. B. Du Bois, author of *Souls of Black Folk,* readily accepted the post as NAACP director of research and also the editorship of its monthly publication, *The Crisis.* Yet he remained a persistently enigmatic figure because his individual genius was never fully reconciled to the organizational complexities and necessities of the Association. In his twenty-four years as editor of *The Crisis,* the journal became both the principal voice of interracial protest and reform and the leading medium for the introduction of talented Negro writers.

The program which Du Bois outlined in the April, 1915

issue was a mixture of the NAACP platform and Du Bois's personal position on public affairs. He heatedly and unequivocally denied the concept of white superiority and anchored his position on the concept of a society that must encourage diversity and pluralism. With biting effect, he noted that patterns of segregation and discrimination literally cut the Negro off from life in the fullest and most fundamental sense. His call for the cooperative uses of the means of production and distribution carried overtones of his personal sympathies for socialism, a view which he shared with several of the white organizers of the NAACP.

In a broader sense, the Du Bois program reflected the spirit of the Progressive Era. Progressives believed in the reaction of an electorate alerted to existing evils by publicity and exposé, and educated to the need for reform by the tactics of meetings and conferences, newspaper and magazine articles, and open public debate. They believed in legal-judicial redress as a means to achieve broad, national reform.

DOCUMENT 63

The Immediate Program of the American Negro*

The immediate program of the American Negro means nothing unless it is mediate to his great ideal and the ultimate ends of his development. We need not waste time by seeking to deceive our enemies into thinking that we are going to be content with a half loaf, or by being willing to lull our friends into a false sense of our indifference and present satisfaction.

The American Negro demands equality—political equality, industrial equality and social equality; and he is never going to rest satisfied with anything less. He demands this in no spirit of braggadocio and with no obsequious envy of others, but as an absolute measure of self-defense and the only one that will assure to the darker races their ultimate survival on earth.

. . . .

* W. E. B. Du Bois, "The Immediate Program of the American Negro," *The Crisis*, IX (April, 1915), pp. 310–12. Reprinted by permission.

These involve both negative and positive sides. They call for freedom on the one hand and power on the other. The Negro must have political freedom; taxation without representation is tyranny. American Negroes of to-day are ruled by tyrants who take what they please in taxes and give what they please in law and administration, in justice and in injustice; and the great mass of black people must stand helpless and voiceless before a condition which has time and time again caused other peoples to fight and die.

The Negro must have industrial freedom. Between the peonage of the rural South, the oppression of shrewd capitalists and the jealousy of certain trade unions, the Negro laborer is the most exploited class in the country, giving more hard toil for less money than any other American, and has less voice in the conditions of his labor.

In social intercourse every effort is being made to-day from the President of the United States and the so-called Church of Christ down to saloons and boot-blacks to segregate, strangle and spiritually starve Negroes so as to give them the least possible chance to know and share civilization.

. . . .

The practical steps to this are clear. First we must fight obstructions; by continual and increasing effort we must first make American courts either build up a body of decisions which will protect the plain legal rights of American citizens or else make them tear down the civil and political rights of all citizens in order to oppress a few. Either result will bring justice in the end. It is lots of fun and most ingenious just now for courts to twist law so as to say I shall not live here or vote there, or marry the woman who wishes to marry me. But when to-morrow these decisions throttle all freedom and overthrow the foundation of democracy and decency, there is going to be some judicial house cleaning.

We must *secondly* seek in legislature and congress remedial legislation; national aid to public school education, the removal of all legal discriminations based simply on race and color, and those marriage laws passed to make the seduction of black girls easy and without legal penalty.

Third the human contact of human beings must be increased; the policy which brings into sympathetic touch and understanding, men and women, rich and poor, capitalist and laborer, Asiatic and European, must bring into closer contact and mutual knowledge the white and black people of this land. It is the most frightful indictment of a country which dares to call itself civilized that it has allowed itself to drift into a state of ignorance where ten million people are coming to believe that all white people are liars and thieves, and the whites in turn to believe that the chief industry of Negroes is raping white women.

Fourth only the publication of the truth repeatedly and incisively and uncompromisingly can secure that change in public opinion which will correct these awful lies.

• • • •

Such is the program of work against obstructions. Let us now turn to constructive effort. This may be summed up under (1) economic co-operation (2) a revival of art and literature (3) political action (4) education and (5) organization.

Under economic co-operation we must strive to spread the idea among colored people that the accumulation of wealth is for social rather than individual ends. We must avoid, in the advancement of the Negro race, the mistakes of ruthless exploitation which have marked modern economic history. To this end we must seek not simply home ownership, small landholding and saving accounts, but also all forms of co-operation, both in production and distribution, profit sharing, building and loan associations, systematic charity for definite, practical ends, systematic migration from mob rule and robbery, to freedom and enfranchisement, the emancipation of women and the abolition of child labor.

In art and literature we should try to loose the tremendous emotional wealth of the Negro and the dramatic strength of his problems through writing, the stage, pageantry and other forms of art. We should resurrect forgotten ancient Negro art and history, and we should set the black man before the world as both a creative artist and a strong subject for artistic treatment.

In political action we should organize the votes of Negroes in such congressional districts as have any number of Negro voters. We should systematically interrogate candidates on matters vital to Negro freedom and uplift. We should train colored voters to reject the bribe of office and to accept only decent legal enactments both for their own uplift and for the uplift of laboring classes of all races and both sexes.

In education we must seek to give colored children free public school training. We must watch with grave suspicion the attempt of those who, under the guise of vocational training, would fasten ignorance and menial service on the Negro for another generation. Our children must not in large numbers, be forced into the servant class; for menial service is still, in the main, little more than an antiquated survival of impossible conditions. It has always been as statistics show, a main cause of bastardy and prostitution and despite its many marvelous exceptions it will never come to the light of decency and honor until the house servant becomes the Servant in the House. It is our duty then, not drastically but persistently, to seek out colored children of ability and genius to open up to them broader, industrial opportunity and above all, to find that Talented Tenth and encourage it by the best and most exhaustive training in order to supply the Negro race and the world with leaders, thinkers and artists.

For the accomplishment of all these ends we must organize. Organization among us already has gone far but it must go much further and higher. Organization is sacrifice. It is sacrifice of opinions, of time, of work and of money, but it is, after all, the cheapest way of buying the most priceless of gifts—freedom and efficiency. I thank God that most of the money that supports the National Association for the Advancement of Colored People comes from black hands; a still larger proportion must so come, and we must not only support but control this and similar organizations and hold them unwaveringly to our objects, our aims and our ideals.

VOTING RIGHTS AND THE GRANDFATHER CLAUSE (1915)

In many southern states, the voting rights granted the Negro under the Fifteenth Amendment (Document 48) were merely a paper guarantee. For nearly a century, a vast arsenal of legislative devices was created to keep the Negro from the polls. And many of them succeeded. Not until the adoption of the Twenty-fourth Amendment in 1964 (Document 88) was the poll tax finally abolished in federal elections. Other devices designed to restrict the Negro franchise were not struck down until the passage of the Federal Voting Rights Act of 1965 (Document 92).

Most of the litigation on Negro franchise rights involved legislation designed to prohibit colored persons from voting in party primaries. These are considered in the key case of *Terry* v. *Adams* (Document 76).

One of the most effective devices to restrict the Negro vote was the establishment or stiffening of literacy requirements. The only disadvantage of literacy tests, from the southern point of view, was that they also barred numerous whites from the polling booths. State statutes and constitutional provisions containing so-called "grandfather clauses" were adopted by Alabama, Georgia, Louisiana, North Carolina, Oklahoma, South Carolina, and Virginia to sidestep the requirements. Most important was the Oklahoma constitutional provision exempting from literacy tests all persons and lineal descendants of all persons who had the right of franchise as of January 1, 1866. Since virtually all Negroes were nonvoters on that date, literacy tests would only be applicable to them. But did such state constitutional provisions meet the federal test of constitutionality under the Fifteenth Amendment? The United States Supreme Court said no. The unanimous Court condemned this voting restriction as one which "recreates and perpetuates the very conditions which the Amendment was intended to destroy" (238 U.S. at 360).

Oklahoma responded with a 1916 statute requiring that all persons who had previously been denied the franchise register within a twelve-day period. Since this obviously applied only to Negroes, and since the "practical difficulties in the administration of such a strict registration provision" would undoubtedly keep most Negroes from the polls, this statute was likewise held unconstitutional; *Lane* v. *Wilson*, 307 U.S. 268 (1939).

DOCUMENT 64

*Guinn and Beal v. United States**

MR. CHIEF JUSTICE WHITE delivered the opinion of the court. . . .

The questions which the court below asks are these:

"1. Was the amendment to the constitution of Oklahoma, heretofore set forth, valid?

"2. Was that amendment void in so far as it attempted to debar from the right or privilege of voting for a qualified candidate for a Member of Congress in Oklahoma, unless they were able to read and write any section of the constitution of Oklahoma, negro citizens of the United States who were otherwise qualified to vote for a qualified candidate for a Member of Congress in that State, but who were not, and none of whose lineal ancestors was, entitled to vote under any form of government on January 1, 1866, or at any time prior thereto, because they were then slaves?"

. . . .

Considering the questions in the light of the text of the suffrage amendment it is apparent that they are twofold because of the twofold character of the provisions as to suffrage which the amendment contains. The first question is concerned with that provision of the amendment which fixes a standard by which the right to vote is given upon conditions existing on January 1, 1866, and relieves those coming within that standard from the standard based on a literacy test which is established by the other provision of the amendment. The second question asks as to the validity of the literacy test and how far, if intrinsically valid, it would continue to exist and be operative in the event the standard based upon January 1, 1866, should be held to be illegal as violative of the Fifteenth Amendment.

. . . .

No question is raised by the Government concerning the validity of the literacy test provided for in the amendment

---

* Supreme Court of the United States, 238 U.S. 347 (1915).

under consideration as an independent standard since the conclusion is plain that that test rests on the exercise of state judgment and therefore cannot be here assailed either by disregarding the State's power to judge on the subject or by testing its motive in enacting the provision.

. . . .

1. *The operation and effect of the Fifteenth Amendment. . . .*

(a) Beyond doubt the Amendment does not take away from the state governments in a general sense the power over suffrage which has belonged to those governments from the beginning and without the possession of which power the whole fabric upon which the division of state and national authority under the Constitution and the organization of both governments rest would be without support and both the authority of the nation and the State would fall to the ground. In fact, the very command of the Amendment recognizes the possession of the general power by the State, since the Amendment seeks to regulate its exercise as to the particular subject with which it deals.

(b) But it is equally beyond the possibility of question that the Amendment in express terms restricts the power of the United States or the States to abridge or deny the right of a citizen of the United States to vote on account of race, color or previous condition of servitude. The restriction is coincident with the power and prevents its exertion in disregard of the command of the Amendment. But while this is true, it is true also that the Amendment does not change, modify or deprive the States of their full power as to suffrage except of course as to the subject with which the Amendment deals and to the extent that obedience to its command is necessary. Thus the authority over suffrage which the States possess and the limitation which the Amendment imposes are coördinate and one may not destroy the other without bringing about the destruction of both.

(c) While in the true sense, therefore, the Amendment gives no right of suffrage, it was long ago recognized that in operation its prohibition might measurably have that effect; that is to say, that as the command of the Amendment was self-executing and reached without legislative action the conditions of discrimination against which it was aimed, the result might arise that as a consequence of the striking down of a discriminating clause a right of suffrage would be enjoyed by reason of the generic character of the provision which would remain after the discrimination was stricken out. . . .

With these principles before us how can there be room for any serious dispute concerning the repugnancy of the standard based upon January 1, 1866 (a date which preceded the adoption of the Fifteenth Amendment), if the suffrage provision fixing that standard is susceptible of the significance which the Government attributes to it? Indeed, there seems no escape from the conclusion that to hold that there was even possibility for dispute on the subject would be but to declare that the Fifteenth Amendment not only had not the self-executing power which it has been recognized to have from the beginning, but that its provisions were wholly inoperative because susceptible of being rendered inapplicable by mere forms of expression embodying no exercise of judgment and resting upon no discernible reason other than the purpose to disregard the prohibitions of the Amendment by creating a standard of voting which on its face was in substance but a revitalization of conditions which when they prevailed in the past had been destroyed by the self-operative force of the Amendment.

2. *The standard of January 1, 1866, fixed in the suffrage amendment and its significance.*

The inquiry of course here is, Does the amendment as to the particular standard which this heading embraces involve the mere refusal to comply with the commands of the Fifteenth Amendment as previously stated? This leads us for the purpose of the analysis to recur to the text of the suffrage amendment. Its opening sentence fixes the literacy standard which is all-inclusive since it is general in its expression and contains no word of discrimination on account of race or color or any other reason. This however is immediately followed by the provisions creating the standard based upon the condition existing on January 1, 1866, and carving out those coming under that standard from the inclusion in the literacy test which would have controlled them but for the exclusion thus expressly provided for. The provision is this·

"But no person who was, on January 1, 1866, or at any

time prior thereto, entitled to vote under any form of government, or who at that time resided in some foreign nation, and no lineal descendant of such person, shall be denied the right to register and vote because of his inability to so read and write sections of such constitution." . . .

It is true it contains no express words of an exclusion from the standard which it establishes of any person on account of race, color, or previous condition of servitude prohibited by the Fifteenth Amendment, but the standard itself inherently brings that result into existence since it is based purely upon a period of time before the enactment of the Fifteenth Amendment and makes that period the controlling and dominant test of the right of suffrage. In other words, we seek in vain for any ground which would sustain any other interpretation but that the provision, recurring to the conditions existing before the Fifteenth Amendment was adopted and the continuance of which the Fifteenth Amendment prohibited, proposed by in substance and effect lifting those conditions over to a period of time after the Amendment to make them the basis of the right to suffrage conferred in direct and positive disregard of the Fifteenth Amendment. And the same result, we are of opinion, is demonstrated by considering whether it is possible to discover any basis of reason for the standard thus fixed other than the purpose above stated. We say this because we are unable to discover how, unless the prohibitions of the Fifteenth Amendment were considered, the slightest reason was afforded for basing the classification upon a period of time prior to the Fifteenth Amendment. Certainly it cannot be said that there was any peculiar necromancy in the time named which engendered attributes affecting the qualification to vote which would not exist at another and different period unless the Fifteenth Amendment was in view. . . .

And it will be so certified.

FRENCH DIRECTIVE ON THE TREATMENT OF BLACK AMERICAN TROOPS (1918)

White segregationists were justified in their fears that the First World War would prove disruptive to settled attitudes and established patterns of racial discrimination. With the nation mobilized for war, the labor shortage on the domestic front offered unprecedented opportunities for Negroes, especially from the South, to step into reasonably well-paid industrial jobs. At the same time, military necessities abroad meant that thousands of Negro troops would be traveling outside of the United States; they would be exposed to the reactions of European whites, markedly different from those they had known. These experiences at home and abroad, accompanied by the sacrifices of Negro troops in action, affected colored Americans and made it understandably impossible for them to accept a return to prewar conditions of discrimination.

W. E. B. Du Bois expressed this view in the May, 1919, issue of *The Crisis* (the monthly publication of the NAACP), when he spoke of American Negro soldiers in the following terms: "Make way for Democracy! We saved it in France, and by the great Jehovah, we will save it in the United States of America, or know the reason why." (*The Crisis,* XVIII [May, 1919], pp. 13–14.) That article so disturbed southern congressmen that they tried to ban *The Crisis;* the journal was briefly withheld from the mails.

During the last stages of the war, American segregationist influence secured the publication of a French military directive which warned against any action on the part of Frenchmen that might be sympathetic to American Negroes, and, therefore, offensive to American whites. The directive declared that Americans were of one mind on the interracial question, and it hinted at Negro vices that were irremediable in nature. French military authorities were urged to remind both their troops and civilian leaders that they should neither fraternize with nor unduly commend Negro troops. The directive suggested that nondiscriminatory behavior toward American Negroes would also offend white French colonials by encouraging the black race generally.

The authorship and distribution of the directive confirm the disproportionate influence which southern whites had in the United States Army and indicate the acquiescence of northern white Americans in patterns of racial discrimination.

DOCUMENT 65

*A French Directive**

[To the] French Military Mission stationed with the American Army. August 7, 1918. Secret information concerning the Black American Troops.

It is important for French officers who have been called upon to exercise command over black American troops, or to live in close contact with them, to have an exact idea of the position occupied by Negroes in the United States. The information set forth in the following communication ought to be given to these officers and it is to their interest to have these matters known and widely disseminated. It will devolve likewise on the French Military Authorities, through the medium of the Civil Authorities, to give information on this subject to the French population residing in the cantonments occupied by American colored troops.

1. The American attitude upon the Negro question may seem a matter for discussion to many French minds. But we French are not in our province if we undertake to discuss what some call "prejudice." *[recognize that] American opinion is unanimous on the "color question," and does not admit of any discussion.*

The increasing number of Negroes in the United States (about 15,000,000) would create for the white race in the Republic a menace of degeneracy were it not that an impassable gulf has been made between them.

As this danger does not exist for the French race, *the French public has become accustomed to treating the Negro with familiarity and indulgence.*

This indulgence and this familiarity *[These] are matters of grievous concern to the Americans. They consider them an affront to their national policy.* They are afraid that contact with the French will inspire in black Americans aspirations which to them (the whites) appear intolerable. *It is of the utmost importance that every effort be made to avoid profoundly estranging American opinion.*

Although a citizen of the United States, the black man is regarded by the white American as an inferior being with

---

* *The Crisis,* XVIII (May, 1919), pp. 16–18. Reprinted by permission.

whom relations of business or service only are possible. The black is constantly being censured for his want of intelligence and discretion, his lack of civic and professional conscience, and for his tendency toward undue familiarity.

The vices of the Negro are a constant menace to the American who has to repress them sternly. For instance, the black American troops in France have, by themselves, given rise to as many complaints for attempted rape as all the rest of the army. And yet the (black American) soldiers sent us have been the choicest with respect to physique and morals, for the number disqualified at the time of mobilization was enormous.

Conclusion

1. We must prevent the rise of any pronounced degree of intimacy between French officers and black officers. We may be courteous and amiable with these last, but we cannot deal with them on the same plane as with the white American officers without deeply wounding the latter. We *must not eat with* [*the blacks*] them, *must not shake hands or seek to talk or meet with them outside of the requirements of military service*.

2. We must not commend too highly the black American troops, particularly in the presence of (white) Americans. It is all right to recognize their good qualities and their services, but only in moderate terms strictly in keeping with the truth.

3. Make a point of keeping the native cantonment population from "spoiling" the Negroes. (White) *Americans become greatly incensed at any public expression of intimacy between white women with black men.* They have recently uttered violent protests against a picture in the "Vie Parisienne" entitled "The Child of the Desert" which shows a (white) woman in a "cabinet particulier" with a Negro. Familiarity on the part of white women with black men is furthermore a source of profound regret to our experienced colonials who see in it an overweening menace to the prestige of the white race.

Military authority cannot intervene directly in this question, but it can through the civil authorities exercise some influence on the population.

[*Signed*] LINARD

THE PROGRAM OF THE NATIONAL ASSOCIATION FOR THE ADVANCEMENT OF COLORED PEOPLE (1920)

Confronted with the peculiar disruptions of the First World War, which had noticeably accelerated the migration of Negroes from rural and southern areas to northern and midwestern metropolitan centers, the NAACP set a new course. Its efforts were concentrated on a comprehensive program of reform that would work principally through Congress and the state legislatures and through the various court systems.

This approach was particularly compatible with the philosophies of the Association's leading figures: W. E. B. Du Bois, James Weldon Johnson, Moorfield Storey, Mary White Ovington, Oswald Garrison Villard, and Joel and Arthur Spingarn. The program of projected activities was anchored on a campaign to publicize existing racial injustices and to shape an enlightened public mind committed to reform. In his great classic, *The American Dilemma*, written in 1944, Gunnar Myrdal declared that "To get publicity is of the highest strategic importance to the Negro people." (New York: Harper and Bros., 1944 [Vol. I, p. 48].) NAACP leaders had fully appreciated this fact from the very inception of their organization.

The program objectives stated in the *Tenth Annual Report* are clear and revealing in themselves. The pervasive theme throughout the document reflects both the intrinsic interracial nature of the organization and presages the resolute position that would characterize so much of the Association's future work: namely, that separate facilities are, by their very nature, inherently conducive to inequality.

DOCUMENT 66

The Tenth Annual Report of the NAACP for the year 1919*

... First and foremost among the objectives for 1920 must be the continued strengthening of the Association's organization and resources. Its general program must be adapted to specific ends. Its chief aims have many times been stated:

1. A vote for every Negro man and woman on the same terms as for white men and women.

2. An equal chance to acquire the kind of an education that will enable the Negro everywhere wisely to use this vote.

3. A fair trial in the courts for all crimes of which he is accused, by judges in whose election he has participated without discrimination because of race.

4. A right to sit upon the jury which passes judgment upon him.

5. Defense against lynching and burning at the hands of mobs.

6. Equal service on railroad and other public carriers. This to mean sleeping car service, dining car service, Pullman service, at the same cost and upon the same terms as other passengers.

7. Equal right to the use of public parks, libraries and other community services for which he is taxed.

8. An equal chance for a livelihood in public and private employment.

9. The abolition of color-hyphenation and the substitution of "straight Americanism." . . .

Lynching must be stopped. Many Americans do not believe that such horrible things happen as do happen when Negroes are lynched and burned at the stake. Lynching can be stopped when we can reach the heart and conscience of the American people. Again, money is needed.

Legal work must be done. Defenseless Negroes are every day denied the "equal protection of the laws" because there is not money enough in the Association's treasury to defend them, either as individuals or as a race.

* New York: NAACP, 1920, pp. 87–91. Reprinted by permission.

Legislation must be watched. Good laws must be promoted wherever that be possible and bad laws opposed and defeated wherever possible. Once more money is essential.

The public must be kept informed. This means that our regular press service under the supervision of a trained newspaper man must be maintained and strengthened. Every opportunity must be sought out to place before the magazine and periodical reading public, constructive articles on every phase of Negro citizenship. . . . That colored people are contributing their fair share to the well-being of America must be made known. . . . That lawabiding colored people are denied the commonest citizenship rights, must be brought home to all Americans who love fair play. Once again, money is needed.

The facts must be gathered and assembled. This requires effort. Facts are not gotten out of one's imagination. Their gathering and interpretation is skilled work. Research workers of a practical experience are needed. Field investigations, in which domain the Association has already made some notable contributions, are essential to good work. More money.

The country must be thoroughly organized. The Association's more than 300 branches are a good beginning. An increased field staff is essential to the upbuilding of this important branch development. A very large percentage of the branch members are colored people. Colored people have less means, and less experience in public organization, than white people. But, they are developing rapidly habits of efficiency in organization. Money, again is needed.

But, not money alone is needed. Men and women are vital to success. Public opinion is the main force upon which the Association relies for a *victory of justice.* Particularly do we seek the active support of all white Americans who realize that a democracy cannot draw the color line in public relations without lasting injury to its best ideals.

THE SUPREME COURT AND THE RIGHT TO A FAIR TRIAL (1923)

In the fall of 1919, Negro sharecroppers in Phillips County, Arkansas, had attempted to improve their economic situation through organizational activities. But fearful whites triggered three days of mob violence—resulting in the deaths of more than two hundred men, women, and children. A court trial of sorts followed. Negroes were excluded from the jury, and Negro witnesses were whipped until they agreed to testify against colored defendants. A white mob threatened violence and lynching if no convictions ensued. The court-appointed defense counsel failed to ask for a change of venue, called no witnesses, and placed no defendants on the witness stand. The entire proceedings lasted less than an hour, and within five minutes the jury voted a dozen Negroes guilty of murder in the first degree. The court sentenced the twelve to death and committed sixty-seven others to long prison terms.

In a series of protracted and dramatic developments, the NAACP eventually secured freedom for all seventy-nine defendants. Working through its Arkansas branch and utilizing the services of two lawyers from the region, white attorney U. S. Bratton and Negro lawyer Scipio Africanus Jones, the Association brought the case to the United States Supreme Court. There Moorfield Storey, a Boston patrician and a former president of the American Bar Association, successfully presented the Negroes' appeal.

The case is important in the law as a transition point in Supreme Court analysis and action. "Indubitably, *Moore* v. *Dempsey* marked the abandonment of the Supreme Court's deference, ... to decisions of State appellate tribunals on issues of constitutionality and the proclamation of its intention no longer to treat as virtually conclusive pronouncements by the latter that proceedings in a trial court were fair." (*Constitution of the United States of America*, Library of Congress edition [Senate Doc. No. 39, 88th Congress, 1st Session] p. 1277.)

The Supreme Court restated its role as the protector of constitutional rights and its responsibility to insure fair trials. As Justice Oliver Wendell Holmes stated in his opinion, "if ... the whole proceeding is a mask ... [and] counsel, jury and judge were swept to the fatal end by the irresistible wave of public passion, and ... the State Courts failed to correct the wrong," then "intervention by the Supreme Court" was demanded.

DOCUMENT 67

*Moore v. Dempsey**

MR. JUSTICE HOLMES delivered the opinion of the Court. This is an appeal from an order of the District Court for the Eastern District of Arkansas dismissing a writ of *habeas corpus* upon demurrer, the presiding judge certifying that there was probable cause for allowing the appeal. There were two cases originally, but by agreement they were consolidated into one. The appellants are five negroes who were convicted of murder in the first degree and sentenced to death by the Court of the State of Arkansas. The ground of the petition for the writ is that the proceedings in the State Court, although a trial in form, were only a form, and that the appellants were hurried to conviction under the pressure of a mob without any regard for their rights and without according to them due process of law. . . .

Shortly after the arrest of the petitioners a mob marched to the jail for the purpose of lynching them but were prevented by the presence of United States troops and the promise of some of the Committee of Seven and other leading officials that if the mob would refrain, as the petition puts it, they would execute those found guilty in the form of law. The Committee's own statement was that the reason that the people refrained from mob violence was "that this Committee gave our citizens their solemn promise that the law would be carried out." According to affidavits of two white men and the colored witnesses on whose testimony the petitioners were convicted, produced by the petitioners since the last decision of the Supreme Court hereafter mentioned, the Committee made good their promise by calling colored witnesses and having them whipped and tortured until they would say what was wanted, among them being the two relied on to prove the petitioners' guilt. However this may be, a grand jury of white men was organized on October 27 with one of the Committee of Seven and, it is alleged, with many of a posse organized to fight the blacks, upon it, and on the morning of the 29th the indictment was returned. On November 3 the petitioners were brought into Court, informed that a certain

---

* Supreme Court of the United States, 261 U.S. 86 (1923).

lawyer was appointed their counsel and were placed on trial before a white jury—blacks being systematically excluded from both grand and petit juries. The Court and neighborhood were thronged with an adverse crowd that threatened the most dangerous consequences to anyone interfering with the desired result. The counsel did not venture to demand delay or a change of venue, to challenge a juryman or to ask for separate trials. He had had no preliminary consultation with the accused, called no witnesses for the defence although they could have been produced, and did not put the defendants on the stand. The trial lasted about three-quarters of an hour and in less than five minutes the jury brought in a verdict of guilty of murder in the first degree. According to the allegations and affidavits there never was a chance for the petitioners to be acquitted; no juryman could have voted for an acquittal and continued to live in Phillips County and if any prisoner by any chance had been acquitted by a jury he could not have escaped the mob. . . .

In *Frank* v. *Mangum,* 237 U.S. 309, 335, it was recognized of course that if in fact a trial is dominated by a mob so that there is an actual interference with the course of justice, there is a departure from due process of law; and that "if the State, supplying no corrective process, carries into execution a judgment of death or imprisonment based upon a verdict thus produced by mob domination, the State deprives the accused of his life or liberty without due process of law." We assume in accordance with that case that the corrective process supplied by the State may be so adequate that interference by *habeas corpus* ought not to be allowed. It certainly is true that mere mistakes of law in the course of a trial are not to be corrected in that way. But if the case is that the whole proceeding is a mask—that counsel, jury and judge were swept to the fatal end by an irresistible wave of public passion, and that the State Courts failed to correct the wrong, neither perfection in the machinery for correction nor the possibility that the trial court and counsel saw no other way of avoiding an immediate outbreak of the mob can prevent this Court from securing to the petitioners their constitutional rights. . . .

Order reversed. The case to stand for hearing before the District Court.

MARCUS GARVEY EXTOLS BLACK NATIONALISM (1925)

Stressing the beauty of and need for racial purity, Marcus Garvey, a Jamaican Negro who had come to the United States in 1916, vehemently denounced all efforts at interracial adjustment and argued instead for a distinct separation of black and white. His Universal Negro Improvement Association served as the organizational instrument through which he planned to lead Negro Americans back to Africa, where they could establish a great nation of their own. Garvey was contemptuous of NAACP leaders. He deemed their attempts at interracial reform dangerous to the purity of the black race and doomed to failure by inevitable white duplicity.

Garvey's black nationalism had particular appeal to the Negro masses. In a day when the Ku Klux Klan had achieved unprecedented national influence, Garvey represented the pressure against interracial amity from the opposite extreme. In an historical sense, Garvey reiterated the general position of the American Colonization Society of the 1820's (Document 22) and the plan for settling Negroes abroad endorsed by President Lincoln, and presaged the separatist proposals of the Black Muslims in the mid-1960's.

Although Garvey's schemes attracted widespread attention and no little support, his personal career was effectively ended with a federal conviction on the charge of using the mails to defraud, a term in the Atlanta penitentiary, and, despite a Presidential pardon, deportation in 1927 as an undesirable alien.

DOCUMENT 68

*The objectives of the Universal Negro Improvement Association**

The declared objects of the association are:
"To establish a Universal Confraternity among the race; to

---

* Amy Jacques-Garvey, ed., *Philosophy and Opinions of Marcus Garvey* (New York: Universal Publishing House, 1925), pp. 38–39. Reprinted by permission.

promote the spirit of pride and love; to reclaim the fallen; to administer to and assist the needy; to assist in civilizing the backward tribes of Africa; to assist in the development of Independent Negro Nations and Communities; to establish a central nation for the race; to establish Commissaries or Agencies in the principal countries and cities of the world for the representation of all Negroes; to promote a conscientious Spiritual worship among the native tribes of Africa; to establish Universities, Colleges, Academies and Schools for the racial education and culture of the people; to work for better conditions among Negroes everywhere."

Supplying a Long Felt Want

The organization of the Universal Negro Improvement Association has supplied among Negroes a long-felt want. Hitherto the other Negro movements in America, with the exception of the Tuskegee effort of Booker T. Washington, sought to teach the Negro to aspire to social equality with the whites, meaning thereby the right to intermarry and fraternize in every social way. This has been the source of much trouble and still some Negro organizations continue to preach this dangerous "race destroying doctrine" added to a program of political agitation and aggression. The Universal Negro Improvement Association on the other hand believes in and teaches the pride and purity of race. We believe that the white race should uphold its racial pride and perpetuate itself, and that the black race should do likewise. We believe that there is room enough in the world for the various race groups to grow and develop by themselves without seeking to destroy the Creator's plan by the constant introduction of mongrel types.

The unfortunate condition of slavery, as imposed upon the Negro, and which caused the mongrelization of the race, should not be legalized and continued now to the harm and detriment of both races.

The time has really come to give the Negro a chance to develop himself to a moral-standard-man, and it is for such an opportunity that the Universal Negro Improvement Association seeks in the creation of an African nation for Negroes, where the greatest latitude would be given to work out this racial ideal.

There are hundreds of thousands of colored people in America who desire race amalgamation and miscegenation as a solution of the race problem. These people are, therefore, opposed to the race pride ideas of black and white; but the thoughtful of both races will naturally ignore the ravings of such persons and honestly work for the solution of a problem that has been forced upon us.

Liberal white America and race loving Negroes are bound to think at this time and thus evolve a program or plan by which there can be a fair and amicable settlement of the question.

We cannot put off the consideration of the matter, for time is pressing on our hands. The educated Negro is making rightful constitutional demands. The great white majority will never grant them, and thus we march on to danger if we do not now stop and adjust the matter.

The time is opportune to regulate the relationship between both races. Let the Negro have a country of his own. Help him to return to his original home, Africa, and there give him the opportunity to climb from the lowest to the highest positions in a state of his own. If not, then the nation will have to hearken to the demand of the aggressive, "social equality" organization, known as the National Association for the Advancement of Colored People, of which W. E. B. DuBois is leader, which declares vehemently for social and political equality, viz.: Negroes and whites in the same hotels, homes, residential districts, public and private places, a Negro as president, members of the Cabinet, Governors of States, Mayors of cities, and leaders of society in the United States. In this agitation, DuBois is ably supported by the "Chicago Defender," a colored newspaper published in Chicago. This paper advocates Negroes in the Cabinet and Senate. All these, as everybody knows, are the Negroes' constitutional rights, but reason dictates that the masses of the white race will never stand by the ascendency of an opposite minority group to the favored positions in a government, society and industry that exist by the will of the majority, hence the demand of the DuBois group of colored leaders will only lead, ultimately, to further disturbances in riots, lynching and mob rule. The only logical solution therefore, is to supply the Negro with opportunities and environments of his own, and there point him to the fullness of his ambition.

THE SCOTTSBORO CASES (1932 and 1935)

Certainly the most sensational trials in the history of the Negro at the American bar of justice were those which took place in the early 1930's, in the little town of Scottsboro, Alabama. So dramatic were these cases that there is a tendency to forget the vital principles of law which were established when twice the cases came before the United States Supreme Court. In *Powell* v. *Alabama*, 287 U.S. 45 (1932), the Supreme Court overturned the convictions on the ground that the constitutional right to counsel had been denied. In *Norris* v. *Alabama*, 294 U.S. 587 (1935), the Supreme Court set aside the convictions because Negroes had been systematically excluded from jury service.

Nine Negroes, two of them boys of thirteen and fourteen, went on trial in 1931, on the charge of raping two white girls on a freight train in which they had all been riding. Eight of them were found guilty and sentenced to death. The Supreme Court of Alabama set aside one of the convictions. The case involving the other seven was heard by the United States Supreme Court in 1932.

There was no real factual question as to the adequacy of counsel at the mass trial in Scottsboro. Young, uneducated, faced with public hostility and in peril of their lives, the nine required the most competent of attorneys. Instead, there had been mere token legal representation. The Supreme Court would not permit the convictions to stand. The Court held that, at least in capital cases, where the accused was unable to employ counsel and was not sufficiently knowledgeable to present his own defense, it was the duty of the trial court to assign appropriate counsel. Failure to do so was a violation of due process of law.

This was the first case in which the Supreme Court held that the right "to have the assistance of counsel," guaranteed against the national government by the Sixth Amendment, was likewise a right guaranteed against state governments by the due process clause of the Fourteenth Amendment.

Two of the seven once again underwent trial in Scottsboro. They were convicted and given the death sentence. Again there was a legal issue for Supreme Court review. In 1935, the high court once more set aside the convictions. As before, there was no real dispute over the facts. Although no Alabama statute discriminated against Negroes as jurors, state practices had systematically and arbitrarily excluded Negroes from the jury lists. This, ruled the Court, was a violation of the equal protection clause of the Fourteenth Amendment.

In the subsequent history of the Scottsboro cases, charges were dropped against five of the nine and the other four were retried and convicted in 1936 and 1937. Three were later paroled and the fourth, who escaped, subsequently died in a Michigan penitentiary.

The Scottsboro affair was, from the beginning, an international scandal. Few believed—or now believe—that the Negro youths were guilty. One of the girls involved was an admitted prostitute and the other's claim to virtue was, at the very least, questionable. All of the accusations were clouded with more than a reasonable doubt, and what passed for evidence was accepted by few besides the vital twelve men who sat in the jury box. Most historians agree that the Scottsboro boys had committed no crime other than being born black.

DOCUMENT 69

Norris v. Alabama*

Mr. Chief Justice Hughes delivered the opinion of the Court.

Petitioner, Clarence Norris, is one of nine negro boys who were indicted in March, 1931, in Jackson County, Alabama, for the crime of rape. On being brought to trial in that county, eight were convicted. The Supreme Court of Alabama reversed the conviction of one of these and affirmed that of seven, including Norris. This Court reversed the judgments of conviction upon the ground that the defendants had been

---

* Supreme Court of the United States, 294 U.S. 587 (1935).

denied due process of law in that the trial court had failed in the light of the circumstances disclosed, and of the inability of the defendants at that time to obtain counsel, to make an effective appointment of counsel to aid them in preparing and presenting their defense. *Powell* v. *Alabama*, 287 U.S. 45.

After the remand, a motion for change of venue was granted and the cases were transferred to Morgan County. Norris was brought to trial in November, 1933. At the outset, a motion was made on his behalf to quash the indictment upon the ground of the exclusion of negroes from juries in Jackson County where the indictment was found. A motion was also made to quash the trial *venire* in Morgan County upon the ground of the exclusion of negroes from juries in that county. In relation to each county, the charge was of long continued, systematic and arbitrary exclusion of qualified negro citizens from service on juries, solely because of their race and color, in violation of the Constitution of the United States. The State joined issue on this charge and after hearing the evidence, which we shall presently review, the trial judge denied both motions, and exception was taken. The trial then proceeded and resulted in the conviction of Norris who was sentenced to death. On appeal, the Supreme Court of the State considered and decided the federal question which Norris had raised, and affirmed the judgment. 229 Ala. 226; 156 So. 556. We granted a writ of certiorari. 293 U.S. 552.

First. There is no controversy as to the constitutional principle involved. That principle, long since declared, was not challenged, but was expressly recognized, by the Supreme Court of the State. Summing up precisely the effect of earlier decisions, this Court thus stated the principle in *Carter* v. *Texas*, 177 U.S. 442, 447, in relation to exclusion from service on grand juries: "Whenever by any action of a State, whether through its legislature, through its courts, or through its executive or administrative officers, all persons of the African race are excluded, solely because of their race or color, from serving as grand jurors in the criminal prosecution of a person of the African race, the equal protection of the laws is denied to him, contrary to the Fourteenth Amendment of the Constitution of the United States.

. . . .

Second. The evidence on the motion to quash the indict-ment. In 1930, the total population of Jackson County, where the indictment was found, was 36,881, of whom 2688 were negroes. The male population over twenty-one years of age numbered 8801, and of these, 666 were negroes.

The qualifications of jurors were thus prescribed by the state statute (Alabama Code, 1923, § 8603): "The jury commission shall place on the jury roll and in the jury box the names of all male citizens of the county who are generally reputed to be honest and intelligent men, and are esteemed in the community for their integrity, good character and sound judgment, but no person must be selected who is under twenty-one or over sixty-five years of age, or, who is an habitual drunkard, or who, being afflicted with a permanent disease or physical weakness is unfit to discharge the duties of a juror, or who cannot read English, or who has ever been convicted of any offense involving moral turpitude. If a per-son cannot read English and has all the other qualifications prescribed herein and is a freeholder or householder, his name may be placed on the jury roll and in the jury box." See Gen. Acts, Alabama, 1931, No. 47, p. 59.

Defendant adduced evidence to support the charge of unconstitutional discrimination in the actual administration of the statute in Jackson County. The testimony, as the state court said, tended to show that "in a long number of years no negro had been called for jury service in that county." It appeared that no negro had served on any grand or petit jury in that county within the memory of witnesses who had lived there all their lives. Testimony to that effect was given by men whose ages ran from fifty to seventy-six years. Their testimony was uncontradicted. It was supported by the testi-mony of officials. The clerk of the jury commission and the clerk of the circuit court had never known of a negro serving on a grand jury in Jackson County. The court reporter, who had not missed a session in that county in twenty-four years, and two jury commissioners testified to the same effect. One of the latter, who was a member of the commission which made up the jury roll for the grand jury which found the indictment, testified that he had "never known of a single instance where any negro sat on any grand or petit jury in the entire history of that county." . . .

The state court rested its decision upon the ground that

even if it were assumed that there was no name of a negro on the jury roll, it was not established that race or color caused the omission. The court pointed out that the statute fixed a high standard of qualifications for jurors (*Green* v. *State*, 73 Ala. 26; *State* v. *Curtis*, 210 Ala. 1; 97 So. 291) and that the jury commission was vested with a wide discretion. The court adverted to the fact that more white citizens possessing age qualifications had been omitted from the jury roll than the entire negro population of the county, and regarded the testimony as being to the effect that "the matter of race, color, politics, religion or fraternal affiliations" had not been discussed by the commission and had not entered into their consideration, and that no one had been excluded because of race or color. . . .

We are of the opinion that the evidence required a different result from that reached in the state court. We think that the evidence that for a generation or longer no negro had been called for service on any jury in Jackson County, that there were negroes qualified for jury service, that according to the practice of the jury commission their names would normally appear on the preliminary list of male citizens of the requisite age but that no names of negroes were placed on the jury roll, and the testimony with respect to the lack of appropriate consideration of the qualifications of negroes, established the discrimination which the Constitution forbids. The motion to quash the indictment upon that ground should have been granted.

• • • •

We are concerned only with the federal question which we have discussed, and in view of the denial of the federal right suitably asserted, the judgment must be reversed and the cause remanded for further proceedings not inconsistent with this opinion.

Reversed.

THE GAVAGAN ANTILYNCHING BILL (1937)

A prime legislative goal of the NAACP in the period from World War I to the end of the Truman Administration was the passage of a federal antilynching law. Three times—in 1922, 1937, and 1940—such a bill was passed by the House of Representatives, only to die in the Senate because of a southern filibuster, actual or threatened.

While the National Association for the Advancement of Colored People failed in its legislative objective, the antilynching campaigns advanced the cause of civil rights. Calling public attention to the existence of such mob violence reduced lynching in practice. Furthermore, with the public more responsive, Congress and the White House were induced to work for interracial reforms.

A prototype of these antilynching measures was the bill introduced by New York Congressman Joseph Gavagan in 1937. Like the other antilynching bills sponsored by the NAACP during the twenties and thirties, the Gavagan Bill sought a monetary penalty on the county or counties in which the abduction and lynching occurred and a fine and jail term for public officials whose delinquency permitted the lynching to take place. During the Truman years, the Association's antilynching bill sought punitive action directly against the members of the mob.

DOCUMENT 70

*The Gavagan Bill**

An Act. To assure to persons within the jurisdiction of every State the equal protection of the laws, and to punish the crime of lynching.

Be it enacted by the Senate and House of Representatives of the United States of America in Congress assembled, That, for the purposes of this Act, the phrase "mob or riotous assemblage," when used in this Act, shall mean an assemblage composed of three or more persons acting in concert, without authority of law, to kill or injure any person in the custody of any peace officer, with the purpose or consequence of depriving such person of due process of law or the equal protection of the laws.

Sec. 2. If any State or governmental subdivision thereof

---

* *Public Bills,* 75th Congress, 1st Session, V, H.R. 1507, April 19, 1937 (Library of Congress).

fails, neglects, or refuses to provide and maintain protection to the life or person of any individual within its jurisdiction against a mob or riotous assemblage, whether by way of preventing or punishing the acts thereof, such State shall by reason of such failure, neglect, or refusal be deemed to have denied to such person due process of law and the equal protection of the laws of the State, and to the end that the protection guaranteed to persons within the jurisdictions of the several States, or to citizens of the United States, by the Constitution of the United States, may be secured, the provisions of this Act are enacted.

SEC. 3. (a) Any officer or employee of any State or governmental subdivision thereof who is charged with the duty or who possesses the power or authority as such officer or employee to protect the life or person of any individual injured or put to death by any mob or riotous assemblage or any officer or employee of any State or governmental subdivision thereof having any such individual in his custody, who fails, neglects, or refuses to make all diligent efforts to protect such individual from being so injured or being put to death, or any officer or employee of any State or governmental subdivision thereof charged with the duty of apprehending, keeping in custody, or prosecuting any person participating in such mob or riotous assemblage who fails, neglects, or refuses to make all diligent efforts to perform his duty in apprehending, keeping in custody, or prosecuting to final judgment under the laws of such State all persons so participating, shall be guilty of a felony, and upon conviction thereof shall be punished by a fine not exceeding $5,000 or by imprisonment not exceeding five years, or by both such fine and imprisonment.

(b) Any officer or employee of any State or governmental subdivision thereof, acting as such officer or employee under authority of State law, having in his custody or control a prisoner, who shall conspire, combine, or confederate with any person who is a member of a mob or riotous assemblage to injure or put such prisoner to death without authority of law, or who shall conspire, combine, or confederate with any person to suffer such prisoner to be taken or obtained from his custody or control to be injured or put to death by a mob or riotous assemblage shall be guilty of a felony, and those who so conspire, combine, or confederate with such officer or employee shall likewise be guilty of a felony. On conviction the parties participating therein·shall be punished by imprisonment of not less than five years or not more than twenty-five years.

SEC. 4. The District Court of the United States judicial district wherein the person is injured or put to death by a mob or riotous assemblage shall have jurisdiction to try and to punish, in accordance with the laws of the State where the injury is inflicted or the homicide is committed, any and all persons who participate therein: *Provided,* That it is first made to appear to such court (1) that the officers of the State charged with the duty of apprehending, prosecuting, and punishing such offenders under the laws of the State shall have failed, neglected, or refused to apprehend, prosecute, or punish such offenders; or (2) that the jurors obtainable for service in the State court having jurisdiction of the offense are so strongly opposed to such punishment that there is probability that those guilty of the offense will not be punished in such State court. A failure for more than thirty days after the commission of such an offense to apprehend or to indict the persons guilty thereof, or a failure diligently to prosecute such persons, shall be sufficient to constitute prima facie evidence of the failure, neglect, or refusal described in the above proviso.

SEC. 5. Any county in which a person is seriously injured or put to death by a mob or riotous assemblage shall be liable to the injured person or the legal representatives of such person for a sum not less than $2,000 nor more than $10,000 as liquidated damages, which sum may be recovered in a civil action against such county in the United States District Court of the judicial district wherein such person is put to the injury or death. Such action shall be brought and prosecuted by the United States district attorney of the district in the United States District Court for such district. If such amount awarded be not paid upon recovery of a judgment therefor, such court shall have jurisdiction to enforce payment thereof by levy of execution upon any property of the county, or may otherwise compel payment thereof by mandamus or other appropriate process; and any officer of such county or other person who disobeys or fails to comply with any lawful order of the court in the premises shall be liable to punishment as for contempt and to any other penalty provided by law therefor. The amount recovered shall be exempt from all claims by creditors of the deceased. The amount recovered upon such judgment shall be paid to the injured person, or where death resulted, distributed in accordance with the laws governing the distribution of an intestate decedent's assets then in effect in the State wherein such death occurred.

SEC. 6. In the event that any person so put to death shall have been transported by such mob or riotous assemblage from one county to another county during the time intervening between his seizure and putting to death, the county in which he is seized and the county in which he is put to death shall be jointly and severally liable to pay the forfeiture herein provided. Any district judge of the United States District Court of the judicial district wherein any suit or prosecution is instituted under the provisions of this Act, may by order direct that such suit or prosecution be tried in any place in such district as he may designate in such order. . . .

Passed the House of Representatives, April 15, 1937.

VII

War, and Cold War: Executive and Judicial Responses
1941–1958

Under NAACP leadership, the objective of the Negro protest movement during the interwar years, 1915 to 1941, had been to seek reform through legal and judicial processes. This approach prevailed until the emergence of direct, nonviolent action in the 1960's.

In the years 1941 to 1958, the continued use of legal-judicial tactics elicited far-reaching executive and judicial responses on the part of the federal government. By contrast, Congress still maintained a position of inaction until 1957.

The extent of executive and judicial reform is understandable in light of three phenomena: Negro spokesmen had, to a degree, reeducated the nation to the necessity for change in the interwar years; military demands and labor shortages during the Second World War had opened new opportunities to Negro citizens; and the challenge of the Cold War had intensified the need for domestic unity and the enhancement of the nation's image abroad.

From 1941 to 1958, Presidents Roosevelt, Truman, and Eisenhower issued a dozen executive orders affecting civil rights. These touched upon fair employment practices, federal contracts with private industry, employment and advancement opportunities in federal service, integration in the armed forces, and the implementation of a federal court order for school desegregation. The United States Supreme Court heard and ruled upon a wide range of cases related to civil rights, and its decisions on voting, interstate travel, housing covenants, higher education, and public school desegregation were resoundingly favorable to the Negro's plea for reform.

These executive and judicial responses alarmed southern whites and their conservative counterparts throughout the nation, who decried interference with state and local affairs and denounced any surrender to minority-group protest. Opponents of civil rights openly expressed their resentment against executive policy and initiated a relentless campaign to discredit the Supreme Court. Some even went so far as to allege that the winds of change originated with Communist agitators and subversives seeking to disrupt America's established order. Diehard southerners supported segregationist organizations, including the Ku Klux Klan with its tendencies to mob action, and the White Citizens' Council with its appeals to states' rights, southern regionalism, and obstructive legislative tactics.

While voices of conservative reaction induced delay, they did not represent the general spirit of the nation in the years 1941 to 1958. The constant pressure of the Negro protest movement, coupled with the realities of change at home and abroad, inexorably forced American society to recognize the necessity of interracial reform. But still undecided was how much interracial reform would be forthcoming and how fast it should be achieved. Was interracial justice to be denied because of white sentiments that the Negro was expecting too much or moving too fast?

PRESIDENT ROOSEVELT'S FAIR EMPLOYMENT PRACTICES COMMITTEE (1941)

Increasingly strained international relations had forced the United States to military preparedness as early as 1938, and, despite isolationist objections, activities which anticipated ever-growing involvement in the world struggle were well underway by the summer of 1941. One immediate effect was the intensified production of defense and military equipment. American Negroes were distressed that they did not secure a fair share of the new and expanded employment opportunities that resulted.

Early in 1941, A. Philip Randolph, president of the Brotherhood of Sleeping Car Porters, proposed a mass march on the nation's capital to protest against discrimination in hiring. Anti-Semitism and other fascist atrocities in Europe had sensitized the world to the most blatant aspects of religious and racial injustice. It seemed particularly timely to make the point that American democracy could not tolerate racism. In addition, the maturing strength of the NAACP, the fledgling program of the National Negro Congress, sporadic but vocal pressures from the Communist party, and the steady but not wholly effective efforts of liberals generally affirmed the logic of striking for some formal governmental action on the matter of discrimination.

President Roosevelt responded on June 25, 1941, with Executive Order 8802, which established the Committee on Fair Employment Practices within the Office of Production Management. The order was limited to employment and vocational training programs in defense industries and governmental defense contracts. The President declined to issue a broader order, as Negro spokesmen had wished, which would also have barred discrimination in the military services. The FEPC was empowered to investigate and recommend, but it lacked enforcement powers. The Committee functioned throughout World War II, with somewhat altered powers granted by Executive Order 9346 (May 27, 1943 [8 F.R. 7183]); it died in peacetime, largely because of Congressional opposition. Not until the Civil Rights Act of 1964 (Document 89) did the Senate and House of Representatives respond to appeals for comprehensive statutory enactment of fair employment provisions.

Franklin D. Roosevelt's Executive Order 8802 has remained a singularly important document, whatever may have been its limitations in practice. However, like so much of what white America does for the Negro, the order was given grudgingly in response to domestic pressures and in the face of increasing international complications; once again, the nation had responded to the question of interracial injustice, not on the intrinsic merit of the Negro's case, but rather on the grounds of expediency.

DOCUMENT 71

Executive Order 8802, June 25, 1941[*]

Reaffirming Policy of Full Participation in the Defense Program by All Persons, Regardless of Race, Creed, Color, or National Origin, and Directing Certain Action in Furtherance of Said Policy

Whereas it is the policy of the United States to encourage full participation in the national defense program by all citizens of the United States, regardless of race, creed, color, or national origin, in the firm belief that the democratic way of life within the Nation can be defended successfully only with the help and support of all groups within its borders; and

Whereas there is evidence that available and needed workers have been barred from employment in industries engaged in defense production solely because of considerations of race, creed, color, or national origin, to the detriment of workers' morale and of national unity:

Now, therefore, by virtue of the authority vested in me by the Constitution and the statutes, and as a prerequisite to the successful conduct of our national defense production effort, I do hereby reaffirm the policy of the United States that there shall be no discrimination in the employment of workers in defense industries or government because of race, creed, color, or national origin, and I do hereby declare that it is the duty of employers and of labor organizations, in furtherance of said policy and of this order, to provide for the full and equitable participation of all workers in defense industries, without discrimination because of race, creed, color, or national origin;

And it is hereby ordered as follows:

1. All departments and agencies of the Government of the United States concerned with vocational and training programs for defense production shall take special measures appropriate to assure that such programs are administered without discrimination because of race, creed, color, or national origin;

[*] 6 Fed. Reg. 3109 (1941).

2. All contracting agencies of the Government of the United States shall include in all defense contracts hereafter negotiated by them a provision obligating the contractor not to discriminate against any worker because of race, creed, color, or national origin;

3. There is established in the Office of Production Management a Committee on Fair Employment Practice, which shall consist of a chairman and four other members to be appointed by the President. The Chairman and members of the Committee shall serve as such without compensation but shall be entitled to actual and necessary transportation, subsistence and other expenses incidental to performance of their duties. The Committee shall receive and investigate complaints of discrimination in violation of the provisions of this order and shall take appropriate steps to redress grievances which it finds to be valid. The Committee shall also recommend to the several departments and agencies of the Government of the United States and to the President all measures which may be deemed by it necessary or proper to effectuate the provisions of this order.

FRANKLIN D. ROOSEVELT

THE WHITE HOUSE
June 25, 1941

SCREWS V. UNITED STATES—MURDER AND THE FOURTEENTH AMENDMENT (1945)

After the Supreme Court invalidated the 1875 Civil Rights Act (Document 47) in the Civil Rights Cases (Document 54), the principal federal laws for the protection of the Negro were embodied in what are now Sections 241 and 242 of Title 18 of the United States Code.

Section 241 (51) (19) provides penalties for conspiracy "to injure, oppress, threaten, or intimidate any citizen in the free exercise or enjoyment of any right or privilege secured him by the Constitution or laws of the United States. . . ." It also has the Ku Klux Klan provision, making it a crime for "two or more persons [to] go in disguise on the highway" to interfere with such civil rights. Under Section 242 (52) (20), punishments are prescribed for any person who "under color of any law . . . willfully subjects any inhabitant of any State . . . to the deprivation of any rights, privileges, or immunities secured or protected by the Constitution . . . by reason of his color, or race. . . ."

An indictment charging Georgia Sheriff Screws of a crime under Section 242 (52) (20) came before the Supreme Court in 1945. Screws had actually committed murder, brutally beating to death a Negro who had allegedly stolen a tire. But since it was impossible to secure a murder conviction against the sheriff in the Georgia state courts, the United States attorney took the novel approach of proceeding under the federal statute. Screws was charged with *willfully* depriving the deceased of a right protected by the Constitution—"the right not to be deprived of *life* without due process of law." (Emphasis added.) The accused was convicted by the federal trial court.

The nine men of the Supreme Court were forcibly reminded of the basic principle that a penal statute is unconstitutional where it "either forbids or requires the doing of an act in terms so vague that men of common intelligence must necessarily guess at its meaning and differ as to its application." *Connally* v. *General Construction Co.,* 269 U.S. 385, 391 (1926).

Four justices in the eventual majority opinion concluded that the lower court jury should have been instructed in the element of *willfulness* before they could vote a conviction, and thus recommended remanding the case for a new trial. Three justices denied the federal government's power to act against Screws. Only two justices expressed the view that the conviction of the lower court should be affirmed, but one of these finally voted with the block of four for a remand in order to avoid a stalemate.

The use and interpretation of Sections 241 and 242 became an important issue again in the 1966 cases of *United States* v. *Price,* and *United States* v. *Guest* (Document 94). These involved prosecutions arising out of the murders of three civil rights workers in Philadelphia, Mississippi, in 1964, and the murder of Lemuel A. Penn, a Negro reserve officer, while he was driving through Georgia on his way to Washington, D.C., after a tour of military duty.

DOCUMENT 72

Screws v. United States*

MR. JUSTICE DOUGLAS announced the judgment of the Court and delivered the following opinion, in which the CHIEF JUSTICE, MR. JUSTICE BLACK and MR. JUSTICE REED concur. . . .

I

We are met at the outset with the claim that § 20 is unconstitutional, insofar as it makes criminal acts in violation of the due process clause of the Fourteenth Amendment. The argument runs as follows: It is true that this Act as construed in *United States* v. *Classic*, 313 U.S. 299, 328, was upheld in its application to certain ballot box frauds committed by state officials. But in that case the constitutional rights protected were the rights to vote specifically guaranteed by Art. I, § 2 and § 4 of the Constitution. Here there is no ascertainable standard of guilt. There have been conflicting views in the Court as to the proper construction of the due process clause. The majority have quite consistently construed it in broad general terms. . . .

It is said that the Act must be read as if it contained those broad and fluid definitions of due process and that if it is so read it provides no ascertainable standard of guilt. It is pointed out that in *United States* v. *Cohen Grocery Co.*, 255 U.S. 81, 89, an Act of Congress was struck down, the enforcement of which would have been "the exact equivalent of an effort to carry out a statute which in terms merely penalized and punished all acts detrimental to the public interest when unjust and unreasonable in the estimation of the court and jury." . . .

The serious character of that challenge to the constitutionality of the Act is emphasized if the customary standard of guilt for statutory crimes is taken. As we shall see, specific intent is at times required. . . . But the general rule was stated in *Ellis* v. *United States*, 206 U.S. 246, 257, as follows: "If a man intentionally adopts certain conduct in certain circumstances known to him, and that conduct is forbidden by the law under those circumstances, he intentionally breaks the law

---

* Supreme Court of the United States, 325 U.S. 91 (1945).

in the only sense in which the law ever considers intent." . . . Under that test a local law enforcement officer violates § 20 and commits a federal offense for which he can be sent to the penitentiary if he does an act which some court later holds deprives a person of due process of law. And he is a criminal though his motive was pure and though his purpose was unrelated to the disregard of any constitutional guarantee. The treacherous ground on which state officials—police, prosecutors, legislators, and judges—would walk is indicated by the character and closeness of decisions of this Court interpreting the due process clause of the Fourteenth Amendment.

. . . .

Those who enforced local law today might not know for many months (and meanwhile could not find out) whether what they did deprived some one of due process of law. The enforcement of a criminal statute so construed would indeed cast law enforcement agencies loose at their own risk on a vast uncharted sea.

If such a construction is not necessary, it should be avoided. This Court has consistently favored that interpretation of legislation which supports its constitutionality. . . . That reason is impelling here so that if at all possible § 20 may be allowed to serve its great purpose—the protection of the individual in his civil liberties.

SEC. 20 was enacted to enforce the Fourteenth Amendment. It derives from § 2 of the Civil Rights Act of April 9, 1866. 14 Stat. 27. Senator Trumbull, chairman of the Senate Judiciary Committee which reported the bill, stated that its purpose was "to protect all persons in the United States in their civil rights, and furnish the means of their vindication." Cong. Globe, 39th Cong., 1st Sess., p. 211. In origin it was an antidiscrimination measure (as its language indicated), framed to protect Negroes in their newly won rights. See Flack, The Adoption of the Fourteenth Amendment (1908), p. 21. It was amended by § 17 of the Act of May 31, 1870, 16 Stat. 144, and made applicable to "any inhabitant of any State or Territory." The prohibition against the "deprivation of any rights, privileges, or immunities, secured or protected by the Constitution and laws of the United States" was introduced by the revisers in 1874. R.S. § 5510. Those words were taken over from § 1 of the Act of April 20, 1871, 17 Stat. 13 (the so-called Ku-Klux Act) which provided civil suits for redress of such wrongs. See Cong. Rec., 43d Cong., 1st Sess., p. 828. The 1874 revision was applicable to any person who under color of law, etc., "subjects, or causes to be subjected" any inhabitant to the deprivation of any rights, etc. The requirement for a "willful" violation was introduced by the draftsmen of the Criminal Code of 1909. Act of March 4, 1909, 35 Stat. 1092. And we are told "willfully" was added to § 20 in order to make the section "less severe." 43 Cong. Rec., 60th Cong., 2d Sess., p. 3599.

We hesitate to say that when Congress sought to enforce the Fourteenth Amendment in this fashion it did a vain thing. We hesitate to conclude that for 80 years this effort of Congress, renewed several times, to protect the important rights of the individual guaranteed by the Fourteenth Amendment has been an idle gesture. Yet if the Act falls by reason of vagueness so far as due process of law is concerned, there would seem to be a similar lack of specificity when the privileges and immunities clause (*Madden* v. *Kentucky*, 309 U.S. 83) and the equal protection clause (*Smith* v. *Texas*, 311 U.S. 128; *Hill* v. *Texas*, 316 U.S. 400) of the Fourteenth Amendment are involved. Only if no construction can save the Act from this claim of unconstitutionality are we willing to reach that result. We do not reach it, for we are of the view that if § 20 is confined more narrowly than the lower courts confined it, it can be preserved as one of the sanctions to the great rights which the Fourteenth Amendment was designed to secure.

II

We recently pointed out that "willful" is a word "of many meanings, its construction often being influenced by its context." . . . the word denotes an act which is intentional rather than accidental. . . . But "when used in a criminal statute it generally means an act done with a bad purpose." . . . In that event something more is required than the doing of the act proscribed by the statute. . . . "An evil motive to accomplish that which the statute condemns becomes a constituent element of the crime." And that issue must be submitted to the jury under appropriate instructions. . . .

An analysis of the cases in which "willfully" has been held to connote more than an act which is voluntary or intentional would not prove helpful as each turns on its own peculiar facts. Those cases, however, make clear that if we construe "willfully" in § 20 as connoting a purpose to deprive a person of a specific constitutional right, we would introduce no innovation. The Court, indeed, has recognized that the requirement of a specific intent to do a prohibited act may avoid those consequences to the accused which may otherwise render a vague or indefinite statute invalid. The constitutional vice in such a statute is the essential injustice to the accused of placing him on trial for an offense, the nature of which the statute does not define and hence of which it gives no warning. See *United States* v. *Cohen Grocery Co., supra*. But where the punishment imposed is only for an act knowingly done with the purpose of doing that which the statute prohibits, the accused cannot be said to suffer from lack of warning or knowledge that the act which he does is a violation of law. The requirement that the act must be willful or purposeful may not render certain, for all purposes, a statutory definition of the crime which is in some respects uncertain. But it does relieve the statute of the objection that it punishes without warning an offense of which the accused was unaware. . . .

It is said, however, that this construction of the Act will not save it from the infirmity of vagueness since neither a law enforcement official nor a trial judge can know with sufficient definiteness the range of rights that are constitutional. But that criticism is wide of the mark. For the specific intent required by the Act is an intent to deprive a person of a right which has been made specific either by the express terms of the Constitution or laws of the United States or by decisions interpreting them. Take the case of a local officer who persists in enforcing a type of ordinance which the Court has held invalid as violative of the guarantees of free speech or freedom of worship. Or a local official continues to select juries in a manner which flies in the teeth of decisions of the Court. If those acts are done willfully, how can the officer possibly claim that he had no fair warning that his acts were prohibited by the statute? He violates the statute not merely because he has a bad purpose but because he acts in defiance of announced rules of law. He who defies a decision interpreting the Constitution knows precisely what he is doing. If sane, he hardly may be heard to say that he knew not what he did. Of course, willful conduct cannot make definite that which is undefined. But willful violators of constitutional requirements, which have been defined, certainly are in no position to say that they had no adequate advance notice that they would be visited with punishment. When they act willfully in the sense in which we use the word, they act in open defiance or in reckless disregard of a constitutional requirement which has been made specific and definite. When they are convicted for so acting, they are not punished for violating an unknowable something.

. . . .

The difficulty here is that this question of intent was not submitted to the jury with the proper instructions. The court charged that petitioners acted illegally if they applied more force than was necessary to make the arrest effectual or to protect themselves from the prisoner's alleged assault. But in view of our construction of the word "willfully" the jury should have been further instructed that it was not sufficient that petitioners had a generally bad purpose. To convict it was necessary for them to find that petitioners had the purpose to deprive the prisoner of a constitutional right, e. g. the right to be tried by a court rather than by ordeal. And in determining whether that requisite bad purpose was present the jury would be entitled to consider all the attendant circumstances—the malice of petitioners, the weapons used in the assault, its character and duration, the provocation, if any, and the like.

. . . .

III

It is said, however, that petitioners did not act "under color of any law" within the meaning of § 20 of the Criminal Code. We disagree. We are of the view that petitioners acted under "color" of law in making the arrest of Robert Hall and in assaulting him. They were officers of the law who made the arrest. By their own admissions they assaulted Hall in order to protect themselves and to keep their prisoner from escaping. It was their duty under Georgia law to make the arrest effective. Hence, their conduct comes within the statute.

Some of the arguments which have been advanced in support of the contrary conclusion suggest that the question under § 20 is whether Congress has made it a federal offense for a state officer to violate the law of his State. But there is no warrant for treating the question in state law terms. The problem is not whether state law has been violated but whether an inhabitant of a State has been deprived of a federal right by one who acts under "color of any law." He who acts under "color" of law may be a federal officer or a state officer. He may act under "color" of federal law or of state law. The statute does not come into play merely because the federal law or the state law under which the officer purports to act is violated. It is applicable when and only when someone is deprived of a federal right by that action. The fact that it is also a violation of state law does not make it any the less a federal offense punishable as such. Nor does its punishment by federal authority encroach on state authority or relieve the state from its responsibility for punishing state offenses. . . .

Since there must be a new trial, the judgment below is

Reversed.

Mr. Justice Rutledge, concurring in the result.

For the compelling reason stated at the end of this opinion I concur in reversing the judgment and remanding the cause for further proceedings. But for that reason, my views would require that my vote be cast to affirm the judgment, for the reasons stated by Mr. Justice Murphy and others I feel forced, in the peculiar situation, to state. . . .

There could be no clearer violation of the Amendment or the statute. No act could be more final or complete, to denude the victim of rights secured by the Amendment's very terms. Those rights so destroyed cannot be restored. Nor could the part played by the state's power in causing their destruction be lessened, though other organs were now to repudiate what was done. The state's law might thus be vindicated. If so, the vindication could only sustain, it could not detract from the federal power. Nor could it restore what the federal power shielded. Neither acquittal nor conviction, though affirmed by the state's highest court, could resurrect what the wrongful use of state power has annihilated. There was in this case abuse of state power, which for the Amendment's great purposes was state action, final in the last degree, depriving the victim of his liberty and his life without due process of law. . . .

Lying beneath all the surface arguments is a deeper implication, which comprehends them. It goes to federal power. It is that Congress could not in so many words denounce as a federal crime the intentional and wrongful taking of an individual's life or liberty by a state official acting in abuse of his official function and applying to the deed all the power of his office. This is the ultimate purport of the notions that state action is not involved and that the crime is against the state alone, not the nation. It is reflected also in the idea that the statute can protect the victim in his many procedural rights encompassed in the right to a fair trial before condemnation, but cannot protect him in the right which comprehends all others, the right to life itself.

Suffice it to say that if these ideas did not pass from the American scene once and for all, as I think they did, upon adoption of the Amendment without more, they have long since done so. Violation of state law there may be. But from this no immunity to federal authority can arise where any part of the Constitution has made it supreme. To the Constitution state officials and the states themselves owe first obligation. The federal power lacks no strength to reach their malfeasance in office when it infringes constitutional rights. If that is a great power, it is one generated by the Constitution and the Amendments, to which the states have assented and their officials owe prime allegiance.

The right not to be deprived of life or liberty by a state officer who takes it by abuse of his office and its power is such a right. To secure these rights is not beyond federal power. This §§ 19 and 20 have done, in a manner history long since has validated.

Accordingly, I would affirm the judgment.

My convictions are as I have stated them. Were it possible for me to adhere to them in my vote, and for the Court at the same time to dispose of the cause, I would act accordingly. The Court, however, is divided in opinion. If each member accords his vote to his belief, the case cannot have disposition. Stalemate should not prevail for any reason, however compelling, in a criminal cause or, if avoidable, in any other. My views concerning appropriate disposition are more nearly in accord with those stated by MR. JUSTICE DOUGLAS, in which three other members of the Court concur, than they are with the views of my dissenting brethren who favor outright reversal. Accordingly, in order that disposition may be made of this case, my vote has been cast to reverse the decision of the Court of Appeals and remand the cause to the District Court for further proceedings in accordance with the disposition required by the opinion of MR. JUSTICE DOUGLAS.

MR. JUSTICE MURPHY, dissenting. . . .

It is axiomatic, of course, that a criminal statute must give a clear and unmistakable warning as to the acts which will subject one to criminal punishment. And courts are without power to supply that which Congress has left vague. But this salutary principle does not mean that if a statute is vague as to certain criminal acts but definite as to others the entire statute must fall. Nor does it mean that in the first case involving the statute to come before us we must delineate all the prohibited acts that are obscure and all those that are explicit. . . .

It is an illusion to say that the real issue in this case is the alleged failure of § 20 fully to warn the state officials that their actions were illegal. The Constitution, § 20 and their own consciences told them that. They knew that they lacked any mandate or authority to take human life unnecessarily or without due process of law in the course of their duties. They knew that their excessive and abusive use of authority would only subvert the ends of justice. The significant question, rather, is whether law enforcement officers and those entrusted with authority shall be allowed to violate with impunity the clear constitutional rights of the inarticulate and the friendless. Too often unpopular minorities, such as Negroes, are unable to find effective refuge from the cruelties of bigoted and ruthless authority. States are undoubtedly capable of punishing their officers who commit such outrages. But where, as here, the states are unwilling for some reason to prosecute such crimes the federal government must step in unless constitutional guarantees are to become atrophied.

This necessary intervention, however, will be futile if courts disregard reality and misuse the principle that criminal statutes must be clear and definite. Here state officers have violated with reckless abandon a plain constitutional right of an American citizen. The two courts below have found and the record demonstrates that the trial was fair and the evidence of guilt clear. And § 20 unmistakably outlaws such actions by state officers. We should therefore affirm the judgment.

Mr. Justice Roberts, Mr. Justice Frankfurter and Mr. Justice Jackson, dissenting. . . .

Of course the petitioners are punishable. The only issue is whether Georgia alone has the power and duty to punish, or whether this patently local crime can be made the basis of a federal prosecution. The practical question is whether the States should be relieved from responsibility to bring their law officers to book for homicide, by allowing prosecutions in the federal courts for a relatively minor offense carrying a short sentence. The legal question is whether, for the purpose of accomplishing this relaxation of State responsibility, hitherto settled principles for the protection of civil liberties shall be bent and tortured. . . .

The Fourteenth Amendment prohibited a State from so acting as to deprive persons of new federal rights defined by it. Section 5 of the Amendment specifically authorized enabling legislation to enforce that prohibition. Since a State can act only through its officers, Congress provided for the prosecution of any officer who deprives others of their guaranteed rights and denied such an officer the right to defend by claiming the authority of the State for his action. In short, Congress said that no State can empower an officer to commit acts which the Constitution forbade the State from authorizing, whether such unauthorized command be given for the State by its legislative or judicial voice, or by a custom contradicting the written law. . . . The present prosecution is not based on an officer's claim that that for which the United States seeks his punishment was commanded or authorized by the law of his State. On the contrary, the present prosecution is based on the theory that Congress made it a federal offense for a State officer to violate the explicit law of his State. We are asked to construe legislation which was intended to effectuate prohibitions against States for defiance of the Constitution, to be equally applicable where a State duly obeys the Constitution, but an officer flouts State law and is unquestionably subject to punishment by the State for his disobedience.

So to read § 20 disregards not merely the normal function

of language to express ideas appropriately. It fails not merely to leave to the States the province of local crime enforcement, that the proper balance of political forces in our federalism requires. It does both, heedless of the Congressional purpose, clearly evinced even during the feverish Reconstruction days, to leave undisturbed the power and the duty of the States to enforce their criminal law by restricting federal authority to the punishment only of those persons who violate federal rights under claim of State authority and not by exerting federal authority against offenders of State authority. Such a distortion of federal power devised against recalcitrant State authority never entered the minds of the proponents of the legislation.

. . . .

But assuming unreservedly that conduct such as that now before us, perpetrated by State officers in flagrant defiance of State law, may be attributed to the State under the Fourteenth Amendment, this does not make it action under "color of any law." Section 20 is much narrower than the power of Congress. Even though Congress might have swept within the federal criminal law any action that could be deemed within the vast reach of the Fourteenth Amendment, Congress did not do so. The presuppositions of our federal system, the pronouncements of the statesmen who shaped this legislation, and the normal meaning of language powerfully counsel against attributing to Congress intrusion into the sphere of criminal law traditionally and naturally reserved for the States alone. When due account is taken of the considerations that have heretofore controlled the political and legal relations between the States and the National Government, there is not the slightest warrant in the reason of things for torturing language plainly designed for nullifying a claim of acting under a State law that conflicts with the Constitution so as to apply to situations where State law is in conformity with the Constitution and local misconduct is in undisputed violation of that State law. In the absence of clear direction by Congress we should leave to the States the enforcement of their criminal law, and not relieve States of the responsibility for vindicating wrongdoing that is essentially local or weaken the habits of local law enforcement by tempting reliance on federal authority for an occasional unpleasant task of local enforcement. . . .

Since the majority of the Court do not share this conviction that the action of the Georgia peace officers was not perpetrated under color of law, we, too, must consider the constitutionality of § 20. All but two members of the Court apparently agree that insofar as § 20 purports to subject men to punishment for crime it fails to define what conduct is made criminal. As misuse of the criminal machinery is one of the most potent and familiar instruments of arbitrary government, proper regard for the rational requirement of definiteness in criminal statutes is basic to civil liberties. As such it is included in the constitutional guaranty of due process of law. But four members of the Court are of the opinion that this plain constitutional principle of definiteness in criminal statutes may be replaced by an elaborate scheme of constitutional exegesis whereby that which Congress has not defined the courts can define from time to time, with varying and conflicting definiteness in the decisions, and that, in any event, an undefined range of conduct may become sufficiently definite if only such undefined conduct is committed "willfully."

* * * *

Under the construction proposed for § 20, in order for a jury to convict, it would be necessary "to find that petitioners had the purpose to deprive the prisoner of a constitutional right, e. g. the right to be tried by a court rather than by ordeal." There is no question that Congress could provide for a penalty against deprivation by State officials "acting under color of any law" of "the right to be tried by a court rather than by ordeal." But we cannot restrict the problem raised by § 20 to the validity of penalizing a deprivation of this specific constitutional right. We are dealing with the reach of the statute, for Congress has not particularized as the Court now particularizes. Such transforming interpolation is not interpretation. And that is recognized by the sentence just quoted, namely, that the jury in order to convict under § 20 must find that an accused "had the purpose to deprive" another "of a constitutional right," giving *this* specific constitutional right as "e. g.," by way of illustration. Hence a judge would have to define to the jury what the constitutional rights are deprivation of which is prohibited by § 20. If that is a legal question as to which the jury must take instruction from the court, at least the trial court must be possessed of the means of knowing with sufficient definiteness the range of "rights" that are "constitutional." The court can hardly be helped out in determining that legal question by leaving it to the jury to decide whether the act was "willfully" committed. . . .

The complicated and subtle problems for law enforcement raised by the Court's decision emphasize the conclusion that § 20 was never designed for the use to which it has now been fashioned. The Government admits that it is appropriate to leave the punishment of such crimes as this to local authorities. Regard for this wisdom in federal-State relations was not left by Congress to executive discretion. It is, we are convinced, embodied in the statute itself.

PRESIDENT TRUMAN'S CIVIL RIGHTS PROGRAM (1946–1948)

To a more limited extent, the post-World War II period witnessed an increase in lynching and mob violence that paralleled the wave of terrorism and race riots at the close of the First World War. After a sequential pattern of decline in the years 1943 to 1945, the number of reported lynchings rose to six in 1946. (*The Statistical History of the United States from Colonial Times to the Present* [Stamford, Conn.: Fairfield Publishers, 1965], p. 218.) The nation was further shocked in 1946 and 1947 by reports of racial terror in Minden, Louisiana; Monroe, Georgia; Batesburg and Greenville, South Carolina; and Columbia, Tennessee. These incidents ran directly counter to Negro expectations that wartime experiences would lead to effective peacetime reforms.

In September, 1946, Walter White, NAACP Executive Secretary, led a delegation to the White House to plead with President Truman for forthright and effective executive action on behalf of colored Americans. The President responded in

December with Executive Order 9808, in which he established the President's Committee on Civil Rights. Such White House initiative circumvented the kind of Congressional procedures which had obstructed the passage of antilynching, fair employment practices, and antipoll tax measures. The Committee was empowered to investigate the status of civil rights and to submit a report, with recommendations, to the President. The President's Committee on Civil Rights undertook its tasks with dispatch. Within a year the group submitted a report based on comprehensive research, accompanied by an impressive range of fundamental recommendations for remedial action. Although the proposals were rejected by Congress, they constituted the basic legislative objectives sought by interracial reformers during the twenty years that followed.

The Committee's report, entitled *To Secure These Rights*, was clearly the product of a period in American life that had witnessed massive tensions and disruptions. The Depression, the Second World War, and the start of the Cold War had sharpened the public's awareness of the inequitable and obsolescent practices characterizing domestic race relations. The Committee could thus justify its appeals for redress on a variety of grounds, including moral, civil, and economic necessity at home, and international urgency abroad. The recommendations for action were both procedural and substantive, calling for joint efforts by federal and state governments.

President Truman incorporated the basic recommendations of the Committee in his special message to Congress on February 2, 1948. Congress, however, refused to act.

What motivated the President to take such bold initiative became a topic of debate. Critics then and later charged Truman with crass political maneuvering in an election year; some said that impending pressures from the Left—both within and without the Democratic party—had forced him to pander to voters in northern and midwestern metropolitan areas. Others credited him with the sincere intention of shaping fundamental reforms. Still others believed that he had chosen racial reform as a prime program with which his name and presidency might be identified in history.

DOCUMENTS 73

Executive Order 9808, December 5, 1946, Establishing the President's Committee on Civil Rights*

Whereas the preservation of civil rights guaranteed by the Constitution is essential to domestic tranquility, national security, the general welfare, and the continued existence of our free institutions; and

Whereas the action of individuals who take the law into their own hands and inflict summary punishment and wreak personal vengeance is subversive of our democratic system of law enforcement and public criminal justice, and gravely threatens our form of government; and

Whereas it is essential that all possible steps be taken to safeguard our civil rights:

Now, therefore, by virtue of the authority vested in me as President of the United States by the Constitution and the statutes of the United States, it is hereby ordered as follows:

1. There is hereby created a committee to be known as the President's Committee on Civil Rights, which shall be composed of the following-named members, who shall serve without compensation:

Mr. C. E. Wilson, chairman; Mrs. Sadie T. Alexander, Mr. James B. Carey, Mr. John S. Dickey, Mr. Morris L. Ernst, Rabbi Roland B. Gittelsohn, Dr. Frank P. Graham, The Most Reverend Francis J. Haas, Mr. Charles Luckman, Mr. Francis P. Matthews, Mr. Franklin D. Roosevelt, Jr., The Right Reverend Henry Knox Sherrill, Mr. Boris Shishkin, Mrs. M. E. Tilly, Mr. Channing H. Tobias.

2. The Committee is authorized on behalf of the President to inquire into and to determine whether and in what respect current law-enforcement measures and the authority and means possessed by Federal, State, and local governments may be strengthened and improved to safeguard the civil rights of the people.

3. All executive departments and agencies of the Federal Government are authorized and directed to cooperate with

---

* 11 Fed. Reg. 14153 (1946).

the Committee in its work, and to furnish the Committee such information or the services of such persons as the Committee may require in the performance of its duties.

4. When requested by the Committee to do so, persons employed in any of the executive departments and agencies of the Federal Government shall testify before the Committee and shall make available for the use of the Committee such documents and other information as the Committee may require.

5. The Committee shall make a report of its studies to the President in writing, and shall in particular make recommendations with respect to the adoption or establishment, by legislation or otherwise, of more adequate and effective means and procedures for the protection of the civil rights of the people of the United States.

6. Upon rendition of its report to the President, the Committee shall cease to exist, unless otherwise determined by further Executive Order.

HARRY S TRUMAN

THE WHITE HOUSE
December 5, 1946

*A program of action: the Committee's Recommendations**

The Time Is Now

Twice before in American history the nation has found it necessary to review the state of its civil rights. The first time was during the 15 years between 1776 and 1791, from the drafting of the Declaration of Independence through the Articles of Confederation experiment to the writing of the Constitution and the Bill of Rights. It was then that the distinctively American heritage was finally distilled from earlier views of liberty. The second time was when the Union was temporarily sundered over the question of whether it could exist "half-slave" and "half-free."

It is our profound conviction that we have come to a time

* *To Secure These Rights* (Washington, D.C.: U.S. Government Printing Office, 1947), pp. 139–73.

for a third re-examination of the situation, and a sustained drive ahead. Our reasons for believing this are those of conscience, of self-interest, and of survival in a threatening world. Or to put it another way, we have a moral reason, an economic reason, and an international reason for believing that the time for action is now.

The Moral Reason

We have considered the American heritage of freedom at some length. We need no further justification for a broad and immediate program than the need to reaffirm our faith in the traditional American morality. The pervasive gap between our aims and what we actually do is creating a kind of moral dry rot which eats away at the emotional and rational bases of democratic beliefs. There are times when the difference between what we preach about civil rights and what we practice is shockingly illustrated by individual outrages. There are times when the whole structure of our ideology is made ridiculous by individual instances. And there are certain continuing, quiet, omnipresent practices which do irreparable damage to our beliefs.

As examples of "moral erosion" there are the consequences of suffrage limitations in the South. The fact that Negroes and many whites have not been allowed to vote in some states has actually sapped the morality underlying universal suffrage. Many men in public and private life do not believe that those who have been kept from voting are capable of self rule. They finally convince themselves that disfranchised people do not really have the right to vote.

Wartime segregation in the armed forces is another instance of how a social pattern may wreak moral havoc. Practically all white officers and enlisted men in all branches of service saw Negro military personnel performing only the most menial functions. They saw Negroes recruited for the common defense treated as men apart and distinct from themselves. As a result, men who might otherwise have maintained the equalitarian morality of their forebears were given reason to look down on their fellow citizens. This has been sharply illustrated by the Army study discussed previously, in which white servicemen expressed great surprise at the excellent performance of Negroes who joined them in the firing line.

Even now, very few people know of the successful experiment with integrated combat units. Yet it is important in explaining why some Negro troops did not do well; it is proof that equal treatment can produce equal performance.

. . . .

It is impossible to decide who suffers the greatest moral damage from our civil rights transgressions, because all of us are hurt. That is certainly true of those who are victimized. Their belief in the basic truth of the American promise is undermined. But they do have the realization, galling as it sometimes is, of being morally in the right. The damage to those who are responsible for these violations of our moral standards may well be greater. They, too, have been reared to honor the command of "free and equal." And all of us must share in the shame at the growth of hypocrisies like the "automatic" marble champion. All of us must endure the cynicism about democratic values which our failures breed.

The United States can no longer countenance these burdens on its common conscience, these inroads on its moral fiber.

The Economic Reason

One of the principal economic problems facing us and the rest of the world is achieving maximum production and continued prosperity. The loss of a huge, potential market for goods is a direct result of the economic discrimination which is practiced against many of our minority groups. A sort of vicious circle is produced. Discrimination depresses the wages and income of minority groups. As a result, their purchasing power is curtailed and markets are reduced. Reduced markets result in reduced production. This cuts down employment, which of course means lower wages and still fewer job opportunities. Rising fear, prejudice, and insecurity aggravate the very discrimination in employment which sets the vicious circle in motion.

Minority groups are not the sole victims of this economic waste; its impact is inevitably felt by the entire population.

. . . .

Discrimination imposes a direct cost upon our economy through the wasteful duplication and many facilities and services required by the "separate but equal" policy. That the resources of the South are sorely strained by the burden of a double system of schools and other public services has already been indicated. Segregation is also economically wasteful for private business. Public transportation companies must often provide duplicate facilities to serve majority and minority groups separately. Places of public accommodation and recreation reject business when it comes in the form of unwanted persons. Stores reduce their sales by turning away minority customers. Factories must provide separate locker rooms, pay windows, drinking fountains, and washrooms for the different groups.

. . . .

Similarly, the rates of disease, crime, and fires are disproportionately great in areas which are economically depressed as compared with wealthier areas. Many of the prominent American minorities are confined—by economic discrimination, by law, by restrictive covenants, and by social pressure—to the most dilapidated, undesirable locations. Property in these locations yields a smaller return in taxes, which is seldom sufficient to meet the inordinately high cost of public services in depressed areas. The majority pays a high price in taxes for the low status of minorities.

. . . .

. . . It is not at all surprising that a people relegated to second-class citizenship should behave as second-class citizens. This is true, in varying degrees, of all of our minorities. What we have lost in money, production, invention, citizenship, and leadership as the price for damaged, thwarted personalities—these are beyond estimate.

The United States can no longer afford this heavy drain upon its human wealth, its national competence.

The International Reason

Our position in the postwar world is so vital to the future that our smallest actions have far-reaching effects. We have come to know that our own security in a highly inter-dependent world is inextricably tied to the security and well-being of all people and all countries. Our foreign policy is designed to make the United States an enormous, positive influence for peace and progress throughout the world. We have tried to let nothing, not even extreme political differences between ourselves and foreign nations, stand in the way of this goal. But our domestic civil rights shortcomings are a serious obstacle.

. . . .

We cannot escape the fact that our civil rights record has been an issue in world politics. The world's press and radio are full of it. This Committee has seen a multitude of samples. We and our friends have been, and are, stressing our achievements. Those with competing philosophies have stressed—and are shamelessly distorting—our shortcomings. They have not only tried to create hostility toward us among specific nations, races, and religious groups. They have tried to prove our democracy an empty fraud, and our nation a consistent oppressor of underprivileged people. This may seem ludicrous to Americans, but it is sufficiently important to worry our friends.

. . . .

. . . Our achievements in building and maintaining a state dedicated to the fundamentals of freedom have already served as a guide for those seeking the best road from chaos to liberty and prosperity. But it is not indelibly written that democracy will encompass the world. We are convinced that our way of life—the free way of life—holds a promise of hope for all people. We have what is perhaps the greatest responsibility ever placed upon a people to keep this promise alive. Only still greater achievements will do it.

The United States is not so strong, the final triumph of the democratic ideal is not so inevitable that we can ignore what the world thinks of us or our record.

President Truman's Message to Congress, February 2, 1948[*]

In the State of the Union Message on January 7, 1948, I spoke of five great goals toward which we should strive in our constant effort to strengthen our democracy and improve the welfare of our people. The first of these is to secure fully our essential human rights. I am now presenting to the Congress my recommendations for legislation to carry us forward toward that goal.

This Nation was founded by men and women who sought these shores that they might enjoy greater freedom and greater opportunity than they had known before. The founders of the United States proclaimed to the world the American belief that all men are created equal, and that governments are instituted to secure the inalienable rights with which all men are endowed.

· · · ·

We believe that all men are created equal and that they have the right to equal justice under law.

We believe that all men have the right to freedom of thought and of expression and the right to worship as they please.

We believe that all men are entitled to equal opportunities for jobs, for homes, for good health and for education.

We believe that all men should have a voice in their government and that government should protect, not usurp, the rights of the people.

These are the basic civil rights which are the source and the support of our democracy.

Today, the American people enjoy more freedom and opportunity than ever before. Never in our history has there been better reason to hope for the complete realization of the ideals of liberty and equality.

· · · ·

[*] U.S. House of Representatives, *Civil Rights Program Message from the President of the United States*, 80th Congress, 2nd Session, (House Doc. 516).

The Federal Government has a clear duty to see that Constitutional guarantees of individual liberties and of equal protection under the laws are not denied or abridged anywhere in our Union. That duty is shared by all three branches of the Government, but it can be fulfilled only if the Congress enacts modern, comprehensive civil rights laws, adequate to the needs of the day, and demonstrating our continuing faith in the free way of life.

I recommend, therefore, that the Congress enact legislation at this session directed toward the following specific objectives:

1. Establishing a permanent Commission on Civil Rights, a Joint Congressional Committee on Civil Rights, and a Civil Rights Division in the Department of Justice.

2. Strengthening existing civil rights statutes.

3. Providing Federal protection against lynching.

4. Protecting more adequately the right to vote.

5. Establishing a Fair Employment Practice Commission to prevent unfair discrimination in employment.

6. Prohibiting discrimination in interstate transportation facilities.

7. Providing home-rule and suffrage in Presidential elections for the residents of the District of Columbia.

8. Providing Statehood for Hawaii and Alaska and a greater measure of self-government for our island possessions.

9. Equalizing the opportunities for residents of the United States to become naturalized citizens.

10. Settling the evacuation claims of Japanese-Americans.

Strengthening the Government Organization

As a first step, we must strengthen the organization of the Federal Government in order to enforce civil rights legislation more adequately and to watch over the state of our traditional liberties.

I recommend that the Congress establish a permanent Commission on Civil Rights reporting to the President. The Commission should continuously review our civil rights policies and practices, study specific problems, and make recommendations to the President at frequent intervals. It should work with other agencies of the Federal Government, with state and local governments, and with private organizations.

I also suggest that the Congress establish a Joint Congressional Committee on Civil Rights. This Committee should make a continuing study of legislative matters relating to civil rights and should consider means of improving respect for and enforcement of those rights.

. . . .

A specific Federal measure is needed to deal with the crime of lynching—against which I cannot speak too strongly. It is a principle of our democracy, written into our Constitution, that every person accused of an offense against the law shall have a fair, orderly trial in an impartial court. We have made great progress toward this end, but I regret to say that lynching has not yet finally disappeared from our land. So long as one person walks in fear of lynching, we shall not have achieved equal justice under law. I call upon the Congress to take decisive action against this crime.

Protecting the Right to Vote

Under the Constitution, the right of all properly qualified citizens to vote is beyond question. Yet the exercise of this right is still subject to interference. Some individuals are prevented from voting by isolated acts of intimidation. Some whole groups are prevented by outmoded policies prevailing in certain states or communities.

We need stronger statutory protection of the right to vote. I urge the Congress to enact legislation forbidding interference by public officers or private persons with the right of qualified citizens to participate in primary, special and general elections in which Federal officers are to be chosen. This legislation should extend to elections for state as well as Federal officers insofar as interference with the right to vote results from discriminatory action by public officers based on race, color, or other unreasonable classification.

Requirements for the payment of poll taxes also interfere with the right to vote. There are still seven states which, by their constitutions, place this barrier between their citizens and the ballot box. The American people would welcome voluntary action on the part of these states to remove this barrier. Nevertheless, I believe the Congress should enact measures insuring that the right to vote in elections for Federal officers shall not be contingent upon the payment of taxes.

I wish to make it clear that the enactment of the measures I have recommended will in no sense result in Federal conduct of elections. They are designed to give qualified citizens Federal protection of their right to vote. The actual conduct of elections, as always, will remain the responsibility of State governments.

Fair Employment Practice Commission

We in the United States believe that all men are entitled to equality of opportunity. Racial, religious and other invidious forms of discrimination deprive the individual of an equal chance to develop and utilize his talents and to enjoy the rewards of his efforts.

Once more I repeat my request that the Congress enact fair employment practice legislation prohibiting discrimination in employment based on race, color, religion or national origin. The legislation should create a Fair Employment Practice Commission with authority to prevent discrimination by employers and labor unions, trade and professional associations, and government agencies and employment bureaus. The degree of effectiveness which the wartime Fair Employment Practice Committee attained shows that it is possible to equalize job opportunity by government action and thus to eliminate the influence of prejudice in employment.

Interstate Transportation

The channels of interstate commerce should be open to all Americans on a basis of complete equality. The Supreme Court has recently declared unconstitutional state laws requiring segregation on public carriers in interstate travel. Company regulations must not be allowed to replace unconstitutional state laws. I urge the Congress to prohibit discrimination and segregation, in the use of interstate transportation facilities, by both public officers and the employees of private companies.

. . . .

The position of the United States in the world today makes it especially urgent that we adopt these measures to secure for all our people their essential rights.

The peoples of the world are faced with the choice of freedom or enslavement, a choice between a form of government which harnesses the state in the service of the individual and a form of government which chains the individual to the needs of the state.

• • • •

We know that our democracy is not perfect. But we do know that it offers a fuller, freer, happier life to our people than any totalitarian nation has ever offered.

If we wish to inspire the peoples of the world whose freedom is in jeopardy, if we wish to restore hope to those who have already lost their civil liberties, if we wish to fulfill the promise that is ours, we must correct the remaining imperfections in our practice of democracy.

We know the way. We need only the will.

INTEGRATION IN THE ARMED SERVICES (1948)

During World War II and the Cold War, the United States has been actively committed to freedom and the protection of individual and national rights throughout the world. In this context, military units charged with the task of implementing those commitments, but organized on the basis of skin color, not only made poor sense functionally but represented an inconsistency which damaged the nation's worldwide image.

Realizing that he could get no cooperation from Congress, President Truman again chose the tactics of executive action to remedy the traditional pattern of discrimination in the armed services. Executive Order 9981 of July, 1948, established the President's Committee on Equality of Treatment and Opportunity in the Armed Services, with authority to inquire into discriminatory practices and to make recommendations for change.

The order was merely a beginning. Military custom, sustained by civilian predilections toward segregation, could not be altered in one stroke. The several branches of the armed services, their multiple divisions and units, and the major military, naval, and civilian authorities responsible for the nation's defense complex wrestled with the problem in varying degrees of earnestness, equanimity, and efficiency. The report of the President's Committee, *Freedom to Serve*, offered guidelines for action.

While the Directive issued by the Secretary of Defense in April, 1949 was an official step toward the fulfillment of the President's original order, it was the harsh realities of the Korean War that accelerated the pace of integration within fighting units.

DOCUMENT(S) 74

Executive Order 9981, July 26, 1948[*]

Whereas it is essential that there be maintained in the armed services of the United States the highest standards of democracy, with equality of treatment and opportunity for all those who serve in our country's defense:

Now, therefore, by virtue of the authority vested in me as President of the United States, by the Constitution and the statutes of the United States, and as Commander in Chief of the armed services, it is hereby ordered as follows:

1. It is hereby declared to be the policy of the President that there shall be equality of treatment and opportunity for all persons in the armed forces without regard to race, color, religion, or national origin. This policy shall be put into effect as rapidly as possible, having due regard to the time required to effectuate any necessary changes without impairing efficiency or morale.

2. There shall be created in the National Military Establishment an advisory committee to be known as the President's Committee on Equality of Treatment and Opportunity in the Armed Services, which shall be composed of seven members to be designated by the President.

3. The Committee is authorized on behalf of the President

---

[*] 13 Fed. Reg. 4313 (1948).

to examine into the rules, procedures, and practices of the armed services in order to determine in what respect such rules, procedures, and practices may be altered or improved with a view to carrying out the policy of this order. The Committee shall confer and advise with the Secretary of Defense, the Secretary of the Army, the Secretary of the Navy, and the Secretary of the Air Force, and shall make such recommendations to the President and to said Secretaries as in the judgment of the Committee will effectuate the policy hereof.

4. All executive departments and agencies of the Federal Government are authorized and directed to cooperate with the Committee in its work, and to furnish the Committee such information or the services of such persons as the Committee may require in the performance of its duties.

5. When requested by the Committee to do so, persons in the armed services or in any of the executive departments and agencies of the Federal Government shall testify before the Committee and shall make available for the use of the Committee such documents and other information as the Committee may require.

6. The Committee shall continue to exist until such time as the President shall terminate its existence by Executive order.

HARRY S TRUMAN

THE WHITE HOUSE
July 26, 1948

*Directive issued by Secretary of Defense Louis Johnson on April 6, 1949 to Army, Navy, and Air Force to review their personnel practices**

MEMORANDUM FOR: the Secretary of the Army, the Secretary of the Navy, the Secretary of the Air Force, [and] Chairman, Personnel Policy Board

SUBJECT: Equality of Treatment and Opportunity in the Armed Services

* From release issued by National Military Establishment, Office of Public Information, Washington, D.C., April 20, 1949.

1. a. It is the policy of the National Military Establishment that there shall be equality of treatment and opportunity for all persons in the Armed Services without regard to race, color, religion, or national origin.

b. To assist in achieving uniform application of this policy, the following supplemental policies are announced:

(1) To meet the requirements of the Services for qualified individuals, all personnel will be considered on the basis of individual merit and ability and must qualify according to the prescribed standards for enlistment, attendance at schools, promotion, assignment to specific duties, etc.

(2) All individuals, regardless of race, will be accorded equal opportunity for appointment, advancement, professional improvement, promotion and retention in their respective components of the National Military Establishment.

(3) Some units may continue to be manned with Negro personnel; however, all Negroes will not necessarily be assigned to Negro units. Qualified Negro personnel shall be assigned to fill any type of position vacancy in organizations or overhead installations without regard to race.

2. Each Department is directed to examine its present practices and determine what forward steps can and should be made in the light of this policy and in view of Executive Order 9981, dated July 26, 1948, which directs that this policy shall be put into effect as rapidly as possible with due regard to the time required to effectuate any necessary changes without impairing efficiency or morale.

3. Following the completion of this study, each Department shall state, in writing, its own detailed implementation of the general policy stated herein and such supplemental policies as may be determined by each Service to meet its own specific needs. These statements shall be submitted to the Chairman of the Personnel Policy Board, Office of the Secretary of Defense, not later than 1 May 1949.

/s/ Louis Johnson

SHELLEY V. KRAEMER—ON SEGREGATED HOUSING (1948)

As far back as 1917, the Supreme Court had taken affirmative action against what was then—in both the North and the the South—one of the most common methods of maintaining housing discrimination. In the case of *Buchanan* v. *Warley*, 245 U.S. 60 (1917), the unanimous Court declared unconstitutional a city zoning ordinance that prohibited Negroes from living on so-called white blocks. This resulted in the increased use of private deeds, contracts, and agreements restricting the ownership of certain real property solely to members of the white race. The questions in *Shelley* v. *Kraemer* were whether such *private* arrangements could be used to maintain segregated housing patterns—and how they might be enforced.

In the absence of specific *state* legislation condemning these private property agreements, they appeared on the surface to have all the trappings of legality. Voluntary, private discrimination falls under no prohibition of the United States Constitution. Only discriminatory state action—only the action of a state through one of its myriad agencies—can suffer constitutional disability. This was readily conceded by the unanimous Court in *Shelley* v. *Kraemer*. The Fourteenth Amendment, wrote Chief Justice Fred M. Vinson, "erects no shield against merely private conduct, however discriminatory or wrongful."

Thus—again absent a state or local enactment—there is nothing a court can do to void voluntary compliance with a purely private, restrictive housing agreement. But suppose one of the private parties breaks that agreement and is sued for breach of contract? Here, according to *Shelley* v. *Kraemer*, the court must counter discrimination by refusing to act. Such real estate arrangements may not be constitutionally enforced through the judicial process. The "coercive power of government" may not be used to deny the enjoyment of property rights "on the grounds of race or color," wrote the Chief Justice. Action by a court (or by a legislature, or a town council, or a school board, or a deputy sheriff) is state action

—and state participation in a discriminatory scheme violates the equal protection clause of the Fourteenth Amendment.

This is a decision of far-reaching significance; its influence will undoubtedly be felt in a generation of litigation yet to come. The state and its multiplicity of agencies become increasingly involved with the lives of their citizens. At what point does a tenuous involvement by the state in a private contract warrant a judicial declaration that it constitutes state action? At what point will the relationship between the state and the private discrimination be vulnerable to a judicial declaration of unconstitutionality?

Two subsequent cases further nullified the effectiveness of these property restrictions. A restrictive covenant in the District of Columbia was struck down as violative of the due process clause of the Fifth Amendment in *Hurd* v. *Hodge*, 334 U.S. 24 (1948). And in *Barrows* v. *Jackson*, 346 U.S. 249 (1953), it was held that one party to a restrictive covenant may not recover damages in a court suit against another party who broke the covenant.

The meaning of *Shelley* v. *Kraemer* became a matter of debate once again in the sit-in cases of the 1960's (Document 87).

DOCUMENT 75

Shelley v. Kraemer*

MR. CHIEF JUSTICE VINSON delivered the opinion of the Court.

These cases present for our consideration questions relating to the validity of court enforcement of private agreements, generally described as restrictive covenants, which have as their purpose the exclusion of persons of designated race or color from the ownership or occupancy of real property. Basic constitutional issues of obvious importance have been raised.

The first of these cases comes to this Court on certiorari to the Supreme Court of Missouri. On February 16, 1911, thirty out of a total of thirty-nine owners of property fronting both sides of Labadie Avenue between Taylor Avenue and

---

* Supreme Court of the United States, 334 U.S. 1 (1948).

Cora Avenue in the city of St. Louis, signed an agreement, which was subsequently recorded, providing in part:

> ... the said property is hereby restricted to the use and occupancy for the term of Fifty (50) years from this date, so that it shall be a condition all the time and whether recited and referred to as [*sic*] not in subsequent conveyances and shall attach to the land as a condition precedent to the sale of the same, that hereafter no part of said property or any portion thereof shall be, for said term of Fifty-years, occupied by any person not of the Caucasian race, it being intended hereby to restrict the use of said property for said period of time against the occupancy as owners or tenants of any portion of said property for resident or other purpose by people of the Negro or Mongolian Race.

. . . .

On August 11, 1945, pursuant to a contract of sale, petitioners Shelley, who are Negroes, for valuable consideration received from one Fitzgerald a warranty deed to the parcel in question. The trial court found that petitioners had no actual knowledge of the restrictive agreement at the time of the purchase.

On October 9, 1945, respondents, as owners of other property subject to the terms of the restrictive covenant, brought suit in the Circuit Court of the city of St. Louis praying that petitioners Shelley be restrained from taking possession of the property and that judgment be entered divesting title out of petitioners Shelley and revesting title in the immediate grantor or in such other person as the court should direct. The trial court denied the requested relief on the ground that the restrictive agreement, upon which respondents based their action, had never become final and complete because it was the intention of the parties to that agreement that it was not to become effective until signed by all property owners in the district, and signatures of all the owners had never been obtained.

The Supreme Court of Missouri sitting *en banc* reversed and directed the trial court to grant the relief for which respondents had prayed. That court held the agreement effective and concluded that enforcement of its provisions violated no rights guaranteed to petitioners by the Federal Constitution.

At the time the court rendered its decision, petitioners were occupying the property in question.

The second of the cases under consideration comes to this Court from the Supreme Court of Michigan. The circumstances presented do not differ materially from the Missouri case.

. . . .

Petitioners have placed primary reliance on their contentions, first raised in the state courts, that judicial enforcement of the restrictive agreements in these cases has violated rights guaranteed to petitioners by the Fourteenth Amendment of the Federal Constitution and Acts of Congress passed pursuant to that Amendment. Specifically, petitioners urge that they have been denied the equal protection of the laws, deprived of property without due process of law, and have been denied privileges and immunities of citizens of the United States. We pass to a consideration of those issues.

I

Whether the equal protection clause of the Fourteenth Amendment inhibits judicial enforcement by state courts of restrictive covenants based on race or color is a question which this Court has not heretofore been called upon to consider.

. . . .

It should be observed that these covenants do not seek to proscribe any particular use of the affected properties. Use of the properties for residential occupancy, as such, is not forbidden. The restrictions of these agreements, rather, are directed toward a designated class of persons and seek to determine who may and who may not own or make use of the properties for residential purposes. The excluded class is defined wholly in terms of race or color; "simply that and nothing more."

It cannot be doubted that among the civil rights intended to be protected from discriminatory state action by the Fourteenth Amendment are the rights to acquire, enjoy, own and dispose of property. Equality in the enjoyment of property rights was regarded by the framers of that Amendment as an essential pre-condition to the realization of other basic civil rights and liberties which the Amendment was intended to guarantee. Thus, § 1978 of the Revised Statutes, derived from § 1 of the Civil Rights Act of 1866 which was enacted by Congress while the Fourteenth Amendment was also under consideration, provides: "All citizens of the United States shall have the same right, in every State and Territory, as is enjoyed by white citizens thereof to inherit, purchase, lease, sell, hold, and convey real and personal property." This Court has given specific recognition to the same principle. *Buchanan* v. *Warley*, 245 U.S. 60 (1917).

It is likewise clear that restrictions on the right of occupancy of the sort sought to be created by the private agreements in these cases could not be squared with the requirements of the Fourteenth Amendment if imposed by state statute or local ordinance. We do not understand respondents to urge the contrary. In the case of *Buchanan* v. *Warley, supra,* a unanimous Court declared unconstitutional the provisions of a city ordinance which denied to colored persons the right to occupy houses in blocks in which the greater number of houses were occupied by white persons, and imposed similar restrictions on white persons with respect to blocks in which the greater number of houses were occupied by colored persons. During the course of the opinion in that case, this Court stated: "The Fourteenth Amendment and these statutes enacted in furtherance of its purpose operate to qualify and entitle a colored man to acquire property without state legislation discriminating against him solely because of color." . . .

But the present cases, unlike those just discussed, do not involve action by state legislatures or city councils. Here the particular patterns of discrimination and the areas in which the restrictions are to operate, are determined, in the first instance, by the terms of agreements among private individuals. Participation of the State consists in the enforcement of the restrictions so defined. The crucial issue with which we are here confronted is whether this distinction removes these cases from the operation of the prohibitory provisions of the Fourteenth Amendment.

Since the decision of this Court in the *Civil Rights Cases*, 109 U.S. 3 (1883), the principle has become firmly embedded in our constitutional law that the action inhibited by the first section of the Fourteenth Amendment is only such action as may fairly be said to be that of the States. That Amendment erects no shield against merely private conduct, however discriminatory or wrongful.

We conclude, therefore, that the restrictive agreements standing alone cannot be regarded as violative of any rights guaranteed to petitioners by the Fourteenth Amendment. So long as the purposes of those agreements are effectuated by voluntary adherence to their terms, it would appear clear that there has been no action by the State and the provisions of the Amendment have not been violated. . . .

But here there was more. These are cases in which the purposes of the agreements were secured only by judicial enforcement by state courts of the restrictive terms of the agreements. The respondents urge that judicial enforcement of private agreements does not amount to state action; or, in any event, the participation of the State is so attenuated in character as not to amount to state action within the meaning of the Fourteenth Amendment. Finally, it is suggested, even if the States in these cases may be deemed to have acted in the constitutional sense, their action did not deprive petitioners of rights guaranteed by the Fourteenth Amendment. We move to a consideration of these matters.

II

That the action of state courts and judicial officers in their official capacities is to be regarded as action of the State within the meaning of the Fourteenth Amendment, is a proposition which has long been established by decisions of this Court. . . .

The short of the matter is that from the time of the adoption of the Fourteenth Amendment until the present, it has been the consistent ruling of this Court that the action of the States of which the Amendment has reference includes action of state courts and state judicial officials. Although, in construing the terms of the Fourteenth Amendment, differences have from time to time been expressed as to whether particular types of state action may be said to offend the Amendment's prohibitory provisions, it has never been suggested that state court action is immunized from the operation of those provisions simply because the act is that of the judicial branch of the state government.

III

Against this background of judicial construction, extending over a period of some three-quarters of a century, we are called upon to consider whether enforcement by state courts of the restrictive agreements in these cases may be deemed to be the acts of those States; and, if so, whether that action has denied these petitioners the equal protection of the laws which the Amendment was intended to insure.

We have no doubt that there has been state action in these cases in the full and complete sense of the phrase. The undisputed facts disclose that petitioners were willing purchasers of properties upon which they desired to establish homes. The owners of the properties were willing sellers; and contracts of sale were accordingly consummated. It is clear that but for the active intervention of the state courts, supported by the full panoply of state power, petitioners would have been free to occupy the properties in question without restraint.

These are not cases, as has been suggested, in which the States have merely abstained from action, leaving private individuals free to impose such discriminations as they see fit. Rather, these are cases in which the States have made available to such individuals the full coercive power of government to deny to petitioners, on the grounds of race or color, the enjoyment of property rights in premises which petitioners are willing and financially able to acquire and which the grantors are willing to sell. The difference between judicial enforcement and nonenforcement of the restrictive covenants is the difference to petitioners between being denied rights of property available to other members of the community and being accorded full enjoyment of those rights on an equal footing.

The enforcement of the restrictive agreements by the state courts in these cases was directed pursuant to the common-law policy of the States as formulated by those courts in earlier decisions.

. . . .

We hold that in granting judicial enforcement of the restrictive agreements in these cases, the States have denied petitioners the equal protection of the laws and that, therefore, the action of the state courts cannot stand. . . .

Respondents urge, however, that since the state courts stand ready to enforce restrictive covenants excluding white persons from the ownership or occupancy of property covered by such agreements, enforcement of covenants excluding colored persons may not be deemed a denial of equal protection of the laws to the colored persons who are thereby affected. This contention does not bear scrutiny. The parties have directed our attention to no case in which a court, state or federal, has been called upon to enforce a covenant excluding members of the white majority from ownership or occupancy of real property on grounds of race or color. But there are more fundamental considerations. The rights created by the first section of the Fourteenth Amendment are, by its terms, guaranteed to the individual. The rights established are personal rights. It is, therefore, no answer to these petitioners to say that the courts may also be induced to deny white persons rights of ownership and occupancy on grounds of race or color. Equal protection of the laws is not achieved through indiscriminate imposition of inequalities.

Nor do we find merit in the suggestion that property owners who are parties to these agreements are denied equal protection of the laws if denied access to the courts to enforce the terms of restrictive covenants and to assert property rights which the state courts have held to be created by such agreements. The Constitution confers upon no individual the right to demand action by the State which results in the denial of equal protection of the laws to other individuals. And it would appear beyond question that the power of the State to create and enforce property interests must be exercised within the boundaries defined by the Fourteenth Amendment. . . .

For the reasons stated, the judgment of the Supreme Court of Missouri and the judgment of the Supreme Court of Michigan must be reversed.

Reversed.

TEXAS WHITE PRIMARY CASES (1927–1953)

In the ever-continuing legal maneuvers to restrict Negro voting rights granted by the Fifteenth Amendment (Document 48), many Southern states passed laws and adopted practices to deny Negroes the right of franchise in the Democratic primaries. These were, after all, the only important elections in the once Solid South. But, one after another, each of these devices was struck down by the Supreme Court.

Texas white primary litigation was before the Supreme Court five times between 1927 and 1953. In *Nixon* v. *Herndon*, 273 U.S. 536 (1927), the Court declared unconstitutional a 1923 statute providing that "in no event shall a negro be eligible to participate in a Democratic party primary election held in the state of Texas." In response—and in an attempt to eliminate state action on its restrictive voting practices—Texas then passed a statute giving its political parties the power to prescribe voter qualifications for their primaries. When the subsequent party regulations likewise barred the Negro from the polls, this statute was declared unconstitutional in *Nixon* v. *Condon*, 286 U.S. 73 (1932). Texas then repealed its laws restricting membership in political parties and left the matter to the parties themselves without providing for it in statutory form.

In *Grovey* v. *Townsend*, 295 U.S. 45 (1935), the Supreme Court temporarily altered its position. It upheld the validity of a resolution of the state Democratic convention which limited primary voting to whites. This, reasoned the Supreme Court of 1935, did not constitute state action. That decision was to last for only nine years.

Smith v. *Allwright*, 321 U.S. 649 (1944), specifically overruled *Grovey* v. *Townsend*. The Court wrote: "The privilege of membership in a party may be . . . no concern of a state. But when, as here, that privilege is also the essential qualification for voting in a primary to select nominees for a general election, the state makes the action of the party the action of the state."

Once more, Texas sought a restrictive device to perpetuate the white primary. The state Democratic party officially divested itself of the responsibility of selecting nominees. It transferred this duty to the privately operated Jaybird Association, whose membership was limited to whites. Whether the Jaybird primaries constituted state action was the issue before the Court in the fifth and last of these cases, *Terry* v. *Adams*. The answer was yes. A divided Supreme Court ruled that Negroes could not be barred from voting in the Jaybird elections.

DOCUMENT 76

*Terry v. Adams**

MR. JUSTICE BLACK announced the judgment of the Court and an opinion in which MR. JUSTICE DOUGLAS and MR. JUSTICE BURTON join.

In *Smith* v. *Allwright*, 321 U.S. 649, we held that rules of the Democratic Party of Texas excluding Negroes from voting in the party's primaries violated the Fifteenth Amendment. While no state law directed such exclusion, our decision pointed out that many party activities were subject to considerable statutory control. This case raises questions concerning the constitutional power of a Texas county political organization called the Jaybird Democratic Association or Jaybird Party to exclude Negroes from its primaries on racial grounds. The Jaybirds deny that their racial exclusions violate the Fifteenth Amendment. They contend that the Amendment applies only to elections or primaries held under state regulation, that their association is not regulated by the state at all, and that it is not a political party but a self-government voluntary club. The District Court held the Jaybird racial discriminations invalid and entered judgment accordingly. 90 F. Supp. 595. The Court of Appeals reversed, holding that there was no constitutional or congressional bar to the admitted discriminatory exclusion of Negroes because Jaybird's primaries were not to any extent state controlled. 193 F. 2d 600. We granted certiorari. 344 U.S. 883.

There was evidence that:

The Jaybird Association or Party was organized in 1889. Its membership was then and always has been limited to white people; they are automatically members if their names appear on the official list of county voters. It has been run like other political parties with an executive committee named from the county's voting precincts. Expenses of the party are paid by the assessment of candidates for office in its primaries. Candi-

---

* Supreme Court of the United States, 345 U.S. 461 (1953).

dates for county offices submit their names to the Jaybird Committee in accordance with the normal practice followed by regular political parties all over the country. Advertisements and posters proclaim that these candidates are running subject to the action of the Jaybird primary. While there is no legal compulsion on successful Jaybird candidates to enter Democratic primaries, they have nearly always done so and with few exceptions since 1889 have run and won without opposition in the Democratic primaries and the general elections that followed. Thus the party has been the dominant political group in the county since organization, having endorsed every county-wide official elected since 1889.

It is apparent that Jaybird activities follow a plan purposefully designed to exclude Negroes from voting and at the same time to escape the Fifteenth Amendment's command that the right of citizens to vote shall neither be denied nor abridged on account of race. These were the admitted party purposes according to the . . . testimony of the Jaybird's president.

. . . .

The [Fifteenth] Amendment bans racial discrimination in voting by both state and nation. It thus establishes a national policy, obviously applicable to the right of Negroes not to be discriminated against as voters in elections to determine public governmental policies or to select public officials, national, state, or local. . . .

Clearly the Amendment includes any election in which public issues are decided or public officials selected. Just as clearly the Amendment excludes social or business clubs. . . .

It is significant that precisely the same qualifications as those prescribed by Texas entitling electors to vote at county-operated primaries are adopted as the sole qualifications entitling electors to vote at the county-wide Jaybird primaries with a single proviso—Negroes are excluded. Everyone concedes that such a proviso in the county-operated primaries would be unconstitutional. The Jaybird Party thus brings into being and holds precisely the kind of election that the Fifteenth Amendment seeks to prevent. When it produces the equivalent of the prohibited election, the damage has been done.

For a state to permit such a duplication of its election

processes is to permit a flagrant abuse of those processes to defeat the purposes of the Fifteenth Amendment. The use of the county-operated primary to ratify the result of the prohibited election merely compounds the offense. It violates the Fifteenth Amendment for a state, by such circumvention, to permit within its borders the use of any device that produces an equivalent of the prohibited election.

. . . .

We reverse the Court of Appeals' judgment reversing that of the District Court. We affirm the District Court's holding that the combined Jaybird-Democratic-general election machinery has deprived these petitioners of their right to vote on account of their race and color. The case is remanded to the District Court to enter such orders and decrees as are necessary and proper under the jurisdiction it has retained under 28 U.S.C. § 2202. In exercising this jurisdiction, the Court is left free to hold hearings to consider and determine what provisions are essential to afford Negro citizens of Fort Bend County full protection from future discriminatory Jaybird-Democratic-general election practices which deprive citizens of voting rights because of their color.

Reversed and remanded.

Mr. Justice Frankfurter. . . .
Close analysis of what it is that the Fifteenth Amendment prohibits must be made before it can be determined what the relevant line is in the situation presented by this case. The Fifteenth Amendment, not the Fourteenth, outlawed discrimination on the basis of race or color with respect to the right to vote. Concretely, of course, it was directed against attempts to bar Negroes from having the same political franchise as white folk. "The right of citizens of the United States to vote shall not be denied or abridged by the United States or by any State on account of race, color, or previous condition of servitude." U.S. Const., Amend. XV, § 1. The command against such denial or abridgment is directed to the United States and to the individual States. Therefore, violation of this Amendment and the enactments passed in enforcement of it must involve the United States or a State. In this case the conduct that is assailed pertains to the election of local

Texas officials. To find a denial or abridgment of the guaranteed voting right to colored citizens of Texas solely because they are colored, one must find that the State has had a hand in it.

The State, in these situations, must mean not private citizens but those clothed with the authority and the influence which official position affords. The application of the prohibition of the Fifteenth Amendment to "any State" is translated by legal jargon to read "State action." This phrase gives rise to a false direction in that it implies some impressive machinery or deliberate conduct normally associated with what orators call a sovereign state. The vital requirement is State responsibility—that somewhere, somehow, to some extent, there be an infusion of conduct by officials, panoplied with State power, into any scheme by which colored citizens are denied voting rights merely because they are colored.

. . . .

The legal significance of the Jaybird primary must be tested against the cases which, in an endeavor to screen what is effectively an exertion of State authority in preventing Negroes from exercising their constitutional right of franchise, have pierced the various manifestations of astuteness. In the last of the series, *Smith* v. *Allwright,* 321 U.S. 649, we held that the State regulation there of primaries conducted by a political party made the party "required to follow these legislative directions an agency of the State in so far as it determines the participants in a primary election." *Id.*, at 663. Alternative routes have been suggested for concluding that the Jaybird primary is "so slight a change in form," *id.*, at 661, that the result should not differ in substance from that of *Smith* v. *Allwright.* The District Court found that the Jaybird Association is a political party within the meaning of the Texas legislation regulating the administration of primaries by political parties; it said that the Association could not avoid that result by holding its primary on a different date and by utilizing different methods than those prescribed by the statutes. . . .

The State of Texas has entered into a comprehensive scheme of regulation of political primaries, including procedures by which election officials shall be chosen. The county election officials are thus clothed with the authority of the State to secure observance of the State's interest in "fair methods and a fair expression" of preferences in the selection of nominees. . . . If the Jaybird Association, although not a political party, is a device to defeat the law of Texas regulating primaries, and if the electoral officials, clothed with State power in the county, share in that subversion, they cannot divest themselves of the State authority and help as participants in the scheme. Unlawful administration of a State statute fair on its face may be shown "by extrinsic evidence showing a discriminatory design to favor one individual or class over another not to be inferred from the action itself," *Snowden* v. *Hughes*, 321 U.S. 1, 8; here, the county election officials aid in this subversion of the State's official scheme of which they are trustees, by helping as participants in the scheme. . . .

It does not follow, however, that the relief granted below was proper. Since the vice of this situation is not that the Jaybird primary itself is the primary discriminatorily conducted under State law but is that the determination there made becomes, in fact, the determination in the Democratic primary by virtue of the participation and acquiescence of State authorities, a federal court cannot require that petitioners be allowed to vote in the Jaybird primary. The evil here is that the State, through the action and abdication of those whom it has clothed with authority, has permitted white voters to go through a procedure which predetermines the legally devised primary. To say that Negroes should be allowed to vote in the Jaybird primary would be to say that the State is under a duty to see to it that Negroes may vote in that primary. We cannot tell the State that it must participate in and regulate this primary; we cannot tell the State what machinery it will use. But a court of equity can free the lawful political agency from the combination that subverts its capacity to function. What must be done is that this county be rid of the means by which the unlawful "usage," R. S. § 2004, 8 U.S.C. § 31, in this case asserts itself.

. . . .

MR. JUSTICE CLARK, with whom THE CHIEF JUSTICE,

Mr. Justice Reed, and Mr. Justice Jackson join, concurring. . . .

We agree with Chief District Judge Kennerly that the Jaybird Democratic Association is a political party whose activities fall within the Fifteenth Amendment's self-executing ban. See *Guinn* v. *United States,* 238 U.S. 347, 363 (1915); *Myers* v. *Anderson,* 238 U.S. 368, 379–380 (1915). Not every private club, association or league organized to influence public candidacies or political action must conform to the Constitution's restrictions on political parties. Certainly a large area of freedom permits peaceable assembly and concerted private action for political purposes to be exercised separately by white and colored citizens alike. More, however, is involved here.

. . . .

Quite evidently the Jaybird Democratic Association operates as an auxiliary of the local Democratic Party organization, selecting its nominees and using its machinery for carrying out an admitted design of destroying the weight and effect of Negro ballots in Fort Bend County. To be sure, the Democratic primary and the general election are nominally open to the colored elector. But his must be an empty vote cast after the real decisions are made. And because the Jaybird-indorsed nominee meets no opposition in the Democratic primary, the Negro minority's vote is nullified at the sole stage of the local political process where the bargaining and interplay of rival political forces would make it count.

The Jaybird Democratic Association device, as a result, strikes to the core of the electoral process in Fort Bend County. Whether viewed as a separate political organization or as an adjunct of the local Democratic Party, the Jaybird Democratic Association is the decisive power in the county's recognized electoral process. Over the years its balloting has emerged as the locus of effective political choice. Consonant with the broad and lofty aims of its Framers, the Fifteenth Amendment, as the Fourteenth, "refers to exertions of state power in all forms." *Shelley* v. *Kraemer,* 334 U.S. 1, 20 (1948). Accordingly, when a state structures its electoral apparatus in a form which devolves upon a political organization the uncontested choice of public officials, that organization itself, in whatever disguise, takes on those attributes of government which draw the Constitution's safeguards into play. *Smith* v. *Allwright, supra,* at 664; cf. *United States* v. *Classic,* 313 U.S. 299, 324 (1941); *Lane* v. *Wilson,* 307 U.S. 268, 275 (1939).

In sum, we believe that the activities of the Jaybird Democratic Association fall within the broad principle laid down in *Smith* v. *Allwright, supra.* For that reason we join the judgment of the Court.

Mr. Justice Minton, dissenting.

I am not concerned in the least as to what happens to the Jaybirds or their unworthy scheme. I am concerned about what this Court says is state action within the meaning of the Fifteenth Amendment to the Constitution. For, after all, this Court has power to redress a wrong under that Amendment only if the wrong is done by the State. That has been the holding of this Court since the earliest cases. The Chief Justice for a unanimous Court in the recent case of *Shelley* v. *Kraemer,* 334 U.S. 1, 13, stated the law as follows:

Since the decision of this Court in the *Civil Rights Cases,* 109 U.S. 3 (1883), the principle has become firmly embedded in our constitutional law that the action inhibited by the first section of the Fourteenth Amendment is only such action as may fairly be said to be that of the States. *That Amendment erects no shield against merely private conduct, however discriminatory or wrongful.* (Emphasis supplied.) *

As I understand Mr. Justice Black's opinion, he would have this Court redress the wrong even if it was individual action alone. I can understand that praiseworthy position, but it seems to me it is not in accord with the Constitution. State action must be shown.

Mr. Justice Frankfurter recognizes that it must be state action but he seems to think it is enough to constitute state action if a state official participates in the Jaybird primary. That I cannot follow. For it seems clear to me that everything done by a person who is an official is not done officially and

---

* The Fifteenth Amendment as here involved is also directed at state action only.

as a representative of the State. However, I find nothing in this record that shows the state or county officials participating in the Jaybird primary.

Mr. Justice Clark seems to recognize that state action must be shown. He finds state action in assumption, not in facts. This record will be searched in vain for one iota of state action sufficient to support an anemic inference that the Jaybird Association is in any way associated with or forms a part of or cooperates in any manner with the Democratic Party of the County or State, or with the State. It calls itself the Jaybird Democratic Association because its interest is only in the candidates of the Democratic Party in the county, a position understandable in Texas. It is a gratuitous assumption on the part of Mr. Justice Clark that: "Quite evidently the Jaybird Democratic Association operates as an auxiliary of the local Democratic Party organization, selecting its nominees and using its machinery for carrying out an admitted design of destroying the weight and effect of Negro ballots in Fort Bend County." . . .

Neither is there any more evidence that the Jaybird Association avails itself of or conforms in any manner to any law of the State of Texas. . . . Even if it be said to be a political organization, the Jaybird Association avails itself of no state law open to political organizations, such as Art. 3163.

However, its action is not forbidden by the law of the State of Texas. Does such failure of the State to act to prevent individuals from doing what they have the right as individuals to do amount to state action? I venture the opinion it does not.

Mr. Justice Clark's opinion agrees with District Judge Kennerly that this Jaybird Democratic Association is a political party whose activities fall within the Fifteenth Amendment's self-executing ban. In the same paragraph, he admits that not all meetings for political action come under the constitutional ban. Surely white or colored members of any political faith or economic belief may hold caucuses. It is only when the State by action of its legislative bodies or action of some of its officials in their official capacity cooperates with such political party or gives it direction in its activities that the Federal Constitution may come into play. A political organization not using state machinery or depending upon state law to authorize what it does could not be within the ban of the

Fifteenth Amendment. As the stipulation quoted shows, the Jaybird Association did not attempt to conform or in any way to comply with the statutes of Texas covering primaries. No action of any legislative or quasi-legislative body or of any state official or agency ever in any manner denied the vote to Negroes, even in the Jaybird primaries.

So it seems to me clear there is no state action, and the Jaybird Democratic Association is in no sense a part of the Democratic Party. If it is a political organization, it has made no attempt to use the State, or the State to use it, to carry on its poll.

. . . .

I do not understand that concerted action of individuals which is successful somehow becomes state action. However, the candidates endorsed by the Jaybird Association have several times been defeated in primaries and elections. Usually but not always since 1938, only the Jaybird-endorsed candidate has been on the Democratic official ballot in the County.

In the instant case, the State of Texas has provided for elections and primaries. This is separate and apart and wholly unrelated to the Jaybird Association's activities. Its activities are confined to one County where a group of citizens have appointed themselves the censors of those who would run for public offices. Apparently so far they have succeeded in convincing the voters of this County in most instances that their supported candidates should win. This seems to differ very little from situations common in many other places far north of the Mason-Dixon line, such as areas where a candidate must obtain the approval of a religious group. In other localities, candidates are carefully selected by both parties to give proper weight to Jew, Protestant and Catholic, and certain posts are considered the sole possession of certain ethnic groups. The propriety of these practices is something the courts sensibly have left to the good or bad judgment of the electorate. It must be recognized that elections and other public business are influenced by all sorts of pressures from carefully organized groups. We have pressure from labor unions, from the National Association of Manufacturers, from the Silver Shirts, from the National Association for the Advancement of Colored People, from the Ku Klux Klan and others. Far from the activities of these groups being properly labeled as state action, under either the Fourteenth or the Fifteenth Amendment, they are to be considered as attempts to influence or obtain state action.

．．．．

In this case the majority have found that this pressure group's work does constitute state action. The basis of this conclusion is rather difficult to ascertain. Apparently it derives mainly from a dislike of the goals of the Jaybird Association. I share that dislike. I fail to see how it makes state action. I would affirm.

BROWN V. BOARD OF EDUCATION OF TOPEKA: THE PREDECESSOR CASES (1938–1950)

State-imposed racial discrimination was struck down as unconstitutional per se in the landmark case of *Brown* v. *Board of Education of Topeka*, 1954 (Document 78). The precise decision was: (a) since all legislation necessarily involves classification, the equal protection clause of the Fourteenth Amendment (Document 46) cannot demand absolute equality; state laws and practices protecting people according to age, sex, and the like are constitutionally valid; (b) discriminatory state action will be upheld providing that it is reasonable; a statute devoted exclusively to regulating the working hours of women is not violative of the equal protection clause, because of the real differences between male and female and the reasonableness of the legislative purpose in protecting the latter; (c) discriminatory racial practices are inherently unreasonable; a racial classification can have no reasonable relation to any legislative purpose; therefore any state-imposed classification based on race is unconstitutional per se as violative of the equal protection mandate.

The last case in which the Supreme Court had expressly upheld a segregation law or any other type of racial classification was in 1927, in *Gong Lum* v. *Rice*, 275 U.S. 78. And all that the nine men did there was to accept the finding of the

Mississippi courts that, for purposes of the public education laws, all those who were not white could be classified as members of the colored race. Since the state had no separate schools for Mongolians, it was held that Martha Lum, a Chinese resident of Mississippi, could be required to attend a colored rather than a white school.

The Japanese relocation regulations in the early days of World War II had strong racial overtones. But the case which sustained this program was justified on the grounds of military necessity. As Justice Hugo L. Black wrote in *Korematsu* v. *United States*, 323 U.S. 214, 216 (1944): "Korematsu was not excluded from the Military Area because of hostility to him or his race. He *was* excluded because we are at war with the Japanese Empire."

Numerous Supreme Court decisions between 1927 and 1954 contained strong language condemning racial discrimination. But there were four specific cases which even more clearly indicated the trend. On four separate occasions between 1938 and 1950, a Negro sought admittance to a white graduate school; four times the Supreme Court ordered the admission. The cases were *Missouri ex rel. Gaines* v. *Canada; Sipuel* v. *Board of Regents*, 332 U.S. 631 (1948); *Sweatt* v. *Painter* (Document 77); and *McLaurin* v. *Oklahoma State Regents*, 339 U.S. 637 (1950).

While the decisions did not expressly overturn the separate-but-equal formula, the holdings testified to the substantial inequality which existed between the white schools and the Negro schools.

The approach of the Supreme Court in these four cases, its willingness to find an existing inequality, and its consistent refusal to uphold a racial classification paved the way for the inevitable *Brown* decision. Excerpts from the Court's opinion in two of the cases follow.

DOCUMENT(S) 77

Missouri ex rel. Gaines v. Canada*

MR. CHIEF JUSTICE HUGHES delivered the opinion of the Court. . . .

---

* Supreme Court of the United States, 305 U.S. 337 (1938).

Petitioner is a citizen of Missouri. In August, 1935, he was graduated with a degree of Bachelor of Arts at the Lincoln University, an institution maintained by the State of Missouri for the higher education of negroes. That University has no law school. Upon the filing of his application for admission to the law school of the University of Missouri, the registrar advised him to communicate with the president of Lincoln University and the latter directed petitioner's attention to § 9622 of the Revised Statutes of Missouri (1929), providing as follows:

SEC. 9622. *May arrange for attendance at university of any adjacent state—Tuition fees.* Pending the full development of the Lincoln university, the board of curators shall have the authority to arrange for the attendance of negro residents of the state of Missouri at the university of any adjacent state to take any course or to study any subjects provided for at the state university of Missouri, and which are not taught at the Lincoln university and to pay the reasonable tuition fees for such attendance; *provided* that whenever the board of curators deem it advisable they shall have the power to open any necessary school or department (Laws 1921, p. 86, § 7).

Petitioner was advised to apply to the State Superintendent of Schools for aid under that statute. It was admitted on the trial that petitioner's "work and credits at the Lincoln University would qualify him for admission to the School of Law of the University of Missouri if he were found otherwise eligible." He was refused admission upon the ground that it was "contrary to the constitution, laws and public policy of the State to admit a negro as a student in the University of Missouri." . . .

It is manifest that this discrimination, . . . would constitute a denial of equal protection. That was the conclusion of the Court of Appeals of Maryland in circumstances substantially similar in that aspect. University of Maryland v. Murray, 169 Md. 478; 182 A. 590. It there appeared that the State of Maryland had "undertaken the function of education in the law" but had "omitted students of one race from the only adequate provision made for it, and omitted them solely because of their color"; that if those students were to be offered "equal treatment in the performance of the function,

they must, at present, be admitted to the one school provided."
Id., p. 489. A provision for scholarships to enable negroes to
attend colleges outside the State, mainly for the purpose
of professional studies, was found to be inadequate (Id., pp.
485, 486) and the question, "whether with aid in any amount
it is sufficient to send the negroes outside the State for legal
education," the Court of Appeals found it unnecessary to discuss. Accordingly, a writ of mandamus to admit the applicant
was issued to the officers and regents of the University of
Maryland as the agents of the State entrusted with the conduct
of that institution.

The Supreme Court of Missouri in the instant case has distinguished the decision in Maryland upon the grounds—(1)
that in Missouri, but not in Maryland, there is "a legislative
declaration of a purpose to establish a law school for negroes
at Lincoln University whenever necessary or practical"; and
(2) that, "pending the establishment of such a school, adequate provision has been made for the legal education of
negro students in recognized schools outside of this State."
113 S.W.2d, p. 791.

As to the first ground, it appears that the policy of establishing a law school at Lincoln University has not yet ripened
into an actual establishment, and it cannot be said that a mere
declaration of purpose, still unfulfilled, is enough. . . .

The state court stresses the advantages that are afforded by
the law schools of the adjacent States, Kansas, Nebraska,
Iowa and Illinois, which admit non-resident negroes. . . .
Petitioner insists that for one intending to practice in Missouri
there are special advantages in attending a law school there,
both in relation to the opportunities for the particular study
of Missouri law and for the observation of the local courts,
and also in view of the prestige of the Missouri law school
among the citizens of the State, his prospective clients. Proceeding with its examination of relative advantages, the state
court found that the difference in distances to be traveled
afforded no substantial ground of complaint and that there
was an adequate appropriation to meet the full tuition fees
which petitioner would have to pay.

We think that these matters are beside the point. The basic
consideration is not as to what sort of opportunities other
States provide, or whether they are as good as those in
Missouri, but as to what opportunities Missouri itself furnishes

to white students and denies to negroes solely upon the ground of color. The admissibility of laws separating the races in the enjoyment of privileges afforded by the State rests wholly upon the equality of the privileges which the laws give to the separated groups within the State. The question here is not of a duty of the State to supply legal training, or of the quality of the training which it does supply, but of its duty when it provides such training to furnish it to the residents of the State upon the basis of an equality of right. By the operation of the laws of Missouri a privilege has been created for white law students which is denied to negroes by reason of their race. The white resident is afforded legal education within the State; the negro resident having the same qualifications is refused it there and must go outside the State to obtain it. That is a denial of the equality of legal right to the enjoyment of the privilege which the State has set up, and the provision for the payment of tuition fees in another State does not remove the discrimination.

. . . .

Here, petitioner's right was a personal one. It was as an individual that he was entitled to the equal protection of the laws, and the State was bound to furnish him within its borders facilities for legal education substantially equal to those which the State there afforded for persons of the white race, whether or not other negroes sought the same opportunity.

. . . .

The judgment of the Supreme Court of Missouri is reversed and the cause is remanded for further proceedings not inconsistent with this opinion.

Reversed.

Sweatt v. Painter *

MR. CHIEF JUSTICE VINSON delivered the opinion of the Court.

---

* Supreme Court of the United States, 339 U.S. 629 (1950).

This case and *McLaurin* v. *Oklahoma State Regents* [339 U.S. 637] present different aspects of this general question: To what extent does the Equal Protection Clause of the Fourteenth Amendment limit the power of a state to distinguish between students of different races in professional and graduate education in a state university? Broader issues have been urged for our consideration, but we adhere to the principle of deciding constitutional questions only in the context of the particular case before the Court. We have frequently reiterated that this Court will decide constitutional questions only when necessary to the disposition of the case at hand, and that such decisions will be drawn as narrowly as possible. . . .

In the instant case, petitioner filed an application for admission to the University of Texas Law School for the February, 1946 term. His application was rejected solely because he is a Negro. Petitioner thereupon brought this suit for mandamus against the appropriate school officials, respondents here, to compel his admission. At that time, there was no law school in Texas which admitted Negroes.

The state trial court recognized that the action of the State in denying petitioner the opportunity to gain a legal education while granting it to others deprived him of the equal protection of the laws guaranteed by the Fourteenth Amendment. The court did not grant the relief requested, however, but continued the case for six months to allow the State to supply substantially equal facilities. At the expiration of the six months, in December, 1946, the court denied the writ on the showing that the authorized university officials had adopted an order calling for the opening of a law school for Negroes the following February. While petitioner's appeal was pending, such a school was made available, but petitioner refused to register therein. The Texas Court of Civil Appeals set aside the trial court's judgment and ordered the cause "remanded generally to the trial court for further proceedings without prejudice to the rights of any party to this suit."

On remand, a hearing was held on the issue of the equality of the educational facilities at the newly established school as compared with the University of Texas Law School. Finding that the new school offered petitioner "privileges, advantages, and opportunities for the study of law substantially equivalent to those offered by the State to white students at the University of Texas," the trial court denied mandamus. The Court of Civil Appeals affirmed. 210 S.W.2d 442 (1948). Petitioner's application for a writ of error was denied by the Texas Supreme Court. We granted certiorari, 338 U.S. 865 (1949), because of the manifest importance of the constitutional issues involved.

The University of Texas Law School, from which petitioner was excluded, was staffed by a faculty of sixteen full-time and three part-time professors, some of whom are nationally recognized authorities in their field. Its student body numbered 850. The library contained over 65,000 volumes. Among the other facilities available to the students were a law review, moot court facilities, scholarship funds, and Order of the Coif affiliation. The school's alumni occupy the most distinguished positions in the private practice of the law and in the public life of the State. It may properly be considered one of the nation's ranking law schools.

The law school for Negroes which was to have opened in February, 1947, would have had no independent faculty or library. The teaching was to be carried on by four members of the University of Texas Law School faculty, who were to maintain their offices at the University of Texas while teaching at both institutions. Few of the 10,000 volumes ordered for the library had arrived; nor was there any full-time librarian. The school lacked accreditation.

Since the trial of this case, respondents report the opening of a law school at the Texas State University for Negroes. It is apparently on the road to full accreditation. It has a faculty of five full-time professors; a student body of 23; a library of some 16,500 volumes serviced by a full-time staff; a practice court and legal aid association; and one alumnus who has become a member of the Texas Bar.

Whether the University of Texas Law School is compared with the original or the new law school for Negroes, we cannot find substantial equality in the educational opportunities offered white and Negro law students by the State. In terms of number of the faculty, variety of courses and opportunity for specialization, size of the student body, scope of the library, availability of law review and similar activities, the University of Texas Law School is superior. What is more important, the University of Texas Law School possesses to a far greater degree those qualities which are incapable of objective measurement but which make for greatness in a law school. Such qualities, to name but a few, include reputation of the faculty, experience of the administration, position and influence of the alumni, standing in the community, traditions and prestige. It is difficult to believe that one who had a free choice between these law schools would consider the question close.

Moreover, although the law is a highly learned profession, we are well aware that it is an intensely practical one. The law school, the proving ground for legal learning and practice, cannot be effective in isolation from the individuals and institutions with which the law interacts. Few students and no one who has practiced law would choose to study in an academic vacuum, removed from the interplay of ideas and the exchange of views with which the law is concerned. The law school to which Texas is willing to admit petitioner excludes from its student body members of the racial groups which number 85% of the population of the State and include most of the lawyers, witnesses, jurors, judges and other officials with whom petitioner will inevitably be dealing when he becomes a member of the Texas Bar. With such a substantial and significant segment of society excluded, we cannot conclude that the education offered petitioner is substantially equal to that which he would receive if admitted to the University of Texas Law School.

It may be argued that excluding petitioner from that school is no different from excluding white students from the new law school. This contention overlooks realities. It is unlikely that a member of a group so decisively in the majority, attending a school with rich traditions and prestige which only a history of consistently maintained excellence could command, would claim that the opportunities afforded him for legal education were unequal to those held open to petitioner. That such a claim, if made, would be dishonored by the State, is no answer. "Equal protection of the laws is not achieved through indiscriminate imposition of inequalities." *Shelley* v. *Kraemer*, 334 U.S. 1, 22 (1948).

It is fundamental that these cases concern rights which are personal and present. This Court has stated unanimously that "The State must provide [legal education] for [petitioner] in conformity with the equal protection clause of the Fourteenth Amendment and provide it as soon as it does for applicants of any other group." *Sipuel* v. *Board of Regents,* 332 U.S. 631, 633 (1948). That case "did not present the issue whether a state might not satisfy the equal protection clause of the Fourteenth Amendment by establishing a separate law school for Negroes." . . . In *Missouri ex rel. Gaines* v. *Canada,* 305 U.S. 337, 351 (1938), the Court, speaking through Chief Justice Hughes, declared that "petitioner's right was a personal one. It was as an individual that he was entitled to the equal protection of the laws, and the State was bound to furnish him within its borders facilities for legal education substantially equal to those which the State there afforded for persons of the white race, whether or not other negroes sought the same opportunity." These are the only cases in this Court which present the issue of the constitutional validity of race distinctions in state-supported graduate and professional education.

In accordance with these cases, petitioner may claim his full constitutional right: legal education equivalent to that offered by the State to students of other races. Such education is not available to him in a separate law school as offered by the State. We cannot, therefore, agree with respondents that the doctrine of *Plessy* v. *Ferguson,* 163 U.S. 537 (1896), requires affirmance of the judgment below. Nor need we reach petitioner's contention that *Plessy* v. *Ferguson* should be re-examined in the light of contemporary knowledge respecting the purposes of the Fourteenth Amendment and the effects of racial segregation. . . .

We hold that the Equal Protection Clause of the Fourteenth Amendment requires that petitioner be admitted to the University of Texas Law School. The judgment is reversed and the cause is remanded for proceedings not inconsistent with this opinion.

Reversed.

SCHOOL SEGREGATION CASES (1953–1955)

No document in the history of civil rights and the American Negro approaches the significance of the unanimous 1954 Supreme Court opinion in *Brown* v. *Board of Education of Topeka,* 347 U.S. 483. All state-imposed racial discrimination was struck down as unconstitutional per se under the equal protection clause of the Fourteenth Amendment, climaxing more than two centuries of litigation on the legal status of the Negro. The *Brown* case marked the opening of a new era in the legal struggle for Negro equality.

"Probably no decision in the history of the Court has directly concerned so many individuals," *The New York Times* wrote on May 18, 1954. "At the time of the Brown case, segregation in the schools was required by law in seventeen states and the District of Columbia. In this area there were over 8,000,000 white and 2,500,000 Negro school children enrolled in approximately 35,000 white schools and 15,000 Negro schools."

Five separate legal actions made up the School Segregation Cases, the least important of which was the suit involving Oliver Brown and the Board of Education of Topeka. Brown was merely the first name in alphabetical order in the first case on the Supreme Court docket for the 1953 October term. The Delaware case of *Gebhart* v. *Belton* was certainly more important. And far more significant were the South Carolina case of *Briggs* v. *Elliott* and the Virginia case of *Davis* v. *County School Board of Prince Edward County*. The fifth suit was *Bolling* v. *Sharpe*, which challenged the validity of segregation in the public schools of the District of Columbia.

Ten years after *Brown* v. *Board of Education of Topeka*, the constitutional declaration against school segregation was still only a paper right. The Segregation-Desegregation Status Table prepared by the Southern Education Reporting Service for the school year 1964–1965 revealed the success of the South in avoiding the Supreme Court mandate. Only 2.14 percent of the nearly three million Negroes in southern schools were receiving anything approaching a desegregated education. The percentage, however, had risen to 59.2 in the Border States.

Dissatisfied with desegregation delays, the Supreme Court spoke strongly in three cases in 1963 and 1964. In *Watson* v. *Memphis*, 373 U.S. 526 (1963), the unanimous Court denounced the policy of gradual desegregation of the city's recreational facilities and ordered immediate integration. And in *Calhoun* v. *Latimer*, 377 U.S. 263 (1964), the trial court was ordered to consider whether Atlanta's school desegregation program was proceeding fast enough.

Far more significant was the decision in *Griffin* v. *Prince Edward School Board*, 377 U.S. 218 (1964), one of the original cases that made up *Brown* v. *Board of Education of Topeka*. There the response to the judicial mandate had been to close the public schools. White children attended a purported "private" school supported by public funds, but from 1959 to 1963, no Negro child attended any school at all in the county. Justice Hugo L. Black spoke for the Court in declaring that the situation reflected "entirely too much deliberation and not enough speed." In a seven to two decision, Prince Edward County was ordered to reopen its public schools on a desegregated basis, and the federal district court was authorized to require the school authorities "to exercise the power that is theirs to levy taxes to raise funds" for the purpose.

School desegregation was to proceed at a faster pace with the enactment of Title VI of the Civil Rights Act of 1964 (Document 89) and the issuance of the 1966 Desegregation Guidelines by the Department of Health, Education, and Welfare (Document 95).

The first Supreme Court decision in *Brown* v. *Board of Education of Topeka* was handed down on October 8, 1952, 344 U.S. 1 (1952). Before the Court at that time were the Kansas and South Carolina actions, which had been set for argument, and a statement of jurisdiction in the Virginia suit. The Supreme Court also noted that the District of Columbia case was pending in a lower federal court. The decision was to continue the cases on the docket so that the arguments might be heard together. On November 10, 1952, certiorari was granted in the District of Columbia case of *Bolling* v. *Sharpe*, 344 U.S. 873 (1952), and on November 24, 1952, certiorari was granted in the Delaware case of *Gebhart* v. *Belton*, 344 U.S. 891 (1952). Also on November 24, 1952, the Supreme Court handed down another ruling in *Brown* v. *Board of Education of Topeka*, 344 U.S. 141 (1952), requesting the State of Kansas to present its views in the forthcoming legal argument. Thus the five cases were consolidated.

On June 8, 1953, the decision was handed down in *Brown* v. *Board of Education of Topeka*, 345 U.S. 972 (1953). This decision was an order assigning the case for reargument and requesting counsel "to discuss particularly" five questions (Document 78). Numerous briefs were prepared in advance of the reargument, including several by the United States Government and *amicus curiae* briefs of the attorneys general of many of the southern states. The most comprehensive summaries of argument were set forth in the briefs of the National Association for the Advancement of Colored People and of South Carolina in *Briggs* v. *Elliott*.

Reargument lasted three days. Before the high tribunal on December 7 to 9, 1953, came some of the foremost talent at the American bar. Thurgood Marshall, now a Justice of the Supreme Court, pleaded the cause of desegregation as chief counsel of the NAACP. Chief spokesman for the South was New York lawyer John W. Davis, Democratic nominee for President of the United States in 1924, representing South Carolina in *Briggs* v. *Elliott*.

The principal decision, handed down on May 17, 1954 (347 U.S. 483), held that state-imposed school segregation was unconstitutional under the Fourteenth Amendment's equal protection clause. Thus disposed of were the Kansas, Delaware, South Carolina, and Virginia cases. But a separate decision was required for the District of Columbia case of *Bolling* v. *Sharpe*, 347 U.S. 497 (1954), delivered that same day. The District of Columbia is under federal authority, and the powers of the United States Government are not restricted by an equal protection clause. The Supreme Court, however, reached the same unanimous conclusion, holding school segregation invalid under the Fifth Amendment's due process clause.

The 1954 determination set forth the constitutional principle, but said nothing about enforcement. The implementation decision was handed down a year later in *Brown* v. *Board of Education of Topeka*, 349 U.S. 294 (1955). This was the mandate ordering school desegregation "with all deliberate speed," requiring "good faith compliance at the earliest practicable date."

Both the South Carolina and Virginia controversies came before the courts again and both rendered important decisions. In *Briggs* v. *Elliott*, 132 F.Supp. 766, 767 (E.D.S.C. 1955), the Federal District Court in South Carolina had this to say: "Whatever may have been the views of this court as to law when the case was originally before us, it is our duty now to accept the law as declared by the Supreme Court." The *Briggs* v. *Elliott* decision has been cited over and over again by southern courts for its explanation of the meaning of the 1954 decision in *Brown* v. *Board of Education of Topeka*. It is one of the principal cases standing for the position that only state-imposed segregation has been declared invalid, and that there is nothing in the Constitution that requires integration or "takes away from the people freedom to choose the schools they attend."

The Virginia case came before the Supreme Court for the last time in 1964, in *Griffin* v. *Prince Edward School Board*.

Brown v. *Board of Education of Topeka* was a school segregation case, and as such its technical holding was limited to a constitutional declaration outlawing racial segregation in the public schools. It required later Supreme Court rulings to provide the full meaning of the *Brown* decision that all state-imposed racial discrimination is unconstitutional per se. Relying specifically on the 1954 Brown determination, the Supreme Court in 1955 declared segregation invalid on public beaches in Maryland and on public golf courses in Georgia. The cases were *Mayor and City Council of Baltimore* v. *Dawson*, 350 U.S. 877 (1955); and *Holmes* v. *Atlanta*, 350 U.S. 879 (1955).

In *Gayle* v. *Browder*, 352 U.S. 903 (1956), the Court declared the unconstitutionality of state statutes requiring racial segregation on the buses of Montgomery, Alabama. It was this transportation case which finally overruled *Plessy* v. *Ferguson*, (Document 58) and its separate-but-equal doctrine.

DOCUMENT(S) 78

Brown v. Board of Education of Topeka[*]

Miscellaneous Orders

No. 8.   BROWN ET AL *v*. BOARD OF EDUCATION OF TOPEKA ET AL.;

No. 101.   BRIGGS ET AL. *v*. ELLIOTT ET AL., MEMBERS OF BOARD OF TRUSTEES OF SCHOOL DISTRICT #22, ET AL.;

No. 191.   DAVIS ET AL. *v*. COUNTY SCHOOL BOARD OF PRINCE EDWARD COUNTY ET AL.;

---

[*] Supreme Court of the United States, 345 U.S. 972 (1953).

No. 413. Bolling et al. *v.* Sharpe et al.; and
No. 448. Gebhart et al. *v.* Belton et al.

Each of these cases is ordered restored to the docket and is
assigned for reargument on Monday, October 12, next. In
their briefs and on oral argument counsel are requested to discuss particularly the following questions insofar as they are
relevant to the respective cases:

1. What evidence is there that the Congress which submitted and the State legislatures and conventions which ratified the Fourteenth Amendment contemplated or did not
contemplate, understood or did not understand, that it would
abolish segregation in public schools?

2. If neither the Congress in submitting nor the States in
ratifying the Fourteenth Amendment understood that compliance with it would require the immediate abolition of
segregation in public schools, was it nevertheless the understanding of the framers of the Amendment

(*a*) that future Congresses might, in the exercise of their
power under section 5 of the Amendment, abolish such segregation, or

(*b*) that it would be within the judicial power, in light of
future conditions, to construe the Amendment as abolishing
such segregation of its own force?

3. On the assumption that the answers to questions 2 (*a*)
and (*b*) do not dispose of the issue, is it within the judicial
power, in construing the Amendment, to abolish segregation
in public schools?

4. Assuming it is decided that segregation in public schools
violates the Fourteenth Amendment

(*a*) would a decree necessarily follow providing that,
within the limits set by normal geographic school districting,
Negro children should forthwith be admitted to schools of
their choice, or

(*b*) may this Court, in the exercise of its equity powers,
permit an effective gradual adjustment to be brought about
from existing segregated systems to a system not based on
color distinctions?

5. On the assumption on which questions 4 (*a*) and (*b*)
are based, and assuming further that this Court will exercise
its equity powers to the end described in question 4 (*b*),

(*a*) should this Court formulate detailed decrees in these cases;

(*b*) if so, what specific issues should the decrees reach;

(*c*) should this Court appoint a special master to hear evidence with a view to recommending specific terms for such decrees;

(*d*) should this Court remand to the courts of first instance with directions to frame decrees in these cases, and if so what general directions should the decrees of this Court include and what procedures should the courts of first instance follow in arriving at the specific terms of more detailed decrees?

The Attorney General of the United States is invited to take part in the oral argument and to file an additional brief if he so desires.

NAACP Brief*

Summary of Argument

These cases consolidated for argument before this Court present in different factual contexts essentially the same ultimate legal questions.

The substantive question common to all is whether a state can, consistently with the Constitution, exclude children, solely on the ground that they are Negroes, from public schools which otherwise they would be qualified to attend. It is the thesis of this brief, submitted on behalf of the excluded children, that the answer to the question is in the negative: the Fourteenth Amendment prevents states from according differential treatment to American children on the basis of their color or race. Both the legal precedents and the judicial theories, discussed in Part I hereof, and the evidence concerning the intent of the framers of the Fourteenth Amendment and the understanding of the Congress and the ratifying states, developed in Part II hereof, support this proposition.

Denying this thesis, the school authorities, relying in part on language originating in this Court's opinion in *Plessy* v.

---

* Brief for Appellants in Nos. 1, 2, and 4 and for Respondents in No. 10; from the briefs on reargument submitted to the Supreme Court, October term, 1953.

Ferguson, 163 U.S. 537, urge that exclusion of Negroes, *qua* Negroes, from designated public schools is permissible when the excluded children are afforded admittance to other schools especially reserved for Negroes, *qua* Negroes, if such schools are equal.

The procedural question common to all the cases is the role to be played, and the time-table to be followed, by this Court and the lower courts in directing an end to the challenged exclusion, in the event that this Court determines, with respect to the substantive question, that exclusion of Negroes, *qua* Negroes, from public schools contravenes the Constitution.

The importance to our American democracy of the substantive question can hardly be overstated. The question is whether a nation founded on the proposition that "all men are created equal" is honoring its commitments to grant "due process of law" and "the equal protection of the laws" to all within its borders when it, or one of its constituent states, confers or denies benefits on the basis of color or race.

1. Distinctions drawn by state authorities on the basis of color or race violate the Fourteenth Amendment. *Shelley* v. *Kraemer*, 334 U.S. 1; *Buchanan* v. *Warley*, 245 U.S. 60. This has been held to be true even as to the conduct of public educational institutions. *Sweatt* v. *Painter*, 339 U.S. 629; *McLaurin* v. *Oklahoma State Regents*, 339 U.S. 637. Whatever other purposes the Fourteenth Amendment may have had, it is indisputable that its primary purpose was to complete the emancipation provided by the Thirteenth Amendment by ensuring to the Negro equality before the law. The *Slaughter-House Cases*, 16 Wall. 36; *Strauder* v. *West Virginia*, 100 U.S. 303.

2. Even if the Fourteenth Amendment did not *per se* invalidate racial distinctions as a matter of law, the racial segregation challenged in the instant cases would run afoul of the conventional test established for application of the equal protection clause because the racial classifications here have no reasonable relation to any valid legislative purpose. See *Quaker City Cab Co.* v. *Pennsylvania*, 277 U.S. 389; *Truax* v. *Raich*, 239 U.S. 33; *Smith* v. *Cahoon*, 283 U.S. 553; *Mayflower Farms* v. *Ten Eyck*, 297 U.S. 266; *Skinner* v. *Oklahoma*, 316 U.S. 535. See also *Tunstall* v. *Brotherhood of Locomotive Firemen*, 323 U.S. 210; *Steele* v. *Louisville & Nashville R. R. Co.*, 323 U.S. 192.

3. Appraisal of the facts requires rejection of the contention of the school authorities. The educational detriment involved in racially constricting a student's associations has already been recognized by this Court. *Sweatt* v. *Painter,* 339 U.S. 629; *McLaurin* v. *Oklahoma State Regents,* 339 U.S. 637.

4. The argument that the requirements of the Fourteenth Amendment are met by providing alternative schools rests, finally, on reiteration of the separate but equal doctrine enunciated in *Plessy* v. *Ferguson.*

Were these ordinary cases, it might be enough to say that the *Plessy* case can be distinguished—that it involved only segregation in transportation. But these are not ordinary cases, and in deference to their importance it seems more fitting to meet the *Plessy* doctrine head-on and to declare that doctrine erroneous.

Candor requires recognition that the plain purpose and effect of segregated education is to perpetuate an inferior status for Negroes which is America's sorry heritage from slavery. But the primary purpose of the Fourteenth Amendment was to deprive the states of *all* power to perpetuate such a caste system.

5. The first and second of the five questions propounded by this Court requested enlightment as to whether the Congress which submitted, and the state legislatures and conventions which ratified, the Fourteenth Amendment contemplated or understood that it would prohibit segregation in public schools, either of its own force or through subsequent legislative or judicial action. The evidence, both in Congress and in the legislatures of the ratifying states, reflects the substantial intent of the Amendment's proponents and the substantial understanding of its opponents that the Fourteenth Amendment would, of its own force, proscribe all forms of state-imposed racial distinctions, thus necessarily including all racial segregation in public education.

The Fourteenth Amendment was actually the culmination of the determined efforts of the Radical Republican majority in Congress to incorporate into our fundamental law the well-defined equalitarian principle of complete equality for all without regard to race or color. The debates in the 39th Congress and succeeding Congresses clearly reveal the intention that the Fourteenth Amendment would work a revolutionary change in our state-federal relationship by denying to the states the power to distinguish on the basis of race.

The Civil Rights Bill of 1866, as originally proposed, possessed scope sufficiently broad in the opinion of many Congressmen to entirely destroy all state legislation based on race. A great majority of the Republican Radicals—who later formulated the Fourteenth Amendment—understood and intended that the Bill would prohibit segregated schools. Opponents of the measure shared this understanding. The scope of this legislation was narrowed because it was known that the Fourteenth Amendment was in process of preparation and would itself have scope exceeding that of the original draft of the Civil Rights Bill.

6. The evidence makes clear that it was the intent of the proponents of the Fourteenth Amendment, and the substantial understanding of its opponents, that it would, of its own force, prohibit all state action predicated upon race or color. The intention of the framers with respect to any specific example of caste state action—in the instant cases, segregated education—cannot be determined solely on the basis of a tabulation of contemporaneous statements mentioning the specific practice. The framers were formulating a constitutional provision setting broad standards for determination of the relationship of the state to the individual. In the nature of things they could not list all the specific categories of existing and prospective state activity which were to come within the constitutional prohibitions. The broad general purpose of the Amendment—obliteration of race and color distinctions—is clearly established by the evidence. So far as there was consideration of the Amendment's impact upon the undeveloped educational systems then existing, both proponents and opponents of the Amendment understood that it would proscribe all racial segregation in public education.

7. While the Amendment conferred upon Congress the power to enforce its prohibitions, members of the 39th Congress and those of subsequent Congresses made it clear that the framers understood and intended that the Fourteenth Amendment was self-executing and particularly pointed out that the federal judiciary had authority to enforce its prohibitions without Congressional implementation.

8. The evidence as to the understanding of the states is equally convincing. Each of the eleven states that had

seceded from the Union ratified the Amendment, and concurrently eliminated racial distinctions from its laws, and adopted a constitution free of requirement or specific authorization of segregated schools. Many rejected proposals for segregated schools, and none enacted a school segregation law until after readmission. The significance of these facts is manifest from the consideration that ten of these states, which were required, as a condition of readmission, to ratify the Amendment and to modify their constitutions and laws in conformity therewith, considered that the Amendment required them to remove all racial distinctions from their existing and prospective laws, including those pertaining to public education.

Twenty-two of the twenty-six Union states also ratified the Amendment. Although unfettered by congressional surveillance, the overwhelming majority of the Union states acted with an understanding that it prohibited racially segregated schools and necessitated conformity of their school laws to secure consistency with that understanding.

9. In short, the historical evidence fully sustains this Court's conclusion in the *Slaughter Houses Cases*, 16 Wall. 36, 81, that the Fourteenth Amendment was designed to take from the states all power to enforce caste or class distinctions.

10. The Court in its fourth and fifth questions assumes that segregation is declared unconstitutional and inquires as to whether relief should be granted immediately or gradually. Appellants, recognizing the possibility of delay of a purely administrative character, do not ask for the impossible. No cogent reasons justifying further exercise of equitable discretion, however, have as yet been produced.

It has been indirectly suggested in the briefs and oral argument of appellees that some such reasons exist. Two plans were suggested by the United States in its Brief as *Amicus Curiae*. We have analyzed each of these plans as well as appellees' briefs and oral argument and find nothing there of sufficient merit on which this Court, in the exercise of its equity power, could predicate a decree permitting an effective gradual adjustment from segregated to non-segregated school systems. Nor have we been able to find any other reasons or plans sufficient to warrant the exercise of such equitable discretion in these cases. Therefore, in the present posture of these cases, appellants are unable to suggest any compelling reasons for this Court to postpone relief.

South Carolina Brief[*]

Summary of Argument

Answering the First Question: The overwhelming preponderance of the evidence demonstrates that the Congress which submitted and the State legislatures which ratified the Fourteenth Amendment did not contemplate and did not understand that it would abolish segregation in public schools.

Answering the Second Question: It was not the understanding of the framers of the Amendment that future Congresses might, in the exercise of their power under Section 5 of the Amendment, abolish segregation in public schools; nor was it the understanding of the framers of the Amendment that it would be within the judicial power, in the light of future conditions, to construe the Amendment as abolishing segregation in public schools of its own force.

Answering the Third Question: It is not within the judicial power to construe the Fourteenth Amendment adversely to the understanding of its framers, as abolishing segregation in the public schools. Moreover, if, in construing the Amendment, the principle of stare decisis is applied, controlling precedents preclude a construction which would abolish or forbid segregation in the public schools. Even if the principle of stare decisis and the controlling precedents be abandoned, and the effect of the Amendment upon public school segregation be examined de novo, under established standards of equal protection the Amendment may not be construed to abolish or forbid segregation as a matter of law and a priori in all cases. Rather, each case of such segregation must be decided upon the facts presented in the record of that case; and unless the record establishes by clear and convincing evidence that school segregation could not conceivably be warranted by local conditions in the particular case, the Fourteenth Amendment may not be construed to abolish segregation in that case.

Answering the Fourth Question: Assuming that it is decided—improperly, as we contend—that segregation in public

---

[*] Harry Briggs, Jr. v. R. W. Elliott, Chairman, J. D. Carson, Members of Board of Trustees of School District No. 22, Clarendon Co., S.C.

schools violates the Fourteenth Amendment, a decree would not necessarily follow providing that, within the limits set by normal geographical school districting, Negro children should forthwith be admitted to schools of their own choice. This Court, in the exercise of its equity powers, may permit an effective gradual adjustment to be brought about from existing segregated systems to a system not based on color distinctions.

Answering the Fifth Question: Again assuming it is decided —improperly, as we contend—that segregation in public schools violates the Fourteenth Amendment, this Court should not, and indeed could not, formulate a detailed decree in this case; nor should this Court appoint a special master to hear evidence with a view to recommending specific terms for such a decree. Rather, this Court should remand the question to the District Court for further proceedings in conformity with this Court's opinion.

The answers to these questions in appellants' brief rest on certain fundamental fallacies. These are:

First, the fallacy that the antislavery crusade was directed against segregation in schools, whereas the fact is that its thrust was against the institution of slavery. By elaborating the philosophical background of the anti-slavery movement, and repeatedly referring to its broad general purposes, appellants seek to create the impression that segregation in schools was totally at variance with the purposes of that movement. But no amount of argument on a general plane, and no invocation of "ethico-moral-religious-natural rights" (Br. 205) or "Judeo-Christian ethic" (Br. 204) can obscure the fundamental fact that the crusade was directed to the abolition of slavery and not to the objective of setting up mixed schools for white and colored children or enforced commingling of any other kind. The problem before this Court is not the legal or moral justification for slavery; rather, the issue to be resolved is whether the people of the State of South Carolina may, in the exercise of their judgment based on first-hand knowledge of local conditions, decide that the state objective of free public education is best served by a system consisting of separate schools for white and colored children. That question is to be answered in the light of well-settled principles governing the application of the Fourteenth Amendment, and not by general theoretical notions put forward during the antislavery crusade.

Nor is the issue to be resolved on the basis of general statements plucked from their contexts in the debates of Congress or the opinions of this Court. In short, one of the principal fallacies of appellants' brief lies in the fact that it seeks to solve the specific issue of school segregation by addressing itself not to the constitutionality of the practice itself, but rather to broad generalizations.

Another fundamental fallacy in appellants' brief is the assumption that, in the years following the Civil War, the Radical Republicans spoke for Congress as a whole. Nothing could be more misleading. The attitude of Congress towards school segregation during these years must be derived from the action which the Congress as a whole actually took, not only at the time when it proposed the Fourteenth Amendment in 1866, but during the surrounding years. That is the only reliable standard by which to evaluate the opinion of Congress, and the application of that standard shows beyond all peradventure that segregated schooling was not intended to be within the reach of the Fourteenth Amendment—either by the Congress which proposed the Amendment to the States, or by succeeding Congresses.

If we were to adopt the views of the Radical Republicans as representing the views of Congress as a whole, history would have to be rewritten. Surely Congress as a whole did not endorse the vituperative views of Thaddeus Stevens who characterized President Johnson as an "alien enemy, a citizen of a foreign state," or of Charles Sumner who called him "an insolent drunken brute in comparison with which Caligula's horse was respectable." Morison and Commager, 2 *The Growth of the American Republic* 39 (1950).

Still another fundamental fallacy in appellants' argument is the notion that all racial distinctions are "an irrational basis for government action" (Br. 22). The fallacy here has two prongs, the first of which is an apparent effort to smother the fundamental constitutional question by repeated references to "abhorrence of race as a premise for governmental action," "racism," "a state scheme of racism" and the like (Br. 25, 30, 31). This tyranny of words in no way advances resolution of the issue, but rather appears to be an attempt to divert attention from the fundamental constitutional problem at hand, which is to be judged by the application of well-settled principles governing the effect of the Constitution on the police power of the State of South Carolina.

The second prong of this fallacy is appellants' theory that the separate but equal doctrine, as enunciated in *Plessy v. Ferguson,* is an aberration inconsistent with the main stream of cases adjudicated before and since that decision. It is true that *Plessy v. Ferguson* was a case of first impression for the Supreme Court of the United States, so far as the enunciation of the separate but equal doctrine was concerned. But other courts, both State and Federal, had already approved that doctrine long before the Plessy case was decided. The leading decisions on the question had been handed down by the courts of New York, Ohio, Indiana, California and Massachusetts.

We shall more fully explore each of these fallacies and others in appellants' position in answer to the specific questions of the Court.

Briggs v. Elliott[*]

Oral Argument

. . . We have in South Carolina a case, as Mr. [Thurgood] Marshall [NAACP counsel representing the Negro litigants] has so positively admitted, with no remaining question of inequality at all, and the naked question is whether a separation of the races in the primary and secondary schools, which are the subject of this particular case, is of itself per se a violation of the Fourteenth Amendment.

Now, turning to our answers, let me state what we say as to each one of them. The first question was: What evidence is there that the Congress which submitted and the State legislatures which ratified the Fourteenth Amendment contemplated or did not contemplate, understood or did not understand, that it would abolish segregation in public schools? We answer: The overwhelming preponderance of the evidence demonstrates that the Congress which submitted and the State

---

[*] Argument delivered before the Supreme Court by Counsel John W. Davis on behalf of the State of South Carolina, December 7, 1953. (Private printing.)

legislatures which ratified the Fourteenth Amendment did not contemplate and did not understand that it would abolish segregation in public schools. . . .

The second question: If neither the Congress in submitting nor the States in ratifying the Fourteenth Amendment understood that compliance with it would require the immediate abolition of segregation in public schools, was it nevertheless the understanding of the framers of the Amendment (a) that future Congresses might, in the exercise of their power under Section 5 of the Amendment, abolish segregation, or (b), that it would be within the judicial power, in light of future conditions, to construe the Amendment as abolishing such segregation of its own force?

And to that we answer (a): It was not the understanding of the framers of the Amendment that future Congresses might, in the exercise of their power under Section 5 of the Amendment, abolish segregation in public schools.

And (b): It was not the understanding of the framers of the Amendment that it would be within the judicial power, in light of future conditions, to construe the Amendment as abolishing segregation in public schools of its own force. . . .

The third question: On the assumption that the answers to questions 2 (a) and (b) do not dispose of the issue, is it within the judicial power, in construing the Amendment, to abolish segregation in the public schools? And we answer: It is not within the judicial power to construe the Fourteenth Amendment adversely to the understanding of its framers as abolishing segregation in the public schools. Before we answer, we preface that with an expression of the extreme difficulty we have in making the initial assumption on which that question is based, for in our humble judgment the answers to questions 1 and 2 (a) and (b) do dispose of the issue in this case and dispose of it in the clearest and most emphatic manner.

We go on in our answer: Moreover, if in construing the Amendment the principle of stare decisis is applied, controlling precedents preclude a construction which would abolish segregation in the public schools. Now we are cognizant of what this Court has said, not once but several times, and what some of us have heard outside the Court as to the scope of stare decisis in constitutional matters; and it has been accepted that, where there is a pronounced dissent from previous opinions in constitutional matters, mere difficulty in amendment leads the Court to bow to that change of opinion more than it would in matters of purely private rights. But be that doctrine what it may, somewhere, sometime, to every principle comes a moment of repose when the decision has been so often announced, so confidently relied upon, so long continued, that it passes the limits of judicial discretion and disturbance.

That is the opinion which we held when we filed our former brief in this case. We relied on the fact that this Court had not once but seven times, I think it is, pronounced in favor of the separate but equal doctrine. We relied on the fact that the courts of last appeal of some sixteen or eighteen States have passed upon the validity of the separate but equal doctrine vis-à-vis the Fourteenth Amendment. We relied on the fact that Congress has continuously since 1862 segregated its schools in the District of Columbia. We relied on the fact that 23 of the ratifying States—I think my figures are right, I am not sure—had by legislative action evinced their conviction that the Fourteenth Amendment was not offended by segregation. And we said in effect—and I am bold enough to repeat it here now—that, in the language of Judge Parker in his opinion below, after that had been the consistent history for over three quarters of a century, it was late indeed in the day to disturb it on any theoretical or sociological basis. We stand on that proposition.

Then we go on: Even if the principle of stare decisis and controlling precedents be denied, and the effect of the Amendment upon public school segregation be examined de novo, the doctrine of reasonable classification would protect this doctrine from any charge that is brought against it.

In Clarendon School District No. 1 in South Carolina, with which this case alone is concerned, there were, in the last report that got into this record, something over a year or a year and a half ago, 2,799 registered Negro children of school age. There were 295 whites. And the State has now provided those 2,800 Negro children with schools as good in every particular. In fact, because of their being newer, they may even be better. There are good teachers and the same curriculum as in the schools for the 295 whites.

Who is going to disturb that situation? If they were to be reassorted or commingled, who knows how that could best be done? If it is done on a mathematical basis, with 30 children to a room as a maximum, which I believe is the accepted standard in pedagogy, you would have 27 Negro children and 3 whites in one school room. Would that make the children any happier? Would they learn any more quickly? Would their lives be more serene?

Children of that age are not the most considerate animals in the world, as we all know. Would the terrible psychological disaster being wrought, according to some of these witnesses, to the colored child be removed if he had three white children sitting somewhere in the same school room? Would white children be prevented from getting a distorted idea of racial relations if they sat with 27 Negro children? I have posed that question because it is one that cannot be overlooked.

You say that is racism. Well, it is not racism to recognize that for 60 centuries or more humanity has been discussing questions of race and race tension. Say that we make special provisions for the aboriginal Indian population of this country. It is not racism. Say that 29 States have miscegenation statutes now in force which they believe are of beneficial protection to both races. And what of racial distinctions in our immigration and naturalization laws? Disraeli said, 'No man will treat with indifference the principle of race. It is the key to history.' And it is not necessary to enter into any comparison of faculties or possibilities. You recognize differences which race implants in the human animal.

Now, I want to spend some time on the fourth and fifth questions. They give us little disturbance, and I don't feel they will greatly disturb the Court.

As to the question of the right of the Court to postpone the remedy, we think that inheres in every court of equity, and there has been no question about it as to power.

The fifth question is whether the Court should formulate a decree. We find nothing here on which this Court could formulate a decree. Nor do we think the Court below has any power to formulate a decree reciting in what manner these schools are to be altered, if at all, and what course the State of South Carolina shall take concerning it. Your Honors do not sit, and cannot sit, as a glorified Board of Education for the State of South Carolina or any other State. Neither can the District Court.

Assuming (in the language of the old treaties about war, "it is not to be expected and may God forbid") that the Court should find that the Statutes of the State of South Carolina violate the Constitution, it can so declare. If it should find that inequality is being practiced in the schools, it can enjoin its continuance. Neither this Court nor any other court, I respectfully submit, can sit in the chairs of the legislature of South Carolina and mold its educational system; and if it is found to be in its present form unacceptable, the State of South Carolina must devise the alternative. It establishes the schools, it pays the funds, and it has the sole power to educate its citizens. What it would do under these adverse circumstances, I don't know. I do know, if the testimony is to be believed, that the result would not be pleasing.

Let me say this for the State of South Carolina. It does not come here, as Thad Stevens would have wished, in sackcloth and ashes. It believes that its legislation is not offensive to the Constitution of the United States. It is confident of its good faith and intention to produce equality for all of its children of whatever race or color. It is convinced that the happiness, the progress and the welfare of these children is best promoted in segregated schools, and it thinks it a thousand pities that, by this controversy, there should be urged the return to an experiment which gives no more promise of success today than when it was written into their Constitution during what we have called "the tragic era." . . .

Here is equal education, not promised, not prophesied, but present. Shall it be thrown away on some fancied question of racial prestige? . . .

Brown v. Board of Education of Topeka*

Opinion on Segregation Laws

No. 1. Appeal from the United States District Court for the District of Kansas.**

MR. CHIEF JUSTICE WARREN delivered the opinion of the Court.

These cases come to us from the States of Kansas, South Carolina, Virginia, and Delaware. They are premised on different facts and different local conditions, but a common legal question justifies their consideration together in this consolidated opinion.[1]

In each of the cases, minors of the Negro race, through their legal representatives, seek the aid of the courts in obtaining admission to the public schools of their community on a non-segregated basis. In each instance, they have been denied admission to schools attended by white children under laws requiring or permitting segregation according to race. This segregation was alleged to deprive the plaintiffs of the equal protection of the laws under the Fourteenth Amendment. In each of the cases other than the Delaware case, a three-judge federal district court denied relief to the plaintiffs on the so-called "separate but equal" doctrine announced by this Court in *Plessy* v. *Ferguson,* 163 U.S. 537. . . . Under that doctrine, equality of treatment is accorded when the races are provided substantially equal facilities, even though these facilities be separate. In the Delaware case, the Supreme Court of Delaware adhered to that doctrine, but ordered that the plaintiffs be admitted to the white schools because of their superiority to the Negro schools.

---

* Supreme Court of the United States, 347 U.S. 483 (1954).

** Together with No. 2, *Briggs et al.* v. *Elliott et al.,* on appeal from the United States District Court for the Eastern District of South Carolina, argued December 9–10, 1952, reargued December 7–8, 1953; No. 4, *Davis et al.* v. *County School Board of Prince Edward County, Virginia, et al.,* on appeal from the United States District Court for the Eastern District of Virginia, argued December 10, 1952, reargued December 7–8, 1953; and No. 10, *Gebhart et al.* v. *Belton et al.,* on certiorari to the Supreme Court of Delaware, argued December 11, 1952, reargued December 9, 1953.

The plaintiffs contend that segregated public schools are not "equal" and cannot be made "equal," and that hence they are deprived of the equal protection of the laws. Because of the obvious importance of the question presented, the Court took jurisdiction.[2] Argument was heard in the 1952 Term, and reargument was heard this Term on certain questions propounded by the Court.[3]

Reargument was largely devoted to the circumstances surrounding the adoption of the Fourteenth Amendment in 1868. It covered exhaustively consideration of the Amendment in Congress, ratification by the states, then existing practices in racial segregation, and the views of proponents and opponents of the Amendment. This discussion and our own investigation convince us that, although these sources cast some light, it is not enough to resolve the problem with which we are faced. At best, they are inconclusive. The most avid proponents of the post-War Amendments undoubtedly intended them to remove all legal distinctions among "all persons born or naturalized in the United States." Their opponents, just as certainly, were antagonistic to both the letter and the spirit of the Amendments and wished them to have the most limited effect. What others in Congress and the state legislatures had in mind cannot be determined with any degree of certainty.

An additional reason for the inconclusive nature of the Amendment's history, with respect to segregated schools, is the status of public education at that time.[4] In the South, the movement toward free common schools, supported by general taxation, had not yet taken hold. Education of white children was largely in the hands of private groups. Education of Negroes was almost nonexistent, and practically all of the race were illiterate. In fact, any education of Negroes was forbidden by law in some states. Today, in contrast, many Negroes have achieved outstanding success in the arts and sciences as well as in the business and professional world. It is true that public school education at the time of the Amendment had advanced further in the North, but the effect of the Amendment on Northern States was generally ignored in the congressional debates. Even in the North, the conditions of public education did not approximate those existing today. The curriculum was usually rudimentary; ungraded schools were common in rural areas; the school term was but three months a year in many states; and compulsory school attendance was virtually unknown. As a consequence, it is not surprising that there should be so little in the history of the Fourteenth Amendment relating to its intended effect on public education.

In the first cases in this Court construing the Fourteenth Amendment, decided shortly after its adoption, the Court interpreted it as proscribing all state-imposed discriminations against the Negro race.[5] The doctrine of "separate but equal" did not make its appearance in this Court until 1896 in the case of *Plessy* v. *Ferguson, supra,* involving not education but transportation.[6] American courts have since labored with the doctrine for over half a century. In this Court, there have been six cases involving the "separate but equal" doctrine in the field of public education.[7] In *Cumming* v. *County Board of Education,* 175 U.S. 528, and *Gong Lum* v. *Rice,* 275 U.S. 78, the validity of the doctrine itself was not challenged.[8] In more recent cases, all on the graduate school level, inequality was found in that specific benefits enjoyed by white students were denied to Negro students of the same educational qualifications. *Missouri ex rel. Gaines* v. *Canada,* 305 U.S. 337; *Sipuel* v. *Oklahoma,* 332 U.S. 631; *Sweatt* v. *Painter,* 339 U.S. 629; *McLaurin* v. *Oklahoma State Regents,* 339 U.S. 637. In none of these cases was it necessary to re-examine the doctrine to grant relief to the Negro plaintiff. And in *Sweatt* v. *Painter, supra,* the Court expressly reserved decision on the question whether *Plessy* v. *Ferguson* should be held inapplicable to public education.

In the instant cases, that question is directly presented. Here, unlike *Sweatt* v. *Painter,* there are findings below that the Negro and white schools involved have been equalized, or are being equalized, with respect to buildings, curricula, qualifications and salaries of teachers, and other "tangible" factors.[9] Our decision, therefore, cannot turn on merely a comparison of these tangible factors in the Negro and white schools involved in each of the cases. We must look instead to the effect of segregation itself on public education.

In approaching this problem, we cannot turn the clock back to 1868 when the Amendment was adopted, or even to 1896 when *Plessy* v. *Ferguson* was written. We must consider public education in the light of its full development and its present place in American life throughout the Nation. Only in this way can it be determined if segregation in public schools deprives these plaintiffs of the equal protection of the laws.

Today, education is perhaps the most important function of state and local governments. Compulsory school attendance laws and the great expenditures for education both demonstrate our recognition of the importance of education to our democratic society. It is required in the performance of our most basic public responsibilities, even service in the armed forces. It is the very foundation of good citizenship. Today it is a principal instrument in awakening the child to cultural values, in preparing him for later professional training, and in helping him to adjust normally to his environment. In these days, it is doubtful that any child may reasonably be expected to succeed in life if he is denied the opportunity of an education. Such an opportunity, where the state has undertaken to provide it, is a right which must be made available to all on equal terms.

We come then to the question presented: Does segregation of children in public schools solely on the basis of race, even though the physical facilities and other "tangible" factors may be equal, deprive the children of the minority group of equal education opportunities? We believe that it does.

In *Sweatt* v. *Painter, supra,* in finding that a segregated law school for Negroes could not provide them equal educational opportunities, this Court relied in large part on "those qualities which are incapable of objective measurement but which make for greatness in a law school." In *McLaurin* v. *Oklahoma State Regents, supra,* the Court, in requiring that a Negro admitted to a white graduate school be treated like all other students, again resorted to intangible considerations: ". . . his ability to study, to engage in discussions and exchange views with other students, and, in general, to learn his profession." Such considerations apply with added force to children in grade and high schools. To separate them from others of similar age and qualifications solely because of their race generates a feeling of inferiority as to their status in the community that may affect their hearts and minds in a way unlikely ever to be undone. The effect of this separation on their educational opportunities was well stated by a finding in the Kansas case by a court which nevertheless felt compelled to rule against the Negro plaintiffs:

Segregation of white and colored children in public schools has a detrimental effect upon the colored children.

The impact is greater when it has the sanction of the law; for the policy of separating the races is usually interpreted as denoting the inferiority of the negro group. A sense of inferiority affects the motivation of the child to learn. Segregation with the sanction of law, therefore, has a tendency to [retard] the educational and mental development of negro children and to deprive them of some of the benefits they would receive in a racial[ly] integrated school system.[10]

Whatever may have been the extent of psychological knowledge at the time of *Plessy* v. *Ferguson,* this finding is amply supported by modern authority.[11] Any language in *Plessy* v. *Ferguson* contrary to this finding is rejected.

We conclude that in the field of public education the doctrine of "separate but equal" has no place. Separate educational facilities are inherently unequal. Therefore, we hold that the plaintiffs and others similarly situated for whom the actions have been brought are, by reason of the segregation complained of, deprived of the equal protection of the laws guaranteed by the Fourteenth Amendment. This disposition makes unnecessary any discussion whether such segregation also violates the Due Process Clause of the Fourteenth Amendment.[12]

Because these are class actions, because of the wide applicability of this decision, and because of the great variety of local conditions, the formulation of decrees in these cases presents problems of considerable complexity. On reargument, the consideration of appropriate relief was necessarily subordinated to the primary question—the constitutionality of segregation in public education. We have now announced that such segregation is a denial of the equal protection of the laws. In order that we may have the full assistance of the parties in formulating decrees, the cases will be restored to the docket, and the parties are requested to present further argument on Questions 4 and 5 previously propounded by the Court for the reargument this Term.[13] The Attorney General of the United States is again invited to participate. The Attorneys General of the states requiring or permitting segregation in public education will also be permitted to appear as *amici curiae* upon request to do so by September 15, 1954, and submission of briefs by October 1, 1954.[14]

It is so ordered.

1. In the Kansas case, *Brown* v. *Board of Education,* the plaintiffs are Negro children of elementary school age residing in Topeka. They brought this action in the United States District Court for the District of Kansas to enjoin enforcement of a Kansas statute which permits, but does not require, cities of more than 15,000 population to maintain separate school facilities for Negro and white students. Kan.Gen.Stat. § 72–1724 (1949). Pursuant to that authority, the Topeka Board of Education elected to establish segregated elementary schools. Other public schools in the community, however, are operated on a nonsegregated basis. The three-judge District Court, convened under 28 U.S.C. §§ 2281 and 2284, found that segregation in public education has a detrimental effect upon Negro children, but denied relief on the ground that the Negro and white schools were substantially equal with respect to buildings, transportation, curricula, and educational qualifications of teachers. 98 F.Supp. 797. The case is here on direct appeal under 28 U.S.C. § 1253.

In the South Carolina case, *Briggs* v. *Elliott,* the plaintiffs are Negro children of both elementary and high school age residing in Clarendon County. They brought this action in the United States District Court for the Eastern District of South Carolina to enjoin enforcement of provisions in the state constitution and statutory code which require the segregation of Negroes and whites in public schools. S.C.Const., Art. XI, § 7; S.C.Code § 5377 (1942). The three-judge District Court, convened under 28 U.S.C. §§ 2281 and 2284, denied the requested relief. The court found that the Negro schools were inferior to the white schools and ordered the defendants to begin immediately to equalize the facilities. But the court sustained the validity of the contested provisions and denied the plaintiffs admission to the white schools during the equalization program. 98 F.Supp. 529. This Court vacated the District Court's judgment and remanded the case for the purpose of obtaining the court's views on a report filed by the defendants concerning the progress made in the equalization program. 342 U.S. 350. On remand, the District Court found that substantial equality had been achieved except for buildings and that the defendants were proceeding to rectify this inequality as well. 103 F.Supp. 920. The case is again here on direct appeal under 28 U.S.C. § 1253.

In the Virginia case, *Davis* v. *County School Board,* the plaintiffs are Negro children of high school age residing in Prince Edward County. They brought this action in the United States District Court for the Eastern District of Virginia to enjoin enforcement of provisions in the state constitution and statutory code which require the segregation of Negroes and whites in public schools. Va. Const., § 140; Va. Code § 22–221 (1950). The three-judge District Court, convened under 28 U.S.C. §§ 2281 and 2284, denied the requested relief. The court found the Negro school inferior in physical plant, curricula, and transportation, and ordered the defendants forthwith to provide substantially equal curricula and transportation and to "proceed with all reasonable diligence and dispatch to remove" the inequality in physical plant. But as in the South Carolina case, the court sustained the validity of the contested provisions and denied the plaintiffs admission to the white schools during the equalization program. 103 F.Supp. 337. The case is here on direct appeal under 28 U.S.C. § 1253.

In the Delaware case, *Gebhart* v. *Belton,* the plaintiffs are Negro children of both elementary and high school age residing in New Castle County. They brought this action in the Delaware Court of Chancery to enjoin enforcement of provisions in the state constitution and statutory code which require the segregation of Negroes and whites in public schools. Del.Const. Art. X, § 2; Del.Rev.Code § 2631 (1935). The Chancellor gave judgment for the plaintiffs and ordered their immediate admission to schools previously attended only by white children, on the ground that the Negro schools were inferior with respect to teacher training, pupil-teacher ratio, extracurricular activities, physical plant, and time and distance involved in travel. 87 A.2d 862. The Chancellor also found that segregation itself results in an inferior education for Negro children (see note 10, *infra),* but did not rest his decision on that ground. *Id.,* at page 865. The Chancellor's decree was affirmed by the Supreme Court of Delaware, which intimated, however, that the defendants might be able to obtain a modification of the decree after equalization of the Negro and white schools had been accomplished. 91 A.2d 137, 152. The defendants, contending only that the Delaware courts had erred in ordering the immediate admission of the Negro plaintiffs to the white schools, applied to this Court for certiorari. The writ was granted, 344 U.S. 891. . . . The plaintiffs, who were successful below, did not submit a cross-petition.

2. 344 U.S. 1, 141, 891.

3. 345 U.S. 972. The Attorney General of the United States participated both Terms as *amicus curiae.*

4. For a general study of the development of public education prior to the Amendment, see Butts and Cremin, A History of Education in American Culture (1953), Pts. I, II; Cubberley, Public Education in the United States (1934 ed.) cc. II–XII. School practices current at the time of the adoption of the Fourteenth Amendment are described in Butts and Cremin, *supra,* at 269–275; Cubberley, *supra,* at 288–339, 408–431; Knight, Public Education in the South (1922), cc. VIII, IX. See also H. Ex. Doc. No. 315, 41st Cong., 2d Sess. (1871). Although the demand for free public schools followed substantially the same pattern in both the North and the South, the development in the South did not begin to gain momentum until about 1850, some twenty years after that in the North. The reasons for the somewhat slower development in the South (*e.g.,* the rural character of the South and the different regional attitudes toward state assistance) are well explained in Cubberley, *supra,* at 408–423. In the country as a whole, but particularly in the South, the War virtually stopped all progress in public

education. *Id.*, at 427-428. The low status of Negro education in all sections of the country, both before and immediately after the War, is described in Beale, A History of Freedom of Teaching in American Schools (1941), 112–132, 175–195. Compulsory school attendance laws were not generally adopted until after the ratification of the Fourteenth Amendment, and it was not until 1918 that such laws were in force in all the states. Cubberley, *supra,* at 563–565.

5. *Slaughter-House Cases,* 16 Wall. 36, 67–72 (1873); *Strauder* v. *West Virginia,* 100 U.S. 303, 307–308 (1880): "It ordains that no State shall deprive any person of life, liberty, or property, without due process of law, or deny to any person within its jurisdiction the equal protection of the laws. What is this but declaring that the law in the States shall be the same for the black as for the white; that all persons, whether colored or white, shall stand equal before the laws of the States, and, in regard to the colored race, for whose protection the amendment was primarily designed, that no discrimination shall be made against them by law because of their color? The words of the amendment, it is true, are prohibitory, but they contain a necessary implication of a positive immunity, or right, most valuable to the colored race,—the right to exemption from unfriendly legislation against them distinctively as colored,—exemption from legal discriminations, implying inferiority in civil society, lessening the security of their enjoyment of the rights which others enjoy, and discriminations which are steps towards reducing them to the condition of a subject race."
See also *Virginia* v. *Rives,* 100 U.S. 313, 318 (1880); *Ex parte Virginia,* 100 U.S. 339, 344–345 (1880).

6. The doctrine apparently originated in *Roberts* v. *City of Boston,* 59 Mass. 198, 206 (1850), upholding school segregation against attack as being violative of a state constitutional guarantee of equality. Segregation in Boston public schools was eliminated in 1855. Mass. Acts 1855, c. 256. But elsewhere in the North segregation in public education has persisted in some communities until recent years. It is apparent that such segregation has long been a nationwide problem, not merely one of sectional concern.

7. See also *Berea College* v. *Kentucky* 211 U.S. 45 (1908).

8. In the *Cumming* case, Negro taxpayers sought an injunction requiring the defendant school board to discontinue the operation of a high school for white children until the board resumed operation of a high school for Negro children. Similarly, in the *Gong Lum* case, the plaintiff, a child of Chinese descent, contended only that state authorities had misapplied the doctrine by classifying him with Negro children and requiring him to attend a Negro school.

9. In the Kansas case, the court below found substantial equality as to all such factors. 98 F.Supp. 797, 798. In the South Carolina case, the court below found that the defendants were proceeding

"promptly and in good faith to comply with the court's decree." 103 F.Supp. 920, 921. In the Virginia case, the court below noted that the equalization program was already "afoot and progressing" (103 F.Supp. 337, 341); since then, we have been advised, in the Virginia Attorney General's brief on reargument, that the program has now been completed. In the Delaware case, the court below similarly noted that the state's equalization program was well under way. 91 A.2d 137, 149.

10. A similar finding was made in the Delaware case: "I conclude from the testimony that in our Delaware society, State-imposed segregation in education itself results in the Negro children, as a class, receiving educational opportunities which are substantially inferior to those available to white children otherwise similarly situated." 87 A.2d 862, 865.

11. K. B. Clark, Effect of Prejudice and Discrimination on Personality Development (Midcentury White House Conference on Children and Youth, 1950); Witmer and Kotinsky, Personality in the Making (1952), c. VI; Deutscher and Chein, The Psychological Effects of Enforced Segregation: A Survey of Social Science Opinion, 26 J.Psychol. 259 (1948); Chein, What are the Psychological Effects of Segregation Under Conditions of Equal Facilities? 3 Int. J. Opinion and Attitude Res. 229 (1949); Brameld, Educational Costs, in Discrimination and National Welfare (MacIver, ed., 1949), 44–48; Frazier, The Negro in the United States (1949), 674–681. And see generally Myrdal, An American Dilemma (1944).

12. See Bolling v. Sharpe, Post, p. 497, concerning the Due Process Clause of the Fifth Amendment.

13. "4. Assuming it is decided that segregation in public schools violates the Fourteenth Amendment

"(a) would a decree necessarily follow providing that, within the limits set by normal geographic school districting, Negro children should forthwith be admitted to schools of their choice, or

"(b) may this Court, in the exercise of its equity powers, permit an effective gradual adjustment to be brought about from existing segregated systems to a system not based on color distinctions?

"5. On the assumption on which questions 4(a) and (b) are based, and assuming further that this Court will exercise its equity powers to the end described in question 4(b).

"(a) should this Court formulate detailed decrees in these cases;

"(b) if so, what specific issues should the decree reach;

"(c) should this Court appoint a special master to hear evidence with a view to recommending specific terms for such decrees;

"(d) should this Court remand to the courts of first instance with directions to frame decrees in these cases, and if so what general directions should the decrees of this Court include and what procedures should the courts of first instance follow in arriving at the specific terms of more detailed decrees?"

14. See Rule 42, Revised Rules of this Court (effective July 1, 1954).

Bolling v. Sharpe[*]

District of Columbia: Companion Case

MR. CHIEF JUSTICE WARREN delivered the opinion of the court.

This case challenges the validity of segregation in the public schools of the District of Columbia. The petitioners, minors of the Negro race, allege that such segregation deprives them of due process of law under the Fifth Amendment. They were refused admission to a public school attended by white children solely because of their race. They sought the aid of the District Court for the District of Columbia in obtaining admission. That court dismissed their complaint. The Court granted a writ of certiorari before judgment in the Court of Appeals because of the importance of the constitutional question presented. 344 U.S. 873. . . .

We have this day held that the Equal Protection Clause of the Fourteenth Amendment prohibits the states from maintaining racially segregated public schools.[1] The legal problem in the District of Columbia is somewhat different, however. The Fifth Amendment, which is applicable in the District of Columbia, does not contain an equal protection clause as does the Fourteenth Amendment which applies only to the states. But the concepts of equal protection and due process, both stemming from our American ideal of fairness, are not mutually exclusive. The "equal protection of the laws" is a more explicit safeguard of prohibited unfairness than "due process of law," and, therefore, we do not imply that the two are always interchangeable phrases. But, as this Court has recognized, discrimination may be so unjustifiable as to be violative of due process.[2]

Classifications based solely upon race must be scrutinized with particular care, since they are contrary to our traditions and hence constitutionally suspect.[3] As long ago as 1896, this Court declared the principle "that the constitution of the United States, in its present form, forbids, so far as civil and political rights are concerned, discrimination by the general government, or by the states, against any citizen because of

---

[*] Supreme Court of the United States, 347 U.S. 497 (1954).

his race." [4] And in *Buchanan* v. *Warley*, 245 U.S. 60, . . . the Court held that a statute which limited the right of a property owner to convey his property to a person of another race was, as an unreasonable discrimination, a denial of due process of law.

Although the Court has not assumed to define "liberty" with any great precision, that term is not confined to mere freedom from bodily restraint. Liberty under law extends to the full range of conduct which the individual is free to pursue, and it cannot be restricted except for a proper governmental objective. Segregation in public education is not reasonably related to any proper governmental objective, and thus it imposes on Negro children of the District of Columbia a burden that constitutes an arbitrary deprivation of their liberty in violation of the Due Process Clause.

In view of our decision that the Constitution prohibits the states from maintaining racially segregated public schools, it would be unthinkable that the same Constitution would impose a lesser duty on the Federal Government.[5] We hold that racial segregation in the public schools of the District of Columbia is a denial of the due process of law guaranteed by the Fifth Amendment to the Constitution.

For the reasons set out in *Brown* v. *Board of Education*, this case will be restored to the docket for reargument on Questions 4 and 5 previously propounded by the Court. 345 U.S. 972. . . .

It is so ordered.

---

1. *Brown* v. *Board of Education*, 347 U.S. 483.

2. *Detroit Bank* v. *United States*, 317 U.S. 329; *Currin* v. *Wallace*, 306 U.S. 1, 13–14; *Steward Machine Co.* v. *Davis*, 301 U.S. 548, 585.

3. *Korematsu* v. *United States*, 323 U.S. 214, 216; *Hirabayashi* v. *United States*, 320 U.S. 81, 100.

4. *Gibson* v. *Mississippi*, 162 U.S. 565, 591. Cf. *Steele* v. *Louisville & Nashville R.R. Co.*, 323 U.S. 192, 198–199.

5. Cf. *Hurd* v. *Hodge*, 334 U.S. 24.

Brown v. Board of Education of Topeka[*]

Enforcement Decree

No. 1 Appeal from the United States District Court for the District of Kansas.[**]

MR. CHIEF JUSTICE WARREN delivered the opinion of the Court.

These cases were decided on May 17, 1954. The opinions of that date [1] declaring the fundamental principle that racial discrimination in public education is unconstitutional, are incorporated herein by reference. All provisions of federal, state, or local law requiring or permitting such discrimination must yield to this principle. There remains for consideration the manner in which relief is to be accorded.

Because these cases arose under different local conditions and their disposition will involve a variety of local problems, we requested further argument on the question of relief.[2] In view of the nationwide importance of the decision, we invited the Attorney General of the United States and the Attorneys General of all states requiring or permitting racial discrimination in public education to present their views on that question. The parties, the United States, and the States of Florida, North Carolina, Arkansas, Oklahoma, Maryland, and Texas filed briefs and participated in the oral argument.

These presentations were informative and helpful to the Court in its consideration of the complexities arising from the transition to a system of public education freed of racial discrimination. The presentations also demonstrated that substantial steps to eliminate racial discrimination in public schools have already been taken, not only in some of the

---

[*] Supreme Court of the United States, 349 U.S. 294 (1955).

[**] Together with No. 2, *Briggs et al.* v. *Elliott et al.*, on appeal from the United States District Court for the Eastern District of South Carolina; No. 3, *Davis et al.* v. *County School Board of Prince Edward County, Virginia, et al.*, on appeal from the United States District Court for the Eastern District of Virginia; No. 4, *Bolling et al.* v. *Sharpe et al.*, on certiorari to the United States Court of Appeals for the District of Columbia Circuit; and No. 5, *Gebhart et al.* v. *Belton et al.*, on certiorari to the Supreme Court of Delaware.

communities in which these cases arose, but in some of the states appearing as *amici curiae,* and in other states as well. Substantial progress has been made in the District of Columbia and in the communities in Kansas and Delaware involved in this litigation. The defendants in the cases coming to us from South Carolina and Virginia are awaiting the decision of this Court concerning relief.

Full implementation of these constitutional principles may require solution of varied local school problems. School authorities have the primary responsibility for elucidating, assessing, and solving these problems; courts will have to consider whether the action of school authorities constitutes good faith implementation of the governing constitutional principles. Because of their proximity to local conditions and the possible need for further hearings, the courts which originally heard these cases can best perform this judicial appraisal. Accordingly, we believe it appropriate to remand the cases to those courts.[3]

In fashioning and effectuating the decrees, the courts will be guided by equitable principles. Traditionally, equity has been characterized by a practical flexibility in shaping its remedies [4] and by a facility for adjusting and reconciling public and private needs.[5] These cases call for the exercise of these traditional attributes of equity power. At stake is the personal interest of the plaintiffs in admission to public schools as soon as practicable on a nondiscriminatory basis. To effectuate this interest may call for elimination of a variety of obstacles in making the transition to school systems operated in accordance with the constitutional principles set forth in our May 17, 1954, decision. Courts of equity may properly take into account the public interest in the elimination of such obstacles in a systematic and effective manner. But it should go without saying that the vitality of these constitutional principles cannot be allowed to yield simply because of disagreement with them.

While giving weight to these public and private considerations, the courts will require that the defendants make a prompt and reasonable start toward full compliance with our May 17, 1954, ruling. Once such a start has been made, the courts may find that additional time is necessary to carry out the ruling in an effective manner. The burden rests upon the defendants to establish that such time is necessary in the public interest and is consistent with good faith compliance at the earliest practicable date. To that end, the courts may consider problems related to administration, arising from the physical condition of the school plant, the school transportation system, personnel, revision of school districts and attendance areas into compact units to achieve a system of determining admission to the public schools on a nonracial basis, and revision of local laws and regulations which may be necessary in solving the foregoing problems. They will also consider the adequacy of any plans the defendants may propose to meet these problems and to effectuate a transition to a racially nondiscriminatory school system. During this period of transition, the courts will retain jurisdiction of these cases.

The judgments below, except that in the Delaware case, are accordingly reversed and the cases are remanded to the District Courts to take such proceedings and enter such orders and decrees consistent with this opinion as are necessary and proper to admit to public schools on a racially nondiscriminatory basis with all deliberate speed the parties to these cases. The judgment in the Delaware case—ordering the immediate admission of the plaintiffs to schools previously attended only by white children—is affirmed on the basis of the principles stated in our May 17, 1954, opinion, but the case is remanded to the Supreme Court of Delaware for such further proceedings as that Court may deem necessary in light of this opinion.

It is so ordered.

---

1. 347 U.S. 483; 347 U.S. 497.

2. Further argument was requested on the following questions, 347 U.S. 483, 495–496, n. 13, previously propounded by the Court:

"4. Assuming it is decided that segregation in public schools violates the Fourteenth Amendment

"(a) would a decree necessarily follow providing that, within the limits set by normal geographic school districting, Negro children should forthwith be admitted to schools of their choice, or

"(b) may this Court, in the exercise of its equity powers, permit an effective gradual adjustment to be brought about from existing segregated systems to a system not based on color distinctions?

"5. On the assumption on which questions 4(a) and (b) are based, and assuming further that this Court will exercise its equity powers to the end described in question 4(b),

"(a) should this Court formulate detailed decrees in these cases;

"(b) if so, what specific issues should the decrees reach;

"(c) should this Court appoint a special master to hear evidence with a view to recommending specific terms for such decrees;

"(d) should this Court remand to the courts of first instance with directions to frame decrees in these cases, and if so what general directions should the decrees of this Court include and what procedures should the courts of first instance follow in arriving at the specific terms of more detailed decrees?"

3. The cases coming to us from Kansas, South Carolina, and Virginia were originally heard by three-judge District Courts convened under 28 U.S.C. §§ 2281 and 2284. These cases will accordingly be remanded to those three-judge courts. See *Briggs* v. *Elliott*, 342 U.S. 350.

4. See *Alexander* v. *Hillman*, 296 U.S. 222, 239.

5. See *Hecht Co.* v. *Bowles*, 321 U.S. 321, 329–330.

REACTIONS TO BROWN V. BOARD OF EDUCATION OF TOPEKA (1955–1956)

The school segregation decisions of 1954 and 1955 were the culmination of the NAACP's legal struggle, begun in the 1920's, against segregated education. Armed only with the Supreme Court's vague mandates that desegregation must proceed "with all deliberate speed" and "at the earliest possible date," the NAACP responded to the decisions with a program of positive, practical implementation.

Effective compliance with the Supreme Court's rulings rested on an indeterminable number of variants, including the tenacity of southern states in seeking avoidance and delay, the resources of civil rights advocates, the goodwill of the dominant white majority, and the persistence of the Negro community. In issuing its recommendations to facilitate desegregation programs, the NAACP urged the cooperation of public officials, the federal courts, and the Negro community. The Association recommended the three-pronged approach of legal action, political pressure, and public education.

The principal NAACP weapon, legal redress, proved in practice a painfully slow and costly tactic; its results were surprisingly ineffective in securing more than token compliance in the next dozen years. It was this agonizing process of victory on a case-to-case basis which induced a younger generation of activists to turn to mass, nonviolent protest in the 1960's (Documents 86 and 96).

Congressional opposition to the school segregation decisions was formalized on March 12, 1956, when a group of senators and congressmen from the eleven states of the Old Confederacy signed and presented to Congress a statement which became known as the Southern Manifesto. The document was largely the work of Senator Sam J. Ervin, Jr., of North Carolina. The Manifesto echoed the statements of southern white spokesmen in decrying the Supreme Court's abuse of judicial power, and it put the signatories on record as endorsing resistance to the Court's decisions on segregated education.

Just as southern state legislators had pointed to their efforts to improve the facilities of Negro schools, so did the Manifesto declare that relations between the races had been satisfactory until the Brown case. Interestingly, the signatories could not secure the concurrence of colleagues in Kentucky, Missouri, West Virginia, Oklahoma, Maryland, and Delaware, even though those states had also had segregated education prior to 1954.

DOCUMENT(S) 79

Statement of the Emergency Southwide NAACP Conference, Atlanta, Georgia, June 4, 1955 and directives to the branches*

We, the State Conference officials of the NAACP, representing 16 Southern states and the District of Columbia have met here today, on June 4, 1955, to map a program of action to make full use of the two historic decisions of the Supreme Court desegregating public schools.

We adopt and approve the staff memorandum interpreting the May 31 decision and we authorize our branches in every state to act to secure desegregation beginning next September, by filing petitions with their school boards requesting the "prompt" beginning set forth in the May 31 opinion. In the absence of any affirmative actions by school boards by the opening of schools in September, 1955, our branches will take whatever action is necessary to get the school board to initiate the process of desegregation. To this end, we are sending the following 8-point directive to all of our branches.

To the recalcitrant states determined to flout the Constitution we say: maintenance of segregated schools is unconsti-

---

* The Crisis, LXII (June–July, 1955), pp. 337–340, 381. Reprinted by permission.

tutional and all state laws and practices to the contrary "must yield" to this principle of desegregation. This is the law of the land which applies to every state, county, city and hamlet. There will be no local option on this. Whenever and wherever a state or county refuses to recognize this principle, our answer will be the same as the legal action begun here in Atlanta on June 3, 1955.

· · · ·

Directives to the Branches

On May 17, 1954, the United States Supreme Court in a historic decision outlawed racial segregation in public schools. On May 31, 1955, in another unanimous decision, the Court ordered "good faith compliance" with this decision "at the earliest practicable date" and made the lower federal courts guardians in the enforcement of this order and arbiters as to whether good faith is being practiced by school authorities.

A sampling of sentiment throughout the country indicates a generally favorable reaction to the May 31 decision, with Kentucky, Oklahoma, Maryland, Missouri, Delaware and West Virginia promising full compliance. There will be resistance in the rest of the South in varying degrees, but make no mistake about it, this decision in no way cuts back on the May 17 pronouncement. Indeed, the May 31 decision merely affords to law-abiding public officials an easy method to conform to the Constitution of the United States. The decision places a challenge on the good faith of the public officials, on the militancy of Negroes and on the integrity of the federal courts.

For our part, we must be prepared to meet the challenge in a forthright manner. Our branches must seek to determine in each community whether the school board is prepared to make a prompt and reasonable start towards integration of the public schools and whether it will proceed with good faith towards full compliance with the May 31 decision at the earliest practicable date. Promises unaccompanied by concrete action are meaningless; nor can there be concern with the attitudes of individuals towards a change in the school system. Segregated schools are illegal, and the Court is merely allowing school boards time to get their houses in order. It does not allow time to procrastinate, stall or evade. It is the job of our branches to see to it that each school board begins to deal with the problem of providing non-discriminatory education. To that end we suggest that each of our branches take the following steps:

1. File at once a petition with each school board, calling attention to the May 31 decision, requesting that the school board act in accordance with that decision and offering the services of the branch to help the board in solving this problem.

2. Follow up the petition with periodic inquiries of the board seeking to determine what steps it is making to comply with the Supreme Court decision.

3. All during June, July, August and September, and thereafter, through meetings, forums, debates, conferences, etc., use every opportunity to explain what the May 31 decision means, and be sure to emphasize that the ultimate determination as to the length of time it will take for desegregation to become a fact in the community is not in the hands of the politicians or the school board officials but in the hands of the federal courts.

4. Organize the parents in the community so that as many as possible will be familiar with the procedure when and if law suits are begun in behalf of plaintiffs and parents.

5. Seek the support of individuals and community groups, particularly in the white community, through churches, labor organizations, civic organizations and personal contact.

6. When announcement is made of the plans adopted by your school board, get the exact text of the school board's pronouncements and notify the State Conference and the National Office at once so that you will have the benefit of their views as to whether the plan is one which will provide for effective desegregation. It is very important that branches not proceed at this stage without consultation with State offices and the National office.

7. If no plans are announced or no steps towards desegregation taken by the time school begins this fall, 1955, the time for a law suit has arrived. At this stage court action is essential because only in this way does the mandate of the Supreme Court that [there be] a prompt and reasonable start towards full compliance become fully operative on the school boards in question.

8. At this stage the matter will be turned over to the Legal Department and it will proceed with the matter in court. . . .

The Southern Manifesto: Declaration of Constitutional Principles*

The unwarranted decision of the Supreme Court in the public school cases is now bearing the fruit always produced when men substitute naked power for established law.

The Founding Fathers gave us a Constitution of checks and balances because they realized the inescapable lesson of history that no man or group of men can be safely entrusted with unlimited power. They framed this Constitution with its provisions for change by amendment in order to secure the fundamentals of government against the dangers of temporary popular passion or the personal predilections of public office-holders.

We regard the decision of the Supreme Court in the school cases as a clear abuse of judicial power. It climaxes a trend in the Federal Judiciary undertaking to legislate, in derogation of the authority of Congress, and to encroach upon the reserved rights of the States and the people.

The original Constitution does not mention education. Neither does the 14th amendment nor any other amendment. The debates preceding the submission of the 14th amendment clearly show that there was no intent that it should affect the system of education maintained by the States.

. . . .

In the case of *Plessy* v. *Ferguson* in 1896 the Supreme Court expressly declared that under the 14th amendment no person was denied any of his rights if the States provided separate but equal public facilities. This decision has been followed in many other cases. It is notable that the Supreme Court, speaking through Chief Justice Taft, a former President of the United States, unanimously declared in 1927 in *Lum* v. *Rice* that the "separate but equal" principle is "within the discretion of the State in regulating its public schools and does not conflict with the 14th amendment."

This interpretation, restated time and again, became a part

---

* *Congressional Record*, 84th Congress, 2nd Session, March 12, 1956, pp. 4460–61, 4515–16.

of the life of the people of many of the States and confirmed their habits, customs, traditions, and way of life. It is founded on elemental humanity and common sense, for parents should not be deprived by Government of the right to direct the lives and education of their own children. . . .

This unwarranted exercise of power by the Court, contrary to the Constitution, is creating chaos and confusion in the States principally affected. It is destroying the amicable relations between the white and Negro races that have been created through 90 years of patient effort by the good people of both races. It has planted hatred and suspicion where there has been heretofore friendship and understanding.

Without regard to the consent of the governed, outside agitators are threatening immediate and revolutionary changes in our public-school systems. If done, this is certain to destroy the system of public education in some of the States.

With the gravest concern for the explosive and dangerous condition created by this decision and inflamed by outside meddlers:

We reaffirm our reliance on the Constitution as the fundamental law of the land.

We decry the Supreme Court's encroachments on rights reserved to the States and to the people, contrary to established law, and to the Constitution.

We commend the motives of those States which have declared the intention to resist forced integration by any lawful means.

We appeal to the States and people who are not directly affected by these decisions to consider the constitutional principles involved against the time when they too, on issues vital to them, may be the victims of judicial encroachment.

Even though we constitute a minority in the present Congress, we have full faith that a majority of the American people believe in the dual system of government which has enabled us to achieve our greatness and will in time demand that the reserved rights of the States and of the people be made secure against judicial usurpation.

We pledge ourselves to use all lawful means to bring about a reversal of this decision which is contrary to the Constitution and to prevent the use of force in its implementation.

In this trying period, as we all seek to right this wrong, we appeal to our people not to be provoked by the agitators and troublemakers invading our States and to scrupulously refrain from disorder and lawless acts. . . .

THE LITTLE ROCK CRISIS (1957–1958)

Reactions to the School Segregation Cases took many forms. The 1954 decision in *Brown* v. *Board of Education of Topeka*, 347 U.S. 483, had declared unconstitutional the laws of twenty-one states and the District of Columbia which required or permitted some variety of racial segregation in the schools. Action was thus demanded of the school boards in twenty-two jurisdictions.

Four states had merely permitted racial discrimination under local option laws, and the reaction in these four (Arizona, Kansas, New Mexico, and Wyoming) was ready compliance. The District of Columbia and Delaware, Kentucky, Maryland, Missouri, Oklahoma, and West Virginia likewise complied without any appreciable opposition. Ten states adopted patterns of avoidance, evasion, and delay under color of law— seeking judicial acceptance of pupil assignment laws, private schools supported with public monies, and other lawyer- created stratagems designed to avoid integration. Of these ten, North Carolina, Tennessee, and Texas ended their legal opposition by 1957. Alabama, Mississippi, and South Carolina forestalled or ignored federal court action. And Florida, Georgia, Louisiana, and Virginia engaged in a continuing series of courtroom battles, using every possible device in the legal armament.

In Arkansas there was violence. It was not expected violence. The Little Rock school board had worked out a detailed and comprehensive desegregation plan in compliance with local federal court decrees, and nine Negro children were scheduled for admission to the high school on September 3, 1957. Arkansas Governor Orval Faubus acted first; National Guard units were ordered to Central High School on the previous day to forestall the school board plan. Little Rock became a national issue.

Three weeks later, President Dwight D. Eisenhower issued an executive order authorizing the use of federal troops to enforce the federal court orders. And soldiers stood on the high school steps to insure the admission of the nine Negro children and to protect them on their way to and from the school. On the night of September 24, 1957, President Eisenhower addressed a worried nation on the importance of his action at Little Rock.

Because of local hostility, the school board petitioned for a delay in its desegregation program. And because of the importance of the issue, the Supreme Court held a special term to hear argument. Delay was denied in the unanimous decision in *Cooper* v. *Aaron*, 358 U.S. 1 (1958).

DOCUMENT(S) 80

*Executive Order 10730, September 24, 1957**

Executive Order providing assistance for the removal of an obstruction of justice within the state of Arkansas

Whereas on Sept. 23, 1957, I issued Proclamation No. 3204 reading in part as follows:

"Whereas certain persons in the state of Arkansas, Individually and in unlawful assemblages, combinations, and conspiracies, have wilfully obstructed the enforcement of orders of the United States District Court for the Eastern District of Arkansas with respect to matters relating to enrollment and attendance at public schools, particularly at Central High School, located in Little Rock school district, Little Rock, Arkansas: and

"Whereas such wilful obstruction of justice hinders the execution of the laws of that state and of the United States, and makes it impracticable to enforce such laws by the ordinary course of judicial proceeding; and

"Whereas such obstruction of justice constitutes a denial of the equal protection of the laws secured by the Constitution of the United States and impedes the course of justice under those laws;

"Now, therefore, I, Dwight D. Eisenhower, President of the United States, under and by virtue of the authority vested in

---

* 22 Fed. Reg. 7628 (1957).

me by the Constitution and statutes of the United States, including Chapter 15 of Title 10 of the United States Code, particularly Sections 332, 333 and 334 thereof, do command all persons engaged in such obstruction of justice to cease and desist therefrom, and to disperse forthwith"; and

Whereas the command contained in that proclamation has not been obeyed and willful obstruction of enforcement of said court orders still exists and threatens to continue:

Now, therefore, by virtue of the authority vested in me by the Constitution and statutes of the United States, including Chapter 15 of Title 10, particularly Sections 332, 333 and 334 thereof, and Section 301 of Title 3 of the United States Code, it is hereby ordered as follows:

SECTION 1. I hereby authorize and direct the Secretary of Defense to order into the active military service of the United States as he may deem appropriate to carry out the purposes of this order, any or all of the units of the National Guard of the United States and of the Air National Guard of the United States within the state of Arkansas to serve in the active military service of the United States for an indefinite period and until relieved by appropriate orders.

SECTION 2. The Secretary of Defense is authorized and directed to take all appropriate steps to enforce any orders of the United States District Court for the Eastern District of Arkansas for the removal of obstruction of justice in the state of Arkansas with respect to matters relating to enrollment and attendance at public schools in the Little Rock School District, Little Rock, Arkansas. To carry out the provisions of this section, the Secretary of Defense is authorized to use the units, and members thereof, ordered into the active military service of the United States pursuant to Section 1 of this order.

SECTION 3. In furtherance of the enforcement of the aforementioned orders of the United States District Court for the Eastern District of Arkansas, the Secretary of Defense is authorized to use such of the armed forces of the United States as he may deem necessary.

SECTION 4. The Secretary of Defense is authorized to delegate to the Secretary of the Army or the Secretary of the Air

Force, or both, any of the authority conferred upon him by this order.

DWIGHT D. EISENHOWER

Eisenhower's Address on the situation in Little Rock, September 24, 1957*

My Fellow Citizens. . . . I must speak to you about the serious situation that has arisen in Little Rock. . . . In that city, under the leadership of demagogic extremists, disorderly mobs have deliberately prevented the carrying out of proper orders from a federal court. Local authorities have not eliminated that violent opposition and, under the law, I yesterday issued a proclamation calling upon the mob to disperse.

This morning the mob again gathered in front of the Central High School of Little Rock, obviously for the purpose of again preventing the carrying out of the court's order relating to the admission of Negro children to that school.

Whenever normal agencies prove inadequate to the task and it becomes necessary for the executive branch of the federal government to use its powers and authority to uphold federal courts, the President's responsibility is inescapable.

In accordance with that responsibility, I have today issued an Executive Order directing the use of troops under federal authority to aid in the execution of federal law at Little Rock, Arkansas. This became necessary when my Proclamation of yesterday was not observed, and the obstruction of justice still continues.

It is important that the reasons for my action be understood by all our citizens.

As you know, the Supreme Court of the United States has decided that separate public educational facilities for the races are inherently unequal and therefore compulsory school segregation laws are unconstitutional. . . .

During the past several years, many communities in our southern states have instituted public school plans for gradual progress in the enrollment and attendance of school children of all races in order to bring themselves into compliance with the law of the land.

---

* *The New York Times,* September 25, 1957, p. 14.

They thus demonstrated to the world that we are a nation in which laws, not men, are supreme.

. . . .

Now, let me make it very clear that federal troops are not being used to relieve local and state authorities of their primary duty to preserve the peace and order of the community. . . .

The proper use of the powers of the Executive Branch to enforce the orders of a federal court is limited to extraordinary and compelling circumstances. Manifestly, such an extreme situation has been created in Little Rock. This challenge must be met and with such measures as will preserve to the people as a whole their lawfully protected rights in a climate permitting their free and fair exercise.

The overwhelming majority of our people in every section of the country are united in their respect for observance of the law—even in those cases where they may disagree with that law. . . .

A foundation of our American way of life is our national respect for law.

In the South, as elsewhere, citizens are keenly aware of the tremendous disservice that has been done to the people of Arkansas in the eyes of the nation, and that has been done to the nation in the eyes of the world.

At a time when we face grave situations abroad because of the hatred that communism bears toward a system of government based on human rights, it would be difficult to exaggerate the harm that is being done to the prestige and influence, and indeed to the safety, of our nation and the world.

Our enemies are gloating over this incident and using it everywhere to misrepresent our whole nation. We are portrayed as a violator of those standards of conduct which the peoples of the world united to proclaim in the Charter of the United Nations. There they affirmed "faith in fundamental human rights" and "in the dignity and worth of the human person" and they did so "without distinction as to race, sex, language or religion."

And so, with deep confidence, I call upon the citizens of the State of Arkansas to assist in bringing to an immediate end all interference with the law and its processes. If resistance to the federal court orders ceases at once, the further presence of federal troops will be unnecessary and the City of Little Rock will return to its normal habits of peace and order and a blot upon the fair name and high honor of our nation in the world will be removed.

Thus will be restored the image of America and of all its parts as one nation, indivisible, with liberty and justice for all.

Cooper v. Aaron*

Opinion of the Court by THE CHIEF JUSTICE, MR. JUSTICE BLACK, MR. JUSTICE FRANKFURTER, MR. JUSTICE DOUGLAS, MR. JUSTICE BURTON, MR. JUSTICE CLARK, MR. JUSTICE HARLAN, MR. JUSTICE BRENNAN, and MR. JUSTICE WHITTAKER.

As this case reaches us it raises questions of the highest importance to the maintenance of our federal system of government. It necessarily involves a claim by the Governor and Legislature of a State that there is no duty on state officials to obey federal court orders resting on this Court's considered interpretation of the United States Constitution. Specifically it involves actions by the Governor and Legislature of Arkansas upon the premise that they are not bound by our holding in *Brown* v. *Board of Education,* 347 U.S. 483. That holding was that the Fourteenth Amendment forbids States to use their governmental powers to bar children on racial grounds from attending schools where there is state participation through any arrangement, management, funds or property. We are urged to uphold a suspension of the Little Rock School Board's plan to do away with segregated public schools in Little Rock until state laws and efforts to upset and nullify our holding in *Brown* v. *Board of Education* have been further challenged and tested in the courts. We reject these contentions.

The case was argued before us on September 11, 1958. On the following day we unanimously affirmed the judgment of the Court of Appeals for the Eighth Circuit, 257 F. 2d 33, which had reversed a judgment of the District Court for the Eastern District of Arkansas, 163 F. Supp. 13. The District

---

* Supreme Court of the United States, 358 U.S. 1 (1958).

Court had granted the application of the petitioners, the Little Rock School Board and School Superintendent, to suspend for two and one-half years the operation of the School Board's court-approved desegregation program. In order that the School Board might know, without doubt, its duty in this regard before the opening of school, which had been set for the following Monday, September 15, 1958, we immediately issued the judgment, reserving the expression of our supporting views to a later date. This opinion of all of the members of the Court embodies those views.

The following are the facts and circumstances so far as necessary to show how the legal questions are presented. . . .

On May 20, 1954, three days after the first *Brown* opinion, the Little Rock District School Board adopted, and on May 23, 1954, made public, a statement of policy entitled "Supreme Court Decision—Segregation in Public Schools." In this statement the Board recognized that "It is our responsibility to comply with Federal Constitution Requirements and we intend to do so when the Supreme Court of the United States outlines the method to be followed."

Thereafter the Board undertook studies of the administrative problems confronting the transition to a desegregated public school system at Little Rock. It instructed the Superintendent of Schools to prepare a plan for desegregation, and approved such a plan on May 24, 1955, seven days before the second *Brown* opinion. The plan provided for desegregation at the senior high school level (grades 10 through 12) as the first stage. Desegregation at the junior high and elementary levels was to follow. It was contemplated that desegregation at the high school level would commence in the fall of 1957, and the expectation was that complete desegregation of the school system would be accomplished by 1963. Following the adoption of this plan, the Superintendent of Schools discussed it with a large number of citizen groups in the city. As a result of these discussions, the Board reached the conclusion that "a large majority of the residents" of Little Rock were of "the belief . . . that the Plan, although objectionable in principle," from the point of view of those supporting segregated schools, "was still the best for the interests of all pupils in the District."

Upon challenge by a group of Negro plaintiffs desiring more rapid completion of the desegregation process, the

District Court upheld the School Board's plan, *Aaron* v. *Cooper*, 143 F. Supp. 855. The Court of Appeals affirmed. 243 F. 2d 361. Review of that judgment was not sought here.

While the School Board was thus going forward with its preparation for desegregating the Little Rock school system, other state authorities, in contrast, were actively pursuing a program designed to perpetuate in Arkansas the system of racial segregation which this Court had held violated the Fourteenth Amendment. First came, in November 1956, an amendment to the State Constitution flatly commanding the Arkansas General Assembly to oppose "in every Constitutional manner the Un-constitutional desegregation decisions of May 17, 1954 and May 31, 1955 of the United States Supreme Court," Ark. Const., Amend. 44, and, through the initiative, a pupil assignment law, Ark. Stat. 80–1519 to 80–1524. Pursuant to this state constitutional command, a law relieving school children from compulsory attendance at racially mixed schools, Ark. Stat. 80–1525, and a law establishing a State Sovereignty Commission, Ark. Stat. 6–801 to 6–824, were enacted by the General Assembly in February 1957.

The School Board and the Superintendent of Schools nevertheless continued with preparations to carry out the first stage of the desegregation program. Nine Negro children were scheduled for admission in September 1957 to Central High School, which has more than two thousand students. Various administrative measures, designed to assure the smooth transition of this first stage of desegregation, were undertaken.

On September 2, 1957, the day before these Negro students were to enter Central High, the school authorities were met with drastic opposing action on the part of the Governor of Arkansas who dispatched units of the Arkansas National Guard to the Central High School grounds and placed the school "off limits" to colored students. As found by the District Court in subsequent proceedings, the Governor's action had not been requested by the school authorities, and was entirely unheralded. The findings were these:

Up to this time [September 2], no crowds had gathered about Central High School and no acts of violence or threats of violence in connection with the carrying out of the plan had occurred. Nevertheless, out of an abundance of caution, the school authorities had frequently conferred with the Mayor and Chief of Police of

Little Rock about taking appropriate steps by the Little Rock police to prevent any possible disturbances or acts of violence in connection with the attendance of the 9 colored students at Central High School. The Mayor considered that the Little Rock police force could adaquately cope with any incidents which might arise at the opening of school. The Mayor, the Chief of Police, and the school authorities made no request to the Governor or any representative of his for State assistance in maintaining peace and order at Central High School. Neither the Governor nor any other official of the State government consulted with the Little Rock authorities about whether the Little Rock police were prepared to cope with any incidents which might arise at the school, about any need for State assistance in maintaining peace and order, or about stationing the Arkansas National Guard at Central High School. *Aaron* v. *Cooper*, 156 F. Supp. 220, 225.

The Board's petition for postponement in this proceeding states: "The effect of that action [of the Governor] was to harden the core of opposition to the Plan and cause many persons who theretofore had reluctantly accepted the Plan to believe there was some power in the State of Arkansas which, when exerted, could nullify the Federal law and permit disobedience of the decree of this [District] Court, and from that date hostility to the Plan was increased and criticism of the officials of the [School] District has become more bitter and unrestrained." The Governor's action caused the School Board to request the Negro students on September 2 not to attend the high school "until the legal dilemma was solved." The next day, September 3, 1957, the Board petitioned the District Court for instructions, and the court, after a hearing, found that the Board's request of the Negro students to stay away from the high school had been made because of the stationing of the military guards by the state authorities. The court determined that this was not a reason for departing from the approved plan, and ordered the School Board and Superintendent to proceed with it.

On the morning of the next day, September 4, 1957, the Negro children attempted to enter the high school but, as the District Court later found, units of the Arkansas National Guard "acting pursuant to the Governor's order, stood shoulder to shoulder at the school grounds and thereby forcibly prevented the 9 Negro students . . . from entering," as they continued to do every school day during the following three weeks. 156 F. Supp., at 225.

That same day, September 4, 1957, the United States Attorney for the Eastern District of Arkansas was requested by the District Court to begin an immediate investigation in order to fix responsibility for the interference with the orderly implementation of the District Court's direction to carry out the desegregation program. Three days later, September 7, the District Court denied a petition of the School Board and the Superintendent of Schools for an order temporarily suspending continuance of the program.

Upon completion of the United States Attorney's investigation, he and the Attorney General of the United States, at the District Court's request, entered the proceedings and filed a petition on behalf of the United States, as *amicus curiae*, to enjoin the Governor of Arkansas and officers of the Arkansas National Guard from further attempts to prevent obedience to the court's order. After hearings on the petition, the District Court found that the School Board's plan had been obstructed by the Governor through the use of National Guard troops, and granted a preliminary injunction on September 20, 1957, enjoining the Governor and the officers of the Guard from preventing the attendance of Negro children at Central High School, and from otherwise obstructing or interfering with the orders of the court in connection with the plan. 156 F. Supp. 220, affirmed, *Faubus* v. *United States*, 254 F. 2d 797. The National Guard was then withdrawn from the school.

The next school day was Monday, September 23, 1957. The Negro children entered the high school that morning under the protection of the Little Rock Police Department and members of the Arkansas State Police. But the officers caused the children to be removed from the school during the morning because they had difficulty controlling a large and demonstrating crowd which had gathered at the high school. 163 F. Supp., at 16. On September 25, however, the President of the United States dispatched federal troops to Central High School and admission of the Negro students to the school was thereby effected. Regular army troops continued at the high school until November 27, 1957. They were then replaced by federalized National Guardsmen who remained throughout the balance of the school year. Eight of the Negro students remained in attendance at the school throughout the school year.

We come now to the aspect of the proceedings presently before us. On February 20, 1958, the School Board and the Superintendent of Schools filed a petition in the District Court seeking a postponement of their program for desegregation. Their position in essence was that because of extreme public hostility, which they stated had been engendered largely by the official attitudes and actions of the Governor and the Legislature, the maintenance of a sound educational program at Central High School, with the Negro students in attendance, would be impossible. The Board therefore proposed that the Negro students already admitted to the school be withdrawn and sent to segregated schools, and that all further steps to carry out the Board's desegregation program be postponed for a period later suggested by the Board to be two and one-half years.

After a hearing the District Court granted the relief requested by the Board. Among other things the court found that the past year at Central High School had been attended by conditions of "chaos, bedlam and turmoil"; that there were "repeated incidents of more or less serious violence directed against the Negro students and their property"; that there was "tension and unrest among the school administrators, the class-room teachers, the pupils, and the latter's parents, which inevitably had an adverse effect upon the educational program"; that a school official was threatened with violence; that a "serious financial burden" had been cast on the School District; that the education of the students had suffered "and under existing conditions will continue to suffer"; that the Board would continue to need "military assistance or its equivalent"; that the local police department would not be able "to detail enough men to afford the necessary protection"; and that the situation was "intolerable." 163 F. Supp., at 20–26. . . .

In affirming the judgment of the Court of Appeals which reversed the District Court we have accepted without reservation the position of the School Board, the Superintendent of Schools, and their counsel that they displayed entire good faith in the conduct of these proceedings and in dealing with the unfortunate and distressing sequence of events which has been outlined. We likewise have accepted the findings of the

District Court as to the conditions at Central High School during the 1957–1958 school year, and also the findings that the educational progress of all the students, white and colored, of that school has suffered and will continue to suffer if the conditions which prevailed last year are permitted to continue.

The significance of these findings, however, is to be considered in light of the fact, indisputably revealed by the record before us, that the conditions they depict are directly traceable to the actions of legislators and executive officials of the State of Arkansas, taken in their official capacities, which reflect their own determination to resist this Court's decision in the *Brown* case and which have brought about violent resistance to that decision in Arkansas. In its petition for certiorari filed in this Court, the School Board itself describes the situation in this language: "The legislative, executive, and judicial departments of the state government opposed the desegregation of Little Rock schools by enacting laws, calling out troops, making statements villifying federal law and federal courts, and failing to utilize state law enforcement agencies and judicial processes to maintain public peace."

One may well sympathize with the position of the Board in the face of the frustrating conditions which have confronted it, but, regardless of the Board's good faith, the actions of the other state agencies responsible for those conditions compel us to reject the Board's legal position. Had Central High School been under the direct management of the State itself, it could hardly be suggested that those immediately in charge of the school should be heard to assert their own good faith as a legal excuse for delay in implementing the constitutional rights of these respondents, when vindication of those rights was rendered difficult or impossible by the actions of other state officials. The situation here is in no different posture because the members of the School Board and the Superintendent of Schools are local officials; from the point of view of the Fourteenth Amendment, they stand in this litigation as the agents of the State.

The constitutional rights of respondents are not to be sacrificed or yielded to the violence and disorder which have followed upon the actions of the Governor and Legislature. As this Court said some 41 years ago in a unanimous opinion in a case involving another aspect of racial segregation: "It is urged that this proposed segregation will promote the public peace by preventing race conflicts. Desirable as this is, and important as is the preservation of the public peace, this aim cannot be accomplished by laws or ordinances which deny rights created or protected by the Federal Constitution." *Buchanan* v. *Warley*, 245 U.S. 60, 81. Thus law and order are not here to be preserved by depriving the Negro children of their constitutional rights. The record before us clearly establishes that the growth of the Board's difficulties to a magnitude beyond its unaided power to control is the product of state action. Those difficulties, as counsel for the Board forthrightly conceded on the oral argument in this Court, can also be brought under control by state action.

The controlling legal principles are plain. The command of the Fourteenth Amendment is that no "State" shall deny to any person within its jurisdiction the equal protection of the laws. "A State acts by its legislative, its executive, or its judicial authorities. It can act in no other way. The constitutional provision, therefore, must mean that no agency of the State, or of the officers or agents by whom its powers are exerted, shall deny to any person within its jurisdiction the equal protection of the laws. Whoever, by virtue of public position under a State government, . . . denies or takes away the equal protection of the laws, violates the constitutional inhibition; and as he acts in the name and for the State, and is clothed with the State's power, his act is that of the State. This must be so, or the constitutional prohibition has no meaning." *Ex parte Virginia*, 100 U.S. 339, 347. Thus the prohibitions of the Fourteenth Amendment extend to all action of the State denying equal protection of the laws; whatever the agency of the State taking the action, see *Virginia* v. *Rives*, 100 U.S. 313; *Pennsylvania* v. *Board of Directors of City Trusts of Philadelphia*, 353 U.S. 230; *Shelley* v. *Kraemer*, 334 U.S. 1; or whatever the guise in which it is taken, see *Derrington* v. *Plummer*, 240 F. 2d 922; *Department of Conservation and Development* v. *Tate*, 231 F. 2d 615. In short, the constitutional rights of children not to be discriminated against in school admission on grounds of race or color declared by this Court in the *Brown* case can neither be nullified openly and directly by state legislators or state executive or judicial officers, nor nullified indirectly by them through evasive schemes for segregation whether attempted "ingeniously or ingenuously." *Smith* v. *Texas*, 311 U.S. 128, 132.

What has been said, in the light of the facts developed, is enough to dispose of the case. However, we should answer the premise of the actions of the Governor and Legislature that they are not bound by our holding in the *Brown* case. It is necessary only to recall some basic constitutional propositions which are settled doctrine.

Article VI of the Constitution makes the Constitution the "supreme Law of the Land." In 1803, Chief Justice Marshall, speaking for a unanimous Court, referring to the Constitution as "the fundamental and paramount law of the nation," declared in the notable case of *Marbury* v. *Madison*, 1 Cranch 137, 177, that "It is emphatically the province and duty of the judicial department to say what the law is." This decision declared the basic principle that the federal judiciary is supreme in the exposition of the law of the Constitution, and that principle has ever since been respected by this Court and the Country as a permanent and indispensable feature of our constitutional system. It follows that the interpretation of the Fourteenth Amendment enunciated by this Court in the *Brown* case is the supreme law of the land, and Art. VI of the Constitution makes it of binding effect on the States "any Thing in the Constitution or Laws of any State to the Contrary notwithstanding." Every state legislator and executive and judicial officer is solemnly committed by oath taken pursuant to Art. VI, cl. 3, "to support this Constitution." Chief Justice Taney, speaking for a unanimous Court in 1859, said that this requirement reflected the framers' "anxiety to preserve it [the Constitution] in full force, in all its powers, and to guard against resistance to or evasion of its authority, on the part of a State. . . ." *Ableman* v. *Booth*, 21 How. 506, 524.

No state legislator or executive or judicial officer can war against the Constitution without violating his undertaking to support it. Chief Justice Marshall spoke for a unanimous Court in saying that: "If the legislatures of the several states may, at will, annul the judgments of the courts of the United States, and destroy the rights acquired under those judgments, the constitution itself becomes a solemn mockery. . . ." *United States* v. *Peters*, 5 Cranch 115, 136. A Governor who asserts a power to nullify a federal court order is similarly restrained. If he had such power, said Chief Justice Hughes, in 1932, also for a unanimous Court, "it is manifest that the fiat of a state Governor, and not the Constitution of the United States, would be a supreme law of the land; that the restrictions of the Federal Constitution upon the exercise of state power would be but impotent phrases. . . ." *Sterling* v. *Constantin*, 287 U.S. 378, 397–398.

It is, of course, quite true that the responsibility for public education is primarily the concern of the States, but it is equally true that such responsibilities, like all other state activity, must be exercised consistently with federal constitutional requirements as they apply to state action. The Constitution created a government dedicated to equal justice under law. The Fourteenth Amendment embodied and emphasized that ideal. State support of segregated schools through any arrangement, management, funds, or property cannot be squared with the Amendment's command that no State shall deny to any person within its jurisdiction the equal protection of the laws. The right of a student not to be segregated on racial grounds in schools so maintained is indeed so fundamental and pervasive that it is embraced in the concept of due process of law. *Bolling* v. *Sharpe*, 347 U.S. 497. The basic decision in *Brown* was unanimously reached by this Court only after the case had been briefed and twice argued and the issues had been given the most serious consideration. Since the first *Brown* opinion three new Justices have come to the Court. They are at one with the Justices still on the Court who participated in that basic decision as to its correctness, and that decision is now unanimously reaffirmed. The principles announced in that decision and the obedience of the States to them, according to the command of the Constitution, are indispensable for the protection of the freedoms guaranteed by our fundamental charter for all of us. Our constitutional ideal of equal justice under law is thus made a living truth.

VIII

Civil Rights and
the Congressional
Response
1957–1968

The period 1957 to 1968 witnessed the most dramatic series of changes in the status of the Negro in America since the Civil War and Reconstruction. Finally roused to action, the United States Congress passed four significant pieces of legislation touching on voting, school desegregation, fair employment practices, and public accommodation. These were designed to overcome local and state obstruction which had obdurately defied the implementation of federal executive and judicial action.

It was also during the years 1957 to 1968 that the tempo and demands of the Negro protest movement intensified. A younger generation, angered by continued delays on the part of segregationists, disheartened by the high costs of extensive litigation, and suspicious of the intentions and sincerity of public leaders, turned to the tactics of nonviolent, direct action. "Putting their bodies on the line," these young activists worked through Martin Luther King's Southern Christian Leadership Conference, the Congress of Racial Equality, and the Student Nonviolent Coordinating Committee, and left to the older, more established NAACP the procedural techniques of lobbying and litigation.

This was also the period of the Black Muslims and the Black Power advocates. While it would be a mistake to over-rate Black Muslim influence, its program of black separatism —not unlike that of Marcus Garvey's forty years before— indicated that not all Negroes enthusiastically accepted the goals of interracial reform through integration.

Another element within the Negro community had become convinced by the mid-1960's that the Negro must first secure conscious self-respect and an economic and political power base before he could hope to deal effectively with the dominant white majority. These Black Power advocates were quickly misunderstood in both the white and the Negro communities. The suggestion that the Negro must first secure political and economic leverage was generally met with disbelief and scorn, and the idea was discredited as part of some wild scheme bred of a mixture of race hatred and self-interest. The deliberate statements of Stokely Carmichael, spokesman for Black Power advocates, and a simple review of the tactics and attitudes employed in the past by other groups seeking social, political, and economic reform would suggest that the nation at large had missed the real implications of Black Power. What this misunderstanding will mean for the further evolution of race relations, remains to be seen.

Despite obvious advances toward interracial reform, the nation has come only partway. In many respects, the situation of the Negro in America is deteriorating. Overt discrimination, confirmed by state and local law, persists. Worse, because of its subtle and inexorable nature, is the pattern of de facto segregation and discrimination which characterizes so much of American life North and South. In the past quarter century the Negro has achieved his legal rights, but he has yet to win a full role in the social and economic life of the nation. A vicious circle of residential segregation, job discrimination, inferior educational opportunities, limited mobility, and, in many cases, a crippled self-image are affixing upon a new generation of Negroes the kind of economic and psychic damage that no executive order, court decision, or piece of federal legislation can readily correct. In part the urban riots of recent years reflect the anger and frustration created by these conditions.

In the seventeenth century, the Negro was brought to America in bondage to meet a simple labor shortage; in the contemporary, automated, technological, sophisticated economy, he need no longer and can no longer fill such a role. He thus faces a new type of economic and social bondage from which he cannot be freed by legal action.

Although the period 1957 to 1968 had been one of ferment, federal response, and genuine hope, it drew to a close in an atmosphere of gnawing uncertainty.

THE CIVIL RIGHTS ACT (1957)

A number of factors combined to require affirmative civil rights action at the start of President Eisenhower's second term. Persistent southern efforts had successfully forestalled implementation of *Brown* v. *Board of Education of Topeka*. Moreover, segregationist and states' rights opposition had encouraged the formation of such organized groups as the White Citizens' Councils and the initiation of such unorganized violence as the kidnap-lynching of fourteen-year-old Emmett Till at Money, Mississippi, in the summer of 1955. At the same time, Negroes were exerting increasing voting power in the nation's metropolitan areas.

The need for Congressional action was dramatized by the Montgomery, Alabama, bus boycott begun in late 1955. Under the leadership of Dr. Martin Luther King, Jr., and the Reverend F. L. Shuttlesworth, a year-long but successful and legally sustained battle was waged in the very heart of the segregationist South. Perhaps more important, the civil rights movement had found a new charismatic leader in the figure of Dr. King.

The law enacted by the 85th Congress on September 9, 1957, was the first civil rights bill since 1875 (Document 47). It was not a far-reaching measure in substance, but it was a clear indication that the legislative branch was at last undertaking responsibilities that had been previously left to the executive and the judiciary.

The 1957 act established a nonpartisan Civil Rights Commission empowered to gather evidence on voting violations. The act also strengthened certain civil rights provisions of the United States Code and authorized the Justice Department to initiate action to counter irregularities in federal elections.

Nondiscriminatory qualifications were prescribed for the selection of federal jurors.

DOCUMENT 81

*An act to provide means of further securing and protecting the civil rights of persons within the jurisdiction of the United States**

Be it enacted by the Senate and House of Representatives of the United States of America in Congress assembled,

PART I—ESTABLISHMENT OF THE COMMISSION ON CIVIL RIGHTS

SEC. 101. (a) There is created in the executive branch of the Government a Commission on Civil Rights (hereinafter called the "Commission").

(b) The Commission shall be composed of six members who shall be appointed by the President by and with the advice and consent of the Senate. Not more than three of the members shall at any one time be of the same political party.

(c) The President shall designate one of the members of the Commission as Chairman and one as Vice Chairman. The Vice Chairman shall act as Chairman in the absence or disability of the Chairman, or in the event of a vacancy in that office. . . .

Rules of Procedure of the Commission

SEC. 102. (a) The Chairman or one designated by him to act as Chairman at a hearing of the Commission shall announce in an opening statement the subject of the hearing.

(b) A copy of the Commission's rules shall be made available to the witness before the Commission.

(c) Witnesses at the hearings may be accompanied by their own counsel for the purpose of advising them concerning their constitutional rights.

---

* 71 Stat. 634 (1957).

(d) The Chairman or Acting Chairman may punish breaches of order and decorum and unprofessional ethics on the part of counsel, by censure and exclusion from the hearings.

(e) If the Commission determines that evidence or testimony at any hearing may tend to defame, degrade, or incriminate any person, it shall (1) receive such evidence or testimony in executive session; (2) afford such person an opportunity voluntarily to appear as a witness; and (3) receive and dispose of requests from such person to subpena additional witnesses.

(f) Except as provided in sections 102 and 105 (f) of this Act, the Chairman shall receive and the Commission shall dispose of requests to subpena additional witnesses.

(g) No evidence or testimony taken in executive session may be released or used in public sessions without the consent of the Commission. Whoever releases or uses in public without the consent of the Commission evidence or testimony taken in executive session shall be fined not more than $1,000, or imprisoned for not more than one year.

(h) In the discretion of the Commission, witnesses may submit brief and pertinent sworn statements in writing for inclusion in the record. The Commission is the sole judge of the pertinency of testimony and evidence adduced at its hearings.

. . . .

(k) The Commission shall not issue any subpena for the attendance and testimony of witnesses or for the production of written or other matter which would require the presence of the party subpenaed at a hearing to be held outside of the State, wherein the witness is found or resides or transacts business.

. . . .

Duties of the Commission

Sec. 104. (a) The Commission shall—
(1) investigate allegations in writing under oath or affirmation that certain citizens of the United States are being

deprived of their right to vote and have that vote counted by reason of their color, race, religion, or national origin; which writing, under oath or affirmation, shall set forth the facts upon which such belief or beliefs are based;

(2) study and collect information concerning legal developments constituting a denial of equal protection of the laws under the Constitution; and

(3) appraise the laws and policies of the Federal Government with respect to equal protection of the laws under the Constitution.

(b) The Commission shall submit interim reports to the President and to the Congress at such times as either the Commission or the President shall deem desirable, and shall submit to the President and to the Congress a final and comprehensive report of its activities, findings, and recommendations not later than two years from the date of the enactment of this Act.

(c) Sixty days after the submission of its final report and recommendations the Commission shall cease to exist.

. . . .

Part II—To Provide for an Additional Assistant Attorney General

Sec. 111. There shall be in the Department of Justice one additional Assistant Attorney General, who shall be appointed by the President, by and with the advice and consent of the Senate, who shall assist the Attorney General in the performance of his duties, and who shall receive compensation at the rate prescribed by law for other Assistant Attorneys General.

. . . .

Part IV—To Provide Means of Further Securing and Protecting the Right To Vote

Sec. 131. Section 2004 of the Revised Statutes (42 U.S.C. 1971), is amended as follows:

(a) Amend the catch line of said section to read, "Voting rights".

(b) Designate its present text with the subsection symbol "(a)".

(c) Add, immediately following the present text, four new sub-sections to read as follows:

"(b) No person, whether acting under color of law or otherwise, shall intimidate, threaten, coerce, or attempt to intimidate, threaten, or coerce any other person for the purpose of interfering with the right of such other person to vote or to vote as he may choose, or of causing such other person to vote for, or not to vote for, any candidate for the office of President, Vice President, presidential elector, Member of the Senate, or Member of the House of Representatives, Delegates or Commissioners from the Territories or possessions, at any general, special, or primary election held solely or in part for the purpose of selecting or electing any such candidate.

"(c) Whenever any person has engaged or there are reasonable grounds to believe that any person is about to engage in any act or practice which would deprive any other person of any right or privilege secured by subsection (a) or (b), the Attorney General may institute for the United States, or in the name of the United States, a civil action or other proper proceeding for preventive relief, including an application for a permanent or temporary injunction, restraining order, or other order. In any proceeding hereunder the United States shall be liable for costs the same as a private person.

"(d) The district courts of the United States shall have jurisdiction of proceedings instituted pursuant to this section and shall exercise the same without regard to whether the party aggrieved shall have exhausted any administrative or other remedies that may be provided by law.

"(e) Any person cited for an alleged contempt under this Act shall be allowed to make his full defense by counsel learned in the law; and the court before which he is cited or tried, or some judge thereof, shall immediately, upon his request, assign to him such counsel, not exceeding two, as he may desire, who shall have free access to him at all reasonable hours. He shall be allowed, in his defense to make any proof that he can produce by lawful witnesses, and shall have the like process of the court to compel his witnesses to appear at his trial or hearing, as is usually granted to compel witnesses to appear on behalf of the prosecution. If such person shall be found by the court to be financially unable to provide for such counsel, it shall be the duty of the court to provide such counsel."

PART V—TO PROVIDE TRIAL BY JURY FOR PROCEEDINGS TO PUNISH CRIMINAL CONTEMPTS OF COURT GROWING OUT OF CIVIL RIGHTS CASES AND TO AMEND THE JUDICIAL CODE RELATING TO FEDERAL JURY QUALIFICATIONS

SEC. 151. In all cases of criminal contempt arising under the provisions of this Act, the accused, upon conviction, shall be punished by fine or imprisonment or both: *Provided however,* That in case the accused is a natural person the fine to be paid shall not exceed the sum of $1,000, nor shall imprisonment exceed the term of six months: *Provided further,* That in any such proceeding for criminal contempt, at the discretion of the judge, the accused may be tried with or without a jury: *Provided further, however,* That in the event such proceeding for criminal contempt be tried before a judge without a jury and the sentence of the court upon conviction is a fine in excess of the sum of $300 or imprisonment in excess of forty-five days, the accused in said proceeding, upon demand therefor, shall be entitled to a trial de novo before a jury, which shall conform as near as may be to the practice in other criminal cases. . . .

SEC. 152. Section 1861, title 28, of the United States Code is hereby amended to read as follows:

"§ 1861. Qualifications of Federal jurors

"Any citizen of the United States who has attained the age of twenty-one years and who has resided for a period of one year within the judicial district, is competent to serve as a grand or petit juror unless—

"(1) He has been convicted in a State or Federal court of record of a crime punishable by imprisonment for more than one year and his civil rights have not been restored by pardon or amnesty.

"(2) He is unable to read, write, speak, and understand the English language.

"(3) He is incapable, by reason of mental or physical infirmities to render efficient jury service."

SEC. 161. This Act may be cited as the "Civil Rights Act of 1957".

APPROVED, September 9, 1957.

THE CIVIL RIGHTS ACT (1960)

When four students from North Carolina A. and T. College decided to sit-in at a segregated lunch counter in Greensboro, North Carolina, in early 1960, the contemporary civil rights movement was fully launched. Within a matter of weeks, the sit-in was an established protest tactic, augmented by mass demonstrations and rallies throughout the South and by supportive picketing and demonstrations outside the South. The constitutional validity of this tactic was later upheld by the Supreme Court in several cases (Document 87).

Faced with this unprecedented phenomenon of mass, non-violent protest, disturbed by the summary arrests and the violent, ill-treatment visited upon the demonstrators, and mindful of the bombings that had destroyed homes, churches, and schools identified with the protest movement, the nation again looked to Washington for deliberate action.

The future political composition of the federal government was an open question in the spring of 1960. President Eisenhower's second administration had been marred by an extended recession and by a resounding liberal and Democratic victory in the Congressional elections of 1958. The impending Presidential elections and the need for both major parties to demonstrate a capacity for decisive liberal leadership made it politically advantageous to pass the second federal civil rights enactment within three years.

The Civil Rights Act of 1960 (passed May 6, 1960) was designed to impede interracial violence without eroding the power and authority of local and state officials. The act called for the preservation of records in federal elections and established referees who could facilitate voting in concert with the courts and the Justice Department. If a "pattern or practice" of discrimination existed, the Justice Department was empowered to take action on behalf of an injured voter.

DOCUMENT 82

An act to enforce constitutional rights, and for other purposes[*]

Be it enacted by the Senate and House of Representatives of the United States of America in Congress assembled, That this Act may be cited as the "Civil Rights Act of 1960." . . .

TITLE II

Flight to avoid prosecution for damaging or destroying any building or other real or personal property; and, illegal transportation, use or possession of explosives; and, threats or false information concerning attempts to damage or destroy real or personal property by fire or explosives

SEC. 201. Chapter 49 of title 18, United States Code, is amended by adding at the end thereof a new section as follows:

"§ 1074. Flight to avoid prosecution for damaging or destroying any building or other real or personal property

"(a) Whoever moves or travels in interstate or foreign commerce with intent either (1) to avoid prosecution, or custody, or confinement after conviction, under the laws of the place from which he flees, for willfully attempting to or damaging or destroying by fire or explosive any building, structure, facility, vehicle, dwelling house, synagogue, church, religious center or educational institution, public or private, or (2) to avoid giving testimony in any criminal proceeding relating to any such offense shall be fined not more than $5,000 or imprisoned not more than five years, or both."

. . . .

SEC. 203. Chapter 39 of title 18 of the United States Code is amended by adding at the end thereof the following new section: "§ 837. Explosives; illegal use or possession; and, threats or false information concerning attempts to damage

---

* 74 Stat. 86 (1960).

or destroy real or personal property by fire or explosives."

. . . .

"(b) Whoever transports or aids and abets another in transporting in interstate or foreign commerce any explosive, with the knowledge or intent that it will be used to damage or destroy any building or other real or personal property for the purpose of interfering with its use for educational, religious, charitable, residential, business, or civic objectives or of intimidating any person pursuing such objectives, shall be subject to imprisonment for not more than one year, or a fine of not more than $1,000, or both; and if personal injury results shall be subject to imprisonment for not more than ten years or a fine of not more than $10,000, or both; and if death results shall be subject to imprisonment for any term of years or for life, but the court may impose the death penalty if the jury so recommends."

. . . .

SEC. 204. The analysis of chapter 39 of title 18 is amended by adding thereto the following: "837. Explosives; illegal use or possession; and threats or false information concerning attempts to damage or destroy real or personal property by fire or explosives."

TITLE III

Federal Election Records

SEC. 301. Every officer of election shall retain and preserve, for a period of twenty-two months from the date of any general, special, or primary election of which candidates for the office of President, Vice President, presidential elector, Member of the Senate, Member of the House of Representatives, or Resident Commissioner from the Commonwealth of Puerto Rico are voted for, all records and papers which come into his possession relating to any application, registration, payment of poll tax, or other act requisite to voting in such election, except that, when required by law, such records and papers may be delivered to another officer of election and except that, if a State or the Commonwealth of Puerto Rico designates a custodian to retain and preserve these records and papers at a specified place, then such records and papers may be deposited with such custodian, and the duty to retain and preserve any record or paper so deposited shall devolve upon such custodian. Any officer of election or custodian who willfully fails to comply with this section shall be fined not more than $1,000 or imprisoned not more than one year, or both.

SEC. 302. Any person, whether or not an officer of election or custodian, who willfully steals, destroys, conceals, mutilates, or alters any record or paper required by section 301 to be retained and preserved shall be fined not more than $1,000 or imprisoned not more than one year, or both.

SEC. 303. Any record or paper required by section 301 to be retained and preserved shall, upon demand in writing by the Attorney General or his representative directed to the person having custody, possession, or control of such record or paper, be made available for inspection, reproduction, and copying at the principal office of such custodian by the Attorney General or his representative. This demand shall contain a statement of the basis and the purpose therefor.

. . . .

TITLE IV

Extension of Powers of the Civil Rights Commission

SEC. 401. Section 105 of the Civil Rights Act of 1957 (42 U.S.C. Supp. V 1975d) (71 Stat. 635) is amended by adding the following new subsection at the end thereof:

"(h) Without limiting the generality of the foregoing, each member of the Commission shall have the power and authority to administer oaths or take statements of witnesses under affirmation."

. . . .

TITLE VI

SEC. 601. That section 2004 of the Revised Statutes (42

U.S.C. 1971), as amended by section 131 of the Civil Rights Act of 1957 (71 Stat. 637), is amended as follows:

. . . .

"The court may appoint one or more persons who are qualified voters in the judicial district, to be known as voting referees, who shall subscribe to the oath of office required by Revised Statutes, section 1757; (5 U.S.C. 16) to serve for such period as the court shall determine, to receive such applications and to take evidence and report to the court findings as to whether or not at any election or elections (1) any such applicant is qualified under State law to vote, and (2) he has since the finding by the court heretofore specified been (a) deprived of or denied under color of law the opportunity to register to vote or otherwise to qualify to vote, or (b) found not qualified to vote by any person acting under color of law. In a proceeding before a voting referee, the applicant shall be heard ex parte at such times and places as the court shall direct. His statement under oath shall be prima facie evidence as to his age, residence, and his prior efforts to register or otherwise qualify to vote. Where proof of literacy or an understanding of other subjects is required by valid provisions of State law, the answer of the applicant, if written, shall be included in such report to the court; if oral, it shall be taken down stenographically and a transcription included in such report to the court.

"Upon receipt of such report, the court shall cause the Attorney General to transmit a copy thereof to the State attorney general and to each party to such proceeding together with an order to show cause within ten days, or such shorter time as the court may fix, why an order of the court should not be entered in accordance with such report. Upon the expiration of such period, such order shall be entered unless prior to that time there has been filed with the court and served upon all parties a statement of exceptions to such report. Exceptions as to matters of fact shall be considered only if supported by a duly verified copy of a public record or by affidavit of persons having personal knowledge of such facts or by statements or matters contained in such report; those relating to matters of law shall be supported by an appropriate memorandum of law. The issues of fact and law raised by such exceptions shall be determined by the court or, if the due and speedy administration of justice requires, they may be referred to the voting referee to determine in accordance with procedures prescribed by the court. A hearing as to an issue of fact shall be held only in the event that the proof in support of the exception disclose the existence of a genuine issue of material fact. The applicant's literacy and understanding of other subjects shall be determined solely on the basis of answers included in the report of the voting referee."

. . . .

"When used in the subsection, the word 'vote' includes all action necessary to make a vote effective, but not limited to, registration or other action required by State law prerequisite to voting, casting a ballot, and having such ballot counted and included in the appropriate totals of votes cast with respect to candidates for public office and propositions for which votes are received in an election; the words 'affected area' shall mean any subdivision of the State in which the laws of the State relating to voting are or have been to any extent administered by a person found in the proceedings to have violated subsection (a); and the words 'qualified under State law' shall mean qualified according to the laws, customs, or usages of the State, and shall not, in any event, imply qualifications more stringent than those used by the persons found in the proceeding to have violated subsection (a) in qualifying persons other than those of the race or color against which the pattern or practice of discrimination was found to exist."

(b) Add the following sentence at the end of subsection (c):

"Whenever, in a proceeding instituted under this subsection any official of a State or subdivision thereof is alleged to have committed any act or practice constituting a deprivation of any right or privilege secured by subsection (a), the act or practice shall also be deemed that of the State and the State may be joined as a party defendant and, if, prior to the institution of such proceeding, such official has resigned or has been relieved of his office and no successor has assumed such office, the proceeding may be instituted against the State." . . .

Approved, May 6, 1960.

PRESIDENT KENNEDY ON NEGRO RIGHTS (1963)

The question of Negro attendance at state-supported institutions of higher education was not a new issue in the summer of 1962. The Supreme Court had decided several landmark cases on that question in the years from 1938 to 1950. But continued contempt of federal court rulings marked the conduct of Mississippi and Alabama officials when Negro James Meredith applied for admission to "Ole Miss" in 1962, and when two Negroes, Vivian Malone and James Hood, sought to enter the University of Alabama for the 1963 summer session. The civil rights movement had advanced at too fast a pace to permit the nation to ignore the issue, and President John F. Kennedy was too vigorous a leader to allow southern officials to defy the federal courts.

In opposing Meredith's admission, Mississippi Governor Ross Barnett even had himself appointed University Registrar. He specifically refused to obey a federal court order enjoining interference with Meredith's enrollment. On September 30, 1962, President Kennedy issued a proclamation demanding Mississippi's compliance with the federal courts, and that evening he addressed the nation on radio and television. His speech was temperate but firm. White Mississippians—both on and off campus—refused to cooperate; violence ensued. Under the protection of federal marshals and the Mississippi National Guard, federalized by the President, Meredith was enrolled.

The following spring, Governor George Wallace took action to block the enrollment of Vivian Malone and James Hood at the University of Alabama. President Kennedy again responded swiftly with the use of federal authority.

On the evening of June 11, 1963, the President once more addressed the nation. He began with a recital of that day's events at the University of Alabama, but took the occasion to deliver a comprehensive, far-ranging address on the status of the Negro in America and the absolute need for wide-scale reform. He informed the nation and the Congress that he was about to ask for extensive federal legislation as a means of redressing the multiple injustices suffered by Negroes. The speech helped launch a protracted effort that culminated, after the President's death in November, in the passage of the Civil Rights Act of 1964 (Document 89).

Presidential pronouncements could not preclude southern violence. On the day following Kennedy's address, the nation was shocked by the assassination of Medgar W. Evers, NAACP field secretary in Mississippi, in front of his Jackson home.

DOCUMENT 83

*President Kennedy's Civil Rights Address**

Good evening my fellow citizens.

This afternoon, following a series of threats and defiant statements, the presence of Alabama National Guardsmen was required on the University of Alabama to carry out the final and unequivocal order of the United States District Court of the Northern District of Alabama.

That order called for the admission of two clearly qualified young Alabama residents who happen to have been born Negro.

That they were admitted peacefully on the campus is due in good measure to the conduct of the students of the University of Alabama who met their responsibilities in a constructive way.

I hope that every American, regardless of where he lives, will stop and examine his conscience about this and other related incidents.

This nation was founded by men of many nations and backgrounds. It was founded on the principle that all men are created equal, and that the rights of every man are diminished when the rights of one man are threatened.

Today we are committed to a worldwide struggle to promote and protect the rights of all who wish to be free. And when Americans are sent to Vietnam or West Berlin we do not ask for whites only.

It ought to be possible, therefore, for American students of any color to attend any public institution they select without having to be backed up by troops. It ought to be possible

---

* *The New York Times,* June 12, 1963, p. 20.

for American consumers of any color to receive equal service in places of public accommodation, such as hotels and restaurants, and theaters and retail stores without being forced to resort to demonstrations in the street.

And it ought to be possible for American citizens of any color to register and to vote in a free election without interference or fear of reprisal.

It ought to be possible, in short, for every American to enjoy the privileges of being American without regard to his race or his color.

In short, every American ought to have the right to be treated as he would wish to be treated, as one would wish his children to be treated. But this is not the case.

The Negro baby born in America today, regardless of the section or the state in which he is born, has about one-half as much chance of completing a high school as a white baby, born in the same place, on the same day; one-third as much chance of completing college; one-third as much chance of becoming a professional man; twice as much chance of becoming unemployed; about one-seventh as much chance of earning $10,000 a year; a life expectancy which is seven years shorter and the prospects of earning only half as much.

This is not a sectional issue. Difficulties over segregation and discrimination exist in every city, in every state of the Union, producing in many cities a rising tide of discontent that threatens the public safety.

Nor is this a partisan issue. In a time of domestic crisis, men of goodwill and generosity should be able to unite regardless of party or politics.

This is not even a legal or legislative issue alone. It is better to settle these matters in the courts than on the streets, and new laws are needed at every level. But law alone cannot make men see right.

We are confronted primarily with a moral issue. It is as clear as the American Constitution. The heart of the question is whether all Americans are to be afforded equal rights and equal opportunities; whether we are going to treat our fellow Americans as we want to be treated.

If an American, because his skin is dark, cannot eat lunch in a restaurant open to the public; if he cannot send his children to the best public school available; if he cannot vote for the public officials who represent him; if, in short, he cannot enjoy the full and free life which all of us want, then who among us would be content to have the color of his skin changed and stand in his place?

Who among us would then be content with the counsels of patience and delay. One hundred years of delay have passed since President Lincoln freed the slaves, yet their heirs, their grandsons, are not fully free. They are not yet freed from the bonds of injustice; they are not yet freed from social and economic oppression.

And this nation, for all its hopes and all its boasts, will not be fully free until all its citizens are free.

We preach freedom around the world, and we mean it. And we cherish our freedom here at home. But are we to say to the world—and much more importantly to each other—that this is the land of the free, except for the Negroes; that we have no second-class citizens, except Negroes; that we have no class or caste system, no ghettos, no master race, except with respect to Negroes.

• • • •

The fires of frustration and discord are burning in every city, North and South. Where legal remedies are not at hand, redress is sought in the streets in demonstrations, parades and protests, which create tensions and threaten violence—and threaten lives.

We face, therefore, a moral crisis as a country and a people. It cannot be met by repressive police action. It cannot be left to increased demonstrations in the streets. It cannot be quieted by token moves or talk. It is a time to act in the Congress, in your state and local legislative body, and, above all, in all of our daily lives.

It is not enough to pin the blame on others, to say this is a problem of one section of the country or another, or deplore the facts that we face. A great change is at hand, and our task, our obligation is to make that revolution, that change peaceful and constructive for all.

Those who do nothing are inviting shame as well as violence. Those who act boldly are recognizing right as well as reality.

• • • •

I am, therefore, asking the Congress to enact legislation

giving all Americans the right to be served in facilities which are open to the public—hotels, restaurants and theaters, retail stores and similar establishments. This seems to me to be an elementary right.

Its denial is an arbitrary indignity that no American in 1963 should have to endure, but many do.

I have recently met with scores of business leaders, urging them to take voluntary action to end this discrimination. And I've been encouraged by their response. And in the last two weeks over 75 cities have seen progress made in desegregating these kinds of facilities.

But many are unwilling to act alone. And for this reason nationwide legislation is needed, if we are to move this problem from the streets to the courts.

I'm also asking Congress to authorize the Federal Government to participate more fully in lawsuits designed to end segregation in public education. We have succeeded in persuading many districts to desegregate voluntarily. Dozens have admitted Negroes without violence.

Today a Negro is attending a state-supported institution in every one of our 50 states. But the pace is very slow.

Too many Negro children entering segregated grade schools at the time of the Supreme Court's decision nine years ago will enter segregated high schools this fall, having suffered a loss which can never be restored.

The lack of an adequate education denies the Negro a chance to get a decent job. The orderly implementation of the Supreme Court decision therefore, cannot be left solely to those who may not have the economic resources to carry their legal action or who may be subject to harassment.

Other features will be also requested, including greater protection for the right to vote.

But legislation, I repeat, cannot solve this problem alone. It must be solved in the homes of every American in every community across our country.

In this respect, I want to pay tribute to those citizens, North and South, who've been working in their communities to make life better for all.

They are acting not out of a sense of legal duty but out of a sense of human decency. Like our soldiers and sailors in all parts of the world, they are meeting freedom's challenge on the firing line and I salute them for their honor—their courage. . . .

NAACP V. BUTTON (1963)

Under the implementation mandate of *Brown* v. *Board of Education of Topeka*, 1955 (Document 78), desegregation enforcement became the responsibility of the federal district courts. But, unlike a legislative body, a court cannot initiate affirmative action. A court is powerless to act unless an actual case is before it for decision; if there are no plaintiffs to institute desegregation suits, there is nothing a judicial body can do. Thus one aspect of Southern resistance has been to discourage litigation. In practical terms, this meant seeking ways to keep the legally oriented National Association for the Advancement of Colored People out of the South.

The NAACP is a New York nonprofit membership corporation. Outside of New York it is, in the eyes of the law, a foreign corporation. Thus, according to southern legal tacticians, it must register in the southern states in which it conducts its activities. Since registration involves the submission of membership lists and raises the probability of individual reprisals, the NAACP has opposed this requirement.

This issue was before the Supreme Court in *NAACP* v. *Alabama*, 357 U.S. 449 (1958). (Also entitled *NAACP* v. *Alabama ex rel Patterson*.) There the unanimous Court reversed an order of the Alabama courts to submit such lists. Justice John Marshall Harlan wrote: "We hold that the immunity from state scrutiny of membership lists which the Association claims on behalf of its members is here so related to the right of the members to pursue their lawful private interest privately and to associate freely with others in so doing as to come within the protection of the Fourteenth Amendment."

The controversy reached the Supreme Court for the fourth time in 1964. The case was also entitled *NAACP* v. *Alabama* or, to avoid confusion, *NAACP* v. *Alabama, ex rel Flowers*, 377 U.S. 288 (1964). It arose out of an order of the Alabama courts barring the NAACP from doing business in that state. Again Justice Harlan spoke for a unanimous Court in striking down the state restriction.

Virginia took another approach to disqualify the NAACP. It attempted to include the Association's activities within the ban of a state statute against "the improper solicitation of any legal or professional business." The Supreme Court reversed the ruling, holding that the activities of the NAACP "are modes of expression and association protected by the First and Fourteenth Amendments." This time Justice Harlan dissented, joined by Justices Tom Clark and Potter Stewart.

DOCUMENT 84

NAACP v. Button[*]

MR. JUSTICE BRENNAN delivered the opinion of the Court.
This case originated in companion suits by the National Association for the Advancement of Colored People, Inc. (NAACP), and the NAACP Legal Defense and Educational Fund, Inc. (Defense Fund), brought in 1957 in the United States District Court for the Eastern District of Virginia. The suits sought to restrain the enforcement of Chapters 31, 32, 33, 35 and 36 of the Virginia Acts of Assembly, 1956 Extra Sessions, on the ground that the statutes, as applied to the activities of the plaintiffs, violated the Fourteenth Amendment. . . .

There is no substantial dispute as to the facts; the dispute centers about the constitutionality under the Fourteenth Amendment of Chapter 33, as construed and applied by the Virginia Supreme Court of Appeals to include NAACP's activities within the statute's ban against "the improper solicitation of any legal or professional business."

The NAACP was formed in 1909 and incorporated under New York law as a nonprofit membership corporation in 1911. It maintains its headquarters in New York and presently has some 1,000 active unincorporated branches throughout the Nation. The corporation is licensed to do business in Virginia, and has 89 branches there. The Virginia branches are organized into the Virginia State Conference of NAACP Branches (the Conference), an unincorporated association, which in 1957 had some 13,500 members. The activities of the Conference are financed jointly by the national organization and the local branches from contributions and membership dues.

---

[*] Supreme Court of the United States, 371 U.S. 415 (1963).

NAACP policy, binding upon local branches and conferences, is set by the annual national convention.

The basic aims and purposes of NAACP are to secure the elimination of all racial barriers which deprive Negro citizens of the privileges and burdens of equal citizenship rights in the United States. To this end the Association engages in extensive educational and lobbying activities. It also devotes much of its funds and energies to an extensive program of assisting certain kinds of litigation on behalf of its declared purposes. For more than 10 years, the Virginia Conference has concentrated upon financing litigation aimed at ending racial segregation in the public schools of the Commonwealth.

The Conference ordinarily will finance only cases in which the assisted litigant retains an NAACP staff lawyer to represent him. The Conference maintains a legal staff of 15 attorneys, all of whom are Negroes and members of the NAACP. The staff is elected at the Conference's annual convention. Each legal staff member must agree to abide by the policies of the NAACP, which, insofar as they pertain to professional services, limit the kinds of litigation which the NAACP will assist. Thus the NAACP will not underwrite ordinary damages actions, criminal actions in which the defendant raises no question of possible racial discrimination, or suits in which the plaintiff seeks separate but equal rather than fully desegregated public school facilities. The staff decides whether a litigant, who may or may not be an NAACP member, is entitled to NAACP assistance. The Conference defrays all expenses of litigation in an assisted case, and usually, although not always, pays each lawyer on the case a per diem fee not to exceed $60, plus out-of-pocket expenses. The assisted litigant receives no money from the Conference or the staff lawyers. The staff member may not accept, from the litigant or any other source, any other compensation for his services in an NAACP-assisted case. None of the staff receives a salary or retainer from the NAACP; the per diem fee is paid only for professional services in a particular case. This per diem payment is smaller than the compensation ordinarily received for equivalent private professional work. The actual conduct of assisted litigation is under the control of the attorney, although the NAACP continues to be concerned that the outcome of the lawsuit should be consistent with NAACP's policies already described. A client is free at any time to withdraw from an action.

. . . .

Statutory regulation of unethical and nonprofessional conduct by attorneys has been in force in Virginia since 1849. These provisions outlaw, *inter alia,* solicitation of legal business in the form of "running" or "capping." Prior to 1956, however, no attempt was made to proscribe under such regulations the activities of the NAACP, which had been carried on openly for many years in substantially the manner described. In 1956, however, the legislature amended, by the addition of Chapter 33, the provisions of the Virginia Code forbidding solicitation of legal business by a "runner" or "capper" to include, in the definition of "runner" or "capper," an agent for an individual or organization which retains a lawyer in connection with an action to which it is not a party and in which it has no pecuniary right or liability. The Virginia Supreme Court of Appeals held that the chapter's purpose "was to strengthen the existing statutes to further control the evils of solicitation of legal business. . . ." 202 Va., at 154, 116 S.E. 2d, at 65. The court held that the activities of NAACP, the Virginia Conference, the Defense Fund, and the lawyers furnished by them, fell within, and could constitutionally be proscribed by, the chapter's expanded definition of improper solicitation of legal business, and also violated Canons 35 and 47 of the American Bar Association's Canons of Professional Ethics, which the court had adopted in 1938.** . . .

** 171 Va., pp. xxxii–xxxv (1938). Canon 35 reads in part as follows:

"Intermediaries.—The professional services of a lawyer should not be controlled or exploited by any lay agency, personal or corporate, which intervenes between client and lawyer. A lawyer's responsibilities and qualifications are individual. He should avoid all relations which direct the performance of his duties by or in the interest of such intermediary. A lawyer's relation to his client should be personal, and the responsibility should be direct to the client. Charitable societies rendering aid to the indigent are not deemed such intermediaries." Canon 47 reads as follows:

"Aiding the Unauthorized Practice of Law.—No lawyer shall permit his professional services, or his name, to be used in aid of, or to make possible, the unauthorized practice of law by any lay agency, personal or corporate."

Petitioner challenges the decision of the Supreme Court of Appeals on many grounds. But we reach only one: . . .

We reverse the judgment of the Virginia Supreme Court of Appeals. We hold that the activities of the NAACP, its affiliates and legal staff shown on this record are modes of expression and association protected by the First and Fourteenth Amendments which Virginia may not prohibit, under its power to regulate the legal profession, as improper solicitation of legal business violative of Chapter 33 and the Canons of Professional Ethics.

A

We meet at the outset the contention that "solicitation" is wholly outside the area of freedoms protected by the First Amendment. To this contention there are two answers. The first is that a State cannot foreclose the exercise of constitutional rights by mere labels. The second is that abstract discussion is not the only species of communication which the Constitution protects; the First Amendment also protects vigorous advocacy, certainly of lawful ends, against governmental intrusion. . . . In the context of NAACP objectives, litigation is not a technique of resolving private differences; it is a means for achieving the lawful objectives of equality of treatment by all government, federal, state and local, for the members of the Negro community in this country. It is thus a form of political expression. Groups which find themselves unable to achieve their objections through the ballot frequently turn to the courts. Just as it was true of the opponents of New Deal legislation during the 1930's, for example, no less is it true of the Negro minority today. And under the conditions of modern government, litigation may well be the sole practicable avenue open to a minority to petition for redress of grievances. . . .

The NAACP is not a conventional political party; but the litigation it assists, while serving to vindicate the legal rights of members of the American Negro community, at the same time and perhaps more importantly, makes possible the distinctive contribution of a minority group to the ideas and beliefs of our society. For such a group, association for litigation may be the most effective form of political association.

B

Our concern is with the impact of enforcement of Chapter 33 upon First Amendment freedoms. We start, of course, from the decree of the [Virginia] Supreme Court of Appeals. . . .

. . . .

We conclude that under Chapter 33, as authoritatively construed by the Supreme Court of Appeals, a person who advises another that his legal rights have been infringed and refers him to a particular attorney or group of attorneys (for example, to the Virginia Conference's legal staff) for assistance has committed a crime, as has the attorney who knowingly renders assistance under such circumstances. There thus inheres in the statute the gravest danger of smothering all discussion looking to the eventual institution of litigation on behalf of the rights of members of an unpopular minority. Lawyers on the legal staff or even mere NAACP members or sympathizers would understandably hesitate, at an NAACP meeting or on any other occasion, to do what the decree purports to allow, namely, acquaint "persons with what they believe to be their legal rights and . . . [advise] them to assert their rights by commencing or further prosecuting a suit. . . ." For if the lawyers, members or sympathizers also appeared in or had any connection with any litigation supported with NAACP funds contributed under the provision of the decree by which the NAACP is not prohibited "from contributing money to persons to assist them in commencing or further prosecuting such suits," they plainly would risk (if lawyers) disbarment proceedings and, lawyers and nonlawyers alike, criminal prosecution for the offense of "solicitation," to which the Virginia court gave so broad and uncertain a meaning. It makes no difference whether such prosecutions or proceedings would actually be commenced. It is enough that a vague and broad statute lends itself to selective enforcement against unpopular causes. We cannot close our eyes to the fact that the militant Negro civil rights movement has engendered the intense resentment and opposition of the politically dominant white community of Virginia; litigation assisted by the NAACP has been bitterly fought. In such circumstances, a statute broadly curtailing group activity leading to litigation may easily become a weapon of oppression, however even-handed its terms appear. Its mere existence could well freeze out of existence all such activity on behalf of the civil rights of Negro citizens. . . .

We hold that Chapter 33 as construed violates the Fourteenth Amendment by unduly inhibiting protected freedoms of expression and association.

. . . .

C

The second contention is that Virginia has a subordinating interest in the regulation of the legal profession, embodied in Chapter 33, which justifies limiting petitioner's First Amendment rights. Specifically, Virginia contends that the NAACP's activities in furtherance of litigation, being "improper solicitation" under the state statute, fall within the traditional purview of state regulation of professional conduct. However, the State's attempt to equate the activities of the NAACP and its lawyers with common-law barratry, maintenance and champerty, and to outlaw them accordingly, cannot obscure the serious encroachment worked by Chapter 33 upon protected freedoms of expression. The decisions of this Court have consistently held that only a compelling state interest in the regulation of a subject within the State's constitutional power to regulate can justify limiting First Amendment freedoms. Thus it is no answer to the constitutional claims asserted by petitioner to say, as the Virginia Supreme Court of Appeals has said, that the purpose of these regulations was merely to insure high professional standards and not to curtail free expression. For a State may not, under the guise of prohibiting professional misconduct, ignore constitutional rights.

. . . .

There has been no showing of a serious danger here of professionally reprehensible conflicts of interest which rules against solicitation frequently seek to prevent. This is so partly because no monetary stakes are involved, and so there is no danger that the attorney will desert or subvert the paramount interests of his client to enrich himself or an outside sponsor. And the aims and interests of NAACP have not been shown to conflict with those of its members and nonmember Negro litigants; compare *NAACP* v. *Alabama ex rel. Patterson,* 357 U.S. 449, 459, where we said:

[the NAACP] and its members are in every practical sense identical. The Association, which provides in its constitution that "[a]ny person who is in accordance with [its] principles and policies . . ." may become a member, is but the medium through which its individual members seek to make more effective the expression of their own views." See also *Harrison* v. *NAACP*, 360 U.S. 167, 177. . . .

We conclude that although the petitioner has amply shown that its activities fall within the First Amendment's protections, the State has failed to advance any substantial regulatory interest, in the form of substantive evils flowing from petitioner's activities, which can justify the broad prohibitions which it has imposed. Nothing that this record shows as to the nature and purpose of NAACP activities permits an inference of any injurious intervention in or control of litigation which would constitutionally authorize the application of Chapter 33 to those activities. *A fortiori,* nothing in this record justifies the breadth and vagueness of the Virginia Supreme Court of Appeals' decree.

A final observation is in order. Because our disposition is rested on the First Amendment as absorbed in the Fourteenth, we do not reach the considerations of race or racial discrimination which are the predicate of petitioner's challenge to the statute under the Equal Protection Clause. That the petitioner happens to be engaged in activities of expression and association on behalf of the rights of Negro children to equal opportunity is constitutionally irrelevant to the ground of our decision. The course of our decisions in the First Amendment area makes plain that its protections would apply as fully to those who would arouse our society against the objectives of the petitioner. . . . For the Constitution protects expression and association without regard to the race, creed, or political or religious affiliation of the members of the group which invokes its shield, or to the truth, popularity, or social utility of the ideas and beliefs which are offered.

Reversed.

• • • •

MR. JUSTICE HARLAN, whom MR. JUSTICE CLARK and MR. JUSTICE STEWART join, dissenting.

No member of this Court would disagree that the validity of state action claimed to infringe rights assured by the Fourteenth Amendment is to be judged by the same basic constitutional standards whether or not racial problems are involved. No worse setback could befall the great principles established by *Brown* v. *Board of Education,* 347 U.S. 483, than to give fair-minded persons reason to think otherwise. With all respect, I believe that the striking down of this Virginia statute cannot be squared with accepted constitutional doctrine in the domain of state regulatory power over the legal profession. . . .

FREEDOM TO THE FREE—REPORT OF THE UNITED STATES COMMISSION ON CIVIL RIGHTS (1963)

The American Negro specifically and the nation generally were sensitive to the fact that 1963 would mark the centennial of President Lincoln's Emancipation Proclamation (Document 41). The United States Civil Rights Commission, established originally under the Civil Rights Act of 1957 (Document 81), commemorated the occasion with its report to the President. Entitled *Freedom to the Free,* the report was devoted to an extensive and comprehensive historical review of the role and status of the Negro in America from colonial times to midtwentieth century. The final section, "The Task Ahead," commented on the reactions of the French nobleman Alexis de Tocqueville to his American visit from 1831 to 1832. De Tocqueville had pessimistically foreseen only two alternatives in the interracial situation—either the perpetuation of slavery, or emancipation followed by increasing racial tension and bitterness. The Commission, weighing de Tocqueville's alternatives, found them wanting in mid-twentieth century and

pointed to the existence of a much more complex range of
problems and potentials than the French visitor had anticipated. With prescience, the Commission distinguished between
the prohibitions facing the Negro in the South and the inequities challenging him in the North. To the Commission,
the hundred years since emancipation were but the commencement of the ongoing responsibilities facing the nation.

DOCUMENT 85

The Task Ahead*

. . . Tocqueville was correct in his assessment. Slavery pre-
cipitated civil war, but it was a war fought between North and
South, not between Negro and white. He also was correct in
his judgment that emancipation was not a panacea—its immediate effect was to intensify prejudice, and to bring the
Negro a freedom more fictional than real. To the end of the
19th century and well into the 20th, the legally-free Negro
citizen was denied the franchise, excluded from public office,
assigned to inferior and separate schools, herded into ghettos,
directed to the back of the bus, treated unequally in the
courts of justice, and segregated in his illness, his worship, and
even in his death.

Up to this point in time and history, Tocqueville's predic-
tions were confirmed. His view that whites and Negroes could
exist together on the American continent only as masters and
slaves or as armed combatants seemed confirmed by failure of
the United States to pass its first major post-Emancipation test
—the reconciliation of the two races in the Reconstruction era.
By the time that emancipation had been achieved, the venom
of racism had so infected the body politic that the Government had become incapable of enforcing the new civil rights
legislation. Moreover, the gap in Federal enforcement had only
in rare instances been filled by the States. This was the long,
dark night for civil rights in America, a period in which the
American people refused to commit themselves to the principle of equal protection under the law.

---

* *Freedom to the Free*, February 12, 1963 (A Report to the
President by the United States Commission on Civil Rights [Wash-
ington, D.C.: U.S. Government Printing Office, 1963], pp. 201–07).

Yet if Tocqueville was accurate in predicting that slavery would precipitate armed conflict, he was wrong in his judgment that the only alternative to slavery was the "extirpation" of either race. Not only have both white and Negro survived; they have shown a remarkable capacity to work together for their common benefit. A significant factor in creating this capacity has been the Negro's demonstrated ability to rise from slavery and become an educated contributor to himself and the community.

The first decades of the 20th century saw profound social and economic changes that were to have a significant impact on the struggle for equal rights. The migration of the Negro from farm to city, and from South to North presented him with new opportunities but it also confronted him with new problems. In an atmosphere of indifference or even hostility, the Negro assumed a greater part of the burden in the struggle for equal rights. He formed his own private organizations to champion the cause of civil rights; he sought higher education and entered the professions; he used the political process as a tool for the achievement of economic and social gains; and he fought for his country on foreign shores. Yet the presence of qualified Negroes in ever increasing numbers often only heightened the unwillingness of many Americans to grant the Negro that equality to which the law said he was entitled, and which the Negro increasingly asserted he deserved.

Important gains were wrought out of the crucibles of depression and world war with government support for private initiative, but they did little more than set the stage for more insistent demands by a minority group which had been called upon for equal sacrifice, but had continued to receive unequal rewards.

Another major factor in the reawakening of Americans to an interest in civil rights has been the Nation's profound involvement in international affairs and the realization that America's prestige in a world torn between ideologies often rests heavily on its performance in living up to its avowed principles of democracy. This new external pressure has brought about a searching reconsideration of the meaning of the Declaration of Independence and the Bill of Rights.

America's new position of world leadership has encouraged action by private groups and government at all levels. It has similarly heightened the interest of the American business community in the condition of the Negro. The interest has been expressed in several divergent ways. One involves the potential of the Negro as buyer to generate a substantial increase in consumption of goods and services.

The business community is also conscious of the studies which show that slum sections of the city yield only about six percent of its total tax receipts but absorb about 45 percent of the total cost of municipal services. And the businessman is growing increasingly aware that refusal to hire qualified Negroes for positions of responsibility is a waste of manpower resources and talent.

As the century following emancipation draws to a close, more forces are working for the realization of civil rights for all Americans than ever before in history. Government is active in every branch and at every level, if not in every region. Voluntary associations in the field have multiplied at such a rate that it is difficult to catalog them. In this swirl of social change, a new pattern is emerging. While it does not reveal solutions to the problems it poses, it offers an increasingly clear portrait of the differing character of civil rights problems which must be met in different regions of the country.

In the South, the problem may be characterized generally as resistance to the established law of the land and to social change. The irresistible force is moving the object which was thought to be immovable; progress is slow and often painful, but it is steady and it appears to be inevitable. In the North, the issue is not one of resistance to law. It is here that segregation and discrimination are usually *de facto* rather than *de jure*, and it is here that the last battle for equal rights may be fought in America. The "gentlemen's agreement" that bars the minority citizen from housing outside the ghetto; the employment practices that often hold him in a menial status, regardless of his capabilities; and the overburdened neighborhood schools, which deprive him of an adequate education, despite his ambitions—these are the subtler forms of denial and the more difficult to eliminate.

Beyond these factors, which are largely ones of public attitude, there is the increasing problem of physical change. The minority person has been anxious to flee the confines of rural life for the promise of the city. In the rural areas, change often comes slowly and customs may linger beyond their validity.

The city, by contrast, provides a climate for the generation and acceptance of new ideas. Yet contemporary history has demonstrated that the growing city becomes a significant menace to minority rights when its physical facilities, public services, and private opportunities fall behind the demands generated by the population.

As a city dweller, the Negro seemingly should gain from efforts to replace dilapidated housing and neighborhoods, to achieve efficient transportation systems, and to make the city a center of community and culture. Instead such projects have often exacerbated the problems of minority residents. The fixing of highway routes and selection of sites for large-scale housing projects, parks, and civic centers historically follow the path of least resistance. This path frequently leads across the depressed neighborhood of the minority person. When old housing is eliminated without providing adequate replacement units for its residents, the result is more overcrowding of the remaining minority neighborhoods. And there, because of the custom of assigning pupils to the schools in the neighborhoods in which they live, the minority child receives an inferior education in a crowded and segregated school.

Thus one paradox gives rise to another. The Negro suffers from the denial of his rights in the rural area because it refuses to change. He suffers from denials in the city because it must change. In the South, he has struggled to get into the neighborhood school. In the North, he is fighting to get out of it. While he seeks and has largely found identification with the mainstream of American life, he has suffered more than others from its occupational and technological dislocations.

As a Nation, we have solved Tocqueville's paradox of a free society's dependence upon a system of slavery. In doing so, we have been presented with new paradoxes for which we have not yet evolved solutions. We have come a far journey from a distant era in the 100 years since the Emancipation Proclamation. At the beginning of it, there was slavery. At the end there is citizenship. Citizenship, however, is a fragile word with an ambivalent meaning. The condition of citizenship is not yet full-blown or fully realized for the American Negro. There is still more ground to cover.

The final chapter in the struggle for equality has yet to be written.

MARTIN LUTHER KING, JR.: LETTER FROM A BIRMINGHAM JAIL (1963)

Dissatisfied with the status of the Negro one hundred years after emancipation, Martin Luther King's Southern Christian Leadership Conference, with its commitment to direct, nonviolent action, decided upon the bold stroke of attacking segregation in its most prominent fortress—Birmingham, Alabama. Carefully laid plans led to the opening of the campaign on April 3, 1963, the day after the city's municipal elections. The civil rights movement underwent a dramatic transition as the nation watched the dignity of protest and the brutality of segregationist retaliation in Birmingham.

Working in conjunction with civil rights leaders in Birmingham, King coordinated an overall campaign designed to attack segregation by the use of sit-ins, picketing, demonstrations, and rallies. Led by Eugene "Bull" Connor, the city responded with mass arrests, and the use of police dogs, nightsticks, and high-pressure fire hoses. On April 12, Dr. King defied a local judge's injunction to bar Negro protest marches, and was promptly arrested and jailed.

With the issues sharply drawn before the eyes of the nation, eight leading white clergymen in Birmingham—Catholic, Protestant, and Jewish—openly denounced King as an outside agitator and advised Birmingham Negroes to withdraw their support of his crusade. King replied with his "Letter"—an authentic American classic in its own time.

He denied that anyone could be classified as an "outsider" when injustice was being visited upon human beings. He explained the tactics of nonviolent, direct action, its need and justification in Birmingham, and the degree of love, courage, and self-sacrifice that must characterize its implementation. He lamented the failure of southern moderates and churchmen to rectify a situation of continuing injustice.

The direct confrontation between the Negro protest movement and southern resistance, with the entire nation as witness, had been consummated—just as King had hoped it would be.

DOCUMENT 86

Letter from Birmingham Jail*

April 16, 1963

My Dear Fellow Clergymen:

While confined here in the Birmingham city jail, I came across your recent statement calling my present activities "unwise and untimely." Seldom do I pause to answer criticism of my work and ideas. If I sought to answer all the criticisms that cross my desk, my secretaries would have little time for anything other than such correspondence in the course of the day, and I would have no time for constructive work. But since I feel that you are men of genuine good will and that your criticisms are sincerely set forth, I want to try to answer your statement in what I hope will be patient and reasonable terms.

I think I should indicate why I am here in Birmingham, since you have been influenced by the view which argues against "outsiders coming in." I have the honor of serving as president of the Southern Christian Leadership Conference, an organization operating in every southern state, with headquarters in Atlanta, Georgia. We have some eighty-five affiliated organizations across the South, and one of them is the Alabama Christian Movement for Human Rights. Frequently we share staff, educational and financial resources with our affiliates. Several months ago the affiliate here in Birmingham asked us to be on call to engage in a nonviolent direct-action program if such were deemed necessary. We readily consented, and when the hour came we lived up to our promise. So I, along with several members of my staff, am here because I was invited here. I am here because I have organizational ties here.

But more basically, I am in Birmingham because injustice is here. Just as the prophets of the eighth century B.C. left their villages and carried their "thus saith the Lord" far beyond the boundaries of their home towns, and just as the Apostle Paul left his village of Tarsus and carried the gospel of Jesus Christ

---

* Martin Luther King, Jr., *Why We Can't Wait* (New York: Harper & Row, 1964), pp. 77–100. Copyright, ©, 1963, by Martin Luther King, Jr. Abridgment reprinted by permission of Harper & Row, Publishers.

to the far corners of the Greco-Roman world, so am I compelled to carry the gospel of freedom beyond my own home town. Like Paul, I must constantly respond to the Macedonian call for aid.

Moreover, I am cognizant of the interrelatedness of all communities and states. I cannot sit idly by in Atlanta and not be concerned about what happens in Birmingham. Injustice anywhere is a threat to justice everywhere. We are caught in an inescapable network of mutuality, tied in a single garment of destiny. Whatever affects one directly, affects all indirectly. Never again can we afford to live with the narrow, provincial "outside agitator" idea. Anyone who lives inside the United States can never be considered an outsider anywhere within its bounds.

You deplore the demonstrations taking place in Birmingham. But your statement, I am sorry to say, fails to express a similar concern for the conditions that brought about the demonstrations. I am sure that none of you would want to rest content with the superficial kind of social analysis that deals merely with effects and does not grapple with underlying causes. It is unfortunate that demonstrations are taking place in Birmingham, but it is even more unfortunate that the city's white power structure left the Negro community with no alternative.

In any nonviolent campaign there are four basic steps: collection of the facts to determine whether injustices exist; negotiation; self-purification; and direct action. We have gone through all these steps in Birmingham. There can be no gainsaying the fact that racial injustice engulfs this community. Birmingham is probably the most thoroughly segregated city in the United States. Its ugly record of brutality is widely known. Negroes have experienced grossly unjust treatment in the courts. There have been more unsolved bombings of Negro homes and churches in Birmingham than in any other city in the nation. These are the hard, brutal facts of the case. On the basis of these conditions, Negro leaders sought to negotiate with the city fathers. But the latter consistently refused to engage in good-faith negotiation.

. . . .

You may well ask: "Why direct action? Why sit-ins, marches and so forth? Isn't negotiation a better path?" You are quite right in calling for negotiation. Indeed, this is the very purpose of direct action. Nonviolent direct action seeks to create such a crisis and foster such a tension that a community which has constantly refused to negotiate is forced to confront the issue. It seeks so to dramatize the issue that it can no longer be ignored. My citing the creation of tension as part of the work of the nonviolent-resister may sound rather shocking. But I must confess that I am not afraid of the word "tension." I have earnestly opposed violent tension, but there is a type of constructive, nonviolent tension which is necessary for growth. Just as Socrates felt that it was necessary to create a tension in the mind so that individuals could rise from the bondage of myths and half-truths to the unfettered realm of creative analysis and objective appraisal, so must we see the need for non-violent gadflies to create the kind of tension in society that will help men rise from the dark depths of prejudice and racism to the majestic heights of understanding and brotherhood.

The purpose of our direct-action program is to create a situation so crisis-packed that it will inevitably open the door to negotiation. I therefore concur with you in your call for negotiation. Too long has our beloved Southland been bogged down in a tragic effort to live in monologue rather than dialogue.

• • • •

We have waited for more than 340 years for our constitutional and God-given rights. The nations of Asia and Africa are moving with jetlike speed toward gaining political independence, but we still creep at horse-and-buggy pace toward gaining a cup of coffee at a lunch counter. Perhaps it is easy for those who have never felt the stinging darts of segregation to say, "Wait." But when you have seen vicious mobs lynch your mothers and fathers at will and drown your sisters and brothers at whim; when you have seen hate-filled policemen curse, kick and even kill your black brothers and sisters; when you see the vast majority of your twenty million Negro brothers smothering in an airtight cage of poverty in the midst of an affluent society; when you suddenly find your tongue twisted and your speech stammering as you seek to explain to your six-year-old daughter why she can't go to the public amusement park that has just been advertised on television, and see tears welling up in her eyes when she is told that Funtown is closed to colored children, and see ominous clouds of inferiority beginning to form in her little mental sky, and see her beginning to distort her personality by developing an unconscious bitterness toward white people; when you have to concoct an answer for a five-year-old son who is asking: "Daddy, why do white people treat colored people so mean?"; when you take a cross-country drive and find it necessary to sleep night after night in the uncomfortable corners of your automobile because no motel will accept you; when you are humiliated day in and day out by nagging signs reading "white" and "colored"; when your first name becomes "nigger," your middle name becomes "boy" (however old you are) and your last name becomes "John," and your wife and mother are never given the respected title "Mrs."; when you are harried by day and haunted by night by the fact that you are a Negro, living constantly at tiptoe stance, never quite knowing what to expect next, and are plagued with inner fears and outer resentments; when you are forever fighting a degenerating sense of "nobodiness"—then you will understand why we find it difficult to wait. There comes a time when the cup of endurance runs over, and men are no longer willing to be plunged into the abyss of despair. I hope, sirs, you can understand our legitimate and unavoidable impatience.

. . . .

I must make two honest confessions to you, my Christian and Jewish brothers. First, I must confess that over the past few years I have been gravely disappointed with the white moderate. I have almost reached the regrettable conclusion that the Negro's great stumbling block in his stride toward freedom is not the White Citizen's Counciler or the Ku Klux Klanner, but the white moderate, who is more devoted to "order" than to justice; who prefers a negative peace which is the absence of tension to a positive peace which is the presence of justice; who constantly says: "I agree with you in the goal you seek, but I cannot agree with your methods of direct action"; who paternalistically believes he can set the timetable for another man's freedom; who lives by a mythical concept of time and who constantly advises the Negro to wait for a "more convenient season." Shallow understanding from people of good will is more frustrating than absolute misunderstanding from people of ill will. Lukewarm acceptance is much more bewildering than outright rejection.

I had hoped that the white moderate would understand that law and order exist for the purpose of establishing justice and that when they fail in this purpose they become the dangerously structured dams that block the flow of social progress. I had hoped that the white moderate would understand that the present tension in the South is a necessary phase of the transition from an obnoxious negative peace, in which the Negro passively accepted his unjust plight, to a substantive and positive peace, in which all men will respect the dignity and worth of human personality. Actually, we who engage in nonviolent direct action are not the creators of tension. We merely bring to the surface the hidden tension that is already alive. We bring it out in the open, where it can be seen and dealt with. Like a boil that can never be cured so long as it is covered up but must be opened with all its ugliness to the natural medicines of air and light, injustice must be exposed, with all the tension its exposure creates, to the light of human conscience and the air of national opinion before it can be cured.

. . . .

Oppressed people cannot remain oppressed forever. The yearning for freedom eventually manifests itself, and that is what has happened to the American Negro. Something within has reminded him of his birthright of freedom, and something without has reminded him that it can be gained. Consciously or unconsciously, he has been caught up by the *Zeitgeist*, and with his black brothers of Africa and his brown and yellow brothers of Asia, South America and the Caribbean, the United States Negro is moving with a sense of great urgency toward the promised land of racial justice. If one recognizes this vital urge that has engulfed the Negro community, one should readily understand why public demonstrations are taking place. The Negro has many pent-up resentments and latent frustrations, and he must release them. So let him march; let him make prayer pilgrimages to the city hall; let him go on freedom rides—and try to understand why he must do so. If his repressed emotions are not released in nonviolent ways, they will seek expression through violence; this is not a threat but a fact of history. So I have not said to my people: "Get rid of your discontent." Rather, I have tried to say that this normal and healthy discontent can be channeled into the creative outlet of nonviolent direct action. And now this approach is being termed extremist.

. . . .

Let me take note of my other major disappointment. I have been so greatly disappointed with the white church and its leadership. Of course, there are some notable exceptions. I am not unmindful of the fact that each of you has taken some significant stands on this issue. I commend you, Reverend Stallings, for your Christian stand on this past Sunday, in welcoming Negroes to your worship service on a nonsegregated basis. I commend the Catholic leaders of this state for integrating Spring Hill College several years ago.

But despite these notable exceptions, I must honestly reiterate that I have been disappointed with the church. I do not say this as one of those negative critics who can always find something wrong with the church. I say this as a minister of the gospel, who loves the church; who was nurtured in its bosom; who has been sustained by its spiritual blessings and who will remain true to it as long as the cord of life shall lengthen.

When I was suddenly catapulted into the leadership of the bus protest in Montgomery, Alabama, a few years ago, I felt we would be supported by the white church. I felt that the white ministers, priests and rabbis of the South would be among our strongest allies. Instead, some have been outright opponents, refusing to understand the freedom movement and misrepresenting its leaders; all too many others have been more cautious than courageous and have remained silent behind the anesthetizing security of stained-glass windows.

In spite of my shattered dreams, I came to Birmingham with the hope that the white religious leadership of this community would see the justice of our cause and, with deep moral concern, would serve as the channel through which our just grievances could reach the power structure. I had hoped that each of you would understand. But again I have been disappointed.

I have heard numerous southern religious leaders admonish their worshipers to comply with a desegregation decision because it is the law, but I have longed to hear white ministers declare: "Follow this decree because integration is morally right and because the Negro is your brother." In the midst of blatant injustices inflicted upon the Negro, I have watched white churchmen stand on the sideline and mouth pious irrelevancies and sanctimonious trivialities. In the midst of a mighty struggle to rid our nation of racial and economic injustice, I have heard many ministers say: "Those are social issues, with which the gospel has no real concern." And I have watched many churches commit themselves to a completely otherworldly religion which makes a strange, un-Biblical distinction between body and soul, between the sacred and the secular.

. . . .

Before closing I feel impelled to mention one other point in your statement that has troubled me profoundly. You warmly commended the Birmingham police force for keeping "order" and "preventing violence." I doubt that you would have so warmly commended the police force if you had seen its dogs sinking their teeth into unarmed, nonviolent Negroes. I doubt that you would so quickly commend the policemen if you were to observe their ugly and inhumane treatment of Negroes here in the city jail; if you were to watch them push and curse old Negro women and young Negro girls; if you were to see them slap and kick old Negro men and young boys; if you were to observe them, as they did on two occasions, refuse to give us food because we wanted to sing our grace together. I cannot join you in your praise of the Birmingham police department.

It is true that the police have exercised a degree of discipline in handling the demonstrators. In this sense they have conducted themselves rather "nonviolently" in public. But for what purpose? To preserve the evil system of segregation. Over the past few years I have consistently preached that nonviolence demands that the means we use must be as pure as the ends we seek. I have tried to make clear that it is wrong to use immoral means to attain moral ends. But now I must affirm that it is just as wrong, or perhaps even more so, to use moral means to preserve immoral ends. Perhaps Mr. Connor and his policemen have been rather nonviolent in public, as was Chief Pritchett in Albany, Georgia, but they have used the moral means of nonviolence to maintain the immoral end of racial injustice. As T. S. Eliot has said: "The last temptation is the greatest treason: To do the right deed for the wrong reason."

. . . .

Never before have I written so long a letter. I'm afraid it is much too long to take your precious time. I can assure you that it would have been much shorter if I had been writing from a comfortable desk, but what else can one do when he is alone in a narrow jail cell, other than write long letters, think long thoughts and pray long prayers?

If I have said anything in this letter that overstates the truth and indicates an unreasonable impatience, I beg you to forgive me. If I have said anything that understates the truth and indicates my having a patience that allows me to settle for anything less than brotherhood, I beg God to forgive me.

I hope this letter finds you strong in the faith. I also hope that circumstances will soon make it possible for me to meet each of you, not as an integrationist or a civil-rights leader but as a fellow clergyman and a Christian brother. Let us all hope that the dark clouds of racial prejudice will soon pass away and the deep fog of misunderstanding will be lifted from our fear-drenched communities, and in some not too distant tomorrow the radiant stars of love and brotherhood will shine over our great nation with all their scintillating beauty.

Yours for the cause of Peace and Brotherhood,
MARTIN LUTHER KING, JR.

THE SIT-IN CASES (1961–1964)

Ten days prior to the passage of the Civil Rights Act of 1964 (Document 89), the Supreme Court spoke for the third time on the sit-in problem. The first time had been in 1961, when the principal statement was made in *Garner* v. *Louisiana*, 368 U.S. 157, a case which set aside sit-in convictions based on breach of the peace statutes. In 1963, in the principal case of *Peterson* v. *Greenville*, 373 U.S. 244, the Supreme Court had reversed sit-in convictions based on criminal trespass statutes. In 1964, the Court considered criminal trespass statutes once more in the principal case of *Bell* v. *Maryland*.

Before the Supreme Court was a vital question of constitutional law, one which Justice William O. Douglas termed "the basic issue of the right of public accommodation under the Fourteenth Amendment." In this respect, Justice Hugo L. Black agreed. He described the crucial, ultimate issue as "whether the Fourteenth Amendment, of itself, forbids a state to enforce its trespass laws to convict a person who comes into a privately owned restaurant, is told that because of his color he will not be served, and over the owner's protest refuses to leave."

Only four members of the Court voted to decide this ultimate issue. One was Justice Douglas who voted "to reverse the judgments of conviction outright." Justices Black, John Marshall Harlan, and Byron R. White also asserted that a decision be reached on the ultimate question. They voted, however, to affirm the convictions. In their view the Fourteenth Amendment does not forbid trespass convictions against sit-ins.

Justice Arthur J. Goldberg, speaking for himself and Chief Justice Earl Warren, declared that the basic issue should not be considered by the Court. Then he added these words: "Since, however, the dissent [of Justices Black, Harlan, and White] at length discusses this constitutional issue and reaches a conclusion with which I profoundly disagree, I am impelled to state the reasons for my conviction that the constitution guarantees to all Americans the right to be treated as equal members of the community with respect to public accommodations." However, Justice Goldberg and Chief Justice Warren voted to concur with the official opinion of the Court.

Delivering the Court's opinion, Justice William J. Brennan, Jr. pointed out that Baltimore had enacted a public accommodations ordinance subsequent to the sit-ins. Thus, under Maryland law at the time of decision, the refusal of a Negro to leave a so-called white restaurant would not constitute a crime. Accordingly, the case was remanded to the state court to consider the effect of the ordinance on the convictions.

The case is far more important for what was said rather than for what was done. While the final answer has yet to be judicially determined, the battle lines have been drawn.

Other Supreme Court cases which considered convictions for sit-ins and demonstrations were *Edwards* v. *South Caro-*

lina, 372 U.S. 229 (1963); *Cox* v. *Louisiana,* 379 U.S. 536
(1965); *Brown* v. *Louisiana,* 383 U.S. 131 (1966); and *Adderly* v. *Florida,* 385 U.S. 39 (1966).

DOCUMENT 87

*Bell v. Maryland**

Mr. Justice Brennan delivered the opinion of the Court.

Petitioners, 12 Negro students, were convicted in a Maryland state court as a result of their participation in a "sit-in" demonstration at Hooper's restaurant in the City of Baltimore in 1960. The convictions were based on a record showing in summary that a group of 15 to 20 Negro students, including petitioners, went to Hooper's restaurant to engage in what their counsel describes as a "sit-in protest" because the restaurant would not serve Negroes. The "hostess," on orders of Mr. Hooper, the president of the corporation owning the restaurant, told them, "solely on the basis of their color," that they would not be served. Petitioners did not leave when requested to by the hostess and the manager; instead they went to tables, took seats, and refused to leave, insisting that they be served. On orders of Mr. Hooper the police were called, but they advised that a warrant would be necessary before they could arrest petitioners. Mr. Hooper then went to the police station and swore out warrants, and petitioners were accordingly arrested.

The statute under which the convictions were obtained was the Maryland criminal trespass law, § 577 of Art. 27 of the Maryland Code, 1957 edition, under which it is a misdemeanor to "enter upon or cross over the land, premises or private property of any person or persons in this State after having been duly notified by the owner or his agent not to do so." The convictions were affirmed by the Maryland Court of Appeals, 227 Md. 302, 176 A. 2d 771 (1962), and we granted certiorari. 374 U.S. 805.

We do not reach the questions that have been argued under the Equal Protection and Due Process Clauses of the Fourteenth Amendment. It appears that a significant change has

---

* Supreme Court of the United States, 378 U.S. 226 (1964).

taken place in the applicable law of Maryland since these convictions were affirmed by the Court of Appeals. Under this Court's settled practice in such circumstances, the judgments must consequently be vacated and reversed and the case remanded so that the state court may consider the effect of the supervening change in state law.

Petitioners' convictions were affirmed by the Maryland Court of Appeals on January 9, 1962. Since that date, Maryland has enacted laws that abolish the crime of which petitioners were convicted. These laws accord petitioners a right to be served in Hooper's restaurant, and make unlawful conduct like that of Hooper's president and hostess in refusing them service because of their race. On June 8, 1962, the City of Baltimore enacted its Ordinance No. 1249, adding § 10A to Art. 14A of the Batlimore City Code (1950 ed.) The ordinance, which by its terms took effect from the date of its enactment, prohibits owners and operators of Baltimore places of public accommodation, including resaturants, from denying their services or facilities to any person because of his race. A similar "public accommodations law," applicable to Baltimore City and Baltimore County though not to some of the State's other counties, was adopted by the State Legislature on March 29, 1963. Art. 49B Md. Code § 11 (1963 Supp.). This statute went into effect on June 1, 1963, as provided by § 4 of the Act, Acts 1963, c. 227. The statute provides that:

It is unlawful for an owner or operator of a place of public accommodation or an agent or employee of said owner or operator, because of the race, creed, color, or national origin of any person, to refuse, withhold from, or deny to such person any of the accommodations, advantages, facilities and privileges of such place of public accommodation. For the purpose of this subtitle, a place of public accommodation means any hotel, restaurant, inn, motel or an establishment commonly known or recognized as regularly engaged in the business of providing sleeping accommodations, or serving food, or both, for a consideration, and which is open to the general public . . . .

It is clear from these enactments that petitioners' conduct in entering or crossing over the premises of Hooper's restaurant after being notified not to do so because of their race would not be a crime today; on the contrary, the law of Baltimore and of Maryland now vindicates their conduct and recognizes it as the exercise of a right, directing the law's prohibition not at them but at the restaurant owner or manager who seeks to deny them service because of their race.

An examination of Maryland decisions indicates that under the common law of Maryland, the supervening enactment of these statutes abolishing the crime for which petitioners were convicted would cause the Maryland Court of Appeals at this time to reverse the convictions and order the indictments dismissed. . . .

It is not for us, however, to decide this question of Maryland law, or to reach a conclusion as to how the Maryland Court of Appeals would decide it. Such a course would be inconsistent with our tradition of deference to state courts on questions of state law. Nor is it for us to ignore the supervening change in state law and proceed to decide the federal constitutional questions presented by this case. To do so would be to decide questions which, because of the possibility that the state court would now reverse the convictions, are not necessarily presented for decision. Such a course would be inconsistent with our constitutional inability to render advisory opinions, and with our consequent policy of refusing to decide a federal question in a case that might be controlled by a state ground of decision. See *Murdock* v. *Memphis*, 20 Wall. 590, 634–636. To avoid these pitfalls—to let issues of state law be decided by state courts and to preserve our policy of avoiding gratuitous decisions of federal questions—we have long followed a uniform practice where a supervening event raises a question of state law pertaining to a case pending on review here. That practice is to vacate and reverse the judgment and remand the case to the state court, so that it may reconsider it in the light of the supervening change in state law.

The rule was authoritatively stated and applied in *Missouri ex rel. Wabash R. Co.* v. *Public Service Comm'n*, 273 U.S. 126, a case where the supervening event was—as it is here—enactment of new state legislation asserted to change the law under which the case had been decided by the highest state court. . . .

Accordingly, the judgment of the Maryland Court of Appeals should be vacated and the case remanded to that court, and to this end the judgment is

Reversed and remanded.

Mr. Justice Douglas, with whom Mr. Justice Goldberg concurs as respects Parts II–V, for reversing and directing dismissal of the indictment.

I

I reach the merits of this controversy. The issue is ripe for decision and petitioners, who have been convicted of asking for service in Hooper's restaurant, are entitled to an answer to their complaint here and now.

On this the last day of the Term, we studiously avoid decision of the basic issue of the right of public accommodation under the Fourteenth Amendment, remanding the case to the state court for reconsideration in light of an issue of state law.

This case was argued October 14 and 15, 1963—over eight months ago. The record of the case is simple, the constitutional guidelines well marked, the precedents marshalled. Though the Court is divided, the preparation of opinions laying bare the differences does not require even two months, let alone eight. Moreover, a majority reach the merits of the issue. Why then should a minority prevent a resolution of the differing views? . . .

The whole Nation has to face the issue; Congress is conscientiously considering it; some municipalities have had to make it their first order of concern; law enforcement officials are deeply implicated, North as well as South; the question is at the root of demonstrations, unrest, riots, and violence in various areas. The issue in other words consumes the public attention. Yet we stand mute, avoiding decision of the basic issue by an obvious pretense.

The clash between Negro customers and white restaurant owners is clear; each group claims protection by the Constitution and tenders the Fourteenth Amendment as justification for its action. Yet we leave resolution of the conflict to others, when, if our voice were heard, the issues for the Congress and for the public would become clear and precise. The Court was created to sit in troubled times as well as in peaceful days.

. . . .

II

The issue in this case, according to those who would affirm, is whether a person's "personal prejudices" may dictate the way in which he uses his property and whether he can enlist the aid of the State to enforce those "personal prejudices." With all respect, that is not the real issue. The corporation that owns this restaurant did not refuse service to these Negroes because "it" did not like Negroes. The reason "it" refused service was because "it" thought "it" could make more money by running a segregated restaurant. . . .

Here, as in most of the sit-in cases before us, the refusal of service did not reflect "personal prejudices" but business reasons. Were we today to hold that segregated restaurants, whose racial policies were enforced by a State, violated the Equal Protection Clause, all restaurants would be on an equal footing and the reasons given in this and most of the companion cases for refusing service to Negroes would evaporate. Moreover, when corporate restaurateurs are involved, whose "personal prejudices" are being protected? The stockholders'? The directors'? The officers'? The managers'? The truth is, I think, that the corporate interest is in making money, not in protecting "personal prejudices."

III . . .

I now assume that the issue is the one stated by those who would affirm. The case in that posture deals with a relic of slavery—an institution that has cast a long shadow across the land, resulting today in a second-class citizenship in this area of public accommodations.

. . . .

The Black Codes were a substitute for slavery; segregation was a substitute for the Black Codes; the discrimination in these sit-in cases is a relic of slavery. . . .

When one citizen because of his race, creed, or color is denied the privilege of being treated as any other citizen in places of public accommodation, we have classes of citizenship, one being more degrading than the other. That is at war with the one class of citizenship created by the Thirteenth, Fourteenth, and Fifteenth Amendments. . . .

IV

The problem in this case, and in the other sit-in cases before us, is presented as though it involved the situation of "a private operator conducting his own business on his own premises and exercising his own judgment" as to whom he will admit to the premises.

The property involved is not, however, a man's home or his yard or even his fields. Private property is involved, but it is property that is serving the public. As my Brother GOLDBERG says, it is a "civil" right, not a "social" right, with which we deal. Here it is a restaurant refusing service to a Negro. But so far as principle and law are concerned it might just as well be a hospital refusing admission to a sick or injured Negro . . . or a drugstore refusing antibiotics to a Negro, or a bus denying transportation to a Negro, or a telephone company refusing to install a telephone in a Negro's home.

The problem with which we deal has no relation to opening or closing the door of one's home. The home of course is the essence of privacy, in no way dedicated to public use, in no way extending an invitation to the public. Some businesses, like the classical country store where the owner lives overhead or in the rear, make the store an extension, so to speak, of the home. But such is not this case. The facts of these sit-in cases have little resemblance to any institution of property which we customarily associate with privacy.

. . . .

There is no specific provision in the Constitution which protects rights of privacy and enables restaurant owners to refuse service to Negroes. The word "property" is, indeed, not often used in the Constitution, though as a matter of experience and practice we are committed to free enterprise. . . .

Apartheid, however, is barred by the common law as respects innkeepers and common carriers. There were, to be sure, criminal statutes that regulated the common callings. But the civil remedies were made by judges who had no written constitution. We, on the other hand, live under a constitution that proclaims equal protection under the law. Why then, even in the absence of a statute, should *apartheid* be given constitutional sanction in the restaurant field? . . . The duty of common carriers to carry all, regardless of race, creed, or color, was in part the product of the inventive genius of judges. See *Lombard* v. *Louisiana*, 373 U.S., at 275–277. We should make that body of law the common law of the Thirteenth and Fourteenth Amendments so to speak. Restaurants in the modern setting are as essential to travelers as inns and carriers. . . .

V . . .

State judicial action is as clearly "state" action as state administrative action. Indeed, we held in *Shelley* v. *Kraemer*, 334 U.S. 1, 20, that "State action, as that phrase is understood for the purposes of the Fourteenth Amendment, refers to exertions of state power in all forms."

. . . .

I would reverse these judgments of conviction outright, as these Negroes in asking for service in Hooper's restaurant were only demanding what was their constitutional right.

MR. JUSTICE GOLDBERG, with whom THE CHIEF JUSTICE joins, and with whom MR. JUSTICE DOUGLAS joins as to Parts II–V, concurring.

I

I join in the opinion and the judgment of the Court and would therefore have no occasion under ordinary circumstances to express my views on the underlying constitutional issue. Since, however, the dissent at length discusses this constitutional issue and reaches a conclusion with which I profoundly disagree, I am impelled to state the reasons for my conviction that the Constitution guarantees to all Americans the right to be treated as equal members of the community wih respect to public accommodations.

II . . .

The dissent argues that the Constitution permits American citizens to be denied access to places of public accommodation solely because of their race or color. Such a view does not do justice to a Constitution which is color blind and to the Court's decision in *Brown* v. *Board of Education*, which affirmed the right of all Americans to public equality. We cannot blind ourselves to the consequences of a constitutional interpretation which would permit citizens to be turned away by all the restaurants, or by the only restaurant, in town. The denial of the constitutional right of Negroes to access to places of public accommodation would perpetuate a caste system in the United States.

The Thirteenth, Fourteenth and Fifteenth Amendments do not permit Negroes to be considered as second-class citizens in any aspect of our public life. . . .

III . . .

The historical evidence amply supports the conclusion of the Government, stated by the Solicitor General in this Court, that:

it is an inescapable inference that Congress, in recommending the Fourteenth Amendment, expected to remove the disabilities barring Negroes from the public conveyances and places of public accommodation with which they were familiar, and thus to assure Negroes an equal right to enjoy these aspects of the public life of the community.

The first sentence of § 1 of the Fourteenth Amendment, the spirit of which pervades all the Civil War Amendments, was obviously designed to overrule *Dred Scott* v. *Sandford*, 19 How. 393, and to ensure that the constitutional concept of citizenship with all attendant rights and privileges would henceforth embrace Negroes. It follows that Negroes as citizens necessarily became entitled to share the right, customarily possessed by other citizens, of access to public accommodations. The history of the affirmative obligations existing at common law serves partly to explain the negative—"deny to any person"—language of the Fourteenth Amendment. For it was assumed that under state law, when the Negro's disability as a citizen was removed, he would be assured the same public civil rights that the law had guaranteed white persons. . . .

In the present case the responsibility of the judiciary in applying the principles of the Fourteenth Amendment is clear. The State of Maryland has failed to protect petitioners' constitutional right to public accommodations and is now prosecuting them for attempting to exercise that right. The decision of Maryland's highest court in sustaining these trespass convictions cannot be described as "neutral," for the decision is as affirmative in effect as if the State had enacted an unconstitutional law explicitly authorizing racial discrimination in places of public accommodation. A State, obligated under the Fourteenth Amendment to maintain a system of law in which Negroes are not denied protection in their claim to be treated as equal members of the community, may not use its criminal trespass laws to frustrate the constitutionally granted right. Nor, it should be added, may a State frustrate this right by legitimating a proprietor's attempt at self-help. To permit self-help would be to disregard the principle that "[t]oday, no less than 50 years ago, the solution to the problems growing out of race relations 'cannot be promoted by depriving citizens of their constitutional rights and privileges,' *Buchanan* v. *Warley* . . . 245 U.S., at 80–81." *Watson* v. *City of Memphis,* 373 U.S. 526, 539. As declared in *Cooper* v. *Aaron,* 358 U.S. 1, 16, "law and order are not . . . to be preserved by depriving the Negro . . . of [his] constitutional rights." . . .

IV

My Brother DOUGLAS convincingly demonstrates that the dissent has constructed a straw man by suggesting that this case involves "a property owner's right to choose his social or business associates." . . .

V

In my view the historical evidence demonstrates that the traditional rights of access to places of public accommodation were quite familiar to Congressmen and to the general public who naturally assumed that the Fourteenth Amendment extended these traditional rights to Negroes. But even if the historical evidence were not as convincing as I believe it to be, the logic of *Brown* v. *Board of Education*, 347 U.S. 483, based as it was on the fundamental principle of constitutional interpretation proclaimed by Chief Justice Marshall, requires that petitioners' claim be sustained. . . .

Mr. Justice Black, with whom Mr. Justice Harlan and Mr. Justice White join, dissenting.

This case does not involve the constitutionality of any existing or proposed state or federal legislation requiring restaurant owners to serve people without regard to color. The crucial issue which the case does present but which the Court does not decide is whether the Fourteenth Amendment, of itself, forbids a State to enforce its trespass laws to convict a person who comes into a privately owned restaurant, is told that because of his color he will not be served, and over the owner's protest refuses to leave. We dissent from the Court's refusal to decide that question. For reasons stated, we think that the question should be decided and that the Fourteenth Amendment does not forbid this application of a State's trespass laws. . . .

We agree that this Court has power, with or without deciding the constitutional questions, to remand the case for the Maryland Court of Appeals to decide the state question as to whether the convictions should be set aside and the prosecutions abated because of the new laws. But as the cases cited by the Court recognize, our question is not one of power to take this action but of whether we should. And the Maryland court would be equally free to give petitioners the benefit of any rights they have growing out of the new law whether we upheld the trespass statute and affirmed, or refused to pass upon its validity at this time. . . .

Section 1 of the Fourteenth Amendment provides in part: "No State shall . . . deprive any person of life, liberty, or property, without due process of law; nor deny to any person within its jurisdiction the equal protection of the laws." This section of the Amendment, unlike other sections, is a prohibition against certain conduct only when done by a State—"state action" as it has come to be known—and "erects no shield against merely private conduct, however discriminatory or wrongful." *Shelley* v. *Kraemer*, 334 U.S. 1, 13 (1948). . . .

Petitioners, but not the Solicitor General, contend that their conviction for trespass under the state statute was by itself the kind of discriminatory state action forbidden by the Fourteenth Amendment. This contention, on its face, has plausibility when considered along with general statements to the effect that under the Amendment forbidden "state action" may be that of the Judicial as well as of the Legislative or Executive Branch of Government. But a mechanical application of the Fourteenth Amendment to this case cannot survive analysis. The Amendment does not forbid a State to prosecute for crimes committed against a person or his property, however prejudiced or narrow the victim's views may be. Nor can whatever prejudice and bigotry the victim of a crime may have be automatically attributed to the State that prosecutes. Such a doctrine would not only be based on a fiction; it would also severely handicap a State's efforts to maintain a peaceful and orderly society. Our society has put its trust in a system of criminal laws to punish lawless conduct. To avert personal feuds and violent brawls it has led its people to believe and expect that wrongs against them will be vindicated in the courts. Instead of attempting to take the law into their own hands, people have been taught to call for police protection to protect their rights wherever possible. It would betray our whole plan for a tranquil and orderly society to say that a citizen, because of his personal prejudices, habits, attitudes, or beliefs, is cast outside the law's protection and cannot call for the aid of officers sworn to uphold the law and preserve the peace. The worst citizen no less than the best is entitled to equal protection of the laws of his State and of his Nation. None of our past cases justifies reading the Fourteenth Amendment in a way that might well penalize citizens who are law-abiding enough to call upon the law and its officers for protection instead of using their own physical strength or dangerous weapons to preserve their rights. . . .

It seems pretty clear that the reason judicial enforcement of the restrictive covenants in *Shelley* was deemed state action was not merely the fact that a state court had acted, but rather that it had acted "to deny to petitioners, on the grounds of race or color, the enjoyment of property rights in premises which petitioners are willing and financially able to acquire and which the grantors are willing to sell." 334 U.S., at 19. In other words, this Court held that state enforcement of the covenants had the effect of denying to the parties their federally guaranteed right to own, occupy, enjoy, and use their property without regard to race or color. Thus, the line of cases from *Buchanan* through *Shelley* establishes these propositions: (1) When an owner of property is willing to sell and a would-be purchaser is willing to buy, then the Civil Rights Act of 1866, which gives all persons the same right to "inherit, purchase, lease, sell, hold, and convey" property, prohibits a State, whether through its legislature, executive, or judiciary, from preventing the sale on the grounds of the race or color of one of the parties. *Shelley* v. *Kraemer, supra*, 334 U.S., at 19. (2) Once a person has become a property owner, then he acquires all the rights that go with ownership: "the free use, enjoyment, and disposal of a person's acquisitions without control or diminution save by the law of the land." *Buchanan* v. *Warley, supra*, 245 U.S., at 74. This means that the property owner may, in the absence of a valid statute forbidding it, sell his property to whom he pleases and admit to that property whom he will; so long as *both* parties are willing parties, then the principles stated in *Buchanan* and *Shelley* protect this right. But equally, when one party is unwilling, as when the property owner chooses *not* to sell to a particular person or *not* to admit that person, then, as this Court emphasized in *Buchanan*, he is entitled to rely on the guarantee of due process of law, that is, "law of the land," to protect his free use and enjoyment of property and to know that only by valid legislation, passed pursuant to some constitutional grant of power, can anyone disturb this free use. But petitioners here would have us hold that, despite the absence of any valid statute restricting the use of his property, the owner of Hooper's restaurant in Baltimore must not be accorded the same federally guaranteed right to occupy, enjoy, and use property given to the parties in *Buchanan* and *Shelley;* instead, petitioners would have us say that Hooper's federal right must be cut down and he must be compelled—though no statute said he must—to allow people to force their way into his restaurant and remain there over his protest. We cannot subscribe to such a mutilating, one-sided interpretation of federal guarantees the very heart of which is equal treatment under law to all. We must never forget that the Fourteenth Amendment protects "life, liberty, or property" of all people generally, not just some people's "life," some people's "liberty," and some kinds of "property."

. . . .

This Court has done much in carrying out its solemn duty to protect people from unlawful discrimination. And it will, of course, continue to carry out this duty in the future as it has in the past. But the Fourteenth Amendment of itself does not compel either a black man or a white man running his own private business to trade with anyone else against his will. We do not believe that Section 1 of the Fourteenth Amendment was written or designed to interfere with a storekeeper's right to choose his customers or with a property owner's right to choose his social or business associates, so long as he does not run counter to valid state or federal regulation. The case before us does not involve the power of the Congress to pass a law compelling privately owned businesses to refrain from discrimination on the basis of race and to trade with all if they trade with any. We express no views as to the power of Congress, acting under one or another provision of the Constitution, to prevent racial discrimination in the operation of privately owned business, nor upon any particular form of legislation to that end. Our sole conclusion is that Section 1 of the Fourteenth Amendment, standing alone, does not prohibit privately owned restaurants from choosing their own customers. It does not destroy what has until very recently been universally recognized in this country as the unchallenged right of a man who owns a business to run the business in his own way so long as some valid regulatory statute does not tell him to do otherwise. . . .

THE ANTIPOLL TAX AMENDMENT (1964)

For twenty-five years, civil rights leaders had sought to end the poll tax requirement in federal elections. Southern states had used this device as an instrument to disfranchise Negro voters, and even, in some instances, economically depressed white voters. Negro spokesmen and their liberal allies in the 1940's had fought for a Congressional bill outlawing the poll tax, and such a measure had been an integral part of the Truman civil rights package (Document 73). Unable in the past to get the bill beyond a southern filibuster or the threat of a filibuster in the Senate, civil rights advocates of the 1960's chose the equally uncertain path of constitutional amendment. The momentum of the civil rights movement proved sufficient to carry the measure, and the poll tax was finally eliminated in federal elections by the adoption of the Twenty-fourth Amendment, on February 5, 1964.

Two years later the Supreme Court, in *Harper* v. *Virginia Board of Elections*, 383 U.S. 663 (1966), held the poll tax unconstitutional in state elections as a violation of the equal protection clause of the Fourteenth Amendment.

DOCUMENT 88

*Twenty-Fourth Amendment**

Voter Qualifications in Federal Elections

SECTION 1. The right of citizens of the United States to vote in any primary or other election for President or Vice President, for elections for President or Vice President, or for Senator or Representative in Congress, shall not be denied or abridged by the United States or any State by reason of failure to pay any poll tax or other tax.

SECTION 2. The Congress shall have power to enforce this article by appropriate legislation.

THE CIVIL RIGHTS ACT (1964)

On July 2, 1964, Congress enacted the most comprehensive piece of civil rights legislation ever proposed. A bipartisan majority had passed the bill in the House on February 10, and the nation watched with intense fascination as the Senate made the measure its chief order of business for the next four

---

* Small, Jayson, and Corwin, eds., *The Constitution of the United States of America* (Washington, D.C.; U.S. Government Printing Office, 1964), p. 1383.

months. On June 10, supporters of the bill rallied sufficient votes to choke off the extended southern filibuster. This was the first time since 1917, when the Senate had initially adopted rules for limiting debate, that cloture was successfully invoked for a civil rights measure. Indeed, cloture had been voted only five other times, up to that point. The fact that northern Republicans were willing to abandon their traditional coalition with southern Democrats made cloture possible, and Senate Minority Leader Everett Dirksen of Illinois explained his party's action by proclaiming, "This is an idea whose time has come. It will not be stayed. It will not be denied."

The new law was structured to insure maximum rights for Negroes in as many areas of public life as possible. Separate titles touched on voting, public accommodations, public facilities, education, and fair employment practices. The powers of the Civil Rights Commission were extended, and provisions were made for the establishment of two other agencies that would facilitate the implementation of the act: the Equal Employment Opportunity Commission and the Community Relations Service. The fair employment provisions were to be instituted over a three-year period, and the act also made it mandatory that all federally sponsored programs and participants in such programs clearly state their compliance with the nondiscrimination provisions of Title VI. The Department of Health, Education, and Welfare was authorized to assist school districts, through funds and training institutes, with their desegregation problems. The comprehensive report demanded of the Commissioner of Education in Section 402 was published in 1966, as *Equality of Educational Opportunity* (Washington, D.C.: U.S. Government Printing Office, 1966).

Because of the unusual importance of this law, the Supreme Court took virtually immediate action to decide the cases testing its constitutionality. Congressional authority to pass such a law was upheld in *Heart of Atlanta Motel* v. *United States* (Document 90), decided only five months after the act was passed.

DOCUMENT 89

> *An act to enforce the constitutional right to vote, to confer jurisdiction upon the district courts of the United States to provide injunctive relief against discrimination in public accommodations, to authorize the Attorney General to institute suits to protect constitutional rights in public facilities and public education, to extend the Commission on Civil Rights, to prevent discrimination in federally assisted programs, to establish a Commission on Equal Employment Opportunity, and for other purposes**[*]

Be it enacted by the Senate and House of Representatives of the United States of America in Congress assembled, That this Act may be cited as the "Civil Rights Act of 1964."

Title I
Voting Rights . . .

SEC. 101. . . . "(2) No person acting under color of law shall—

"(A) in determining whether any individual is qualified under State law or laws to vote in any Federal election, apply any standard, practice, or procedure different from the standards, practices, or procedures applied under such law or laws to other individuals within the same county, parish, or similar political subdivision who have been found by State officials to be qualified to vote;

"(B) deny the right of any individual to vote in any Federal election because of an error or omission on any record or paper relating to any application, registration, or other act requisite to voting, if such error or omission is not material in determining whether such individual is qualified under State law to vote in such election; or

---

[*] 78 Stat. 241 (1964).

"(C) employ any literacy test as a qualification for voting in any Federal election unless (i) such test is administered to each individual and is conducted wholly in writing, and (ii) a certified copy of the test and of the answers given by the individual is furnished to him within twenty-five days of the submission of his request made within the period of time during which records and papers are required to be retained and preserved pursuant to title III of the Civil Rights Act of 1960 (42 U.S.C. 1974–74e; 74 Stat. 88): *Provided, however,* That the Attorney General may enter into agreements with appropriate State or local authorities that preparation, conduct, and maintenance of such tests in accordance with the provisions as are necessary in the preparation, conduct, and maintenance of such tests for persons who are blind or otherwise physically handicapped, meet the purposes of this subparagraph and constitute compliance therewith.

"(3) For purposes of this subsection—

"(A) the term 'vote' shall have the same meaning as in subsection (e) of this section;

"(B) the phrase 'literacy test' includes any test of the ability to read, write, understand, or interpret any matter."

(b) Insert immediately following the period at the end of the first sentence of subsection (c) the following new sentence: "If in any such proceeding literacy is a relevant fact there shall be a rebuttable presumption that any person who has not been adjudged an incompetent and who has completed the sixth grade in a public school in, or a private school accredited by, any State or territory, the District of Columbia, or the Commonwealth of Puerto Rico where instruction is carried on predominantly in the English language, possesses sufficient literacy, comprehension, and intelligence to vote in any Federal election."

(c) Add the following subsection "(f)" and designate the present subsection "(f)" as subsection "(g)":

"(f) When used in subsection (a) or (c) of this section, the words 'Federal election' shall mean any general, special, or primary election held solely or in part for the purpose of electing or selecting any candidate for the office of President, Vice President, presidential elector, Member of the Senate, or Member of the House of Representatives."

(d) Add the following subsection "(h)":

"(h)" In any proceeding instituted by the United States in

any district court of the United States under this section in which the Attorney General requests a finding of a pattern or practice of discrimination pursuant to subsection (e) of this section the Attorney General, at the time he files the complaint, or any defendant in the proceeding, within twenty days after service upon him of the complaint, may file with the clerk of such court a request that a court of three judges be convened to hear and determine the entire case. A copy of the request for a three-judge court shall be immediately furnished by such clerk to the chief judge of the circuit (or in his absence, the presiding circuit judge of the circuit) in which the case is pending. Upon receipt of the copy of such request it shall be the duty of the chief judge of the circuit or the presiding circuit judge, as the case may be, to designate immediately three judges in such circuit, of whom at least one shall be a circuit judge and another of whom shall be a district judge of the court in which the proceeding was instituted, to hear and determine such case, and it shall be the duty of the judges so designated to assign the case for hearing at the earliest practicable date, to participate in the hearing and determination thereof, and to cause the case to be in every way expedited. An appeal from the final judgment of such court will lie to the Supreme Court."

· · · ·

"It shall be the duty of the judge designated pursuant to this section to assign the case for hearing at the earliest practicable date and to cause the case to be in every way expedited."

TITLE II
INJUNCTIVE RELIEF AGAINST DISCRIMINATION IN PLACES OF PUBLIC ACCOMMODATION

SEC. 201. (a) All persons shall be entitled to the full and equal enjoyment of the goods, services, facilities, privileges, advantages, and accommodations of any place of public accommodation, as defined in this section, without discrimination or segregation on the ground of race, color, religion, or national origin.

(b) Each of the following establishments which serves the

public is a place of public accommodation within the meaning of this title if its operations affect commerce, or if discrimination or segregation by it is supported by State action:

(1) any inn, hotel, motel, or other establishment which provides lodging to transient guests, other than an establishment located within a building which contains not more than five rooms for rent or hire and which is actually occupied by the proprietor of such establishment as his residence;

(2) any restaurant, cafeteria, lunchroom, lunch counter, soda fountain, or other facility principally engaged in selling food for consumption on the premises, including, but not limited to, any such facility located on the premises of any retail establishment; or any gasoline station;

(3) any motion picture house, theater, concert hall, sports arena, stadium or other place of exhibition or entertainment; and

(4) any establishment (A)(i) which is physically located within the premises of any establishment otherwise covered by this subsection, or (ii) within the premises of which is physically located any such covered establishment, and (B) which holds itself out as serving patrons of such covered establishment.

(c) The operations of an establishment affect commerce within the meaning of this title if (1) it is one of the establishments described in paragraph (1) of subsection (b); (2) in the case of an establishment described in paragraph (2) of subsection (b), it serves or offers to serve interstate travelers or a substantial portion of the food which it serves, or gasoline or other products which it sells, has moved in commerce; (3) in the case of an establishment described in paragraph (3) of subsection (b), it customarily presents films, performances, athletic teams, exhibitions, or other sources of entertainment which move in commerce; and (4) in the case of an establishment described in paragraph (4) of subsection (b), it is physically located within the premises of, or there is physically located within its premises, an establishment the operations of which affect commerce within the meaning of this subsection. For purposes of this section, "commerce" means travel, trade, traffic, commerce, transportation, or communication among the several States, or between the District of Columbia and any State, or between any foreign country or any territory or possession and any State or the District of Columbia, or between points in the same State but through any other State or the District of Columbia, or between points in the same State but through any other State or the District of Columbia or a foreign country.

(d) Discrimination or segregation by an establishment is supported by State action within the meaning of this title if such discrimination or segregation (1) is carried on under color of any law, statute, ordinance, or regulation; or (2) is carried on under color of any custom or usage required or enforced by officials of the State or political subdivision thereof; or (3) is required by action of the State or political subdivision thereof.

(e) The provisions of this title shall not apply to a private club or other establishment not in fact open to the public, except to the extent that the facilities of such establishment are made available to the customers or patrons of an establishment within the scope of subsection (b).

Sec. 202. All persons shall be entitled to be free, at any establishment or place, from discrimination or segregation of any kind on the ground of race, color, religion, or national origin, if such discrimination or segregation is or purports to be required by any law, statute, ordinance, regulation, rule, or order of a State or any agency or political subdivision thereof.

Sec. 203. No person shall (a) withhold, deny, or attempt to withhold or deny, or deprive or attempt to deprive, any person of any right or privilege secured by section 201 or 202, or (b) intimidate, threaten, or coerce, or attempt to intimidate, threaten, or coerce any person with the purpose of interfering with any right or privilege secured by section 201 or 202, or (c) punish or attempt to punish any person for exercising or attempting to exercise any right or privilege secured by section 201 or 202.

Sec. 204. (a) Whenever any person has engaged or there are reasonable grounds to believe that any person is about to engage in any act or practice prohibited by section 203, a civil action for preventive relief, including an application for a permanent or temporary injunction, restraining order, or other order, may be instituted by the person aggrieved and, upon timely application, the court may, in its discretion, permit the Attorney General to intervene in such civil action if he certifies that the case is of general public importance. Upon application by the complainant and in such circumstances as the court may deem just, the court may appoint an attorney for such complainant and may authorize the commencement of the civil action without the payment of fees, costs, or security.

. . . .

(d) In the case of an alleged act or practice prohibited by this title which occurs in a State, or political subdivision of a State, which has no State or local law prohibiting such act or practice, a civil action may be brought under subsection (a): *Provided,* That the court may refer the matter to the Community Relations Service established by title X of this Act for as long as the court believes there is a reasonable possibility of obtaining voluntary compliance, but for not more than sixty days: *Provided further,* That upon expiration of such sixty-day period, the court may extend such period for an additional period, not to exceed a cumulative total of one hundred and twenty days, if it believes there then exists a reasonable possibility of securing voluntary compliance.

SEC. 205. The Service is authorized to make a full investigation of any complaint referred to it by the court under section 204(d) and may hold such hearings with respect thereto as may be necessary.

. . . .

SEC. 206. (a) Whenever the Attorney General has reasonable cause to believe that any person or group of persons is engaged in a pattern or practice of resistance to the full enjoyment of any of the rights secured by this title, and that the pattern or practice is of such a nature and is intended to deny the full exercise of the rights herein described, the Attorney General may bring a civil action in the appropriate district court of the United States by filing with it a complaint (1) signed by him (or in his absence the Acting Attorney General), (2) setting forth facts pertaining to such pattern or practice, and (3) requesting such preventive relief, including an application for a permanent or temporary injunction, restraining order or other order against the person or persons responsible for such pattern or practice, as he deems necessary to insure the full enjoyment of the rights herein described.

. . . .

Title III—Desegregation of Public Facilities

Sec. 301. (a) Whenever the Attorney General receives a complaint in writing signed by an individual to the effect that he is being deprived of or threatened with the loss of his right to the equal protection of the laws, on account of his race, color, religion, or national origin, by being denied equal utilization of any public facility which is owned, operated, or managed by or on behalf of any State or subdivision thereof, other than a public school or public college as defined in section 401 of title IV hereof, and the Attorney General believes the complaint is meritorious and certifies that the signer or signers of such complaint are unable, in his judgment, to initiate and maintain appropriate legal proceedings for relief and that the institution of an action will materially further the orderly progress of desegregation in public facilities, the Attorney General is authorized to institute for or in the name of the United States a civil action in any appropriate district court of the United States against such parties and for such relief as may be appropriate, and such court shall have and shall exercise jurisdiction of proceedings instituted pursuant to this section. The Attorney General may implead as defendants such additional parties as are or become necessary to the grant of effective relief hereunder.

. . . .

Title IV—Desegregation of Public Education

Definitions

Sec. 401. As used in this title—

(a) "Commissioner" means the Commissioner of Education.

(b) "Desegregation" means the assignment of students to public schools and within such schools without regard to their race, color, religion, or national origin, but "desegregation" shall not mean the assignment of students to public schools in order to overcome racial imbalance.

(c) "Public school" means any elementary or secondary educational institution, and "public college" means any institution of higher education or any technical or vocational school above the secondary school level, provided that such public school or public college is operated by a State, subdivision of a State, or governmental agency within a State, or operated wholly or predominantly from or through the use of governmental funds or property, or funds or property derived from a governmental source.

(d) "School board" means any agency or agencies which administer a system of one or more public schools and any other agency which is responsible for the assignment of students to or within such system.

Survey and Report of Educational Opportunities

Sec. 402. The Commissioner shall conduct a survey and make a report to the President and the Congress, within two years of the enactment of this title, concerning the lack of availability of equal educational opportunities for individuals by reason of race, color, religion, or national origin in public educational institutions at all levels in the United States, its territories and possessions, and the District of Columbia.

Technical Assistance

Sec. 403. The Commissioner is authorized, upon the application of any school board, State, municipality, school district, or other governmental unit legally responsible for operating a public school or schools, to render technical assistance to such applicant in the preparation, adoption, and implementation of plans for the desegregation of public schools. Such technical assistance may, among other activities, include making available to such agencies information regarding effective methods of coping with special educational problems occasioned by desegregation, and making available to such agencies personnel of the Office of Education or other persons specially equipped to advise and assist them in coping with such problems.

Training Institutes

SEC. 404. The Commissioner is authorized to arrange, through grants or contracts, with institutions of higher education for the operation of short-term or regular session institutes for special training designed to improve the ability of teachers, supervisors, counselors, and other elementary or secondary school personnel to deal effectively with special educational problems occasioned by desegregation. Individuals who attend such an institute on a full-time basis may be paid stipends for the period of their attendance at such institute in amounts specified by the Commissioner in regulations, including allowances for travel to attend such institute.

Grants

SEC. 405. (a) The Commissioner is authorized, upon application of a school board, to make grants to such board to pay, in whole or in part, the cost of—

(1) giving to teachers and other school personnel inservice training in dealing with problems incident to desegregation, and

(2) employing specialists to advise in problems incident to desegregation.

(b) In determining whether to make a grant, and in fixing the amount thereof and the terms and conditions on which it will be made, the Commissioner shall take into consideration the amount available for grants under this section and the other applications which are pending before him; the financial condition of the applicant and the other resources available to it; the nature, extent, and gravity of its problems incident to desegregation; and such other factors as he finds relevant.

. . . .

Suits by the Attorney General

SEC. 407. (a) Whenever the Attorney General receives a complaint in writing—

(1) signed by a parent or group of parents to the effect

that his or their minor children, as members of a class of persons similarly situated, are being deprived by a school board of the equal protection of the laws, or

(2) signed by an individual, or his parent, to the effect that he has been denied admission to or not permitted to continue in attendance at a public college by reason of race, color, religion, or national origin,

and the Attorney General believes the complaint is meritorious and certifies that the signer or signers of such complaint are unable, in his judgment, to initiate and maintain appropriate legal proceedings for relief and that the institution of an action will materially further the orderly achievement of desegregation in public education, the Attorney General is authorized, after giving notice of such complaint to the appropriate school board or college authority and after certifying that he is satisfied that such board or authority has had a reasonable time to adjust the conditions alleged in such complaint, to institute for or in the name of the United States a civil action in any appropriate district court of the United States against such parties and for such relief as may be appropriate, and such court shall have and shall exercise jurisdiction of proceedings instituted pursuant to this section, provided that nothing herein shall empower any official or court of the United States to issue any order seeking to achieve a racial balance in any school by requiring the transportation of pupils or students from one school to another or one school district to another in order to achieve such racial balance, or otherwise enlarge the existing power of the court to insure compliance with constitutional standards. The Attorney General may implead as defendants such additional parties as are or become necessary to the grant of effective relief hereunder.

(b) The Attorney General may deem a person or persons unable to initiate and maintain appropriate legal proceedings within the meaning of subsection (a) of this section when such person or persons are unable, either directly or through other interested persons or organizations, to bear the expense of the litigation or to obtain effective legal representation; or whenever he is satisfied that the institution of such litigation would jeopardize the personal safety, employment, or economic standing of such person or persons, their families, or their property.

. . . .

Title V—Commission on Civil Rights

Sec. 501. Section 102 of the Civil Rights Act of 1957 (42 U.S.C. 1975a; 71 Stat. 634) is amended to read as follows: . . .

"Sec. 102. (k) The Commission shall not issue any subpena for the attendance and testimony of witnesses or for the production of written or other matter which would require the presence of the party subpenaed at a hearing to be held outside of the State wherein the witness is found or resides or is domiciled or transacts business, or has appointed an agent for receipt of service of process except that, in any event, the Commission may issue subpenas for the attendance and testimony of witnesses and the production of written or other matter at a hearing held within fifty miles of the place where the witness is found or resides or is domiciled or transacts business or has appointed an agent for receipt of service of process." . . .

Duties of the Commission

"Sec. 104. (a) The Commission shall—

"(1) investigate allegations in writing under oath or affirmation that certain citizens of the United States are being deprived of their right to vote and have that vote counted by reason of their color, race, religion, or national origin; which writing, under oath or affirmation, shall set forth the facts upon which such belief or beliefs are based;

"(2) study and collect information concerning legal developments constituting a denial of equal protection of the laws under the Constitution because of race, color, religion or national origin or in the administration of justice;

"(3) appraise the laws and policies of the Federal Government with respect to denials of equal protection of the laws under the Constitution because of race, color, religion or national origin or in the administration of justice;

"(4) serve as a national clearinghouse for information in respect to denials of equal protection of the laws because of race, color, religion or national origin, including but not limited to the fields of voting, education, housing, employment, the use of public facilities, and transportation, or in the administration of justice;

"(5) investigate allegations, made in writing and under oath or affirmation, that citizens of the United States are unlawfully being accorded or denied the right to vote, or to have their votes properly counted, in any election of presidential electors, Members of the United States Senate, or of the House of Representatives, as a result of any patterns or practice of fraud or discrimination in the conduct of such election; and

"(6) Nothing in this or any other Act shall be construed as authorizing the Commission, its Advisory Committees, or any person under its supervision or control to inquire into or investigate any membership practices or internal operations of any fraternal organization, any college or university fraternity or sorority, any private club or any religious organization."

(b) Section 104(b) of the Civil Rights Act of 1957 (42 U.S.C. 1975c(b); 71 Stat. 635), as amended, is further amended by striking out the present subsection "(b)" and by substituting therefor:

"(b) The Commission shall submit interim reports to the President and to the Congress at such times as the Commission, the Congress or the President shall deem desirable, and shall submit to the President and to the Congress a final report of its activities, findings, and recommendations not later than January 31, 1968." . . .

Title VI—Nondiscrimination in Federally Assisted Programs

Sec. 601. No person in the United States shall, on the ground of race, color, or national origin, be excluded from participation in, be denied the benefits of, or be subjected to discrimination under any program or activity receiving Federal financial assistance.

Sec. 602. Each Federal department and agency which is empowered to extend Federal financial assistance to any program or activity, by way of grant, loan, or contract other than a contract of insurance or guaranty, is authorized and directed to effectuate the provisions of section 601 with respect to such program or activity by issuing rules, regulations, or orders of general applicability which shall be consistent with achievement of the objectives of the statute authorizing the financial assistance in connection with which the action is taken. No such rule, regulation, or order shall become effective unless and until approved by the President. Compliance with any requirement adopted pursuant to this section may be effected (1) by the termination of or refusal to grant or to continue assistance under such program or activity to any recipient as to whom there has been an express finding on the record, after opportunity for hearing, of a failure to comply with such requirement, but such termination or refusal shall be limited to the particular political entity, or part thereof, or other recipient as to whom such a finding has been made and, shall be limited in its effect to the particular program, or part thereof, in which such non-compliance has been so found, or (2) by any other means authorized by law: *Provided, however,* That no such action shall be taken until the department or agency concerned has advised the appropriate person or persons of the failure to comply with the requirement and has determined that compliance cannot be secured by voluntary means. In the case of any action terminating, or refusing to grant or continue, assistance because of failure to comply with a requirement imposed pursuant to this section, the head of the Federal department or agency shall file with the committees of the House and Senate having legislative jurisdiction over the program or activity involved a full written report of the circumstances and the grounds for such action. No such action shall become effective until thirty days have elapsed after the filing of such report.

Sec. 603. Any department or agency action taken pursuant to section 602 shall be subject to such judicial review as may otherwise be provided by law for similar action taken by such department or agency on other grounds. In the case of action, not otherwise subject to judicial review, terminating or refusing to grant or to continue financial assistance upon a finding of failure to comply with any requirement imposed pursuant to section 602, any person aggrieved (including any State or political subdivision thereof and any agency of either) may obtain judicial review of such action in accordance with section 10 of the Administrative Procedure Act, and such action shall not be deemed committed to unreviewable agency discretion within the meaning of that section.

Sec. 604. Nothing contained in this title shall be construed to authorize action under this title by any department or agency with respect to any employment practice of any employer, employment agency, or labor organization except where a primary objective of the Federal financial assistance is to provide employment.

Sec. 605. Nothing in this title shall add to or detract from any existing authority with respect to any program or activity under which Federal financial assistance is extended by way of a contract of insurance or guaranty.

· · · ·

Title VII—Equal Employment Opportunity

Discrimination Because of Race, Color, Religion, Sex, or National Origin

Sec. 703. (a) It shall be an unlawful employment practice for an employer—

(1) to fail or refuse to hire or to discharge any individual, or otherwise to discriminate against any individual with respect to his compensation, terms, conditions, or privileges of employment, because of such individual's race, color, religion, sex, or national origin; or

(2) to limit, segregate, or classify his employees in any way which would deprive or tend to deprive any individual of employment opportunities or otherwise adversely affect his status as an employee, because of such individual's race, color, religion, sex, or national origin.

(b) It shall be an unlawful employment practice for an employment agency to fail or refuse to refer for employment, or otherwise to discriminate against, any individual because of his race, color, religion, sex, or national origin, or to classify or refer for employment any individual on the basis of his race, color, religion, sex, or national origin.

(c) It shall be an unlawful employment practice for a labor organization—

(1) to exclude or to expel from its membership, or otherwise to discriminate against, any individual because of his race, color, religion, sex, or national origin;

(2) to limit, segregate, or classify its membership, or to classify or fail or refuse to refer for employment any individual, in any way which would deprive or tend to deprive any individual of employment opportunities, or would limit such employment opportunities or otherwise adversely affect his status as an employee or as an applicant for employment, because of such individual's race, color, religion, sex, or national origin; or

(3) to cause or attempt to cause an employer to discriminate against an individual in violation of this section.

(d) It shall be an unlawful employment practice for any employer, labor organization, or joint labor-management committee controlling apprenticeship or other training or retraining, including on-the-job training programs, to discriminate against any individual because of his race, color, religion, sex, or national origin in admission to, or employment in, any program established to provide apprenticeship or other training.

(e) Notwithstanding any other provision of this title, (1) it shall not be an unlawful employment practice for an employer to hire and employ employees, for an employment agency to classify, or refer for employment any individual, for a labor organization to classify its membership or to classify or refer for employment any individual, or for an employer, labor organization, or joint labor-management committee controlling apprenticeship or other training or retraining programs to admit or employ any individual in any such program, on the basis of his religion, sex, or national origin in those certain instances where religion, sex, or national origin is a bona fide occupational qualification reasonably necessary to the normal operation of that particular business or enterprise, and (2) it shall not be an unlawful employment practice for a school, college, university, or other educational institution or institution of learning to hire and employ employees of a particular religion if such school, college, university, or other educational institution or institution of learning is, in whole or in substantial part, owned, supported, controlled, or managed by a particular religion or by a particular religious corporation, association, or society, or if the curriculum of such school, college, university, or other educational institution or institution of learning is directed toward the propagation of a particular religion.

(f) As used in this title, the phrase "unlawful employment practice" shall not be deemed to include any action or measure taken by an employer, labor organization, joint labor-management committee, or employment agency with respect to an individual who is a member of the Communist Party of the United States or of any other organization required to register as a Communist-action or Communist-front organization by final order of the Subversive Activities Control Board pursuant to the Subversive Activities Control Act of 1950.

(g) Notwithstanding any other provision of this title, it shall not be an unlawful employment practice for an employer to fail or refuse to hire and employ any individual for any position, for an employer to discharge any individual from any position, or for an employment agency to fail or refuse to refer any individual for employment in any position, or for a labor organization to fail or refuse to refer any individual for employment in any position, if—

(1) the occupancy of such position, or access to the premises in or upon which any part of the duties of such position is performed, or is to be performed, is subject to any requirement imposed in the interest of the national security of the United States under any security program in effect pursuant to or administered under any statute of the United States or any Executive order of the President; and

(2) such individual has not fulfilled or has ceased to fulfill that requirement.

(h) Notwithstanding any other provision of this title, it shall not be an unlawful employment practice for an employer to apply different standards of compensation, or different terms, conditions, or privileges of employment pursuant to a bona fide seniority or merit system, or a system which measures earnings by quantity or quality of production or to employees who work in different locations, provided that such differences are not the result of an intention to discriminate because of race, color, religion, sex, or national origin, nor shall it be an unlawful employment practice for an employer to give and to act upon the results of any professionally developed ability test provided that such test, its administration or action upon the results is not designed, intended or used to discriminate because of race, color, religion, sex or national origin. It shall not be an unlawful employment practice under this title for any employer to differentiate upon the basis of sex in determining the amount of the wages or compensation paid or to be paid to employees of such employer if such differentiation is authorized by the provisions of section 6(d) of the Fair Labor Standards Act of 1938, as amended (29 U.S.C. 206(d)).

. . . .

Equal Employment Opportunity Commission

SEC. 705 (a) There is hereby created a Commission to be known as the Equal Employment Opportunity Commission, which shall be composed of five members, not more than three of whom shall be members of the same political party, who shall be appointed by the President by and with the advice and consent of the Senate. One of the original members shall be appointed for a term of one year, one for a term of two years, one for a term of three years, one for a term of four years, and one for a term of five years, beginning from the date of enactment of this title, but their successors shall be appointed for terms of five years each, except that any individual chosen to fill a vacancy shall be appointed only for the unexpired term of the member whom he shall succeed. The President shall designate one member to serve as Chairman of the Commission, and one member to serve as Vice Chairman. The Chairman shall be responsible on behalf of the Commission for the administrative operations of the Commission, and shall appoint, in accordance with the civil service laws, such officers, agents, attorneys, and employees as it deems necessary to assist it in the performance of its functions and to fix their compensation in accordance with the Classification Act of 1949, as amended. The Vice Chairman shall act as Chairman in the absence or disability of the Chairman or in the event of a vacancy in that office.

o o w w

(g) The Commission shall have power—
   (1) to cooperate with and, with their consent, utilize

regional, State, local, and other agencies, both public and private, and individuals;

(2) to pay to witnesses whose depositions are taken or who are summoned before the Commission or any of its agents the same witness and mileage fees as are paid to witnesses in the courts of the United States;

(3) to furnish to persons subject to this title such technical assistance as they may request to further their compliance with this title or an order issued thereunder;

(4) upon the request of (i) any employer, whose employees or some of them, or (ii) any labor organization, whose members or some of them, refuse or threaten to refuse to cooperate in effectuating the provisions of this title, to assist in such effectuation by conciliation or such other remedial action as is provided by this title;

(5) to make such technical studies as are appropriate to effectuate the purposes and policies of this title and to make the results of such studies available to the public;

(6) to refer matters to the Attorney General with recommendations for intervention in a civil action brought by an aggrieved party under section 706, or for the institution of a civil action by the Attorney General under section 707, and to advise, consult, and assist the Attorney General on such matters.

. . . .

Prevention of Unlawful Employment Practices

SEC. 706. (a) Whenever it is charged in writing under oath by a person claiming to be aggrieved, or a written charge has been filed by a member of the Commission where he has reasonable cause to believe a violation of this title has occurred (and such charge sets forth the facts upon which it is based) that an employer, employment agency, or labor organization has engaged in an unlawful employment practice, the Commission shall furnish such employer, employment agency, or labor organization (hereinafter referred to as the "respondent") with a copy of such charge and shall make an investigation of such charge provided that such charge shall not be made public by the Commission. If the Commission shall determine, after such investigation, that there is reasonable cause to believe that the charge is true, the Commission shall endeavor to eliminate any such alleged unlawful employment practice by informal methods of conference, conciliation, and persuasion. Nothing said or done during and as a part of such endeavors may be made public by the Commission without the written consent of the parties, or used as evidence in a subsequent proceeding. Any officer or employee of the Commission, who shall make public in any manner whatever any information in violation of this subsection shall be deemed guilty of a misdemeanor and upon conviction thereof shall be fined not more than $1,000 or imprisoned not more than one year.

(b) In the case of an alleged unlawful employment practice occurring in a State, or political subdivision of a State, which has a State or local law prohibiting the unlawful employment practice alleged and establishing or authorizing a State or local authority to grant or seek relief from such practice or to institute criminal proceedings with respect thereto upon receiving notice thereof, no charge may be filed under subsection (a) by the person aggrieved before the expiration of sixty days after proceedings have been commenced under the State or local law, unless such proceedings have been earlier terminated, provided that such sixty-day period shall be extended to one hundred and twenty days during the first year after the effective date of such State or local law. If any requirement for the commencement of such proceedings is imposed by a State or local authority other than a requirement of the filing of a written and signed statement of the facts upon which the proceeding is based, the proceeding shall be deemed to have been commenced for the purposes of this subsection at the time such statement is sent by registered mail to the appropriate State or local authority.

. . . .

SEC. 707. (a) Whenever the Attorney General has reasonable cause to believe that any person or group of persons is engaged in a pattern or practice of resistance to the full enjoyment of any of the rights secured by this title, and that the pattern or practice is of such a nature and is intended to deny the full exercise of the rights herein described, the

Attorney General may bring a civil action in the appropriate district court of the United States by filing with it a complaint (1) signed by him (or in his absence the Acting Attorney General), (2) setting forth facts pertaining to such pattern or practice, and (3) requesting such relief, including an application for a permanent or temporary injunction, restraining order or other order against the person or persons responsible for such pattern or practice, as he deems necessary to insure the full enjoyment of the rights herein described.

(b) The district courts of the United States shall have and shall exercise jurisdiction of proceedings instituted pursuant to this section, and in any such proceeding the Attorney General may file with the clerk of such court a request that a court of three judges be convened to hear and determine the case. Such request by the Attorney General shall be accompanied by a certificate that, in his opinion, the case is of general public importance. A copy of the certificate and request for a three-judge court shall be immediately furnished by such clerk to the chief judge of the circuit (or in his absence, the presiding circuit judge of the circuit) in which the case is pending. Upon receipt of such request it shall be the duty of the chief judge of the circuit or the presiding circuit judge, as the case may be, to designate immediately three judges in such circuit, of whom at least one shall be a circuit judge and another of whom shall be a district judge of the court in which the proceeding was instituted, to hear and determine such case, and it shall be the duty of the judges so designated to assign the case for hearing at the earliest practicable date, to participate in the hearing and determination thereof, and to cause the case to be in every way expedited. An appeal from the final judgment of such court will lie to the Supreme Court.

. . . .

Effect on State Laws

SEC. 708. Nothing in this title shall be deemed to exempt or relieve any person from any liability, duty, penalty, or punishment provided by any present or future law of any State or political subdivision of a State, other than any such law which purports to require or permit the doing of any act which would be an unlawful employment practice under this title.

Investigations, Inspections, Records, State Agencies

SEC. 709. (a) In connection with any investigation of a charge filed under section 706, the Commission or its designated representative shall at all reasonable times have access to, for the purpose of examination, and the right to copy any evidence of any person being investigated or proceeded against that relates to unlawful employment practices covered by this title and is relevant to the charge under investigation.

. . . .

Notices To Be Posted

SEC. 711. (a) Every employer, employment agency, and labor organization, as the case may be, shall post and keep posted in conspicuous places upon its premises where notices to employees, applicants for employment, and members are customarily posted a notice to be prepared or approved by the Commission setting forth excerpts from or, summaries of, the pertinent provisions of this title and information pertinent to the filing of a complaint.

(b) A willful violation of this section shall be punishable by a fine of not more than $100 for each separate offense.

. . . .

Forcibly Resisting the Commission or Its Representatives

SEC. 714. The provisions of section 111, title 18, United States Code, shall apply to officers, agents, and employees of the Commission in the performance of their official duties.

Special Study by Secretary of Labor

SEC. 715. The Secretary of Labor shall make a full and complete study of the factors which might tend to result in discrimination in employment because of age and of the consequences of such discrimination on the economy and individuals affected. The Secretary of Labor shall make a report to the Congress not later than June 30, 1965, containing the results of such study and shall include in such report such recommendations for legislation to prevent arbitrary discrimination in employment because of age as he determines advisable.

. . . .

Title VIII—Registration and Voting Statistics

Sec. 801. The Secretary of Commerce shall promptly conduct a survey to compile registration and voting statistics in such geographic areas as may be recommended by the Commission on Civil Rights. Such a survey and compilation shall, to the extent recommended by the Commission on Civil Rights, only include a count of persons of voting age by race, color, and national origin, and determination of the extent to which such persons are registered to vote, and have voted in any statewide primary or general election in which the Members of the United States House of Representatives are nominated or elected, since January 1, 1960. Such information shall also be collected and compiled in connection with the Nineteenth Decennial Census, and at such other times as the Congress may prescribe. The provisions of section 9 and chapter 7 of title 13, United States Code shall apply to any survey, collection, or compilation of registration and voting statistics carried out under this title: *Provided, however,* That no person shall be compelled to disclose his race, color, national origin, or questioned about his political party affiliation, how he voted, or the reasons therefore, nor shall any penalty be imposed for his failure or refusal to make such disclosure. Every person interrogated orally, by written survey or questionnaire or by any other means with respect to such information shall be fully advised with respect to his right to fail or refuse to furnish such information.

Title IX—Intervention and Procedure After Removal in Civil Rights Cases

Sec. 901. Title 28 of the United States Code, section 1447(d), is amended to read as follows:

"An order remanding a case to the State court from which it was removed is not reviewable on appeal or otherwise, except that an order remanding a case to the State court from which it was removed pursuant to section 1443 of this title shall be reviewable by appeal or otherwise."

Sec. 902. Whenever an action has been commenced in any court of the United States seeking relief from the denial of equal protection of the laws under the fourteenth amendment to the Constitution on account of race, color, religion, or national origin, the Attorney General for or in the name of the United States may intervene in such action upon timely application if the Attorney General certifies that the case is of general public importance. In such action the United States shall be entitled to the same relief as if it had instituted the action.

Title X—Establishment of Community Relations Service

Sec. 1001. (a) There is hereby established in and as a part of the Department of Commerce a Community Relations Service (hereinafter referred to as the "Service"), which shall be headed by a Director who shall be appointed by the President with the advice and consent of the Senate for a term of four years. The Director is authorized to appoint, subject to the civil service laws and regulations, such other personnel as may be necessary to enable the Service to carry out its functions and duties, and to fix their compensation in accordance with the Classification Act of 1949, as amended. The Director is further authorized to procure services as authorized by section 15 of the Act of August 2, 1946 (60 Stat. 810; 5 U.S.C. 55(a)), but at rates for individuals not in excess of $75 per diem.

(b) Section 106(a) of the Federal Executive Pay Act of 1956, as amended (5 U.S.C. 2205(a)), is further amended by adding the following clause thereto:

"(52) Director, Community Relations Service."

Sec. 1002. It shall be the function of the Service to provide assistance to communities and persons therein in resolving disputes, disagreements, or difficulties relating to discriminatory practices based on race, color, or national origin which impair the rights of persons in such communities under the Constitution or laws of the United States or which affect or may affect interstate commerce. The Service may offer its services in cases of such disputes, disagreements, or difficulties whenever, in its judgment, peaceful relations among the citizens of the community involved are threatened thereby, and it may offer its services either upon its own motion or upon the request of an appropriate State or local official or other interested person.

SEC. 1003. (a) The Service shall, whenever possible, in performing its functions, seek and utilize the cooperation of appropriate State or local, public, or private agencies. . . .

SEC. 1004. Subject to the provisions of sections 205 and 1003(b), the Director shall, on or before January 31 of each year, submit to the Congress a report of the activities of the Service during the preceding fiscal year.

TITLE XI—MISCELLANEOUS

SEC. 1101. In any proceeding for criminal contempt arising under title II, III, IV, V, VI, or VII of this Act, the accused, upon demand therefor, shall be entitled to a trial by jury, which shall conform as near as may be to the practice in criminal cases. Upon conviction, the accused shall not be fined more than $1,000 or imprisoned for more than six months.

This section shall not apply to contempts committed in the presence of the court, or so near thereto as to obstruct the administration of justice, nor to the misbehavior, misconduct, or disobedience of any officer of the court in respect to writs, orders, or process of the court. No person shall be convicted of criminal contempt hereunder unless the act or omission constituting such contempt shall have been intentional, as required in other cases of criminal contempt.

Nor shall anything herein be construed to deprive courts of their power, by civil contempt proceedings, without a jury, to secure compliance with or to prevent obstruction of, as distinguished from punishment for violations of, any lawful writ, process, order, rule, decree, or command of the court in accordance with the prevailing usages of law and equity, including the power of detention.

Sec. 1102. No person should be put twice in jeopardy under the laws of the United States for the same act or omission. For this reason, an acquittal or conviction in a prosecution for a specific crime under the laws of the United States shall bar a proceeding for criminal contempt, which is based upon the same act or omission and which arises under the provisions of this Act; and an acquittal or conviction in a proceeding for criminal contempt, which arises under the provisions of this Act, shall bar a prosecution for a specific crime under the laws of the United States based upon the same act or omission.

Sec. 1103. Nothing in this Act shall be construed to deny, impair, or otherwise affect any right or authority of the Attorney General or of the United States or any agency or officer thereof under existing law to institute or intervene in any action or proceeding.

Sec. 1104. Nothing contained in any title of this Act shall be construed as indicating an intent on the part of Congress to occupy the field in which any such title operates to the exclusion of State laws on the same subject matter, nor shall any provision of this Act be construed as invalidating any provision of State law unless such provision is inconsistent with any of the purposes of this Act, or any provision thereof.

Sec. 1105. There are hereby authorized to be appropriated such sums as are necessary to carry out the provisions of this Act.

Sec. 1106. If any provision of this Act or the application thereof to any person or circumstances is held invalid, the remainder of the Act and the application of the provision to other persons not similarly situated or to other circumstances shall not be affected thereby.

Approved, July 2, 1964.

EQUALITY IN ACCOMMODATIONS (1964)

On the day before Independence Day, 1964, Atlanta restaurant owner Lester Maddox brandished a pistol as he refused service to three Negro divinity students. At the same time, that city's Heart of Atlanta Motel was denying the use of its facilities to Negro interstate travelers. And in Birmingham, Alabama, Ollie's Barbecue continued its "whites-only" policy in the small enterprise that had little if any interstate traffic, but which served food that had come from out of state.

All three enterprises argued before the federal district courts that the accommodations sections of the Civil Rights Act of 1964 (Document 89) were unconstitutional. The federal court in Birmingham agreed. The court sitting in Atlanta, however, sustained the validity of the enactment in regard to both the motel and restaurateur Maddox. As a result of procedural error, the Maddox case was not ready for review as the Supreme Court moved swiftly to resolve the conflicting determinations of the lower courts. The Court delivered its decisions before year's end in *Heart of Atlanta Motel* v. *United States* and *Katzenbach* v. *McClung*, 379 U.S. 294 (1964).

While unanimously upholding the constitutionality of the 1964 Civil Rights Act, the members of the Court disagreed in their reasoning in the principal case—that involving the Atlanta motel. The majority held that the act was valid as a proper exercise of the federal government's commerce power under Article I, Section 8, Clause 3 of the Constitution (Document 17). Justice Hugo L. Black stated that the statute was valid under both the commerce power and the "necessary and proper clause" of Article I, Section 8, Clause 8 of the Constitution. Justice William O. Douglas concurred, but added that he preferred to base constitutionality on the power conferred on Congress by Section 5 of the Fourteenth Amendment (Document 46). And Justice Arthur J. Goldberg contended that Congress had the necessary power to enact the statute under both the commerce power clause and the Fourteenth Amendment.

Lester Maddox made good his threat to close his restaurant

rather than submit to a judicial integration order. He entered politics. In January, 1967, he became Governor of Georgia.

DOCUMENT 90

Heart of Atlanta Motel v. United States *

MR. JUSTICE CLARK delivered the opinion of the Court.

This is a declaratory judgment action, 28 U.S.C. § 2201 and § 2202 (1958 ed.), attacking the constitutionality of Title II of the Civil Rights Act of 1964, 78 Stat. 241, 243. . . . A three-judge court, empaneled under § 206 (b) as well as 28 U.S.C. § 2282 (1958 ed.), sustained the validity of the Act and issued a permanent injunction on appellees' counterclaim restraining appellant from continuing to violate the Act which remains in effect on order of MR. JUSTICE BLACK, 85 S. Ct. 1. We affirm the judgment.

1. The Factual Background and Contentions of the Parties

The case comes here on admissions and stipulated facts. Appellant owns and operates the Heart of Atlanta Motel which has 216 rooms available to transient guests. The motel is located on Courtland Street, two blocks from downtown Peachtree Street. It is readily accessible to interstate highways 75 and 85 and state highways 23 and 41. Appellant solicits patronage from outside the State of Georgia through various national advertising media, including magazines of national circulation; it maintains over 50 billboards and highway signs within the State, soliciting patronage for the motel; it accepts convention trade from outside Georgia and approximately 75% of its registered guests are from out of State. Prior to passage of the Act the motel had followed a practice of refusing to rent rooms to Negroes, and it alleged that it intended to continue to do so. In an effort to perpetuate that policy this suit was filed.

The appellant contends that Congress in passing this Act exceeded its power to regulate commerce under Art. I, § 8, cl. 3, of the Constitution of the United States; that the Act violates the Fifth Amendment because appellant is deprived

---

* Supreme Court of the United States, 379 U.S. 241 (1964).

of the right to choose its customers and operate its business as it wishes, resulting in a taking of its liberty and property without due process of law and a taking of its property without just compensation; and, finally, that by requiring appellant to rent available rooms to Negroes against its will, Congress is subjecting it to involuntary servitude in contravention of the Thirteenth Amendment.

The appellees counter that the unavailability to Negroes of adequate accommodations interferes significantly with interstate travel, and that Congress, under the Commerce Clause, has power to remove such obstructions and restraints; that the Fifth Amendment does not forbid reasonable regulation and that consequential damage does not constitute a "taking" within the meaning of that amendment; that the Thirteenth Amendment claim fails because it is entirely frivolous to say that an amendment directed to the abolition of human bondage and the removal of widespread disabilities associated with slavery places discrimination in public accommodations beyond the reach of both federal and state law. . . .

2. The History of the Act . . .

The Act as finally adopted was most comprehensive, undertaking to prevent through peaceful and voluntary settlement discrimination in voting, as well as in places of accommodation and public facilities, federally secured programs and in employment. Since Title II is the only portion under attack here, we confine our consideration to those public accommodation provisions.

3. Title II of the Act [See Document 90] . . .

4. Application of Title II to Heart of Atlanta Motel

It is admitted that the operation of the motel brings it within the provisions of § 201 (a) of the Act and that appellant refused to provide lodging for transient Negroes because of their race or color and that it intends to continue that policy unless restrained.

The sole question posed is, therefore; the constitutionality of the Civil Rights Act of 1964 as applied to these facts. The legislative history of the Act indicates that Congress based the Act on § 5 and the Equal Protection Clause of the Fourteenth

Amendment as well as its power to regulate interstate commerce under Art. I § 8, cl. 3, of the Constitution.

The Senate Commerce Committee made it quite clear that the fundamental object of Title II was to vindicate "the deprivation of personal dignity that surely accompanies denials of equal access to public establishments." At the same time, however, it noted that such an objective has been and could be readily achieved "by congressional action based on the commerce power of the Constitution." S. Rep. No. 872, *supra*, at 16–17. Our study of the legislative record, made in the light of prior cases, has brought us to the conclusion that Congress possessed ample power in this regard, and we have therefore not considered the other grounds relied upon. This is not to say that the remaining authority upon which it acted was not adequate, a question upon which we do not pass, but merely that since the commerce power is sufficient for our decision here we have considered it alone. Nor is § 201 (d) or § 202, having to do with state action, involved here and we do not pass upon either of those sections.

5. The Civil Rights Cases, 109 U.S. 3 (1883), and their Application

In light of our grounds for decision, it might be well at the outset to discuss the *Civil Rights Cases, supra,* which declared provisions of the Civil Rights Act of 1875 unconstitutional. 18 Stat. 335, 336. We think that decision inapposite, and without precedential value in determining the constitutionality of the present Act. Unlike Title II of the present legislation, the 1875 Act broadly proscribed discrimination in "inns, public conveyances on land or water, theaters, and other places of public amusement," without limiting the categories of affected businesses to those impinging upon interstate commerce. In contrast, the applicability of Title II is carefully limited to enterprises having a direct and substantial relation to the interstate flow of goods and people, except where state action is involved. Further, the fact that certain kinds of businesses may not in 1875 have been sufficiently involved in interstate commerce to warrant bringing them within the ambit of the commerce power is not necessarily dispositive of the same question today. Our populace had not reached its present mobility, nor were facilities, goods and services circulating as readily in interstate commerce as they are today. Although the principles which we apply today are those first formulated by Chief Justice Marshall in *Gibbons* v. *Ogden,* 9 Wheat. 1 (1824), the conditions of transportation and commerce have changed dramatically, and we must apply those principles to the present state of commerce. The sheer increase in volume of interstate traffic alone would give discriminatory practices which inhibit travel a far larger impact upon the Nation's commerce than such practices had on the economy of another day. Finally, there is language in the *Civil Rights Cases* which indicates that the Court did not fully consider whether the 1875 Act could be sustained as an exercise of the commerce power. Though the Court observed that "no one will contend that the power to pass it was contained in the Constitution before the adoption of the last three amendments [Thirteenth, Fourteenth, and Fifteenth]," the Court went on specifically to note that the Act was not "conceived" in terms of the commerce power and expressly pointed out:

Of course, these remarks [as to lack of congressional power] do not apply to those cases in which Congress is clothed with direct and plenary powers of legislation over the whole subject, accompanied with an express or implied denial of such power to the States, as in the regulation of commerce with foreign nations, among the several States, and with the Indian tribes. . . . In these cases Congress has power to pass laws for regulating the subjects specified in every detail, and the conduct and transactions of individuals in respect thereof. At 18.

Since the commerce power was not relied on by the Government and was without support in the record it is understandable that the Court narrowed its inquiry and excluded the Commerce Clause as a possible source of power. In any event, it is clear that such a limitation renders the opinion devoid of authority for the proposition that the Commerce Clause gives no power to Congress to regulate discriminatory practices now found substantially to affect interstate commerce. We, therefore, conclude that the *Civil Rights Cases* have no relevance to the basis of decision here where the Act explicitly relies upon the commerce power, and where the record is filled with testimony of obstructions and restraints resulting from the discriminations found to be existing. We now pass to that phase of the case.

6. The Basis of Congressional Action

While the Act as adopted carried no congressional findings the record of its passage through each house is replete with evidence of the burdens that discrimination by race or color places upon interstate commerce.

. . . .

7. The Power of Congress Over Interstate Travel

The power of Congress to deal with these obstructions depends on the meaning of the Commerce Clause. . . .

In short, the determinative test of the exercise of power by the Congress under the Commerce Clause is simply whether the activity sought to be regulated is "commerce which concerns more States than one" and has a real and substantial relation to the national interest. Let us now turn to this facet of the problem. . . .

That Congress was legislating against moral wrongs in many of these areas [in prior legislation] rendered its enactments no less valid. In framing Title II of this Act Congress was also dealing with what it considered a moral problem. But that fact does not detract from the overwhelming evidence of the disruptive effect that racial discrimination has had on commercial intercourse. It was this burden which empowered Congress to enact appropriate legislation, and, given this basis for the exercise of its power, Congress was not restricted by the fact that the particular obstruction to interstate commerce with which it was dealing was also deemed a moral and social wrong.

It is said that the operation of the motel here is of a purely local character. But, assuming this to be true, "[i]f it is interstate commerce that feels the pinch, it does not matter how local the operation which applies the squeeze." . . . Thus the power of Congress to promote interstate commerce also includes the power to regulate the local incidents thereof, including local activities in both States of origin and destination, which might have a substantial and harmful effect upon that commerce. One need only examine the evidence which we have discussed above to see that Congress may—as it has—prohibit racial discrimination by motels serving travelers, however "local" their operations may appear.

Nor does the Act deprive appellant of liberty or property under the Fifth Amendment. The commerce power invoked here by the Congress is a specific and plenary one authorized by the Constitution itself. The only questions are: (1) whether Congress had a rational basis for findings that racial discrimination by motels affected commerce, and (2) if it had such a basis, whether the means it selected to eliminate that evil are reasonable and appropriate. If they are, appellant has no "right" to select its guests as it sees fit, free from governmental regulation.

There is nothing novel about such legislation. Thirty-two States now have it on their books either by statute or executive order and many cities provide such regulation. Some of these Acts go back fourscore years. It has been repeatedly held by this Court that such laws do not violate the Due Process Clause of the Fourteenth Amendment. Perhaps the first such holding was in the *Civil Rights Cases* themselves, where Mr. Justice Bradley for the Court inferentially found that innkeepers, "by the laws of all the States, so far as we are aware, are bound, to the extent of their facilities, to furnish proper accommodation to all unobjectionable persons who in good faith apply for them." At 25. . . .

It is doubtful if in the long run appellant will suffer economic loss as a result of the Act. Experience is to the contrary where discrimination is completely obliterated as to all public accommodations. But whether this be true or not is of no consequence since this Court has specifically held that the fact that a "member of the class which is regulated may suffer economic losses not shared by others . . . has never been a barrier" to such legislation. . . . Likewise in a long line of cases this Court has rejected the claim that the prohibition of racial discrimination in public accommodations interferes with personal liberty. See *District of Columbia* v. *John R. Thompson Co.*, 346 U.S. 100 (1953), and cases there cited, where we concluded that Congress had delegated law-making power to the District of Columbia "as broad as the police power of a state" which included the power to adopt "a law prohibiting discriminations against Negroes by the owners and managers of restaurants in the District of Columbia." At 110. Neither do we find any merit in the claim that the Act is a taking of property without just compensation. The cases are to the contrary. . . .

We find no merit in the remainder of appellant's contentions, including that of "involuntary servitude." As we have seen, 32 States prohibit racial discrimination in public accommodations. These laws but codify the common-law innkeeper rule which long predated the Thirteenth Amendment. It is difficult to believe that the Amendment was intended to abrogate this principle. Indeed, the opinion of the Court in the *Civil Rights Cases* is to the contrary as we have seen, it having noted with approval the laws of "all the States" prohibiting discrimination. We could not say that the requirements of the Act in this regard are in any way "akin to African slavery." *Butler* v. *Perry,* 240 U.S. 328, 332 (1916).

We, therefore, conclude that the action of the Congress in the adoption of the Act as applied here to a motel which concededly serves interstate travelers is within the power granted it by the Commerce Clause of the Constitution, as interpreted by this Court for 140 years. It may be argued that Congress could have pursued other methods to eliminate the obstructions it found in interstate commerce caused by racial discrimination. But this is a matter of policy that rests entirely with the Congress not with the courts. How obstructions in commerce may be removed—what means are to be employed—is within the sound and exclusive discretion of the Congress. It is subject only to one caveat—that the means chosen by it must be reasonably adapted to the end permitted by the Constitution. We cannot say that its choice here was not so adapted. The Constitution requires no more.

Affirmed.

PRESIDENT JOHNSON'S COMMENCEMENT ADDRESS AT HOWARD UNIVERSITY (1965)

Lyndon B. Johnson's address at the Howard University commencement exercises on June 4, 1965, moved far beyond any commitment to interracial reform ever proposed by a Chief Executive. The President asserted that the solution exceeded the bounds of legalistic and procedural reform. Substantive redress, he said, demanded a total effort of unprecedented dimensions to overcome generations of oppression and impoverishment.

Within five months of the Howard Address, however, its brightest promises were in severe jeopardy. Escalation of the war in Vietnam increasingly drained Executive energies and federal resources. Urban riots—such as those in the Watts section of Los Angeles—nurtured overt white resistance to further interracial reform. Moreover, advocates of Black Power—whether or not properly understood and interpreted—helped create divisions among Negro spokesmen and their white supporters.

Whether the Howard Address represents a promising new phase in the civil rights struggle or stands merely as a valedictory remains to be determined.

DOCUMENT 91

Text of President Johnson's commencement address, Howard University, Washington, D.C., June 4, 1965[*]

Our earth is the home of revolution.

In every corner of every continent men charged with hope contend with ancient ways in pursuit of justice. They reach for the newest of weapons to realize the oldest of dreams: that each may walk in freedom and pride, stretching his talents, enjoying the fruits of the earth.

Our enemies may occasionally seize the day of change. But it is the banner of our revolution they take. And our own future is linked to this process of swift and turbulent change in many lands. But nothing, in any country, touches us more profoundly, nothing is more freighted with meaning for our own destiny, than the revolution of the Negro American.

In far too many ways American Negroes have been another nation: deprived of freedom, crippled by hatred, the doors of opportunity closed to hope.

In our time change has come to this nation too. Heroically,

---

[*] White House Press Release.

the American Negro—acting with impressive restraint—has peacefully protested and marched, entered the courtrooms and the seats of government, demanding a justice long denied. The voice of the Negro was the call to action. But it is a tribute to America that, once aroused, the courts and the Congress, the President and most of the people, have been the allies of progress.

Thus we have seen the high court of the country declare that discrimination based on race was repugnant to the Constitution, and therefore void. We have seen—in 1957, 1960, and again in 1964—the first civil rights legislation in almost a century.

As majority leader I helped guide two of these bills through the Senate. And, as your President, I was proud to sign the third.

And soon we will have the fourth new law, guaranteeing every American the right to vote.

No act of my administration will give me greater satisfaction than the day when my signature makes this bill too the law of the land.

The voting rights bill will be the latest, and among the most important, in a long series of victories. But this victory—as Winston Churchill said of another triumph for freedom—"is not the end. It is not even the beginning of the end. But it is, perhaps, the end of the beginning."

That beginning is freedom; and the barriers to that freedom are tumbling. Freedom is the right to share, fully and equally, in American society—to vote, to hold a job, to enter a public place, to go to school. It is the right to be treated, in every part of our national life, as a man equal in dignity and promise to all others.

But freedom is not enough. You do not wipe away the scars of centuries by saying: Now, you are free to go where you want, do as you desire, and choose the leaders you please.

You do not take a man who, for years, has been hobbled by chains, liberate him, bring him to the starting line of a race, saying "you are free to compete with all the others," and still justly believe you have been completely fair.

Thus it is not enough to open the gates of opportunity. All our citizens must have the ability to walk through those gates.

This is the next and the more profound stage of the battle for civil rights. We seek not just freedom but opportunity—

not just legal equity but human ability—not just equality as a right and a theory, but equality as a fact and a result.

For the task is to give twenty million Negroes the same chance as every other American to learn and grow—to work and share in society—to develop their abilities—physical, mental and spiritual, and to pursue their individual happiness.

To this end equal opportunity is essential, but not enough. Men and women of all races are born with the same range of abilities. But ability is not just the product of birth. It is stretched or stunted by the family you live with, and the neighborhood you live in—by the school you go to, and the poverty or richness of your surroundings. It is the product of a hundred unseen forces playing upon the infant, the child, and the man.

This graduating class at Howard University is witness to the indomitable determination of the Negro American to win his way in American life.

The number of Negroes in schools of high learning has almost doubled in fifteen years. The number of nonwhite professional workers has more than doubled in ten years. The median income of Negro college women now exceeds that of white college women. And these are the enormous accomplishments of distinguished individual Negroes—many of them graduates of this institution.

These are proud and impressive achievements. But they only tell the story of a growing middle class minority, steadily narrowing the gap between them and their white counterparts.

But for the great majority of Negro Americans—the poor, the unemployed, the uprooted and dispossessed—there is a grimmer story. They still are another nation. Despite the court orders and the laws, the victories and speeches, for them the walls are rising and the gulf is widening.

Here are some of the facts of this American failure.

Thirty five years ago the rate of unemployment for Negroes and whites was about the same. Today the Negro rate is twice as high.

In 1948 the 8 per cent unemployment rate for Negro teenage boys was actually less than that of whites. By last year it had grown to 23 per cent, as against 13 per cent for whites.

Between 1949 and 1959, the income of Negro men relative to white men declined in every section of the country. From 1952 to 1963 the median income of Negro families compared to white actually dropped from 57 per cent to 53 per cent.

In the years 1955–57, 22 per cent of experienced Negro workers were out of work at some time during the year. In 1961–63 that proportion had soared to 29 per cent.

Since 1947 the number of white families living in poverty has decreased 27 per cent while the number of poor non-white families went down only 3 per cent.

The infant mortality of nonwhites in 1940 was 70 per cent greater than whites. Twenty-two years later it was 90 per cent greater.

Moreover, the isolation of Negro from white communities is increasing, rather than diminishing as Negroes crowd into the central cities—becoming a city within a city.

Of course Negro Americans as well as white Americans have shared in our rising national abundance. But the harsh fact of the matter is that in the battle for true equality too many are losing ground.

We are not completely sure why this is. The causes are complex and subtle. But we do know the two broad basic reasons. And we know we have to act.

First, Negroes are trapped—as many whites are trapped—in inherited, gateless poverty. They lack training and skills. They are shut in slums, without decent medical care. Private and public poverty combine to cripple their capacities.

We are attacking these evils through our poverty program, our education program, our health program and a dozen more —aimed at the root causes of poverty.

We will increase, and accelerate, and broaden this attack in years to come, until this most enduring of foes yields to our unyielding will.

But there is a *second* cause—more difficult to explain, more deeply grounded, more desperate in its force. It is the devastating heritage of long years of slavery; and a century of oppression, hatred and injustice.

For Negro poverty is not white poverty. Many of its causes and many of its cures are the same. But there are differences —deep, corrosive, obstinate differences—radiating painful roots into the community, the family, and the nature of the individual.

These differences are not racial differences. They are solely and simply the consequence of ancient brutality, past injustice, and present prejudice. They are anguishing to observe. For the

Negro they are a reminder of oppression. For the white they are a reminder of guilt. But they must be faced, and dealt with, and overcome; if we are to reach the time when the only difference between Negroes and whites is the color of their skin.

Nor can we find a complete answer in the experience of other American minorities. They made a valiant, and largely successful effort to emerge from poverty and prejudice. The Negro, like these others, will have to rely mostly on his own efforts. But he cannot do it alone. For they did not have the heritage of centuries to overcome. They did not have a cultural tradition which had been twisted and battered by endless years of hatred and hopelessness. Nor were they excluded because of race or color—a feeling whose dark intensity is matched by no other prejudice in our society.

Nor can these differences be understood as isolated infirmities. They are a seamless web. They cause each other. They result from each other. They reinforce each other. Much of the Negro community is buried under a blanket of history and circumstance. It is not a lasting solution to lift just one corner. We must stand on all sides and raise the entire cover if we are to liberate our fellow citizens.

One of the differences is the increased concentration of Negroes in our cities. More than 73 per cent of all Negroes live in urban areas compared with less than 70 per cent of whites. Most of them live in slums. And most of them live together; a separated people. Men are shaped by their world. When it is a world of decay ringed by an invisible wall—when escape is arduous and uncertain, and the saving pressures of a more hopeful society are unknown—it can cripple the youth and desolate the man.

There is also the burden a dark skin can add to the search for a productive place in society. Unemployment strikes most swiftly and broadly at the Negro. This burden erodes hope. Blighted hope breeds despair. Despair brings indifference to the learning which offers a way out. And despair coupled with indifference is often the source of destructive rebellion against the fabric of society.

There is also the lacerating hurt of early collision with white hatred or prejudice, distaste or condescension. Other groups have felt similar intolerance. But success and achievement could wipe it away. They do not change the color of a man's skin. I have seen this uncomprehending pain in the eyes of young Mexican-American school children. It can be overcome. But, for many, the wounds are always open.

Perhaps most important—its influence radiating to every part of life—is the breakdown of the Negro family structure. For this, most of all, white America must accept responsibility. It flows from centuries of oppression and persecution of the Negro man. It flows from the long years of degradation and discrimination which have attacked his dignity and assaulted his ability to provide for his family.

This, too, is not pleasant to look upon. But it must be faced by those whose serious intent is to improve the life of all Americans.

Only a minority—less than half—of all Negro children reach the age of 18 having lived all their lives with both parents. At this moment, today, little less than two thirds are living with both parents. Probably a majority of all Negro children receive federally-aided public assistance during their childhood.

The family is the cornerstone of our society. More than any other force it shapes the attitude, the hopes, the ambitions, and the values of the child. When the family collapses the child is usually damaged. When it happens on a massive scale the community itself is crippled.

Unless we work to strengthen the family—to create conditions under which most parents will stay together—all the rest: schools and playgrounds, public assistance and private concern—will not be enough to cut completely the circle of despair and deprivation.

There is no single easy answer to all these problems.

Jobs are part of the answer. They bring the income which permits a man to provide for his family.

Decent homes in decent surroundings and a chance to learn are part of the answer.

Welfare and social programs better designed to hold families together are part of the answer.

Care for the sick is part of the answer.

An understanding heart by all Americans is also part of the answer.

To all these fronts—and a dozen more—I will dedicate the expanding efforts of my administration.

But there are other answers still to be found. Nor do we

fully understand all the problems. Therefore, this fall, I intend to call a White House Conference of scholars, experts, Negro leaders, and officials at every level of government.

Its theme and title: *"To Fulfill These Rights."*

Its object: to help the American Negro fulfill the rights which—after the long time of injustice—he is finally about to secure.

—to move beyond opportunity to achievement.

—to shatter forever, not only the barriers of law and public practice, but the walls which bound the condition of man by the color of his skin.

—to dissolve, as best we can, the antique enmities of the heart which diminish the holder, divide the great democracy, and do wrong to the children of God.

I pledge this will be a chief goal of my Administration, and of my program next year, and in years to come.

I hope it will be part of the program of all America.

For what is justice?

It is to fulfill the fair expectations of man.

Thus, American justice is a very special thing. For, from the first, this has been a land of towering expectations. It was to be a nation where each man would be ruled by the common consent of all—enshrined in law, given life by institutions, guided by men themselves subject to its rule. And all—of every station and origin—would be touched equally in obligation and in liberty.

Beyond the law lay the land. It was a rich land, glowing with more abundant promise than ever man had seen. Here, unlike any place yet known, all were to share the harvest.

And beyond this was the dignity of man. Each could become whatever his qualities of mind and spirit would permit —to strive, to seek, and, if he could, to find his happiness.

This is American justice. We have pursued it faithfully to the edge of our imperfections. And we have failed to find it for the American Negro.

It is the glorious opportunity of this generation to end the one huge wrong of the American nation—and in so doing to find America for ourselves, with the same immense thrill of discovery which gripped those who first began to realize that here, at last, was a home for freedom.

All it will take is for all of us to understand what this country is and what it must become.

The Scripture promises: "I shall light a candle of understanding in thine heart, which shall not be put out."

Together, and with millions more, we can light that candle of understanding in the heart of America.

And, once lit, it will never go out.

THE VOTING RIGHTS ACT (1965)

The march from Selma to Montgomery, Alabama, in March, 1965, marred by the violent deaths of the Reverend James Reeb and Mrs. Viola Liuzzo, convinced the nation at large that additional federal legislation was necessary to guarantee Negro voting rights. On March 15, President Johnson addressed a joint session of Congress to request a new voting law. "The real hero of this struggle," he said, "is the American Negro. His actions and protests, his courage to risk safety and even to risk his life, have awakened the conscience of this nation."

The Voting Rights Act of 1965 provided for the assignment of federal examiners to conduct registration and observe voting in states or counties where patterns of discrimination existed. The law suspended literacy tests and other discriminatory devices employed in any federal, state, local, general, or primary election in the states of Alabama, Alaska, Georgia, Louisiana, Mississippi, South Carolina, and Virginia, and in at least twenty-six counties of North Carolina. These areas were identified on the basis of the legislative stipulation that this act could apply to any state or political subdivision which (1) had maintained a test or device as prerequisite to voting as of November 1, 1964, and (2) had a total voting-age population with less than fifty percent registered or actually voting in the 1964 Presidential election.

While the main thrust of the act was concerned with the plight of Negro voters, implementation was designed to aid the economically impoverished, the poorly educated, and the non-English-speaking minorities as well.

DOCUMENT 92

An act to enforce the Fifteenth Amendment to the Constitution of the United States, and for other purposes*

Be it enacted by the Senate and House of Representatives of the United States of America in Congress assembled, That this Act shall be known as the "Voting Rights Act of 1965"

SEC. 2. No voting qualification or prerequisite to voting, or standard, practice, or procedure shall be imposed or applied by any State or political subdivision to deny or abridge the right of any citizen of the United States to vote on account of race or color.

. . . .

(c) If in any proceeding instituted by the Attorney General under any statute to enforce the guarantees of the fifteenth amendment in any State or political subdivision the court finds that violations of the fifteenth amendment justifying equitable relief have occurred within the territory of such State or political subdivision, the court, in addition to such relief as it may grant, shall retain jurisdiction for such period as it may deem appropriate and during such period no voting qualification or prerequisite to voting, or standard, practice, or procedure with respect to voting different from that in force or effect at the time the proceeding was commenced shall be enforced unless and until the court finds that such qualification, prerequisite, standard, practice, or procedure does not have the purpose and will not have the effect of denying or abridging the right to vote on account of race or color: *Provided,* That such qualification, prerequisite, standard, practice, or procedure may be enforced if the qualification, prerequisite, standard, practice, or procedure has been submitted by the chief legal officer or other appropriate official of such State or subdivision to the Attorney General and the Attorney General has not interposed an objection within sixty days after such submission, except that neither the court's finding nor the Attorney General's failure to object shall bar a subsequent action to enjoin en-

---

* 79 Stat. 437 (1965).

forcement of such qualification, prerequisite, standard, practice, or procedure.

Sec. 4. (a) To assure that the right of citizens of the United States to vote is not denied or abridged on account of race or color, no citizen shall be denied the right to vote in any Federal, State, or local election because of his failure to comply with any test or device in any State with respect to which the determinations have been made under subsection (b) or in any political subdivision with respect to which such determinations have been made as a separate unit, unless the United States District Court for the District of Columbia in an action for a declaratory judgment brought by such State or subdivision against the United States has determined that no such test or device has been used during the five years preceding the filing of the action for the purpose or with the effect of denying or abridging the right to vote on account of race or color: *Provided,* That no such declaratory judgment shall issue with respect to any plaintiff for a period of five years after the entry of a final judgment of any court of the United States, other than the denial of a declaratory judgment under this section, whether entered prior to or after the enactment of this Act, determining that denials or abridgments of the right to vote on account of race or color through the use of such tests or devices have occurred anywhere in the territory of such plaintiff.

. . . .

(b) The provisions of subsection (a) shall apply in any State or in any political subdivision of a state which (1) the Attorney General determines maintained on November 1, 1964, any test or device, and with respect to which (2) the Director of the Census determines that less than 50 per centum of the persons of voting age residing therein were registered on November 1, 1964, or that less than 50 per centum of such persons voted in the presidential election of November 1964.

. . . .

(c) The phrase "test or device" shall mean any requirement that a person as a prerequisite for voting or registration for voting (1) demonstrate the ability to read, write, understand, or interpret any matter, (2) demonstrate any educational achievement or his knowledge of any particular subject, (3) possess good moral character, or (4) prove his qualifications by the voucher of registered voters or members of any other class.

(d) For purposes of this section no State or political subdivision shall be determined to have engaged in the use of tests or devices for the purpose or with the effect of denying or abridging the right to vote on account of race or color if (1) incidents of such use have been few in number and have been promptly and effectively corrected by State or local action, (2) the continuing effect of such incidents has been eliminated, and (3) there is no reasonable probability of their recurrence in the future.

(e) (1) Congress hereby declares that to secure the rights under the fourteenth amendment of persons educated in American-flag schools in which the predominant classroom language was other than English, it is necessary to prohibit the States from conditioning the right to vote of such persons on ability to read, write, understand, or interpret any matter in the English language.

(2) No person who demonstrates that he has successfully completed the sixth primary grade in a public school in, or a private school accredited by, any State or territory, the District of Columbia, or the Commonwealth of Puerto Rico in which the predominant classroom language was other than English, shall be denied the right to vote in any Federal, State, or local election because of his inability to read, write, understand, or interpret any matter in the English language, except that in States in which State law provides that a different level of education is presumptive of literacy, he shall demonstrate that he has successfully completed an equivalent level of education in a public school in, or a private school accredited by, any State or territory, the District of Columbia, or the Commonwealth of Puerto Rico in which the predominant classroom language was other than English.

. . . .

SEC. 6. Whenever (a) a court has authorized the appointment of examiners pursuant to the provisions of section 3(a), or (b) unless a declaratory judgment has been rendered under section 4(a), the Attorney General certifies with respect to any political subdivision named in, or included within the scope of, determinations made under section 4(b) that (1) he has received complaints in writing from twenty or more residents of such political subdivision alleging that they have been denied the right to vote under color of law on account of race or color, and that he believes such complaints to be meritorious, or (2) that in his judgment (considering, among other factors, whether the ratio of nonwhite persons to white persons registered to vote within such subdivision appears to him to be reasonably attributable to violations of the fifteenth amendment or whether substantial evidence exists that bona fide efforts are being made within such subdivision to comply with the fifteenth amendment), the appointment of examiners is otherwise necessary to enforce the guarantees of the fifteenth amendment, the Civil Service Commission shall appoint as many examiners for such subdivision as it may deem appropriate to prepare and maintain lists of persons eligible to vote in Federal, State, and local elections. Such examiners, hearing officers provided for in section 9(a), and other persons deemed necessary by the Commission to carry out the provisions and purposes of this Act shall be appointed, compensated, and separated without regard to the provisions of any statute administered by the Civil Service Commission, and service under this Act shall not be considered employment for the purposes of any statute administered by the Civil Service Commission, except the provisions of section 9 of the Act of August 2, 1939, as amended (5 U.S.C. 118i), prohibiting partisan political activity: *Provided*, That the Commission is authorized, after consulting the head of the appropriate department or agency, to designate suitable persons in the official service of the United States, with their consent. to serve in these positions. Examiners and hearing officers shall have the power to administer oaths.

• • • •

SEC. 8. Whenever an examiner is serving under this Act in any political subdivision, the Civil Service Commission may assign, at the request of the Attorney General, one or more persons, who may be officers of the United States, (1) to enter and attend at any place for holding an election in such subdivision for the purpose of observing whether persons who are

entitled to vote are being permitted to vote, and (2) to enter
and attend at any place for tabulating the votes cast at any
election held in such subdivision for the purpose of observing
whether votes cast by persons entitled to vote are being properly tabulated. Such persons so assigned shall report to an
examiner appointed for such political subdivision, to the Attorney General, and if the appointment of examiners has been
authorized pursuant to section 3(a), to the court.

. . . .

SEC. 10. (a) The Congress finds that the requirement of the
payment of a poll tax as a precondition to voting (i) precludes
persons of limited means from voting or imposes unreasonable
financial hardship upon such persons as a precondition to their
exercise of the franchise, (ii) does not bear a reasonable relationship to any legitimate State interest in the conduct of elections, and (iii) in some areas has the purpose or effect of denying persons the right to vote because of race or color. Upon
the basis of these findings, Congress declares that the constitutional right of citizens to vote is denied or abridged in some
areas by the requirement of the payment of a poll tax as a
precondition to voting.

. . . .

SEC. 11. (a) No person acting under color of law shall fail
or refuse to permit any person to vote who is entitled to vote
under any provision of this Act or is otherwise qualified to
vote, or willfully fail or refuse to tabulate, count, and report
such person's vote.

(b) No person, whether acting under color of law or otherwise, shall intimidate, threaten, or coerce, or attempt to intimidate, threaten, or coerce any person for voting or attempting to vote, or intimidate, threaten, or coerce, or attempt to
intimidate, threaten, or coerce any person for urging or aiding
any person to vote or attempt to vote, or intimidate, threaten,
or coerce any person for exercising any powers or duties under
section 3(a), 6, 8, 9, 10, or 12(e).

(c) Whoever knowingly or willfully gives false information
as to his name, address, or period of residence in the voting
district for the purpose of establishing his eligibility to register

or vote, or conspires with another individual for the purpose of encouraging his false registration to vote or illegal voting, or pays or offers to pay or accepts payment either for registration to vote or for voting shall be fined not more than $10,000 or imprisoned not more than five years, or both: *Provided, however,* That this provision shall be applicable only to general, special, or primary elections held solely or in part for the purpose of selecting or electing any candidate for the office of President, Vice President, presidential elector, Member of the United States Senate, Member of the United States House of Representatives, or Delegates or Commissioners from the territories or possessions, or Resident Commissioner of the Commonwealth of Puerto Rico.

(d) Whoever, in any matter within the jurisdiction of an examiner or hearing officer knowingly and willfully falsifies or conceals a material fact, or makes any false, fictitious, or fraudulent statements or representations, or makes or uses any false writing or document knowing the same to contain any false, fictitious, or fraudulent statement or entry, shall be fined not more than $10,000 or imprisoned not more than five years, or both.

Sec. 12. (a) Whoever shall deprive or attempt to deprive any person of any right secured by section 2, 3, 4, 5, 7, or 10 or shall violate section 11 (a) or (b), shall be fined not more than $5,000, or imprisoned not more than five years, or both.

(b) Whoever, within a year following an election in a political subdivision in which an examiner has been appointed (1) destroys, defaces, mutilates, or otherwise alters the marking of a paper ballot which has been cast in such election, or (2) alters any official record of voting in such election tabulated from a voting machine or otherwise, shall be fined not more than $5,000, or imprisoned not more than five years, or both. . . .

SOUTH CAROLINA V. KATZENBACH (1966)

Turning the paper rights granted by the Fifteenth Amendment (Document 48) into rights in practice became a basic Congressional objective in the period of legislative action begun in 1957. Provisions designed to secure Negro voting rights were incorporated into the Civil Rights Acts of 1957, 1960, and 1964 (Documents 81, 82, and 89).

Southern legal stratagems, however, continued to delay non-discriminatory treatment at the polls. And while each of these legal devices was struck down as unconstitutional, it was impossible to achieve comprehensive franchise equality on a case-by-case basis.

Congress responded with the Voting Rights Act of 1965 (Document 92), which had a long series of complex and comprehensive enforcement provisions. But were they constitutional? The Supreme Court responded with a unanimous yes, save for a dissent in part by Justice Hugo L. Black. But the Court was careful to point out that "only some of the many portions of the Act" were before it for decision. As Justice William J. Brennan, Jr., wrote: "Judicial review of these (other) sections must await subsequent litigation."

DOCUMENT 93

South Carolina v. Katzenbach*

MR. CHIEF JUSTICE WARREN delivered the opinion of the Court.

By leave of the Court, 382 U.S. 898, South Carolina has filed a bill of complaint, seeking a declaration that selected provisions of the Voting Rights Act of 1965 violate the Federal Constitution, and asking for an injunction against enforcement of these provisions by the Attorney General. . . .

The Voting Rights Act was designed by Congress to banish the blight of racial discrimination in voting, which has infected the electoral process in parts of our country for nearly a century. The Act creates stringent new remedies for voting discrimination where it persists on a pervasive scale, and in addition the statute strengthens existing remedies for pockets of voting discrimination elsewhere in the country. Congress assumed the power to prescribe these remedies from § 2 of the Fifteenth Amendment, which authorizes the National Legislature to effectuate by "appropriate" measures the constitutional prohibition against racial discrimination in voting. We

---

* Supreme Court of the United States, 383 U.S. 301 (1966).

hold that the sections of the Act which are properly before us are an appropriate means for carrying out Congress' constitutional responsibilities and are consonant with all other provisions of the Constitution. We therefore deny South Carolina's request that enforcement of these sections of the Act be enjoined.

I

The constitutional propriety of the Voting Rights Act of 1965 must be judged with reference to the historical experience which it reflects. . . .

Two points emerge vividly from the voluminous legislative history of the Act contained in the committee hearings and floor debates. First: Congress felt itself confronted by an insidious and pervasive evil which had been perpetuated in certain parts of our country through unremitting and ingenious defiance of the Constitution. Second: Congress concluded that the unsuccessful remedies which it had prescribed in the past would have to be replaced by sterner and more elaborate measures in order to satisfy the clear commands of the Fifteenth Amendment.

. . . .

The course of . . . Fifteenth Amendment litigation in this Court demonstrates the variety and persistence of . . . institutions designed to deprive Negroes of the right to vote. Grandfather clauses were invalidated in *Guinn* v. *United States*, 238 U.S. 347, and *Myers* v. *Anderson*, 238 U.S. 368. Procedural hurdles were struck down in *Lane* v. *Wilson*, 307 U.S. 268. The white primary was outlawed in *Smith* v. *Allwright*, 321 U.S. 649, and *Terry* v. *Adams*, 345 U.S. 461. Improper challenges were nullified in *United States* v. *Thomas*, 362 U.S. 58. Racial gerrymandering was forbidden by *Gomillion* v. *Lightfoot*, 364 U.S. 339. Finally, discriminatory application of voting tests was condemned in *Schnell* v. *Davis*, 336 U.S. 933; *Alabama* v. *United States*, 371 U.S. 37; and *Louisiana* v. *United States*, 380 U.S. 145.

According to the evidence in recent Justice Department

voting suits, the latter stratagem is now the principal method used to bar Negroes from the polls.

. . . .

In recent years, Congress has repeatedly tried to cope with the problem by facilitating case-by-case litigation against voting discrimination. The Civil Rights Act of 1957 authorized the Attorney General to seek injunction against public and private interference with the right to vote on racial grounds. Perfecting amendments in the Civil Rights Act of 1960 permitted the joinder of States as parties defendant, gave the Attorney General access to local voting records, and authorized courts to register voters in areas of systematic discrimination. Title I of the Civil Rights Act of 1964 expedited the hearing of voting cases before three-judge courts and outlawed some of the tactics used to disqualify Negroes from voting in federal elections.

Despite the earnest efforts of the Justice Department and of many federal judges, these new laws have done little to cure the problem of voting discrimination. According to estimates by the Attorney General during hearings on the Act, registration of voting-age Negroes in Alabama rose only from 14.2% to 19.4% between 1958 and 1964; in Louisiana it barely inched ahead from 31.7% to 31.8% between 1956 and 1965; and in Mississippi it increased only from 4.4% to 6.4% between 1954 and 1964. In each instance, registration of voting-age whites ran roughly 50 percentage points or more ahead of Negro registration. . . .

II

The Voting Rights Act of 1965 reflects Congress' firm intention to rid the country of racial discrimination in voting.

. . . .

At the outset, we emphasize that only some of the many portions of the Act are properly before us. South Carolina has not challenged §§ 2, 3, 4 (e), 6 (a), 8, 10, 12 (d) and (e), 13 (b), and other miscellaneous provisions having nothing to do with this lawsuit. Judicial review of these sections must await subsequent litigation. . . .

III

These provisions of the Voting Rights Act of 1965 are challenged on the fundamental ground that they exceed the powers of Congress and encroach on an area reserved to the States by the Constitution. South Carolina and certain of the *amici curiae* also attack specific sections of the Act for more particular reasons. They argue that the coverage formula prescribed in § 4 (a)–(d) violates the principle of the equality of States, denies due process by employing an invalid presumption and by barring judicial review of administrative findings, constitutes a forbidden bill of attainder, and impairs the separation of powers by adjudicating guilt through legislation. They claim that the review of new voting rules required in § 5 infringes Article III by directing the District Court to issue advisory opinions. They contend that the assignment of federal examiners authorized in § 6 (b) abridges due process by precluding judicial review of administrative findings and impairs the separation of powers by giving the Attorney General judicial functions; also that the challenge procedure prescribed in § 9 denies due process on account of its speed. Finally, South Carolina and certain of the *amici curiae* maintain that §§ 4 (a) and 5, buttressed by § 14 (b) of the Act, abridge due process by limiting litigation to a distant forum.

Some of these contentions may be dismissed at the outset. The word "person" in the context of the Due Process Clause of the Fifth Amendment cannot, by any reasonable mode of interpretation, be expanded to encompass the States of the Union, and to our knowledge this has never been done by any court. . . . The objections to the Act which are raised under these provisions may therefore be considered only as additional aspects of the basic question presented by the case: Has Congress exercised its powers under the Fifteenth Amendment in an appropriate manner with relation to the States?

The ground rules for resolving this question are clear. The language and purpose of the Fifteenth Amendment, the prior decisions construing its several provisions, and the general doctrines of constitutional interpretation, all point to one fundamental principle. As against the reserved powers of the States, Congress may use any rational means to effectuate the constitutional prohibition of racial discrimination in voting. Cf. our rulings last Term, sustaining Title II of the Civil Rights Act of 1964, in *Heart of Atlanta Motel* v. *United States,* 379 U.S. 241, 258–259, 261–262; and *Katzenbach* v. *McClung,* 379 U.S. 294, 303–304. We turn now to a more detailed description of the standards which govern our review of the Act.

Section 1 of the Fifteenth Amendment declares that "[t]he right of citizens of the United States to vote shall not be denied or abridged by the United States or by any State on account of race, color, or previous conditon of servitude." This declaration has always been treated as self-executing and has repeatedly been construed, without further legislative specification, to invalidate state voting qualifications or procedures which are discriminatory on their face or in practice.

. . . .

South Carolina contends that the cases cited above are precedents only for the authority of the judiciary to strike down state statutes and procedures—that to allow an exercise of this authority by Congress would be to rob the courts of their rightful constitutional role. On the contrary, § 2 of the Fifteenth Amendment expressly declares that "Congress shall have power to enforce this article by appropriate legislation." By adding this authorization, the Framers indicated that Congress was to be chiefly responsible for implementing the rights created in § 1. "It is the power of Congress which has been enlarged. Congress is authorized to *enforce* the prohibitions by appropriate legislation. Some legislation is contemplated to make the [Civil War] amendments fully effective." *Ex parte Virginia,* 100 U.S. 339, 345. Accordingly, in addition to the courts, Congress has full remedial powers to effectuate the constitutional prohibition against racial discrimination in voting.

Congress has repeatedly exercised these powers in the past, and its enactments have repeatedly been upheld. For recent examples, see the Civil Rights Act of 1957, which was sustained in *United States* v. *Raines,* 362 U.S. 17; *United States* v. *Thomas, supra;* and *Hannah* v. *Larche,* 363 U.S. 420; and the Civil Rights Act of 1960, which was upheld in *Alabama* v. *United States, supra; Louisiana* v. *United States, supra;* and *United States* v. *Mississippi,* 380 U.S. 128. On the rare occasions when the Court has found an unconstitutional exercise of these powers, in its opinion Congress had attacked evils not comprehended by the Fifteenth Amendment. See *United States* v. *Reese,* 92 U.S. 214; *James* v. *Bowman,* 190 U.S. 127.

. . . .

We therefore reject South Carolina's argument that Congress may appropriately do no more than to forbid violations of the Fifteenth Amendment in general terms—that the task of fashioning specific remedies or of applying them to particular localities must necessarily be left entirely to the courts. Congress is not circumscribed by any such artificial rules under § 2 of the Fifteenth Amendment. . . .

IV

Congress exercised its authority under the Fifteenth Amendment in an inventive manner when it enacted the Voting Rights Act of 1965. First: The measure prescribes remedies for voting discrimination which go into effect without any need for prior adjudication. This was clearly a legitimate response to the problem, for which there is ample precedent under other constitutional provisions. See *Katzenbach* v. *McClung,* 379 U.S. 294, 302–304; *United States* v. *Darby,* 312 U.S. 100, 120–121. Congress had found that case-by-case litigation was inadequate to combat widespread and persistent discrimination in voting, because of the inordinate amount of time and energy required to overcome the obstructionist tactics invariably encountered in these lawsuits. After enduring nearly a century of systematic resistance to the Fifteenth Amendment, Congress might well decide to shift the advantage of time and inertia from the perpetrators of the evil to its victims. The question remains, of course, whether the specific remedies prescribed in the Act were an appropriate means of combatting the evil, and to this question we shall presently address ourselves.

Second: The Act intentionally confines these remedies to a

small number of States and political subdivisions which in most instances were familiar to Congress by name. This, too, was a permissible method of dealing with the problem. Congress had learned that substantial voting discrimination presently occurs in certain sections of the country, and it knew no way of accurately forecasting whether the evil might spread elsewhere in the future. In acceptable legislative fashion, Congress chose to limit its attention to the geographic areas where immediate action seemed necessary. . . . The doctrine of the equality of States, invoked by South Carolina, does not bar this approach, for that doctrine applies only to the terms upon which States are admitted to the Union, and not to the remedies for local evils which have subsequently appeared. . . .

Coverage Formula

We now consider the related question of whether the specific States and political subdivisions within § 4 (b) of the Act were an appropriate target for the new remedies. South Carolina contends that the coverage formula is awkwardly designed in a number of respects and that it disregards various local conditions which have nothing to do with racial discrimination. These arguments, however, are largely beside the point. Congress began work with reliable evidence of actual voting discrimination in a great majority of the States and political subdivisions affected by the new remedies of the Act. The formula eventually evolved to describe these areas was relevant to the problem of voting discrimination, and Congress was therefore entitled to infer a significant danger of the evil in the few remaining States and political subdivisions covered by § 4 (b) of the Act. No more was required to justify the application to these areas of Congress' express powers under the Fifteenth Amendment. . . .

To be specific, the new remedies of the Act are imposed on three States—Alabama, Louisiana, and Mississippi—in which federal courts have repeatedly found substantial voting discrimination. Section 4 (b) of the Act also embraces two other States—Georgia and South Carolina—plus large portions of a third State—North Carolina—for which there was more fragmentary evidence of recent voting discrimination mainly adduced by the Justice Department and the Civil Rights Commission. All of these areas were appropriately subjected to the new remedies. In identifying past evils, Congress obviously may avail itself of information from any probative source.

. . . .

The Act bars direct judicial review of the findings by the Attorney General and the Director of the Census which trigger application of the coverage formula. We reject the claim by Alabama as *amicus curiae* that this provision is invalid because it allows the new remedies of the Act to be imposed in an arbitrary way. The Court has already permitted Congress to withdraw judicial review of administrative determinations in numerous cases involving the statutory rights of private parties. . . .

Suspension of Tests

We now arrive at consideration of the specific remedies prescribed by the Act for areas included within the coverage formula. South Carolina assails the temporary suspension of existing voting qualifications, reciting the rule laid down by *Lassiter* v. *Northampton County Bd. of Elections*, 360 U.S. 45, that literacy tests and related devices are not in themselves contrary to the Fifteenth Amendment. In that very case, however, the Court went on to say, "Of course a literacy test, fair on its face, may be employed to perpetuate that discrimination which the Fifteenth Amendment was designed to uproot." *Id.*, at 53. The record shows that in most of the States covered by the Act, including South Carolina, various tests and devices have been instituted with the purpose of disenfranchising Negroes, have been framed in such a way as to facilitate this aim, and have been administered in a discriminatory fashion for many years. Under these circumstances, the Fifteenth Amendment has clearly been violated. See *Louisiana* v. *United States*, 380 U.S. 145; *Alabama* v. *United States*, 371 U.S. 37; *Schnell* v. *Davis*, 336 U.S. 933.

The Act suspends literacy tests and similar devices for a period of five years from the last occurrence of substantial voting discrimination. This was a legitimate response to the problem, for which there is ample precedent in Fifteenth Amendment cases. *Ibid.* Underlying the response was the feeling that States and political subdivisions which had been allowing white illiterates to vote for years could not sincerely complain about "dilution" of their electorates through the registration of Negro illiterates. Congress knew that continuance of the tests and devices in use at the present time, no matter how fairly administered in the future, would freeze the effect of past discrimination in favor of unqualified white registrants. Congress permissibly rejected the alternative of requiring a complete re-registration of all voters, believing that this would be too harsh on many whites who had enjoyed the franchise for their entire adult lives.

. . . .

Federal Examiners

The Act authorizes the appointment of federal examiners to list qualified applicants who are thereafter entitled to vote, subject to an expeditious challenge procedure. This was clearly an appropriate response to the problem, closely related to remedies authorized in prior cases. See *Alabama* v. *United States, supra; United States* v. *Thomas*, 362 U.S. 58. In many of the political subdivisions covered by § 4 (b) of the Act, voting officials have persistently employed a variety of procedural tactics to deny Negroes the franchise, often in direct defiance or evasion of federal court decrees. Congress realized that merely to suspend voting rules which have been misused or are subject to misuse might leave this localized evil undisturbed. As for the briskness of the challenge procedure, Congress knew that in some of the areas affected, challenges had been persistently employed to harass registered Negroes. It chose to forestall this abuse, at the same time providing alternative ways for removing persons listed through error or fraud. In addition to the judicial challenge procedure, § 7 (d) allows for the removal of names by the examiner himself, and § 11 (c) makes it a crime to obtain a listing through fraud.

In recognition of the fact that there were political subdivisions covered by § 4 (b) of the Act in which the appointment of federal examiners might be unnecessary, Congress assigned the Attorney General the task of determining the localities to which examiners should be sent. There is no warrant for the claim, asserted by Georgia as *amicus curiae*, that the Attorney General is free to use this power in an arbitrary fashion, without regard to the purposes of the Act. Section

6 (b) sets adequate standards to guide the exercise of his discretion, by directing him to calculate the registration ratio of nonwhites to whites, and to weigh evidence of good-faith efforts to avoid possible voting discrimination. At the same time, the special termination procedures of § 13 (a) provide indirect judicial review for the political subdivisions affected, assuring the withdrawal of federal examiners from areas where they are clearly not needed. . . .

After enduring nearly a century of widespread resistance to the Fifteenth Amendment, Congress has marshalled an array of potent weapons against the evil, with authority in the Attorney General to employ them effectively. Many of the areas directly affected by this development have indicated their willingness to abide by any restraints legitimately imposed upon them. We here hold that the portions of the Voting Rights Act properly before us are a valid means for carrying out the commands of the Fifteenth Amendment. Hopefully, millions of non-white Americans will now be able to participate for the first time on an equal basis in the government under which they live. We may finally look forward to the day when truly "[t]he right of citizens of the United States to vote shall not be denied or abridged by the United States or by any State on account of race, color, or previous condition of servitude."

The bill of complaint is

Dismissed.

UNITED STATES V. PRICE (1966)

For many weeks in 1964, the name "Philadelphia" was more often identified with the little town in Mississippi than with the great metropolis in Pennsylvania. The nation and the world had been shocked by the brutal killings of three civil rights workers—suddenly released from detention in the county jail in the Mississippi town so that they might be murdered. James Chaney, Andrew Goodman, and Michael Schwerner entered the history books as martyred freedom fighters; Deputy Sheriff Cecil Ray Price and seventeen other defendants faced prosecution that eventually led to Supreme Court action.

Another shocking and senseless murder demanded a Supreme Court decision at the same time. The victim was reserve officer Lemuel A. Penn, a Negro who had been killed while driving through Georgia on his way to Washington, D.C., after a tour of military duty. Involved where Herbert Guest and five fellow conspirators from Athens, Georgia.

The accused were not prosecuted for murder in either case. A state prosecution for murder would have been impossible in Mississippi, and two of the alleged killers of Colonel Penn had already been found not guilty of murder in a Georgia court. The two cases that came before the Supreme Court were prosecutions under Sections 241 and 242 of Title 18 of the United States Code.

These sections were based upon provisions in the Civil Rights Acts of the Reconstruction period (Document 47) which had survived Supreme Court declarations of unconstitutionality. Section 241 provides federal penalties for conspiracy "to injure, oppress, threaten, or intimidate any citizen in the free exercise or enjoyment of any right or privilege secured him by the Constitution or laws of the United States. . . ." Under Section 242, punishments are prescribed for any person who "under color of any law . . . willfully subjects any inhabitant of the State . . . to the deprivation of any rights, privileges, or immunities secured or protected by the Constitution . . . by reason of his color, or race. . . ."

The Supreme Court spoke twice in the companion cases of *United States* v. *Price* and *United States* v. *Guest,* 383 U.S. 745 (1966). Again it considered the arguments raised twenty-one years before in *Screws* v. *United States* (Document 72). This time the Court went further in extending the coverage of the federal law, relaxing the requirement as to the extent of state participation necessary to invoke the Fourteenth Amendment. Lower federal courts had dismissed the indictments; the Supreme Court reversed and remanded the cases for trial. In October of 1967, Deputy Sheriff Price and six other defendants were found guilty by a federal jury in Meridian, Mississippi.

While there was unanimity in sustaining the validity of the Section 241 indictment in the *Guest* case, four separate opinions were written presenting different constitutional analyses and different grounds for decision. Perhaps most significant was the statement made by Justice Tom C. Clark in a concurring opinion, in which he was joined by Justices Hugo

L. Black and Abe Fortas. Justice Clark wrote: "[T]here now can be no doubt that the specific language of § 5 [of the Fourteenth Amendment] empowers the Congress to enact laws punishing all conspiracies—with or without state action—that interfere with Fourteenth Amendment rights." This view was also expressed in the opinion of Justice William J. Brennan, Jr., in which he was joined by Chief Justice Earl Warren and Justice William O. Douglas. But while six justices took this position, the opinion of the Court written by Justice Potter Stewart did not deal with this question. Justice Stewart's opinion construed Section 241 to require proof of active participation by state officers in an alleged conspiracy.

Set forth here is the opinion in *United States* v. *Price*, unanimous except for the sentence by Justice Black objecting to reliance by the other justices on the *Williams* case.

DOCUMENT 94

*United States v. Price**

Mr. Justice Fortas delivered the opinion of the Court.

These are direct appeals from the dismissal in part of two indictments returned by the United States Grand Jury for the Southern District of Mississippi. The indictments allege assaults by the accused persons upon the rights of the asserted victims to due process of law under the Fourteenth Amendment. The indictment in No. 59 charges 18 persons with violations of 18 U.S.C. § 241 (1964 ed.). In No. 60, the same 18 persons are charged with offenses based upon 18 U.S.C. § 242 (1964 ed.). These are among the so-called civil rights statutes which have come to us from Reconstruction days, the period in our history which also produced the Thirteenth, Fourteenth, and Fifteenth Amendments to the Constitution.

The sole question presented in these appeals is whether the specified statutes make criminal the conduct for which the individuals were indicted. It is an issue of construction, not of constitutional power. We have no doubt of "the power of Congress to enforce by appropriate criminal sanction every right guaranteed by the Due Process Clause of the Fourteenth Amendment." *United States* v. *Williams*, 341 U.S. 70, 72.

* Supreme Court of the United States, 383 U.S. 787 (1966).

The events upon which the charges are based, as alleged in the indictments, are as follows: On June 21, 1964, Cecil Ray Price, the Deputy Sheriff of Neshoba County, Mississippi, detained Michael Henry Schwerner, James Earl Chaney and Andrew Goodman in the Neshoba County jail located in Philadelphia, Mississippi. He released them in the dark of that night. He then proceeded by automobile on Highway 19 to intercept his erstwhile wards. He removed the three men from their automobile, placed them in an official automobile of the Neshoba County Sheriff's office, and transported them to a place on an unpaved road.

These acts, it is alleged, were part of a plan and conspiracy whereby the three men were intercepted by the 18 defendants, including Deputy Sheriff Price, Sheriff Rainey and Patrolman Willis of the Philadelphia, Mississippi, Police Department. The purpose and intent of the release from custody and the interception, according to the charge, were to "punish" the three men. The defendants, it is alleged, "did wilfully assault, shoot and kill" each of the three. And, the charge continues, the bodies of the three victims were transported by one of the defendants from the rendezvous on the unpaved road to the vicinity of the construction site of an earthen dam approximately five miles southwest of Philadelphia, Mississippi.

These are federal and not state indictments. They do not charge as crimes the alleged assaults or murders. The indictments are framed to fit the stated federal statutes, and the question before us is whether the attempt of the draftsman for the Grand Jury in Mississippi has been successful: whether the indictments charge offenses against the various defendants which may be prosecuted under the designated federal statutes.

We shall deal first with the indictment in No. 60, based on § 242 of the Criminal Code, and then with the indictment in No. 59, under § 241. We do this for ease of exposition and because § 242 was enacted by the Congress about four years prior to § 241. Section 242 was enacted in 1866; § 241 in 1870.

I. No. 60

Section 242 defines a misdemeanor, punishable by fine of not more than $1,000 or imprisonment for not more than one year, or both. So far as here significant, it provides punishment for "Whoever, under color of any law, statute, ordinance, regulation, or custom, willfully subjects any inhabitant of any State . . . to the deprivation of any rights, privileges, or immunities secured or protected by the Constitution or laws of the United States. . . ."

The indictment in No. 60 contains four counts, each of which names as defendants the three officials and 15 non-official persons. The First Count charges, on the basis of allegations substantially as set forth above, that all of the defendants conspired "to wilfully subject" Schwerner, Chaney and Goodman "to the deprivation of their right, privilege and immunity secured and protected by the Fourteenth Amendment to the Constitution of the United States not to be summarily punished without due process of law by persons acting under color of the laws of the State of Mississippi." This is said to constitute a conspiracy to violate § 242, and therefore an offense under 18 U.S.C. § 371 (1964 ed.). The latter section, the general conspiracy statute, makes it a crime to conspire to commit any offense against the United States. The penalty for violation is the same as for direct violation of § 242 —that is, it is a misdemeanor.

On a motion to dismiss, the District Court sustained this First Count as to all defendants. As to the sheriff, deputy sheriff and patrolman, the court recognized that each was clearly alleged to have been acting "under color of law" as required by § 242. As to the private persons, the District Court held that "[I]t is immaterial to the conspiracy that these private individuals were not acting under color of law" because the count charges that they were conspiring with persons who were so acting. . . .

The Second, Third and Fourth Counts of the indictment in No. 60 charge all of the defendants, not with conspiracy, but with substantive violations of § 242. Each of these counts charges that the defendants, acting "under color of the laws of the State of Mississippi," "did wilfully assault, shoot and kill" Schwerner, Chaney and Goodman, respectively, "for the purpose and with the intent" of punishing each of the three and that the defendants "did thereby wilfully deprive" each "of rights, privileges and immunities secured and protected by the Constitution and the laws of the United States"—namely, due process of law.

The District Court held these counts of the indictment valid as to the sheriff, deputy sheriff and patrolman. But it dismissed them as against the nonofficial defendants because the counts do not charge that the latter were "officers in fact, or de facto in anything allegedly done by them 'under color of law.'"

We note that by sustaining these counts against the three officers, the court again necessarily concluded that an offense under § 242 is properly stated by allegations of willful deprivation, under color of law, of life and liberty without due process of law. We agree. No other result would be permissible under the decisions of this Court. *Screws* v. *United States,* 325 U.S. 91; . . .

But we cannot agree that the Second, Third or Fourth Counts may be dismissed as against the nonofficial defendants. Section 242 applies only where a person indicted has acted "under color" of law. Private persons, jointly engaged with state officials in the prohibited action, are acting "under color" of law for purposes of the statute. To act "under color" of law does not require that the accused be an officer of the State. It is enough that he is a willful participant in joint activity with the State or its agents.

In the present case, according to the indictment, the brutal joint adventure was made possible by state detention and calculated release of the prisoners by an officer of the State. This action, clearly attributable to the State, was part of the monstrous design described by the indictment. State officers participated in every phase of the alleged venture: the release from jail, the interception, assault and murder. It was a joint activity, from start to finish. Those who took advantage of participation by state officers in accomplishment of the foul purpose alleged must suffer the consequences of that participation. In effect, if the allegations are true, they were participants in official lawlessness, acting in willful concert with state officers and hence under color of law. . . .

Accordingly, we reverse the dismissal of the Second, Third and Fourth Counts of the indictment in No. 60 and remand for trial.

II. No. 59

No. 59 charges each of the 18 defendants with a felony—a violation of § 241. This indictment is in one count. It charges that the defendants "conspired together . . . to injure, oppress, threaten and intimidate" Schwerner, Chaney and Goodman "in the free exercise and enjoyment of the right and privilege secured to them by the Fourteenth Amendment to the Constitution of the United States not to be deprived of life or liberty without due process of law by persons acting under color of the laws of Mississippi." The indictment alleges that it was the purpose of the conspiracy that Deputy Sheriff Price would release Schwerner, Chaney and Goodman from custody in the Neshoba County jail at such time that Price and the other 17 defendants "could and would intercept" them "and threaten, assault, shoot and kill them." The penalty under § 241 is a fine of not more than $5,000, or imprisonment for not more than 10 years or both. . . .

The District Court dismissed the indictment as to all defendants. In effect, although § 241 includes rights or privileges secured by the Constitution or laws of the United States without qualification or limitation, the court held that it does not include rights protected by the Fourteenth Amendment.

It will be recalled that in No. 60 the District Court held that § 242 included the denial of Fourteenth Amendment rights—the same right to due process involved in the indictment under § 241. Both include rights or privileges secured by the Constitution or laws of the United States. Neither is qualified or limited. Each includes, presumably, *all* of the Constitution and laws of the United States. To the reader of the two sections, versed only in the English language, it may seem bewildering that the two sections could be so differently read. . . .

There is no doubt that the indictment in No. 59 sets forth a conspiracy within the ambit of the Fourteenth Amendment. Like the indictment in No. 60, *supra*, it alleges that the defendants acted "under color of law" and that the conspiracy included action by the State through its law enforcement officers to punish the alleged victims without due process of law in violation of the Fourteenth Amendment's direct admonition to the States. . . .

This is an allegation of state action which, beyond dispute, brings the conspiracy within the ambit of the Fourteenth Amendment. It is an allegation of official, state participation in murder, accomplished by and through its officers with the participation of others. It is an allegation that the State, without the semblance of due process of law as required of it by the Fourteenth Amendment, used its sovereign power and office to release the victims from jail so that they were not charged and tried as required by law, but instead could be intercepted and killed. If the Fourteenth Amendment forbids denial of counsel, it clearly denounces denial of any trial at all.

As we have consistently held "The Fourteenth Amendment protects the individual against *state action*, not against wrongs done by *individuals*." *Williams* I, 341 U.S., at 92 (opinion of DOUGLAS, J.). In the present case, the participation by law enforcement officers, as alleged in the indictment, is clearly state action, as we have discussed, and it is therefore within the scope of the Fourteenth Amendment. . . .

In [the historical] context, it is hardly conceivable that Congress intended § 241 to apply only to a narrow and relatively unimportant category of rights. We cannot doubt that the purpose and effect of § 241 was to reach assaults upon rights under the entire Constitution, including the Thirteenth, Fourteenth and Fifteenth Amendments, and not merely under part of it. . . .

The present application of the statutes at issue does not raise fundamental questions of federal-state relationships. We are here concerned with allegations which squarely and indisputably involve state action in direct violation of the mandate of the Fourteenth Amendment—that no State shall deprive any person of life or liberty without due process of law. This is a direct, traditional concern of the Federal Government. It is an area in which the federal interest has existed for at least a century, and in which federal participation has intensified as part of a renewed emphasis upon civil rights. . . . Today, a decision interpreting a federal law in accordance with its historical design, to punish denials by state action of constitutional rights of the person can hardly be regarded as adversely affecting "the wise adjustment between State responsibility and national control. . . ." *Williams* I, 341 U.S., at 73 (opinion of Frankfurter, J.). In any event, the problem, being statutory and not constitutional, is ultimately, as it was in the beginning, susceptible of congressional disposition.

Reversed and remanded.

SCHOOL DESEGREGATION GUIDELINES (1966)

Acting under the Civil Rights Act of 1964 (Document 89), the Office of Education of the United States Department of Health, Education, and Welfare has periodically issued guidelines to help achieve the required desegregation of students, faculty, and facilities in the nation's schools. While guidelines do not specify a particular school desegregation plan, each school system is required to adopt that plan best suited to accomplish desegregation "as quickly as possible." The USOE also insists that evidence of compliance with Title VI of the 1964 Civil Rights Act is a prerequisite for receipt of federal funds.

Reactions to the Office of Education guidelines varied in different parts of the South, but Governor George Wallace of Alabama quickly became the leading spokesman of states' rights, segregationist opposition. In September, 1966, he secured the passage of an Alabama enactment declaring the federal guidelines unconstitutional and null and void within the state. The legislation also provided that no local school system—whatever its attitudes and existing agreements with USOE—could comply with the federal guidelines. The Alabama law established a Governor's Commission to implement the new legislation. It also provided for state funds to replace federal monies lost to Alabama school systems because of their rejection of the federal guidelines.

In December, 1966, Commissioner Harold Howe II defended the USOE guidelines before a special subcommittee of the House Judiciary Committee. A few days later, on December 29, the United States Court of Appeals for the Fifth Circuit, which includes Alabama, upheld the constitutionality of the guidelines in *United States* v. *Jefferson County Board of Education.*

DOCUMENT(S) 95

*Guidelines for school desegregation, a summary explanation . . . , March 1, 1966**

THE 1966 TITLE VI GUIDELINES FOR SCHOOL DESEGRATION

The 1966 Guidelines require:
1. Substantial achievements under free choice desegregation plans,
2. Significant progress in desegregation of teachers and staff,
3. Progress in closing of small, inadequate schools established for Negro students or other minority groups,
4. Simplified procedures and periodic reports from school districts to measure progress in implementing desegregation plans.

ASSURANCE

To be eligible for Federal funds, each school system must assure the Commissioner that it will abide by Title VI of the Civil Rights Act. The type of assurance varies with the nature of the school system:

Desegregated Systems

A school district that never had or has already eliminated a segregated system submits an assurance of full compliance by HEW Form 441.

Dual School Systems

School systems that are working toward desegregation submit either a Federal court order for desegregation or a voluntary desegregation plan. School systems with voluntary plans file Form 441–B, which provides that a school system's voluntary desegregation plan will be carried out in accordance with the standards outlined in the 1966 Guidelines.

---

* Department of Health, Education, and Welfare; Office of Education (Washington, D.C.: U.S. Government Printing Office, 1966).

Performance

Any compliance assurance or plan is essentially a statement of intent, and is not a substitute for performance. The Commissioner may require additional assurance or evidence of performance if he has cause to believe that a school system is not living up to its original assurance.

TYPES OF PLAN

No single type of desegregation plan fits all school systems. Each school system is responsible for selecting the plan best suited to accomplish desegregation as quickly as possible. However, if the Commissioner has cause to believe a plan will not work in a particular district or has evidence that a previously accepted plan is failing, he may require the adoption of a different plan.

A. General Requirements

The school system—not the State or Federal Government—is responsible for making its plan work. The system must inform the community of its plan, solicit community support, and take the necessary steps to protect all persons exercising their rights under the plan.

The Guidelines require periodic reports to help the Commissioner determine a system's progress under its plan. These reports include data on student and faculty assignment by race and school; notification of any changes the system seeks to make in its plan; and descriptions of special circumstances hampering the progress of desegregation.

B. Attendance Zone Plans

Under this type of plan, students are assigned to schools within a school system according to their area of residence. The school system must establish a single set of attendance zones, and then assign students to schools serving their zone regardless of race, color, or national origin.

Students with special educational needs—handicapped children, for example—can be assigned to a school outside their normal attendance zone.

C. Free Choice Plans

These plans require students to choose their own school, regardless of where they live. The expectation is that students of each race will choose the same school and thus break down the dual school pattern.

Every student and his parent *must* choose a school *each* year . . . in most cases 4 or 5 months before the school year begins. The school system must ensure that this choice is free, and that students and parents can choose in safety and without fear of reprisal.

School systems must make significant progress in eliminating the dual school pattern under free choice plans. Progress in the transfer of students from segregated schools will be measured in relation to achievements of prior years and will be judged in accordance with the Federal court rule that school districts which start late must move faster in desegregating their schools.

DESEGREGATION OF FACULTY

The 1965 Guidelines required at least a first step toward faculty desegregation through integrated staff meetings in the first year. The 1966 Guidelines require actual desegregation in the school staff.

In general, school systems with separate white and Negro faculties must either assign staff in such a way as to produce some faculty integration in every school, or use some other pattern of staff assignment which will make comparable progress in bringing about staff desegregation successfully.

The 1966 Guidelines also include safeguards against discriminatory hiring, firing, promotion, and extension of tenure. They do not violate a system's right to administer its staff according to professional criteria, but they do require that such practices not result in discrimination by race, color, or national origin.

Desegregation of Facilities

Any facility or activity—including athletics, transportation, parent-teacher or student assemblies, extracurricular programs, special educational opportunities—identifiable as being school-related must be open to all appropriate persons without discrimination.

Summary

The basic concept behind the design of the 1966 Guidelines is substantial progress in each district beyond what it achieved under the 1965 Guidelines.

The basic criterion for the Commissioner's interpretation of these Guidelines is measurable evidence of progress and good faith effort to eliminate the dual school system as quickly as possible.

*Alabama legislation in reaction to the Federal desegregation guidelines**

Enrolled, An Act, To preserve the integrity of the local public school systems against unlawful encroachment in the administration and control of local schools, to provide for the determination by the courts or the justices of the Supreme Court of Alabama of the legality of requirements for Federal financial assistance to local school systems, to provide financial assistance in the operation and administration of the public schools when federal assistance is withdrawn by reason of the failure or refusal to make an agreement, adopt a plan or perform some act not required by law, and to appropriate state funds for such purpose; and to provide for the method of making payments from such appropriation; to provide for a Commission, which with the Governor, is authorized to assist but not interfere with local, City and County Boards of Education.

---

* H. 446 of the State of Alabama, September 2, 1966. (Mimeographed copy sent to the editors by the Governor's office.)

(PREAMBLE)

WHEREAS, the Legislature of Alabama is authorized to establish, organize, and maintain a system of schools throughout the State for the benefit of the children of the State, and the Legislature has from time to time made provisions for the continued operation of an efficient school system within the State by the appropriation of public money; and

WHEREAS, public confidence in the local school systems is being destroyed by the recent attempt by the United States Department of Health, Education and Welfare to control the internal operation of the local schools in Alabama, by issuing certain so-called "guidelines"; and

WHEREAS, following the guidelines will either effectively destroy the public schools or destroy the quality of education offered in the public schools; and

WHEREAS, it is immoral and repugnant for agencies of the Federal government to use Federal money appropriated for educational purposes to interfere with the administration and operation of the local public schools by duly constituted authorities; and . . .

WHEREAS, it appears that agents of the Department of Health, Education and Welfare will continue to use threats, intimidation and coercion in an attempt to get local school boards to agree to administrative procedures not required or authorized by law; and

WHEREAS, the time has come when the citizens of Alabama are no longer willing to abide by such infringements of constitutionally guaranteed personal rights and freedoms; and

WHEREAS, the Legislature of the State of Alabama under the Constitution of Alabama has the authority and the duty to require or impose conditions or procedures deemed necessary to maintain a system of public schools throughout the State for the benefit of the children of school age and to preserve peace and order in the public schools of this State; now, therefore

BE IT ENACTED BY THE LEGISLATURE OF ALABAMA:

SECTION 1. The Legislature finds and declares that the Revised Statement of Policies for School Desegregation Plans (March 1966—Title 45, Part 181, CFR, as printed in the

Federal Register in Volume 31, No. 69, on April 9, 1966) (herein called the "guidelines") purporting to have been issued by the United States Department of Health, Education and Welfare under Title VI of the Civil Rights Act of 1964, exceed the authority granted by the Civil Rights Act of 1964, are unreasonable, arbitrary, capricious, and unconstitutional and interfere with the performance of the duty imposed upon the local city and county Boards of Education in the State of Alabama to operate and supervise the schools within their jurisdiction for the benefit of the children of school age therein residing. Any agreement or assurance of compliance with the guidelines heretofore made or given by a local county or city Board of Education is null and void and shall have no binding effect. No local county or city Board of Education shall have the authority to give any assurance of compliance with the guidelines or to enter into any other agreement with any agency of the government of the United States which would obligate such local city or county Board of Education to adopt any plan for desegregation which requires the assignment of students to public schools in order to overcome racial imbalance or which would authorize any agent of the United States to take any unlawful action with respect to any employment practice of such board or to take other action not required by law. . . .

SECTION 3. Any city or county Board of Education may in its discretion, by the adoption of a resolution, agreed to by a majority of all of its members, request the Governor and the Governor's Commission to stand in the place and stead of such board in any matters pertaining to requests for federal financial assistance, either grants or loans, and as to any agreement or assurance of compliance or requirement in connection therewith and as to any enforcement action relating thereto, which may be designated in such request. Any city or county Board of Education which has requested the Governor and the Governor's Commission to stand in its place and stead may by resolution agreed to by a majority of all the members of said board revoke such request under any authority delegated thereby to the Governor and the Governor's Commission.

SECTION 4. Whenever any federal financial assistance grant, loan or contract which would accrue to a local city or county Board of Education under any existing federal educational assistance program is withheld from any local public school system or if payment thereof is deferred because of the failure or refusal of the City or County Board of Education or the Governor and the Governor's Commission acting in the place and stead of any city or county Board of Education to subscribe to or agree to abide by any assurance of compliance with the "guidelines" or any other requirement by any agency of the federal government in connection with the federal financial assistance program, which the justices of the Supreme Court or a majority of them or any court having jurisdiction shall declare to be invalid, the State of Alabama shall make up or replace such loss by the allocation of state funds to such board. Such sum or sums as may be necessary for this purpose and for the purpose of defraying the reasonable and necessary expenses of the Commission in carrying out the purpose of this act are hereby appropriated from any funds in the State Treasury to the credit of the Alabama Special Educational Trust Fund.

• • • •

SECTION 5. There shall be created and established a State agency to be known as the Governor's Commission. The function of such Commission shall be to aid in and be jointly responsible with the Governor for the administration of this Act. The Commission shall be composed of not exceeding 160 persons of good repute who are qualified electors of the State and representative of the citizens in the various counties of the State and who shall be appointed by the Governor with the advice and consent of the Senate. The members of the Commission shall be appointed for initial terms ending November 15, 1966 and their successors shall be appointed for terms ending on the 15th day of each second year thereafter. The Commission may appoint an executive committee and empower said committee to act for it and in its place and stead.

SECTION 6. The Governor and the Governor's Commission are authorized to institute in the name of the State of Alabama such proceedings in such courts as to them may appear desirable to contest the validity of the guidelines and of any other rules, regulations or requirements of any Federal agency for the operation of local schools or school systems and of any Act of Congress making provision or requirements for such operation, and to request the opinions of the Justices of the Supreme Court or a majority of them concerning any such matter. The Governor and the Commission may employ counsel.

APPROVED, September 2, 1966.

. . . .

BLACK POWER (1966)

Since the summer of 1966, the "Black Power" slogan has obsessed the nation. The term stemmed from the comparatively mild statements of Stokely Carmichael and Floyd McKissick, the newly installed leaders of the Student Nonviolent Coordinating Committee and the Congress of Racial Equality, respectively. But misunderstanding and a refusal to seek understanding made it a term that inspired fear in the white community. Convinced that federal civil rights legislation would not be totally effectual, and that it was, after all, simply another aspect of the white power structure, Carmichael and McKissick sought to rally Negroes to action on their own behalf.

The Black Power philosophy sprang from the experiences of SNCC and CORE field workers who had assumed the burdens of the civil rights movement at the community level throughout the rural South and in northern metropolitan areas. They had already witnessed and suffered too much brutality and had seen too much economic impoverishment to endorse the standard procedures readily accepted by most liberal Americans as evidences of reform. They argued that Negroes must develop a base of political and economic power from which to identify and define their own needs in their own terms. Black Americans must be able to demand justice and bargain from a position of strength when dealing with the dominant white majority.

White America tended to confuse Black Power with the strident and racist position advocated by the Black Muslims of Elijah Muhammed. In late September, 1966, Stokely Carmichael drafted an explanation of Black Power, in which he denied that it involved racial hatred and racial separatism. Carmichael defined it as a philosophy and a strategy of self-perception and self-help designed to offer black Americans choices for action and the opportunity to live with dignity within an interracial society.

DOCUMENT 96

*"What We Want," by Stokely Carmichael**

One of the tragedies of the struggle against racism is that up to now there has been no national organization which could speak to the growing militancy of young black people in the urban ghetto. There has been only a civil rights movement, whose tone of voice was adapted to an audience of liberal whites. It served as a sort of buffer zone between them and angry young blacks. None of its so-called leaders could go into a rioting community and be listened to. In a sense, I blame ourselves—together with the mass media—for what has happened in Watts, Harlem, Chicago, Cleveland, Omaha. Each time the people in those cities saw Martin Luther King get slapped, they became angry; when they saw four little black girls bombed to death, they were angrier; and when nothing happened, they were steaming. We had nothing to offer that they could see, except to go out and be beaten again. We helped to build their frustration.

For too many years, black Americans marched and had their heads broken and got shot. They were saying to the country, "Look, you guys are supposed to be nice guys and we are only going to do what we are supposed to do—why do you beat us up, why don't you give us what we ask, why don't you straighten yourselves out?" After years of this, we are at almost the same point—because we demonstrated from a position of weakness. We cannot be expected any longer to march and have our heads broken in order to say to whites: come on, you're nice guys. For you are not nice guys. We have found you out.

An organization which claims to speak for the needs of a

---

* Copyright 1966, The Student Nonviolent Coordinating Committee. Reprinted by permission from *The New York Review of Books*, Vol. VII, No. 4 (September 22, 1966), pp. 5, 6, and 8.

community—as does the Student Nonviolent Coordinating Committee—must speak in the tone of that community, not as somebody else's buffer zone. This is the significance of black power as a slogan. For once, black people are going to use the words they want to use—not just the words whites want to hear. And they will do this no matter how often the press tries to stop the use of the slogan by equating it with racism or separatism.

An organization which claims to be working for the needs of a community—as SNCC does—must work to provide that community with a position of strength from which to make its voice heard. This is the significance of black power beyond the slogan.

Black power can be clearly defined for those who do not attach the fears of white America to their questions about it. We should begin with the basic fact that black Americans have two problems: they are poor and they are black. All other problems arise from this two-sided reality: lack of education, the so-called apathy of black men. Any program to end racism must address itself to that double reality. . . .

All of the efforts were attempts to win black power. Then, in Alabama, the opportunity came to see how blacks could be organized on an independent party basis. An unusual Alabama law provides that any group of citizens can nominate candidates for county office and, if they win 20 per cent of the vote, may be recognized as a county political party. The same then applies on a state level. SNCC went to organize in several counties such as Lowndes, where black people —who form 80 per cent of the population and have an average annual income of $943—felt they could accomplish nothing within the framework of the Alabama Democratic Party because of its racism and because the qualifying fee for this year's elections was raised from $50 to $500 in order to prevent most Negroes from becoming candidates. On May 3, five new county "freedom organizations" convened and nominated candidates for the offices of sheriff, tax assessor, members of the school boards. These men and women are up for election in November—if they live until then. Their ballot symbol is the black panther: a bold, beautiful animal, representing the strength and dignity of black demands today. A man needs a black panther on his side when he and his family must endure—as hundreds of Alabamians have endured—loss of job, eviction, starvation, and sometimes death, for political activity. He may also need a gun and SNCC reaffirms the right of black men everywhere to defend themselves when threatened or attacked. As for initiating the use of violence, we hope that such programs as ours will make that unnecessary; but it is not for us to tell black communities whether they can or cannot use any particular form of action to resolve their problems. Responsibility for the use of violence by black men, whether in self-defense or initiated by them, lies with the white community.

This is the specific historical experience from which SNCC's call for "black power" emerged on the Mississippi march last July. But the concept of "black power" is not a recent or isolated phenomenon: It has grown out of the ferment of agitation and activity by different people and organizations in many black communities over the years. Our last year of work in Alabama added a new concrete possibility. In Lowndes county, for example, black power will mean that if a Negro is elected sheriff, he can end police brutality. If a black man is elected tax assessor, he can collect and channel funds for the building of better roads and schools serving black people—thus advancing the move from political power into the economic arena. In such areas as Lowndes, where black men have a majority, they will attempt to use it to exercise control. This is what they seek: control. Where Negroes lack a majority, black power means proper representation and sharing of control. It means the creation of power bases from which black people can work to change statewide or nationwide patterns of oppression through pressure from strength—instead of weakness. Politically, black power means what it has always meant to SNCC: the coming-together of black people to elect representatives and *to force those representatives to speak to their needs*. It does not mean merely putting black faces into office. A man or woman who is black and from the slums cannot be automatically expected to speak to the needs of black people. Most of the black politicians we see around the country today are not what SNCC means by black power. The power must be that of a community, and emanate from there. . . .

Ultimately, the economic foundations of this country must be shaken if black people are to control their lives. The colonies of the United States—and this includes the black ghettoes within its borders, north and south—must be liberated. For a century, this nation has been like an octopus of exploitation, its tentacles stretching from Mississippi and Harlem to South America, the Middle East, southern Africa, and Vietnam; the form of exploitation varies from area to area but the essential result has been the same—a powerful few have been maintained and enriched at the expense of the poor and voiceless colored masses. This pattern must be broken. As its grip loosens here and there around the world, the hopes of black Americans become more realistic. For racism to die, a totally different America must be born.

This is what the white society does not wish to face; this is why that society prefers to talk about integration. But integration speaks not at all to the problem of poverty, only to the problem of blackness. Integration today means the man who "makes it," leaving his black brothers behind in the ghetto as fast as his new sports car will take him. It has no relevance to the Harlem wino or to the cottonpicker making three dollars a day. As a lady I know in Alabama once said, "the food that Ralph Bunche eats doesn't fill my stomach."

Integration, moreover, speaks to the problem of blackness in a despicable way. As a goal, it has been based on complete acceptance of the fact that *in order to have* a decent house or education, blacks must move into a white neighborhood or send their children to a white school. This reinforces, among both black and white, the idea that "white" is automatically better and "black" is by definition inferior. This is why integration is a subterfuge for the maintenance of white supremacy. It allows the nation to focus on a handful of Southern children who get into white schools, at great price, and to ignore the 94 per cent who are left behind in unimproved all-black schools. Such situations will not change until black people have power—to control their own school boards, in this case. Then Negroes become equal in a way that means something, and integration ceases to be a one-way street. Then integration doesn't mean draining skills and energies from the ghetto into white neighborhoods; then it can mean white people moving from Beverly Hills into Watts, white people joining the Lowndes County Freedom Organization. Then integration becomes relevant. . . .

To most whites, black power seems to mean that the

Mau Mau are coming to the suburbs at night. The Mau Mau are coming, and whites must stop them. Articles appear about plots to "get Whitey," creating an atmosphere in which "law and order must be maintained." Once again, responsibility is shifted from the oppressor to the oppressed. Other whites chide, "Don't forget—you're only 10 per cent of the population; if you get too smart, we'll wipe you out." If they are liberals, they complain, "what about me?—don't you want my help any more?" These are people supposedly concerned about black Americans, but today they think first of themselves, of their feelings of rejection. Or they admonish, "you can't get anywhere without coalitions," without considering the problems of coalition with whom?; on what terms (coalescing from weakness can mean absorption, betrayal)?; when? Or they accuse us of "polarizing the races" by our calls for black unity, when the true responsibility for polarization lies with whites who will not accept their responsibility as the majority power for making the democratic process work. . . .

Whites will not see that I, for example, as a person oppressed because of my blackness, have common cause with other blacks who are oppressed because of blackness. This is not to say that there are no white people who see things as I do, but that it is black people I must speak to first. It must be the oppressed to whom SNCC addresses itself primarily, not to friends from the oppressing group.

From birth, black people are told a set of lies about themselves. We are told that we are lazy—yet I drive through the Delta area of Mississippi and watch black people picking cotton in the hot sun for fourteen hours. We are told, "If you work hard, you'll succeed"—but if that were true, black people would own this country. We are oppressed because we are black—not because we are ignorant, not because we are lazy, not because we're stupid (and got good rhythm), but because we're black. . . .

The need for psychological equality is the reason why SNCC today believes that blacks must organize in the black community. Only black people can convey the revolutionary idea that black people are able to do things themselves. Only they can help create in the community an aroused and continuing black consciousness that will provide the basis for political strength. In the past, white allies have furthered white supremacy without the whites involved realizing it—or wanting it, I think. Black people must do things for themselves; they must get poverty money they will control and spend themselves, they must conduct tutorial programs themselves so that black children can identify with black people. This is one reason Africa has such importance: The reality of black men ruling their own nations gives blacks elsewhere a sense of possibility, of power, which they do not now have.

This does not mean we don't welcome help, or friends. But we want the right to decide whether anyone is, in fact, our friend. In the past, black Americans have been almost the only people whom everybody and his momma could jump up and call their friends. We have been tokens, symbols, objects—as I was in high school to many young whites, who liked having "a Negro friend." We want to decide who is our friend, and we will not accept someone who comes to us and says: "If you do X, Y, and Z, then I'll help you." We will not be told whom we should choose as allies. We will not be isolated from any group or nation except by our own choice. We cannot have the oppressors telling the oppressed how to rid themselves of the oppressor. . . .

There is a vital job to be done among poor whites. We hope to see, eventually, a coalition between poor blacks and poor whites. That is the only coalition which seems acceptable to us, and we see such a coalition as the major internal instrument of change in American society. SNCC has tried several times to organize poor whites; we are trying again now, with an initial training program in Tennessee. It is purely academic today to talk about bringing poor blacks and whites together, but the job of creating a poor-white power bloc must be attempted. The main responsibility for it falls upon whites. Black and white can work together in the white community where possible; it is not possible, however, to go into a poor Southern town and talk about integration. Poor whites everywhere are becoming more hostile—not less—partly because they see the nation's attention focussed on black poverty and nobody coming to them. Too many young middle-class Americans, like some sort of Pepsi generation, have wanted to come alive through the black community; they've wanted to be where the action is—and the action has been in the black community.

Black people do not want to "take over" this country. They don't want to "get whitey"; they just want to get him off their backs, as the saying goes. It was for example the exploitation by Jewish landlords and merchants which first created black resentment toward Jews—not Judaism. The white man is irrelevant to blacks, except as an oppressive force. Blacks want to be in his place, yes, but not in order to terrorize and lynch and starve him. They want to be in his place because that is where a decent life can be had. . . .

As for white America, perhaps it can stop crying out against "black supremacy," "black nationalism," "racism in reverse," and begin facing reality. The reality is that this nation, from top to bottom, is racist; that racism is not primarily a problem of "human relations" but of an exploitation maintained—either actively or through silence—by the society as a whole. Camus and Sartre have asked, can a man condemn himself? Can whites, particularly liberal whites, condemn themselves? Can they stop blaming us, and blame their own system? Are they capable of the shame which might become a revolutionary emotion?

We have found that they usually cannot condemn themselves, and so we have done it. But the rebuilding of this society, if at all possible, is basically the responsibility of whites—not blacks. We won't fight to save the present society, in Vietnam or anywhere else. We are just going to work, in the way *we* see fit, and on goals *we* define, not for civil rights but for all our human rights.

RACIAL ISOLATION IN THE PUBLIC SCHOOLS (1967)

Mere possession of legislatively or judicially ordained rights is only the preliminary goal in the achievement of interracial equality. The mobile, automated, technological America of the mid-twentieth century demands education and economic opportunity to make legal rights meaningful. The nation has yet to direct its efforts to this end.

In a vigorous dissent against this inaction, the United States Commission on Civil Rights released its two-volume report, *Racial Isolation in the Public Schools,* in February, 1967.

It pointed out that the nation was falling behind in providing meaningful equality for its black citizens despite the legislative victories and favorable judicial decisions. De facto school segregation, inextricably tied to residential, occupational, and economic discrimination, was increasing, dooming another generation of black Americans to second-class citizenship.

The Commission set forth its various findings and offered initial recommendations for public and private action.

DOCUMENT 97

Racial Isolation in the Public Schools, February 20, 1967*

RACIAL ISOLATION: EXTENT AND CONTEXT

Extent

1. Racial isolation in the public schools is intense throughout the United States. In the Nation's metropolitan areas, where two-thirds of both the Negro and white population now live, it is most severe. Seventy-five percent of the Negro elementary students in the Nation's cities are in schools with enrollments that are nearly all-Negro (90 percent or more Negro), while 83 percent of the white students are in nearly all-white schools. Nearly nine of every 10 Negro elementary students in the cities attend majority-Negro schools.

2. This high level of racial separation in city schools exists whether the city is large or small, whether the proportion of Negro enrollment is large or small, and whether the city is located North or South.

Trends

3. Racial isolation in the public schools has been increasing. Over recent years Negro elementary school enrollment in northern city school systems has increased, as have the number and proportion of Negro elementary students in majority-

---

* Report of the United States Commission on Civil Rights, Vol. I (Washington, D.C.: U.S. Government Printing Office, 1967), pp. 199–204, 209–12.

Negro and nearly all-Negro schools. Most of this increase has been absorbed in schools which are now more than 90 percent Negro, and almost the entire increase in schools which are now majority-Negro. There is evidence to suggest that once a school becomes almost half- or majority-Negro, it tends rapidly to become nearly all-Negro.

4. In Southern and border cities, although the proportion of Negroes in all-Negro schools has decreased since the 1954 Supreme Court decision in *Brown* v. *Board of Education,* a rising Negro enrollment, combined with only slight desegregation, has produced a substantial increase in the number of Negroes attending nearly all-Negro schools.

Population Movements in Metropolitan Areas

5. The Nation's metropolitan area populations are growing and are becoming increasingly separated by race. Between 1940 and 1960, the increase of Negroes in metropolitan areas occurred mainly in the central cities while the white increase occurred mainly in the suburbs. These trends are continuing.

6. The trends are reflected among school-age children.

(*a*) By 1960, four of every five nonwhite school-age children in metropolitan areas lived in central cities while nearly three of every five white children lived in the suburbs.

(*b*) Negro schoolchildren in metropolitan areas increasingly are attending central city schools and white children, suburban schools.

(*c*) A substantial number of major cities have elementary school enrollments that are more than half-Negro.

Causes of Racial Isolation

Metropolitan Dimensions

1. The Nation's metropolitan area populations also are becoming increasingly separated socially and economically. There are widening disparities in income and educational level between families in the cities and families in the suburbs. People who live in the suburbs increasingly are more wealthy and better educated than people who live in the cities.

2. The increasing racial, social, and economic separation

is reflected in the schools. School districts in metropolitan areas generally do not encompass both central city and suburban residents. Thus, central city and suburban school districts, like the cities and suburbs themselves, enclose separate racial, economic, and social groups.

3. Racial, social, and economic separation between city and suburb is attributable in large part to housing policies and practices of both private industry and government at all levels.

(*a*) The practices of the private housing industry have been discriminatory and the housing produced in the suburbs generally has been at prices only the relatively affluent can afford.

(*b*) Local governments in suburban areas share the responsibility for residential segregation. Residential segregation has been established through such means as racially restrictive zoning ordinances, racially restrictive covenants capable of judicial enforcement, administrative determinations on building permits, inspection standards and location of sewer and water facilities, and use of the power of eminent domain, suburban zoning, and land use requirements to keep Negroes from entering all-white communities.

(*c*) Federal housing policy has contributed to racial segregation in metropolitan areas through past discriminatory practices. Present nondiscrimination policies and laws are insufficient to counteract the effects of past policy.

(*d*) Laws and policies governing low- and moderate-income housing programs, including public housing, the FHA 221(d) (3) program, and the rent supplement program, serve to confine the poor and the nonwhite to the central city. Under each of these programs, suburban jurisdictions hold a special veto power.

4. Racial and economic isolation between city and suburban school systems is reinforced by disparities of wealth between cities and suburbs and the manner in which schools are financed.

(*a*) Schools are financed by property tax levies which make education dependent on the wealth of the community.

(*b*) Suburbs with increasing industry and increasing numbers of affluent people have a large tax base and are able to finance their schools with less effort.

(*c*) Cities with shrinking industry, a disproportionate share of the poor, and increasing costs for non-educational services to both residents and nonresidents, are less able to provide the required revenue for schools.

(d) State educational aid for schools, though designed to equalize, often does not succeed in closing the gap between city and suburban school districts.

(e) Federal aid at present levels in most instances is insufficient to close the gap between central city school districts and those of more affluent suburbs.

(f) These disparities provide further inducement to many white families to leave the city.

Racial Isolation and the Central City

5. Within cities, as within metropolitan areas, there is a high degree of residential segregation—reflected in the schools—for which responsibility is shared by both the private housing industry and government.

(a) The discriminatory practices of city landlords, lending institutions, and real estate brokers have contributed to the residential confinement of Negroes.

(b) State and local governments have contributed to the pattern of increasing residential segregation through such past discriminatory practices as racial zoning ordinances and racially restrictive covenants capable of judicial enforcement. Current practices in such matters as the location of low-rent public housing projects, and the displacement of large numbers of low-income nonwhite families through local improvement programs also are intensifying residential segregation.

(c) Federal housing programs and policies serve to intensify racial concentrations in cities. Federal policies governing low- and moderate-income housing programs such as low-rent public housing and FHA 221(d)(3) do not promote the location of housing outside areas of intense racial concentration. Federal urban renewal policy is insufficiently concerned with the impact of relocation on racial concentrations within cities.

6. Individual choice contributes to the maintenance of residential segregation, although the impact of such choice is difficult to assess since the housing market has been restricted.

7. In all central cities, as compared to their suburbs, non-

public schools absorb a disproportionately large segment of the white school population; nonwhites, however, whether in city or suburbs, attend public schools almost exclusively.

Educational Policies and Practices

8. The policies and practices of city school systems have a marked impact on the racial composition of schools.

(*a*) Geographical zoning, the most commonly used form of student assignment in northern cities, has contributed to the creation and maintenance of racially and socially homogeneous schools.

(*b*) School authorities exercise broad discretion in determining school attendance areas, which in most communities are not prescribed by reference to well-defined neighborhoods or by specific guidelines based on the optimum size of schools.

(*c*) In determining such discretionary matters as the location and size of schools, and the boundaries of attendance areas, the decisions of school officials may serve either to intensify or reduce racial concentrations. Although there have been only a few instances where purposeful segregation has been judicially determined to exist in the North, apparently neutral decisions by school officials in these areas frequently have had the effect of reinforcing racial separation of students.

(*d*) In Southern and border cities, similar decisions of school officials, combined with a high degree of residential racial concentration and remnants of legally compelled segregation, have had the effect of perpetuating racial isolation in the schools.

RACIAL ISOLATION AND THE OUTCOMES OF EDUCATION

1. There are marked disparities in the outcomes of education for Negro and white Americans. Negro students typically do not achieve as well in school as white students. The longer they are in school the further they fall behind. Negroes are enrolled less often in college than whites and are much more likely to attend high schools which send a relatively small proportion of their graduates to college. Negroes with college education are less likely than similarly educated whites to be employed in white-collar trades. Negroes with college education earn less on the average than high-school educated

whites. These disparities result, in part, from factors that influence the achievement, aspirations, and attitudes of school children.

2. There is a strong relationship between the achievement and attitudes of a school child and the economic circumstances and educational background of his family. Relevant factors that contribute to this relationship include the material deprivation and inadequate health care that children from backgrounds of poverty often experience, the fact that disadvantaged children frequently have less facility in verbal and written communication—the chief vehicle by which schools measure student achievement—and the inability of parents in poor neighborhoods to become as involved in school affairs and affect school policy as much as more affluent parents.

3. The social class of a student's schoolmates—as measured by the economic circumstances and educational background of their families—also strongly influences his achievement and attitudes. Regardless of his own family background, an individual student achieves better in schools where most of his fellow students are from advantaged backgrounds than in schools where most of his fellow students are from disadvantaged backgrounds. The relationship between a student's achievement and the social class composition of his school grows stronger as the student progresses through school.

4. Negro students are much more likely than white students to attend schools in which a majority of the students are disadvantaged. The social class composition of the schools is more important to the achievement and attitudes of Negro students than whites.

5. There are noticeable differences in the quality of schools which Negroes attend and those which whites attend. Negro students are less likely than whites to attend schools that have well-stocked libraries. Negro students also are less likely to attend schools which offer advanced courses in subjects such as science and languages and are more likely to be in overcrowded schools than white students. There is some relationship between such disparities and the achievement of Negro students.

6. The quality of teaching has an important influence on the achievement of students, both advantaged and disadvantaged. Negro students are more likely than white students to have teachers with low verbal achievement, to have sub-

stitute teachers, and to have teachers who are dissatisfied with their school assignment.

7. The relationship between the quality of teaching and the achievement of Negro students generally is greater in majority-Negro schools than in majority-white schools. Negro students in majority-white schools with poorer teachers generally achieve better than similar Negro students in majority-Negro schools with better teachers.

8. There is also a relationship between the racial composition of schools and the achievement and attitudes of most Negro students, which exists when all other factors are taken into account.

(a) Disadvantaged Negro students in school with a majority of equally disadvantaged white students achieve better than Negro students in school with a majority of equally disadvantaged Negro students.

(b) Differences are even greater when disadvantaged Negro students in school with a majority of disadvantaged Negro students are compared with similarly disadvantaged Negro students in school with a majority of advantaged white students. The difference in achievement for 12th-grade students amounts to more than two entire grade levels.

(c) Negroes in predominantly Negro schools tend to have lower educational aspirations and more frequently express a sense of inability to influence their futures by their own choices than Negro students with similar backgrounds attending majority-white schools. Their fellow students are less likely to offer academic stimulation.

(d) Predominantly Negro schools generally are regarded by the community as inferior institutions. Negro students in such schools are sensitive to such views and often come to share them. Teachers and administrative staff frequently recognize or share the community's view and communicate it to the students. This stigma affects the achievement and attitudes of Negro students.

9. The effects of racial composition of schools are cumulative. The longer Negro students are in desegregated schools, the better are their academic achievement and their attitudes. Conversely, there is a growing deficit for Negroes who remain in racially isolated schools.

10. Racial isolation in school limits job opportunities for Negroes. In general, Negro adults who attend desegregated

schools tend to have higher incomes and more often fill white-collar jobs than Negro adults who went to racially isolated schools.

11. Racial isolation is self-perpetuating. School attendance in racial isolation generates attitudes on the part of both Negroes and whites which tend to alienate them from members of the other race. These attitudes are reflected in behavior. Negroes who attended majority-white schools are more likely to reside in interracial neighborhoods, to have children in majority-white schools, and to have white friends. Similarly, white persons who attended school with Negroes are more likely to live in an interracial neighborhood, to have children who attend school with Negroes, and to have Negro friends.

. . . .

Recommendations

This report describes conditions that result in injustices to children and require immediate attention and action. The responsibility for corrective action rests with government at all levels and with citizens and organizations throughout the Nation. We must commit ourselves as a Nation to the establishment of equal educational opportunity of high quality for all children. *As an important means of fulfilling this national goal, the Commission recommends that the President and the Congress give immediate and urgent consideration to new legislation for the purpose of removing present racial imbalances from our public schools, thus to eliminate the dire effects of racial isolation which this report describes, and at long last, providing real equality of educational opportunity by integrating presently deprived American children of all races into a totally improved public educational system.*

Without attempting to outline needed legislation in great detail, our study of the problem convinces the Commission that new legislation must embody the following essential principles:

1. *Congress should establish a uniform standard providing for the elimination of racial isolation in the schools.*

Since large numbers of Negro children suffer harmful effects that are attributable in part to the racial composition of schools they attend, legislation should provide for the elimination of schools in which such harm generally occurs. No standard of general applicability will fit every case precisely; some schools with a large proportion of Negro students may not in fact produce harmful effects while others with a smaller proportion may be schools in which students are disadvantaged because of their race. But the alternative to establishing such a standard is to require a time-consuming and ineffective effort to determine on a case-by-case basis the schools in which harm occurs. As it has in analogous situations, Congress should deal with this problem by establishing reasonable and practical standards which will correct the injustice without intruding unnecessarily into areas where no corrective action is needed.

In prescribing a reasonable standard, there is much to commend the criterion already adopted by the legislature in Massachusetts and the Commissioner of Education of New York, defining as racially imbalanced, schools in which Negro pupils constitute more than 50 percent of the total enrollment. It was found in this report that when Negro students in schools with more than 50 percent Negro enrollment were compared with similarly situated Negro students in schools with a majority-white enrollment, there were significant differences in attitude and performance. It is the schools that have a majority-Negro enrollment that tend to be regarded and treated by the community as segregated and inferior schools. Although there are many factors involved, the racial composition of schools that are majority-Negro in enrollment tends to be less stable than that of majority-white schools and to be subject to more rapid change.

Similar arguments might be advanced for a standard which would deviate slightly from a 50-percent criterion, but a standard set significantly higher would not be adequate to deal with the problem and probably would not result in lasting solutions.

2. Congress should vest in each of the 50 States responsibility for meeting the standard it establishes and should allow the States maximum flexibility in devising appropriate remedies. It also should provide financial and technical assistance to the States in planning such remedies.

It would be unwise for the Federal Government to attempt to prescribe any single solution or set of solutions for the entire Nation. There is a broad range of techniques which are capable of achieving education of high quality in integrated public schools. Each State should be free to adopt solutions best suited to the particular needs of its individual communities.

At the same time it is clear that the responsibility should be placed upon the States rather than the individual school districts. The States, and not individual communities alone, have the capacity to develop and implement plans adequate to the objective. The States have assumed the responsibility for providing public education for all of their citizens and for establishing the basic conditions under which it is offered. Responsibility for achieving the goal of high-quality integrated education can and should be placed upon the States under terms which afford broad scope for local initiative. But in many jurisdictions, particularly the major cities, solutions are not possible without the cooperation of neighboring communities. The States possess the authority and the means for securing cooperation, by consolidating or reorganizing school districts or by providing for appropriate joint arrangements between school districts.

To help the States in devising appropriate remedies, the Federal Government should provide technical and financial assistance.

3. *The legislation should include programs of substantial financial assistance to provide for construction of new facilities and improvement in the quality of education in all schools.*

In many cases, particularly in the major cities, integrating the public schools will require the construction of new facilities designed both to serve a larger student population and to be accessible to all children in the area to be served. Substantial Federal assistance is needed to supplement the resources of States and localities in building new schools of this kind and providing higher quality education for all children. Federal assistance also can be helpful in encouraging cooperative arrangements between States which provide education services to the same metropolitan area and between separate school districts in a metropolitan area. In addition, Federal financial assistance now available under programs such as aid for mass transportation and community facilities should be utilized in ways which will advance the goal of integration.

Regardless of whether the achievement of integration requires new facilities, Federal financial assistance is needed for programs to improve the quality of education. States and localities should have broad discretion to develop programs best suited to their needs. Programs that are among the most promising involve steps—such as the reduction of pupil-teacher ratios, the establishment of ungraded classes and team teaching, and the introduction of specialized remedial instruction—which enable teachers to give more attention to the individual needs of children. Funds also could be used for purposes such as assisting the training of teachers, developing new educational techniques, and improving curriculum.

4. *Congress should provide for adequate time in which to accomplish the objectives of the legislation.*

It is clear that equal opportunity in education cannot be achieved overnight. Particularly in the large cities where problems of providing equal educational opportunity have seemed so intractable, time will be necessary for such matters as educational and physical planning, assembling and acquiring land, and building new facilities. However, since the problem is urgent a prompt start must be made toward finding solutions, progress must be continuous and substantial, and there must be some assurance that the job will be completed as quickly as possible. The time has come to put less emphasis on "deliberate" and more on "speed."

The goals of equal educational opportunity and equal housing opportunity are inseparable. Progress toward the achievement of one goal necessarily will facilitate achievement of the other. Failure to make progress toward the achievement of either goal will handicap efforts to achieve the other. *The Commission recommends, therefore, that the President and Congress give consideration to legislation which will:*

5. *Prohibit discrimination in the sale or rental of housing, and*

6. *Expand programs of Federal assistance designed to increase the supply of housing throughout metropolitan areas within the means of low- and moderate-income families.*

Additional funds should be provided for programs such as the rent supplement program and FHA 221 (d) (3), and these two programs should be amended to permit private enterprise to participate in them free from the special veto power now held by local governments under present Federal statutes.

In addition, *the Commission recommends that the Department of Housing and Urban Development:*

7. *Require as a condition for approval of applications for low- and moderate-income housing projects that the sites will be selected and the projects planned in a nondiscriminatory manner that will contribute to reducing residential racial concentrations and eliminating racial isolation in the schools.*

8. *Require as a condition for approval of urban renewal projects that relocation will be planned in a nondiscriminatory manner that will contribute to reducing residential racial concentrations and eliminating racial isolation in the schools.*

U. S. RIOT COMMISSION REPORT— OFFICIAL SUMMARY (1968)

White America—and Black America as well—was alarmed, frightened, discouraged, and surprised by the events of the "long hot summer" of 1967. But there should have been no surprise over the outbreak of riots in Newark, Detroit, and Cleveland and in more than a score of smaller cities. Perhaps the nation should have been surprised that three hundred years of racial inequities had not produced more serious riots much earlier.

The official response to the riots was President Lyndon B. Johnson's Executive Order 11365 of July 29, 1967, establishing a National Advisory Commission on Civil Disorders. Appointment of the eleven-man Commission, however, was actually made two days earlier in a major Presidential address to the nation. The President declared:

"The Commission will investigate the origins of the recent disorders in our cities. It will make recommendations—to me, to the Congress, to the State Governors, and to the Mayors—for measures to prevent or contain such disasters in the future." And, at the time he issued the Executive Order, the President charged the Commission with finding the answers to "three basic questions about these riots": "What happened? Why did it happen? What can be done to prevent it from happening again and again?"

Acting with unusual efficiency and dispatch, the Commission completed its comprehensive and compelling Report in a scant seven months. And on February 29, 1968, Americans were warned that, "Our nation is moving toward two societies, one black, one white—separate and unequal."

Taken seriously and implemented efficiently, the Commission's recommendations can provide the basic guide for effecting the initial actions which must be taken throughout the nation—essential actions en route to any meaningful changes in the conditions facing black Americans and in white attitudes now reinforcing those conditions. The Report sorely tests the public will for change.

Yet there was really nothing new, startling, or unusual in the Report. As Dr. Kenneth B. Clark pointed out in his testimony before the Commission, the nation had already had at its disposal a long and steady stream of reports on interracial riots, violence, and injustice. Indeed, the U.S. Commission on Civil Rights had also warned the country of the brutalizing and pervasive effects of racial discrimination in its Report of February, 1967 (see Document 97).

What made the Commission recommendations so significant is that they represented the work of moderates. Chaired by the then Illinois Governor Otto Kerner, with New York Mayor John V. Lindsay as Vice Chairman, its Negro members were Senator Edward W. Brooke of Massachusetts and Roy Wilkins of the NAACP. Conspicuous by their absence were such activists as Martin Luther King (see Document 86) and Stokely Carmichael (see Document 96).

DOCUMENT 98

Report of the National Advisory Commission on Civil Disorders*

SUMMARY OF REPORT

INTRODUCTION

The summer of 1967 again brought racial disorders to American cities, and with them shock, fear and bewilderment to the nation.

The worst came during a two-week period in July, first in Newark and then in Detroit. Each set off a chain reaction in neighboring communities.

On July 28, 1967, the President of the United States established this Commission and directed us to answer three basic questions:

What happened?
Why did it happen?
What can be done to prevent it from happening again?

To respond to these questions, we have undertaken a broad range of studies and investigations. We have visited the riot cities; we have heard many witnesses; we have sought the counsel of experts across the country.

This is our basic conclusion: Our nation is moving toward two societies, one black, one white—separate and unequal.

Reaction to last summer's disorders has quickened the movement and deepened the division. Discrimination and segregation have long permeated much of American life; they now threaten the future of every American.

This deepening racial division is not inevitable. The movement apart can be reversed. Choice is still possible. Our principal task is to define that choice and to press for a national resolution.

To pursue our present course will involve the continuing polarization of the American community and, ultimately, the destruction of basic democratic values.

---

* Washington, D.C.; U.S. Government Printing Office, 1968, pp. 1–13.

The alternative is not blind repression or capitulation to lawlessness. It is the realization of common opportunities for all within a single society.

This alternative will require a commitment to national action—compassionate, massive and sustained, backed by the resources of the most powerful and the richest nation on this earth. From every American it will require new attitudes, new understanding, and, above all, new will.

The vital needs of the nation must be met; hard choices must be made, and, if necessary, new taxes enacted.

Violence cannot build a better society. Disruption and disorder nourish repression, not justice. They strike at the freedom of every citizen. The community cannot—it will not—tolerate coercion and mob rule.

Violence and destruction must be ended—in the streets of the ghetto and in the lives of people.

Segregation and poverty have created in the racial ghetto a destructive environment totally unknown to most white Americans.

What white Americans have never fully understood—but what the Negro can never forget—is that white society is deeply implicated in the ghetto. White institutions created it, white institutions maintain it, and white society condones it.

It is time now to turn with all the purpose at our command to the major unfinished business of this Nation. It is time to adopt strategies for action that will produce quick and visible progress. It is time to make good the promises of American democracy to all citizens—urban and rural, black and white, Spanish-surname, American Indian, and every minority group.

Our recommendations embrace three basic principles:

- To mount programs on a scale equal to the dimension of the problems;
- To aim these programs for high impact in the immediate future in order to close the gap between promise and performance;
- To undertake new initiatives and experiments that can change the system of failure and frustration that now dominates the ghetto and weakens our society.

These programs will require unprecedented levels of funding and performance, but they neither probe deeper nor demand more than the problems which called them forth. There can be no higher priority for national action and no higher claim on the nation's conscience.

We issue this Report now, five months before the date called for by the President. Much remains that can be learned. Continued study is essential.

As Commissioners we have worked together with a sense of the greatest urgency and have sought to compose whatever differences exist among us. Some differences remain. But the gravity of the problem and the pressing need for action are too clear to allow further delay in the issuance of this Report.

Part I

WHAT HAPPENED?

Chapter 1

Profiles of Disorder

The Report contains profiles of a selection of the disorders that took place during the summer of 1967. These profiles are designed to indicate how the disorders happened, who participated in them, and how local officials, police forces, and the National Guard responded. Illustrative excerpts follow:

Newark

. . . It was decided to attempt to channel the energies of the people into a nonviolent protest. While Lofton promised the crowd that a full investigation would be made of the Smith incident, the other Negro leaders began urging those on the scene to form a line of march toward the city hall.

Some persons joined the line of march. Others milled about in the narrow street. From the dark grounds of the housing project came a barrage of rocks. Some of them fell among the crowd. Others hit persons in the line of march. Many smashed the windows of the police station. The rock throwing, it was believed, was the work of youngsters; approximately 2,500 children lived in the housing project.

Almost at the same time, an old car was set afire in a parking lot. The line of march began to disintegrate. The police, their heads protected by World War I-type helmets, sallied forth to disperse the crowd. A fire engine, arriving on the scene, was pelted with rocks. As police drove people away from the station, they scattered in all directions.

A few minutes later a nearby liquor store was broken into. Some persons, seeing a caravan of cabs appear at city hall to protest Smith's arrest, interpreted this as evidence that the disturbance had been organized and generated rumors to that effect.

However, only a few stores were looted. Within a short period of time, the disorder appeared to have run its course.

. . . .

. . . On Saturday, July 15, [Director of Police Dominick] Spina received a report of snipers in a housing project. When he arrived he saw approximately 100 National Guardsmen and police officers crouching behind vehicles, hiding in corners and lying on the ground around the edge of the courtyard.

Since everything appeared quiet and it was broad daylight, Spina walked directly down the middle of the street. Nothing happened. As he came to the last building of the complex, he heard a shot. All around him the troopers jumped, believing themselves to be under sniper fire. A moment later a young Guardsman ran from behind a building.

The Director of Police went over and asked him if he had fired the shot. The soldier said, "Yes," he had fired to scare a man away from a window; that his orders were to keep everyone away from windows.

Spina said he told the soldier: "Do you know what you just did? You have now created a state of hysteria. Every Guardsman up and down this street and every state policeman and every city policeman that is present thinks that somebody just fired a shot and that it is probably a sniper."

A short time later more "gunshots" were heard. Investigating, Spina came upon a Puerto Rican sitting on a wall. In reply to a question as to whether he knew "where the firing is coming from?" the man said:

"That's no firing. That's fireworks. If you look up to the fourth floor, you will see the people who are throwing down these cherry bombs."

By this time four truckloads of National Guardsmen had arrived and troopers and policemen were again crouched everywhere looking for a sniper. The Director of Police remained at the scene for three hours, and the only shot fired was the one by the Guardsman.

Nevertheless, at six o'clock that evening two columns of National Guardsmen and state troopers were directing mass fire at the Hayes Housing Project in response to what they believed were snipers. . . .

Detroit

. . . A spirit of carefree nihilism was taking hold. To riot and destroy appeared more and more to become ends in themselves. Late Sunday afternoon it appeared to one observer that the young people were "dancing amidst the flames."

A Negro plainclothes officer was standing at an intersection when a man threw a Molotov cocktail into a business establishment at the corner. In the heat of the afternoon, fanned by the 20 to 25 m.p.h. winds of both Sunday and Monday, the fire reached the home next door within minutes. As residents uselessly sprayed the flames with garden hoses, the fire jumped from roof to roof of adjacent two- and three-story buildings. Within the hour the entire block was in flames. The ninth house in the burning row belonged to the arsonist who had thrown the Molotov cocktail. . . .

. . . .

. . . Employed as a private guard, 55-year-old Julius L. Dorsey, a Negro, was standing in front of a market when accosted by two Negro men, and a woman. They demanded he permit them to loot the market. He ignored their demands. They began to berate him. He asked a neighbor to call the police. As the argument grew more heated, Dorsey fired three shots from his pistol into the air.

The police radio reported: "Looters—they have rifles." A patrol car driven by a police officer and carrying three National Guardsmen arrived. As the looters fled, the law enforcement personnel opened fire. When the firing ceased, one person lay dead.

He was Julius L. Dorsey. . . .

. . . .

. . . As the riot alternately waxed and waned, one area of the ghetto remained insulated. On the northeast side the residents of some 150 square blocks inhabited by 21,000 persons had, in 1966, banded together in the Positive Neighborhood Action Committee (PNAC). With professional help from the Institute of Urban Dynamics, they had organized block clubs and made plans for the improvement of the neighborhood. . . .

When the riot broke out, the residents, through the block clubs, were able to organize quickly. Youngsters, agreeing to stay in the neighborhood, participated in detouring traffic. While many persons reportedly sympathized with the idea of a rebellion against the "system," only two small fires were set—one in an empty building.

． ． ． ．

. . . According to Lt. Gen. Throckmorton and Col. Bolling, the city, at this time, was saturated with fear. The National Guardsmen were afraid, and the police were afraid. Numerous persons, the majority of them Negroes, were being injured by gunshots of undetermined origin. The general and his staff felt that the major task of the troops was to reduce the fear and restore an air of normalcy.

In order to accomplish this, every effort was made to establish contact and rapport between the troops and the residents. The soldiers—20 percent of whom were Negro—began helping to clean up the streets, collect garbage, and trace persons who had disappeared in the confusion. Residents in the neighborhoods responded with soup and sandwiches for the troops. In areas where the National Guard tried to establish rapport with the citizens, there was a similar response.

New Brunswick

. . . A short time later, elements of the crowd—an older and rougher one than the night before—appeared in front of the police station. The participants wanted to see the mayor.

Mayor [Patricia] Sheehan went out onto the steps of the station. Using a bullhorn, she talked to the people and asked that she be given an opportunity to correct conditions. The crowd was boisterous. Some persons challenged the mayor. But, finally, the opinion, "She's new! Give her a chance!" prevailed.

A demand was issued by people in the crowd that all persons arrested the previous night be released. Told that this already had been done, the people were suspicious. They asked to be allowed to inspect the jail cells.

It was agreed to permit representatives of the people to look in the cells to satisfy themselves that everyone had been released.

The crowd dispersed. The New Brunswick riot had failed to materialize.

Chapter 2

Patterns of Disorder

The "typical" riot did not take place. The disorders of 1967 were unusual, irregular, complex and unpredictable social processes. Like most human events, they did not unfold in an orderly sequence. However, an analysis of our survey information leads to some conclusions about the riot process.

In general:

- The civil disorders of 1967 involved Negroes acting against local symbols of white American society, authority and property in Negro neighborhoods—rather than against white persons.
- Of 164 disorders reported during the first 9 months of 1967, eight (5 percent) were major in terms of violence and damage; 33 (20 percent) were serious but not major; 123 (75 percent) were minor and undoubtedly would not have received national attention as riots had the nation not been sensitized by the more serious outbreaks.
- In the 75 disorders studied by a Senate subcommittee, 83 deaths were reported. Eighty-two percent of the deaths and more than half the injuries occurred in Newark and Detroit. About 10 percent of the dead and 36 percent of the injured were public employees, primarily law officers and firemen. The overwhelming majority of the persons killed or injured in all the disorders were Negro civilians.
- Initial damage estimates were greatly exaggerated. In Detroit, newspaper damage estimates at first ranged from $200 million to $500 million; the highest recent estimate is $45 million. In Newark, early estimates ranged from $15 to $25 million. A month later damage was estimated at $10.2 million, 80 percent in inventory losses.

In the 24 disorders in 23 cities which we surveyed:

- The final incident before the outbreak of disorder, and the initial violence itself, generally took place in the evening or at night at a place in which it was normal for many people to be on the streets.
- Violence usually occurred almost immediately following the occurrence of the final precipitating incident, and then escalated rapidly. With but few exceptions, violence subsided during the day, and flared rapidly again at night. The night-day cycles continued through the early period of the major disorders.
- Disorder generally began with rock and bottle throwing and window breaking. Once store windows were broken, looting usually followed.
- Disorder did not erupt as a result of a single "triggering" or "precipitating" incident. Instead, it was generated out of an increasingly disturbed social atmosphere, in which typically a series of tension-heightening incidents over a period of weeks or months became linked in the minds of many in the Negro community with a reservoir of underlying grievances. At some point in the mounting tension, a further incident—in itself often routine or trivial—became the breaking point and the tension spilled over into violence.
- "Prior" incidents, which increased tensions and ultimately led to violence, were police actions in almost half the cases; police actions were "final" incidents before the outbreak of violence in 12 of the 24 surveyed disorders.
- No particular control tactic was successful in every situation. The varied effectiveness of control techniques emphasizes the need for advance training, planning, adequate intelligence systems, and knowledge of the ghetto community.
- Negotiations between Negroes—including young militants as well as older Negro leaders—and white officials concerning "terms of peace" occurred during virtually all the disorders surveyed. In many cases, these negotiations involved discussion of underlying grievances as well as the handling of the disorder by control authorities.
- The typical rioter was a teenager or young adult, a life-long resident of the city in which he rioted, a high school dropout; he was, nevertheless, somewhat better educated than his nonrioting Negro neighbor, and was usually un-

deremployed or employed in a menial job. He was proud of his race, extremely hostile to both whites and middle-class Negroes and, although informed about politics, highly distrustful of the political system.

A Detroit survey revealed that approximately 11 percent of the total residents of two riot areas admitted participation in the rioting, 20 to 25 percent identified themselves as "by-standers," over 16 percent identified themselves as "counter-rioters" who urged rioters to "cool it," and the remaining 48 to 53 percent said they were at home or elsewhere and did not participate. In a survey of Negro males between the ages of 15 and 35 residing in the disturbance area in Newark, about 45 percent identified themselves as rioters, and about 55 percent as "noninvolved."

- Most rioters were young Negro males. Nearly 53 percent of arrestees were between 15 and 24 years of age; nearly 81 percent between 15 and 35.
- In Detroit and Newark about 74 percent of the rioters were brought up in the North. In contrast, of the non-involved, 36 percent in Detroit and 52 percent in Newark were brought up in the North.
- What the rioters appeared to be seeking was fuller par-ticipation in the social order and the material benefits enjoyed by the majority of American citizens. Rather than rejecting the American system, they were anxious to ob-tain a place for themselves in it.
- Numerous Negro counter-rioters walked the streets urg-ing rioters to "cool it." The typical counter-rioter was better educated and had higher income than either the rioter or the noninvolved.
- The proportion of Negroes in local government was sub-stantially smaller than the Negro proportion of popula-tion. Only three of the 20 cities studied had more than one Negro legislator; none had ever had a Negro mayor or city manager. In only four cities did Negroes hold other important policy-making positions or serve as heads of municipal departments.
- Although almost all cities had some sort of formal griev-ance mechanism for handling citizen complaints, this

typically was regarded by Negroes as ineffective and was generally ignored.

- Although specific grievances varied from city to city, at least 12 deeply held grievances can be identified and ranked into three levels of relative intensity:

First Level of Intensity
1. Police practices
2. Unemployment and underemployment
3. Inadequate housing

Second Level of Intensity
4. Inadequate education
5. Poor recreation facilities and programs
6. Ineffectiveness of the political structure and grievance mechanisms

Third Level of Intensity
7. Disrespectful white attitudes
8. Discriminatory administration of justice
9. Inadequacy of federal programs
10. Inadequacy of municipal services
11. Discriminatory consumer and credit practices
12. Inadequate welfare programs

- The results of a three-city survey of various federal programs—manpower, education, housing, welfare and community action—indicate that, despite substantial expenditures, the number of persons assisted constitute only a fraction of those in need.

The background of disorder is often as complex and difficult to analyze as the disorder itself. But we find that certain general conclusions can be drawn:

- Social and economic conditions in the riot cities constituted a clear pattern of severe disadvantage for Negroes compared with whites, whether the Negroes lived in the area where the riot took place or outside it. Negroes had completed fewer years of education and fewer had attended high school. Negroes were twice as likely to be unemployed and three times as likely to be in unskilled and service jobs. Negroes averaged 70 percent of the income earned by whites and were more than twice as likely to be living in poverty. Although housing cost Negroes relatively more, they had worse housing—three times as likely to be overcrowded and substandard. When compared to white suburbs, the relative disadvantage is even more pronounced.

A study of the aftermath of disorder leads to disturbing conclusions. We find that, despite the institution of some post-riot programs:

* Little basic change in the conditions underlying the outbreak of disorder has taken place. Actions to ameliorate Negro grievances have been limited and sporadic; with but few exceptions, they have not significantly reduced tensions.
* In several cities, the principal official response has been to train and equip the police with more sophisticated weapons.
* In several cities, increasing polarization is evident, with continuing breakdown of interracial communication, and growth of white segregationist or black separatist groups.

Chapter 3

Organized Activity

The President directed the Commission to investigate "to what extent, if any, there has been planning or organization in any of the riots."

To carry out this part of the President's charge, the Commission established a special investigative staff supplementing the field teams that made the general examination of the riots in 23 cities. The unit examined data collected by federal agencies and congressional committees, including thousands of documents supplied by the Federal Bureau of Investigation, gathered and evaluated information from local and state law enforcement agencies and officials, and conducted its own field investigation in selected cities.

On the basis of all the information collected, the Commission concludes that:

* The urban disorders of the summer of 1967 were not caused by, nor were they the consequence of, any organized plan or "conspiracy."

Specifically, the Commission has found no evidence that all or any of the disorders or the incidents that led to them were planned or directed by any organization or group, international, national or local.

Militant organizations, local and national, and individual agitators, who repeatedly forecast and called for violence, were active in the spring and summer of 1967. We believe that they sought to encourage violence, and that they helped to create an atmosphere that contributed to the outbreak of disorder.

We recognize that the continuation of disorders and the polarization of the races would provide fertile ground for organized exploitation in the future.

Investigations of organized activity are continuing at all levels of government, including committees of Congress. These investigations relate not only to the disorders of 1967 but also to the actions of groups and individuals, particularly in schools and colleges, during this last fall and winter. The Commission has cooperated in these investigations. They should continue.

Part II

WHY DID IT HAPPEN?

Chapter 4

The Basic Causes

In addressing the question "Why did it happen?" we shift our focus from the local to the national scene, from the particular events of the summer of 1967 to the factors within the society at large that created a mood of violence among many urban Negroes.

These factors are complex and interacting; they vary significantly in their effect from city to city and from year to year; and the consequences of one disorder, generating new grievances and new demands, become the causes of the next. Thus was created the "thicket of tension, conflicting evidence and extreme opinions" cited by the President.

Despite these complexities, certain fundamental matters

are clear. Of these, the most fundamental is the racial attitude and behavior of white Americans toward black Americans.

Race prejudice has shaped our history decisively; it now threatens to affect our future.

White racism is essentially responsible for the explosive mixture which has been accumulating in our cities since the end of World War II. Among the ingredients of this mixture are:

- *Pervasive discrimination and segregation* in employment, education and housing, which have resulted in the continuing exclusion of great numbers of Negroes from the benefits of economic progress.
- *Black in-migration and white exodus,* which have produced the massive and growing concentrations of impoverished Negroes in our major cities, creating a growing crisis of deteriorating facilities and services and unmet human needs.
- *The black ghettos,* where segregation and poverty converge on the young to destroy opportunity and enforce failure. Crime, drug addiction, dependency on welfare, and bitterness and resentment against society in general and white society in particular are the result.

At the same time, most whites and some Negroes outside the ghetto have prospered to a degree unparalleled in the history of civilization. Through television and other media, this affluence has been endlessly flaunted before the eyes of the Negro poor and the jobless ghetto youth.

Yet these facts alone cannot be said to have caused the disorders. Recently, other powerful ingredients have begun to catalyze the mixture:

- *Frustrated hopes* are the residue of the unfulfilled expectations aroused by the great judicial and legislative victories of the civil rights movement and the dramatic struggle for equal rights in the South.
- *A climate that tends toward approval and encouragement of violence* as a form of protest has been created by white terrorism directed against nonviolent protest; by the open defiance of law and federal authority by state and local officials resisting desegregation; and by some protest groups engaging in civil disobedience who

turn their backs on nonviolence, go beyond the constitutionally protected rights of petition and free assembly,
and resort to violence to attempt to compel alteration
of laws and policies with which they disagree.

- *The frustrations of powerlessness* have led some Negroes
to the conviction that there is no effective alternative
to violence as a means of achieving redress of grievances,
and of "moving the system." These frustrations are
reflected in alienation and hostility toward the institutions of law and government and the white society
which controls them, and in the reach toward racial
consciousness and solidarity reflected in the slogan
"Black Power."

- *A new mood* has sprung up among Negroes, particularly
among the young, in which self-esteem and enhanced
racial pride are replacing apathy and submission to
"the system."

- *The police are not merely a "spark" factor.* To some
Negroes police have come to symbolize white power,
white racism and white repression. And the fact is
that many police do reflect and express these white
attitudes. The atmosphere of hostility and cynicism
is reinforced by a widespread belief among Negroes
in the existence of police brutality and in a "double
standard" of justice and protection—one for Negroes
and one for whites.

. . . .

To this point, we have attempted only to identify the prime
components of the "explosive mixture." In the chapters that
follow we seek to analyze them in the perspective of history.
Their meaning, however, is already clear:

In the summer of 1967, we have seen in our cities a chain
reaction of racial violence. If we are heedless, none of us
shall escape the consequences.

Chapter 5

Rejection and Protest: An Historical Sketch

The causes of recent racial disorders are embedded in a tangle of issues and circumstances—social, economic, political and psychological—which arise out of the historical pattern of Negro-white relations in America.

In this chapter we trace the pattern, identify the recurrent themes of Negro protest and, most importantly, provide a perspective on the protest activities of the present era.

We describe the Negro's experience in America and the development of slavery as an institution. We show his persistent striving for equality in the face of rigidly maintained social, economic and educational barriers, and repeated mob violence. We portray the ebb and flow of the doctrinal tides —accommodation, separatism, and self-help—and their relationship to the current theme of Black Power. We conclude:

- The Black Power advocates of today consciously feel that they are the most militant group in the Negro protest movement. Yet they have retreated from a direct confrontation with American society on the issue of integration and, by preaching separatism, unconsciously function as an accommodation to white racism. Much of their economic program, as well as their interest in Negro history, self-help, racial solidarity and separation, is reminiscent of Booker T. Washington. The rhetoric is different, but the programs are remarkably similar.

Chapter 6

The Formation of the Racial Ghettos[1]

Throughout the 20th century the Negro population of the United States has been moving steadily from rural areas to

[1] The term "ghetto" as used in this Report refers to an area within a city characterized by poverty and acute social disorganization and inhabited by members of a racial or ethnic group under conditions of involuntary segregation.

urban and from South to North and West. In 1910, 91 percent of the nation's 9.8 million Negroes lived in the South and only 27 percent of American Negroes lived in cities of 2,500 persons or more. Between 1910 and 1966 the total Negro population more than doubled, reaching 21.5 million, and the number living in metropolitan areas rose more than five-fold (from 2.6 million to 14.8 million). The number outside the South rose elevenfold (from 885,000 to 9.7 million).

Negro migration from the South has resulted from the expectation of thousands of new and highly paid jobs for unskilled workers in the North and the shift to mechanized farming in the South. However, the Negro migration is small when compared to earlier waves of European immigrants. Even between 1960 and 1966, there were 1.8 million immigrants from abroad compared to the 613,000 Negroes who arrived in the North and West from the South.

As a result of the growing number of Negroes in urban areas, natural increase has replaced migration as the primary source of Negro population increase in the cities. Nevertheless, Negro migration from the South will continue unless economic conditions there change dramatically.

Basic data concerning Negro urbanization trends indicate that:

- Almost all Negro population growth (98 percent from 1950 to 1966) is occurring within metropolitan areas, primarily within central cities.[2]
- The vast majority of white population growth (78 percent from 1960 to 1966) is occurring in suburban portions of metropolitan areas. Since 1960, white central-city population has declined by 1.3 million.
- As a result, central cities are becoming more heavily Negro while the suburban fringes around them remain almost entirely white.
- The twelve largest central cities now contain over two-thirds of the Negro population outside the South, and almost one-third of the Negro total in the United States.

Within the cities, Negroes have been excluded from white

---

[2] A "central city" is the largest city of a standard metropolitan statistical area, that is, a metropolitan area containing at least one city of at least 50,000 inhabitants.

residential areas through discriminatory practices. Just as significant is the withdrawal of white families from, or their refusal to enter, neighborhoods where Negroes are moving or already residing. About 20 percent of the urban population of the United States changes residence every year. The refusal of whites to move into "changing" areas when vacancies occur means that most vacancies eventually are occupied by Negroes.

The result, according to a recent study, is that in 1960 the average segregation index for 207 of the largest U.S. cities was 86.2. In other words, to create an unsegregated population distribution, an average of over 86 percent of all Negroes would have to change their place of residence within the city.

Chapter 7

Unemployment, Family Structure and Social Disorganization

Although there have been gains in Negro income nationally, and a decline in the number of Negroes below the "poverty level," the condition of Negroes in the central city remains in a state of crisis. Between 2 and 2.5 million Negroes—16 to 20 percent of the total Negro population of all central cities—live in squalor and deprivation in ghetto neighborhoods.

Employment is a key problem. It not only controls the present for the Negro American but, in a most profound way, it is creating the future as well. Yet, despite continuing economic growth and declining national unemployment rates, the unemployment rate for Negroes in 1967 was more than double that for whites.

Equally important is the undesirable nature of many jobs open to Negroes and other minorities. Negro men are more than three times as likely as white men to be in low-paying, unskilled or service jobs. This concentration of male Negro employment at the lowest end of the occupational scale is the single most important cause of poverty among Negroes.

In one study of low-income neighborhoods, the "sub-employment rate," including both unemployment and under-employment, was about 33 percent, or 8.8 times greater than the overall unemployment rate for all U.S. workers.

Employment problems, aggravated by the constant arrival of new unemployed migrants, many of them from depressed rural areas, create persistent poverty in the ghetto. In 1966, about 11.9 percent of the nation's whites and 40.6 percent of its nonwhites were below the "poverty level" defined by the Social Security Administration (in 1966, $3,335 per year for an urban family of four). Over 40 percent of the nonwhites below the poverty level live in the central cities.

Employment problems have drastic social impact in the ghetto. Men who are chronically unemployed or employed in the lowest status jobs are often unable or unwilling to remain with their families. The handicap imposed on children growing up without fathers in an atmosphere of deprivation is increased as mothers are forced to work to provide support.

The culture of poverty that results from unemployment and family breakup generates a system of ruthless, exploitative relationships within the ghetto. Prostitution, dope addiction, and crime create an environmental "jungle" characterized by personal insecurity and tension. Children growing up under such conditions are likely participants in civil disorder.

Chapter 8

Conditions of Life in the Racial Ghetto

A striking difference in environment from that of white, middle-class Americans profoundly influences the lives of residents of the ghetto.

Crime rates, consistently higher than in other areas, create a pronounced sense of insecurity. For example, in one city one low-income Negro district had 35 times as many serious crimes against persons as a high-income white district. Unless drastic steps are taken, the crime problems in poverty areas are likely to continue to multiply as the growing youth and rapid urbanization of the population outstrip police resources.

Poor health and sanitation conditions in the ghetto result in higher mortality rates, a higher incidence of major diseases and lower availability and utilization of medical services. The infant mortality rate for nonwhite babies under the age of one month is 58 percent higher than for whites; for one to 12 months it is almost three times as high. The level of sanitation in the ghetto is far below that in high-income areas. Garbage collection is often inadequate. Of an estimated 14,000 cases of rat bite in the United States in 1965, most were in ghetto neighborhoods.

Ghetto residents believe they are exploited by local merchants; and evidence substantiates some of these beliefs. A study conducted in one city by the Federal Trade Commission showed that higher prices were charged for goods sold in ghetto stores than in other areas.

Lack of knowledge regarding credit purchasing creates special pitfalls for the disadvantaged. In many states garnishment practices compound these difficulties by allowing creditors to deprive individuals of their wages without hearing or trial.

Chapter 9

Comparing the Immigrant and Negro Experience

In this chapter, we address ourselves to a fundamental question that many white Americans are asking: Why have so many Negroes, unlike the European immigrants, been unable to escape from the ghetto and from poverty?

We believe the following factors play a part:

- *The Maturing Economy:* When the European immigrants arrived, they gained an economic foothold by providing the unskilled labor needed by industry. Unlike the immigrant, the Negro migrant found little opportunity in the city. The economy, by then matured, had little use for the unskilled labor he had to offer.
- *The Disability of Race:* The structure of discrimination has stringently narrowed opportunities for the Negro and restricted his prospects. European immigrants suffered from discrimination, but never so pervasively.
- *Entry into the Political System:* The immigrants usually settled in rapidly growing cities with powerful and expanding political machines, which traded economic ad-

vantages for political support. Ward-level grievance machinery, as well as personal representation, enabled the immigrant to make his voice heard and his power felt.

By the time the Negro arrived, these political machines were no longer so powerful or so well equipped to provide jobs or other favors and were unwilling to share their remaining influence with Negroes.

- *Cultural Factors:* Coming from societies with a low standard of living and at a time when job aspirations were low, the immigrants sensed little deprivation in being forced to take the less desirable and poorer paying jobs. Their large and cohesive families contributed to total income. Their vision of the future—one that led to a life outside of the ghetto—provided the incentive necessary to endure the present.

Although Negro men worked as hard as the immigrants, they were unable to support their families. The entrepreneurial opportunities had vanished. As a result of slavery and long periods of unemployment, the Negro family structure had become matriarchal; the males played a secondary and marginal family role—one which offered little compensation for their hard and unrewarding labor. Above all, segregation denied Negroes access to good jobs and the opportunity to leave the ghetto. For them, the future seemed to lead only to a dead end.

Today, whites tend to exaggerate how well and quickly they escaped from poverty. The fact is that immigrants who came from rural backgrounds, as many Negroes do, are only now, after three generations, finally beginning to move into the middle class.

By contrast, Negroes began concentrating in the city less than two generations ago, and under much less favorable conditions. Although some Negroes have escaped poverty, few have been able to escape the urban ghetto.

Part III

WHAT CAN BE DONE?

Chapter 10

The Community Response

Our investigation of the 1967 riot cities establishes that virtually every major episode of violence was foreshadowed by an accumulation of unresolved grievances and by widespread dissatisfaction among Negroes with the unwillingness and inability of local government to respond.

Overcoming these conditions is essential for community support of law enforcement and civil order. City governments need new and more vital channels of communication to the residents of the ghetto; they need to improve their capacity to respond effectively to community needs before they become community grievances; and they need to provide opportunity for meaningful involvement of ghetto residents in shaping policies and programs which affect the community.

The Commission recommends that local governments:

* Develop Neighborhood Action Task Forces as joint community-government efforts through which more effective communication can be achieved, and the delivery of city services to ghetto residents improved.

* Establish comprehensive grievance-response mechanisms in order to bring all public agencies under public scrutiny.

* Bring the institutions of local government closer to the people they serve by establishing neighborhood outlets for local, state and federal administrative and public service agencies.

* Expand opportunities for ghetto residents to participate in the formulation of public policy and the implementation of programs affecting them through improved political representation, creation of institutional channels for community action, expansion of legal services, and legislative hearings on ghetto problems.

In this effort, city governments will require state and federal support.

The Commission recommends:

- State and federal financial assistance for mayors and city councils to support the research, consultants, staff and other resources needed to respond effectively to federal program initiatives.
- State cooperation in providing municipalities with the jurisdictional tools needed to deal with their problems; a fuller measure of financial aid to urban areas; and the focusing of the interests of suburban communities on the physical, social and cultural environment of the central city.

Chapter 11

Police and the Community

The abrasive relationship between the police and minority communities has been a major—and explosive—source of grievance, tension and disorder. The blame must be shared by the total society.

The police are faced with demands for increased protection and service in the ghetto. Yet the aggressive patrol practices thought necessary to meet these demands themselves create tension and hostility. The resulting grievances have been further aggravated by the lack of effective mechanisms for handling complaints against the police. Special programs for bettering police-community relations have been instituted but these alone are not enough. Police administrators, with the guidance of public officials, and the support of the entire community, must take vigorous action to improve law enforcement and to decrease the potential for disorder.

The Commission recommends that city government and police authorities:

- Review police operations in the ghetto to ensure proper conduct by police officers, and eliminate abrasive practices.
- Provide more adequate police protection to ghetto resi-

dents to eliminate their high sense of insecurity, and the belief in the existence of a dual standard of law enforcement.

- Establish fair and effective mechanisms for the redress of grievances against the police, and other municipal employees.

- Develop and adopt policy guidelines to assist officers in making critical decisions in areas where police conduct can create tension.

- Develop and use innovative programs to ensure widespread community support for law enforcement.

- Recruit more Negroes into the regular police force and review promotion policies to ensure fair promotion for Negro officers.

- Establish a "Community Service Officer" program to attract ghetto youths between the ages of 17 and 21 to police work. These junior officers would perform duties in ghetto neighborhoods but would not have full police authority. The federal government should provide support equal to 90 percent of the costs of employing CSOs on the basis of one for every ten regular officers.

Chapter 12

Control of Disorder

Preserving civil peace is the first responsibility of government. Unless the rule of law prevails, our society will lack not only order but also the environment essential to social and economic progress.

The maintenance of civil order cannot be left to the police alone. The police need guidance, as well as support, from mayors and other public officials. It is the responsibility of public officials to determine proper police policies, support adequate police standards for personnel and performance, and participate in planning for the control of disorders.

To maintain control of incidents which could lead to disorders, the Commission recommends that local officials:

- Assign seasoned, well-trained policemen and supervisory officers to patrol ghetto areas, and to respond to disturbances.

- Develop plans which will quickly muster maximum police manpower and highly qualified senior commanders at the outbreak of disorders.

- Provide special training in the prevention of disorders, and prepare police for riot control and for operation in units, with adequate command and control and field communication for proper discipline and effectiveness.

- Develop guidelines governing the use of control equipment and provide alternatives to the use of lethal weapons. Federal support for research in this area is needed.

- Establish an intelligence system to provide police and other public officials with reliable information that may help to prevent the outbreak of a disorder and to institute effective control measures in the event a riot erupts.

- Develop continuing contacts with ghetto residents to make use of the forces for order which exist within the community.

- Establish machinery for neutralizing rumors, and enabling Negro leaders and residents to obtain the facts. Create special rumor details to collect, evaluate, and dispel rumors that may lead to a civil disorder.

The Commission believes there is a grave danger that some communities may resort to the indiscriminate and excessive use of force. The harmful effects of overreaction are incalculable. The Commission condemns moves to equip police departments with mass destruction weapons, such as automatic rifles, machine guns and tanks. Weapons which are designed to destroy, not to control, have no place in densely populated urban communities.

The Commission recommends that the federal government share in the financing of programs for improvement of police forces both in their normal law enforcement activities as well as in their response to civil disorders.

To assist government authorities in planning their response to civil disorder, this report contains a Supplement on Control of Disorder. It deals with specific problems encountered during riot-control operations, and includes:

- Assessment of the present capabilities of police, National

Guard and Army forces to control major riots, and recommendations for improvement.

- Recommended means by which the control operations of those forces may be coordinated with the response of other agencies, such as fire departments, and with the community at large.
- Recommendations for review and revision of federal, state and local laws needed to provide the framework for control efforts and for the call-up and interrelated action of public safety forces.

Chapter 13

The Administration of Justice Under Emergency Conditions

In many of the cities which experienced disorders last summer, there were recurring breakdowns in the mechanisms for processing, prosecuting and protecting arrested persons. These resulted mainly from long-standing structural deficiencies in criminal court systems, and from the failure of communities to anticipate and plan for the emergency demands of civil disorders.

In part, because of this, there were few successful prosecutions for serious crimes committed during the riots. In those cities where mass arrests occurred many arrestees were deprived of basic legal rights.

The Commission recommends that the cities and states:

- Undertake reform of the lower courts so as to improve the quality of justice rendered under normal conditions.
- Plan comprehensive measures by which the criminal justice system may be supplemented during civil disorders so that its deliberative functions are protected, and the quality of justice is maintained.

Such emergency plans require broad community participation and dedicated leadership by the bench and bar. They should include:

- Laws sufficient to deter and punish riot conduct.

- Additional judges, bail and probation officers, and clerical staff.
- Arrangements for volunteer lawyers to help prosecutors and to represent riot defendants at every stage of proceedings.
- Policies to ensure proper and individual bail, arraignment, pre-trial, trial and sentencing proceedings.
- Adequate emergency processing and detention facilities.

Chapter 14

Damages: Repair and Compensation

The Commission recommends that the federal government:

- Amend the Federal Disaster Act—which now applies only to natural disasters—to permit federal emergency food and medical assistance to cities during major civil disorders, and provide long-term economic assistance afterwards.
- With the cooperation of the states, create incentives for the private insurance industry to provide more adequate property-insurance coverage in inner-city areas.

The Commission endorses the report of the National Advisory Panel on Insurance in Riot-Affected Areas: "Meeting the Insurance Crisis of Our Cities."

Chapter 15

The News Media and the Riots

In his charge to the Commission, the President asked: "What effect do the mass media have on the riots?"

The Commission determined that the answer to the President's question did not lie solely in the performance of the press and broadcasters in reporting the riots. Our analysis had to consider also the overall treatment by the media of the Negro ghettos, community relations, racial attitudes, and poverty—day by day and month by month, year in and year out.

A wide range of interviews with government officials, law enforcement authorities, media personnel and other citizens, including ghetto residents, as well as a quantitative analysis of riot coverage and a special conference with industry representatives leads us to conclude that:

- Despite instances of sensationalism, inaccuracy and distortion, newspapers, radio and television tried on the whole to give a balanced, factual account of the 1967 disorders.
- Elements of the news media failed to portray accurately the scale and character of the violence that occurred last summer. The overall effect was, we believe, an exaggeration of both mood and event.
- Important segments of the media failed to report adequately on the causes and consequences of civil disorders and on the underlying problems of race relations. They have not communicated to the majority of their audience —which is white—a sense of the degradation, misery and hopelessness of life in the ghetto.

These failings must be corrected, and the improvement must come from within the industry. Freedom of the press is not the issue. Any effort to impose governmental restrictions would be inconsistent with fundamental constitutional precepts.

We have seen evidence that the news media are becoming aware of and concerned about their performance in this field. As that concern grows, coverage will improve. But much more must be done, and it must be done soon.

The Commission recommends that the media:

- Expand coverage of the Negro community and of race problems through permanent assignment of reporters familiar with urban and racial affairs, and through establishment of more and better links with the Negro community.
- Integrate Negroes and Negro activities into all aspects of coverage and content, including newspaper articles and television programming. The news media must publish newspapers and produce programs that recognize

the existence and activities of Negroes as a group within the community and as a part of the larger community.

- Recruit more Negroes into journalism and broadcasting and promote those who are qualified to positions of significant responsibility. Recruitment should begin in high schools and continue through college; where necessary, aid for training should be provided.

- Improve coordination with police in reporting riot news through advance planning, and cooperate with the police in the designation of police information officers, establishment of information centers, and development of mutually acceptable guidelines for riot reporting and the conduct of media personnel.

- Accelerate efforts to ensure accurate and responsible reporting of riot and racial news, through adoption by all news-gathering organizations of stringent internal staff guidelines.

- Cooperate in the establishment of a privately organized and funded Institute of Urban Communications to train and educate journalists in urban affairs, recruit and train more Negro journalists, develop methods for improving police–press relations, review coverage of riots and racial issues, and support continuing research in the urban field.

Chapter 16

The Future
of the Cities

By 1985, the Negro population in central cities is expected to increase by 68 percent to approximately 20.3 million. Coupled with the continued exodus of white families to the suburbs, this growth will produce majority Negro populations in many of the nation's largest cities.

The future of these cities, and of their burgeoning Negro populations, is grim. Most new employment opportunities are being created in suburbs and outlying areas. This trend will continue unless important changes in public policy are made.

In prospect, therefore, is further deterioration of already inadequate municipal tax bases in the face of increasing demands for public services, and continuing unemployment and poverty among the urban Negro population:

Three choices are open to the nation:

- We can maintain present policies, continuing both the proportion of the nation's resources now allocated to programs for the unemployed and the disadvantaged, and the inadequate and failing effort to achieve an integrated society.
- We can adopt a policy of "enrichment" aimed at improving dramatically the quality of ghetto life while abandoning integration as a goal.
- We can pursue integration by combining ghetto "enrichment" with policies which will encourage Negro movement out of central-city areas.

The first choice, continuance of present policies, has ominous consequences for our society. The share of the nation's resources now allocated to programs for the disadvantaged is insufficient to arrest the deterioration of life in central-city ghettos. Under such conditions, a rising proportion of Negroes may come to see in the deprivation and segregation they experience, a justification for violent protest, or for extending support to now isolated extremists who advocate civil disruption. Large-scale and continuing violence could result, followed by white retaliation, and, ultimately, the separation of the two communities in a garrison state.

Even if violence does not occur, the consequences are unacceptable. Development of a racially integrated society, extraordinarily difficult today, will be virtually impossible when the present black central-city population of 12.1 million has grown to almost 21 million.

To continue present policies is to make permanent the division of our country into two societies; one, largely Negro and poor, located in the central cities; the other, predominantly white and affluent, located in the suburbs and in outlying areas.

The second choice, ghetto enrichment coupled with abandonment of integration, is also unacceptable. It is another way of choosing a permanently divided country. Moreover, equality cannot be achieved under conditions of nearly complete separation. In a country where the economy, and particularly the resources of employment, are predominantly white, a policy of separation can only relegate Negroes to a permanently inferior economic status.

We believe that the only possible choice for America is the third—a policy which combines ghetto enrichment with programs designed to encourage integration of substantial numbers of Negroes into the society outside the ghetto.

Enrichment must be an important adjunct to integration, for no matter how ambitious or energetic the program, few Negroes now living in central cities can be quickly integrated. In the meantime, large-scale improvement in the quality of ghetto life is essential.

But this can be no more than an interim strategy. Programs must be developed which will permit substantial Negro movement out of the ghettos. The primary goal must be a single society, in which every citizen will be free to live and work according to his capabilities and desires, not his color.

Chapter 17

Recommendations for National Action

Introduction

No American—white or black—can escape the consequences of the continuing social and economic decay of our major cities.

Only a commitment to national action on an unprecedented scale can shape a future compatible with the historic ideals of American society.

The great productivity of our economy, and a federal revenue system which is highly responsive to economic growth, can provide the resources.

The major need is to generate new will—the will to tax ourselves to the extent necessary to meet the vital needs of the nation.

We have set forth goals and proposed strategies to reach those goals. We discuss and recommend programs not to commit each of us to specific parts of such programs but to illustrate the type and dimension of action needed.

The major goal is the creation of a true union—a single

society and a single American identity. Toward that goal, we propose the following objectives for national action:

- Opening up opportunities to those who are restricted by racial segregation and discrimination and eliminating all barriers to their choice of jobs, education and housing.
- Removing the frustration of powerlessness among the disadvantaged by providing the means for them to deal with the problems that affect their own lives and by increasing the capacity of our public and private institutions to respond to these problems.
- Increasing communication across racial lines to destroy stereotypes, to halt polarization, end distrust and hostility and create common ground for efforts toward public order and social justice.

We propose these aims to fulfill our pledge of equality and to meet the fundamental needs of a democratic and civilized society—domestic peace and social justice.

Employment

Pervasive unemployment and underemployment are the most persistent and serious grievances in the Negro ghetto. They are inextricably linked to the problem of civil disorder.

Despite growing federal expenditures for manpower development and training programs and sustained general economic prosperity and increasing demands for skilled workers, about two million—white and nonwhite—are permanently unemployed. About ten million are underemployed, of whom 6.5 million work full time for wages below the poverty line.

The 500,000 "hard-core" unemployed in the central cities who lack a basic education and are unable to hold a steady job are made up in large part of Negro males between the ages of 18 and 25. In the riot cities which we surveyed, Negroes were three times as likely as whites to hold unskilled jobs, which are often part time, seasonal, low-paying and "dead end."

Negro males between the ages of 15 and 25 predominated among the rioters. More than 20 percent of the rioters were unemployed, and many who were employed held intermittent, low-status, unskilled jobs which they regarded as below their education and ability.

The Commission recommends that the federal government:

- Undertake joint efforts with cities and states to consolidate existing manpower programs to avoid fragmentation and duplication.
- Take immediate action to create 2,000,000 new jobs over the next three years—one million in the public sector and one million in the private sector—to absorb the hard-core unemployed and materially reduce the level of underemployment for all workers, black and white. We propose 250,000 public sector and 300,000 private sector jobs in the first year.
- Provide on-the-job training by both public and private employers with reimbursement to private employers for the extra costs of training the hard-core unemployed, by contract or by tax credits.
- Provide tax and other incentives to investment in rural as well as urban poverty areas in order to offer to the rural poor an alternative to migration to urban centers.
- Take new and vigorous action to remove artificial barriers to employment and promotion, including not only racial discrimination but, in certain cases, arrest records or lack of a high school diploma. Strengthen those agencies such as the Equal Employment Opportunity Commission, charged with eliminating discriminatory practices, and provide full support for Title VI of the 1964 Civil Rights Act allowing federal grant-in-aid funds to be withheld from activities which discriminate on grounds of color or race.

The Commission commends the recent public commitment of the National Council of the Building and Construction Trades Unions, AFL–CIO, to encourage and recruit Negro membership in apprenticeship programs. This commitment should be intensified and implemented.

Education

Education in a democratic society must equip children to develop their potential and to participate fully in American life. For the community at large, the schools have discharged this responsibility well. But for many minorities, and particularly for the children of the ghetto, the schools have failed to provide the educational experience which could overcome the effects of discrimination and deprivation.

This failure is one of the persistent sources of grievance and resentment within the Negro community. The hostility of Negro parents and students toward the school system is generating increasing conflict and causing disruption within many city school districts. But the most dramatic evidence of the relationship between educational practices and civil disorders lies in the high incidence of riot participation by ghetto youth who have not completed high school.

The bleak record of public education for ghetto children is growing worse. In the critical skills—verbal and reading ability—Negro students are falling farther behind whites with each year of school completed. The high unemployment and underemployment rate for Negro youth is evidence, in part, of the growing educational crisis.

We support integration as the priority education strategy; it is essential to the future of American society. In this last summer's disorders we have seen the consequences of racial isolation at all levels, and of attitudes toward race, on both sides, produced by three centuries of myth, ignorance and bias. It is indispensable that opportunities for interaction between the races be expanded.

We recognize that the growing dominance of pupils from disadvantaged minorities in city-school populations will not soon be reversed. No matter how great the effort toward desegregation, many children of the ghetto will not, within their school careers, attend integrated schools.

If existing disadvantages are not to be perpetuated, we must drastically improve the quality of ghetto education. Equality of results with all-white schools must be the goal.

To implement these strategies, the Commission recommends:

- Sharply increased efforts to eliminate de facto segregation in our schools through substantial federal aid to school systems seeking to desegregate either within the system or in cooperation with neighboring school systems.
- Elimination of racial discrimination in Northern as well as Southern schools by vigorous application of Title VI of the Civil Rights Act of 1964.
- Extension of quality early childhood education to every disadvantaged child in the country.

- Efforts to improve dramatically schools serving disadvantaged children through substantial federal funding of year-round quality compensatory education programs, improved teaching, and expanded experimentation and research.
- Elimination of illiteracy through greater federal support for adult basic education.
- Enlarged opportunities for parent and community participation in the public schools.
- Reoriented vocational education emphasizing work-experience training and the involvement of business and industry.
- Expanded opportunities for higher education through increased federal assistance to disadvantaged students.
- Revision of state aid formulas to assure more per student aid to districts having a high proportion of disadvantaged school-age children.

The Welfare System

Our present system of public welfare is designed to save money instead of people, and tragically ends up doing neither. This system has two critical deficiencies:

First, it excludes large numbers of persons who are in great need, and who, if provided a decent level of support, might be able to become more productive and self-sufficient. No federal funds are available for millions of men and women who are needy but neither aged, handicapped nor the parents of minor children.

Second, for those who are included, the system provides assistance well below the minimum necessary for a decent level of existence, and imposes restrictions that encourage continued dependency on welfare and undermine self-respect.

A welter of statutory requirements and administrative practices and regulations operate to remind recipients that they are considered untrustworthy, promiscuous and lazy. Residence requirements prevent assistance to people in need who are newly arrived in the state. Searches of recipients' homes violate privacy. Inadequate social services compound the problems.

The Commission recommends that the federal government, acting with state and local governments where necessary, reform the existing welfare system to:

- Establish, for recipients in existing welfare categories, uniform national standards of assistance at least as high as the annual "poverty level" of income, now set by the Social Security Administration at $3,335 for an urban family of four.
- Require that all states receiving federal welfare contributions participate in the Aid to Families with Dependent Children–Unemployed Parents program (AFDC–UP) that permits assistance to families with both father and mother in the home, thus aiding the family while it is still intact.
- Bear a substantially greater portion of all welfare costs— at least 90 percent of total payments.
- Increase incentives for seeking employment and job training, but remove restrictions recently enacted by the Congress that would compel mothers of young children to work.
- Provide more adequate social services through neighborhood centers and through family-planning programs.
- Remove the freeze placed by the 1967 welfare amendments on the percentage of children in a state that can be covered by federal assistance.
- Eliminate residence requirements.

As a long-range goal, the Commission recommends that the federal government seek to develop a national system of income supplementation based strictly on need with two broad and basic purposes:

- To provide, for those who can work or who do work, any necessary supplements in such a way as to develop incentives for fuller employment;
- To provide, for those who cannot work and for mothers who decide to remain with their children, a minimum standard of decent living, and aid in saving children from the prison of poverty that has held their parents.

A broad system of supplementation would involve substantially greater federal expenditures than anything now contemplated. The cost will range widely depending on the standard of need accepted as the "basic allowance" to individuals and families, and on the rate at which additional income above this level is taxed. Yet if the deepening cycle of poverty and dependence on welfare can be broken, if the children of the poor can be given the opportunity to scale the wall that now separates them from the rest of society, the return on this investment will be great indeed.

Housing

After more than three decades of fragmented and grossly underfunded federal housing programs, nearly six million substandard housing units remain occupied in the United States.

The housing problem is particularly acute in the Negro ghettos. Nearly two-thirds of all nonwhite families living in the central cities today live in neighborhoods marked by substandard housing and general urban blight. Two major factors are responsible.

First: Many ghetto residents simply cannot pay the rent necessary to support decent housing. In Detroit, for example, over 40 percent of the nonwhite-occupied units in 1960 required rent of over 35 percent of the tenants' income.

Second: Discrimination prevents access to many nonslum areas, particularly the suburbs, where good housing exists. In addition, by creating a "back pressure" in the racial ghettos, it makes it possible for landlords to break up apartments for denser occupancy, and keeps prices and rents of deteriorated ghetto housing higher than they would be in a truly free market.

To date, federal programs have been able to do comparatively little to provide housing for the disadvantaged. In the 31-year history of subsidized federal housing, only about 800,000 units have been constructed, with recent production averaging about 50,000 units a year. By comparison, over a period only three years longer, FHA insurance guarantees have made possible the construction of over ten million middle- and upper-income units.

Two points are fundamental to the Commission's recommendations:

First: Federal housing programs must be given a new thrust aimed at overcoming the prevailing patterns of racial segregation. If this is not done, those programs will continue to concentrate the most impoverished and dependent segments of the population into the central-city ghettos where there is already a critical gap between the needs of the population and the public resources to deal with them.

Second: The private sector must be brought into the production and financing of low- and moderate-rental housing to supply the capabilities and capital necessary to meet the housing needs of the nation.

The Commission recommends that the federal government:

- Enact a comprehensive and enforceable federal open-housing law to cover the sale or rental of all housing, including single-family homes.
- Reorient federal housing programs to place more low- and moderate-income housing outside of ghetto areas.
- Bring within the reach of low and moderate income families within the next five years, six million new and existing units of decent housing, beginning with 600,000 units in the next year.

To reach this goal we recommend:

- Expansion and modification of the rent supplement program to permit use of supplements for existing housing, thus greatly increasing the reach of the program.
- Expansion and modification of the below-market interest-rate program to enlarge the interest subsidy to all sponsors and provide interest-free loans to nonprofit sponsors to cover pre-construction costs, and permit sale of projects to nonprofit corporations, cooperatives, or condominiums.
- Creation of an ownership supplement program similar to present rent supplements, to make home ownership possible for low-income families.
- Federal writedown of interest rates on loans to private builders constructing moderate-rent housing.
- Expansion of the public housing program, with emphasis on small units on scattered sites, and leasing and "turnkey" programs.
- Expansion of the Model Cities program.
- Expansion and reorientation of the urban renewal program to give priority to projects directly assisting low-income households to obtain adequate housing.

CONCLUSION

One of the first witnesses to be invited to appear before this Commission was Dr. Kenneth B. Clark, a distinguished and perceptive scholar. Referring to the reports of earlier riot commissions, he said:

> I read that report . . . of the 1919 riot in Chicago, and it is as if I were reading the report of the investigating committee on the Harlem riot of '35, the report of the investigating committee on the Harlem riot of '43, the report of the McCone Commission on the Watts riot.
>
> I must again in candor say to you members of this commission —it is a kind of Alice in Wonderland—with the same moving picture re-shown over and over again, the same analysis, the same recommendations, and the same inaction.

These words come to our minds as we conclude this Report. We have provided an honest beginning. But we have uncovered no startling truths, no unique insights, no simple solutions. The destruction and the bitterness of racial disorder, the harsh polemics of black revolt and white repression have been seen and heard before in this country.

It is time now to end the destruction and the violence, not only in the streets of the ghetto but in the lives of people.

Index

Index

Prepared by Jessie L. Matthews, Rutgers Law Library, Camden, N.J. All numbers given are page numbers.

659

The Diary of the American Revolution

Compiled by Frank Moore

*Edited, Abridged, and with an Introduction
by John Anthony Scott*

A rare collection of reports and opinion from British, Tory and Revolutionary sources, 1775 to 1781

"A thoroughly enlightening and entertaining edition ... the selections from colonial newspapers—on-the-spot stories, political essays, diatribes, humorous features—are wonderfully vivid reading."

—Publishers' Weekly

Illustrated with eight steel engravings, ten facsimile broadsides, and augmented with ballads and songs.

Hardcover   19645 $7.95

Living Documents in American History

Edited and with Introductions by John Anthony Scott

Two rich and provocative collections of original documents—letters, essays, sermons, manifestos, speeches, court cases, and songs—tracing the struggle for interracial democracy in the United States.

Volume I

From Earliest Colonial Times to the Civil War

Including: An Account of the Slave Trade / The Massachusetts Body of Liberties / The Lincoln-Douglas Debates / as well as numerous documents of The Great Awakening, and America's surge westward.

Hardcover   98088 $5.95   Paperback   W•1040   90¢

Volume II

From Reconstruction to the Outbreak of World War I

Including: The Radical, Moderate and Conservative positions on Reconstruction / Andrew Carnegie on Wealth / The Civil Rights Cases of 1883 / as well as major contributions from The Gilded Age, America's rise as a world power, and the Progressive Era.

Hardcover   42699 $7.95

WSP
🏠 WASHINGTON SQUARE PRESS, INC.